MIDDLE-CLASS
LIFEBOAT

MIDDLE-CLASS LIFEBOAT

Careers and Life Choices for Navigating a Changing Economy

PAUL & SARAH EDWARDS

THOMAS NELSON
Since 1798

NASHVILLE   DALLAS   MEXICO CITY   RIO DE JANEIRO   BEIJING

Published in Nashville, Tennessee by Thomas Nelson. Thomas Nelson is a registered trademark of Thomas Nelson, Inc.

Some people's names and their locations mentioned in this book have been changed upon their request for privacy.

Thomas Nelson, Inc. titles may be purchased in bulk for educational, business, fund-raising, or sales promotional use. For information, please e-mail SpecialMarkets@ThomasNelson.com.

Library of Congress Cataloging-in-Publication Data

Edwards, Paul, 1940–
    Middle class lifeboat : three safeguards to secure your financial future now / by Paul and Sarah Edwards.
      p. cm.
    Includes bibliographical references and index.
    ISBN 978-0-7852-2052-7
    1. Finance, Personal. 2. Budgets, Personal. 3. Quality of life. 4. Middle class. I. Edwards, Sarah (Sarah A.) II. Title.
    HG179.E388 2008
    332.024—dc22

2007037604

Printed in the United States of America

07 08 09 10 11 RRD 6 5 4 3 2 1

We dedicate this book to the millions of people who are searching for the way to improve their lives by taking their futures into their own hands, and we hope the ideas and guidance shared here will make their journey through the seas of personal and economic change simpler and easier.

CONTENTS

PART I – RIDING THE WAVES OF A SEA CHANGE

PART II – SAFEGUARDING YOUR LIVELIHOOD: 50+ WAYS TO BECOME FINANCIALLY SELF-SUFFICIENT WHETHER THE ECONOMY IS UP OR DOWN

Chapter Three

Chapter Four

PART III – SAFEGUARDING YOUR QUALITY OF LIFE: NINE OFF-THE-MAP LIFESTYLE CHOICES FOR INCREASING SATISFACTION WHILE LOWERING THE COST OF LIVING

PART IV – SAFEGUARDING YOUR ABILITY TO AFFORD THE LIFE YOU SEEK– NINE CASHLESS WAYS TO EXTEND YOUR INCOME, WORK LESS, AND LIVE MORE

To be middle class in America once meant living well and having financial security. But today that comfortable and contented lifestyle is harder to achieve and maintain.

Parade magazine survey

PART I

Riding the Waves of a Sea Change

Opportunity beckons! But, oh, how it can be disguised. It's not your imagination. For those of us in the middle class, it *is* harder to find and keep a good-paying job with dependable benefits. It *is* harder to retire comfortably. It *is* more difficult to make ends meet, and life *is* ever more stressed, complicated, and harried. Most likely you've been noticing this pinch and are feeling somewhat, or maybe a lot, bothered—or at least uncertain about what it means for your future, your bank balance, and what your life will be like if something doesn't change.

We first started to notice this shift several years ago. It seemed we were working harder and harder to maintain the lifestyle we'd achieved. Although we've always enjoyed our work writing, speaking, consulting, and broadcasting, our days were growing ever more complicated and stressful. At first we thought we just needed to work a little harder, manage our efforts effectively, and everything would even out again. That's what we assumed—until we began interviewing hundreds of people from several dozen different fields we've been following for more than a decade.

As we talked with person after person in one field after another, it was clear what we were experiencing was neither particular to us nor passing. Almost everyone we talked to was working harder and feeling stressed about how to find a better balance between personal desires and daily economic pressures.

Don't worry, though; this book is not about how bad times are. The economic *sea change* in our economy that's making life more difficult for middle-class workers offers new, creative opportunities and challenges as we transition from a job-based corporate economy. Most importantly, the book is about what those opportunities are and how we can ride through the waves of change and continue to enjoy the promise, security, and gratification a middle-class lifestyle has long represented.

The term *sea change* is one of the most evocative phrases in the English language. It refers to a profound transformation. Not just a readjustment or little shift, but a radical change in fundamental character and structure. There have been other economic sea changes over the course of history, such as when we changed from hunters and gatherers to farmers and herders, or when we moved from an agrarian life in small villages to an urban life in large cities. Similarly, life changed radically when factory work was eclipsed by information and service work. But such major shifts are not common.

Most economic changes are incremental, allowing new generations of people to gradually shift the way they live and work. The creation of an American middle class, for example, was itself a gradual change, dating from before the time Tocqueville visited America in 1831 and wrote about the novelty of a country composed of an "innumerable crowd who are . . . not exactly rich nor yet quite poor." In his notes Tocqueville marveled, "The whole society seems to have turned into one middle class." This economic middle grew gradually and then burgeoned after World War II when it became possible to have a middle-class life on a working-class wage. During that era, instead of asking why some people were rich, as Adam Smith did in *Wealth of Nations*, scholars began for the first time in history to explore why some people were still poor.

But compared to this kind of gradual evolution, a sea change happens relatively quickly and catches us off guard. Such unexpected shifts are confusing and disorienting, because we're no longer able to count on things working the way we expect. Best-laid plans go out the window, and we're not sure just what to replace them with in such an unfamiliar and uncertain economy. As a thirty-nine-year-old worker in the auto parts industry put it when the company where he'd worked for ten years to qualify for full-pay benefits declared bankruptcy, "The hardest part of all this is that there was no warning. If we could have had a couple of years' warning, we could adjust our lifestyle." Instead he found his life turned upside down virtually overnight.

While these huge shifts come on suddenly, adjusting to them personally isn't always as rapid. It takes some time and effort. The way things have been done begins to crumble in the wake of a sea change, but the new structures and economic safeguards for how things will be are not in place yet. Even younger workers with more flexibility can get caught in choppy economic waters. But it is this very uncertainty that provides such a wealth of new opportunities. The upside of a sea change is that if we understand what's happening and see the signs of what's coming, we can participate in shaping the quality and kind of lives we and our children will be living as the new economy comes to the fore.

That's the goal of this book. Part I provides a snapshot of what we're dealing with, offers four steps we can take to survive and thrive in the evolving new economy, and discusses how Parts II, III, and IV will supply a wealth of choices for how we can safeguard our income, our lifestyle, and our ability to afford our lives.

*Many Americans are upset about the direction
of their lives, but find it difficult to imagine
how their course could be altered.*
Harwood Group. *Futurist* magazine,
September–October 2004

CHAPTER ONE

Surviving and Thriving in New Economic Realities

Viewed one by one, the signs of the economic sea change going on around us don't seem all that significant at first. They may seem more like the result of unwise personal decisions, a misguided public policy, or a market aberration. But considered as a whole, they reflect a confluence of forces beyond the scope of any single personal, political, or economic decision, and their impact can jolt us into action. Here are a few of the signs furrowing many a brow these days. They cause people like you to make some changes—as we and many others have been doing over the past few years—in how we live and work. At the very least, the signs prompt us to begin looking for possible new choices.

For example, how many of the following changes, or the impending possibility of them, are already affecting you, your family, friends, or neighbors?

- ❑ Longer work hours
- ❑ Increased workload without additional compensation
- ❑ Layoffs, closures, or required pay cuts
- ❑ Fewer or no vacation and/or sick days
- ❑ Increased health insurance costs or no health insurance benefits
- ❑ Loss or freezing of retirement benefits
- ❑ Lower return or loss of investment income
- ❑ Increased cost of gasoline and/or cost of heating and cooling a home
- ❑ Increased cost of day care
- ❑ Longer waits to find a new job
- ❑ Available jobs paying less than previous ones laid off from

❑ Jobs being offshored to workers in another country

❑ Higher personal debt to keep up one's lifestyle

❑ Reduced or no government benefits to get through a tough time

❑ Need to shop more at box discount stores and outlet centers

❑ Inability to save as much or not at all

❑ Little or no discretionary income for things one once enjoyed

❑ Less time to devote to the aspects of life you value or enjoy most

We don't want to dwell on the statistics available to show how common and widespread these signs have become recently. In fact, we hope your reaction is that it's not all that bad for you yet. Hopefully it won't ever be. By international standards we in the American middle class are still living well, but a review of a variety of surveys of middle-class Americans over the past few years sheds light on a growing unease beneath our apparent prosperity. They reflect a disquieting rise of concern about such things as being able to:

❑ Keep or replace a job

❑ Pay the bills each month

❑ Get ahead financially

❑ Obtain affordable quality health care

❑ Finance a college education

❑ Provide for a comfortable retirement

❑ Have time off for family, friends, vacations, relaxation

All such things were once considered relatively secure aspects of a middle-class life, yet over half of us express concern for the first time in generations that economic circumstance will be worse for our children and future generations. The Gallup Worry Index, which tracks public fears on economic issues, showed us as an anxious nation, recording as of this writing its highest anxiety reading ever.

If you would like to read more about the findings of these studies and others we mention in this chapter, you will find them listed under Studies in the LEARN MORE section at the end of the chapter.

A Federal Reserve Board Survey of Consumer Finances offers a detailed portrait of the financial balance sheet of the typical U.S. family:

▶ About $3,800 in the bank

▶ No retirement account, but living next to neighbors who have about $35,000 in a retirement account

▶ No mutual funds, stocks, or bonds

▶ Own a house worth $160,000, on which $95,000 is owed

▶ An income of more than $43,000 a year, but unable to pay off a $2,200 credit card balance

One way many of us have managed to stay afloat so far, despite such concerns, is by living on credit. Credit card debt is at an all-time high, averaging $9,312 per household. But how much more debt can we carry, and how much stress does our growing debt load add for the 80 percent of us who are already overstressed from juggling family and work? With minimum monthly payments and no additional borrowing, it will take an average of ten years to pay off such a debt, and the overall cost will be almost double the original amount borrowed. So is it any wonder 81 percent of people polled report experiencing some type of financial difficulty?

Analysis of household income over the past fifteen years tells us that "good economic times" today are little better for most of us than what would have been considered "bad times" back then. But again, our aim is not to focus on economic woes. You have undoubtedly already read or heard plenty about the thin economic margin so many of us balance on and what could happen were it to suddenly disappear.

Our goal is to emphasize that, for reasons beyond our personal control, many of the benefits we've come to rely upon to maintain a secure and comfortable middle-class lifestyle are slipping away, leaving us with the challenge of how to fill in the gaps. With three out of four working people believing it is becoming harder today to achieve the American Dream, many are already finding exciting and imaginative ways to do just that. When polled, nearly half of Americans say they've begun making voluntary changes to address forces that are threatening their way of life. They are building an economic lifeboat for:

- Financial security and a sense of control over their future
- Dependable work that is interesting and meaningful
- A simpler life, with fewer work hours
- More time for loved ones, personal interests, and community
- Less pressure, stress, and complexity in their lives
- A greater sense of autonomy and freedom within a close, stable community

How they are doing this, and how you can do it too, is precisely what this book will address. Here are the four essential steps we need to take starting right away:

Four Steps to Securing Your Own Middle-Class Lifeboat^{sm}

First, we must educate ourselves as to just what is happening and understand the forces that are shaping the changes around us. Otherwise we will neither recognize the safeguards we must put into place nor see the many new opportunities that are open to us. Next, we must decide how we will safeguard our livelihoods to assure that we have a secure, dependable, and rewarding source of income we can rely upon in the evolving new economy. Then we need to make positive changes in the way we live to safeguard the quality of our life. Finally, we need to make sure we can afford to make the changes we want to make and enjoy pursuing them.

So let's begin by looking at just what is happening. What are the forces driving this economic sea change? How might they affect you, and what changes might they motivate you to consider making?

Step One to Securing Your Own Middle-Class Lifeboat^{sm}:
Understand What's Happening and the Personal Changes It's Inspiring

Life has always been a struggle for the poor. The rich have always weathered change with less difficulty than the rest of us. But the middle class holds a unique and sometimes precarious position somewhere between the extremes of rich and poor, a place where we may never feel as financially secure as the rich, but where we can rest assured that if we do a good job at our work, we can enjoy a comfortable life. For most, such a life includes a nice home, good schools for our children, material comforts, being cared for in our old age—all the things that add up to making us feel sufficiently successful and satisfied.

Right now 92 percent of Americans define themselves as somewhere in the middle class, but most of us don't think it's as easy to stay there as it once was. Whereas 95 percent of voters believe you could enjoy a solid middle-class lifestyle twenty-five years ago if you worked hard and played by the rules, today less than half belief that, says a Douglas E. Schoen poll. Instead, most of us believe our numbers are shrinking.

Analysts agree. They are noticing that as the global economy progresses, our vast middle class is decreasing at a rate of 5 to 6 percent each year, and the gap between the rich and the poor is widening. Already, the most recent Census Bureau figures show that the richest fifth of U.S. households received 50.4 percent of all national income, the highest level since they began compiling such data in 1967, while the poorest fifth got just 3.4 percent. Loss of middle-income jobs has been well documented for some time, but Census Bureau data now shows that middle class neighborhoods are disappearing at an even faster rate than comparable jobs.

Such patterns are common in times of large-scale economic change. When the United States shifted quickly from agrarian times—when wealth was distributed relatively evenly—to the industrial era, the gap between rich and poor in some urban areas left the wealthiest 4 percent of the population in control of as much as two-thirds of a city's wealth.

In other words, in such times as these, pressure to hold one's own economically increases. Obviously we don't want to slip into poverty, but we don't want to work ourselves into the ground either just to stay where we are. So what are the forces catalyzing the economic sea change that are making life more difficult, raising anxiety, and propelling us to question if our way of life is as secure as we would like it? Here are six of the key interrelated forces that are churning up our economic seas.

1. Globalization. The increasing integration of worldwide markets for goods, services, and capital over the past decade is one of the key forces driving the changes we're experiencing. It means that we in the United States are now sharing many of the traditional well-paying jobs with workers in other countries. More U.S. jobs, including those in start-up companies, are being "offshored," that is, sent to other countries, like China, India, Mexico, the Philippines, and Eastern European nations, where workers are paid far less and have fewer benefits. This includes white-collar jobs once thought to be secure, such as analysts, accountants, customer service reps, engineers, graphic and software designers, marketers, programmers, and even some medical specialties. Economic analysts predict the offshored share of such jobs could double in the next three years.

> *Pasadena Now, an online newspaper, advertised on their Web site: "We are seeking a newspaper journalist based in India to report on city government and political scene in Pasadena, California."*

2. Othersourcing. An increasing numbers of jobs that were once done by people are now being done by nonhuman means (such as automation, digitalization, and robotization) for example making bank deposits, checking-in for flights at airports, moving cameras on television sets, and checking out merchandise at retail stores. Keep in mind that by using labor-saving technology, companies can continue to profit and grow without adding jobs. Management guru Tom Peters predicts that between these first two forces, 90 percent of the white-collar jobs we know today may no longer exist within the next dozen years.

3. Growing dominance of multinational corporations. In a democratic society such as ours, an important role of national government is to intervene in the marketplace when necessary to assure economic stability—good jobs at decent wages and strong, safe, and secure families and communities. One effect of globalization, however, has been the rise of multinational corporations and financial institutions not subject to the jurisdictional controls of our national government. This lack of jurisdiction weakens our government's ability to provide a counterbalancing role in maintaining economic stability. These financial institutions can operate beyond the reach of public accountability, making our role as consumers more important to society than our role as citizens or workers. In this position, our voice is often confined to little more than choosing which products to purchase from among these corporations.

4. Dwindling natural resources. Growing international competition for dwindling natural resources is yet another factor in the economic sea change. The United States, Europe, and Japan have been using 80 percent of the world's natural resources, some of which are becoming depleted by rapid population growth and increased standards of living. Now economies in other countries are expanding too, and we must compete with them for these vital resources. Companies in India, China, and South Korea, for example, are competing with U.S. companies for oil supplies in countries as far and wide as Myanmar, Canada, Russia and the many nations of Africa.

Such competition means U.S. business and industry must pay more for things they've long enjoyed at a low cost, such as oil, gasoline, natural gas, water, and everything we consume that requires such resources. These costs are, of course, passed on to us as consumers. More than half of Americans polled say, for example, that rising fuel costs are causing them financial hardship. Six in ten report they're cutting back on discretionary spending as a result of higher gasoline and energy prices.

Also, as costs of commodities rise, businesses that can no longer compete are forced to close, while others feel compelled to make major cuts in their work force and/or benefits. Federal, state, and local government services are also affected by these rising costs, and recent cutbacks in such programs as Medicare, Social Security, job training, and unemployment compensation are expected to continue.

5. A cultural shift in social responsibility. Such cuts in the private and public sector revenue mean that we as individuals and families are increasingly left to shoulder more of the cost for economic safeguards once provided by our employers or the government. We find ourselves required to:

- pay all or a larger part of our health care costs
- manage our own retirement funds in place of guaranteed pensions
- assume the risk that accompanies such investments
- cover the costs of an economic crisis, such as being laid off, injured on the job, becoming seriously ill, or providing care for ill or disabled family members

This shift is having a particularly profound effect on the family. Long thought of as the backbone of economic security and stability, marriage and family are becoming an economic risk. Married couples and families are more likely to file bankruptcy, lose their homes, and fall behind on their credit card debt than are singles. "We're not used to thinking of children as an economic liability," says Jacob S. Hacker, author of *The Great Risk Shift*, "but fully one quarter of 'poverty spells' originate with the birth of a child." The Census Bureau tells us that for the first time, households headed by singles outnumber those headed by married ones. Also a first, 51 percent of adult women and nearly 50 percent of men now live without a spouse. This shift in the epicenter of risk is not just a U.S. phenomenon—it is occurring across the Western world.

Basics Cost More

Some vital expense categories have far outstripped the consumer price index. Percentage changes from September 1986 to September 2006:

▶ College tuition	289.5%
▶ Hospital services	280.4%
▶ Drugs	177.6%
▶ Medical care	173.5%
▶ Doctor services	137.3%
▶ Energy	131.9%
▶ Housing	83.6%
▶ Fuels	81.9%
▶ Food and beverages	78.8%
▶ Eggs	58.1%
▶ Electricity	53.0%
▶ New car	23.0%
▶ Apparel	12.6%

Source: Bureau of Labor Statistics

6. Rising cost of essentials. While many things, such as T-shirts, digital cameras, video phones, and computers are becoming cheaper, most of our fixed costs, the essentials we *must* have, such as housing, utilities, gasoline, transportation, health care, child care, medication, and education, are becoming progressively more expensive. "Families are being forced to live beyond their means, just to pay for the basics, such as housing and health care," says Christian Weller, a senior economist for the Center for American Progress.

The average homeowner spends more than a fifth of his or her total annual income to pay the mortgage, property taxes, homeowner's insurance, and utilities. More than a third of homeowners spend more than 30 percent of their annual income on mortgage payments alone. With the U.S. population aging and living longer, rising health care costs are of particular concern. Over the past year, the cost of health care premiums rose to an annual average of $11,500 for a family plan, according to the Kaiser Family Foundation. This doubling in only seven years is twice as fast as the overall inflation rate and salary increases. A Watson Wyatt study reports "a vast majority of employers are planning to cut or eliminate health coverage for current and future retirees." In fact, health care costs borne by both workers and retirees are expected to keep on increasing, says Paul Fronstin of Employee Benefits Research Institute.

While we can easily cut back on or do without a larger T-shirt wardrobe and forego the newest electronic device, living without the essentials is a much greater challenge we'd prefer not to contemplate. Yet some of us are already facing trade-offs we'd rather not make. Do I drive an hour each way to work from a larger home we can afford, or does the family stay in a cramped apartment closer to work? Does gas money come before regular family dental care, savings for college, or funds for a much-needed vacation? Do I reduce how often I take my prescription medicine, let it go unfilled, or make the credit card payment?

The prospect of having to make such trade-offs is spurring people like those you will meet in this book to step out of this discomfort zone and create new lives for themselves that safeguard their livelihoods and the quality of their lives.

Personal Changes Inspired by These Forces: As we contemplate the full impact of these changes, it becomes clear that some of us may not be able to continue living and working in the costly ways we do today, and most of us won't want to. We're seeking lives that cost less in terms of our health, happiness, and future well-being. In other words, we need to find what could be called "sustainable" ways of living. We invite you to consider careers and ways of living that allow you to enjoy a secure source of income outside the hyperconsumerism that keeps us buried in debt, working too hard, and diminishing our overall sense of satisfaction.

Sustainable Living Defined: Simply put, "sustainable" means that which can be maintained over time. In this context we are referring to living and working in ways that don't jeopardize our security, health, and well-being over time, as well as that of our families, communities, and the natural resources we rely on to live a good life.

So "sustainable" would be the opposite of "I just can't keep this up." That's how Becky Kowalski put it when she told us she had to find an alternative to her daily schedule. It involves driving her eight-year-old daughter to a private special education school in one part of the city, then heading off through heavy, smog-laden traffic to her job in another part of town, then back through the traffic to get her daughter after work, and home again across town where she can afford to live. A single mother, Becky makes what most of us would consider a lot of money, yet she worries constantly about whether she will be able to continue paying for her daughter's private school with special education and tutoring. She worries if she can keep up with escalating rent increases. But most of all, she worries about her daughter's emotional and academic problems and that she only sees her mother when she's rushed, exhausted, harried, and on edge. "I wish she had a better mother," Becky confessed sadly.

Sustainable would be a counter to feeling as if "there has to be another way," as Lee Lyons expressed it when he was laid off from his job of thirty-three years just months before his retirement vested. "I never saw it coming," he said, proceeding to explain how disappointed he felt when he realized that at his age he not only wasn't going to find a job that paid what he had been earning, but he wasn't going to be able to find a job for half his past wage. In fact, at his age, it appeared he wasn't going to be able to find any full-time job. Not long after this realization, Lee suffered a heart attack. After a series of heart surgeries, he is now disabled. To make ends meet, his wife, who had been approaching retirement from her job, rented an apartment in another city, where she could take a higher paying job. Her new job requires near full-time travel. Whenever possible, she sees her husband on weekends.

Another word for sustainable might be *affordable*. That is, living and working in a way we can afford to keep doing without:

- ▶ Going bankrupt or deeper in debt.
- ▶ Suffering from one or more of the chronic stress-related illnesses so common today. Conditions ranging from high blood pressure and heart disease to obesity and diabetes are all becoming more prevalent and striking at ever-younger ages.
- ▶ Depleting our environment of the vital resources that sustain us, such as clean air and pure water, or despoiling it so we will be susceptible to the growing number of environmentally related illnesses, such as asthma, cancer, autoimmune diseases, and psychiatric or developmental problems like ADHD or autism.

Because individual circumstances, needs, and desires differ, the changes individuals and families want to make to safeguard their middle-class lives are different as well. The task before us is to make innovative choices that will work for us personally. That means being explorative, bold, and creative, as well as willing to look beyond the usual way things have been to what could be.

Tina Alvarado, 43, for example, was living in a small apartment working as a leasing specialist in San Diego, California, one of the largest and most desirable, but also most expensive, metropolitan areas in the United States. Visiting friends in Helena, Alabama, outside of Birmingham, she realized what a toll the high costs, long commutes, and tension-filled hours on the job were taking on her health and happiness. They had left her feeling stressed, isolated, and unhappy. At age forty-three, she also faced the reality that, with the escalating cost of housing in her metro area, she was never going to be able to own her own home. In fact, the average mortgage payment there is more than double the average rent.

The sense of community and personal friendship Tina experienced among her friends in Helena, especially at their church, was the biggest draw for her. "I knew I needed to make a big change," she recalls. Within the year, even though she didn't have a job offer in hand, she gathered the courage to quit her job and relocate. It was a daring move, she admits. It required a great deal of faith. But Alabama has a diversified economy coupled with a relatively low cost of living, reasonable housing prices, and low property taxes and utility costs.

Six months later Tina had not only found a job, but she'd also found her dream job with a dream company. "I love this job," she says. "I want to keep this job until I retire." And she is now the proud owner of her own home. Her new home cost less than a tenth of the average home price in San Diego. But, best of all, she no longer feels alone and isolated. In the church community that drew her there, she has found the close friendships and deeply spiritual life she had been missing in San Diego.

The Blanchards decided to make a more dramatic change. Katy, 57, a fiber artist, and Rick, 62, a landscape architect, had lived their whole lives in a metro area, but they yearned for a simpler way of life closer to nature—somewhere Katy could grow dye plants for her artwork. They took a trip across the western United States in search of their dream location and found fifty-six acres of land outside of Abiquiu, New Mexico. As appealing as living on this beautiful site was, when it came to actually leaving city life behind, Rick, who was telecommuting to an employer in another metro area, hesitated. He was worried about the financial repercussions of such drastic change, until his banker convinced him they'd be much better off living in a less expensive area like Abiquiu.

The Blanchards now live there "off the grid," relying on solar power for electricity and water from the well on their property. Katy continues to knit and weave but also grows dye plants and indigenous medicinal herbs and teaches these lost arts to others. Rick still telecommutes to his California employer. "I knew that if we stayed where we were, we'd have to work our tails off forever," Katy explains. "Every cell in my body told me I needed to do this, and we are very happy we did! It's a blast."

Peter and Susan Baylies of North Andover, New Hampshire, made a far less drastic, but equally unusual choice. Until Peter was laid off from his job at Digital

Equipment Corporation, he and Susan were juggling the financial, physical, and psychological stresses of a typical two-career couple with a new baby. Once Peter was home full-time while looking for a new job, it didn't take long to realize how much easier life was for everyone in the family. Going against convention, they decided that Peter wouldn't take another job. Instead he became a stay-at-home dad. Susan, an elementary school teacher, became the primary breadwinner, and Peter takes care of their two boys, now ages nine and twelve. One surprise they had not anticipated was just how much money they've saved with Peter working at home, especially on day care costs. Their choice has worked so well that Peter began publishing a newsletter for other stay-at-home dads and has written a book called *The Stay-at-Home Dad Handbook* with Jessica Toonkel.

Of course, your own choices might be quite different from any of these. What's increasingly clear is that we in the middle class can't simply wait and hope economic forces, investments, or government policies will protect us. We must begin now to make new choices, and fortunately there are many possibilities, from making simple adjustments to major alterations. Like Tina, Katy, Rick, Peter, Susan, and many others you will meet in the following chapters, we need to start looking at our own discomfort zones and deciding what level of changes would be comfortable and attractive to us.

Consider, for example, your own level of discomfort with your financial circumstances right now. Where would you place your discomfort level on a scale of one to ten, with zero being none at all and ten being at absolute wit's end?

0——1——2——3——4——5——6——7——8——9——10

How about your present quality of life? How much are financial, career, and lifestyle pressures detracting from your ability to enjoy your daily life? How uncomfortable have these pressures become for you?

0——1——2——3——4——5——6——7——8——9——10

Given the level of discomfort you are feeling, how much of a change might you be willing to consider making?

❏ *A Little*: *Simplifying Your Life.* Mini-sizing your current life to make it easier, simpler, or more secure, for example, spending less, paying off debt, making small changes in your spending priorities, moving to a smaller home in the same area, or deciding what's most important to you and then rearranging your schedule(s) to put things first in your day, the way Peter and Susan have done.

❏ *Quite a Bit: Redesigning Your Life.* Making a more significant change such as taking a less stressful, more secure job; cutting back the hours you work to focus more on home, family, or community; telecommuting instead of driving to work; starting a full- or part-time sustainable independent career; or relocating to a lower-cost city or state, the way Tina has done.

❑ *A Whole Lot: Transforming Your Life.* Making a head-turning change, as Katy and Rick have done, something quite beyond what people customarily consider, such as moving to a remote location or another country, living and working on the land or off the grid, farming in your urban backyard, setting up a shared living arrangement with others, or living and working full-time on the road from your RV.

As you reflect on how much change you might consider, should you want to learn more about the forces creating the sea change we're undergoing and how they might affect you, you'll find a wealth of resources for exploring them further in the LEARN MORE section at the end of this chapter.

"The challenge we face today. . . is how to engage in the global economy without decimating our own middle class . . . The logic of global capitalism as currently practiced is to drive down work- ers' wages, weaken their bargaining power, and strip away their social protections in both rich and poor countries, while simulta- neously encouraging . . . the excesses of debt-driven con- sumerism."

The Optimistic Progressive

Step Two to Securing Your Own Middle-Class Lifeboat℠: Safeguarding Your Livelihood

The more we understand about the changes our economy is undergoing, the clearer it becomes that to safeguard our livelihood, we each need to have a reli- able source of independent income that's not dependent on having a corporate job, a corporate pension plan, reliable investments, or the continuation of Social Security benefits. This does not mean we all have to go out and quit our jobs, as long as we have good ones. Nor does it mean we should discontinue or cut back our retirement savings and investment plans. It simply means we need to have a full- or part-time independent income in the household to:

- ► supplement possible benefit or salary cuts
- ► offset rising prices
- ► reduce debt

- serve as a safety net to fall back on and build from should your job suddenly be downsized, eliminated, or offshored
- protect against changes in pension, investment, or Social Security plans
- supplement other retirement income when that time comes

On the other hand, if you've already been downsized, laid off, or outsourced one time too many, don't like the jobs available to you, or find your salaried position too stressful, uncertain, and unrewarding, you may well be attracted to the flexibility, assurance, choice, and freedom of having a full-time independent income.

What's important to remember in this economy is that in order to survive and meet their legal obligation, corporations must put profits first. For them, employees are "costs," so when competition rises, they need to use every means to limit their costs. Our salaries and benefits are highly vulnerable in any company that must jockey to survive in a world marketplace where using the cheapest labor and providing the fewest possible benefits are rewarded.

It's even more important to remember, though, that our situation in this economy is by no means hopeless. We may feel totally dependent on having a job with benefits, but that's because we have forgotten that it's possible to support ourselves independently. Having a self-sustaining independent income, or what today would be called being self-employed, may be unusual in today's job-based economy, but it's been only in recent history that the majority of adults have sold their labor for a wage. As recently as 1820, for example, most people supported themselves by selling the *product* of their labor. At that time three out of four Americans were farmers. Each family produced what was needed for household or local use. Even the typical urban worker was a self-employed artisan or craftsperson working with others in the household to produce and sell what they needed.

Only after the Industrial Revolution did most of us lose control over our own means of production from a farm, workshop, or store. Only then did we begin to forego our independence by selling our time and labor as a commodity instead of using or selling what we produced ourselves. By becoming self-employed, full- or part-time, we regain the security of owning our means of production and can assume greater control over what, when, how often, and for how much we work.

With this goal in mind, in Part II we will identify and profile more than fifty sustainable careers that can be done independently or in a job. These careers fall into three sectors that we believe have the greatest potential to remain secure or grow in demand as the new economy evolves:

1. Careers providing basic local services that cannot be outsourced. Chapter 2, 27 Basic Local Services, focuses on hands-on or face-to-face careers needed within local communities. In many ways these will become the most stable and dependable income sources in the new economy because they cannot be offshored, yet people will continue to need and want them. Also, as the costs of oil and gas rise, communities will of necessity want and need to rely more on local products and services.

2. Virtual careers providing niche products and services via a high-speed Internet connection or other means of telecommunication. Chapter 3, 13 Nichable Virtual Products and Services, describes careers you can pursue by serving clients and customers far and wide through computer and/or telephone technology. These careers offer a great deal of flexibility, allowing you, should you choose, to move to a different part of the country, including smaller communities, remote areas, or even another country, while still having access to customers from large population areas or even a worldwide market.

3. Careers addressing new needs arising from the emerging economy. Chapter 4, 14 Products and Services for New Economic Realities, features careers, including "green" careers, that address new needs resulting from the six forces we've described above— from globalization and dwindling natural resources to a shift in social responsibility and rising costs of essentials. While some of these careers may be less established at the moment, they will probably provide the greatest income potential in the future as both the general public and businesses go about adjusting how they live and work to new economic realities.

To identify the fifty-plus careers we selected from these three sectors, we evaluated dozens of possible careers using a *Durability Scale* based on eight criteria for choosing a "sustainable living career" today and in the years to come. We then narrowed down the many possibilities in terms of two factors: first, how well does this career fit into present and emerging economic realities, and second, how well does it fit our personal needs for a simpler, saner, and less harried lifestyle. A final screen included those that scored highest in their likelihood to provide a dependable income while also strengthening one's community and, in turn, society. Here are the eight criteria we used:

Criteria for a Sustainable Living Career

Economic Reality Fit
1. Strong income potential in an established and stable or a new and emerging field that can be pursued as a self-employed individual (if one chooses), in both good times and not-so-good times
2. Resistant to offshoring, that is, it can be done locally or remotely via telecommunications in a specialized niche

3. Not unduly dependent upon discretionary income, that is income remaining after paying for products and services one considers a necessity
4. Not easily replaced by technology

Personal Reality Fit

5. Low start-up costs if the career is being pursued independently
6. Low overhead costs for needed materials and services, including the ability to obtain needed materials, supplies, and help locally and little need for travel or other uses of costly fossil fuels
7. Readily barterable that is, things others want or need but dislike doing, complain about, or don't have needed resources or skills to do themselves) to reduce dependence of producing high levels of income that require overworking
8. Reasonable stress level and flexible hours

Each career profile begins with a set of mini-charts describing how well the career meets these criteria. To further help you evaluate the viability of these careers, we've provided a Durability Rating in each profile. Using a five-point scale, this rating summarizes at-a-glance our projection of how strongly we believe the career will continue to reflect the above criteria in years to come.

In the profile for each career we explain:

▸ What makes it a good choice for the new economy
▸ Income potential
▸ What it involves
▸ Who it serves
▸ What skills or training are needed
▸ What to watch out for
▸ What people who are doing it have to say about it
▸ Other resources you can turn to

As you explore these careers, you will notice there are many meaningful opportunities to apply experience and expertise from existing jobs, trades, and professions in new ways and venues, as well as many newer, emerging, or more cutting-edge opportunities for those who are ready to engage in more pioneering pursuits. None of the careers we've included require advanced degrees or other extensive education. Many such professions and trades, however, are now and will continue to be sustainable for years to come. This is particularly true of professions and trades that involve a hands-on, local service, such as nursing; legal services; practicing allopathic, homeopathic, and chiropractic medicine;

mortuary services; various medical ancillary services, such as phlebotomy and mammography; plumbing; hair, nail, and facial care; the construction trades; psychotherapy; pharmacy; and dental care.

"An affluent society is one in which all people's material wants are easily satisfied."

Marshall Sahlins, Stone-Age Economics

Step Three to Securing Your Own Middle-Class Lifeboat℠: *Safeguarding Your Quality of Life*

While a dependable, independent income is essential to safeguarding a middle-class lifestyle, it alone is not sufficient to preserve our way of life. A middle-class way of life is about more than having money. It is also an emotional state of mind, not having a certain amount of income or material possessions. People with incomes under $35,000 a year to over $350,000 a year consider themselves to be middle class. One in five of those earning more than $100,000 a year report living paycheck-to-paycheck, and a 2007 survey by Discover Financial Services found that 18 percent of them could only continue their current lifestyle for one month or less if they lost their income. So being middle class is about both feeling economically secure and having what we consider to be a good life, or at least being able to look forward to a good life in the future through our continued best efforts.

Surveys show that most of us are still surviving financially, but the physical, social, and emotional price of keeping up with ever-rising costs of having a good life is taking a toll on our sense of well-being. This can be equally true even with an established independent income that protects us from corporate, stock market, or governmental whims and from changes in technology or globalization. If you're working morning, noon, and night with no end in sight to make ends meet, it may look as though you're in the middle class, but you will feel more like you're in the overworking class. To safeguard our quality of life, we also need ways to circumvent the continual demand to spend more and more of our time and energy working to make more and more money. So people are finding ways to live that cost far less, freeing them to work less, and allowing them to do the things they consider the good life.

In Part III of *Middle-Class Lifeboat℠* we feature innovative and imaginative ways people are adjusting how they live to better suit their personal needs and values in view of the uncertainty and changing nature of the economy. Some, for example, are seeking a life that's more family-centered. Eric Mack was traveling to 150 business meetings a year for his work. This left him little time to be with his wife, Kathy, and their four young daughters. Even moving his work home didn't help because he was always on the road. He and Kathy decided on what was, for them, a better way. They moved to what we call a nearby faraway place, a small mountain village an hour from a nearby urban area where Eric could afford to take on fewer clients, work fewer hours, buy a larger home, and homeschool their daughters.

Others are tired of working hard at jobs they don't enjoy just so they can live a high-maintenance lifestyle. Carolyn and John Grace, for example, were successful Boston lawyers making what they refer to as "lawyer's money," but summer vacations to Swans Island, Maine, with their four children showed them a simpler, slower, more pleasant way of life. By saving and learning a new craft during evenings, they pulled together the resources and knowledge to move to Swans Island, where they became vintage blanket weavers using wool from local sheep ranches (www.swansislandblanket.com).

Still others want to retire, but they can't unless they find a less costly way to live. When Chris and Al Kocourek married, Al had already retired, and they lived in different East Coast cities. They wanted to relocate somewhere they could retire without the cold winters, humid summers, and high cost of living. But they also wanted the cultural sophistication and quality of services available in Manhattan or Santa Fe, just without the high costs. Their solution was to move to San Miguel, Mexico. There they enjoy what for them is a near-perfect climate, seventies and eighties during the day and fifties at night, a walking city of galleries, and a wealth of cultural events and lecture series. They also have the benefit of excellent health care services. Here they pay for needed medical care out-of-pocket for far less per visit than their monthly health insurance premiums in the United States, not to mention the co-pays that were an additional cost.

Nine Off-the-Map Lifestyle Choices for Increasing Satisfaction and Lowering Costs

1. Eliminating Stuff That Drags You Down
2. Moving to a Small City or Town
3. Nestling in a Nearby Faraway Place
4. Living Abroad
5. Living Rent-Free
6. Traveling the Land or Sea
7. Bringing Country Living to Town
8. Living Off the Grid
9. Living with Others

Whatever the motivation, many people are stepping out of convention and innovating more rewarding ways to live. Again, as we mentioned, the choices individuals and families are making vary in how much change they are willing to undertake. Not everyone wants to fundamentally change their way of life as these couples have. Some like Gail Sullivan of Baldwin, Georgia, simply want to simplify their lives, putting them on a diet, so to speak—cutting back or getting rid of the things they don't need or even want anymore.

Gail went through her entire house and "purged" anything she no longer needed. "It has been very liberating. My things no longer own me," she told us. "It's like reclaiming my life for what's really important."

Whether you're interested in tweaking, redesigning, or overhauling your life, in Chapters 5 through 13 you'll find nine popular choices people are making to live better for less. You may not have heard of some of these options; others you may be aware of but never considered. We invite you to explore each of them. You may be surprised at what you'll find appealing once you see how others are approaching and enjoying these choices.

Step Four to Securing Your Own Middle-Class Lifeboat℠: *Safeguarding Your Ability to Afford the Life You Seek*

In Part IV, Chapter 14, we describe some new—and some not-so-new—ways people are finding to make sure they have what they want and need without relying so heavily on making lots and lots of money. Today we tend to think we need money for just about everything and anything. But in past times, money was only one of many ways folks were able to attain the wherewithal for a good life.

Nine Cashless Ways to Extend Your Income

▶ Do It Yourself	▶ Lending and Sharing	▶ Bartering
▶ Helping Out	▶ Exchanges or Swaps	▶ Time Banks
▶ Co-ops	▶ Regiving Networks	▶ Local Currencies

Over the past few generations, we've become convinced that cashless alternatives like making or trading for the things we need are somehow not as good or prestigious as paying hard, cold cash. But such a belief can turn us into wage slaves and handcuff us to lives of white, blue, or pink-collar drudgery that may provide lots of material things but leave little time or energy to enjoy them. Chapter 14 invites you to explore some new alternatives for the role money plays in your life and how you might live just as well, or better, with less of it.

Throughout the book, you'll meet lots of people who are making novel choices and you'll discover:

- What these choices involve
- Pros and cons of each
- Practical steps for making such a change
- Mistakes to avoid
- Resources for exploring more

Finding What's Right for You

Be it a sustainable career, a new life choice, cashless alternatives, or some combination thereof, you'll find many possible middle-class lifeboats in the pages that follow. But are they right for you? As with any career and life choice, they each have their pros and cons, so as you read about them we want you to put them to the test. Ask yourself:

- Is this something I could enjoy? If not, will I have a hard time motivating myself to follow through on my intentions to make the proactive and protective changes I want to make?
- Does this choice call on my natural abilities? It is easier to succeed at something you can do well naturally without a lot of strain and irritation.
- How much preparation, training, and resources would I need to make this change? Would I be willing to, even energized about, obtaining new skills and knowledge if need be?
- Am I up for the degree of adventuresomeness this change calls for?
- Do I have the contacts and positioning I need to move gracefully into this change or, if not, am I willing to make contacts and break new ground to carry out this change?
- Does this option truly fit my values, desired lifestyle, and life goals?
- Is this choice suitable for where I live now? Would I need to relocate? Or if I want to relocate, is this choice one that would narrow or expand my opportunities?

In the chapters that follow, we have aimed to provide you with sufficient information to determine the answers to questions like these.

Is the Information in This Book Readily Available on the Internet?

Much of what you will find in this book is available on the Internet. We have provided frequent links where you can find out more. But there is also a ton of other information on the Internet that we didn't include. The advice, suggestions, guidance, and data we've provided carefully distill information from the Internet, along with insights gleaned from thousands of interviews for our books, radio, and television shows and face-to-face conversations, as well as dozens of trend publications we've amassed over thirty years. It took three years to synthesize the ideas and information you'll find between the covers of this book. It's intended to save you many hours of research and help you avoid many mistakes.

Finally, while it's important for you to put the options you are considering to the test, it's also important to give them a chance. When a choice seems attractive or appealing to you at first glance, resist the urge to automatically discard it just because it's unfamiliar, unusual, or seemingly impractical. Many things that would have been impractical and unusual in the past will be quite realistic in the uncertainty of the new economy. Take some time to imagine what your world will be like as globalization, automation, multinational corporations, and rising costs of utilities and basic services reshape your priorities and those of your family, neighbors, and community. Then explore the potential of the options that attract you in the context of the forces that are changing our economy.

We believe you'll find the key information you need to conclude, "Oh, *that* sure isn't for me!" or "Yes, I'm ready for something like *this*!" And we've included plenty of resources you can turn to for advice on where to go next in pursuit of options you'd like to explore further. Should none of the options we describe be quite right for you, chances are they will spur other ideas for how you can create, alter, adjust, or otherwise fashion your own middle-class lifeboat^{sm} for safely riding the waves of today's sea change.

LEARN MORE

Books

- *Affluenza: The All-Consuming Epidemic* by John De Graaf, David Wann, Thomas H. Naylor, Berrett-Koehler Publishers, 2005.
- *PowerDown: Options and Actions for a Post-Carbon World* by Richard E. Heinberg, The New Society Publishers, 2004.
- *Screwed: The Undeclared War Against the Middle Class and What We Can Do About It* by Thom Hartmann, Berrett-Koehler Publishers, 2006.
- *The Corporation: The Pathological Pursuit of Profit and Power* by Joel Bakan, Free Press, 2005.
- *The End of Oil: On the Edge of a Perilous New World* by Paul Roberts, Mariner Books, 2005.
- *The End of Work* by Jeremy Rifkin, Tarcher Putnam, 1995.

- *The Fragile Middle Class: Americans in Debt* by Teresa A. Sullivan, Elizabeth Warren, and Jay Lawrence Westbrook, Yale University Press, 2000.
- *The Great Risk Shift: The Assault on American Jobs, Families, Health Care, and Retirement—and How You Can Fight Back* by Jacob S. Hacker, Oxford University Press, 2006.
- *The Long Emergency: Surviving the Converging Catastrophes of the Twenty-first Century* by James Howard Kunstler, Grove Press, 2006.
- *The Overspent American* by Juliet Schor, Harper Paperbacks, 1999.
- *The Party's Over: Oil, War and the Fate of Industrial Societies* by Richard Heinberg, New Society Publishers, 2005.
- *The Post-Corporate World: Life After Capitalism* by David C. Korten, Berrett-Koehler Publishers, 2000.
- *The Two-Income Trap: Why Middle-Class Mothers and Fathers Are Going Broke* by Elizabeth Warren and Amelia Warren Tyagi, Basic Books, 2003.
- *The Working Life: The Promise and Betrayal of Modern Work* by Joanne B. Ciulla, Three Rivers Press, 2000.
- *The Working Poor: Invisible in America* by David K. Shipler, Vintage, 2004.
- *The World Is Flat: A Brief History of the Twenty-First Century* by Thomas Friedman, Farrar, Straus and Giroux, 2006.
- *Twilight in the Desert: The Coming Saudi Oil Shock and the World Economy* by Matthew R. Simmons, Wiley, 2005.
- *When Corporations Rule the World* by David C. Korten, Berrett-Koehler Publishers, 2002.
- *Unequal Protection: The Rise of Corporate Dominance and the Theft of Human Rights* by Thom Hartmann, Rodale Press, 2002.
- *War on the Middle Class: How the Government, Big Business, and Special Interest Groups Are Waging War on the American Dream and How to Fight Back* by Lou Dobbs, Viking Adult, 2006.
- *Peak Everythin: Waking Up to the Century of Declines* by Richard Heinberg, New Society Publishers.

Documentaries – DVD

- *The Corporation*, Zeitgeist Films, 2005.
- *The End of Suburbia*, The Electric Wallpaper, 2005.

Background on Middle-Class Issues Cited in This Chapter

1. Surveys summarized here include:
   - *The New American Dream Survey*. Widmeyer Research and Polling for the Center for the New American Dream, Washington, D.C. and New York, 2004.
   - *The American Dream Survey: Hope and Fear in Working America,*

Change to Win, Service Employees International Union, UNITE HERE, United Food and Commercial Workers International Union, International Brotherhood of Teamsters, Laborers' International Union of North America, United Brotherhood of Carpenters and Joiners of America and United Farm Workers of America, 2006.

▶ *Is the American Dream Still Possible?* Survey conducted by Mark Clements Research, Inc. for *Parade* magazine, New York, 2006.

▶ *The Vacation Deprivation Survey,* Synovate, Aegis Group for Expedia. London and worldwide, 2003.

▶ *One in Three: Non-elderly Americans Without Health Insurance,* Families USA, Washington, D.C., 2004.

▶ *Career Confidence Index,* Right Management Consulting, Philadelphia, 2005

▶ *Getting Paid in America,* American Payroll Association, San Antonio, TX, 2006.

▶ *Living Paycheck to Paycheck,* Harris Interactive for CareerBuilder.com, Rochester, NY, 2007.

▶ Douglas E. Schoen Survey, *What Do American Voters Really Want?* (2006), for the Aspen Institute, Queenstown, MD, 410-820-5433. www.aspeninstitute.org.

▶ "Study Says More Employers Doing Away with Pensions," reporting on newly released findings of the Department of Labor, Employee Benefit Research Institute. *Los Angeles Times.* July 11, 2007.

▶ "Land of the Overworked and Tired," by Ezra Klein. *Los Angeles Times.* July 15, 2006.

▶ *Decline in Total Wages,* Congressional Budget Office Heath and Human Services Report, April 2007. http://www.cbo.gov/.

▶ *Americans in All Income Groups Worry,* The Gallup Organization, Annual Personal Finance Poll, Washington, D.C., April, 2007.

▶ *Permanent Lower Middle Class*: Asset Limited Income Constrained. "ALIC" Project, a study by Clemson University, VOX Global Mandate and Dollar Financial Corporation, BusinessWire, July 2, 2007.

▶ *Is the American Dream Still Possible?* Survey conducted by Mark Clements Research, Inc. for Parade Magazine, New York, NY, 2006.

▶ *Anger, Anxiety, and Restoring the American Dream*, Lake Research Partners, Washington, DC, 2007.

2. A Federal Reserve Board Survey of Consumer Finances as quoted in "Our Financial Failing" by Neil Irwin, *Washington Post,* Sunday, March 5, 2006.

3. "Credit Card Woes," ABC News, November 20, 2005.

4. "A Rising Tide that Lifts Only Yachts" by Ezra Klein, *LA Times.* May 5, 2006, B12.

5. *The Brand You 50: Or Fifty Ways to Transform Yourself from an 'Employee'*

into a Brand That Shouts Distinction, Commitment, and Passion! by Tom Peters, Knoph, 1999.

6. *The Great Risk Shift: The Assault on American Jobs, Families, Health Care, and Retirement—and How You Can Fight Back* by Jacob S. Hacker. Oxford University, 2006.

7. Bureau of Census, http://www.census.gov.

8. Bureau of Labor Statistics, http://www.bls.gov/.

9. *Middle Class Living on the Edge?* by Debora Vrana. MSN *Money.*

10. *State of America's Housing,* Joint Center for Housing Studies of Harvard University, Cambridge, MA (2005).

11. *Employee Health Benefits: 2006 Annual Survey* by the Henry J. Kaiser Family Foundation, 2006.

12. *Group Benefits and Health Care* by Watson Wyatt Worldwide, Arlington, VA, 2006.

13. *Retirement Confidence Survey,* Paul Fronstin, Director, Health Research and Education Program, Employee Benefits Research Institute, Washington, D.C. (annual release).

14. *The Optimistic Progressive* by Shayne Munger, OpEdNews.com, May 27, 2006.

15. *Money, a Memoir: Women, Emotions, Cash* by Liz Perle, Picador, 2006.

16. *Four-in-Ten Workers Live Paycheck to Paycheck*, a survey by Harris Interactive for Career Builders, 2007.

17. "High Earners Still Struggle" by Stephanie Armour, *USA Today,* June 28, 2007.

When you see a window of
opportunity, leap through it.
Michael Sayer

PART II

Safeguarding Your Livelihood:
50+ Ways to Become Financially Self-Sufficient
Whether the Economy Is Up or Down

The next three chapters provide profiles of fifty-some careers we believe promise a dependable source of income as a middle-class lifeboat[sm]. The particular reasons we believe a career meets this standard is spelled out in each of the profiles. However, all are what we call "sustainable careers" in that they allow us to establish a secure source of income that isn't dependent upon having a corporate job, reliable investments, or the continuation of Social Security benefits.

As you may know, we have written about self-employment and independent careers since the 1980s. This was once a career path of choice for the few, but we firmly believe it has taken on a new level of importance today for most people. Having a reliable full- or part-time source of independent income will be a vital component for anyone wanting to ensure his or her economic security in the future.

Thus, all of the careers we profile in the upcoming three chapters can be and often are pursued independently. Most can be done either on a part-time basis or ramped up to provide a full-time income if necessary or desired. Fortunately, a 2005 Gallup survey tells us that three out of five Americans would prefer to pursue independent careers if given a choice.

If you're one of the other two of five who value the predictability of a regular paycheck, salaried positions are also available within many of these careers, although the pay and benefits for these jobs may be less than other more vulnerable corporate positions. But finding a job in one of the careers we feature, with either a large or small company, is a good way to position yourself to move more easily into working independently should you need or want to at a later time. For information on finding a job and for more salaried jobs, we recommend *Cool Careers for Dummies* by Marty Nemko, now in its third edition.

Some of the careers we've included here appear in our prior books, but this time they have been chosen with an eye to a much different future, one in which economic changes may eliminate as many as one in seven existing jobs each year. So other careers we have written about before are not included here because of economic pressures they're undergoing or pressures we anticipate they will be experiencing during the life of this book. Medical billing, claims assistance, coding, and transcription, for example, while popular careers now, are vulnerable to "othersourcing," either in terms of being automated or offshored. Almost one dollar in three in medical office overhead goes to processing medical bills, so as costs of health care continue to rise, political pressure is mounting to see the medical system streamlined to cut down on paperwork using artificial intelligence for all routine processing tasks such as these. Some of the careers appear to cater to upscale customers, but in all cases they are desired, thus making it possible to barter their services to many people.

Using the Profiles

Each profile has certain features we'd like to introduce you to. First, as we mentioned earlier in Chapter 1, the careers we feature in this section are divided into three key sectors in today's economy:

Chapter 2: 27 Basic Local Services
Chapter 3: 13 Nichable Virtual Products and Services
Chapter 4: 14 Products and Services for New Economic Realities

These three sectors don't necessarily have fixed boundaries. For example, many primarily virtual careers, such as virtual administrative or Web services, can also be provided to local clients, and many primarily locally focused careers, such as sewing and tutoring, can be expanded into online sales or services outside a local community. Some careers, though, are limited to their own sector. You can't repair a broken screen door, rid a house of ants, or sit with a pet via the Internet—at least not yet.

Also as we mentioned earlier, we used a number of specific criteria in select-ing the careers we profile here. Some relate to how well the career fits with the demands of the emerging global economy; others relate to how well it fits with the personal reality of a comfortable middle-class life. While all the careers have been screened through these criteria not all of them meet all the criteria equally. So at the beginning of each profile, you will see a set of two mini-charts that pro-vide an overview to what extent each career meets the criteria we've established:

ECONOMIC REALITY FIT

► Necessary vs. Discretionary	Necessary or No
► Replaceable with Technology	Partially or No
► Offshorable	Partially or No
► Industry Status	Established and Stable, Established and Expanding, or Emerging

PERSONAL REALITY FIT

	Minimal	Moderate	More Than Most
Start-up costs	Under $2,500	$2,501–$7,500	over $7,501
Overhead	Under 20%	20–40%	Over 40%
Potential earnings	Under $20,000	$20,000–$50,000	Over $50,001
Flexible hours	Not so flexible	Somewhat flexible	Very flexible
Computer Skills	None to few	Computer Proficient	Computer-savy
Stress	Stress unusual	Some stress	Frequent stress
Ease of bartering	Occasionally	Common	Popular

Following these two reality fits we provide an at-a-glance Durability Rating using a five-point scale that summarizes our overall projection for how strongly we believe the career will continue to reflect the above criteria in years to come. This rating is represented by a series of muscles; the most robust careers have five muscles, while those with less robust promise will have fewer than five.

Durability Rating

In addition, because all the careers we profile can be pursued as self-employment careers, to make the profiles more helpful to those wishing to choose a dependable independent career, we have also used icons to represent the best marketing methods most commonly used for each career. But just because certain icons appear for a particular career does not mean other marketing methods can't also be effective, just that these are the ones most frequently used.

Marketing Icons

We suggest you place a bookmark on this page so you can refer back to these marketing methods.

Icon 1: Networking. This icon represents face-to-face networking in organizations like the Chamber of Commerce, trade and professional associations, and business referral organizations—any organization in which you can develop relationships with potential customers, gatekeepers who are sources of client referrals, and people in your own field with whom you might collaborate. While the reason for participating in these organizations is to advance your career, the key to networking success lies in Business Network International Founder Ivan Misner's dictum, "Givers gain." Set a goal of meeting five new people at every meeting and event you attend, and think of how you might contribute to their success.

Icon 2: Listing in Directories and Referral Agencies. One of the advantages of most trade and professional associations is being listed on their Web sites, where visitors can find the help they're seeking. You also may be able to list in self-standing directories that aren't related to a particular association. Sometimes basic listings are provided at no cost, but the site will charge for more extensive listings. There are also online referral agencies for some careers. A business with a store location can get a free listing on Google Maps. When your directory listing refers those interested in your service to your Web site rather than your e-mail address, you will get leads.

Icon 3: Posting Flyers. Bulletin boards abound. Try using ones at locations where people who need what you offer frequent, such as grocery stores, churches and temples, community centers, schools, and other establishments. Flyers with telephone number tear-offs on the bottom that people can pull off and take with them will produce more phone calls.

Icon 4: Making Presentations, Speeches, and Teaching. Gatherings ranging from meetings of chambers of commerce and business or civic organizations to local library events and trade shows are opportunities to expose many potential clients to your expertise and work. Since so many people try to market this way, however, having a fresh topic or an unusual approach to your topic will help get bookings. Teaching short courses through local adult-education programs can also attract customers and provide publicity for you through the promotion the sponsor does for the event.

Icon 5: Signage on Your Vehicle and Yourself. You've no doubt contacted someone from the sign on his or her vehicle, and, of course, you've noticed how often someone will ask you what you do. Putting the name of your business, your phone number, your slogan, and your Web address on your car, van, or truck can attract business in the course of daily life, without extra effort. If appropriate to your clientele, you can also make yourself into a billboard for your business by wearing a T-shirt, sweatshirt, cap, or button that displays your logo and phone number. Be sure to make your phone number and Web address large enough for people to read.

Icon 6: Referrals from Competitors. Not only can competitors provide you with a wealth of information, but they can also be a source of business. You might be able to handle their overload or be referred for specialty work they do not do. Be ready to return the favor and refer business to others when you get overloaded or when a potential customer needs something special that you don't provide. Developing relationships with colleagues can enable you to jointly bid projects you or they would not undertake alone.

Icon 7: Referrals from Past Customers. Getting referrals from satisfied customers is golden. Often they don't come automatically, however. So be sure to let your customers know that you appreciate referrals. You also can ask for testimonial letters from satisfied clients for use on your Web site and in portfolios. Thanking referral sources encourages future referrals. You can express your appreciation with a handwritten thank-you note, or you may show it in tangible form with a gift of food, a product you sell, gift certificates, or by offering a discount on future work for them.

Icon 8: Advertising on Local Search Engines. One out of every four online searches begins with seeking a local product or service. Advertising on a local search site is cost-effective because you're not paying to reach the world. Yahoo! (http://local.yahoo.com), Google (http://local.google.com), and Amazon (www.a9.com) offer the most popular local search services. Another popular choice is to use Internet yellow page directories, such as InfoSpace, Anywho, Smartpages, Switchboard, SuperPages, and Yellowpages. You can learn more about local search at www.localsearchguide.org.

 Icon 9: Social Networking on the Web. While increasingly social networking on sites like MySpace are being used for business and career purposes, we're primarily referring to sites that have a career and business focus, such as:

- www.ecademy.com
- www.fastcompany.com/cof (*Fast Company* magazine's Company of Friends)
- www.linkedin.com (popular with people in technical fields)
- www.meetup.com (enables face-to-face meetings in one's area)
- www.orkut.com (Google's networking site)
- www.ryze.com
- www.spoke.com
- www.tribe.net

Another form of social networking is answering questions on sites such as Yahoo Answers (http://answers.yahoo.com) and Amazon's Askville (http://askville.amazon.com/askville/CIndex .do?id=5#answers). You can position yourself to have people contact you and thereby develop new business. You can also set up your own social networking site using Ning (www.ning.com) either free if you accept ads or by paying $20 a month.

Participating on these sites is somewhat like cold calling. Developing relationships that lead to business will take time to warm up, and there will be more misses than hits. The people who do best utilize online networking as a way to identify contacts whom they follow up with later using conventional marketing methods, such as meeting for lunch or breakfast.

 Icon 10: Keeping in Contact with Customers. Using e-mail or snail mail to notify past or potential clients of sales, promotions, and newsletters keeps you top-of-mind. To get people to open your

e-mail, the subject line must be intriguing, such as asking a question or giving some attention-grabbing news. Edit what you send to be entirely relevant to your readers, and send yourself a copy. To learn more about using e-mail effectively, you can subscribe to a free newsletter at www.dmnews.com/newsletters.

Icon 11: Tools for the Web and Other Electronic Media. These tools include having a Web site, blog, podcast, e-newsletter, video newsletter, or a Wiki. To get started you can use free or low-cost tools like Microsoft Office Live Basics (http://office .microsoft.com/en-us/officelive/default.aspx) and Constant Contact (www.constantcontact.com). To develop a Web site, blog, or podcast, you can use Apple Computer's iWeb program (www.apple.com/ilife). Google offers free Webmaster tools (www.google.com/services) and blogging software (www.blogger.com). Your Web site also can earn revenue with Google's AdSense (www.google.com/adsense). A clever business name and logo in your signature on MySpace and Spacebook can attract people as well. You can create low-cost TV ads on sites like www.spotrunner.com and www.spotzer.com. Using such tools effectively enables you to reach out to others and allow others to find you.

Icon 12: Writing Articles for print and electronic publications. Depending on what career you are pursuing, this might involve contributing content to a Web site, e-newsletter, local newspaper, or trade/professional publication. In addition to a credit line with your Web site address, ask that a short description of what you do and a photo be included at the close of the article.

A Note About the Usefulness of Associations

A key industry, professional, or trade association can provide a wealth of information on trends, statistical information, future of the industry, and current issues facing the industry. Sometimes this information is readily available at no charge on the association Web site; however, many associations limit key information to members.

Adapting the Profiles to Your Goals and Your Life

Basically, the process of deciding upon a way to support yourself in this new economy is a matter of asking, "how can I help?" How can I enjoyably apply my interests, talents, skills, knowledge, and experience, or those I wish to acquire, to fulfill the needs of people or companies in my community, be they real or virtual?

Ecopsychologist Linda Buzzell has identified seventeen essential sectors of community life that need to be sustained during any major economy change. As you review the career profiles in the next three chapters, think of how you might adapt what you could do to one or more of these sectors:

17 Essential Sectors of Community Life

1. A healthy environment or habitat in which to live and work
2. Healthy, readily available food
3. Ample, clean water
4. Clean air
5. Safe, affordable, nontoxic, energy-efficient shelter
6. Comfortable, affordable, nontoxic, and nonpolluting textiles and clothing
7. Robust commerce and trade that provides good wages, generates profit, and provides for needed products and services while not degrading the natural resources upon which we depend
8. Affordable, energy-efficient travel and transport
9. Security that assures peace and order within local, national, and global communities, including viable plans for addressing natural and manmade emergencies
10. Safe scientific and technological developments that support rather than degrade future resources and communities
11. Affordable and sustainable sources of energy
12. Functional social, political, legal, family, and community support systems
13. Affordable health care for all
14. Dependent care for children, the elderly, and companion animals
15. Education that enables all people to achieve their potential and contribute their talents and abilities in ways that support them, their loved ones, and their communities
16. Arts, entertainment, and communication that enable us to enliven, inspire, and sustain one another
17. Mutually respectful and diverse ways of caring for the human spirit, psyche, and culture

Of course, having a reliable, independent income is not the only aspect of our middle-class lifestyle we want to preserve. We also want to enjoy the life we're securing, so if, like so many others, your goal involves not having to work so hard, perhaps even being able to work less and live with less hassle and stress, then you will want to select a career that enables you to do that in your own way. Part III of this book features nine lifestyle choices many people are making with this goal in mind, and Part IV features nine cashless ways to live a less money-directed life. In keeping with these choices, one of the criteria we used in selecting the careers profiled in the next three chapters is their ability to be easily traded or bartered.

As you seek to put together a career choice that matches your desired lifestyle choices, we suggest doing an informal assessment of both your own needs and the needs of others in the local or virtual community you would like to serve. Here are the kinds of questions you can ask yourself as you go about defining how you can work less, live more simply, and enjoy life more.

A Personal and Community Needs Assessment

1. How many hours do you work now?
2. How many hours would you work if you had a choice?
3. What would you do with your time if you didn't need to earn so much money?
4. On what are you spending the money you currently earn?
5. Which of these expenses would you no longer need if you worked for yourself from home and set your own schedule?
6. What things could and would you do yourself and not have to spend money on if you had the time?
7. How many of the things that you are currently spending your income on could you get by bartering with people you know or might meet?
8. Which of them *do* you purchase locally?
9. Which ones *could* you purchase locally?
10. Which ones could be provided locally if you could identify or recruit the talents of someone local to provide them?
11. What products or services could you provide that people in your community now do without or buy elsewhere?
12. Who specifically in your community has these needs?
13. If you were adequately supported within your local community, what expertise or contributions could you share with others outside your community, online, or via telecommunications?

A locally owned business and the community that it operates in are inextricably linked. The health of one is deeply connected to the health of the other.

Larry Hammel and Gun Denhart,
Growing Local Value

CHAPTER TWO

27 Basic Local Services

Bill Collecting/Collection Services

Easy credit. Few offers are as seductive in our credit- and debt-driven economy. The siren song of "easy credit" or even "free credit" is shouted, whispered, and sung to nearly everyone in our society—from low-income people, college students, single mothers, and immigrants to CEOs, celebrities, and trust-fund babies. Television advertising. Radio advertising. Print. Internet.

Buy now. Pay later. Credit is a wonderful thing. The ability to make purchases on credit allows all of us to function in our modern world. Whether car payments, home payments, furniture payments, or credit card payments, we all rely on the ability to defer payments. Who uses cash anymore except for the simplest purchases? Most people manage their purchases and payments so that they can meet their credit payment obligations. However, there is a small but significant number of people who do not pay their bills. That number increases when the economy is more difficult and the "small print" that accompanies "easy credit" is smaller and packs more of a delayed wallop.

These factors can create a real opportunity for anyone who is tenacious, interested in what makes people tick, sympathetic (to a certain degree), and organized enough to figure out a way to get people to pay down their debts. If your image of a bill collector is some kind of Simon Legree or Dickensonian character who takes pleasure at the inability of people to manage their debts and seems to find joy in denying people home and hearth, then it is time for an image upgrade.

A good bill collector is part stern parent, part counselor, part teacher, and part coach. In short, bill collectors fill a necessary role in our economy, one that often creates more conflict and stress than it should.

The real secret to successful bill collecting is that most people *want* to pay their bills. The vast majority of people who find themselves hearing from bill collectors are people for whom circumstances have overwhelmed their ability to manage their finances. Health crises. Lay-offs. Divorce. Everyone confronts these types of circumstances at one point or another. For those who have relied too much on credit and have left themselves with very little backup, these life challenges present frightening consequences.

This is why bill collecting is the perfect career for someone with the right temperament. There will always be those who are behind on their bills. Appealing to their desire to pay rather than their fear of being behind the eight ball is the key to becoming a successful bill collector.

While the vast majority of bill collecting falls to fairly large agencies, there is a good argument to be made that this is a wonderful time for independents and small agencies to "get in the game."

Large companies are, almost by definition, impersonal. All big companies confront this problem. However, in the case of bill collecting, it poses a particular challenge because of the companies' emphasis on results. This leads them to follow a "bullying" strategy, which, while effective in many cases, actually runs counter to the best way to try to collect bills.

A smart, "problem-solving" approach that remains consistent with the Fair Credit Reporting Act will result in a greater bill-paying response. This kind of approach is almost impossible for large collection agencies to utilize. It relies on the "personal touch"—which you, as an independent, can provide. Perhaps more to the point, larger agencies tend to ignore wonderful collection opportunities because it is not "cost-effective" for them to function otherwise.

For example, studies indicate that up to 20 percent of people who fall behind on their payments will find a way to meet their obligation after a single notice. Because agencies work on a commission basis, usually a percentage of the overdue bill, they will send out that first letter and then, if the bill is below a certain amount, will make no further attempts to collect. Their overhead simply doesn't allow for the tenacious pursuit of smaller bills. However, with your lower overhead, you will be able to collect on all accounts—satisfying your clients and earning enough to keep you comfortably middle class.

While you can seek clients in any business that provides credit to its customers, from home-repair companies to cable television operators to retail stores, you will likely narrow your clients to one or two related fields. You might specialize in consumer debtors or commercial debtors. Whether those clients will be health care providers, rent or mortgage providers, retail stores, or service providers, you will find that your understanding of the client's services and the kinds of people who utilize those services will aid you in being more successful.

As a bill collector, you should have excellent communication skills and have a functional fluency in at least one other language (or have an employee who has language skills). You should have the ability to express empathy with debtors and clients alike. Remember, most people do not want to be debt-ridden. They are most likely in the situation they are in as a result of difficult circumstances, *not* because they are scofflaws. If you are able to negotiate repayment plans that are manageable for the debtor, you will be very successful.

Some states require you to have a license to operate as a bill collector; others require posting a bond; some require both. All bill collectors are obligated to have knowledge of the various federal and state laws that pertain to debt and debt collection, such as:

- The Fair Credit Reporting Act, which deals with handling credit information
- The Fair Debt Collection Practices Act, which prohibits abusive collection practices like lying, making dire threats, and calling late at night
- Postal Regulations that bar identifying an addressee as delinquent in paying a debt on the outside of an envelope or postcard

You should also understand bookkeeping, accounts payable, and accounts receivable. Various software programs are available to help you perform all relevant tasks associated with bill collecting. If you are able to advise debtors about how to budget their resources, you will not only find yourself collecting on debt, but you will also be helping debtors remain debt free in the future.

Other ways to generate income as a bill collector are:

- Collecting rents for absentee owners of commercial and residential buildings.
- Purchasing debt for pennies on the dollar, which you can acquire from companies like Charge-Off Clearinghouse (www.chargeoffclearinghouse .com) or directly from creditors. You keep all that you collect. Another aspect of debt purchasing is managing portfolios of debt, which involves buying, evaluating, locating debtors preparatory to collecting, or selling debt portfolios. This field is growing, according to John Pratt (www.locateservicesllc.com), particularly because of the increasing debts people are incurring from rising medical costs.

Always remember that no one *wants* to be in debt. If you can view debtors as individuals who have found themselves in unwanted circumstances, you will find your job more pleasant and more successful. That said, it will still require persistence to be successful. Follow-up is key. As we mentioned above, only about 20 percent of debtors pay their bills after the initial contact. Tenacity, coupled with empathy, is a winning combination for bill collectors.

Related Careers

Credit Counseling/Guidance. There is a dearth of wise counsel for people to rely on to bring down their debt and to avoid it to begin with. With the knowledge you gain from bill collecting, you could provide this service—both to creditors (as a service to their customers) or directly to debtors.

Judicial Recovery. This is a term used to describe a niche in bill collection work involving collection on court judgments. It involves doing the paperwork and legwork to seize bank accounts, garnish wages, and place liens on or seize personal property.

Skip Tracing. Skip tracing is, simply, finding the debtor. There are a number of people who do their best to hide from creditors. Finding them becomes the task of the skip tracer. Skip tracing is necessary for collection work, but it's also needed by attorneys who specialize in collections law, judgment recovery specialists, debt buyers, and others. Because identity thieves use many of the same tools as legitimate skip tracers, legal restrictions on what skip tracers must do are increasing, so while remaining necessary, the work is becoming more challenging. However, this also means that skip tracers who produce results may be increasingly in demand as others will choose to not risk the legal consequences of missteps in gathering information. A number of books have been written on how to trace people, including the following:

- *Find Anyone Fast,* Richard S. Johnson, Debra Johnson Knox, Military Information Enterprises, 2001.
- *Public Records Online,* Michael L. Sankey, Peter J. Weber, Facts on Demand Press, 2006.
- *You Can Find Anybody!* Joseph Culligan, Jodere Group, 2000.

BILL COLLECTING AT A GLANCE

ECONOMIC REALITY FIT

Necessary vs. Discretionary	Necessary
Replaceable with technology	Partial
Offshorable	No
Industry Status	Established and Stable

PERSONAL REALITY FIT

► Start-up costs	Minimal [Depends on software selected and state requirements for bonding]
► Overhead	Moderate
► Potential earnings	More Than Most
► Flexible hours	Moderate
► Overall stress	More Than Most
► Ease of bartering	More Than Most

Durability Rating

Likely Transferable Skills, Background, Careers
- ► Sales, credit, or collection work
- ► Credit counseling

What to Charge
Commissions range from 25 percent on newer accounts to as much as 50 percent on accounts that are older—at least a year—or accounts that must go to court.

Best Ways to Market Bill Collecting

- ► Contact local businesses that are advertising for bookkeepers or credit managers in the classifieds section of local newspapers or on the Web.
- ► Directly solicit potential clients by telephone or in person. To see doctors, find out which day of the week they see pharmaceutical reps and ask to be placed on the schedule.

Tips for Getting Started
- ► If you have no background in doing collections work, a good way to gain the experience you need is to take a job for several months with a collection agency or, if possible, as a credit manager.
- ► Familiarize yourself with all federal and state requirements. This will include the Fair Credit Reporting Act, the Fair Debt Collection Practices Act, postal regulations, and the laws and requirements in the

state where you will be working. If you are collecting on medical bills, you need to have an understanding of health insurance policies and billing practices as well as HIPAA, which is the Health Insurance Portability and Accountability Act of 1996.

► Develop a contract to use with your clients. You need a signed contract to collect debts.

LEARN MORE

Associations

► American Collectors Association: (952) 926-6547, www.acainternational.org

► International Association of Commercial Collectors, Inc. (IACC): (952) 925-0760, www.commercialcollector.com

Books

► *Debt Purchasing and Investors Guide to Buying Debt,* John Pratt, Rick Shell Morris Publishing, 2005.

► *How to Do Financial Asset Investigations: A Practical Guide for Private Investigators, Collections Personnel, and Asset Recovery Specialists,* Ronald L. Mendell, Charles C. Thomas Publisher Ltd, 2006.

► *How To Get Anything on Anybody Book 3,* Lee Lapin, Intelligence Here 2003.

► *How to Start a Home-Based Collection Agency,* Robert H. Bills, BookSurge Publishing, 2003.

► *Starting a Collection Agency,* Michelle A. Dunn, Never Dunn Publishing LLC, 2006. To order copies, call (603) 357-2922.

Franchise

► National One. This is a collection agency that also offers franchises: (212) 679-2007, www.national1credit.com

Magazines

► *Collector,* ACA International: (952) 926–6547, www.acainternational.org

► *Collection Advisor:* (888) 610-1144, www.collectionadvisor.com

Software

► Debtmaster: (509) 674-7000, www.comtronic.com

► Collect!: (250) 391-0466, www.collect.org

► EZCollector: (888) 439-7638 or (561) 997-9003, www.collectionagencysoftware.com.

Web Sites

- ▶ www.credit-and-collections.com – Credit & Collections offers a free e-book on starting a collections agency.
- ▶ www.insidearm.com – A news site for the collection industry
- ▶ www.startingacollectionagency.com

Cleaning Services

Everything gets dirty. Therefore, everything needs to be cleaned. This obvious (and trivial) truth has combined with a number of social and cultural trends to bring cleaning services into the forefront of opportunities for anyone willing to roll up his (or her!) sleeves and get some dirt under those fingernails.

Our society has long held that "cleanliness is next to godliness." We hold cleanliness to the highest of standards, whether in our homes, our businesses, or our meeting places. We frown on those who do not maintain a neat and tidy home, tend not to do business in places that are not clean, and avoid frequenting places that are dirty.

As it happens, our high standards are not solely the result of our aesthetic preferences. Uncleanliness and sickness seem to go hand in hand. Dust, mold, and other domestic air pollutants have been associated with respiratory illnesses in homes and offices. An unclean workspace is often an unsafe and unhealthy workspace. In short, "clean" often translates into healthier, happier, and safer work and living environments. Legions of homemakers have traditionally devoted hours upon hours to tasks from vacuuming to polishing to scrubbing bathroom floors. But things have changed. While economic demands have conspired with social and demographic trends to make it more difficult for people (traditionally, women) to devote all those hours to cleaning, our lifestyle choices have made many less willing to devote their ever-diminishing "personal time" to tasks like cleaning.

A growing number of people simply prefer not to do the cleaning themselves. Add to that number the growing number of single parents, two-income households, and elderly people living alone—people who do not have the time or the physical capability to do their own cleaning—and it becomes clear that fewer and fewer people are keeping their houses clean. While some may long for the "good old days" when the demands of our economy weren't so great on families, and homemakers could stay in the home to take care of these chores, you can applaud these changes because they represent a tremendous opportunity for you.

Cleaning services run the gamut from home cleaning services that do regular and "routine" cleaning to those that step in for those more demanding jobs—from carpet shampooing to commercial cleaning and even crime-scene clean-up.

As suggested above, cleaning services are needed for more than just homes. Offices, clinics, banks, churches and synagogues, large commercial spaces such as schools and supermarkets, along with every manner of retail space all require regular cleaning. By providing prompt, efficient, and reliable cleaning services, you can easily create a business that will maintain a comfortable middle class lifestyle.

Cleaning services often work flexible and "off" hours. Banks, offices, and nursery or private schools generally prefer that cleaning crews come in during evening or weekend hours. Other nonemergency cleaning jobs can be scheduled throughout the daytime hours.

Cleaning services lend themselves to specialization. Some services will focus on working in homes, providing cleaning services such as dusting and waxing. Others will concentrate on office buildings. Still others will focus on medical clinics. Each type of service has its particular set of needs and demands. Some specializations worth considering, either because of their size or their growth potential, include the following:

- ▶ **Construction Cleanup.** Whenever there's a construction job of any type, cleanup is necessary before occupancy or marketing to lessees. Another positive for this specialty is you can readily identify your potential clients. Don Aslett's book *Construction Cleanup* (Marsh Creek Press, 1997) can help you get started.
- ▶ **Disaster Cleanup.** When people hear "disaster," they usually think hurricane, tornado, or earthquake. However, many smaller, more localized "disasters" occur. Fire. Flood. Smoke. Damage from these and other sources can prove to be traumatic for businesses and homeowners. Being able to provide fast, efficient, and complete cleanup helps minimize the trauma and begins the transition to people feeling comfortable and safe in their homes and businesses again.
- ▶ **Green Cleaning.** Whether because more people are being identified with having allergies and sensitivities to man-made products or because a growing number of people are environmentally conscious, cleaning services that use green cleaning methods—biodegradable, nontoxic products and equipment and supplies such as HEPA vacuum cleaners and microfiber cloths for cleaning surfaces without chemical cleaners—are growing.
- ▶ **Pressure-Cleaning/Water-Blasting.** For the tough jobs and for large areas such as construction sites, industrial-sized equipment mounted on a truck cleans aluminum siding; old brick, cement, and marble on

buildings being restored; farm, industrial, and construction equipment; garbage trucks, airplanes, and boats; parking lots; restaurant freezers and vent hoods; awnings and signs; and air-conditioning units, phone booths, shopping carts, and hotel dumpsters.

▶ **Rubbish Removal.** From rotted fences to soiled carpeting to complete garage cleanups, rubbish removal services attack the cleanup jobs that are too large for the home or business owner. From general rubbish removal, to clearing out the homes of deceased family members, to stripping down offices, factories, houses, or apartments, the rubbish removal service performs a necessary—and much-in-demand—service. Also see Hauling Services on page 86.

▶ **Window Washing.** Window washers have profited from most cleaning services avoiding windows. Window washing can be done part-time or expanded into a good-sized business. The International Window Cleaning Association [(703) 971-7771, www.iwca.org] site makes it obvious that window cleaning is an industry. See the *American Window Cleaner* magazine for more information on this specialization: (510) 233-4011, www.awcmag.com.

▶ **Other specialized cleaning services** include parking lot sweeping, organization and storage solutions, drape and blind cleaning services, furniture refinishing, painting, and "odd jobs."

Of course, there are still more specific areas of specialization—air-duct cleaning, chimney cleaning, crime-scene cleanup, disaster cleanup, power washing exteriors and sidewalks, pool cleaning, stone and masonry cleaning, and window cleaning, just to name a few. In the future, environmentally friendly mobile car wash machines, such as the ones made by the Korean company Seven CarWash, that use steam and as little as a glass of water, will continue to grow in popularity with the public.

Cleaning services have the added benefit of not requiring extensive communication skills. Basic language skills are required so that special instructions can be correctly understood, but an advanced education is not required. However, as more and more clients expect cleaning materials to be "green" or environmentally friendly, you will have to be able to understand the correct and safe uses of various cleaning materials and solvents. Certain cleaning environments, such as public bathrooms and food preparation areas, must be cleaned according to Department of Health guidelines and requirements.

Once you are established for providing cleaning services, you will find that home and business owners will ask you for assistance when they have other jobs on their premises. From snow removal and painting to gardening and floor refinishing, you will be in a position to recommend a network of other professionals, thereby expanding your network of references. Or you may want to enlarge your own business to provide these services to your clients.

CLEANING SERVICES AT A GLANCE

ECONOMIC REALITY FIT

▶ Necessary vs. Discretionary	Both
▶ Replaceable with technology	Limited
▶ Offshorable	No
▶ Industry Status	Established and Enduring

PERSONAL REALITY FIT

▶ Start-up costs	$2,500–$7,500 (depends on materials)
▶ Overhead	Under 20%
▶ Potential earnings	Moderate
▶ Flexible hours	More Than Most
▶ Overall stress	Minimal
▶ Ease of bartering	More Than Most

Durability Rating

Likely Transferable Skills, Background, Careers

For most cleaning services, transferable skills would extend to other "maintenance" type jobs, such as painting, floor refinishing, waxing, simple carpentry, etc. However, if the cleaning service is highly specialized, such as a service that decontaminates "clean rooms" in high-tech plants or uses particular machinery, the skills necessary in those instances might be transferable from other positions, such as equipment maintenance or calibration.

What to Charge

Fees are always higher in cities such as New York City, Chicago, Los Angeles, and Miami, and less in more rural and Midwestern towns and cities. House-cleaning services can be priced by the hour or the job. Hourly rates for house cleaning are generally between $12 and $35. If you are including special jobs, such as silver polishing, washing windows, laundry, or ironing, you should ask more than the basic cleaning charge. Because "green" cleaning services require more skill and use more expensive cleaning materials, pricing should be at the high end of the range.

Cleaning services that charge by the job should assume a four-hour fee minimum. Determine your fee based on a reasonable estimate of how long the job will require—again, with a four-hour fee minimum. If you find it difficult to fairly estimate the time a particular job will require, you can price a job by the size of the facility you will be cleaning. When first establishing your fees, you should check Web sites that post rates and phone other local services to make sure you are not pricing yourself out of a job—or asking too little for your services.

Best Ways to Market Cleaning Services

- Take the time to "canvass" local neighborhoods and local businesses.
- For cleaning services that need to be performed periodically, such as air duct cleaning and chimney sweeping, contact past clients to remind them the time for service is at hand.
- For customers who can pay premium prices, do extras things. For example, in the bedroom, turn down beds and place chocolates on pillows. Satisfy your customer's sense of smell by spraying linens with lavender mist, leaving small bowls of potpourri, and burning essential oils while cleaning. However, because the sense of smell can evoke both positive and negative reactions, it's a good idea to check with customers about this.
- When the work to be done is outdoors and—without trespassing— you can see the work that needs to be done, quote a price on a flyer and leave it behind. Businesses that can use this include window washing, lawn care, gardening and landscaping services, and pooper scooper services.

Tips for Getting Started

- One of the best "first steps" for starting a cleaning service is to take advantage of free training classes given at places such as Home Depot, Lowe's, and janitorial supply stores. These classes will not only familiarize you with cleaning products used by commercial cleaners, but you will also begin to learn about the local market for your services.
- Consider specializing the kind of service you provide, particularly in a new or growing area where you can be the first or only service.
- Take a "step-by-step" approach to building your business. Don't make a significant investment in supplies and equipment. You may discover

after a short time that floor waxing is not for you, but window washing is a breeze.
- ► The flexible scheduling allows you to "ease into" your new business. Evening and weekend cleaning schedules will allow you to make a smooth transition into this new career.
- ► Invest in a pager or cell phone so you don't miss any job opportunities while you're working.

Learn More

Associations

- ► Building Service Contractors Association International is a trade association for commercial cleaning firms, providing certification in a number of specialties: (800) 368-3414 or (703) 359-7090, www.bscai.org.

Books

- ► *The Cleaning Encyclopedia,* Don Aslett, Dell, 1999.
- ► *How to Start a Home-Based Housecleaning Business,* Melinda Morse and Laura Jorstad, Globe Pequot Press, 2005.
- ► *Sales and Marketing for Janitorial Service Businesses,* Forrest L. Farmer, Clean-Pro Industries Inc., 2000.
- ► *Start and Run a Home Cleaning Business,* Susan Bewsey, Self-Counsel Press, 2003.

Magazine

- ► *Cleaner Times* (800) 443-3433 or (501) 280-9111, www.adpub.com/ctimes.

Training and Other Resources

- ► Allergy Clean Environments is a source of allergy-proofing products and also operates Allergy, Air & More retail stores in Texas: www .allergyclean.com.
- ► Cleaning Management Institute is a source of professional training and education, including archived newsletters on its Web site: (518) 783-1281, www.cminstitute.net.
- ► Contact Cleaning Consultants, Inc. publishes dozens of books, videos, and software and provides consulting services: (206) 682-9748, www.cleaningconsultants.com.
- ► Cleaning expert Don Aslett has authored a number of books about the cleaning business. He sells cleaning supplies, such as microfiber cloths, from his Web site, www.donaslett.com.

Community and Corporate Meeting and Event Planning

Despite the convenience of instant messaging, conference calls, Internet chats, and online auctions, people still want to meet one another in the "real." If that meeting garners a sense of community or a sense of participation, in a somewhat old-fashioned sense of the word, more's the better.

This human need means a continuing demand for the skills of event and meeting planners in many kinds of meetings and events. An event or meeting planner organizes business and social events for corporations, communities, and private parties. Corporations hire event planners to put on sales conferences, product announcements, seminars and training workshops, and even employee parties. Hotels and casinos hire meeting planners to plan meetings, weddings (the subject of a separate profile), and other large events. Event and meeting planners can also work independently with a range of clients to plan corporate events from safety fairs to health club events to annual meetings. Sample tasks include booking travel and lodging, establishing menus, and preparing agendas.

Downtown music festivals, art fairs, and open-air produce markets are some examples of burgeoning community-oriented events. They take a lot of coordinating and may not pay as well as the corporate track, but for the right person, this can be a rewarding and creative career.

A good event planner, whether working in a high-powered corporate environment, a fun resort context, or an earthy community market setting, must have excellent communication skills, be very professional, and know where to find high-quality goods and reliable services at the best prices. This career is for on-the-go and people-oriented people only! This work requires a lot of energy and will demand time on the phone, the Internet, and in person negotiating the intricacies of coordinating many people and the personalities, needs, and desires those people bring to the table.

Whether it's catering services or clowns, musicians or multimedia equipment, the event planner is the supreme source of all things "meeting," mandating a high level of organization and professionalism. Clients may be spending tens of thousands of dollars on an event and will expect timeliness, efficiency, and beauty in the face of an onslaught of demands. Letting small details slip can spell disaster. There are myriad software packages on the market designed to facilitate meeting planning. Some even have 3-D room mapping so your client can see what the banquet hall will look like with round tables instead of rectangular ones. This means that computer skills sufficient to use specialized software will make your work considerably easier.

If the event organizing you do is more small-town, community oriented, the same demands will be present. While you might be able to wear your jeans to organize a farmers' market rather than the suit demanded by convention planning, you will still have to coordinate, potentially, hundreds of vendors, dealing with everything from where to park to what they are able to sell. Street fairs and markets probably will involve working with the local chamber of commerce, city council, and other community organizations. This may mean a bit of networking and politicking to make the fair or market a real community effort.

Depending upon the state of the economy, the demand for large on- or off-site meetings fluctuates. A meeting coordinator or event planner may need to diversify, but because of the diversity of this field, the variety of industries and venues that need people with requisite skills offer many possibilities. Providing a specialized service or market segment is another avenue to enter this field. Examples of specializations include:

- Audio/visual services for trade shows and conventions
- Planning destination group travel excursions, such as a white water rafting trip
- Organizing contests, sweepstakes, and games

Related Career

Business Network Organizer. If you have an outgoing personality and would like to make money while you're making contacts and helping other people make contacts, organizing and running a business referral organization is a means for you to do all this. Business referral organizations, networks, or leads clubs are more focused on helping their members develop their businesses and professional practices than traditional service and fraternal organizations like Rotary and the Lions. The sole purpose of a business referral organization is to enable members to give and get referrals. Only one person per business type or profession is eligible to join a group. This is unlike groups spawned by social networking sites like www.meetup.com. You can start your own group from scratch, affiliate with an organization, or acquire a franchise. One franchise organization, Business Network International (www.bni.com), founded in 1985, has over 4,600 chapters in thirty-seven countries. For more information on networking, check out Ivan R. Misner's book *Truth or Delusion? Busting Networking's Biggest Myths*.

MEETING AND EVENT PLANNING AT A GLANCE

ECONOMIC REALITY FIT

▶ Necessary vs. Discretionary	Discretionary
▶ Replaceable with technology	No

▸ Offshorable   No
▸ Industry Status   Established and Enduring

PERSONAL REALITY FIT

▸ Start-up costs   Moderate
▸ Overhead   Moderate
▸ Potential earnings   Moderate
▸ Flexible hours   Moderate
▸ Overall stress   Moderate
▸ Ease of bartering   Moderate

Durability Rating

Likely Transferable Skills, Background, Careers

Public relations, communications, and marketing backgrounds translate nicely into this field. Further, many administrative assistants and executive assistants have some level of experience with this type of planning, in addition to experience with organizing schedules and travel planning.

What to Charge

Fees for event planning vary greatly depending on the nature of the event, the going rate for the area, the number of participants, and special problems like short notice. Fees may be a percentage of the event cost (10 to 20 percent), hourly rates (generally $40 to $75), or flat fees. Private clients expect flat fees. Some planners charge an initial consultation fee that may range from $50 to $150 because some clients go no further than acquiring the planner's ideas. If the planner is providing other services, a package price may be negotiated.

Best Ways to Market Meeting and Event Planning

▸ Contact corporations and associations directly. In the case of corporations, you need to determine how meetings are handled in each corporation to determine who you contact. In many companies, events departments book about half of all corporate meetings. The other 50 percent are the responsibility of the departments that "own" the meetings. In this case, a departmental manager or director is apt to have responsibility. In other companies, executive assistants handle meetings and events and may be very pleased to hand off some or all of these types of tasks to an efficient contractor!

► Join your city's convention and visitor bureau. Membership often entitles participants to inside information about trade shows and a free listing of your company's name in any materials they send out to prospective attendees.

Tips for Getting Started

► If you don't have experience but think your personality and dreams are a good fit with this career, you might work with a hotel or existing event planning company to get some experience. You can also volunteer at a nonprofit organization supporting a cause you believe in (they always need more help!) and gain some experience that way.

► Take on one or more smaller meetings or events without a fee to get referral sources and testimonial letters as well as experience.

► To start a farmers' market or to offer a street fair, a sponsor is required. This is usually a city government or a nonprofit organization. Most markets need a professional market manager to handle the extensive coordination that is required.

► Prepare a brochure to introduce yourself, and make sure you photograph every event you plan for your portfolio. Clients like to see what you can do.

► Join a professional association of meeting planners. You'll get training, get information, and make contacts that may lead to business.

LEARN MORE

Associations

► Meeting Professionals International (MPI) is the largest organization of meeting planners, offering local chapters and certification: (972) 702-3000, www.mpiweb.org

► International Association of Exhibitions and Events represents the interests of trade show and exposition managers. It has a job board on its Web site. (972) 458-8002, www.iaem.org

► The Professional Convention Management Association publishes *Convene* magazine, which conducts and publishes an annual salary survey: (205) 823-7262, www.pcma.org

Books

► *The Business of Event Planning,* Judy Allen, John Wiley, 2002.

▶ *How to Start a Home-Based Event Planning Business,* Jill Moran, Globe Pequot, 2004.
▶ *Start Your Own Event Planning Business,* Krista Turner, Entrepreneur Press, 2004.

Web Sites

▶ www.conworld.net – A portal site for the convention industry
▶ www.corbinball.com/bookmarks – Corbin Ball Associates provides a site with three thousand links
▶ www.expoworld.net – Search tools for reaching virtually all facets of the industry; an associated site is www.conventionbureaus.com

Community Management

While community management of homeowner associations has been around for some time and even has its own trade associations, there are growing demands for management of other aspects of community life. Three of the most promising new career opportunities lie in new types of housing arrangements for seniors, the growing amount of housing that is association governed, and new community efforts arising from the relocalization movement.

Retirement Communities

Popping up across the country, the latest retirement communities are virtual. A virtual community addresses the desire and need of seniors to stay at home, as well as the basic needs that can be furnished through group buying and service links. Group buying and service arrangements frequently come with discounts for community members.

The virtual retirement community works like this: As the operator, you recruit members who pay an annual fee, generally under a thousand dollars. Members come from neighborhoods or developments in close proximity to one another. For an annual fee you offer access to a buying group, perhaps priority service at a health facility, and a list of handypersons and tradespeople who have been checked out and may offer a special rate for community members.

Beacon Hill Village in Boston (www.beaconhillvillage.org) is a prototype for this type of organization. It "contracts for household services (repair, cleaning, errands), transportation (to friends, airports, doctors), concierge services, meals and grocery shopping, and home health care."

If the linkages you offer prove beneficial to the members, you can expect an annual income while maintaining a system of services that takes minimal effort.

Further value is added for members if you provide social organizing, whether theater, movie, or museum trips, card games, or other events.

Still another recent concept is a Naturally Occurring Retirement Community, or NORC. This is a term used to describe a community that is aging in place. It may be a large neighborhood or suburban community that was built to be home to families with children. It would have schools as well as the usual supermarket, other retail outlets, police, fire, and other services. Now, the original owners are aging in place, not wanting to move on. The government has taken notice of these social configurations and is providing grants to nonprofit groups to organize and provide necessary services. There is considerable opportunity in this niche if you have an interest in people fifty-five and older, patience, a positive outlook on life, and a creative streak.

Yet another way of earning in the world of the retired or retiring is in organizing communities inside new retirement villages. This job is part recreation or social director and part salesperson. This position is temporary but not necessarily short-term, as you may start as the first homes in a new development are being occupied and not finish until months after the last home is taken over by its new owner.

Association Management

Since the year 2000, nearly four out of five of all new housing starts have been in association-governed communities. These include homeowner associations, condominiums, cooperatives, and other planned communities. Each ownership method comes with a different method of governance, for example, cooperative, condominium, and homeowner associations. For the community management professional this means varying approaches, too. Regardless of the community governing body or managing agent, the manager's job is the same: servicing the community's needs, which may be a combination of serving as government, community, and business. In fact, a California appellate court described an association as being "a quasi-government entity paralleling in almost every case the powers, duties, and responsibilities of a municipal government."

While homeowner associations are known for their internal conflict, a survey by the respected Zogby organization recently found better than three in four residents are positive about the value and support their community managers provide. A newsletter recently reported that many existing managers are nearing retirement while the number of entities needing management talent is growing.

Relocalization Movement

Another rising opportunity for managers comes in the relocalization movement. Communities developing around this concept are developing self-sufficiency in all areas of community life, including food, power, clothing, and more. All this requires organization and ongoing management. You can learn more about relocalization in Chapter 11 "Relocalization Communities." Another growing phenomenon is discussed in Part III, where you'll learn 9 Cashless Ways to Extend Your Income, Earn Less, and Live More. Some of the new entities, like time banks, utilize full-time coordinators to manage them.

A community manager will need to bring a basket-load of skills to work. Paramount among these will be people skills, as there will be an interesting array of personalities to serve. As the manager you will be called upon to employ others to provide direct services, but you will be held responsible for the actions of those employees.

Leadership is another critical skill. The manager leads or guides the community members in developing and/or directing services. The menu of services will cover all aspects of community life from garbage collection to recreation. The community manager draws on his or her own experience and expertise, as well as that of community members and outside experts.

Over the long term, community management will require knowledge of all kinds of local resources and the building of relationships with community dwellers to keep in touch with the changing interests and needs of community members.

In community management you can be employee, employer, or independent contractor. Existing communities that continue to employ a management firm may be looking for employees, while communities without management firms may seek a manager. Your approach can be shaped by where you want to live or what kind of work you want to do. This is a vast industry that has continuing growth potential as community developers set their sights on new areas.

There is the question of managing a community in which you live. Some within the field advise against this. This requires a strong constitution in a new community as the kinks get worked out in new construction, and community members look for all the promised amenities.

COMMUNITY MANAGEMENT AT A GLANCE

ECONOMIC REALITY FIT

► Necessary vs. Discretionary	Both
► Replaceable with technology	In Part
► Offshorable	No
► Industry Status	Established and Expanding

PERSONAL REALITY FIT

- ► Start-up costs — Minimal
- ► Overhead — Minimal
- ► Potential earnings — Moderate
- ► Flexible hours — Moderate
- ► Overall stress — Moderate
- ► Ease of bartering — Minimal
- ► Computer skills — More Than Most

Durability Rating

Likely Transferable Skills, Background, Careers

Degrees in business administration or public administration are helpful, but there is no specific educational background required to become a community manager. However, many community associations are requiring credentialing of manager and management companies by the Community Associations Institute (www.caionline.org/about/designations.cfm). For retirement communities, teachers who bring skills at organizing groups can make the transition, and social workers and other social service providers will find their professional skills directly transferable.

What to Charge

The average annual compensation for community managers in 2007 was $61,132, according to the Community Association Manager Compensation Salary Survey from the Foundation for Community Association Research. If you are organizing a virtual community with basic services, a $500 initial membership fee would be appropriate.

Best Ways to Market Community Management

- ► To create a virtual retirement community, anticipate canvassing door-to-door.
- ► Post your résumé, and search job listings online. Check out the Job Bank of the Community Association Institute (www.caionline.org) and the American Society of Public Administration (www.publicservicecareers.org).

Tips for Getting Started

▶ Post on the bulletin boards of supermarkets, diners, and bookstores in the area you are focused on.
▶ To gain experience with retirement communities, consider working for one. Research these companies: ATRIA (www.atriaseniorliving .com), Robson (www.robson.com), Pringle (www.pringle.com), and others.

LEARN MORE

Associations

▶ Community Association Institute provides a Career Center, certification, and has local chapters: 703-548-8600, www.caionline .org.
▶ American Association of Retirement Communities: www.the-aarc.org
▶ American Seniors Housing Association: www.seniorhousing.org

Books

▶ *Becoming a Manager*, Linda A. Hill, Harvard Business School Press, 2003.
▶ *On-Site Managers*, Thomas Burgess and Pam Washburn, Community Associations Institute, 2004.
▶ *The New Farmers' Market*, Vance Corum, Marcie Rosenzweig, Eric Gibson, New World Publishing, 2005.
▶ *The Profession of Local Government Management*, Roy E. Green, Praeger Publishers, 1989.
▶ *Senior Living Communities,* Benjamin W. Pearce, The Johns Hopkins University Press, 1998.

Web Sites

▶ www.virtual-retirement.com – National index of retirement communities, senior housing, assisted-living retirement communities, continuing care homes, active-living retirement communities, and nursing homes located in the United States and Canada
▶ www.seculife.com – Seculife International Ltd., a provider of virtual retirement community services in Israel, has developed technology called Carephone, which is part of a social/medical alarm system 011-972-3-515-4420

Errand Services

Don't want to do it. Don't have time to do it. Couldn't figure out *how* to do it even if we wanted to.

We have met the client, and it is us! We are the clients who will make your errand services successful. If you want to truly appreciate the potential in errand services, you need only to appreciate the three statements above. Broadening your potential client base even further, there are people, such as the elderly or the homebound, who require the assistance of errand services simply because they can't do certain things.

We live in a society in which there are nearly 29 million two-career couples struggling to cope with the day-to-day necessities of life. In the past twenty-five years, we have added the equivalent of a month of time per year with our work and commuting schedules. Add to that the fact that many of the things we once turned to for "relaxation and leisure"—from weekend games of tennis to exercise regimens—have become necessities that must fit into our busy schedules.

We rush everyplace. We are constantly minutes behind schedule. We've got five minutes to finish packing to catch the cab to catch a flight to make a meeting . . .

When, in all this rush, do we find time to shop? To go to the DMV? To buy a new suit, pick up the wedding gift, pick up a prescription, order flowers for our anniversary? And heaven help us if we have to get a car to the mechanic!

Enter errand services, sometimes called "personal concierge services." If you are willing and able to pick up groceries, stand in lines, drive to the airport to pick up relatives, order flowers for wives or cigars for husbands, make restaurant reservations, pick up shoes at the shoe repair service—in short, do anything and everything that will simplify our lives—then you can be successful in errand services.

In addition to these basic errands, there are other varieties of errand services you can explore. In the past, only the well-to-do considered the services of a "personal shopper"—a person who was familiar with their particulars (waist size, height, etc.) and their preferences (colors, hemline, choice in accessories, etc.) and who frequented boutiques and department stores to shop for clothes, belts, scarves, blouses—whatever the person might need. But now more and more people need the services of a personal shopper. And not only to save them time. Many personal shoppers go past understanding a client's preferences to recommending what kinds of clothes or accessories are most appropriate in a variety of settings.

In the past, a "gofer" was a regular presence in large corporations. Usually a secretary or other employee low on the totem pole, this person would be sent out to fetch coffee, sandwiches, flowers—whatever was needed. However, now more small- and medium-sized companies have the need for someone to fill that "gofer" role. Without the dispensable employees of a large corporation, they have begun to turn to errand services to do everything from coffee and sandwich deliveries to taking materials to be printed, to picking up dry cleaning, etc.

Something we expect to emerge as energy prices go up and more people live in small towns and rural areas distant from where they can shop to get the best possible prices on things they buy, is paying someone to do buying for the group. This form of aggregate buying can be a steady customer for an errand service.

As a culture, perhaps nothing defines our lack of patience so much as our distaste for standing in lines. This simple task—standing in line and dealing with the bureaucratic annoyances that it generally demands—opens a whole field for errand services. From delivering paperwork to the DMV to dealing with Social Security offices or governmental agencies, errand services do the footwork—or rather, the standing work—that people have neither the time nor inclination to deal with.

Ultimately, errand services work "at the fringes"—doing nearly anything small or large that people can't or won't do themselves and are willing to pay someone else to do. As long as it doesn't run afoul of the law and you're willing to do it, you will find that errand services can afford you a very comfortable, and sometimes entertaining, career and insight into our culture.

To succeed, you will need patience and a high level of interpersonal skills. You should be intelligent and discerning as well as have good communication skills. You must be able to take instructions clearly and well. (No one wants the wrong sandwich or an error on his vanity license plate!) You will need stamina—those same activities that tire others out will form the bulk of your day. You will have to rely on solid organizational skills to manage errands for a number of clients in an efficient manner. Of course, you will need reliable transportation. And finally, although it will appear that you are that "low man on the totem pole," you must be assertive. If you expect to get service quickly for your clients, you will have to have the strong, polite manner that will get others to give you what you need.

ERRAND SERVICES AT A GLANCE

ECONOMIC REALITY FIT

▸ **Necessary vs. Discretionary**   Discretionary
▸ **Replaceable with technology**   Partial

▶ Offshorable	No
▶ Industry Status	Established and Enduring

PERSONAL REALITY FIT

▶ Start-up costs	Minimal
▶ Overhead	Minimal
▶ Potential earnings	Moderate
▶ Flexible hours	More Than Most
▶ Overall stress	More Than Most
▶ Industry Status	Established and Expanding

Durability Rating

Likely Transferable Skills, Background, Careers

In addition to communication and people skills, organizational skills are key to success in errand services.

What to Charge

Charging for errand services is as variable as the errands that you will find yourself engaging in. You will have to decide whether to charge a fixed rate or charge by the hour. Hourly fees range from $25 to $50 per hour. As with every other service career, you will find that rates vary with location and the nature of the task. Rush or emergency requests generally receive a 50 to 100 percent increase over the normal rates and require a one- or two-hour minimum fee that covers drive time to and from the client's location. Transporting people, such as on airport drop-offs and delivery, is usually a flat fee depending on distance, but if you transport people for any service, you will need an endorsement or rider on your vehicle insurance to cover this. If you will be going into people's homes or offices, where valuables are kept, it is wise to obtain business liability insurance.

When planning your fees, account for variability in gas prices, as well as wear and tear on your vehicle. Consider offering discounts to encourage repeat and volume business. This is also called *package pricing*.

Best Ways to Market Errand Services

- Approach small businesses, such as accountants; advertising and public relations agencies; attorneys; auto dealers; doctors; escrow companies; realtors; hospitals; and nursing homes. These businesses frequently need errand services. Fresh donuts, bagels, or cookies will help you to introduce yourself in a pleasing way.
- Distribute brochures that outline your services at charity events and local religious institutions.
- Place classified advertising in local and community newspapers.
- Bid for work on www.domystuff.com. You will pay the site from 7 to 10 percent of your fee.

Tips for Getting Started

- Pick a catchy name for your service. Calling it a concierge service may help get upscale customers.
- Check out what business licenses you will need.
- Make sure your car is in excellent working order.
- Make sure you have any liability insurance coverage that you might need.
- Check out getting bonded to instill confidence in prospective clients.
- Get up-to-date maps of the area where you will be working, or better yet, a portable GPS unit, and still better, an in-car navigation system with a service that overlays current traffic conditions onto your car's navigation system maps.
- Have a cell phone and beeper.

Related Career

Hotel, Corporate, or Lobby Concierge. To gain experience as a concierge, you may consider working for a hotel, a corporation serving its employees, or a real estate management company serving its tenants. You can find out more about this in the following books:

- *The Concierge Manual*, Third Edition, Katharine C. Giovanni, NewRoad Publishing, 2007
- *Ultimate Service*, Holly Stiel and Delta Collins, Prentice Hall College Division, 1994.

Learn More

Association

- International Concierge and Errand Association lists members in a directory; you'll see many examples of catchy names: (800) 934-ICEA or (215) 743-5618, www.iceaweb.org

Books

- *FabJob Guide to Become a Personal Shopper*, Laura Harrison McBride, Peter J. Gallanis, Tag Goulet, 2005. See also www.fabjob.com
- *Get Paid to Shop*, Emily S. Limpkin, Forté Publishing, 1999.
- *How to Start and Operate an Errand Service*, Rob Spina, Legacy Marketing, 2001.

Family Child Care

The ultimate service oriented stay-at-home occupation for a mother of young children may well be family child care operator. This parent has an opportunity to stay home with her own child or children while providing a much-needed service to other parents. Beyond this approach to day care is, of course, the in-home provider who serves only the children of others.

This huge and necessary industry is a result of the changes in the economy as well as the social changes that have significantly altered the need for out-of-home child care. With more women working while still in their childbearing years, and with the increasing distances among family members, the need for someone to "mind" the kids expands. To fill this gap takes energy and a desire to be with children.

Big commercial child-care businesses, such as those offered to employees by corporations, are highly regulated, carry significant insurance loads, and can only make it if they serve large numbers of children. Home-based child-care businesses provide a more intimate setting, often with three to six children, where parents and operators can arrange schedules that meet their needs rather than corporate needs. Home-based day care costs less than commercial child care, meaning that financially pinched parents have less of their paychecks going to pay for child care.

The home-based child-care provider is someone who has developed a set of skills based on the desire to provide a safe and nurturing environment. A child-care provider can follow several paths of specialization, which helps to determine the skill set he or she develops. Providers can define their services for specific age groups, particularly for infants, toddlers, or preschoolers. Each requires knowledge of CPR and first aid, but nutrition, play, naps, learning needs, and abilities are all different. Home-based providers may choose to work with special-needs children or any other group they have identified as needing care in the community they serve.

Artisans of all types can develop niches in this industry. Parents, particularly those of toddlers, may be enticed by a home-based day care operated by a singer or dancer to assure themselves that music or movement will be an important part of their child's days. An artist can offer a very special day care experience centered on paint or other media.

Opening a child-care business will require a license in most states. The licensing requirements vary from jurisdiction to jurisdiction. This will require some research on your part. Determinants may include the number of children you will care for, their ages, the number of adults in the house, and so forth. You will most likely be required to carry insurance. This is an excellent idea—accidents do happen.

No doubt there will be requirements related to safety and cleanliness. In some communities you may find yourself dealing with multiple government agencies. Licensing may also open doors for your business to secure state grants and/or food subsidies from the U.S. Department of Agriculture.

There are a number of businesses that furnish an umbrella operation for small, home-based day care providers. Organizations like Monday Morning America (www.mondayam.com) bring parents and caregivers together, having promised parents that they have checked out and inspected the provider and home. Other sources of information and support are listed below.

CHILD CARE PROVIDER AT A GLANCE
ECONOMIC REALITY FIT

► Necessary vs. Discretionary	Both
► Replaceable with technology	No
► Offshorable	No
► Industry Status	Established and Stable

PERSONAL REALITY FIT

► Start-up costs	Moderate (depends on education background and experience)
► Overhead	Moderate
► Potential earnings	Minimal
► Flexible hours	More Than Most
► Overall stress	More Than Most
► Ease of bartering	More Than Most

Durability Rating

Likely Transferable Skills, Background, Careers

Being a day care provider requires a desire to be with children. Personal traits such as being kind, patient, nurturing, loving, and understanding are a requirement in this business. The ability to multitask is critical when you are with a group of small children. Experience as a teacher, nurse, psychologist, or social worker will help, but most important will be the knowledge of child development that comes with the training for these professions.

What to Charge

Day care fees vary widely with a number of factors. If you are accredited, you may charge more for the assurance parents gain from that. If you specialize in infant care or in the care of special-needs children, you will charge more as well. The best way to set fees is inquire of child care providers in your area, both home-based and those in commercial settings. You may be able to supplement your fees from clients if you are licensed with food subsidies from the U.S. Department of Agriculture that pay for breakfasts, lunches, and snacks.

Best Ways to Market Family Child Care

- ▶ Advertise in local parenting newsletters.
- ▶ Develop relationships with pediatricians, local elementary schools, and other child care providers to gain a referrer base.
- ▶ Reach out to local businesses, particularly the larger ones, who might refer new hires your way. There is also an opportunity to contract with local businesses.
- ▶ Specialize to serve children with learning disabilities, handicaps, or chronic illnesses. Consider catering to parents who want their children to experience a specific curriculum, such as preschool, infant, or religious, or who need after-school care or care at nonstandard times (45 percent of single moms have shift-work jobs).

Tips for Getting Started
- ▶ Speak with other in-home providers.
- ▶ Call your local social services or health department for licensing information.
- ▶ Check with your local zoning board for limitations on home-based businesses or child-care businesses specifically, although some states have laws that override local zoning when child care is offered in the home.
- ▶ Walk through your home with a critical eye; is it safe, and would you want to leave your child here?

▸ Check with your insurer about any special coverage you may need to operate a day care from your home.

Related Career

Shadow Nurse. Children with asthma and sensitivities to common items like peanuts, which can be fatal, can never be fully protected in classrooms by busy, overworked teachers alone. Even something made with peanut oil can produce a fatal anaphylactic reaction. With approximately half of nurses dropping out within five years of graduation, this is an opportunity to utilize their training in a relatively low-stress pursuit.

Learn More

Associations

▸ Canadian Child Care Federation is a bilingual organization with chapters throughout Canada: (800) 858-1412 or (613) 729-5289, www.cccf-fcsge.ca

▸ National Association of Child Care Resource & Referral Agencies is a national network that works with the Department of Defense to provide affordable child care for military personnel: (703) 341-4100, www.naccrra.net

▸ National Association for the Education of Young Children takes public policy positions, has international affiliations, and provides accreditation that enables higher reimbursement from the states: (800) 424-2460 or (202) 232-8777, www.naeyc.org

▸ National Association for Family Child Care is an organization specifically for family child care providers and advocates that also offers accreditation: (801) 269-9338, www.nafcc.org

▸ National Association for Sick Child Daycare conducts research and provides information on the care of sick children: (205) 324-8447, www.nascd.com

Books

▸ *How to Start a Home-Based Day-Care Business*, Shari Steelsmith, Globe Pequot, 2006.

▸ *Family Child Care Marketing Guide,* Tom Copeland, Redleaf Press, 1999.

▸ *Family Child Care Contracts and Policies,* Tom Copeland, Redleaf Press, 2006.

▸ *Opening & Operating a Successful Child Care Center*, Dorothy June Sciarra, Anne Dorsey, Thomson Delmar Learning, 2001.

▸ *The Business of Child Care*, Gail H. Jack, Thomson Delmar Learning, 2004.

Training

You can learn about approved training programs from the licensing agency in your state. From this site funded by the U.S. Department of Health and Human Service's Maternal and Child Health Bureau, you will find links to the licensing agencies in every state: http://nrc.uchsc.edu/STATES/states.htm

Web Sites

- ▶ www.childcareaware.org/en/dailyparent – E-newsletter published by the National Association of Child Care Resource & Referral Agencies
- ▶ www.childcareaware.org. The National Resource Center site includes links to information on licensing regulations in your state. It is funded by the Health Resources and Services Administration (*http://hrsa.gov*).
- ▶ www.resourcesforchildcare.org – A nonprofit organization affiliated with Redleaf National Institute and Redleaf Press, publisher of curriculum, management, and business resources for early-childhood professionals. (651) 641-0305

Handyman/Handywoman

A good handyman (or woman) is hard to find. Considering the increasing amount of remodeling, repairing, and refurbishing of homes, as well as existing old possessions, the need for reliable, knowledgeable, trustworthy, all-around repair people is on the rise.

Some jobs are just too small for a professional contractor, and the homeowner finds himself in a bind to get something repaired, installed, or finished at an affordable price. Sometimes a homeowner wants something done that is not to common design specifications, a specialty tile for example. Contractors are often not interested in training their workers or spending the time to do something that's different. Seniors, choosing to live independently, often need help with tasks they might have handled themselves when younger. So if you're a problem-solver who enjoys fixing things, have the ability to learn quickly, and are willing to do a variety of jobs from minor plumbing repairs to installing a light fixture, you can find yourself very busy.

In our community, a retired law enforcement officer found that quality services offered in a timely manner were scarce. This discovery led him to provide handyman services in the neighborhood. He works four hours a day and is able to stay busy just based on word-of-mouth referrals. He enjoys the challenge of solving unusual problems that have been on the "honey-do" list for too long.

Not just a career for men, one Manhattan mother established a handy-person business that has resulted in the moniker "Blue Collar Martha Stewart." She even designed a lighter-weight tool kit for women, which has been marketed nationally. It might be a bit outside the expectations of the homeowner to have a woman show up with the coveralls and toolbox, but when the skills are there, the stereotypes can change. Highly visible in signaling women's role in home improvement is Be Jane, an online community for female do-it-yourselfers that has become popular with the media. Their Web site (www.bejane.com) has forums, articles, and tricks of the trade.

When you're first starting out you need to be willing to take on all kinds of tasks, like hanging wallpaper, painting, installing flooring, electrical wiring, fixing decking, repairing roofs, cleaning gutters, and replacing tiles. At the same time, you need to be honest about what you can and cannot do. If you haven't done a repair before, you inform the customer, and if the customer is willing, you can offer him or her a price break to cover your learning curve, being ready to pass on work you can't do.

You always want to develop satisfied customers, because future work comes from word-of-mouth referrals and repeat business. Work from owners of fixer-uppers can keep you busy for months or even years. Someone who is reliable about showing up, is pleasant, and shows empathy with a customer's problem contrasts sharply with home improvement contractors, who are the second-largest source of consumer complaints. Being trustworthy, reliable, and having good people skills are just about as important as the ability to turn a wrench.

Once you develop a customer base, you might specialize in interior or exterior work. If you have some experience with electrical jobs and the project is too small for a contractor, you might move outlets or install chandeliers. Small tile change-outs and wood floor repairs are special services that larger installers don't like to bother with. Some people love the meditative task of painting or the challenge of hanging a wallpaper border with invisible seams and perfectly matched patterns. It can be a good idea to consider your interests and then make yourself into a kind of expert for that area. You can also focus on serving individual homeowners, busy professionals, or single older women.

Your tool kit needs to include everything you need to do any service you offer. Also carry basic supplies, like Spackle, sandpaper, and screws, to save time on trips to the hardware store. If the job is a bigger one, you can have the customer purchase supplies like paint or piping in advance.

A handyperson can offer services for simple odd jobs like hanging pictures or painting doors. Slightly heavier work like assembling furniture and adjusting derailed closet doors, might require a bit more strength and know-how. The heaviest work, for example, constructing small walls or installing a new tub and shower faucet, might require a bit more training and a bigger toolbox.

Licensing requirements vary from state to state. Some require that you register your business and have licenses for each type of service you offer if the job exceeds a certain dollar amount. In California, for example, any job from landscaping to tiling that exceeds five hundred dollars requires licensing. Some states require a license based on the kind of work you want to offer. For example, in Massachusetts you can't run wiring or install plugs without a license, but you can work on small appliances that will be plugged into an electrical outlet. Some states require written quotes for jobs over a specified dollar amount. Regardless of licensing, professional liability insurance is a good idea to protect you and your business.

HANDYMAN/HANDYWOMAN AT A GLANCE

ECONOMIC REALITY FIT

► Necessary vs. Discretionary	Both
► Replaceable with technology	No
► Offshorable	No
► Industry Status	Established and Expanding

PERSONAL REALITY FIT

► Start-up costs	Moderate
► Overhead	Moderate
► Potential earnings	Moderate
► Flexible hours	Moderate
► Overall stress	Moderate
► Ease of bartering	More Than Most

Durability Rating

Likely Transferable Skills, Background, Careers

People with experience in construction fields will find an easy transition to this career, but anyone who is skillful at doing a number of different things, is a good problem solver, can figure out where to find answers to mysterious home-related questions, and is reliable will find being a handyperson doable.

What to Charge

Hourly rates vary from $20 in some areas to $80 in large urban centers. Rates also vary by experience and how much the individual is in demand. It's common to charge a minimum fee, say, for four hours. Emergency and after-hours rates may be up to double the regular rate. A rule of thumb is to charge two-thirds the rate of contractors in your area. However, if you must get a license, your rate needs to cover the cost of maintaining a license.

Best Ways to Market Handyman/Handywoman Services

- ▶ Directly solicit customers:
  - » in condominium complexes where owners lack tools even if they know how to make repairs and
  - » in areas where people have second homes and are mostly nonresident but need to have their property looked after and repaired.
- ▶ Leave fliers with real estate offices.
- ▶ Teach short courses on fixing household items through local adult education programs at home improvement stores.

Tips for Getting Started
- ▶ Check state laws and local regulations to determine if you will need a contractor's license and what you can do without one.
- ▶ Tell people you know what you are doing—getting your first customers is key to getting underway. One handyman, active in a local church, worked for half the people in his choir.

Learn More

Books
- ▶ *Handyman In-Your-Pocket*, Richard Allen Young, Thomas J. Glover, Sequoia Publishing Inc, 2001.
- ▶ *Handyman's Handbook*, David Koenigsberg, McGraw-Hill Professional, 2003.
- ▶ *Hassle-Free Handyman*, Brian Kaskavalciyan, Thomas Fall, White Tiger Press, 2004. Written from the point of view of a consumer, this book can help develop your approach to structuring your services.
- ▶ *Markup & Profit: A Contractor's Guide*, Michael C. Stone, Craftsman Book Company, 1999.

Franchises

Entrepreneur magazine identifies a dozen handyman franchises in its Franchise Zone at www.entrepreneur.com/franchises, such as:

- ▸ House Doctors Handyman Service: (800) 319-3359 or (513) 831-0100, www.housedoctors.com
- ▸ Handyman Connection: (800) 884-2639, www.handymanconnection.com

Training

Home improvement retailers feature classes on how to do everything from building planter boxes to building a new deck. You can take advantage of these free or low-cost, half-day classes to develop new skills and augment existing ones. The same retailers offer a vast library of DIY books that show step-by-step processes for even complicated tasks.

Web Sites

- ▸ www.handyman-business.com – Useful links and a starter kit (with software) to help you get your business started.
- ▸ www.handymanplans.com – Find and order project plans from a variety of sources. Plans are mailed, not downloaded.
- ▸ www.naturalhandyman.com – A portal for the handyman world. Listing on this site is free.

Hauling Services

At one time or another, most of us contend with getting rid of big, bulky, heavy things or loads of things. Old appliances, garden trimmings, and debris from the last remodeling project need to be hauled off; new sofas, firewood, and new fruit trees need to be delivered, unloaded, and even put in place. The call for someone who offers a light to medium hauling service is growing commensurate with the busy and varied lifestyles of people.

Most homeowners and even renters don't have the time or the resources (meaning a truck) for transporting things from home and bringing new things in. A manager who works hard all day at her desk may not want to schlep garden debris to the green waste site or even to the curb. She'd be glad to pay someone to come and do this job on an afternoon.

Sometimes the delivery schedule of a department store doesn't coincide with the homeowner's need for a new refrigerator or television set. Somebody who is reliable with a truck and an appliance dolly (plus maybe a helper or two) is welcome, and the money spent to hire this person will be seen as several dollars well spent. A business with a need to move file boxes from the office to storage or from storage to the shredding facility would find a dependable hauling service a real boon.

Likely customers for a hauling service include the elderly, busy professionals, single women, men without trucks and strong (willing) friends to do heavy lifting, and businesses with limited custodial personnel. An interior designer with a client who has furniture that needs reupholstering might contract with you to transport dining chairs or an armoire to the refurbishing facility and then to the client's home after the job is done.

Additional services can supplement income for a hauling service, or they may grow into becoming a specialization if the demand is high enough. Examples include the following:

- ▶ Contractual Work. Possibilities for regular work with a monthly check include making deliveries for a store, picking up inventory or supplies for a company, or delivering small loads for a trucking company. The monthly check can cover up to a set number of loads, with per-load pricing for any additional loads.
- ▶ Firewood Delivery. The need for firewood delivery services is growing. High fuel costs have resulted in big sales of wood stoves. Many people are also interested in the luxurious coziness of a fire in the fireplace. Firewood demand is not limited by region, season, or economics. People from all walks are using it. You should investigate sources and lock in some places to get wood regularly. Mills, the U.S. Forest Service, and construction companies are some possibilities. Wood pellets are also a good choice for hauling because they are most economically purchased by the ton and store charges for delivery may provide a price umbrella for you.
- ▶ Junk Dealing. One person's junk is another's treasure. Capitalizing on this old adage using online auctions, listing services, or selling items at flea markets can really supplement the hourly rate you make hauling the stuff away. People throw away old oil paintings, small appliances that still work but feature dated colors, old light fixtures, and heaps of serviceable clothes. Lots of furniture, appliances, and books are left behind when people move. A flea market shopper might see the funky coffee table, the one your suburban client couldn't stand, as a hip addition to her urban loft, and you might make seventy-five or one hundred dollars on the first guy's trash! You might have to take a truckload to get one sellable item, but keep your eyes peeled and you could have a second, profitable business on your hands.

A strong back and a reliable, clean-looking vehicle are the first requirements. As the business grows, you might hire a crew. They need to be neatly dressed and polite. You might want to have separate trucks for hauling antiques and garbage, or at least make sure you wash out the bed of the truck before you pick up the eight-thousand-dollar dining room table.

As with any service business, you need to be reliable. The number you give people needs to be one you answer when they call. If you say you'll do a job at a certain time, then you need to be as good as your word. A twenty-dollar job that gets delayed, without a courtesy call, for a five-hundred-dollar job can cost you more in lost work through negative advertising than the time it takes to either do the job or make the call.

You should like to be outdoors and have a strong back for this job. A squeamish personality is not a good match. But the flexibility and fresh air should make up for any unsavory loads you might encounter.

HAULING AT A GLANCE

ECONOMIC REALITY FIT

▸	Necessary vs. Discretionary	Both
▸	Replaceable with technology	No
▸	Offshorable	No
▸	Industry Status	Established and Enduring

PERSONAL REALITY FIT

▸	Start-up costs	More Than Most
▸	Overhead	Moderate
▸	Potential earnings	Moderate
▸	Flexible hours	Moderate
▸	Overall stress	Moderate
▸	Ease of bartering	More Than Most

Durability Rating

Likely Transferable Skills, Background, Careers

It's not true that anyone can haul. In addition to having the physical strength and stamina, a positive customer service attitude is vital.

What to Charge

Pricing is usually based on volume (figured on how much of a truckload), time involved loading, number of workers, type of vehicle, and disposal fees. Some haulers price by weight; others price by the item (like sofas, freezers, ranges, and so forth). Some place surcharges on heavier or difficult items. Prices vary geographically with the equivalent of a pickup load, which would occupy only a quarter of a larger truck, ranging from $50 to $150.

Best Ways to Market Hauling Services

> ► Directly solicit to professional organizers, estate sale organizers, and others who help people dispose of things.

Tips for Getting Started

> ► You will need a truck or a large van (preferably with a lift gate), large furniture blankets, rope or bungee cords, and a variety of dollies. If you end up with more than one vehicle for your hauling service, you may be required to store them in a commercial lot; further, zoning laws need to be checked, particularly if you plan to offer additional items like roll-off dumpsters.
>
> ► If you plan to use a truck you already own, convert the liability insurance on your truck to commercial insurance. Otherwise, the insurance company is able to deny coverage for a claim arising from hauling something for pay.
>
> ► Pick a clever name. We once met a man in a workshop who called his hauling business Grunt 'N Dump. He told us he never lacked for calls to haul something.
>
> ► A primary disposal site will be imperative. Depending on what you are hauling (for example, mattresses and construction materials are often deposited in different places than green waste), you may need to make arrangements with the disposal site. One scrap metal place might take appliances, while another dump will not accept them. A little research will help you make efficient work of whatever it is you are hauling.
>
> ► Find out about special permits to transport empty tanks or certain types of debris so you can build those costs into what you charge. You need to be clear about hazardous materials definitions, as most dumps do not accept paint, batteries, and other such materials. If you are caught dumping them, you can incur fines and restrictions on your

business. Specially licensed firms can dispose of hazardous materials if you find them in the load you are hauling.

▶ Check with your county offices to know the requirements for your area.

▶ Some states require special licenses to haul things belonging to other people. Most states have Web sites where this type of information can be found. If you are hauling across state lines, you might have to comply with interstate commerce regulations.

LEARN MORE

Book

▶ *How to Earn $15 to $50 an Hour and More with a Pickup Truck or Van,* Don Lilly, Darian Books, 1999.

Franchise

▶ 1-800-Got-Junk: (877) 408-5865, www.1800gotjunk.com

Home Theater System Installation and Support

Would you like to cash in on an expanding market? Home theater is an ever-improving technology providing a growing market for those who offer high-quality installation service. Offering high-quality service is important and will generate business because many installers are not experts and leave customers with picture and/or sound qualities that do not meet customer expectations. Luai Khouja, who has been installing audio-video since 1989 told us, "One-third of our customers come from negative experiences with others who are either ill-trained or ill-managed."

High Definition Television (HDTV), coupled with the other elements of a home theater environment (speakers, tuner, DVD player, etc.), requires more skill to install than might first be evident. Speakers must be properly placed to get the full effect of surround sound. The TV itself requires placement in the right light, and all components must be tuned to each other and the source, whether cable, satellite, or another provider.

What a purchaser sees in the showroom is usually a TV in a darkened space. When the customer gets it home, the basic calibration is universal, but the customer's room is not. This is where the professional enters. With fees ranging from two hundred to more than one thousand dollars, the expert calibrates the TV, connects and locates components, and provides suggestions for adjustments in furniture positioning and room lighting.

Are you a TV sports fanatic? Have you seen your sport in high definition? The crowded airwaves of today will be more orderly as the digital signal becomes the standard. HDTV is the true driver of the installation industry, set to take off over the next decade.

In the not-too-distant future it will not only be home theater components requiring expert installation, but also the interconnection of the rest of the environment, from kitchen to bedroom to burglar alarm to lawn sprinkler, that will all be inhabited by computer chips. The installer with knowledge and a past relationship will be the one called upon when the time comes to upgrade.

High-end home theater installation and consultation is a business that does not suffer from down turns in the economy. The wealthy continue to seek out the latest in technologies for their homes. Media rooms, in professional settings or large homes, belong to the type of client who will return for service and new technology.

Working at the high end requires a fastidious person who leaves no trace of having been at the customer's home or place of business. A desire for precision in the work must accompany this neatness, as well as an internalization of customer service principles. Luai Khouja (www.takeonetheatersystems.com), who consults with start-ups in addition to installing home theaters on the West Side of Los Angeles, says that while there are opportunities to specialize, "you're not sacrificing by knowing all facets. The core is the media room, but there's also lighting, security, and networking that factor in—in other words, system integration."

With experience and references, an expert home theater installer can land projects that bring in over seventy-five thousand dollars and additional referrals from friends and associates who want the same.

An expert installer can also serve as a personal shopper or shopping consultant if you have the presentation and interpersonal skills to work in this manner. You will have to put your customers' styles and desires ahead of your own, applying your expertise to assist them in their selections.

HOME THEATER INSTALLATION AT A GLANCE

ECONOMIC REALITY FIT

- ▶ Necessary vs. Discretionary — Discretionary
- ▶ Replaceable with technology — No
- ▶ Offshorable — No
- ▶ Industry Status — Established and Expanding

PERSONAL REALITY FIT

- Start-up costs   Minimal (Tools and tranporation),
                        Moderate (Expert tools including meters and
                        analyzers)
- Overhead   Minimal
- Potential earnings   More Than Most
- Flexible hours   More Than Most
- Overall stress   Moderate
- Ease of bartering   Minimal (At the high end), Moderate (Middle
                        income customers)

Durability Rating

Likely Transferable Skills, Background, Careers

Experience in one of the relevant trades—electricity, networking, or acoustics—accompanied by an understanding of not only how sound works but also how to run cables and wires inside walls and under floors—provides a good background for home theater and smart home installation. Computer consultants with a passion for entertainment technology can transition into home theater.

What to Charge

Work is priced by the hour or job. Hourly rates vary by locale, expertise, and demand, typically $50 to $100. Consultants at the very high end who do design work get $300 an hour and subcontract for others to do the actual installation. Routine calibration may be priced by the job, from $100 to $150, but some installers get $400. If more than calibration is needed, further work may be billed at an hourly rate.

Best Ways to Market Home Theater Installation

- Go door-to-door among the retailers in the area you want to serve so that they can see who you are. This is crucial as retailers are apt to be your best source of referrals. High-end audiophile studios will bring you customers who buy the top-of-the-line, expect top-of-the-line service, and will pay top-of-the-line prices.

- ▶ Seek work through image and sound transmission companies (cable, satellite, etc).
- ▶ Develop mutual referral relationships with interior designers and decorators, builders, and architects.
- ▶ Develop sports bars into regular customers.

Tips for Getting Started

- ▶ Getting enough hands-on experience sufficient to do quality work requires up to a year of experience and classroom instruction. Working for an installation company is the best place to get this. Trade shows are a good place to take workshops you can use for certification. Many manufacturers offer free classes to educate you on their product lines.
- ▶ To be in business for yourself, take classes in business management.
- ▶ Getting your initial customers is key to building a clientele, because most of your business is going to come from word-of-mouth referrals.

LEARN MORE

Books

- ▶ *Audio/Video Cable Installer's Pocket Guide*, Stephen H. Lampen, McGraw-Hill Professional, 2002.
- ▶ *Digital Video and HDTV Algorithms and Interfaces*, Charles Poynton, Morgan Kaufmann, 2003.
- ▶ *Home Theater for Dummies*, Danny Briere, Pat Hurley, For Dummies, 2003.
- ▶ *Latest Technology in Automated Home Control: System Design Manual*, Robert N. Bucceri, Silent Servant Inc., 2003.
- ▶ *Newnes Guide to Digital TV*, Richard Brice, Newnes, 2002.
- ▶ *Servicing Digital HDTV Systems*, Bob Goodman, Prompt, 2001.

Magazines

Several dozen magazines serve this vibrant sector of the economy. Among them are:

- ▶ *CE Pro* – Provides forums and downloadable installer guides: www.cepro.com
- ▶ *Electronic House* – Provides directory of installers: www.electronichouse.com
- ▶ *HDTV Magazine* – Offers an active forum: www.hdtvmagazine.com
- ▶ *Home Theater* – Provides archives of past e-newsletters: www.hometheatermag.com

- *Sound & Vision* – Offers forums and free e-newsletter: www
  .soundandvisionmag.com

Training and Certification

- The Consumer Electronic Association's Web site provides links to
  industry certification programs and offers study guides for preparing
  for certification exams: www.ce.org
- CEDIA, a trade association of companies that specialize in designing
  and installing electronic systems for the home, offers workshops and
  certification through its CEDIA University. (800) 669-5329 or (317)
  328-4336, www.cedia.net
- National Coalition for Electronic Education's Web site provides links
  to companies in the electronics industry interested or involved in
  education: www.ncee-edu.org/Links.html
- Planet Installation is a trade association of companies that provides six
  levels of certification ranging from apprentice to master installer:
  www.planetinstallation.com

Web Sites

- www.cnet.com – news, news, and more news
- www.highdefforum.com – attracts many to its communities

Interior Decorating

Many people are opting for renovating and remodeling rather than moving up
the housing ladder, which, coupled with the universal desire to live and work in a
beautiful place and the need for more space for our stuff, has resulted in television shows and entire cable networks dedicated to remodeling and redecorating
projects. Of course, when people move into a new home, redecorating is also at
the top of many people's agendas.

Since Martha Stewart made her debut three decades ago, the notion that the
average person might make his home and workplace a personalized, striking
reflection of his dreams has grown incrementally. While this growing interest in
Do-It-Yourself (DIY) has many people ready to take on the task of transforming
their homes into reflections of their personalities and lifestyles, these trends also
mean that there is a lot of work for talented, creative interior decorators.

The challenge for many consumers comes when they try to figure out,
among the mass of color, texture, pattern, style, and cost options, which ones
will work together, how to get the result they really desire, and what is involved

in completing their projects before they begin. This is where the decorator comes in.

This can be a fun career for a flexible, creative person who enjoys a high level of interaction with a variety of people and is willing to be flexible and somewhat intimate with his or her client. Being an interior decorator definitely requires a fine ability to tease out the true desires of your clients. Working with an array of clients having a range of budgets will call on your creativity and sensitivity to help them make choices they will enjoy living with for years to come.

An interior decorator decides, together with the client, what colors will be used on the walls, what fabrics will be perfect for re-covering that beloved upholstered armchair or auction sofa, how the furniture and accessories should be arranged, and what kind of art and accessories will perfectly express the vision the client has for the space. Usually the decorator's tasks will not include working directly with contractors or planning build-outs. That is the more specialized field of interior *design*.

Interior decorators can practice without formal credentials, but interior designers must have two to five years' postgraduate education and certification by the American Society of Interior Design. They need to be able to read blueprints, understand basic structural considerations to know if removing a wall would damage the integrity of the building, and ensure that fire safety codes are being met. They are also required to develop estimates for remodeling projects that would include construction, fixtures, and decorating.

Other requirements for both designers and decorators are a sense of color coordination, an understanding of various fashion trends, and the ability to develop and communicate with visual presentations the plan for the project. Fortunately there are plenty of software programs that can help with space planning, color coordination, and proposal presentation that give 3-D pictures of the end goal. Many communities offer showcase events where tours of fabulous homes are provided for the price of a ticket. You can also visit real estate open houses in different neighborhoods to see what some people have done.

As in most businesses, specialization is appropriate and desirable. A quickly growing specialty is "interior redesign." Interior redesigners work with lower budgets because redesigning uses existing furniture, flooring, and accessories, rearranging and swapping items from room to room to freshen the look. It may involve some new paint, maybe a reupholstering job, potentially a lot of reorganizing, but mostly it is pulling together what the client already has and loves. Redesigning calls for being nonjudgmental. Interior Redesign has its own association called I.R.I.S. [www.weredesign.com or (866) 388-5208].

Some decorators specialize by working mainly in the commercial sector; some for particular types of businesses, such as restaurants, health care settings, law firms, or offices. Many work with private homes, apartments, and bungalows.

Bed and breakfast establishments are very invested in a kind of cozy hominess that is well served by a creative decorator. If you live in a coastal area, there is even a demand for decorating yachts.

Style can be a specialization, too. From modern to shabby chic, Edwardian to rustic, the requirements of a particular style may not mesh with those of another. If you love a particular look, you could consider specializing in that genre. This could be dangerous, however, if the look is very trendy and goes out of style. If you are flexible and don't mind doing your research, you can probably accommodate any style that interests the client.

To get started as a decorator, build a portfolio with examples of your work. If you are new to the field, try making over one room of your own house in various guises to photograph as examples. For experience, volunteer to do a few projects for family, friends, a church, or other nonprofit. When you get jobs, be sure to document with before and after pictures for your portfolio.

Related Careers

Feng Shui Practitioner. Individuals, businesses, architects, city planners, interior designers, parks and recreation departments, realtors, and schools are consulting practitioners of feng shui and related technologies (Vastu shastra and building biology) to evoke harmony in their surroundings. Realtors have found homes enhanced with feng shui principles sell faster.

Combined with your own aesthetic sense and personal intuition, learning the basics of feng shui will give you an understanding of how to make a space calm, clear, and well balanced. Noteworthy resources include the International Feng Shui Guild [(954) 345-3838, www.internationalfengshuiguild.org]; books like *A Master Course in Feng-Shui* by Eva Wong; and training programs such as those from the Feng Shui Institute of America, which offers a home-study course and professional certification program [(888) 488-3742 or (772) 388-2085, www.windwater.com].

Building biology training and certification can be obtained from the International Institute for Bau-Biologie & Ecology [(772) 461-4371, www.bau-biologieusa.com].

Home Staging. Staging a home so that it is presented at its best when placed on the market results in a quicker sale and a higher price. The notion is that the way your home looks as you live in it and the way it needs to look to sell can be very different. With the volatility of the real estate market, "staging" has become a must for sellers wishing for a quick sale, particularly in a slow market, and a premium price. Staging involves making recommendations for painting, changing furniture arrangement or placement, lighting, landscaping, removing clutter, or adding decorating touches. Some stagers only offer consultation; others rearrange homes and do repairs. Fees for consultation range from $250 to $500, and the cost of having the stager do the work ranges from $2,000 to $4,000. While not required, there are courses available to become an Accredited Staging Professional (ASP), which you can locate at www.stagedhomes.com. The site also sells educational DVDs and the book *Building a Successful Home Staging Business* by Barb Schwarz. Also informative is *The Complete Idiot's Guide to Staging Your Home to Sell*, Julie Dana and Marcia Layton Turner, Alpha, 2007.

Professional Organizer. The professional organizing career has been growing rapidly in part because we have more stuff and less time to keep it findable. Bigger homes mean more spaces to organize. Happily, professional organizers can work miracles.

Organizers do best when they specialize. Some organizers specialize by industry, such as banks, hospitals, law offices, dental and medical practices, etc. Others specialize by focusing on a particular type of task or problem, such as computer data, filing cabinets, time management, wardrobes, collections and other memorabilia, estate sales, finances and bill paying, photographs, garages, attics, basements, closets, kitchens, packing and moving, relocation, and project management.

It's common for organizers to see themselves as hands-on coaches, getting their clients to focus on the end goal. Organizers charge by the hour, with rates ranging from thirty-five to two hundred dollars, or they work by the project. Some organizers make retainer agreements with clients, making themselves available for an agreed upon number of hours over a period of time. Professional organizers can do well during economic downturns by positioning themselves as a way to cut costs and organize remaining staff to be more productive, helping to compensate for lost personnel during downsizing. Resources include:

- National Association of Professional Organizers: (847) 375-4746, www.napo.net
- *Everything You Need to Know About a Career as a Professional Organizer,* Sara Pedersen, Time to Organize, 2006.
- *The Professional Organizer's Complete Business Guide,* Lisa Steinbacher, Eternity Publishing, 2004.
- *Conquering Chaos at Work,* Harriet, Schechter, Fireside Books, 2006.
- *Organized to Be Your Best!* Susan Silver, Adams-Hall Publishing, 2006.

INTERIOR DECORATION AT A GLANCE

ECONOMIC REALITY FIT

Necessary vs. Discretionary	Discretionary
Replaceable with technology	No
Offshorable	No
Industry Status	Established and Expanding

Personal Reality Fit

► Start-up costs	Moderate, More Than Most (Franchise)
► Overhead	Minimal
► Potential earnings	More Than Most
► Flexible hours	Subject to project and client demands
► Overall stress	Moderate
► Ease of bartering	Moderate

Durability Rating

Likely Transferable Skills, Background, Careers

With the needed eye for color and design and the right personality, this field is open.

What to Charge

Decorators charge from $40 to $200 per hour; some require a $500 to $1000 initial deposit. Some decorators mark up on items, such as fabric, floor coverings, and furniture purchased for clients, by 10 to 20 percent; if the decorator buys at a sufficient discount, this still results in a savings for clients.

Best Ways to Market Interior Decoration

- ► Walk around business areas, introducing yourself to commercial clients, such as bed and breakfast inns, art galleries, advertising agencies, law firms, restaurants, spas, and corporate headquarters.
- ► Develop relationships with real estate agents, home builders, and furniture stores to enable you to reach new home buyers. To reach people who are refinancing their homes to remodel them, develop relationships with remodeling contractors and lenders.

Tips for Getting Started

- ► Develop relationships with vendors who supply the kinds of services and products you will use in decorating projects. This includes manufacturers of wall coverings and paint; sources for fabrics and flooring; and painters, plumbers, electricians, and other contractors.

- Obtain a business and resale license so you will be able to buy from designers and showrooms to get the best pricing for products.
- Design and have plenty of attractive leave-off materials, such as fliers, small brochures, and business cards.

LEARN MORE

Associations

- American Society of Interior Designers: (202) 546-3480, www.asid.org
- International Interior Design Association: (888) 799-4432 or (312) 467-1950, www.iida.org

Books

- *How to Start a Home-Based Interior Design Business*, Nita B. Phillips, Suzanne DeWalt, Globe Pequot Press, 2006.
- *Interior Design Course: Principles, Practices, and Techniques for the Aspiring Designer*, Tomris Tangaz, Barron's Educational Series, 2006.
- *The Interior Designer's Guide to Pricing, Estimating, and Budgeting*, Theo Stephan Williams, Allworth Press, 2005.

Franchises

- A Designer's Eye (818) 936-3333, www.adefranchising.com
- Decorating Den Interiors: (800) 332-3367 or (301) 272-1500, www.decoratingden.com
- Decor & You: (800) 477-3326 or (203) 264-3500, www.decorandyou.com

Training

In addition to universities that offer degree or certificate programs in interior design, colleges and schools that offer certificates in interior decoration, and franchises that include training as part of the franchise fee, online programs are available from:

- The Art Institute Online, part of the Art Institute of Pittsburgh: (877) 872-8869 or (412) 291-5100, www.aionline.edu
- Academy of Art College: (800) 544-ARTS or (415) 274-2200, www.academyart.edu
- Interior Decorator, Education Direct: (800) 275-4410), www.education direct.com
- Sheffield School of Interior Design: (212) 661-7270, www.sheffield.edu
- Penn Foster Career School: (570) 961-4014, www.pennfoster.edu

Web Sites

- ▶ www.archdigest.com – *Architectural Digest* magazine
- ▶ www.homefurnish.com/tradeorg.htm – Links to the home furnishings industry
- ▶ www.interiordesign.net – *Interior Design* magazine
- ▶ www.i-d-d.com – Interior Design Directory

Massage and Bodywork

There was a time not so terribly long ago when massage therapy was considered the purview luxury of the rich and famous. Only aristocrats and celebrities could afford to enjoy the exotic mineral waters, mud baths, and pampering that spas had to offer.

No more. If you were to visit a spa—whether for the day or the week—you would rub elbows with people from all walks of life: the bus driver, the stay-at-home mom, and the commodities runner. You would discover that they are all taking advantage of the spa for a hundred different reasons, from the desire for a clean break from their everyday stresses, to the rejuvenation of muscles, joints, and skin, to a way of treating health problems.

However, you no longer have to go to a spa to enjoy the benefits of a good massage. You are just as likely to find a good masseuse in an airport, your local gym, the doctor's office, or in the privacy of your own home as you are at an expensive spa. As the health benefits of massage and other forms of bodywork and relaxation have become clear, more and more people have availed themselves of these "small luxuries" and made them part of their regular routine.

As the numbers of people enjoying the benefits of massage therapy grow, so do the opportunities for intelligent and creative people to build solid careers as massage therapists and other purveyors of physical and mental relaxation techniques.

Many people now view massage therapy as a necessity, not a luxury. More and more companies have brought massage into the workplace. This trend is not the result of companies becoming "new age" or "touchy-feely." Far from it. Companies that provide these services for their employees have their attention focused on productivity and the bottom line. They know that a happy staff is a productive staff. They have found that offering these services not only makes their employees happy, but it also aids in retaining their employees in a competitive job market.

Executives and managers in high-stress fields are discovering that massage reduces stress in their employees, improving morale and productivity. Some studies have indicated that massage also lowers tension and fatigue, making employees more alert and efficient.

Away from the workplace, massage eases the pain of all those baby boomers whose aging joints and muscles ache from being pushed to do the same things that they could do much more easily twenty years ago. Massage has proven itself as a way to relieve pain, slow the heart rate, lower blood pressure, reduce depression, and speed healing and recovery from illness and injury.

Massage therapists work with people who suffer from repetitive stress injuries. There are therapists who specialize in sports massage, baby massage, and facial massage. Others specialize in the populations they work with—from autistic children, to asthmatics, to post-mastectomy patients. Others work with dancers, the elderly, end-of-life patients, and drug and alcohol rehab patients. Massage is a proven benefit to everyone. As a result, your potential clients are nearly countless—from neighbors and friends to the long-haul trucker and the commuter.

BODYWORK AND MASSAGE THERAPY SERVICES AT A GLANCE
ECONOMIC REALITY FIT

► Necessary vs. Discretionary	Discretionary
► Replaceable with technology	No
► Offshorable	No
► Industry Status	Established and Expanding

PERSONAL REALITY FIT

► Start-up costs	More Than Most
► Overhead	Minimal
► Potential earnings	More Than Most
► Flexible hours	More Than Most
► Overall stress	More Than Most
► Ease of bartering	More Than Most

Durability Rating

Likely Transferable Skills, Background, Careers

Massage therapy requires you to have a thorough knowledge of anatomy, physiology, and kinesiology. As such, anyone with a background in these fields and subjects can consider a career in massage therapy. If you have worked in the medical field as an aide or a nurse, you will be able to transfer many of your skills to this field.

Massage is physically demanding in that you will use your physical strength to manipulate your client's muscles and joints. Massage is an intimate—but *not* sexual—form of therapy. You must have effective communication skills to be successful as a massage therapist. If you have a background in a counseling field, those skills can be transferred to massage therapy.

What to Charge

Charging for massage therapy is highly variable. Not only will your fee depend on your own background and ability, but it will also depend on your clientele. If you are setting up a massage table in an airport or doctor's office, you will charge differently than if you are working in a spa. If you are providing in-home services, you will have to take into account your travel costs. After factoring in your overhead, you should earn between $25 and $125 per hour.

Best Ways to Market Massage Therapy

- ▶ Establish a relationship with companies as a "house nurturer"— someone who provides a broad spectrum of services to employees. Companies in hot industries (and governments) that are competing for employees are good targets.
- ▶ Make personal contact. Massage and bodywork involve highly personal relationships with clients. Because of this, getting and retaining clients are often the result of personal contact. Any form of contact, such as networking in organizations, in which you relate to people what you do, will result in a certain number of people saying, "I need that."
- ▶ Set up your table at art shows and fairs.
- ▶ Volunteer at charity events, health fairs, and other public events.
- ▶ Establish relationships with health care facilities, hotels, and other places that may refer clients to you.
- ▶ Approach companies that need to compete for top employees. Massage is increasingly an employee benefit.
- ▶ Combine massage with another type of treatment, such as acupuncture, to attract and keep clients. Massage therapists frequently offer acupressure, aromatherapy, cranial therapy, polarity therapy, reflexology, Reiki, shiatsu, therapeutic touch (t-touch), among others. Keep in mind, however, that everything you offer will require additional training.

Tips for Getting Started

- ▶ Check into whether licensing is required in your state or county. Over thirty states so far have licensed massage, and bills are pending in most of the other states. Each state sets its own criteria, and some counties and cities also regulate massage.

▶ Obtain national certification through the National Certification Board of Therapeutic Massage and Bodywork: (800) 296-0664 or (630) 627-8000, www.ncbtmb.com. Most states that license have adopted this examination as a requirement. In other states, it's a recognized credential. To be eligible for certification requires either graduating from an accredited school or proving an equivalent amount of training and experience. You can find approved providers on the NCTMB Web site, or if your state licenses massage therapists, the licensing agency will list approved education programs in the state on its Web site.

▶ Obtain your training from an accredited school. The largest accrediting organization is the Commission on Massage Therapy Accreditation (www.comta.org). Its site has a directory of schools.

▶ Decide if and in what you will specialize, and then get the additional training, credentials, and experience you need.

▶ Decide whether you will establish a practice in your home, an office, your clients' workplaces and homes, or if you will affiliate with a spa, salon, hotel, health club, hospital, or doctor's office.

Related Careers
Fitness Trainer/Coach

Fitness training was already growing before serious efforts to deal with obesity began. An aging population turns to personal trainers to maintain or improve themselves and to deal with diseases and conditions, such as arthritis, cardiac or musculoskeletal problems, diabetic conditions, disabilities, and pregnancy. A growing specialty for fitness trainers is helping brides get into the kind of physical shape that will enable them to look their best on their wedding day.

Fitness trainers work both for themselves and for clubs. Clients may come to them, or they may go to their clients. Trainers who work on their own meet with clients in gyms or at their clients' homes. Some trainers provide coaching over the phone or Internet. Some fitness trainers organize classes or boot camps to serve bridal clients.

Because the best advertising to potential clients is the trainer's own health and appearance, coaches and trainers need to be physically fit. There are over three hundred certifications for personal trainers available from many organizations, so certification is relatively easy to get in this field. It's inevitable that some certifications are more recognized than others. Credentialing organizations, such as the American Council on Exercise [(858) 279-8227, (800) 825-3636, www.ace-fitness.org] and the National Council on Strength and Fitness (www.ncsf.org), that have been accredited by the National Commission for Certifying Agencies (www.noca.org) are more apt to be recognized by clubs, should you want to work with one.

Yoga Teacher

Yoga provides another means for people to relax and strengthen their muscles. Because of its effectiveness in reducing stress, yoga is employed to reduce the pain of repetitive stress injuries as well as other forms of chronic pain, provide a type of facial, help with PMS, and much more. Many practitioners are people who have benefited from yoga and learn to teach it. As a result, yoga practitioners come from a wide variety of occupational backgrounds. Yoga may be taught to individuals in their homes or in classes of ten or fifteen in places like a local gym, church, or yoga center. Fees for classes vary with class size; however, an instructor should be able to earn, after factoring in costs, between $25 and $75 per hour. For coming to someone's home, $50 is a typical rate. A comprehensive resource center for all things yoga is the Yoga Site (www.yoga-site.com). The site can also be contacted by phone at (877) 964-2748 or (508) 896-4456. To find a registered school or teacher, contact the Yoga Alliance at http://yogaalliance.org/ or (877)964-2255 or (301)868-4700.

Learn More

Associations

- ▶ American Massage Therapy Association (AMTA) is the oldest association of massage therapists and bodyworkers, offering an extensive number of services, including liability insurance: (877) 905-2700 or (847) 864-0123, www.amtamassage.org.
- ▶ Associated Bodywork & Massage Professionals (ABMP) is an alternative organization to AMTA, with its own school accrediting organization, and includes skincare professionals (aestheticians and cosmetologists): (800) 458-2267, www.abmp.com.
- ▶ International Massage Association (IMA) offers lower-cost liability insurance and offers a home study course. The company that owns IMA also operates separate divisions for fifteen other healing modalities: (540) 351-0800, www.imagroup.com.
- ▶ Specialty associations include the American Medical Massage Association, www.americanmedicalmassage.com; the American Organization for Bodywork Therapies of Asia, www.aobta.org; the American Polarity Therapy Association, www.polaritytherapy.org; The Feldenkrais Guild, www.feldenkrais.com; the International Association of Equine Sports Massage Therapists, www.iaespmt.com; the International Somatic Movement Education & Therapy Association, www.ismeta.org; the Rolf Institute, www.rolf.org; and the U.S. Trager Association, www.trager.com.

Books

- *Hands Heal: Communication, Documentation, and Insurance Billing for Manual Therapists,* Diana L. Thompson, Lippincott Williams & Wilkins, 2005.
- *Marketing Massage,* Monica Roseberry, Thomson Delmar Learning, 2001.
- *Massage: A Career at Your Fingertips,* Martin Ashley, Enterprise Publishing, 2005.
- *Massage Therapy: Career Guide for Hands-on Success,* Steve Capellini, Thomson Delmar Learning, 2006.
- *Mosby's Fundamentals of Therapeutic Massage,* Sandy Fritz, Mosby, 2004. Sandy Fritz has also authored *Mosby's Essential Sciences for Therapeutic Massage: Anatomy, Physiology, Biomechanics and Pathology,* 2003.
- *Save Your Hands! Injury Prevention for Massage Therapists,* Lauriann Greene, Robert A. Greene, Gilded Age Press, 2000.
- *The Ethics of Touch: The Hands-on Practitioner's Guide to Creating a Professional, Safe and Enduring Practice,* Cherie M. Sohnen-Moe, Ben E. Benjamin, Lippincott Williams & Wilkins, 2006.
- *Tappan's Handbook of Healing Massage Techniques,* Patricia J. Benjamin, Frances M. Tappan, Prentice Hall, 2004.

Magazines and Journals

- Most of the associations listed previously publish a journal or magazine.
- *Massage Magazine,* (800) 533-4263. The magazine's publishers operate a massage museum in Spokane, Washington.

Mediation

Are you a scrupulously fair person, often intervening in others' troubles? Do you relish an opportunity to settle a dispute equitably? Do people respond positively to you at first meetings? If you've answered yes to these three questions, you can enter the growing field of alternative dispute resolution.

Mediation has grown as an acceptable service for settling disputes for several reasons. Principal among these is the clogged court system that can result in waits of three or more years. Mediation is also gaining popularity because lawyers are very expensive, and some disputes just don't merit the expense.

Mediation has positive aspects that contribute to its increasing use. Mediated solutions are not made part of the public record, as are court proceedings, and the emphasis in mediation is on the disputing parties working toward a solution collaboratively with the mediator rather than in an adversarial format.

Mediation is not to be confused with arbitration. These approaches to dispute resolution are completely different. In arbitration the parties present their sets of facts and opinions to an arbitrator, who then determines the solution on his or her own. Contracts often have provisions for arbitration and often specify the American Arbitration Association as the sole source for the person to play the role of arbitrator. If the process is "binding arbitration," it is just that, binding on both parties.

You've no doubt read newspaper stories of mediators going back and forth between hotel rooms of parties to political disputes, labor disputes, and other major public events. The practice is the same when the parties are individuals as when they are governments or unions: the mediator talks to both sides, looking for the common ground on which to build compromise.

As we have seen, the mediator's role is to bring the parties to a point of agreement on whatever their thorny issue is. The large number of subjects people could possibly disagree on means that mediators must be broadly trained, or they may specialize. Specialties include divorce, child custody, workplace issues, business-to-business disputes, consumer/business disagreements, and many more.

In the workplace you will find yourself mediating disputes about harassment and other human resources matters. You might be called upon to find the solution to a business dispute about the meaning of a contract clause or delivery requirements. Mediators can find themselves developing expertise in fields they never had an interest in or fields in which they worked for an entire career.

A mediator's working conditions can vary. Most common is neutral conference space that must be rented by the mediator; hotel spaces rented by the parties may also work well, with the mediator moving back and forth between the rooms. You could also find yourself mediating in virtual space from your home office.

MEDIATION AT A GLANCE

ECONOMIC REALITY FIT

► Necessary vs. Discretionary	Discretionary
► Replaceable with technology	No
► Offshorable	No
► Industry Status	Established and Expanding

PERSONAL REALITY FIT

► Start-up costs	Minimal
► Overhead	Moderate

► Potential earnings	More Than Most
► Flexible hours	More Than Most
► Overall stress	More Than Most
► Ease of bartering	Minimal

Durability Rating

Likely Transferable Skills, Background, Careers

The professional skills that translate most easily to mediation would be those of an attorney. One could make an excellent case for social workers, psychologists, and other counselors being capable of understanding and using the motivations of opposing parties to reach an acceptable compromise, particularly in domestic and other interpersonal disputes. A person with a lengthy career and the right personality traits will find mediation a satisfying choice of business, and others will see their experience as a valuable bonus.

What to Charge

Mediation can be court ordered. These mediators, if they are lawyers, can charge $150 to $350 an hour or more. Non-attorney mediators are more likely to charge $75 to $150 an hour depending on their expertise in the subject and experience as a mediator. You should be aware of the market in determining your fees. In some parts of the country there are very few trained mediators, and in others the competition is substantial.

Best Ways to Market Mediation

► Join mediation organizations that offer listing services or post listings online.

Tips for Getting Started

► Take courses. Find out about some courses at www.mediationworks.com and www.mediationservices.net (or www.accri.org for commercial products), and try your local college for free or low-cost training.
► Establish yourself in local houses of worship, starting with free services.

► Talk to your own attorney about opportunities in the community or with his/her clients.

LEARN MORE

Associations
► American Arbitration Association: www.adr.org
► Global Arbitration Mediation Association: www.gama.com
► Association for Conflict Resolution: www.acrnet.org
► National Association for Community Mediation: www.mediate.com/nafcm

Books
► *The Mediation Process,* Christopher W. Moore, Jossey-Bass, 2003.
► *A Guide to Divorce Mediation,* Gary J. Friedman, Workman Publishers, 2003.
► *Bringing Peace into the Room,* Daniel Bowling, Ed., Jossey-Bass, 2003.
► *The Handbook of Dispute Resolution,* Michael L. Moffitt, ed., Jossey-Bass, 2005.

Newsletters
► Mediation On-Line, www.adrr.com
► Mediate.com Newsletter, www.mediate.com

Midwife and Doula Services

With the economic shifts in our society have come profound demographic shifts. Not so long ago, it was not unusual to find neighborhoods in which parents, grandparents, aunts, uncles, and cousins all lived within easy traveling distance. But now, grandparents might be thousands of miles from their grandchildren. Aunts and uncles might live hundreds of miles away. A family getting together is reduced to a handful of holidays and family celebrations. There is a tremendous emotional loss in this change. But there is also a very practical loss—one that cries out for conscientious and caring women to repair.

Rather than caring family members or close friends, women have been left with a library of self-help books and a medical establishment to assist them with the profound transition and adjustment of pregnancy, childbirth, and motherhood. In our disjointed society, women are often alone to struggle with the changes childrearing brings about. They long for a calm, caring, knowledgeable, and nurturing presence to guide them and assist them. Doulas and midwives provide these services and others to help with problems that have been recognized as deserving expert attention. First, let's consider the more recognized field of midwifery.

Midwife. Midwives have been around for a long time, and owing to the popularity of natural child birth, the high cost of medical care, and the lack of available health insurance for some, midwives are back in fashion. Midwives deliver more than two-thirds of babies in the world, and in the United States, the number of midwife-assisted births has doubled in the last ten years, reaching nearly one in ten, according to the American College of Nurse-Midwives. While midwives deal with normal births and healthy mothers, their training also enables them to recognize and refer problems of illness and the need for medical intervention to obstetricians. In some respects what they do overlaps with doulas, but the licensing requirements for midwives sets them apart, and their emphasis is on the actual birth.

Midwives play a role before the birth in providing information to the mother and family. After the birth, the midwife may continue to help the mother and the infant for about six weeks until the mother's body returns to normal.

Registered nurses who decide to become nurse midwives can practice in hospitals, while women (and occasionally men) who acquire midwife skills through specialized study or apprenticeship typically deliver babies in nonhospital settings, usually in homes or birth centers.

To become licensed or certified in those states permitting midwifery, one must meet the requirements established by the North American Registry of Midwives (NARM, www.narm.org) to become a certified professional midwife. This involves an examination. NARM's requirements may involve graduating from a program accredited by the Midwifery Education Accreditation Council (www.meacschools.org), becoming certified by the American Midwifery Certification Board (www.amcbmidwife.org), or passing NARM's own competency-based Portfolio Evaluation Process.

While some midwives operate without credentials, this can be problematic both from legal and marketing perspectives. This is particularly a temptation not only in those states that prohibit midwives but also where malpractice insurance premiums for midwives have skyrocketed. Despite this problem, parents' desires for traditional childbearing and concerns about health insurance costs point to a growth of the use of midwives.

Doula. Less well-known than midwives, doulas are also called *birth coaches* and *labor assistants*. There is a huge and growing desire for a woman who serves, true to the Greek origins of the title, as an assistant to a new mother as she negotiates her new and expanded role. The role of the doula is clearly proscribed. She is not a midwife, and she is not a nanny. She has no *medical* role in childbirth, like a midwife, nor is her primary role solely to care for the newborn after birth, like a nanny. Her real role is to *humanize* what should be a profoundly human, not institutionalized, experience—one that modern medicine has too often turned into another medical procedure. In the process, doulas make the transition for new mothers from pregnant woman to parent much more manageable.

Childbirth has proven itself stubbornly resistant to the desire of hospitals and medical staff for efficient and predictable procedures. Too often, whether in reality or just in the perception of the expectant mother, hospital procedures and schedules seek to "trump" the natural process of childbirth. In this situation, fraught with so much emotion and risk, the doula is a vital player. She often serves as the interface between the patient—her client—and medical personnel. On the one hand, she is an advocate for her clients' needs, and on the other, she makes more understandable and less frightening the medical procedures attendant to childbirth. By bridging the space between the needs of the new mother and the procedures of the hospital, the doula contributes to a more positive and satisfying outcome.

As you can imagine, the willingness of the doula to participate in childbirth drama can be extremely rewarding but also exhausting and unpredictable. Labor can last more than thirty hours—that is one long work shift! It is also one of the reasons why there has been a trend toward specialization for doulas. Specialization has allowed doulas to define their role with more precision. Some work with parents-to-be exclusively before and through childbirth, but some doulas find the delivery room almost as physically demanding as the new mother. These doulas opt for the less demanding, but equally necessary, role of post-partum doula, assisting the new mother after her baby is born.

While some doulas assist in finding obstetricians who share the childbirth experience vision with the parents-to-be, most doulas are "hands-on" caregivers, who comfort the mother at whatever stage of the process. They do not provide any clinical skill or participate in any medical aspect of the pregnancy or birth. However, their participation has real medical value. Many doulas assist their clients with pain-relieving breathing techniques to ease the labor experience. They may provide massage therapy for relaxation, sing to the mother, or provide aromatherapy to calm the mother.

Another professional designation coming into use is that of *monitrice*. Monitrices have medical training in nursing or midwifery. Like a birth doula, a monitrice provides personal support for a woman in labor as well as during the third trimester, checking the baby's heart rate and position in the womb, providing counsel, and suggesting exercises that will strengthen and stretch the muscles to ease delivery.

There can be no minimizing the need for doulas nor any doubt to the objective benefit they provide. Numerous studies have shown that mothers report labor to be a more positive experience when a doula is present. The benefit is not only perceptual. Studies have noted that labor is reduced by up to a quarter, requests for pain medication drop by as much as 60 percent, cesarean sections are reduced, and forceps deliveries also go down. Perhaps most importantly, follow-up studies done two months post-partum indicate that women who had a doula with them during birth are more loving and responsive to their babies.

Growing numbers of insurance companies are recognizing the benefits of a doula—both to their clients and to their own bottom line. Insurance companies often cover doula services, although some plans only cover doula services provided through the hospital. Many insurance companies also cover post-partum doula care, particularly companies that operate in states requiring forty-eight hours of post-partum care.

MIDWIFE AND DOULA SERVICES AT A GLANCE

ECONOMIC REALITY FIT

► Necessary vs. Discretionary	Both
► Replaceable with technology	No
► Offshorable	No
► Industry Status	Established and Expanding

PERSONAL REALITY FIT

► Start-up costs	Minimal (depends on educatin and the cost of professional liability insurance)
► Overhead	Moderate (Doula), More Than Most (Midwife)
► Potential earnings	More Than Most
► Flexible hours	More Than Most
► Overall stress	Moderate
► Ease of bartering	More Than Most

Durability Rating

Likely Transferable Skills, Background, Careers

Background knowledge in medical care provides the ability to understand medical procedures, make them understandable to clients, and communicate a client's needs and feelings to medical staff. Being a doula is a task performed exclusively by women, and almost always women who have previously experienced childbirth and motherhood. With additional medical training, a doula can become a midwife and then take an active role in childbirth. Unlike doulas, men can become midwives. About one in fifty midwives are male, according to the American College of Nurse-Midwives.

What to Charge

Generally, the doula will charge a flat fee for her service, and those fees can vary greatly. In establishing a fee, geographic and demographic differences come into play. A doula in Wyoming might ask $400, whereas a doula in New York City might reasonably expect nearly $2,000 for the same service. Some doulas offer a sliding scale. Fees for midwives are more than double those of doulas because of what they do and the cost of malpractice insurance. In some states midwife fees are reimbursable by insurance and subject to what the insurance company will pay.

Best Ways to Market Midwife and Doula Services

> Advertise in local newspapers and newsletters like the Wet Set Gazette, a twenty-page newspaper published through your local Dydee Diaper Service, or local parenting newsletters published by nursery schools, parent groups, diaper services, or other agencies.
> Affiliate with local hospitals and clinics. These contacts will be very useful, as will word-of-mouth recommendations offered by local gynecologists and obstetricians.
> Teach childbirth classes, such as Lamaze (www.lamaz.org). Other organizations that provide training and certification in childbirth education are the American Academy of Husband-Coached Childbirth® (www.bradleybirth.com), Association of Labor Assistants and Childbirth Educators (www.alace.org), Childbirth and Postpartum Professional Association (www.cappa.net), and International Childbirth Education Association (www.icea.org).

---

*Unlike many other professionals, doulas tend to be noncompetitive. Some look for other doulas to work with so that they can provide backup for their clients if they are unavailable or sick when a client goes into labor.

Tips for Getting Started
- Speak with others in the field and ask them about their experiences.
- Speak to your own gynecologist or obstetrician about the possibility of your becoming a doula or midwife.
- If you become a doula, start out as a postpartum doula.
- Visit childbirth classes given by private instructors or the Red Cross.

LEARN MORE

Associations
Doulas
- Association of Labor Assistants and Childbirth Educators offers training and certification: (888) 222-5223 or (617) 441-2500, www.alace.org
- Childbirth and Postpartum Professional Association (CAPPA): 888-MY-CAPPA, www.cappa.net
- Doulas of North America: (888) 788-3662, www.dona.com
- International Childbirth Education Association (ICEA): (952) 854-8660, www.icea.org

Midwives
- Citizens for Midwifery is a nonprofit, grassroots citizen organization dedicated to promoting the model of care provided by midwives: http://cfmidwifery.org
- Midwives Alliance of North America (MANA) is a support organization of midwives: www.mana.org
- National Association of Certified Professional Midwives: (866) 704-9844, www.nacpm.net

Books
Midwives
- *Midwifery: Women's Health Nurse Practitioner Certification Review Guide,* Beth M. Kelsey and Patricia Burkardt, eds., Health Leadership Associates Inc., March 2004.
- *Varney's Midwifery*, Helen Varney Burst, Jones and Bartlett Publishers Inc., 2004

Doulas
- *The Doula Advantage,* Rachel Gurevich, Prima Lifestyles, 2003.
- *Doula Programs*, Paulina Perez, Deaun Thelen, Cutting Edge Press, 1998.
- *Ina May's Guide to Childbirth,* Ina May Gaskin, Bantam, 2003.
- *Nurturing the Family*, Jacqueline Kelleher, Xlibris Corporation, 2002.

Training
Midwives
- ▸ Programs accredited by the Midwifery Education Accreditation Council: (425) 602-3130, www.meacschools.org
- ▸ Programs accredited by the American College of Nurse-Midwives Division of Accreditation: (650) 696-1060, www.midwife.org/careers.cfm?id=86

Doulas
Doula associations listed above either offer training, certification, or list workshops such as those provided by independently owned and operated centers like Birthing from Within (505) 254-4884, www.birthingfromwithin.com and Birthworks (888) 862-4784, www.birthworks.org

Web Sites
Midwives
- ▸ www.mana.org/statechart.html – Provides links to the laws regulating midwives in all fifty states, including states that prohibit midwifery

Doulas
- ▸ www.doula.com – Online childbirth resources
- ▸ www.childbirth.org – Includes a section for doula information
- ▸ www.doulanetwork.com – Directory of doulas

Mobile Services

With all the focus on multitasking, wouldn't it be easier if a lot of the things you need to have done came to you instead of your having to go to them? How much time would it save you if, for example, instead of taking your dog to the groomer, the groomer came to your dog, or instead of rushing home to make a dinner, a personal chef had it waiting for you, or when you go to the parking lot after a day's work, you find your car's oil changed and safety systems inspected?

These are three of the more obvious mobile services available right now in many communities. Stressed office workers can benefit from mobile massage therapy, mobile auto body repair, mobile dent removal, mobile auto glass repair or replacement, or the time-saving service of a personal shopper. You will find more about being a personal shopper in the Errand Services profile. In Shanghai, entrepreneurs are selling clothing from stretch minivans to office workers.

On the grand scale, there are medical services that can now be provided on a mobile basis, including mammography, dentistry, and beyond. Mobile services save people time and money, reduce traffic, and make it easier for everyone to get to the places they do need to go. For you to provide some of these time-saving mobile services may require an occupational or professional license. All will require training or insight. All will require interpersonal and sales skills.

When you take your trade to the road, you have the added expense of acquiring, outfitting, and maintaining a vehicle, but this can offset the cost of an office or storefront while giving you access to customers who may never have come to a fixed location. Some services, such as pet grooming, glass replacement, and screen repair, require special equipment. With some, like mobile mammography, the equipment is expensive and requires technical expertise. On the other hand, the entry cost is low to become a mobile notary public: once you meet the qualifications in your state, all you need is your stamp and your pen. To be a personal shopper you will need a sense of style and an understanding of each client and his/her preferences.

Your market is potentially huge for many mobile services. Working couples have little enough time for each other, and if they have to address these needs outside working hours they have even less. Single parents often go without because there is no time to spare. Executives typically work long hours. As metropolitan areas spread out, access to services becomes more difficult. Some services do not have enough providers to reach out beyond the immediate urban and suburban area.

Providing mobile service can be a new delivery method for your present profession or something completely new resulting from an expertise developed in your pursuit of an avocation. Going mobile will appeal to you if starting late is your preference. Mobile providers can, for the most part, make their own hours. If you like to drive, this is certainly for you.

MOBILE SERVICES AT A GLANCE

ECONOMIC REALITY FIT

► Necessary vs. Discretionary	Discretionary
► Replaceable with technology	No
► Offshorable	No
► Industry Status	Established and Expanding

PERSONAL REALITY FIT

► Start-up costs	Moderate (with vehicle), More Than Most (with vehicle and equipment)

- ▶ Overhead   Moderate
- ▶ Potential earnings   More Than Most
- ▶ Flexible hours   More Than Most
- ▶ Overall stress   Moderate
- ▶ Computer skills   Minimal
- ▶ Ease of bartering   More Than Most

Durability Rating

Likely Transferable Skills, Background, Careers

This is a broad series of enterprises. Two of the most obvious common denominators are people and sales skills. If you are expanding an existing business or changing its mode of delivery and already have a usable vehicle, you have what you need.

What to Charge

Here again the number of possibilities is significant. Some services are priced by the job, some by the day, and as in mobile screen repair, by the square foot. Generally, if you are bringing the service to the customer, saving the customer time, you will charge more than the business they have to take time to visit. A grooming job priced at $35 in a shop might be $50 in a mobile unit. A mobile notary who would get $2.50 a stamp in a storefront might add mileage and a service charge of $20 into the fee. Regional variations in pricing are common. For example, personal chefs, many of whom base their prices on the number of meals per month, may get $11 a meal in Memphis and $16 in New York City.

Best Ways to Market Mobile Services

- ▶ Build business relationships with stationary providers of your same service who can provide referrals for you. For example, mobile screen repairers can get work from screen shops. Other mobile services get customers from other types of businesses who have contact with the kind of customers you want. For example, mobile notaries get a lot of referrals from law offices, title companies, apartment complexes, realtors, and social-service directors of nursing homes and hospitals.
- ▶ Advertise in the magazines/journals/specialty newspapers of

professional groups such as physicians, attorneys, clergy, and others who typically live pressured lives.

► If you're independent as opposed to owning a franchise, create a Web site with photos, testimonial letters, and a listing of your services and fees.

Tips for Getting Started

► Research and obtain any necessary license or certification to transact this business in the community. For example, determine if you need a city business license for each community you intend to serve.

► Refine your expertise in the service to be provided and develop any additional skills necessitated by your newfound mobility.

► Consider getting a used vehicle to save you money. On the other hand, if its fuel efficiency is not good, your up-front savings may be wiped out by gas prices.

LEARN MORE

Associations

► National Dog Groomers Association of America offers certification: (724) 962-1919, www.nationaldoggroomers.com

► American Society for Notaries: (850) 671-5164; www.notaries.org

► National Notary Association offers a home-study course: (800) 876-6827; www.nationalnotary.org

► American Personal Chef Association: (800) 644-8389 or (619) 294-2436, www.personalchef.com

► United States Personal Association: (800) 995-2138, www.uspca.com

Books

► *The Essential Guide to Mobile Business,* Ingrid Vos, Pearson Education, 2001.

► *From Problems to Profits: The Madson Management System for Pet Grooming Businesses,* Madeline Bright Ogle, The Madson Group, 1997.

► *FabJob Guide to Become a Personal Shopper,* Laura Harrison McBride, Peter J. Gallanis, Tag Goulet, 2005. See also www.fabjob.com

► *Get Paid to Shop.* Emily S. Lumpkin, Forte Publishing, 1999.

► *How to Start, Operate and Market a Freelance Notary Signing Agent Business,* Victoria Ring, Graphico Publishing, 2004.

► *The Notary Public,* Jerry Withers, Lulu Press, 2005.

► *Notary Signing Agent Certification Course,* Milton G. Valera, National Notary Association, 2002.

► *A Personal Chef Cooks,* Cheryl Mochau, 1st Books Library, 2003.

Franchises

- ▶ The Glass Doctor: (800) 280-9858, www.glassdoctorfranchise.com
- ▶ Techna Glass: (888) 701-4046, www.technaglass.com
- ▶ The Ding King Training Institute offers a business opportunity, not a franchise: (800) 304-3474, www.dingking.com
- ▶ Aussie Pet Mobile: (949) 234-0680, www.aussiepetmobile.com
- ▶ The Screenmobile: (866) 540-5800, www.screenmobile.com
- ▶ The Screen Machine: (877) 505-1985, www.screen-machine.com

Paralegal

The paralegal profession is projected to grow by as much as 25 percent during the next ten years as paralegals assume more of the work lawyers have done, such as research, drafting contracts and pleadings, and preparing for trials. Today more than a quarter of a million paralegals, who are called legal assistants in some places, are at work either as employees or as self-employed independents, according to the Bureau of Labor Statistics.

Paralegals emerged in the 1960s largely as "faux" lawyers, in that their responsibilities were the practical parts of the law practice, freeing attorneys to work on developing clients, face-to-face negotiation, matters of legal theory, etc. Today paralegals may be the entire firm, providing practical services at lower fees. Paralegals may also be virtual and may specialize.

Today's paralegal is educated, trained, and often certified. You can find college-level courses and training at many community colleges. A large number of private schools now include paralegal training in their catalog and many exclusively train paralegals. Certification can be earned from professional organizations and educational institutions. If you wish to become a practicing paralegal, you must have training.

A paralegal practice can take many forms. To work independently, there are two principal approaches: virtual firm and storefront firm. The storefront paralegal firm has grown in popularity in recent years. In a storefront operation you either operate under the license of an attorney to provide basic legal services or do document preparation in states that allow this without the visible support of a member of the bar. Different states regulate these firms differently, so you must contact the appropriate state agency and often the state bar. A few of the basic legal services include drafting wills and divorce papers and reviewing legal documents, such as leases. As a paralegal you do not offer legal advice. You also cannot charge either hourly or contingency fees.

The virtual paralegal does similar work to the storefront paralegal. A virtual paralegal may provide services to smaller law firms or even overextended large firms. Like any virtual service, you can operate your business for less; your expenses are lower and your hours are your own. So a virtual paralegal can be someone who has a day job or child care responsibilities, because much of this work can be done at night.

Specialization is part of the fun. If you become expert in the practical aspects of one part of the legal profession, you can pursue a particular interest of your own while becoming invaluable to a firm with the same specialization. Criminal Law, Real Estate Law, Commercial Law, and Matrimonial Law are a few examples of general specialties. Within these can be even more specialization: death penalty matters, driving while under the influence, sale or purchase of residential real estate, business mergers or dissolutions, prisoner advocacy, and Medicare matters to name a few.

This is the field for you if you are a detail-oriented person who likes every *i* dotted and every *t* crossed. It's also ideal for a person who has always been interested in the law but didn't have the time or money for law school or for someone who wants to focus on bringing legal services to an underserved part of the community. There is much here to satisfy you.

Related Careers

While not ladders to self-employment, job opportunities are expected to grow for legal secretaries, legal investigators, and victim advocates. Victim advocates assist victims and survivors of crimes, help prepare them for trial, and advocate their needs. Training is available for each of these careers, although employment as a victim advocate may require a bachelor's degree in social work, sociology, psychology, criminal justice, or another social science field as a prerequisite.

Registered nurses can become legal nurse consultants. To pursue this, RNs acquire specialized training or even a law degree. The field has one professional association, the American Association of Legal Nurse Consultants (www.aalnc.org).

We live in a time of increasing specialization, which has given rise to expert witness locators who assist attorneys in finding experts to consult and testify on cases. Experts are required on everything from accident analysis to zero gravity environments.

PARALEGALS AT A GLANCE

Economic Reality Fit

▶ Necessary vs. Discretionary	Both
▶ Replaceable with technology	Partial
▶ Offshorable	No
▶ Industry Status	Established and Expanding

Personal Reality Fit

► Start-up costs	Moderate
► Overhead	Minimal, Moderate (storefront)
► Potential earnings	More Than Most
► Flexible hours	Moderate
► Computer skills	More Than Most
► Overall stress	Moderate
► Ease of bartering	Moderate

Durability Rating

Likely Transferable Skills, Background, Careers

Someone with good research skills or a technical writer will find him- or herself smoothly entering this field. Legal secretaries can move up to paralegal positions with appropriate coursework.

What to Charge

According to industry experts Scott and Lisa Hatch, salaried paralegals earn an average of $48,850 a year. Independent paralegals billing attorneys get $15 to $45 an hour. When you operate a paralegal storefront, fees are often charged by the document or project, and these will vary with the jurisdiction in which you are operating. What local lawyers charge will help you set your fees. Divorce papers in an uncontested divorce will command $300 in some areas and considerably more in others.

Best Ways to Market Paralegal Services

- ► Directly solicit attorneys and office managers of law firms. A 2006 survey by *Legal Assistant Today* magazine found more than two out of three clients of independent paralegals are solo practitioners or small firms.
- ► Hang around law libraries, according to Scott Hatch of Center for Legal Studies, where attorneys become frustrated doing legal research.
- ► Make contact with attorneys and other paralegals at legal functions or organizations. Meet other paralegals at local and state paralegal associations.
- ► Send direct-mail brochures and letters to potential firms.

Tips for Getting Started

▶ Talk to friends or family who are local attorneys. They will know the extent to which in-house paralegals are used.

▶ Determine what you can do in the state in which you live or plan to practice. The states differ in their requirements for education, training, or work experience.

▶ If you plan to go independent, plan to spend two years working in a law firm, corporation, real estate firm, or nonprofit organization to acquire experience and develop a specialization. Working in a law firm will require very long hours and constant pressure, which motivates some paralegals to go independent.

LEARN MORE

Associations

▶ American Alliance of Paralegals Inc. offers certification: www.aapipara .org

▶ National Association of Legal Assistants offers certification as a CLA (Certified Legal Assistant) or a CP (Certified Paralegal). While the examination is the same, in some states one professional designation or the other is favored. (918) 587-6828, www.nala.org

▶ National Federation of Paralegal Associations offers continuing education and a career center: (425) 967-0045, www.paralegals.org.

▶ National Paralegal Association offers a career center: (215) 297-8333, www.nationalparalegal.org.

Books

▶ *How to Land Your First Paralegal Job*, Andrea Wagner, Prentice Hall, 2004.
▶ *Paralegal Career Guide,* Chere B. Estrin, Prentice Hall, 2001.
▶ *Paralegal Career for Dummies*, Scott A. Hatch and Lisa Zimmer Hatch, For Dummies, 2006.

Training

▶ The paralegal organizations listed above and the American Association for Paralegal Education (www.aafpe.org) provide information on choosing a paralegal program. You will want to know what your state's requirements are and what credentials local attorneys value before making a decision. Of course, whether you want a classroom or a distance-learning program, what you want to spend, what you want to learn, and whether the program helps you identify a specialty are among other factors that go into the selection process.

▶ The Center for Legal Studies (www.legalstudies.com) provides distance education courses for over one thousand universities. Its Web site provides candid advice on certification. Below is one of the distance-learning programs for which it provides materials.

　　» The U.S. Department of Agriculture Graduate School offers both classroom and distance-learning courses in paralegal studies that lead to certification: (888) 744-4723 or (202) 314-3300, www.grad.usda.gov.

Franchise

▶ We the People Forms & Service Centers are document preparation stores: (805) 962-4100, www.wethepeopleusa.com

Web Sites

▶ www.legalassistanttoday.com – Offers archives of past articles
▶ www.paralegalgateway.com – A portal with hundreds of links to paralegal resources

Pest Control

Pest control is a lifelong pursuit for most of us. Sometimes seasonal and in some places year round, just about everyone confronts big or little undesirable critters. Globalization has meant that unwanted insects and creatures have come to our shores aboard ships, planes, on people's clothing, and in their luggage. Bedbugs, considered eradicated in the 1950s, have returned. Often these unwanted immigrants have no natural predators. The problems and treatments are becoming more complex, lessening the ability of property owners to do it themselves. Universals like this offer a myriad of career opportunities.

What you choose to pursue and how you choose to do battle with critters is dependent on a number of items. The community in which you plan to do business makes an early decision for you: what pests to target. You won't find many weevils in urban settings or pigeons in farm country. Another early decision will be green or not green? Specifically, will you use chemicals or other methods that—although they may be less expensive and very effective—have negative environmental side effects or inhumane elimination methods, or will you use natural products and methods that trap and relocate?

In most jurisdictions pest control is a licensed business with licensed operators who are required to receive regular training in handling dangerous chemicals. If you go green there may be less regulation. You'll need to check with state and local environmental protection agencies to know for sure.

Pest control has come of age, with broader approaches in use. Integrated pest management now includes such diverse tasks as identifying pests, locating them, blocking them from entering structures, killing them, and educating owners and tenants about sanitation matters and early signs of infestation.

In addition, the tools are changing. The introduction of computer technology to aid in identifying critters can reduce the time you take before implementing action to thwart them. Automated application systems result in reduced risks to operators and tenants. It won't be long before advanced sniffer technologies will identify and locate pests quickly and efficiently.

If you want to go green, there are numerous Web sites and other resources listed on the following pages to assist in your education and training. If you wish to be more traditional, you should sign up for training toward applicator licenses and start out working for an established pest control business. A free and valuable resource about pest control is your state's cooperative extension service.

A certain amount of physicality is required. Pest control operators can spend considerable amounts of time on their hands and knees in crawl spaces or climbing around in attics.

Insurance is an issue in traditional pest control because of the expense. You may have some difficulty getting reasonable insurance protection for your organic-based business because it is not well understood and some compounds may not be well researched. You will need insurance, so work at finding the right company. One agent is LIPCA (www.lipca.com), an all-purpose pest control insurance agent. American Safety Insurance Group (www.americansafetyinsurance.com) also insures pest control operators.

This is also an industry where you could develop your own niche. Location will determine the critters that are the biggest nuisance, and this can change over time with suburban sprawl. You can specialize in the removal of specific pests or removal methods. You can operate a business focused on homeowners, commercial properties, or farms and gardens. This industry has many opportunities to offer.

PEST CONTROL AT A GLANCE

ECONOMIC REALITY FIT

► Necessary vs. Discretionary	Both
► Replaceable with technology	No
► Offshorable	No
► Industry Status	Established and Expanding

Personal Reality Fit

► Start-up costs	Moderate, More Than Most
► Overhead	Moderate
► Potential earnings	More Than Most
► Flexible hours	Moderate
► Overall stress	Minimal
► Ease of bartering	Moderate

Durability Rating

Likely Transferable Skills, Background, Careers

Experience in the building trades will help you identify critter entry and hiding places. Such experience will also protect you in environments of wires and nails like crawl spaces and attics. A biology teacher will find that he/she has easily transferable knowledge for both the identification and elimination parts of this industry.

What to Charge

Parts of the industry are highly competitive and price research will be required. Pest control is usually offered as either a one-shot control application/operation or an annual plan. Individual control application costs are based on time, risk, and expenses, so they are very different from job to job. Termite control is usually a major treatment effort, while trap and release has relatively inexpensive equipment and requires only two visits.

Best Ways to Market Pest Control

- ► Develop relationships with home inspectors and local realtors who are in a position to refer you to customers.
- ► Write a column for the local newspaper and/or community Web site focusing on the pest of the season.

Tips for Getting Started

- ► If you lack experience, find a job or apprenticeship with an established self-employed pest control firm.

> Check with local jurisdictions about necessary business certificates and licenses for pest control applications. Training is required for each pest control category you wish to treat.

Related Career

Lice Removal Service. They've always been with us, and they won't go away without nitpicking. Chemical treatments just don't do the job, because lice have grown resistant to them. According to the National Science Foundation, six to twelve million people are afflicted with head lice each year. Affecting children from every economic class, referrals can come from school nurses, day care centers, pharmacists, doctors, and camps. Some school districts contract for this service. While no particular background is required, cosmetologists are well suited for this work. Treatment of private clients is done in their homes, and it takes two visits to rid someone of lice. Some lice removers charge by the head ($100 to $200), some by the hour ($50 to $75); some charge for the initial inspection of a family to determine if they have a lice infestation.

LEARN MORE

Associations

> National Pest Management Association is the industry trade association: www.pestworld.org

> The Association of Natural Biocontrol Producers is a professional association representing the biological pest management industry: www.anbp.org

Books

> *How to Start and Manage a Pest Control Service Business,* Jerre G. Lewis, Lewis & Renn Associates Inc., 2004.

> *Natural Enemies Handbook,* Mary Louise Flint, Steve H. Driestadt, University of California Press, 1999.

> *PCT Technician's Handbook,* Richard Kramer, Pest Control Technology, 1998.

> *Start Your Own Pest Control Service,* www.125aday.com/books/289/ start-pest-control-service.cfm

> *The Mallis Handbook of Pest Control*, Arnold Mallis, Mallis Products, 2004.

Magazines

> *Rodale's Organic Gardening Magazine* has frequent articles on organic pest control: www.organicgardening.com

> *Pest Control Info* is an e-magazine: www.pestcontrolmag.com

Training

▶ LIPCA, an insurance company, offers training in many states: www.lipca.com

▶ Orkin University Online: (866) 214-2449, www.orkincommercial.com

▶ You can identify other sources of approved providers by contacting your state agency regulating pest control or state land grant university in your area. Links to each state's regulatory agency can be found at http://npic.orst.edu/state1.htm#map.

Web Sites

▶ www.epa.gov – The Environmental Protection Agency (EPA) provides information about pesticides and university programs and also sponsors the National Pesticide Information Center: (800) 858-7378, http://npic.orst.edu.

▶ www.pestinformation.com – Natural pest control information

▶ www.pestcontrolportal.com – Pest control portal

▶ www.termite.com/usa – Pest Control USA provides information and links to pest control companies.

▶ www.pestweb.com – Offers a paid listing service

Pet Services

Pets bring much joy into the lives of millions upon millions of people—young, old, families, singles—they're just plain therapeutic! No matter where you live there are pets in your community. Approximately 70 million homes have pets, and according to the American Pet Product Manufacturers Association, in 2007, Americans are expected to spend $41 billion, only a quarter of it on veterinary care, providing lots of entrepreneurial opportunity. Where dog and cats are not permitted in rented homes or condos, you can find fish and birds and reptiles. Every human environment can make way for a number of types of pets.

There are more than a dozen different ways that you can serve the pet-owning community. Some of the more common pet services are dog walking, pet sitting, pet training, and pet grooming. Pets are such a major factor in our lives that an increasing number of psychotherapists are adding pet bereavement counseling either as a focus for their practice or as a specialty.

With pet sitting, you can take at least two approaches, provider or agency. As an agency for pet sitters you prescreen and schedule sitters for clients, which requires building a large client base. A more upscale version of pet sitting is "pet nanny," which involves devoting full attention to one owner's dog or other pet.

In urban areas dog walking is big business, which can keep a walker busy most of the day at as much as ten dollars per dog per day. It is not uncommon to see a walker with five or more dogs out for a morning or afternoon stroll, and then see the same walker with five more dogs at a different hour the same day.

Sometimes dog walking, pet sitting, and plant sitting are rolled into one job when a regular customer is out of town. We recently used a pet sitter who combines pet sitting with babysitting. Pet sitting should include playtime, feeding, and walking, the latter two on the pet's regular schedule. This requires clients to trust you, so references or a bonded agent will help you develop business.

If you have experience training pets, you can also offer that as a service. Pet training is not only for dogs but also cats and even monkeys. Capuchin monkeys are now used to assist people with disabilities.

There are a number of pet services you can develop on wheels, such as teeth cleaning, grooming, and transportation. The most obscure of these three is transportation, which can take the form of a pet taxi or pet moving services. Very busy people cannot find time to take themselves or their pets to the doctor. They will take the opportunity to have their pets transported to and from appointments when needed. For this operation you will need a number of cages of varying sizes and an appropriate vehicle. This business is best in an urban setting.

Another mobile service that focuses on pets but has very limited contact with animals is pet food and product delivery services. In this business you can also take several approaches. Homes with large pets need large quantities of pet food not typically sold in local stores and not very easy to transport. Offering specialty products not locally available but recommended by area veterinarians is another angle to pursue.

Are you a party animal? Do you enjoy working and playing with animals? There are at least three businesses here: show and demonstrations, animals in your act, and pet therapy services. Schools, clubs, and other organizations are always looking for educational and entertaining demonstrations, particularly of more exotic animals. If you like children as much as you like animals and you have a party act, consider adding animals. There is always the old rabbit trick!

If you like the idea of helping the ill, the lonely, the disabled, and other isolated people, you might consider pet therapy. This involves providing calm, friendly animals for a limited period of time in a setting where they are usually not found. While pet therapy is widely accepted, it is difficult for institutional settings, small or large, to properly care for animals. This is where you enter the picture, not only providing the animal but also supervising.

Veterinary surgery is common and, like people, animals often require extra care after discharge; the owners may not be able to change bandages, administer medication, and perform special exercises for any number of reasons. This form of pet care can most successfully be developed with one or more veterinarians making direct referrals.

If you're a photographer, there's also pet photography. You can add this onto an existing photography business or an existing pet business. It should be a fairly easy sale to someone who is already purchasing services for his or her pet. Artists can also specialize in pet portraits.

Making specialty products for pets has been a way for some people to produce an income in a satisfying way. For example, Steve Mondazzi makes coffins and other pet bereavement products in his home and sells them from his Web site, www.petsweloved.com.

This menu of business possibilities is for an animal lover and extend to services like acupuncture, massage treatments, swim classes, and psychic readings. The ideas in this profile include both inexpensive startups and some that need capital investment. There are jobs for those who enjoy working with their hands and those who just want to be around animals. In pet services there really is something for everyone.

PET SERVICES AT A GLANCE

ECONOMIC REALITY FIT

► Necessary vs. Discretionary	Both
► Replaceable with technology	No
► Offshorable	No
► Industry Status	Established and Stable

PERSONAL REALITY FIT

► Start-up costs	Minimal, Moderate
► Overhead	Minimal
► Potential earnings	Minimal, Moderate
► Flexible hours	More Than Most
► Overall stress	Minimal
► Ease of bartering	More Than Most

Durability Rating

Likely Transferable Skills, Background, Careers

The key attributes for a career with pets is a fondness for animals and a natural ability to relate to them; not to mention skill at communicating with humans about their pets. As Ellen Price of Pet Sitters International told us, "The dogs can be happy, but they're not writing the checks." Any experience in a veterinarian's office will help, as will experience with farm animals or in a pet shelter. Experience in nursing homes or hospitals will assist in developing a pet therapy operation.

What to Charge

Each one of the businesses described in this section has prices determined by the setting, whether it is urban or suburban. Dog walking in a city is most lucrative in an upscale neighborhood where you can charge ten dollars or more per dog per day. Pet sitters charge by the hour, the visit, or the day. Home visits run fifteen to twenty for up to three pets. If you perform additional chores, your rate will raise accordingly.

Best Ways to Market Pet Services

> Establish active referral relationships with anyone whom pet owners might ask about finding someone offering a pet service, such as veterinarians, cleaning services, pet food and pet supply stores, travel agents, and hotel concierges. You can offer to make reciprocal referrals in return. Many times such businesses will give out your business cards to people asking for your services.
> Offer a five or 10 percent discount for first-time customers.

Check out the possibilities for becoming a service provider or obtaining referral work from luxury hotels, resorts, residence clubs, and luxury condominium developments.

Tips for Getting Started

> If your service involves taking animals onto your property or into your home, check with the local jurisdiction for regulations or required licenses.
> Review your insurance needs both for yourself and your business.
> If you are going on the road and crossing county or state lines, make sure you are properly licensed and insured in all jurisdictions. Consider bonding as well.

- Locate distributors of pet foods and supplies to be able to provide these items if any of your customers ask.

Related Career

Yard clean-up after dogs. Some pet owners do not like to clean up after their pets, but they do like to use their backyard. Enter the pooper scooper service. Several times a week for a reasonable fee of fifteen to thirty dollars a week, you will scoop the poop, providing a clean yard for your customer. Some people earn over fifty thousand dollars a year providing a pooper scooper service. This may not be something you want to make a career of, but it may help as supplemental income during a transition. Have a flyer describing your service with a pricing schedule (number of times, weight, and number of dogs). You'll also need to purchase pooper scoopers and trash bags and arrange a disposal site. You can list your service on the Web at www.pooper-scooper.com.

LEARN MORE

Associations

- The Cat Fanciers' Association has a mentor program for breeders and exhibitors: (732) 528-9797, www.cfainc.org
- National Dog Groomers Association of America provides training and certification: (724) 962-2711, www.nationaldoggroomers.com
- National Association of Professional Dog Walkers offers liability insurance and bonding coverage: (866) 899-3633, www.napdw.com

Pet Sitting

- National Association of Professional Pet Sitters offers certification: (856) 439-0324, www.petsitters.org
- Pet Sitters International offers multiple services to members: (336) 983-9222, www.petsit.com

Animal Training

- The American Boarding Kennels Association offers training and certification: (877) 570-7788 or (719) 667-1600, www.abka.org
- American Dog Trainers Network provides links to people who train others to work with animals: www.inch.com/~dogs
- Association of Companion Animal Behavior Counselors offers several levels of certification for working with and training companion animals: http://animalbehaviorcounselors.org
- Association of Pet Dog Trainers has a listing of members and extensive information: (800) 738-3647, www.apdt.com

Books

- *All About Dog Daycare*, Robin K. Bennett, C&R Publishing, 2005.
- *Handbook of Applied Dog Behavior and Training*, three volumes, Steven R. Lindsay and Victoria Lea Voith, Iowa State University Press, 2000, 2001, 2005.
- *How to Start a Home-Based Pet Care Business*, Kathy Salzberg, Globe Pequot, 2006.
- *Pet Sitting for Profit*, Patti J. Moran, Howell Book House, 2006.
- *Professional Techniques for Pet and Animal Photography*, Debrah H. Muska, Amherst Media, 2003.
- *Start Your Own Pet-Sitting Business*, Cheryl Kimball, Entrepreneur Press, 2004.
- *So You Want to Be a Dog Trainer*, Nicole Wilde, Phantom Publishing, 2006.

Training

- Each of the organizations listed in **Associations** either provides training leading to certification or lists sources of training.
- Dr. Ian Dunbar Dog Behavior & Training Seminars: (707) 745-4237, www.puppyworks.com

Franchises

- Doggie Day Pet Service – Offers multiple services for multiple types of pets: (877) 738-7738, www.doggieday.com
- Fetch! Pet Care – A pet sitting and dog walking franchise: www.fetchpet care.com
- Pet Butler – Pet waste cleanup: (800) 738-2885, www.petbutler.com

Web Sites

- www.petgroomer.com – Offers helpful information for pet groomers
- www.petsitcenter.com – A Place for pet sitters

Sewing Services

A timeworn and venerable profession that has spawned names as famous as Betsy Ross and Ralph Lauren involves the sewing and/or weaving of natural or synthetic materials into clothing, symbols, or other usable items. The machinery and implements have changed, the styles have changed, but the basic principles remain the same. Opportunities abound today as they have for centuries, and a major attraction is that many of us already own the principal tool, a sewing machine.

One of these opportunities is designing and making clothing for special occasions and activities, such as wedding party apparel, prom dresses, and costumes of all kinds for dancing, skating, expeditions, musicals, stage productions, re-enactments, and customized theme uniforms for waiters and waitresses. Also, people with special physical needs, such as spine curvature, mastectomy patients, preemies, Down's syndrome children, and wheelchair-bound people have need for clothing tailored to their requirements. For example, clothing that will make dressing and undressing easier and more comfortable like step-in openings or Velcro closings instead of buttons and zippers. Handmade accessories, such as walker caddies, wheelchair totes, and easy-to-access cloth handbags, are also possible ideas.

Other people who have need for custom clothing are members of religious groups with specialized dress customs, businesspeople with nonstandard proportions, and slender women who must go to girls' departments to find clothing that fits. Or how about reproducing people's favorite items of clothing that are out of style or discontinued?

Opportunities lie in choosing a more exotic specialty based on where you live, your skills, and personal interests. For example, if you live in a northern climate you might design a line of stylish muffs and mittens. Today's synthetic furs and materials provide a variety of attractive looks and versatile linings. You might also consider clothing that's wearable art. If you have a special love for animals, you might create custom clothing for pets, such as sweaters, parkas, or holiday costumes. You could also develop a line of pet wear specializing in a particular breed.

Clothing for dolls has a market too. For example, teddy bear collectors Jeanne and Tony Degatano established the Cape May Teddy Bear Co.® (www.capem ayteddybear.com) and sew clothing for teddy bears, ranging from Air Force uniforms to Victorian dresses.

And of course there is custom sewing for home décor as well, from draperies and valances to pillows, bedspreads, duvets, slipcovers, tablecloths, placemats, napkins, pillows, and shams. You could also produce any number of handmade gift items to sell at boutiques, art fairs, bazaars, and on the Web. No matter what products you decide to offer, you should consider selling your merchandise on the Internet to take full advantage of your sales potential.

Creating items for sale or auction at charity or organizational fundraisers is yet another option. By relating the design of your items to the logo or theme of the organization or by offering something quite stunning, be it throws, tiny purses, or ornate bustiers, you can draw a profit for both yourself and the charity.

Doing alteration and tailoring work is another option that can be done at home, in your own storefront, or for dry cleaners, boutiques, and other local retailers. If you can offer quick turnaround and last-minute service, you will most likely find yourself very much appreciated and highly recommended, as people often discover something doesn't fit right before they're preparing for a significant event. With jeans costing in the hundreds of dollars as well as it being a challenge to find a perfect fit, reweaving torn denims has become a growing niche.

Designing and creating custom clothing and other items requires superior sewing skills and will usually involve acquiring special attachments and features for your sewing machine to produce a finely finished look and enable you to work with certain fabrics, such as denim. Fitting and pattern making are yet additional requisite skills. Communication skills are also important, as you need to have a clear understanding and agreement as to what a customer wants and needs before you invest your time and money in materials, design, and creation. A seamstress also needs a keen sensitivity to the needs and circumstances of the customers. For example, many a bride or bridesmaid is overly conscious of her waistline, and a customer with a disability or disfigurement may be especially self-conscious about aspects of his/her appearance.

Besides sewing itself there is also a need for sewing educators. Sewing teachers can run classes or provide private instruction. Your classroom might be one you set up as a "sewing café" where people who like to sew their own clothes can benefit from your expert help. You'll need to provide sewing machines just like Internet cafés provide computers. The Home Sewing Association (www.sewing .org), an organization of business members that support home sewing, offers a course teaching how to become a sewing educator.

Sewing is a creative career, that when done well, can lead to a dedicated following of greatly appreciative clientele. While custom sewing remains an essentially local business because of the need for fitting, if you have a line of items you've developed, you can also sell them on the Web or distribute them via retail outlets.

SEWING SERVICES AT A GLANCE

ECONOMIC REALITY FIT

- ► Necessary vs. Discretionary   Both
- ► Replaceable with technology   Partially
- ► Offshorable   No
- ► Industry Status   Established and Expanding

PERSONAL REALITY FIT

- ► Start-up costs   Minimal, Moderate (depends on equipment)
- ► Overhead   Minimal

► Potential earnings	Moderate
► Flexible hours	Moderate
► Overall stress	Moderate
► Ease of bartering	More Than Most

Durability Rating

Likely Transferable Skills, Background, Careers

Sewing enthusiasts who desire to satisfy customers and are willing to adopt business practices are naturals. Someone with a mind for technical understanding can translate this into making specialty clothing.

What to Charge

Pricing factors to take into account in setting your hourly rate are where you're located, your area's cost of living, the prices of others sewing professionally in your area, your experience, and your speed. Also check out the Web sites of other providers; some post their prices. Of course, if you sell custom items on the Web, you'll need to scout out comparable pricing. Customers want fixed prices, which means estimating your time and the cost of supplies you provide. Keep your eye on the cost of customized clothing offered by companies like Land's End on their Web sites; however, these do not substitute for what you offer to customers who prize personal attention and the unique personal styling a local seamstress provides. Customers generally pay for their own fabric and notions; however, if you do the shopping, you can charge for your time.

Best Ways to Market Sewing Services

► Form your own referral network. An example is Denver's sewing referral network: www.sewingreferralnetwork.com.
► Visit shops and stores related to your specialty and show examples of your work. For example, visit dry cleaners if you do alterations, bridal shops if you work on bridal gowns, wedding planners if you design wedding gowns, vets and pet stores if you make pet clothing, furniture stores and interior designers and decorators if you make home décor items.
► Become a supplier to sites like myshape.com that take orders from customers that are fulfilled by independent designers.

Tips for Getting Started

▶ Determine if you want to be a custom service provider or a manufacturer of similar or identical items.

▶ If you are going to run your business out of your home, contact your village, town, or city government and find out what licenses, if any, are needed.

▶ Make contact with others doing professional sewing in your community; sewers are good networkers and love to share information.

Related Career

Embroidery. Embroidery is an ancient handicraft that can now be done with automatic machinery. The logos you see on baseball caps used for self-promotion or a bejeweled or sequined T-shirt may be the work of an individual embroiderer. There are many kinds of embroidery, and the industry has a national association, Embroidery National Network of Embroidery Professionals: (800) 866-7396 or (330) 678-4887, www.nnep.net. The industry magazine, *Stitches* (www.stitches .com), offers two newsletters on its Web site: *Embroidery Business Insights* and *Stitches Small Business.*

LEARN MORE

Association

▶ Professional Association of Custom Clothiers (PACC) offers local chapters for custom clothing and related businesses: (877) 755-0303 or (443) 755-0303, www.paccprofessionals.org

Books

▶ *The "Business" of Sewing,* Barbara Wright Sykes, Collins Publications, 2005. This is one of a series of books by the same author and publisher. Other titles are: *The "Business" of Sewing, Volume 2; Marketing Your Sewing Business; Pricing Without Fear;* and *Do You Sew for Profit?: A Guide for Wholesale, Retail and Consignment.*

▶ *Sew to Success,* Kathleen Spike, Palmer/Pletsch Publishing, 1995.

Training

▶ Penn Foster Career School offers a distance-learning program in dressmaking and design: (800) 275-4410, www.pennfoster.edu

Web Sites

▶ www.sew-whats-new.com – Offers forums and quilting lessons

Small Town Newspaper Publishing

If you live in a big city, you're no doubt aware that metropolitan newspapers are declining in readership, advertising, and influence. Why then do we include small town newspaper publishing in a book about middle-class survival? The answer is that contrary to what's happening in cities, newspapers in small communities without a local television station are growing in number—and this provides opportunity! Community newspapers, in keeping with the trends we write about in Part II, serve people moving to small towns, metro adjacent communities, edge cities, and nearby faraway places that are either in the shadows of or away from metropolitan media that do not cover their local news.

People want to know the happenings, events, crimes, fires, birth, deaths, and opinions on both sides of issues confronting the community. While there may be a community Web site, it won't contain the breadth or depth a newspaper can provide. So the number of small town newspapers has grown from 5,500 weeklies in the 1960s to over 8,000 today.

Sometimes people moving from a city purchase an existing small town enterprise. This is what Gary Meyer and Patric Hedlund did when moving from Los Angeles to the Frazier Park area to acquire the *Mountain Enterprise*. Or sometimes communities will take up the initiative themselves and create a community-owned newspaper, paying their staff from advertising sales, subscription fees, and donations in order to get the paper off the ground.

When Gary Meyer goes to newspaper conferences, city editors and publishers constantly tell him, "I'd give anything to own a small town paper now." Meyers attributes this to the fact that small town papers are highly profitable in relation to circulation numbers.

Obviously, not every paper succeeds. Arguably, the major difference between papers that make it and those that do not is having an objective publisher with an awesome sense of community responsibility and an ethical backbone of steel. Equally as important, the community must perceive the publisher that way, because people look to their local newspaper for accurate information, but even more for fairness.

The limited number of staff a small newspaper can support brings with it the need to be a jack-of-all-trades, including news gathering, writing, layout, and printing or arranging for printing. You may be called upon to demonstrate a reasonable understanding of subject areas as diverse as gardening, building construction and destruction, and local politics. And working under deadline pressure can't be an anathema to you. So if getting out the news is a personal joy for you, this can be your future. In fact, it could be the most fun you've ever had.

Newspapers, like any other business, require funds to operate. Sources of funds include subscriptions, over-the-counter sales, advertising, and donations. The small town newspaper is often circulated for free to all community members, making advertising revenue critical. Additional sources of revenue may come from printing directories and shoppers guides. Printing services can actually be a side business that provides significant support to the bottom line. The kinds of print jobs you can take depends on your equipment, your staff, and available press time.

Can small town newspapers avoid the electronic age? No. In fact, the *Mountain Enterprise* started its online edition (www.mountainenterprise.com) a few months ago. Meyers says, "Online is the future. You need to put one foot in it firmly now." After only the seventh issue since the launch of the Web site, it has improved advertising revenue. "It will pay for itself in the first couple of months." He advises colleagues to "think of yourself as a *news* publisher, not as *newspaper* publisher."

While the focus of this profile is on newspaper publishing, we have included books about other types of publications, such as magazines, newsletters, and shoppers, in the LEARN MORE section below.

Newspaper publishing is a venerable profession at the heart of the founding fathers' American dream and the First Amendment right of freedom of the press. Being part of continuing this tradition can be personally and professionally fulfilling.

SMALL TOWN NEWSPAPER PUBLISHING AT A GLANCE

ECONOMIC REALITY FIT

► Necessary vs. Discretionary	Discretionary
► Replaceable with technology	Yes
► Offshorable	No
► Industry Status	Established and Stable

PERSONAL REALITY FIT

► Start-up costs	More Than Most
► Overhead	Moderate
► Potential earnings	Moderate
► Flexible hours	Moderate
► Overall stress	More Than Most
► Ease of bartering	More Than Most

Durability Rating

Likely Transferable Skills, Background, Careers

Writers readily transfer to the newspaper business if they have had any journalism experience or tend to write tight, thoroughly researched pieces. English teachers have one of the skill sets required, writing and good grammar. A longtime reader of bigger city papers will have garnered useful insight into this field too. Publishers, however, come from many backgrounds, and the curiosity and discipline to learn what is necessary go a long way.

What to Charge

Newspapers have a number of things they charge for: subscriptions, individual copies, advertising, personals, and classifieds. Each has its own associated expense of effort or money that helps determine the charge. Local papers cost anywhere from nothing to a dollar. Subscriptions to a weekly run between $25 and $50 a year. Advertising rates are quite competitive for display ads and depend on circulation. Rates for personals are often free, and classifieds are billed by the word or by the inch.

Best Ways to Market Small Town Newspaper Publishing

- ▶ If starting a paper from scratch, get local business owners to pledge they will advertise. If seeking donations, involve the community in such tasks as choosing a name for the paper.
- ▶ Be deeply involved in your community.
- ▶ Hire an advertising salesperson.
- ▶ Put your publication on the Web as well as in print.

Tips for Getting Started

- ▶ Carefully assess the need for a local paper. If you are going into competition with an existing paper, is there a big enough community to support you both? Talk with the heads of the major employers in the area.
- ▶ Join your state association of newspaper publishers, attend the conference, and read its publications. Attend workshops and small business education offerings that focus on advertising.
- ▶ To keep costs down, contact the nearest college or university to inquire about offering internships to their students.

LEARN MORE

Associations
- ► Your state newspaper association will probably be the best source of current information you can get. Links to all the state newspaper associations can be found at https://id37.securedata.net/publishers-edge/index_files/State_Industry_Links.htm.
- ► The Newspaper Association of America, while primarily composed of large newspapers, has a Smaller-Market Newspaper Federation that publishes a bimonthly electronic newsletter called *Big Ideas*: www .naa.org.
- ► The National Newspaper Association is the trade association of community newspapers with over 2,500 newspaper members: 573-882-5800, www.nna.org

Books
Newspapers
- ► *Bad News and Good Judgment: A Guide to Reporting on Sensitive Issues in a Small-Town Newspaper,* Jim Pumarlo, Marion Street Press Inc., 2005.
- ► *Community Journalism,* Jock Lauterer, The University of North Carolina Press, 2006.
- ► *How to Publish Weekly Newspapers, Niche-Market Tabloids and Free Circulation Shoppers,* Kitchen-Table Publisher Book, Thomas A. Williams, 2000.

Other Types of Publications
- ► *Publish Your Own Magazine, Guide Book, or Weekly Newspaper,* Thomas A. Williams, Sentient Publications, 2002.
- ► *Starting & Running a Successful Newsletter or Magazine,* Cheryl Woodard, Nolo, 2004.
- ► *How to Start a Magazine,* James Kobak, M. Evans and Company Inc., 2002.

Tax Preparation

The inevitability of taxes coupled with the dislike of both paying them and preparing them makes the tax preparer something of a white knight who ensures we pay only as much as is required and does the tedious work of completing forms for us. And, of course, tax preparers are paid well for providing their services.

Every year millions of tax forms are filed, and a growing proportion are not prepared by the taxpayer; three out of five of us turn to tax practitioners. No wonder! Since 1986, there have been more than 14,400 changes to the tax code. The tax code is becoming more complex each year, and under penalty of perjury we must declare that our return is true, accurate, and complete. Even energy tax credits and deductions can be complicated. Computer tax preparation programs and online tax preparation options have not stopped people from turning to tax professionals. Business is so good that operations like H&R Block and Jackson Hewitt hold classes regularly as a way to recruit new staff.

You can fit into this growing field in a number of ways. The simplest option is as a tax preparer. Although there is much to learn if you take a generalist approach, the majority of individual tax filings are basic; many bookkeepers also prepare taxes. Becoming a tax preparer requires no federal license or certification and nothing in most state jurisdictions beyond the standard local business license required of any business in one's community. California and Oregon are exceptions—in California, state registration is required; in Oregon, a state license. Regardless, in this field, training is everything, and as you will see in the Training section that follows, with a simple Web search, there is plenty of training available.

If you want to have a more sophisticated understanding of tax law, have more extensive training, and be a specially certified tax consultant, you can become an enrolled agent. Here the federal government steps in with a long and difficult exam, but when you pass you gain a special status and the right to appear before the IRS instead of your taxpayer client. This is a benefit for clients and makes it possible for you to get higher fees.

Tax preparation consultants are often called upon, as the amount owed emerges from the pile of receipts and other records, to answer a question like, "What can I do to owe less?" Here you can veer off into consulting. Typical answers would include changing withholdings, moving to tax exempt investments, and so on. You would also advise clients on the tax advantages of alternative energy utilization, social investing, charitable giving arrangements that yield sizable current tax benefits, and businesses that are treated specially in the tax code like farming. Helping clients set up such arrangements could become a business in itself.

Another approach to tax preparation and consultation is tax review. Taxpayers do make mistakes and some are costly. Your business would be to review and re-file for increased refunds or to help people with IRS collection problems.

Taxes are inevitable, but they can provide many opportunities for independent individuals to make a good living. If you work hard and put in the long hours during the four-month tax season, you can be pretty much on your own for the other eight months of the year.

Related Career

Bookkeeping. Despite the growing adoption of accounting software by small businesspeople, bookkeepers manage to stay as busy as they have since the time of ancient Babylonia. Bookkeeping is one task entrepreneurs like to delegate. But even for businesspeople who use accounting software, the need for bookkeepers who do forensic work—that is, identifying and correcting problems that are inherent in or creep in with the use of accounting software—has increased. Bookkeepers can work with their clients' records remotely by accessing their clients' computers. Accountants are not trained to keep a set of books, and as a result they either employ or refer out the bookkeeping for their clients.

Bookkeeping requires a good sense of math and the ability to be thorough, dependable, and accurate. Some bookkeepers will do it all; others specialize in accounts receivable, accounts payable, auditing, or payroll. Others specialize by working with law firms, medical practices, construction companies, or any particular type of business well represented in your area. Typically clients who use outside bookkeepers have fewer than five employees. Bookkeepers can become certified, and this helps in getting work from accountants.

Resources include the American Institute of Professional Bookkeepers [(800) 622-0121, www.aipb.com]; the book *How to Open Your Own In-Home Bookkeeping Service* by Julie A. Mucha-Aydlott; and Web sites such as those listed in the Web sites section that follows. Many community colleges offer courses in accounting, and a growing number of colleges offer distance-learning programs.

TAX PREPARATION AT A GLANCE

ECONOMIC REALITY FIT

► Necessary vs. Discretionary	Necessary
► Replaceable with technology	No
► Offshorable	No
► Industry Status	Established and Expanding

PERSONAL REALITY FIT

► Start-up costs	Moderate
► Overhead	Minimal
► Potential earnings	More Than Most
► Flexible hours	Minimal
► Computer skills	More Than Most
► Overall stress	More Than Most (deadline pressure at tax times)
► Ease of bartering	More Than Most

Durability Rating

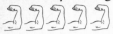

Likely Transferable Skills, Background, Careers

While tax preparation is open to anyone who has the requisite affinity for numbers and details and the patience to master federal and state tax codes, people who have experience in banking, government work, or anything dealing with complex rules and financial information are well suited.

What to Charge

Tax preparers either charge a flat fee per return or by the hour at rates from $50 to $200. A recent survey by the National Society of Accountants found tax preparers charging an average of $110 to prepare a non-itemized 1040 Form and $201 for an itemized 1040 Form with Schedule A. Fees in the Midwest are lower; they are higher in the Northeast, South, and West. Business returns can command fees of up to several thousand dollars.

Independent bookkeepers either charge by the hour or the kind of transaction.

Best Ways to Market Tax Preparation

> ▹ Focus your outreach, including mailings, on new residents and businesses moving into your area.
> ▹ If you are focusing on a niche like teachers, contact their local associations directly to offer your services and/or provide seminars.
> ▹ Seek overload work from CPAs.

Tips for Getting Started

> ▹ Take a class with one of the distance-learning or classroom-training providers.
> ▹ Work part- or fulltime for one of the big preparer outfits for a tax season.
> ▹ Purchase several consumer tax preparation software packages and do your own taxes to learn the nuances of each.
> ▹ Prepare for and take the Enrolled Agents examination. Enrolled agents are able to get double the rates of tax preparers.

LEARN MORE

Associations
- ► National Association of Enrolled Agents: (301) 212-9608, www.naea.org
- ► National Association of Tax Practitioners: (800) 558-3402, www.natptax .com
- ► The National Association of Tax Consultants: (800) 475-2904, www.natctax.com

Book
- ► *Getting Started in Tax Consulting*, Gary Carter, John Wiley & Sons, 2001.

Franchises
- ► Jackson Hewitt: www.jacksonhewitt.com
- ► Tax Centers of America: (800) 555-9936, www.tcoa.net
- ► Liberty Tax Service: www.libertytaxfranchise.com

Training
- ► The H&R Block Income Tax Course: www.hrblock.com
- ► Jackson Hewitt offers classroom and computerized income tax courses: www.jacksonhewitt.com
- ► National Tax Training School offers distance training: (201) 684-0828, www.nattax.com
- ► People's Income Tax Inc.: (804) 204-1040, www.peoplestax.com
- ► Universal Accounting Center: (801) 265-3777, www.universaltax school.com
- ► You can find other sources of training at the California Tax Education Council Web site, which posts lists of approved education providers: www.ctec.org

Web Sites
- ► www.irs.gov/taxpros – The Internal Revenue Service's site for tax professionals
- ► www.sisterstates.com – Links to every state's official tax site
- ► www.taxsites.com and www.el.com/elinks/taxes – Portals with links to information and resources
- ► www.accounting-and-bookkeeping-tips.com
- ► www.allbookkeepingresource.com

Travel Services

People love to travel for new experiences and vacation getaways. Some futurists predict a new surge in travel as boomers reach the age when they have more leisure time and take grandchildren on multi-generational vacations. In the United States alone travel generates an estimated $40,000 a second or 1.3, trillion in economic activity annually, according to the U.S. Department of Commerce. With more travel choices and the complications posed by security, any traveler knows planning is more important than ever before. Whether someone does it for you or you do it yourself, the plan's the thing. Of course, consumers are increasingly planning and booking their own airline tickets, hotel reservations, and packages from travel Web sites, and the airlines no longer pay commissions to travel agents.

Today's opportunities lie in the fact that if someone wants an unusual vacation or a personalized experience, they still need help. As Rick Flesch, vice president of Global Travel International told us, "Internet vendors (like Expedia, Travelocity) can sell three- and four-day packages, but the more people spend on travel, the more they want to be catered to, counseled, and have things taken care of. It's like cutting the grass yourself or having a lawn service do the work." This means they want more than standard packages—they want special experiences.

These needs create many special niches for travel agents to book such experiences. Despite the hundreds, if not thousands, of such possible travel niches, there are many yet to discover and create. A niche can be based on destination, a mode of travel, a sport, an interest in a particular kind of food or wine, an affinity group, a type of experience (such as medical tourism, which helps people find lower cost ways of getting medical procedures performed)—virtually anything and everything, as well as the kind of personal service you provide.

The first place to look for these special niches is to your own interests because no doubt, in a country of 300 million people there are others who share your interests. For example, Kate Delosso specializes in "motherland tours" (www.collectibletours.com) for foreign-born adoptees who want to learn about the lands of their birth. Kelly Monaghan, who has written about being a home-based travel agent, has shared his fascination with Roman ruins by leading tours of Hadrian's Wall in Great Britain. Stuart Wilde manifested his love for the environment by acquiring a herd of llamas and leading Llama Nature Adventures (www.llamaadventures.com) in New Mexico.

Independent travel agents focus a great deal of their attention on cruises, because they pay commissions and because agents are able to book directly with cruise lines. A recent survey by the Outside Sales Support Network of home-based travel agents found better than three out of four consider cruises to be their niche. The survey found tours are the second-largest niche and the second most profitable.

Ecotourism is a rapidly growing niche that involves traveling to places where what's there—forests, mountains, wildlife, or a distinct culture—is the primary draw. The attraction might be watching the penguins march in Antarctica, photographing endangered animals on safari-like trips, watching birds in a cloud forest, watching whales on the Baja coast, or taking in the aurora borealis near the Arctic Circle. These tours are desirable for travel agents because they're more expensive than ordinary travel, and, accordingly, commissions are higher.

In addition to serving as a travel agent, here are some other ways to participate in the travel industry:

- ▶ **Tour packaging** can be done in one of two ways. Either you can simply be the agent—book the hotels, food, and guide services your clients will use—or you can accompany your clients, acting as the guide for their tour, which is what Stuart Wilde does in actually leading the llama tours. Functioning in either way requires knowing the area to be toured well.

- ▶ **Adult education** is a special kind of tour in which participants learn about a topic. The destination may or may not be the topic. For example, while classes on French cooking would most likely take place in France, the setting to learn the ins and outs of digital filmmaking could be on a Caribbean island or in the highlands of Scotland. Conducting classes on cruises is popular. This type of tour is a way in which experts can combine subject-matter expertise with the adventure and pleasure of travel. What you charge participants, of course, has to cover your costs and pay you enough to justify your effort at organizing the tour and teaching your subject.

- ▶ **Travel clubs** enable members to trade the use of their home for the use of another member's home. Running a travel club is a complex business, because you have to be sure the rules are clear and all members are honest. You are covering potentially vast geographic areas, and this presents additional risk. However, as the club manager, you collect an annual fee, and once established the business gets easier to run.

- ▶ **Travel writing and publishing.** Who writes the free information on the Web? Except for review sites, people get paid to do this. In addition, there are travel magazines, guidebooks, newsletters, and much more that are written by travel writers. A major section of every bookstore is the travel section. Most of the books are published by the big houses, but a portion of them are self-published. Other self-published books are published as e-books, and then more than ever, the author's role is to get them sold.

▶ **Operating a bed and breakfast.** If you have a gift for fulfilling other's needs and wishes, you may enjoy operating a bed and breakfast (B&B) inn. Many travelers prefer the personalized attention B&Bs can offer, but your home needs to be in an area that draws travelers. Innkeeping can be a part-time venture, renting out three or fewer rooms to supplement your principal income, or it can be done as a full-time occupation, if you have enough rooms and can keep them occupied a healthy percentage of the time. The more rooms, the better; however, the more licensing requirements you may face. If your location is suitable, renting it for weddings can be a significant source of income, a lot less work, and no license is required. A good resource for anyone interested in this field is the Professional Association of Innkeepers International: (800) 468-7244 or (856) 310-1102, www.paii.org

The travel industry is a service industry—and a big one. You create your own opportunities. You can celebrate your lifelong interest in a subject or place by introducing others to it, or you can operate a Web-based business from home. If any of this appeals to you, the world is waiting.

TRAVEL SERVICES AT A GLANCE

ECONOMIC REALITY FIT

▶ Necessary vs. Discretionary	Discretionary
▶ Replaceable with technology	No
▶ Offshorable	No
▶ Industry Status	Established and Expanding

PERSONAL REALITY FIT

▶ Start-up costs	Minimal
▶ Overhead	Minimal
▶ Potential earnings	Moderate
▶ Flexible hours	More Than Most
▶ Computer skills	Moderate
▶ Overall stress	Minimal
▶ Ease of bartering	Moderate

Durability Rating

Likely Transferable Skills, Background, Careers

Your choice of approach to the travel business will be influenced in part by your feelings about travel. You will need sales skills no matter which business you choose. Teachers can put their professional skills to use as a guide.

What to Charge

The first consideration if you are a tour guide is covering all your expenses, which are charged across the entire group. If you are packaging tours, the markup is between 18 and 25 percent on hotels, events, tours, etc. Unless you are a travel agent or allied with one, have your customers book their own air transportation.

Best Ways to Market Travel Services

- ► Develop strong relationships with organizations and groups that can book the cruises and tours, which are the most profitable products for independent travel agents. This may be church groups or any kind of group with members likely to be interested in your travel specialty.
- ► Offer exceptional services such as home pickup both going and returning from a trip, particularly to your clients with special needs; however, check your vehicle insurance to make sure you're covered to do this.
- ► Participate on sites like www.tripology.com which connects travelers with specialized travel agents. Agents bid on leads.

Tips for Getting Started

- ► To help you identify a travel niche, consider what people are reading and writing in online reviews of their travel experiences. You can do this on sites like www.tripadvisor.com. Look to see what people are enjoying and what they're not!
- ► With people able to learn so much for themselves on the Web, you need to become expert in the options and travel issues related to your niche and its products. This requires considerable initial and ongoing research.
- ► Something we've noticed about everyone we've ever interviewed who

makes money in the travel field is they're really good at making people happy. This translates into referrals.

► You may find it works to offer discounts when one client helps you sign up new clients.

► You'll need both trip insurance and errors and omissions insurance if you're packaging tours.

► Check if your state requires licensing or bonding of travel agents.

LEARN MORE

Associations

► American Society of Travel Agents: (800) 440-ASTA or (703) 739-2782, www.astanet.com

► National Association of Commissioned Travel Agents serves home-based and cruise-oriented agents: (703) 739-6826 or (760) 751-1197, www.nacta.com

► The National Tour Association, operators of escorted bus tours: (800) 682-8886 or (859) 226-4444, www.ntaonline.com

► Network of Entrepreneurs Selling Travel, a marketing group: (888) 245-6378, www.jointhenest.com

► Outside Sales Support Network supports home-based travel agencies, independent contractors, and outside sales travel agents: (800) 452-3198, www.ossn.com

► Travel Industry Association: (202) 408-8422, www.tia.org

► United States Tour Operators Association: (212) 599-6599, www.ustoa.com

Books

► *Conducting Tours*, Marc Mancini, Thomson Delmar Learning, 2000.

► *The Ethical Travel Guide*, Polly Pattullo, Earthscan, May 2006.

► *Home-Based Travel Agent*, Kelly Monaghan, The Intrepid Traveler, 2006.

► *How to Start a Home-Based Travel Agency*, Tom and Joanie Ogg, Tom Ogg and Associates, 2001.

► *Internet Marketing for Your Tourism Business*, Susan Sweeney, Maximum Press, 2000.

► *Niche Tourism*, Marina Novelli, ed., Butterworth-Heinemann, 2005.

Magazines and Newsletter

► *Travel Agent magazine* has archives on its site: www.travelagentcentral .com

▶ *Agent @ Home Magazine*: www.agentathome.com
▶ *Travelwriter Marketletter:* (703) 879-6814, www.travelwriterml.com
▶ *Travel Weekly* newspaper: (303) 470-4445, www.travelweekly.com

Training

▶ The Travel Institute offers textbooks, courses, and certification: (781) 237-0280 or (800) 542-4282, www.thetravelinstitute.com.

Web Sites

▶ www.arccorp.com–The Airlines Reporting Corporation allows independent or at-home agents to become verified travel consultants, which enables the use of ARC's reporting and settlement system.
▶ www.ecotourism.org – The International Ecotourism Society maintains listings of tours, lodges, travel agents, and services by destination (202) 347-9203.
▶ www.travelwriters.com – An online community for professional travel writers, (800) 523-7274.
▶ www.hometravelagency.com – Home-Based Travel Agent resource center, (203) 488-5341.

Tutoring and Adult Education

Today's classrooms are too often crowded beyond the capacity for a single teacher to provide special attention needed by struggling students. Add to this an increased use of standardized testing for high school graduation and entry into colleges, plus intense competition for prized seats in private K–12 schools and the best universities and colleges, and you understand the growing demands for private tutors. And it's not just young people who are seeking help. Adult education is equally on the rise.

At the youngest end of the age spectrum, private preschools and elementary schools have difficult entrance exams and interviews, and the competition for limited spaces is intense. So most parents wanting their children to be accepted into these schools make sure their children get tutored and coached to be sure they do their best. Admission to some private high schools is also subject to competitive testing.

Public schools now must administer standardized testing pursuant to the No Child Left Behind Act, which requires K–12 students to pass a test before advancing to the next grade. The act has also been a boon to tutoring companies, since failing school districts are required to provide free tutoring to their students (subsidized by the federal government). Though independent tutors have perhaps been slightly edged out of the equation by these subsidies, only one in six of the 1.4 million students eligible for tutoring are taking advantage of it, which suggests that in at least some districts there may be opportunity.

College admissions have grown far more competitive than ever before, and both students and parents are willing to do almost anything to get ahead. This includes taking more difficult courses, often through the Advanced Placement and International Baccalaureate programs, which then often requires some degree of outside help or tutoring to help the student to excel. Then there's preparing for college entrance exams, usually the SAT, SAT2, and ACT, and for students seeking National Merit scholarships, there's the PSAT.

Though students at all stages are getting tutored, most academic tutoring is focused on middle- and high-school-age children. Math is the most common subject, but science, foreign languages, reading, history, study skills, and writing are also in demand. Writing is of particular interest now that there's an essay section on college entrance exams, and most colleges and universities require students to submit a personal essay as part of their applications.

Once admitted, college students often require tutoring in subjects they find difficult, such as physics, calculus, biology, and foreign languages. The need for personalized tutelage doesn't end with undergraduate school. College seniors who wish to continue in academic or professional post-graduate schools often need tutoring to score well on such tests as the GRE and LSAT. Those who want to get into a prestigious MBA program are using admissions consultants to coach them with their essays and personal interviews.

Students aren't alone in the market for tutoring. Tutors are helping people with everything from manners and music to sports and speech. Dave Gorrie, for example, gives batting lessons to young people ages eight to eighteen; Andy Mizener offers private pitching lessons, which he's been doing for forty-one years. Special education and ESL (English as a second language) students often need tutors, as do people who wish to improve foreign or regional accents or master pronunciation, grammar, and diction.

An emerging area is teaching what are considered to be "lost arts," which are skills that until recently were thought of as no longer needed, such as boot making, chair caning, canning, crocheting, decorative ironwork, furniture making, growing one's own food, metal casting, needlework, pottery, sewing, tanning, tinning, tracking, weaving, and wood carving.

If income is of primary importance, the most dependable type of tutoring remains the major tests that nearly all high school students take— ACT, which is accepted at all colleges and universities, and the SAT. But it is possible to make a good supplemental income tutoring or teaching topics that are a bit more rarefied. And there are subjects—such as various aspects of using specialized computer software and the Internet—that are as crucial for adults as the SAT is for high schoolers. There's also business writing, which is discussed as a Related Career in the "Writing for a Living" profile in Chapter 3.

Generally students come to an academic tutor's home. For a higher fee some tutors will travel to the student's home. Tutoring in skills such as sports or metal casting requires a special facility where the tutor can work. Usually tutoring is one-on-one. Individual, personal attention is why people will pay well for it, but some tutors also offer small, semi private lessons. However, in working with small groups of five to six students, Christine Dreir, a math tutor/teacher, found that some move ahead and some get lost. "You experience the same issues a classroom teacher does." There is also a technological movement afoot to provide "e-tutoring"—tutoring over the Internet. This has emerged into online teaching and even online education consulting. As the popularity of webcams and real-time interaction grows this may become a preferred method of tutoring.

In 2006 the College Entrance Exam Advisors and Educators (CEEAE) began administering its Educator Proficiency Exam (EPE) to college entrance exam tutors. The online exam tests acumen on the material regularly on the exams and communications proficiency. While it cannot be required, parents can be expected to ask about a prospective tutor's score as word about the exam gets out.

The challenging trends of globalization and othersourcing have placed demands on us and our children as few times before. Your work as a tutor contributes to the preservation of the middle class.

TUTORING AND ADULT EDUCATION AT A GLANCE

ECONOMIC REALITY FIT

► Necessary vs. Discretionary	Discretionary
► Replaceable with technology	Not Completely
► Offshorable	Sometimes
► Industry Status	Established and Expanding

PERSONAL REALITY FIT

► Start-up costs	Minimal
► Overhead	Minimal
► Potential earnings	Moderate, More Than Most (college entrance and beyond)
► Flexible hours	Moderate
► Overall stress	Minimal
► Ease of bartering	More Than Most

Durability Rating

Likely Transferable Skills, Background, Careers

Almost any skill can be used in tutoring and teaching, but generally at least a bachelor's degree in the topic of the tutoring is desirable. But, as described previously, there are very useful and marketable skills in which one would not have a degree, and any background in these is sufficient. If you know it, you can teach it, and more than in almost any other career, your confidence in your own knowledge is the only prerequisite.

What to Charge

For academic tutoring, it is certainly possible to charge a minimum of $50 an hour, and even more if your experience warrants it; however, some tutors charge much less and some much more. Rates vary with subject, grade of the students, experience, your community, and travel time required. Rates for teaching necessary or desirable skills will also vary, while it makes sense to charge less ($25 or $30 an hour) for tutoring in "lost arts."

Best Ways to Market Tutoring

- ▶ Directly contact teachers, school office personnel, counselors, and principals. Also contact psychologists and family counselors who may have in their professional practices children with learning difficulties.
- ▶ Sell your expertise by the minute on the phone using services such as Ether (www.ether.com) and JyvePro (www.jyvepro.com). Clients are billed automatically.

Tips for Getting Started

- ▶ Define a specialization based on a subject and age group. Consider competition in making this decision.
- ▶ If you want to work for a tutoring company, they may be open to training you in subjects in which you have less experience.
- ▶ Certification or its equivalent provides credibility. Make your qualifications clear in whatever advertising you do, articles you write, etc.

- ► Teach adult education classes in local schools to expose you to parents who are apt to have children that are candidates for tutoring.
- ► Home schooling is also a market for tutors.

LEARN MORE

Associations

- ► Association for the Tutoring Profession is a "professional and scholarly association": www.jsu.edu/depart/edprof/atp
- ► Association of Educational Therapists: (800) 286-4267 or (415) 982-2389, www.aetonline.org
- ► Music Teachers National Association: (888) 512-5278 or (513) 421-1420, www.mtna.org
- ► National Tutoring Association provides certification: (863) 529-5206, www.ntatutor.org

Certification

While no states require licensing or certification to tutor students privately, if you wish to work with students whose tutoring is subsidized with government funds, you will need to meet the qualifications established by the school district that administers the money. A teaching credential will always fulfill the standard. Certification is available from the National Tutoring Association and TutorNation.com. To learn about the Educator Proficiency Exam offered by CEEAE, visit www.ceeae.org.

Books

- ► *How to Tutor*, Samuel L. Blumenfeld, Paradigm Company, 1991.
- ► *The Practical Tutor*, Emily Meyer, Louise Z. Smith, Oxford University Press, 1987.
- ► *Tutoring as a Successful Business,* Eileen Kaplan Shapiro, Nateen Publishing, 2001.
- ► *Tutoring Matters*, Jerome Rabow, Tiffani Chin, Nima Fahimian, Temple University Press, 1999.

Franchise

- ► Abrakadoodle®: (703) 871-7356, www.abrakadoodle.com

Training

- ► Lost Arts Preservation Cooperative of Dallas has an apprenticeship program: (214) 565-1055, www.lostarts.com

Wedding Planning and Consulting Services

Marriage is an enduring institution, and because people take pleasure in celebrating love, weddings have turned into an industry with countless options for every possible style of wedding. With couples getting married later in life, often paying for weddings themselves, and both pursuing careers, a wedding planner is a godsend, helping to take the stress out of making preparations and creating a special day the couple can remember joyously for years to come.

The trend has shifted to more formal weddings, but producing a large-scale, one-day event is a considerable task involving many details, like special rules of etiquette that the average couple is unfamiliar with and unprepared to handle on their own. So using a wedding professional reduces this complexity and saves the couple an enormous amount of time. It also saves a lot of money.

A typical wedding usually consists of four bridesmaids, four ushers, music, dancing, and food costing a minimum $15,000. At this writing, the average cost of a wedding is $28,000, and collectively people are spending $72 billion a year to create the wedding day of their dreams, according to Knot.com. By finding the best prices, qualifying for discounts, and steering couples away from costly mistakes, in almost all cases, the wedding professional will save clients more money than what he/she charges in service fees. Such cost savings can be particularly important to couples who are wishing to simplify their lives or who are living on tight budgets, hoping to buy their first home together, move out of a parents' home, or start a family.

Generally wedding professionals, who are called bridal consultants, wedding coordinators, wedding consultants, wedding directors, and wedding planners, play the role for the bride and groom that a contractor plays in building a dream home or a director plays in the making of a movie. The consultant works with the bride and groom and their families to understand what they want and establish a wedding budget. He or she then coordinates the entire production of the wedding, from finding and renting the facilities for the ceremony and reception to negotiating contracts and overseeing the many elements and personnel involved, like photographers, videographers, florists, caterers, travel agents, musicians, and disc jockeys. This means working with and coordinating the efforts of dozens of separate businesses to make the event happen as planned and being at the event itself to see that all goes well. It may even extend to dealing with issues of insurance, luggage for the honeymoon, and home furnishings to set up the couple's first home.

Some couples are choosing to plan a "destination wedding" located at an unusual or exotic venue, such as an extraordinary outdoor setting, a museum, a lighthouse, a theme park, a mansion, or a medieval castle for rent in a distant country. This is creating a niche market for wedding planners who are located in popular destinations. Newer still are wedding planners based at airports providing "weddings to go." Also growing in popularity are "green" weddings. With the right personality, skills, and contacts, this can be an exciting, glamorous, and rewarding career.

WEDDING PLANNING AT A GLANCE

ECONOMIC REALITY FIT

► Necessary vs. Discretionary	Discretionary
► Replaceable with technology	No
► Offshorable	Only at a destination location
► Industry Status	Established and Expanding

PERSONAL REALITY FIT

► Start-up costs	Minimal
► Overhead	Minimal
► Potential earnings	Moderate
► Flexible hours	Minimal
► Overall stress	More Than Most
► Ease of bartering	Moderate

Durability Rating

Likely Transferable Skills, Background, Careers

More important than a particular professional background are the temperament and work characteristics of a wedding professional. As a rule, wedding planners are energetic and peppy and need to be detailed-oriented, creative problem solvers, able to stick to a schedule, and first-rate communicators. They need to have calm nerves under pressure and the talent to soothe tense members of the wedding party and to negotiate with vendors and suppliers. Professional backgrounds that segue into wedding planning include teaching and nursing, because these occupations teach one how to schedule events and manage people. The ability to delegate is essential. If you think you have to do everything by yourself, you may be in a world of hurt.

What to Charge

Wedding coordinators either charge a fee for their time and services by the hour or day, a flat fee, or an actual percentage of the cost of the wedding.

Flat fees are approximately 10 to 15 percent of the wedding budget. If a wedding costs $25,000, a typical fee may be from $2,500 to about $4,000. Because wedding planning is competitive, particularly newer planners are apt to begin at fees in the lower range. If charging by the hour for consultation or by the day for help with the event itself, hourly rates range from $50 to $150 and per diem rates from $300 to $1,200. As you might expect, location and competition influences pricing. While some wedding planners offset much of their fees to their clients by receiving a commission from vendors with whom they have a commissionable arrangement, many wedding professionals frown on this practice.

Wedding coordinators can enhance their revenue by providing extra services, such as selling accessories, coordinating showers, renting tuxedos, and printing invitations. They can continue serving clients by doing anniversary parties and other events for them, their family, and their friends.

Best Ways to Market Wedding Planning

- ▶ Advertise in specialty wedding publications or guides and the wedding supplements to local newspapers.
- ▶ Exhibit at bridal shows or in a smaller community or niche market. You could even set up your own small bridal show.
- ▶ Get repeat business by doing anniversary parties and other events for your clients, their families, and their friends.
- ▶ Provide free consultations for couples, advising them of what will be involved in planning their weddings.

Tips for Getting Started

- ▶ Study trends in weddings and consider specializing your practice by the type of weddings or by focusing on a particular ethnic background or special interest (theme weddings). For example, green or eco-friendly weddings are growing in popularity. Going to bridal shows and expos will give you ideas. You can also take classes, read magazines, and troll the Web for information.
- ▶ Learn the basics of wedding coordination. Sometimes this can be done with a job, other times by apprenticing yourself with an established wedding planner. The Association of Bridal Consultants (listed in the LEARN MORE section that follows) has an internship/apprenticeship program.
- ▶ Plan the wedding of a friend or relative for free or a very low cost so

you can build a portfolio that includes photographs of the wedding and letters of recommendation from your clients and their families.

▸ Get your wardrobe in shape so you will have clothes for meeting with suppliers, clients, and attending the weddings.

▸ Identify suppliers you can rely upon. If you try to do this when you're in the throes of coordinating an actual wedding, your frustration will rise and your hourly rate will go down.

▸ To establish credibility if you are handling client money, consider establishing an escrow account that will assure clients that contractors will be paid.

Related Careers

Bridal Clothing: The wedding gown has to be central to the saying "All brides are beautiful." People anticipating the bride entering the room in a beautiful dress, veiled and beaded, is palpable at even the most casual wedding. Many brides now want unique creations that might combine elements from several gowns they wish to emulate or that reflect a period or regional costume they admire. Custom wedding gowns go for $8,000 to $150,000. This business can be developed either by a skilled seamstress or a designer partnering with a seamstress. See the Sewing Services profile earlier in this chapter.

For the wedding on a budget, a business can be built renting wedding gowns and designer dresses for the mother of the bride and dresses suitable for remarriages. This is what Bev Osbourne has done in the basement rec room of her University Place, Washington, home. She calls her business Nothing to Wear.

Wedding Makeup Artist: A wedding makeup artist specializes in making the bride, the bridal party, and even the groom look good in person and for the photos and videos they want to look at years from now. This requires knowledge of skin types and the ability to work around nervous brides and family members who often seek to supervise the makeup sessions.

Wedding makeup artists do their work over two sessions, one before the wedding for sixty to ninety minutes to show the bride various possibilities for the color scheme that's been selected, and the next session is the day of the wedding, before photos are taken, to do the makeup for the entire bridal party. The makeup artist may either leave or stay on hand to touch up the makeup at various times during the wedding celebration. By doing more than one wedding per weekend, makeup artists can earn seven to eight hundred dollars per week.

LEARN MORE

Associations

▸ Association of Bridal Consultants offers insurance and professional development programs: (860) 355-0464, www.bridalassn.com

- Association for Wedding Professionals International: (800) 242-4461) or (916) 482-3010, www.afwpi.com
- Association of Certified Professional Wedding Consultants: (408) 528-9000, www.acpwc.com
- June Wedding Inc.: (702) 474-9558, www.junewedding.com

Books

- *FabJob Guide to Become a Wedding Planner,* Catherine Goulet, Jan Riddell, 2003. See also www.fabjob.com
- *How to Start a Wedding Planning Business,* Cho Phillips, Sherrie Wilkolaski, e-book, 2003. See also www.lulu.com
- *Start Your Own Wedding Consulting Business,* Eileen Figure Sandlin, Entrepreneur Media Inc., 2003.

Also see the books listed in the Corporate and Community Meeting and Event Planning profile earlier in the chapter.

Training

Most of the associations listed in this section offer courses and accreditation. Also see:

- Penn Foster Career School: www.pennfoster.edu/bridalconsultant
- Professional Career Development Institute: (800) 223-4542 or 770-729-8400, www.pcdi-homestudy.com
- Weddings Beautiful Worldwide: (804) 288-1220, www.weddings beautiful.com

Web Sites

- http://messageboards.ivillage.com/iv-wfwfhwedding – iVillage's wedding and event planner community message board
- www.ethicalweddings.com – a site for listing ethical wedding services and products
- www.greenhotels.com–Green Hotels Association
- www.theknot.com, www.weddingchannel.com, www.weddingsite .com – Portal sites for all things wedding.
- www.portovert.com – E-magazine about green weddings.
- www.weddingbells.com – *Weddingbells* magazine (free)
- www.weddingsolutionssuperstore.com – Wedding products

The new electronic independence recreates the
world in the image of a global village.
Marshall McLuhan, *The Gutenberg Galaxy:*
The Making of Typographic Man

CHAPTER THREE

13 Nichable Virtual Products and Services

The careers profiled in this chapter do not rely on a local population for their clients and customers to the extent those in Chapter 2 do. For example, you can coach, provide customer support, or consult from a mountaintop if you have a broadband Internet connection. These careers enable you to consider living almost anywhere. Another facet of the careers in Chapter 3 is that they generally require being specialized. In fact, it's a disadvantage to try to serve anyone who needs coaching or consulting. The Web rewards you with higher rankings on search engines for distinguishing what you do from the hundreds or even thousands of other people who do something similar. Particularly for the careers in Chapter 3, "finding your niche and scratching it" works.

Coaching Services

Some people regard the field of life coaching as overcrowded because so many people have flocked into it since its debut in the 1990s. But in a fast-changing economy, almost everyone has to reset their goals, solve problems, and identify skills to improve or develop. As a result of the growing amount of *othersourcing* that is squeezing the middle class, two kinds of coaching will be particularly in demand:

> ▶ Creativity coaching helps creative artists pursue their work, but it is also becoming important for anyone in a workforce where left-brain

skills alone will no longer be enough to succeed in the corporate world. This is illustrated by a recent statement General Motors Vice Chairman Bob Lutz made at a shareholders' meeting: "What we've got at GM now is a general comprehension that you can't run this business by the left, intellectual, analytical side of the brain. You have to have a lot of right side, creative input. We are in the arts and entertainment business, and we're putting a huge emphasis on world-class design."

▶ Transition or post–corporate career coaching encompasses helping individuals redefine their life purpose, find a new career, pursue job search strategies, and identify an acceptable balance between their lives and their work. As Dan Pink, author of *A Whole New Mind: Why Right-Brainers Will Rule the Future*, told us, "The shelf life of any specialized knowledge—or even any specialized skills—is so brief that people have to constantly upgrade their abilities. Learning is no longer a pit stop along the track of someone's career." This pace of change is faster than most people can handle on their own, and the role of the post–corporate career coach is to help people identify where they fit in a continually changing economy and how to make repeated transitions. Someone who stays alert to emerging needs such as these and has good interpersonal skills like those we describe in the pages that follow can earn a living in this satisfying field.

Usually successful coaches specialize: sometimes by the desired outcome one helps others achieve, such as creativity or leadership; by the type of problem they help others address, such as fitness or health care; or by the industry they serve. For example, after twenty-four years in commercial real estate, Clara Goldenhar developed a practice helping people in her former industry through career transitions. Coaching was a natural fit for her, she told us. "I had always been sought out for advice. Problem solving was something I did well."

Many people who go into coaching have credentials in already-established fields, such as psychotherapy, accounting, law, career counseling, human-resource development, management consulting, training, theater, financial planning, and even engineering. A fair number of these career migrants identify themselves as coach/consultants; we, however, believe some primary difference exists between coaching and consulting.

First, coaches work with individuals, and the development of their individual potentials is the focus of their efforts. Consultants typically help clients within the context of an organization, although consultants who focus on something specific, such as image or finances, work with individuals. This is not a sharp line, because some coaches work with multiple clients in a group in an organizational setting, though often this is to guide group members in coaching one another.

Consultants more readily render advice and information where coaches pose challenging questions.

Usually coaches will either assist clients in addressing personal issues or business and career issues. Personal coaches focus on career transitions, creativity, quality of life, health and wellness, professional development, parenting skills, relationships, finances, and balancing work with life, among others. Business coaches may work with specific types or sizes of companies and may focus on issues such as business planning, financing, strategic planning, conflict management, team building, partnership relations, management styles, and productivity.

While coaches usually obtain their income from working with individual clients over the phone or in corporations, they also frequently conduct workshops and seminars for large or small groups in weekend retreats and offsite meetings for private or corporate groups. They also write articles for local, regional, and national publications or for wellness, personal development, and coaching Web sites.

Related Career

Stress Management. Stress can lead to depression, and with 42 percent of people reporting that they experience stress in their daily lives, depression is forecast to be the most debilitating illness of high-income individuals over the next twenty years—nearly double the rate of heart disease—according to the World Health Organization's estimate of the *Global Burden of Disease*. Already in affluent South Korea, one in ten Koreans reports considering suicide because of economic distress, according to a survey by South Korea's National Statistical Office. Nature-guided counseling and healing is particularly useful in helping people overcome depression. Without a prior degree in psychotherapy, you can become certified or obtain academic degrees (www.ecopsych.com).

COACHING AT A GLANCE

ECONOMIC REALITY FIT

▹ Necessary vs. Discretionary	Discretionary
▹ Replaceable with technology	No
▹ Offshorable	Because most one-to-one coaching is by phone, cultural limitations are those that are important
▹ Industry Status	Established and Expanding

PERSONAL REALITY FIT

▹ Start-up costs	Minimal
▹ Overhead	Minimal

- ▸ Potential earnings   More Than Most
- ▸ Flexible hours   Moderate
- ▸ Overall stress   Moderate
- ▸ Ease of bartering   Minimal

Durability Rating

Likely Transferable Skills, Background, Careers

As one coach says, "What you bring to coaching are your life and work skills." Any field in which you have experience has potential for a client base when combined with strong interpersonal skills and the ability to form a positive relationship with clients. From baseball to team building, trust is the key to coaching. Clients need to trust a coach in order to honestly reveal themselves. Coaches also need to be able to interpret what clients mean, which is often quite different from what they say. They need to know how to ask questions in a way that provoke clients to expand and clarify their thinking and their choices.

What to Charge

Coaching fees range from $200 to $2,000 a month for three to four thirty- to fifty-minute sessions, with $400 to $600 a month being in the mid-range. Some coaches charge by the project. For example, a weekend team building off-site, depending on the number of participants, can cost from $8,000 to $20,000. The best revenue streams are one-to-one coaching by the month, group coaching by the month (by way of a corporate contract or groups you assemble), workshops, and teleclasses.

Best Ways to Market Coaching

- ▸ Offer sample (free) fifteen- to thirty-minute consultations in person or over the phone. You can also have an online consultation practice whereby people can "chat" with you for a by-the-minute fee.
- ▸ Sell your services by the minute on the phone using services like Ether (www.ether.com) and JyvePro (www.jyvepro.com). Clients are billed automatically.

Tips for Getting Started

- Identify one or more specializations that will enable you to focus your marketing efforts and attract clients. For example, you could offer post–corporate career coaching for people leaving an industry because of disability. A subspecialty might be a particular disability like back injuries. Business coaching for a specific industry or market in a foreign language is another way to specialize, subspecialize, and sub-subspecialize.
- Obtain whatever training you think will be helpful. With dozens and dozens of training programs, find a program that seems closest to preparing you for the type of coaching you plan to do.
- Arrange your finances so you will have the several years it will take to build your practice. Keep in mind most of your clients are going to be people in some form of transition, typically between the ages of thirty-five and fifty-five.

Learn More

Associations and Certification

- International Association of Coaches: www.certifiedcoach.org
- International Coach Federation (ICF): (888) 423-3131 or (859) 219-3580, www.coachfederation.org
- Worldwide Association of Business Coaches: www.wabccoaches.com

Books

- *Coaching with Spirit,* Teri-E Belf, Jossey-Bass/Pfeiffer, 2002.
- *Four Steps to Building a Profitable Coaching Practice: A Complete Marketing Resource Guide for Coaches*, Deborah Brown-Volkman, iUniverse, 2003.
- *Getting Started in Personal and Executive Coaching,* Stephen G. Fairley and Chris E. Stout, John Wiley & Sons, 2003.
- *Therapist as Life Coach: Transforming Your Practice,* Patrick Williams, Deborah C. Davis, W. W. Norton & Company, 2002. Patrick Williams has also coauthored *Total Life Coaching*.

Training

- The site www.peer.ca/coachingschools.html briefly describes almost three hundred schools and gives the prices of their programs and links to their sites. Considerations in choosing a school are how long it's been operating, how many graduates it has produced, and if it relates to the specialization you wish to pursue. For example, if you're interested in creativity coaching, there's the Creativity Coaching Association (www.creativitycoachingassociation.com/cca/programs/certification.shtml).

▶ The Progressive International Coaching Board offers free mentoring to new coaches: www.picb.org

Web

A directory of professional associations, service organizations, support networks, consortiums, and franchises can be found at: www.mentors.ca/coachorgs.html#profs.

Consulting

Many people think of consulting as a second career or a default way of earning a living when they find employment no longer possible or appealing. What distinguishes consulting from other forms of self-employment? Bill Mooney, a renowned trainer of new consultants, has crystallized a definition of consulting in terms of what a consultant does—helping people in organizations solve problems and add value as a result. Value may be increasing profit margin, decreasing costs, improving a process like customer contact, avoiding employee grievances, or creating a new product or service.

Professional consulting has emerged because the time has passed when most organizations could claim at least one "wise man"—an individual with enough strength, stature, wisdom, and insight to provide a guiding hand when the going got tough or to solve what appeared, at first glance, to be an intractable problem. Today, too often executives are as unlikely as middle managers to envision necessary strategic changes or be around long enough to implement necessary steps to solve problems and advance business objectives. Thus companies turn to outside consultants for the insight, discipline, and objectivity required in an increasingly competitive business environment. Huge consulting firms like Accenture, Deloitte, and McKinsey & Company as well as tens of thousands of smaller firms and individual consultants thrive on the consulting needs of the private, nonprofit, and public sectors.

As the economic landscape becomes more challenging, your own corporate position may be threatened, but even if you find yourself "downsized," there may be an upside. While you may be leaving your job, you are bringing your expertise, experience, and years of accrued wisdom. And consulting is one business where the experience and expertise you bring is at the heart of the business. Consulting allows you to turn your experience into an income if your expertise is valuable to someone else and you have techniques for employing your knowledge in ways that benefit and add value to others. The more state-of-the-art your know-how is, the more likely you are to be able to sell it. Experience is your track record of solving problems.

These strengths can be the basis for a rewarding and successful consulting career. Individuals with credible experience and know-how can enter into the market immediately, particularly if they specialize in something in current demand such as:

- ► engineering
- ► graphic design
- ► information technology
- ► management and marketing on a project basis
- ► protocol documentation
- ► writing training manuals

Some consulting arenas needed in good times and bad include business turnaround, crisis management, political campaign consulting, professional practice management, and security consulting (the subject of another profile). Some, like image and marketing consultants, do better when companies are in an expansion mode, but when the economy is hurting, consulting shifts to saving money.

You will most likely be able to find consulting clients in an industry in which you have experience. For example, Tom Edwards (no relative), who worked for Microsoft for thirteen years as a geographer, geoculturalist, cartographer, and geopolitical strategist, is performing the same kind of work but for a broader range of companies.

Invariably when several consultants are competing for the same project, the consultant with industry experience gets the work. However, you also can relate your expertise to emerging technologies and newly enacted laws and regulations that cause organizations to seek consultants for training and implementation. Bill Mooney points out that the three driving forces for hiring consultants are the introduction of new technologies; the need to comply with all forms of regulation, whether it be governmental, corporate financial, environmental, or quality standards; and the necessity to stay competitive.

Change is brewing in the world of consulting, and for some, change means opportunity. Even efforts that begin as a substitution for high-priced consulting contracts can be a chance for individuals or small groups of people with expertise. For example, just as organizations have moved from hiring employees to hiring consultants, firms are now using competitions to get ideas and solve problems. Here are some examples:

- ► Staples wanted new product ideas, so it held a competition seeking new product ideas from customers. For a twenty-five-thousand-dollar grand prize, Staples got 13,700 product concepts.
- ► Eli Lilly, one of the largest of the pharmaceutical giants, created a subsidiary, an e-business venture called InnoCentive (www.innocentive .com), that enables corporations (Seekers) to list biology and chemistry problems they want solved. Scientists and small firms (Solvers)—so far eighty-five thousand of them from 173 countries—propose solutions, and a winner is picked. Prizes can be as much as one hundred thousand dollars.
- ► The Defense Advanced Research Projects Agency (DARPA) held a contest to anyone who could pilot an unmanned vehicle across the Mojave Desert. It took two years of contests to produce a winner of a one-million-dollar prize, but DARPA estimates that by developing this capability with conventional engineering contracts or in-house research, this feat would have taken years.

Consultants can lead their clients to such competitions and help them prepare proposals and submissions. This type of work lends itself to project management work, which is a prominent type of consulting assignment.

As in the DARPA example above, depending on your expertise and the competition, you as a consultant may compete as an entrant. Some competitions often require labs or test facilities. We foresee this will spur consultants to develop their own laboratories for their clients or on a for-hire basis for other consultants and small firms, possibly available on an hourly basis where freelancers ply their skills. Chemist Rita Boggs, PhD, operates her own independent testing laboratory, American Research and Testing Inc. in Gardena, California, which she uses to serve clients.

So we predict that even in the midst of change, consulting will remain intellectually, creatively, and financially rewarding. To be successful, you should bring to bear your broad spectrum of skills and tools. However, bear in mind the fundamental paradox of consulting—as a consultant, you will be advising people of equal intellectual ability who have a much more extensive understanding of the problem confronting their company. In other words, it would not be unreasonable to expect them to be in a stronger position to solve their company's problem than you, yet they are looking to you for a solution! To be an effective consultant, you need to do more than simply "solve problems"—you need to be the calm, wise voice that also offers strategic guidance to the company or corporation you are advising. To effectively guide others toward such solutions, you will have to play a number of roles: counselor, parent figure, psychotherapist, and stern disciplinarian.

The decision to become a consultant should be based on more than finding a "default" career choice. While your motivation to become a consultant may be the result of mid-career factors as varied as the desire to work independently or an economy that threatens the security of your current job and future, even so, you should bring a passion for ideas to consulting, a passion for client service, and a passion for people. Otherwise, even your experience and expertise will not be enough to make consulting a rewarding and successful career choice.

Related Career

Information professional. Originally people in this field were called information brokers, but this proved to be too confining a term for professionals who do work that's more like investigative reporting or market research than commercing in raw data. In time intelligent agents or software that acts on behalf of someone in conducting a search will overtake many of the search aspects of their work, but the core of what they are needed for will largely remain. That core is analyzing huge amounts of information that is relevant to companies and organizations of all types and sizes. And because not all information is available on the public or private Web (like Dialog, LEXIS/NEXIS, and Westlaw) and must be obtained via telephone and personal contact, we expect this profession to last. To some extent, their role may shift to verifying and editing the work of intelligent agents. Frequently information professionals collaborate with consultants. Resources for learning more include the Association of Independent Information Professionals (www.aiip.org); the book *Building & Running a Successful Research Business* by Mary Ellen Bates and Reva Basch; and training from sources like MarketingBase [(800) 544-5924 or (707) 829-9421; www.marketingbase.com].

CONSULTING AT A GLANCE

ECONOMIC REALITY FIT

► Necessary vs. Discretionary	Discretionary
► Replaceable with technology	No
► Offshorable	Possible
► Industry Status	Established and Expanding

PERSONAL REALITY FIT

► Start-up costs	Moderate
► Overhead	Minimal
► Potential earnings	More Than Most

► Flexible hours	More Than Most
► Overall stress	Moderate
► Ease of bartering	Minimal

Durability Rating

Likely Transferable Skills, Background, Careers

As a consultant, you should have an academic and experiential background in the field you will be working within. For example, if you are advising a manufacturing company on ways to make their manufacturing process more efficient, you should not only have an appropriate educational background but also experience in the field of manufacturing. By the same token, if you are being asked to advise a company on improving their "corporate culture," you should have a background that allows you to appropriately address those concerns.

While your background experience will certainly benefit you if you provide consulting only in your field, you will find that your greatest asset is your "business sense" and "people sense." Even in those situations when the problem solving will be fairly specific and will require your knowledge in a field, your life experience and maturity—your ability to read people and interpersonal dynamics (the core of a corporate culture)—will enable you to diagnose/define a problem, articulate a solution, and develop a strategy to implement your solution.

What to Charge

Depending on the situation, you will bill either by the hour, by the project, or on the value or impact of your work. Hourly rates vary with the type of client, your field, and, of course, location. For small businesses and highly competitive fields, billing $75 to $150 an hour is common by individual consultants; $150 to $300 by small firms. For larger companies or specialties that are in high demand, individual consultants can expect to bill $200 and more.

Experienced consultants are able to safely estimate the number of hours a project will require and can quote a project price, which is usually preferred over hourly rates by smaller businesses. Travel expenses and hotel accommodations should be factored into your fee or contracted as a separate expense to the company.

Best Ways to Market Consulting

▶ Maintain and nurture your relationship with past employers, colleagues, and clients—they're the best sources of continuing new business.

▶ Develop relationships that result in referrals from other professionals who are serving the same clientele, such as lawyers, accountants, bankers, vendors in industry, and other consultants with other specializations. You want them to consider referring you as a way of helping their clients.

▶ Offer services remotely. Using webcams, you can expand your pool of prospective clients, provide support services, and reduce travel costs to clients. You can sell your expertise by the minute on the phone using services like Ether (www.ether.com) and JyvePro (www.jyvepro.com). Clients are billed automatically.

▶ Check out Web sites like www.elance.com, www.guru.com, and www.expertmarketplace.com where buyers seeking services look for providers to bid on their projects. If you're willing to bid your services at prices less than what you would charge a local client, these are marketplaces for you.

Tips for Getting Started

▶ Identify a way to specialize that will differentiate you from other consultants, even in the same industry.

▶ Obtain certifications that will enhance your credibility; first, in your chosen field or specialization, and then as a consultant.

▶ Develop a business plan, particularly a marketing plan for the first year, and allow yourself two to four years to reach profitability.

LEARN MORE

Associations

Approximately one hundred fifty associations serve the consulting industry. Out of those:

▶ Most are focused on a particular type of consulting, such as chemical, computer, health care, political consulting, security, and weddings

▶ Some are organized based on particular functions, like marketing, human resources, and computers

▶ Others are geographically focused, like the Society of Professional Consultants in New England, the Association of Professional Consultants (APC) in California, and the Association of Independent Consultants in Toronto

▶ Still others exist as councils within industry and trade associations

Books

- *The Complete Guide to Consulting Success,* Howard L. Shenson, Ted Nicholas, Paul Franklin, Dearborn Trade, 1997.
- *Consulting for Dummies,* Bob Nelson and Peter Economy, For Dummies, 1997.
- *The Consultant's Quick Start Guide,* Elaine Biech, Pfeiffer, 2001.
- *The Consultant's Toolkit,* Mel Silberman, McGraw-Hill Trade, 2000.
- *Flawless Consulting,* Peter Block, Pfeiffer, 1999.
- *Getting Started in Consulting,* Alan Weiss, John Wiley & Sons, 2003. Weiss has a number of other useful titles, such as *Million Dollar Consulting* (Wiley, 2005) and *How to Establish a Unique Brand in the Consulting Profession* (Pfeiffer, 2001).
- *Guerrilla Marketing for Consultants,* Jay Conrad Levinson, Michael W. McLaughlin, John Wiley & Sons, 2004.
- *High-Impact Consulting,* Robert H. Schaffer, Jossey-Bass, 2002.
- *Successful Independent Consulting,* Douglas Florzak, Logical Directions Inc., 2003.
- *The Trusted Advisor,* David Maister, Rob Galford, Charles Green Free Press, 2001.
- For a comprehensive list of relevant books, check out www.consultant coach.com/resources.htm

Certification

- The Institute of Management Consultants (IMC) conducts programs leading to certification: (800) 221-2557, www.imcusa.org.
- Computer Institute of Certification of Computer Professionals: (847)299-4227 or (800-843-8227), www.iccp.org

Training

- The Center For Consulting & Professional Practices: (310) 324-2386, www.consultantcoach.com – The Center was the Southern California licensee of Howard L. Shenson's programs. Shenson was the first person to offer training for consultants. The late Mr. Shenson encouraged us to write our first book, *Working From Home.*
- Most of the consulting associations provide training for their members. For example, the Institute of Management Consultants conducts teleseminars on consulting as a second career.

Web Sites

- www.consultingcentral.com – Home to Kennedy Information, a company that researches and forecasts the market for consulting services. It publishes three print newsletters, three e-newsletters, a national magazine, research reports, and professional books. The company also produces on-site conferences and hosts audio and Web conferences.

▶ www.dmreview.com/portals/portal.cfm?topicId=230017) – DM Review's Consulting Portal offers articles, white papers, lists of books, an "Ask the Expert" archive, and other resources.

▶ http://raintoday.com – Provides articles about marketing consulting

Customer Support

If you like to talk and you're a quick study, you could be an agent for a U.S.-based customer service operation and making money in about a week. In a much-needed turnabout, many U.S. companies are bringing their customer service programs back to the mainland. Small companies are finding that consumers expect more, resulting in a need for more extensive customer support systems. This means opportunity for entrepreneurs.

Time spent with customers results in new sales and referrals when the exchange is a positive one from the customer's perspective. Negative customer service experiences will cost a business a customer as well as potential sales and referrals. In fact, negative experiences account for two out of five customer defections. You can intervene and assure quality experiences as a customer support professional.

There are multiple opportunities in this service industry segment. You can operate independently, selling your services to small businesses. You can operate virtually, developing a network of operators to respond to customer needs. Or you can go to work for another operator like www.alpineaccess.com, www.arise.com, www.five9.com, www.liveops.com, or www.workingsol.com. According to a study by IDC, a Framingham, Massachusetts-based research company, over one hundred thousand people work from home as home care agents, and this is projected to triple by 2010.[1]

Kim Conner, a former chemistry teacher, who now works with Liveops, concluded that when she had her second child, juggling the hours of several part-time jobs didn't work for her any longer. She was up and running providing customer support within a week and a half and deciding on her own hours. In fact, she finds her major challenge is committing to a particular schedule of

---

[1] *Home-Based Agent 2005–2010 Forecast and Analysis: Converging Economic Forces to Drive the Expansion of Homeshoring in the United States* http://www.idc.com/getdoc.jsp?containerId=prUS20036206

hours when she will work. She says, "It's easy to say 'I'm not going to work.'" So she sets goals for herself and then rewards herself when she reaches them. The other challenge is being on your own for technical support. So she has two computers (one of them a notebook) and two Internet service providers. She easily makes up the cost of these by not having downtime. The notebook computer enables her to work from anywhere in her home or even in bed.

Each company has its own way of operating, and entry costs vary. In the case of Arise Virtual Solutions Inc., you need to incorporate, so your start-up cost can run about six hundred dollars. Of course, this means you own your own corporation. If you establish your own service operation, your initial costs will be in the thousands. Your entry cost depends solely on which approach you pursue and whether you operate independently or look to an established operation.

If you're working for someone else, incomes of six to twenty dollars per hour are the range. As you acquire experience, your earnings are more apt to be at the higher end. If you offer technical expertise, your range will expand upward. The hours can be exceptional. You will be setting up your own work hours within the needs of the company and its clients. However, in a 24/7 society, your choice of hours will probably be when you work.

Survey work typically pays seven to ten dollars per hour, while customer support work, which can include incentives, pays more. Survey work is often in the evening, making this a good way to supplement your income.

Customer support personnel are usually independent contractors and receive a Form 1099 at year-end. In this case, you are responsible for filing and paying your estimated taxes.

If you choose to work for a customer service firm, you will be provided with the necessary training. Going it alone means having to study a company and its products until your knowledge is complete.

CUSTOMER SUPPORT AT A GLANCE

ECONOMIC REALITY FIT

► Necessary vs. Discretionary	Both
► Replaceable with technology	Yes
► Offshorable	Yes
► Industry Status	Established and Expanding

PERSONAL REALITY FIT

► Start-up costs	Minimal
► Overhead	Minimal
► Potential earnings	Minimal

- ► Flexible hours　　　　　More Than Most
- ► Overall stress　　　　　Minimal
- ► Ease of bartering　　　　Minimal

Durability Rating

Likely Transferable Skills, Background, Careers

If you've worked the phones in just about any business, you may be comfortable providing customer support. Offering the service to business sectors you've worked in will make you a quick study, able to get up and running quickly. More than any other, sales professionals will fit easily into these positions, because they understand the need for extensive product knowledge and possess the skills to bring a matter to a close.

What to Charge

If you are developing your own business, you can bill by the call, by time, or by the coverage hour. As an independent employing others, you will have to pay the equivalent of at least $6 to $10 an hour.

Best Ways to Market Customer Service

- ► Offer your services to small- to medium-sized businesses, particularly ones you've worked at in the past.
- ► Contact businesses that are advertising for customer support personnel.

Tip for Getting Started

If you have no background in providing customer support, consider working for an existing firm before starting your own service. You will obtain training and gain experience.

LEARN MORE

Association and Training

- ► The International Customer Service Association offers a self-paced training program (called "Through the Customer's Eyes") leading to certification: (800)360-4272 or (312) 321-6800, www.icsa.com

- ▶ The Customer Care Institute offers a two-day training program leading to certification: (404) 352-9291, www.customercare.com
- ▶ The National Association of Call Centers, an industry trade association, has five types of membership: (601) 447-8300, www.nationalcallcenters .org

Books

- ▶ *301 Great Customer Service Ideas*, Nancy Artz, ed., Inc. Publishing, 1997.
- ▶ *Customer Service Training 101*, Renee Evenson, AMACOM Books, 2005.
- ▶ *Customer Service for Dummies*, Karen Leland, Keith Bailey, For Dummies, 2006.
- ▶ *Customer Service on the Internet*, Jim Sterne, John Wiley & Sons, 2000.
- ▶ *Great Customer Service on the Telephone*, Kristin Anderson, AMACOM Books, 1992.
- ▶ *The Big Book of Customer Service Training Games*, Peggy Carlaw, Vasudha K. Deming, McGraw-Hill, 1998.

Web

- ▶ www.customerservicemanager.com – Offers an e-magazine and online community

Disease Management

One of the reasons that Americans live longer than we used to is said to be the significant improvements in the diagnosis and treatment of disease. However, the effectiveness of treatment is limited when patients do not follow the medication regimens they are prescribed. As many as 20 percent of patients in treatment for hypertension are considered noncompliant, meaning they do not take their medication as prescribed. This is caused by a number of factors, including a lack of insurance, the cost of medications, and poor patient education.

An example of the costs addressed here is best exemplified by diabetes. This is a potentially life-threatening illness. When diabetes is not managed, patients can suffer blindness, loss of limbs, and other costly conditions such as heart disease. The operant term is costly. Disease management programs have demonstrated that long-term and acute costs can be reduced. This cheers insurance companies, patients and their families, and folks looking for a career helping people.

Disease management can be defined as proactive management of a chronic medical condition that brings together physicians and support services to assist patients in taking better care of themselves. Disease management programs are most common in the care of persons with diabetes, allergies and asthma, heart disease, and more recently, depression and prenatal care.

Your participation in the disease management industry could take one of several directions: direct patient care as an independent operator, patient care as an agent of an insurance company, direct patient care as an employee of an assisted living operator, and more. Working in this field usually requires specialization in one disease and its management. It means keeping up with the latest successes in management and treatment in professional journals as well as popular sources. The latter is important because this is where patients often get their information. It means having extensive knowledge of local resources for information, supplies, treatment, etc.

Disease management program staff, whether independent or not, are people who can communicate up and down the care chain. Physicians, nurses, home health aides, family members, and neighbors may all be recruited to support a chronically ill client. Your job is to keep them on task and communicating with each other, you, and the patient as necessary.

Disease management programs can be limited to calling the patient on a regular or even scheduled basis to discuss medication compliance, diet, and general health. It may mean making sure diabetes supplies are ordered and delivered or prescriptions reordered and refilled. Disease management will mean educating patients and caretakers about medications, disease complications, limitations, and more. Education may simply take the form of providing literature. More elaborate programs may include group meetings or face-to-face teaching.

Some disease management staff never meet their patients; the relationship is strictly via telephone or across the Internet. There are high-tech programs that provide monitoring and reporting equipment for essential data. In diabetes management a patient's glucose level may be sent from the testing device directly to your computer with alarm systems to alert you when additional action or support is necessary. Blood pressures and other circulatory statistics can be similarly monitored and reported to the disease management professional or program.

While you need extensive knowledge of the disease in which you are specializing, you will also need to demonstrate genuine care for each of your patients and be able to be assertive with the patient and the individuals in their support network.

DISEASE MANAGEMENT AT A GLANCE

ECONOMIC REALITY FIT

► Necessary vs. Discretionary	Both
► Replaceable with technology	Probably not; technology complements human contact

- Offshorable   Possibly
- Industry Status   Established and Expanding

Personal Reality Fit

- Start-up costs   Minimal
- Overhead   Minimal
- Potential earnings   Moderate
- Flexible hours   Moderate
- Overall stress   Minimal
- Ease of bartering   Minimal

Durability Rating

Likely Transferable Skills, Background, Careers

Clearly the most easily transferable skill sets come from nurses, whether registered nurses or practical nurses. Nurse aides and home health aides with specialized experience in a specific disease will also transfer well. Someone living with a chronic disease may wish to work with similarly afflicted people.

What to Charge

Insurance companies often employ disease management staff. These personnel will be paid commensurate with their credentials and their experience. Independent disease management experts can charge by the contact hour, $25 and up, keeping careful records of advocacy as well as face-to-face time.

Best Ways to Market Disease Management

- Approach insurance companies and assisted living providers directly.

Tips for Getting Started

- Research current insurance company and hospital offerings in disease management. Look for opportunities to specialize, such as in one disease, perhaps a rare one, or one monitoring device.

- ► Sign up for all the mailing lists you can find on the Web that address the disease you're focusing on and the patients who have the condition.
- ► Join professional and public associations to have ready access to emerging information about management and treatment.
- ► Contact the local or state Department of Health and ask about disease management initiatives.

LEARN MORE

Associations
- ► Disease Management Association of America: www.dmaa.org
- ► URAC (the "UR" stands for utilization review) offers accreditation for disease management organizations and publishes the *Disease Management Journal*: (202) 216-9006, www.urac.org.

Books
- ► *Chronic Disease Management*, Jim Nuovo, Springer, 2006.
- ► *Dictionary of Disease Management*, Ian Duncan, ed., Disease Management Association of America, 2004.
- ► *Disease Management for Nurse Practitioners*, Lippincott Williams & Wilkins, Springhouse, 2001.
- ► *Disease Management Program Evaluation Guide*, DMAA Outcomes Consolidation Steering Committee, Disease Management Association of America, 2004.
- ► *Disease Management*, Diane Huber, W. B. Saunders Company, 2005.
- ► *Healthcare Professional's Guide to Disease Management*, James B. Couch, Aspen Publishers, 1998.
- ► *The Disease Manager's Handbook*, Rufus Howe, Jones & Bartlett Publishers, 2005.

Web Sites
- ► www.aaaai.org/aadmc – Allergy and Asthma Disease Management Center
- ► www.diabetes.org – American Diabetes Association
- ► www.americanbenefitscouncil.org – American Benefits Council
- ► www.americanheart.org – American Heart Association
- ► www.aafa.org – Asthma & Allergy Foundation of America
- ► http://goldcopd.com – The Global Initiative for Chronic Obstructive Lung Disease

Editorial Services

If you like to read and you're dreaming of a world where you could be paid to do it, you're in luck. Every text that is published also gets edited, and increasingly more and more firms are outsourcing their editorial jobs. Most publishers count on contracting with editors, proofreaders, and indexers to perform this essential job. With good grammatical skills, an eye for details, a computer, a printer, and e-mail, you're ready to set up shop.

Authors hire independent editors for themselves, as publishers have pared down the staff and are unable to offer as much editorial attention as in the past. Aspiring authors are also hiring editors to give their manuscripts the refinement that might lead to publication. In fact, editing and proofreading are two of the most sought-out services on the Web.

You can focus on providing one type of editorial service, such as indexing, which is a specialized skill, or supply several editorial services. The primary types of editorial services include:

- ► Copyediting to correct grammar or improve clarity, double-check a manuscript for consistency and cross-references, and make corrections and style improvements on manuscripts turned in by writers.
- ► Developmental editing to rework a project into a cohesive document by working with the writer to develop ideas and plan the sequence of chapters or sections.
- ► Indexing to create the alphabetical lists at the back of nonfiction and professional books and reference materials. Web indexing is a specialized area.
- ► Line editing to actually rewrite the copy line by line. Usually this is needed when a manuscript needs substantial reworking.
- ► Project editing to manage and hire the other types of editors needed to produce a work.
- ► Proofreading to eliminate typographical errors, misspellings, incorrect punctuation, and mistakes in word usage from manuscripts that are in galley form.

Specializing is a way to develop an editorial business. You can specialize by the type of client served or the kind of content worked on. Types of clients range from general and textbook publishers, book packagers, university presses, advertising agencies and law firms, government agencies and nonprofit organizations, utility companies, and other service or manufacturing organizations. The content can range from fiction or nonfiction to technical or training manuals. Other content can range from business and financial materials to cookbooks. In addition to book publishers, other editorial work can include articles in journals, reports, research papers, and internal corporate documents, such as training materials. The specialization can really depend on your interests.

Editorial work can be done from virtually anywhere, as long as you have Internet access; you can even do your work while traveling. The projects you work on can introduce you to a variety of topics, making it interesting and intellectually stimulating. You'll have the opportunity to read a variety of books and articles before their publication. Editorial work might help you develop your own ideas for a book and to make contacts needed to get your own writing published.

A fact of life for editors is that the publishing cycle continues to speed up, making long nights and lost weekends necessary to meet fast turnaround requirements. Some editorial services specialize in overnight jobs. One has the motto "In by nine, out by five." That means 9 PM and 5 AM. Since most editors work on several projects at once, you should possess a high level of organization. Missing a deadline is a sure way to disappoint a client and perhaps make an entire project fail.

Editors themselves must be able to communicate clearly; their notes and comments conveying suggestions and changes must be graspable and written in good English. A meticulous focus on details is critical. While you're not on a campaign to save the English language, you should not miss grammatical and spelling errors. As Henry Krawitz, who specializes in editing for academic presses, says, "It's not enough just to deliver your work on time. Clients expect a quality piece of work that doesn't require additional cleaning up."

It is a great help if you are able to imagine how the printed word will be arranged in a designed piece, such as a brochure or book cover. Sometimes font types and symbols are used to create graphic interest. Insisting, for example, that the word *and* be spelled out when an ampersand is functioning as a graphic element can be too narrow a focus for an editor.

An editorial career can nicely complement a creative writing career. Since they are related, it keeps you in the writing field, but it doesn't normally drain your creative juices the way a marketing or design job might. Since the work schedule is so flexible, a creative career is also possible, because you can work one project around another. On the other hand, two or three clients who provide steady work can keep you busy full-time.

EDITORIAL SERVICES AT A GLANCE

ECONOMIC REALITY FIT

▶ Necessary vs. Discretionary	Necessary
▶ Replaceable with technology	Probably Not

► Offshorable	Not usually
► Industry Status	Established and Enduring

PERSONAL REALITY FIT

► Start-up costs	Minimal
► Overhead	Minimal
► Potential earnings	Moderate
► Flexible hours	More Than Most
► Overall stress	Moderate (deadline pressure)
► Ease of bartering	Moderate

Durability Rating

Likely Transferable Skills, Background, Careers

People working in the education field, corporations, and governmental agencies often have to develop editorial capabilities as part of a larger job. Administrative personnel and managers, who automatically edit whatever they read, may be suited to editing too. For still others, editing is a sort of instinct. An English or journalism degree is helpful.

What to Charge

Editors can change by the hour, by the project, or by the page, with some editors adjusting their project fee structures based on the type of project. Other influencing factors include specialized expertise required, the industry, the complexity and particular demands of the project, and the turnaround time required by the client.

Clients prefer flat-rate pricing by the project, but it is important to indicate in the initial bid the exact parameters of the fee and what changes or additional work will cost. The more experienced you are at knowing how long a project will take, the better able you will be to quote a flat fee that's based on an accurate assessment of what a given project will involve. In that case, a flat-rate price can be more profitable for you if you're able to work both quickly and accurately and the client does not present difficulty.

A great source for seeing the current range of hourly and other rates by type of work is provided by the Editorial Freelancers Association at www.the-efa.org/res/rates.html. Rates for editorial services currently range from $20 to $65 an hour. However, without prior experience, entry-level rates are lower.

Best Ways to Market Editorial Services

- ► Check ads for freelance work that appear in two trade magazines, *Publishers Weekly* and *Library Journal,* both of which are available in many public libraries. Look also in specific trade magazines for advertisements for writers and editors who know how a specific industry works.
- ► Target your marketing efforts to production, managing, and/or project managers at corporations.
- ► Find work on the Web by listing on a Web site such as www.simply english.com and bidding for work on sites that post projects for freelancers, such as www.elance.com and www.guru.com.
- ► Get to know the in-house editors who are responsible for hiring freelancers at publishing companies, magazines, journals, and newsletters. Personal contacts are the best marketing tool for editorial services. Take them out to lunch to find out what kind of work they usually have available, how they decide whom to pick, and how much they typically pay. Leave your business card and stay in touch on a regular basis so that you remain foremost in their minds. If you specialize in corporate work, get to know copywriters who may be getting contracts for business brochures, annual reports, and other business documents.
- ► Use *Writer's Market* or *Literary Market Place* to locate names and addresses of publishers to whom you can send a résumé and samples of your work. There are also many Web sites that post work for freelancers.

Tips for Getting Started
- ► If you don't have publishing experience and editing is a new career for you, copyediting and proofreading are probably the easiest fields to break into. Both copy editors and proofreaders need to be able to pass a screening test when going for a contract with a publishing house or large organization. The electronic booklet from the American Copy Editors Society (www.copydesk.org) can help prepare you.
- ► Regardless of the area in which you choose to focus, or your industry of interest, you need a portfolio of projects on which you have worked. Book indexers need samples to send production managers in publishing houses. Some people even prepare samples of a book from the publisher's house to show how they can enhance an index.
- ► If you're interested in proofreading, a brief course to learn standard proofreader's marks can help.

▶ Several temp agencies place proofreaders. This is a way to gain experience and build a portfolio.

LEARN MORE

Associations

▶ The American Copy Editors Society has a job bank at www.copydesk .org. Freelance editors qualify only for associate membership.

▶ American Society of Indexers provides links to many professional associations, a sample contract, and special interest groups on its site: (303) 463-2887, www.asindexing.org

▶ Editorial Freelancers Association offers a job list among other resources: (866) 929-5400 or (212) 929-5400, www.the-efa.org

▶ In addition, there are many local or regional organizations for writers and editors, as well as specific associations that serve specializations within the editing field, such as the Association of Art Editors (www.artedit.org), Association of Earth Science Editors (www.aese.org), Council of Biology Editors (www.councilscienceeditors .org), and the National Association of Real Estate Editors (www.naree.org).

Books

▶ *Butcher's Copy-editing,* Judith Butcher, Caroline Drake, Maureen Leach, Cambridge University Press, 2006.

▶ *Copyediting*, Karen Judd, Crisp Learning, 2001.

▶ *The Copy Editor's Handbook*, Amy Einsohn, University of California Press, 2000.

▶ *Indexing Books*, Nancy C. Mulvany, University of Chicago Press, 2005.

▶ *Introduction to Indexing and Abstracting*, Donald B. Cleveland, Ana D. Cleveland, Libraries Unlimited, 2000.

Training

▶ Back-of-the-Book Indexing Course is a videotaped workshop: (877) 408-7299 or (781) 893-0514, www.abbington.com/holbert

▶ The University of Chicago (publisher of the *Chicago Manual of Style*) offers an editorial certification program: The Graham School of General Studies; (773)702-1722, http://grahamschool.uchicago.edu

▶ The U.S. Department of Agriculture Graduate School offers both classroom and distance-learning courses in proofreading and editing that lead to certification: (888) 744-4723 or (202) 314-3300, www.grad.usda.gov

▶ Other distance-learning and classroom courses are available from community colleges and university journalism departments.

Web Sites

▶ www.editorium.com – Program add-ins for Microsoft Word
▶ http://peach.ease.lsoft.com/archives/freelance.html – Online discussion group (Listserv) of freelancers in the publishing industry, including editors, indexers, and proofreaders. Archives of resources dating back to 1998.
▶ www.writers.net – Internet directory of writers, editors, publishers, and literary agents with discussion forums.

Energy Rating and Building Performance Auditing and Rating

New careers have emerged from the efforts of homeowners, commercial property owners, governments, and investors to make homes and commercial buildings more energy efficient. New construction must meet federal and state standards for energy efficiency. This is backed up by tax incentives from the federal and many state governments to spur more energy efficiency for both new and existing homes and buildings. Energy analysts say every one dollar saved in annual energy cost increases a home or building's value by twenty dollars.

Of course, when an energy company raises its rates, which is increasingly frequent, or someone gets a jarring electricity, natural gas, propane, or heating oil bill, people think, "What can I do?"

Many people are turning to professionals to assess their homes and businesses. For about the cost of a home inspection or real estate appraisal, a property owner can learn how he/his can cut their energy use and costs. The professionals who do this go by various names—energy auditors, energy raters, building analysts, and home performance specialists. Building analysts, a.k.a. home performance specialists, take the broadest view of measuring and testing a home with additional technology to ensure energy-saving measures are safe and healthful, which means protecting against such issues as developing mold and radon leakage.

People with a background in knowing how systems operate, such as with computer systems, have a ready ability to conceptualize a home or building as a system. For example, Lee O'Neil had been a home inspector for thirteen years when he inspected a brand-new home in a new development. The following winter when O'Neil's client and his neighbors compared utility bills, the client's energy bills were running at half those of his neighbors. What was the difference? O'Neil's thorough home inspection resulted in the client's home fully complying with the building code. The following November O'Neil acquired his first equipment for performing energy audits, growing a company that is active in a dozen states. Specializing in military base construction has helped Lee grow his business. He is credentialed by the Residential Energy Services Network (RESNET).

At the present time, RESNET raters work mostly on new construction; those with Building Performance Institute (BPI) certification work on existing buildings. If your focus is on new buildings, expect to work the hours contractors work, but if you want to start on a part-time basis, you can confine your hours to weekends by working with existing homes.

What your customer expects varies—builders need a rating based on Energy Star standards; home and building owners need to know how to reduce their energy bills and/or feel more comfortable. Keep in mind, too, the more equipment you use, the more physically demanding the job becomes. For example, blower door units, which are used to test air flow and identify energy leaks, weigh thirty-five to forty pounds.

BPI recognizes specializations in mechanical (heating and cooling), envelope (detecting air leakage and thermal defects in a building's outer shell), building analysis (involving measurement and testing), multifamily buildings, and manufactured housing. Building analysts use more types of technologies and hence require several more weeks of training, and either a background or training (or both) is needed for specialization.

The Harvard Joint Center for Housing Studies estimates at least 70 percent of America's over 100 million existing homes are below modern code. As energy costs spiral upward, owners are seeking ways to save, which begins with an audit. Auditing of commercial buildings is on the rise too. Auditing commercial buildings is often done to satisfy investors in the property or the business. Audits are done in varying degrees of thoroughness, from simple or walk-through audits to comprehensive or investment-grade audits. In-between levels are referred to as general or mini-audits. The more detailed audits involve analyzing utility bills, metering energy-using equipment, and projecting potential savings in terms of return on investment.

While jobs are available with established energy rating and building performance firms, and some cities are hiring energy auditors to go door-to-door, opportunity abounds for people wishing to have their own business. If you enter the field as an employee of a firm, the firm will probably pay the cost of training and provide you with needed equipment. If you become self-employed, you will need to handle these costs yourself, plus marketing your service and obtaining professional insurance. You will also need to decide between the types of certification that are available—to become an energy rater through RESNET or a building analyst through BPI.

ENERGY AUDITING AT A GLANCE

ECONOMIC REALITY FIT

▶ Necessary vs. Discretionary	Necessary
▶ Replaceable with technology	No
▶ Offshorable	No
▶ Industry Status	Established and Expanding

PERSONAL REALITY FIT

▶ Start-up costs	More Than Most (particularly if acquiring an infrared camera)
▶ Overhead	Moderate
▶ Potential earnings	More Than Most
▶ Flexible hours	Moderate
▶ Overall stress	Moderate
▶ Ease of bartering	Moderate

Durability Rating

Likely Transferable Skills, Background, Careers

While construction, home inspection, and weatherization are useful fits for transitioning into this field, people who are passionate about doing something about our growing energy and environmental problems can learn the skills needed from scratch through the many training programs that are available.

What to Charge

For existing homes, audits range from $250 to $500, with $350 being the average. The more tests offered, the higher the charge. Ratings for new homes are negotiated with contractors, and there's a trend to sampling housing developments rather than rating each dwelling unit.

Best Ways to Market Energy Rating

▶ Exhibit at trade and home shows.

▶ Develop referral relationships with realtors, remodeling contractors, and mortgage brokers. An energy rating is needed to qualify for an energy-efficient mortgage.

▶ Develop business relationships with new home builders whom you might meet by joining a home builders association.

▶ Contact company human resource managers and membership committees of organizations, and provide discount coupons for employees and members.

Tips for Getting Started

▶ Obtain references, even if this means doing your first several jobs without a fee

▶ Consider joining the Better Business Bureau, Association for Affordable Housing, and Habitat for Humanity, to get your name out there.

▶ If you cannot afford some testing equipment, contract with another company to do these tests for you.

▶ Enhance the value of what you provide; for example, offering the Energy Star label or providing photos adds to the perceived value of the service.

▶ Identify a specialty or niche.

Related Career

Home Inspection. Virtually any home sold today needs to be inspected by a credentialed home inspector, particularly in states like California, Florida, and Texas that require sellers to disclose any existing problems with their home to prospective buyers and put liability on real estate agents, too. Wise sellers are preemptively having their homes inspected before placing them on the market. But like other real estate businesses that depend on home sales, home inspection depends on the health of the real estate market. Resources include:

▶ Two national associations: American Society of Home Inspectors (ASHI) [(800) 743-2744 or (847) 759-2820, www.ashi.com] and the National Association of Home Inspectors Inc. (NAHI) [(800) 448-3942 or (952) 928-4641, www.nahi.org].

▶ Courses in home inspection are available from community colleges, ASHI, and others.

▶ Recommended books: *Become a Home Inspector!* by Michael A. Pompeii and *The Complete Book of Home Inspection* by Norman Becker.

► Franchises are available from firms like AmeriSpec Home Inspection Service [(800) 426-2270, www.amerispecfranchise.com] and HouseMaster of America [(800) 526-3939, www.housemaster.com].

LEARN MORE

Associations
► Building Performance Institute: (877) 274-1274 or (518) 899-2727, www.bpi.org
► Residential Energy Services Network: (760) 806-3448, www.natresnet.org

Books
► *Insulate and Weatherize*, Bruce Harley, Taunton Press, 2002
► Print and digital guides available at Saturn Resource Management's bookstore at www.srmi.biz/Bookstore.

Magazine
► *Home Energy Magazine*, online edition at www.homeenergy.org; for print, call (510) 524-5405.

Training
► RESNET maintains a National Registry of Accredited Energy Rater Training Providers: www.natresnet.org/programs/training/directory .htm.
► Find links to programs on whole house performance at www .homeenergy.org/contrainingguide/index.html.

Web Sites
► www.dsireusa.org – The Database of State Incentives for Renewable Energy (DSIRE) lists financial incentives by state for energy efficiency.

Grant and Proposal Writing

Combine the prosperity of the last several decades with the social consciousness of the Baby Boom generation, and you have dozens of well-endowed private foundations with money to grant. Most of this money goes to nonprofit organizations offering a range of services from community development to health, education, or research. Further, there are thousands of Request for Proposals (RFPs) issued by various government agencies, targeted to both for-profit companies and nonprofit organizations.

The projects are usually targeted to specific groups or populations in need. For example, clients can include needy rural communities, centers for at-risk youth, or fire safety councils. Or a project could be for research that will advance science, health care, or education to address social or environmental problems.

The kind of detailed development work required for writing a winning grant proposal, though, is often beyond the skill and time availability the organization's staff has to offer. This means there is a continuing need for help in identifying, making contact with, and developing relationships inside granting organizations, as well as writing detailed proposals for exactly how a project will be executed, what money is needed, and how the benefits of the project will be measured. Grant writers can do all of these things.

Some proposal writers are generalists with a broad knowledge of diverse fields, but many are specialists with a background in a single area, such as agriculture, communications, engineering, business, medicine, or another advanced industry. Some writers have enough specific experience in a field that they advise their clients on how to improve upon their original idea for the proposal. They may also help clients conceive of programs that will win in competition with others seeking the same funds. Or they may appeal to newer foundations, for example, those of eBay founders Pierre Omidyar and Jeffrey Skoll, and Google founders Sergey Brin and Larry Page who are funding new models of social entrepreneurship. Here is where the art involved in grant writing comes into play.

As far as actually writing the grant proposal, as one proposal writer told us, "any writer with good skills can do this work, whatever your background. Like lawyers, it doesn't matter who your client is; if you can write logically and can understand the technology enough to explain it, you can do it."

Because there is a lot of competition for grant funds, both from private sources and the government, it is important to understand the mission and goals of the grantor to make sure these align closely with the project for which the grantee needs money.

Clarity and organization are also key factors grant and proposal reviewers appreciate. Because clients must often relay complex details about their project, they tend to use equally complex language. So this kind of detail needs to be skillfully related to the goals of the granting organization. In a sense a grant proposal is like a business plan.

Funding sources have explicit deadlines, so writers need to produce proposals not only clearly and knowledgeably but also quickly. In some cases, the proposal writers will learn about the RFPs before their clients do, so they can bring prospective business to an organization by notifying them of the release of the bid request.

Helping clients get funding is emotionally rewarding work. Some people relish the research aspect; others, the program design; still others, the writing. All delight in the sense of accomplishment from winning and being a part of what comes about as a result of a grant they obtained. And while nonprofit organizations may only be able to pay modest fees up front, if your client base is diverse and you are able to offer a range of services from project development to administration, you can make a nice living while benefiting society as a whole.

Related Career

Contract Compliance Assistance. Once a company has gotten a federal contract, another service a grant writer can offer is to assist them with federal contract compliance. Smaller companies are not staffed to meet the onerous paperwork requirements of holding a government contract, particularly a federal contract. To meet this need a cadre of consultants has emerged who provide this service on a contractual basis. This requires significant experience in administering federal contracts, but usually, the grant administrator for the federal agency granting the funds is happy to work with you to sort out the extensive details.

GRANT AND PROPOSAL WRITING AT A GLANCE

ECONOMIC REALITY FIT

- Necessary vs. Discretionary — Necessary
- Replaceable with technology — No
- Offshorable — Probably not
- Industry Status — Established and Expanding

PERSONAL REALITY FIT

- Start-up costs — Minimal
- Overhead — Minimal
- Potential earnings — Moderate
- Flexible hours — More Than Most
- Computer skills — More Than Most
- Overall stress — More Than Most (deadline pressure)
- Ease of bartering — Moderate

Durability Rating

Likely Transferable Skills, Background, Careers

While industry-specific experience is helpful (aerospace, utility, health care, education), it is not required. The ability to quickly assimilate information and assemble it into a clear, concise document is the most important attribute. Some management experience is also helpful because, while not actually supervising a team, a grant writer is a hub for the information that comes in from various contributors and is responsible to ensure every line item is accurately completed. When working with a number of contributors, the ability to negotiate with people who are often used to working solitarily and may not care to have their writing edited is a real plus.

What to Charge

Grant writers charge an hourly rate from $35 to $85 per hour. A few proposals take one or two days to write, but most can take months to research and create. A successful writer in a specialty area such as energy or business can charge from $2,000 to $10,000 per proposal, depending on length and the amount of funding the company is seeking. Most grant writers do not work on a "contingency basis," meaning that they get paid a percentage if the proposal bid is successful. Since winning is impossible to guarantee, the contingency basis fee might often leave the grant writer in a bad position.

Best Ways to Market Grant Writing

- ▸ Inform past and possible clients of newly released RFPs and other new sources of funding. Combining this with some preliminary research increases your chances of getting hired to pursue the funding.
- ▸ Bid for work on sites like elance.com and guru.com

Tips for Getting Started

- ▸ Take courses to fill in information you don't have.
- ▸ Develop a focus that inspires you. Grant writers need to feel passionate about their projects.
- ▸ To develop a track record, volunteer if necessary to get your first successful proposal under your belt.
- ▸ Develop a marketing plan that will put you into contact with potential clients.

LEARN MORE

Associations

- American Association of Grant Professionals: (913) 788-3000, www.grantprofessionals.org
- American Grant Writers' Association offers courses in grant writing: (727) 366-9334, www.agwa.us
- Association of Fund Raising Professionals http://www.afpnet.org
- Association of Proposal Management Professionals: www.apmp.org
- Society of Research Administrators offers valuable resources: (703) 741-0140, www.srainternational.org

Books

- *Demystifying Grant Seeking*, Larissa Golden Brown, Martin John Brown, Jossey-Bass, 2001.
- *Getting Funded*, Mary S. Hall, Susan Howlett, Continuing Education Press, 2003.
- *Government Assistance Almanac*, J. Robert Dumouchel, Omnigraphics Inc., Annual.
- *Grant Writing For Dummies*, Beverly A. Browning, For Dummies, 2005.
- *Proposal Planning and Writing*, Lynn E. Miner, Jerry Griffith, Greenwood Press, 2003.
- *The Foundation Directory 2006*, David Jacobs, ed., Foundation Center, 2006.
- *U.S. Government Style Manual*. Downloadable at www.gpoaccess.gov/stylemanual/browse.html

Training

- The Foundation Center (more about it below): http://foundationcenter.org/getstarted/learnabout/proposalwriting.html
- The Grantmanship Center provides training in Southern California. Its Web site offers articles and access to the Federal Register. GrantDomain enables users to search government, foundation, and corporate funding sources: (213) 482-9860, www.tgci.com
- H. Silver and Associates is a large training firm with major corporate clients. It offers training seminars in various locations: (310) 563-1240, www.hsilver.com
- Teaching Yourself to be a Grantwriter http://www.grantproposal.com/starting_inner.html
- The U.S. Department of Agriculture Graduate School offers a classroom

course in grant writing: (888) 744-4723 or (202) 314-3300, www.grad.usda.gov

Web Sites

> www.cfda.gov – The online Catalog of Federal Domestic Assistance provides access to a database of all federal programs.

> http://foundationcenter.org – The Foundation Center describes itself as "Your Gateway to Philanthropy on the World Wide Web" and for many grant writers, it is. It offers training and databases of foundation information. Access to their database is available for a fee or for free at many public libraries. Libraries often offer a free, half-day training session on how to use the database to search for appropriate grants. The Foundation's ultimate research resource is a subscription to its Foundation Directory Online Professional at $1,295 per year. For professional use, access begins at $20 per month.

> www.schoolgrants.org – Provides information about educational grant opportunities and links to relevant sites

Private Investigation

Are you fascinated with the investigatory skills you see on *CSI* or *Law and Order*? Are you a fan of the TV private investigators of the past like Magnum or Sam Spade? Do you read the crime stories before the sports in your daily newspaper? A yes to any one of these, or all of them, suggests that being a private or professional investigator (PI) could be a great career for you.

You will need enthusiasm, because investigations are often slow and methodical, and your innate excitement with this work will help to carry you through. Private investigators provide services to a wide array of clients: corporations, private individuals, attorneys, accountants, employment agencies, collection agencies, even newspapers. The field is wide open and can be well paying.

You can be an independent or you can be an employee of an investigation firm or a corporation that keeps you on full-time to investigate fraud, theft, backgrounds, and more. Businesses and their human resources departments require investigations of a number of kinds. Prospective employees are the most fertile source of need. In these matters an HR department wants to know about criminal records and driving records; they want references checked, personal and professional; and they want credentials, degrees, licenses, and certifications verified.

Background checking is also needed by companies considering doing business with another company or individual, by landlords screening tenants, and increasingly by couples who want to do a premarital check on their prospective mates. And if the marriage doesn't work, people often hire PIs to locate assets that one spouse hides from another in a divorce case. Salespeople and corporations are now hiring PIs to search the Web for information, which includes tens of millions of blogs, online résumés, and entries on MySpace that can be used to develop profiles on prospective or actual customers.

Each of the checks enumerated above requires knowledge that you can learn by experimentation on the Internet, online or live classes, or by on-the-job training. You will learn that most states sell their driving record files, that criminal records are not so secure, and that there are online resources that specialize in each of the categories of information. Clients pay PIs to pull all this information together into one document that presents the data they're looking for.

The Magnums and the Sam Spades of the old days were frequently beat up, shot at, and tied up. The work you'll be doing is not at all like that. More often than not, you will spend most of your time online and on the phone. However, as an independent, you can choose the type or types of investigation services you want to offer.

There can be field work. The employee out sick who is suspected of not being so sick may need to be photographed. The compensation case with the injured back might be videotaped doing roof repairs or playing football. And, of course, there's surveillance to catch cheating spouses. These can be accomplished with a long lens or a good zoom lens, video cameras that can be attached to sunglasses or hats or look like pagers, and concealable GPS tracking devices.

Then there's investigating counterfeited goods, such as clothing, cosmetics, handbags, movies, software, and watches, and preventing (or doing) corporate espionage to obtain secrets about what business competitors are doing. "Competitive intelligence is the future for companies to understand their competitor so that they can custom design their own company to be more unique," according to Dakota Michaels of the Spy Academy (see their listing under Training in the LEARN MORE section).

You will need good people skills to be effective at some of this work. Reference checking is all about how you ask for information that could secure a reference that is less than glowing—information your client needs to know. If you're going to be an independent, you'll need to market yourself, too. For all types of investigation, top-notch computer skills are required.

One of the more rewarding investigation businesses is the one that locates people. If you wish to specialize in finding natural birth parents or relatives who have not been heard from in many years, these are both areas that offer significant personal rewards. You will need excellent people skills to manage your clients and cajole agencies that don't want to share information, and you will need an understanding of laws in different jurisdictions if you have to leave your computer and go looking for someone.

Professional investigation is a growing field; our litigious society requires that employees be hired with extreme care, and our mobile society creates new missing persons every day. If you open this door, you will find the potential for fascinating and sometimes exciting work. With so much of the work shifting to the Web, a great deal can be done at any time of the day or night, leaving you much flexibility.

Related Careers

Process Serving. Process serving of lawsuit papers and other legal documents requiring personal service is a career with its own professional association, the National Association of Professional Process Servers (www.napps.com). Another resource is www.servenow.com and its associated Yahoo! group. Both sites have links to the process serving laws and rules of civil procedure in each state. In some states, process servers must be licensed.

Security Consulting. A search on the Web might lead you to think a security consultant advises on alarm systems, but in actuality security consulting embraces a variety of types of expertise and activities. Security consultants assist clients in protecting their employees, building and facilities, client lists, and proprietary technology through:

- Site consulting – Evaluating the design of buildings and spaces
- Technical security consulting – Specifying, selecting, and installing specific security technologies and products
- Systems design – Specifying security needs at the design phase (remodel or initial construction), which may include designing security software and hardware

Security consultants are also called as expert witness in trials involving mishaps like fires, thefts, and break-ins where security breaches are an issue. They also teach and train others, including law enforcement officials, about their field of expertise.

Security consultants' clients include architectural firms, contractors, companies building new buildings, museums, banks, stadiums, city and municipal governments, schools and universities, computer facilities, and many other types of employers. Being certified is an important professional credential for security consultants; ASIS International is a professional association that does this: (703) 519-6200; www.asisonline.org. Books that will introduce you to the field are *Security Consulting* by Charles A. Sennewald and *Introduction to Security* (Butterworth-Heinemann, 2003), by Robert J. Fischer and Gion Green.

Skip Tracing. See the Bill Collecting profile on page 47.

PRIVATE INVESTIGATION AT A GLANCE

ECONOMIC REALITY FIT

▹ Necessary vs. Discretionary	Both
▹ Replaceable with technology	In part
▹ Offshorable	In part
▹ Industry Status	Established and Expanding

PERSONAL REALITY FIT

▹ Start-up costs	Moderate
▹ Overhead	Moderate
▹ Potential earnings	More Than Most
▹ Flexible hours	More Than Most
▹ Overall stress	Minimal
▹ Computer skills	More Than Most
▹ Ease of bartering	Moderate

Durability Rating

Likely Transferable Skills, Background, Careers

Retired law enforcement personnel are naturals for this field. If you have been a process server, you've already attained many of the skills to be good at this. Experience with electronic records at any level of government or with any large corporation will also give you a good start here.

What to Charge

Professional investigative services that locate and identify basic information about individuals are usually billed according to the piece or pieces of data required, often from $15 to $25. If a client requires an extensive report, you will want to charge $150 to $300, which incorporates charges you incur by subcontracting portions of the online work. Hourly fees for surveillance are from $75 to $125 an hour; for other services the range is from $50 to $150 an hour.

Best Ways to Market Private Investigation

- Approach employment agencies and human resource departments with a package of services focused around background checks.
- Directly solicit lawyers, accountants, and insurance companies to generate business.

Tips for Getting Started

- You will need to find out about licensing in your state. Requirements vary significantly. You can find links to each state's laws at www.pimagazine.com/links_Licensing.htm.
- Determine what courses and training you will need; decide if you wish to pursue certification from a professional association.
- PIs like to share with each other, which may explain the large number of associations. Take advantage of this to learn from established PIs.

LEARN MORE

Associations

Dozens of state, regional, national, and international associations serve this industry. You can find links to them at www.pimagazine.com/links.htm. Two of the national organizations are:

- National Association of Legal Investigators: (480) 726-3961, www.nalionline.org
- United States Association of Professional Investigators (USAPI) has a certification program: (866) 958-7274 or (202) 393.5900, www.usapi.org

Books

- *The Complete Idiot's Guide to Private Investigating,* Steven Kerry Brown, Alpha, 2002.
- *How to do Financial Asset Investigations*, Ronald L. Mendell, Charles C. Thomas, 2006.
- *Private Investigation 101*, Norma M. Tillman, Norma Tillman Enterprises, 2006.
- *Private Investigation in the Computer Age*, Bud Jillett, Paladin Press, 2003.
- *Reference Checking for Everyone,* Paul W. Barada, J. Michael McLaughlin, McGraw-Hill, 2004.

Magazine

- *PI Magazine* – Published by the USAPI: (732) 308-3800 or (800) 836-3088, www.pimagazine.com

Training

- ▶ Detective Training Institute: (888) 425-9338 or (949) 492-4420, www.detectivetraining.com
- ▶ Global School of Investigation: (877) 337-0785, www.pvteye.com
- ▶ The Institute of Private Investigation: (888) 659-3897, www.inst.org/pi
- ▶ The Spy Academy: (661) 242-1788, www.dmispy.com/spy_academy.htm
- ▶ For links to additional schools, see www.infoguys.com/schools.cfm.

Web Sites

- ▶ www.detectivehelp.com/pimuseum – The actual PI museum is in San Diego, but you can get a sample of history on this site.
- ▶ www.picoffeeshop.com – Private Eye Coffee Shop offers a forum, blog, and more.
- ▶ www.einvestigator.com, www.infoguys.com, www.pimall.com – PI portal sites
- ▶ www.integrascan.com – Offers searches of criminal and civil records for background checking

Selling Things on the Web

Selling is the biggest of all industries. Some people sell intangible items, things you can't touch, like computer power and many personal and business services. Others sell tangible things, everything from antiques to recreational vehicles. In this profile, though, we're focusing on selling tangibles, because that's where we see opportunities to carve out a new independent career—selling things full- or part-time.

Selling on the Web continues to grow as a percentage of total retail sales. This isn't surprising, because selling is basically about communication—letting people know about something you can provide that you think they need or would enjoy—and the Internet is one vast communications network. Whether it is by Googling for something, going to an auction site, or clicking on a link from any topical site, the Internet is a powerful vehicle for selling.

Since practically every wholesale and retail establishment from a big box store to upscale boutique is selling products on the Internet, the key to being successful there as a private individual is finding products that are novel or not otherwise readily available from multiple sources at discount prices. Often the best way to discover items that meet this criteria is to identify things you and others you know want or need but can't obtain—or at least not readily.

For example, Penny Stewart took up belly dancing to lose weight and decided to sell the things people interested in belly dancing could not readily get (www.pinkgypsy.com). Even if a particular type of product is available, you may have a twist or improvement that will make it sought after. For example, Carolyn and John Grace loved the feel of their grandparents' old-fashioned blankets, but when they tried to buy some with that special texture and feel, they couldn't find any. That was the beginning of Swan Island Blankets (www. swansislandblankets.com). Greg Shugar, a former practicing attorney told us, "After eight long years of trial work, I found my love in designing and selling my own brand of neckwear." He sells them on his site, www.thetiebar.com.

Broadly speaking, there are three ways of getting products to sell on the Web:

- ► Making things yourself, such as the pet coffins Steve Mondazzi makes and sells (www.petsweloved.com), the unique gardening tool Elena Shermata created (www.diggitinc.com), and Andrew Horn's Masonic functional art jewelry (www.mastersjewel.com). (See the Creator of Functional Art profile on page 248.)
- ► Obtaining products made by others, which may range from artwork to sporting goods you buy at wholesale prices and mark up to retail prices. The simplest, and usually the most cost-effective, is to drop ship items, meaning you take the orders, send them to your suppliers with their payment and shipping costs, and they send the item(s) directly to your customers. This saves you from tying up your funds in inventory and storage costs. On the other hand, it probably means a narrower profit margin and no direct control over when and how sales orders are filled. Of course, if you're selling something that does not require a lot of storage space, you can buy a supply and fulfill orders yourself.
- ► Shopping antique stores, estate sales, garage sales, pawnshops, flea markets, and thrift shops. You can also buy at online auctions or directly from vendors who buy large quantities of merchandise they can't or decide not to sell.

Once you've identified what you're going to sell, you have lots of options for how to sell them on the Web. Here are some ideas:

- ► Join the million and a half people worldwide who are earning a part- or full-time living selling on eBay and other auction sites. (Don't kid yourself, eBay has competitors, such as Overstock, Bidville, ePier, and iOffer.)
- ► Get a storefront from providers like Yahoo! Shopping (http:// smallbusiness.yahoo.com/ecommerce), eBay, eBay's Half.com, Monster

Commerce (www.monstercommerce.com), ZlioShops (www.zlio.com) or one of the many mall sites, some of which are specialized. Such providers make it easy and inexpensive for a start-up. Services that are under fifty dollars a month can include storefront, shopping cart, and the ability to do credit card transactions.

▶ Build a storefront on your own Web site, probably with the help of a consultant.

▶ Sell from a mall or gallery, such as www.etsy.com. The site draws shoppers in return for a commission, and you do the shipping.

▶ Use consignment stores, such as iSold It and UPS-affiliated QwikDrop, where you deposit your goods and the store takes care of listing your goods as well as the shipping process. In exchange the company takes about 40 percent of the selling price.

While selling on the Internet does not require the same degree of upbeatness that other kinds of selling does, all sales require tenacity, the ability to take no for an answer and keep going, and an ability to listen well and to identify the needs of the customer and how your product meets those needs. If you're willing to work hard and keep the creative juices flowing, you will do well at selling things.

Related Career

Direct Selling. Approximately 14 million people in the United States alone are selling products and services through direct sales or network marketing companies such as Avon, Country Peddlers, Mary Kay, Pampered Chef, and Shaklee. Two out of three of these sales are made by direct person-to-person contact, but proving that people are social, a fourth of direct sales are made through party plan or group selling, such as at Tupperware, Creative Memories, and Discovery Toys parties. Participants in direct-selling organizations go by various names—distributors, representatives, and consultants—but by whatever name, they're all independent salespeople. The variety of things directly sold keeps growing, but the primary types of what's sold are products for personal care, including cosmetics, skin care, and jewelry; the home, such as cleaning supplies, kitchenware, and decorating items; nutrition, health, and wellness; services like benefit packages, insurance, Internet service, and auto care; and leisure and education, such as books, DVDs, and artwork.

All the people we've ever interviewed who do well in direct selling have great enthusiasm for what they sell; they have upbeat, outgoing personalities. In most companies, making money means recruiting other people to join your "network" or "downline," which is why this type of selling is also called multilevel marketing. In a multilevel organization, people in the upline receive commissions from their downline's sales; some distribution models pay commissions down seven levels. The growth in direct selling in recent years has mostly been outside the United States. Most people who sell directly, seven out of eight, work part-time as a way to supplement their principal income. Some sites to check out are www.dsa.org and www.mlmsurvivor.com. A well-regarded book is *The Wave 4 Way to Building Your Downline*, Richard Poe, Three Rivers, 2000.

SELLING THINGS ON THE WEB AT A GLANCE

ECONOMIC REALITY FIT

► Necessary vs. Discretionary	Selling is Both
► Replaceable with technology	Mostly not
► Offshorable	Mostly not
► Industry Status	Established and Expanding

PERSONAL REALITY FIT

► Start-up costs	Minimal
► Overhead	Minimal (depends on inventory expense)
► Potential earnings	More Than Most
► Flexible hours	More Than Most
► Computer skills	Moderate
► Overall stress	Moderate
► Ease of bartering	Moderate

Durability Rating

Likely Transferable Skills, Background, Careers

People from all walks of life and backgrounds freely move into both Internet selling and direct sales. If you have a special knowledge that relates to salable items, such as collectibles you want to sell, you will slip fairly easily into selling them by using your knowledge and enthusiasm.

What to Charge

If you are planning to sell on auction sites, buyers will determine the prices, although you can set a reserve price (an unstated minimum). If you are developing a retail site, check out what competitors are charging for the same or similar items. Make sure you can make a profit, considering all your overhead costs. Since the prospect of saving money is one of the two primary motivations for people who shop on the Web (convenience is the other one), know that conscientious Web shoppers are doing the same thing as you.

Best Ways to Market Things on the Web

- ▻ Advertise on search engines under a catchy Web site name or the item type you sell.
- ▻ Use the services offered by your Web host to be sure that the search engines are finding you. If your site is not in the first thirty listings, you'll get little traffic from search engines. This is important because almost 40 percent of people are motivated to buy something when they search for it compared to only 7 percent who become motivated from an e-mail.
- ▻ Depending on what you're selling, well-placed print advertising can help you develop customers.
- ▻ On an auction site, list your product in categories where people would look for a similar type of product. Be specific about describing what you are selling; if you are selling something that's been used or remanufactured, candidly describe any flaws or blemishes.
- ▻ Provide first-rate customer service, which means responding promptly to customer questions and comments and shipping what you sell within two or three days after receiving payment. If you're selling on eBay, positive comments mean business; negative ones kill it.
- ▻ Offer multiple ways for people to pay. Five times (55 percent) as many online shoppers pay with credit cards than use PayPal.

Tips for Getting Started

- ▻ Spend considerable time searching the Web looking for other sites that are selling what you want to sell. Determine if there is too much competition, and develop a new twist if possible.
- ▻ Take all the free consultation time you can get from your Web hosting service.
- ▻ If you are going to use an auction site as your principal business, buy some things similar to those you want to sell. See how other sellers are treating customers and see what prices are like.
- ▻ Check out research tools like Terapeak (http://terapeak.com/eBay),

Market Research Wizard (www.worldwidebrands.com), and HammerTap Deep Analysis (www.hammertap.com).

▶ Convenience and lower prices drive shopping on the Web. Convenience translates into speed of service and ease in buying. Ease in buying is about site design, but what you control on a day-to-day basis is speed of service.

LEARN MORE

Books

▶ *eBay PowerSeller Million Dollar Ideas,* Debra and Brad Schepp, McGraw-Hill, 2006.

▶ *How to Start and Run an eBay Consignment Business,* Skip McGrath, McGraw-Hill, 2006.

▶ *Starting a Yahoo! Business for Dummies*, Rob Snell, For Dummies, 2006.

▶ *Starting an Online Business for Dummies*, Greg Holden, For Dummies, 2005.

▶ *The eBay Seller's Tax and Legal Answer Book*, Cliff Ennico, AMACOM Books, 2007.

▶ *Titanium eBay,* Skip McGrath, Alpha, 2006.

Training

▶ *Auction Genius Course©* – Live classes taught on your computer: http://auction-genius-course.com

Web Sites

▶ www.auctionbytes.com – Offers a newsletter, forums, and a blog

▶ http://forums.ebay.com – eBay has scores of Seller and PowerSeller groups you can join.

▶ www.skipmcgrath.com/newsletters – The eBay seller's newsletter

▶ http://smallbusiness.yahoo.com – Yahoo!'s Small Business site offers a free newsletter and StartupNation's media presentation entitled "10 Steps to Open for Business."

Translation and Interpreting Services

The big picture of the world is rapidly changing. As the populations of the countries in the developed world continue to age, the workforces of those countries will continue to shrink. In the coming decades, developing countries will have far larger dependable workforces than those of the main economic powers today. In addition, business is shifting and globalizing, and U.S. companies will begin to confront both foreign companies and increasingly important foreign markets.

It is predicted that the United States will align economically with Canada, the United Kingdom, Latin America, and India. Australia and New Zealand will align with China, Japan, Korea, and the rest of East Asia, while Russia, most of the Middle East, and Africa will align with Europe. Translation will facilitate all these transitions. And you can turn knowledge you've had your entire life—knowledge you might have thought useless or just "cool"—into marketable skills you can use to remain solidly in the middle class as these economic changes occur.

While English is said to be the language of business, people in other countries want contracts drawn up in their local languages. Of course, marketing communication is more effective in the local language, respecting the norms and idioms of the area. At this point, the largest growth in Internet usage is by people accessing in languages other than English. For those people fortunate enough to speak more languages than English, that ability can be the ticket to an interesting and rewarding home business.

Increases in world trade and advances in technology drive the demand for translators and interpreters. Software menus and commands need to be adapted for use in other countries. E-commerce enables even the smallest companies to have access to people all over the globe who don't speak English, provided they can transact business in the languages of these new customers. Even though the eventual target of computer scientists and programmers is to achieve fluent two-way machine translation, it appears at least a decade away. Except for the most repetitive of translation needs, such as real estate contracts, weather forecasting, and technical manuals, automated translation done by computers is not expected to readily replace humans who can master nuance.

People with knowledge of one or more foreign languages can start a translation business. Of the three thousand U.S. translation companies, most are small, home-based operations, launched with a few thousand dollars for basic office equipment. All you need to get started is your know-how, some dictionaries, and a computer. Translators can live almost anywhere and service clients around the world.

As in so many other businesses, specialization is an asset in this field, although some specialties, such as translating literary works, prose, and poetry for publishing houses, usually don't pay well. If you have a technical background of any kind, however, particularly one in a growing technology, you can earn a good living in this high-demand specialty. Another growing specialization is translating the content of Web sites into other languages so companies and organizations can attract more people to their sites.

The world of entertainment needs translators too, doing such things as translating scripts for dubbing, translating stage plays, and subtitling films. As the American film industry begins to depend more and more on foreign markets for their product, this will become even more important. Interpreters can specialize in cross-cultural training for businesspeople, community relations, crisis intervention, or sign language. Conference translation is a possibility for people living in the cities where international organizations are located, such as New York City and Washington DC.

Translation work is incredibly flexible, depending on how many projects you take on and the nature of those assignments. But there will *always* be projects. The "field is booming," says Walter Bacak, executive director of the American Translators Association, and there is little chance that that situation will change. Almost every type of translation allows you to work flexible hours at a location of your choice; you can have a very profitable part-time job working in your pajamas!

Which is not to say that everything is sunshine. Since clients may not be aware of the process of translation or appreciate the time involved, you may encounter sticker shock when you quote your prices. Therefore, in the process of selling your services, you will need to educate your clients in order to reach an equitable business agreement. In many businesses, translators are not adequately reimbursed, considering the substantial time and difficulty of their job. In fact, managing to convince people that they need to hire *you* at *your* price is much of the battle, since the jobs themselves are so plentiful. Walter Bacak says, "The difference between those who are successful and those who are not is business skills."

In addition, the attention drawn to translation recently, both in the real-life examples of CIA translators working to fight terrorism and in major motion pictures such as *The Interpreter*, has made the field more competitive than in the past. And competition is not just coming from fellow Americans, but from lower-cost translators abroad, such as the former Soviet Union, where English was taught extensively. However, firms wanting to protect proprietary technology often prefer American-based firms and freelancers.

In addition to international translation, the immigration boom in the United States has increased the need for translators and interpreters within the country, at courts and in hospitals. Both these kinds of in-person interpreters and translators of written texts are not easily or dependably replaced by technology. Though translation software has gotten more and more sophisticated, Alison Anderson, a translator in San Francisco who specializes in French (http://alison-anderson .com), states that the scuttlebutt among translators is that the software is still catastrophically inaccurate and unable to detect the subtleties of a human translator. As the United States aligns with other nations in loosely defined but powerful economic federations, the job of translation will become more important. If you have the skills, translation and interpreting can be a career that will afford a middle-class lifestyle.

TRANSLATION SERVICES AT A GLANCE

ECONOMIC REALITY FIT

▶ Necessary vs. Discretionary	Necessary
▶ Replaceable with technology	Only in part
▶ Offshorable	No
▶ Industry Status	Established and Enduring

PERSONAL REALITY FIT

▶ Start-up costs	Minimal
▶ Overhead	Minimal
▶ Potential earnings	More Than Most
▶ Flexible hours	More Than Most
▶ Overall stress	Moderate
▶ Ease of bartering	Moderate

Durability Rating

Likely Transferable Skills, Background, Careers

A starting point is fluency in both English and the second language or languages, including colloquialisms and slang. Translators need to be exacting and accurate, because they create a permanent written record. Interpreting requires concentration and focus, being able to comprehend meaning, and being empathetic enough to anticipate what the person speaking is going to say. Having lived in the area of the language in which you will be working to learn the norms and culture of the area is typical of many people doing translating and interpreting. An undergraduate degree in an area other than language, such as business or engineering, along with a master's degree in the primary language you will be translating are helpful.

What to Charge

Pricing may be by the word, by the hour, or by the job. Pricing by the word may be either by the source or target language, with a range as wide as ten cents to twenty cents a word. When in-depth knowledge of a field is needed, such as for legal, medical, scientific, and technical translation, higher fees can be commanded. Fees are higher for high-demand languages and for more complex assignments. Interpreters earn $329 a day working in the federal courts, with half-day minimums.

Best Ways to Market Translation Services

- ▶ Directly solicit work from law firms, public relations firms, immigration service agencies, health care providers, and companies operating internationally.
- ▶ Network with other translators for work they can refer or subcontract. Consider jointly proposing to handle the translation work for a company as a consortium.
- ▶ Seek work on the Web. For example, www.translationpeople.com advertises for translators on its site as well as posting notices of other sources of translation work. You can also bid for translation assignments on sites like elance.com and guru.com
- ▶ Volunteer your work in organizations that reach out to ethnic audiences.

Tips for Getting Started

- ▶ Subcontract or be employed by an existing translation service or agency.
- ▶ Determine what the local sources of work are in your area. Keep in mind that in some companies, the marketing department and the purchasing department may each hire translators independently of one another.
- ▶ If you are going into court translation, obtain any necessary certification. Certification is required for interpreting some languages in federal courts (currently Haitian Creole, Navajo, and Spanish). Some state courts also require certification. You also will need to understand court procedures.
- ▶ If you are going to do commercial translation, invest in software like that made by SDL Trados (www.translationzone.com). Trados offers certification, and licensees can post a profile in its "Find a Translator" database.

LEARN MORE

Associations

- ► American Translators Association (ATA) offers accreditation and liability insurance, provides a searchable directory of members, and has chapters and affiliated groups. A model contract is available on its Web site (703) 683-6100, www.atanet.org
- ► American Literary Translators Association: (972) 883-209, www.literarytranslators.org. The Association of Canadian Literary Translators can be found at www.attlc-ltac.org
- ► Chartered Institute of Linguists is a British-based organization that offers certification: www.iol.org.uk. Another UK-based association is the Institute of Translation and Interpreting: www.iti.org.uk/indexMain.html
- ► International Association of Conference Interpreters: www.aiic.net
- ► The National Association of Judiciary Interpreters and Translators: (206) 267-2300, www.najit.org
- ► The Translators and Interpreters Guild functions as a nationwide labor union for freelance and in-house translators and interpreters: (301) 563-6450, www.trans-interp-guild.org
- ► Yahoo! has a number of applicable groups; some require membership in a professional organization for admission: http://groups.yahoo.com

Books

- ► *Becoming a Translator,* Doug Robinson, Routledge, 2003.
- ► *The Craft of Translation*, John Biguenet and Rainer Schulte eds., University of Chicago Press, 1989.
- ► *Getting Started: A Newcomer's Guide to Translation and Interpretation*, American Translators Association (www.atanet.org).
- ► *Interpretation: Techniques and Exercises*, James Nolan, Multilingual Matters Limited, 2005.

Courses and Training

A number of university continuing education programs, community colleges, and proprietary institutions offer certification programs. The American Translators Association (www.atanet.org) publishes *Park's Guide to Translating and Interpreting Programs in North America*, a directory of institutions offering translator/interpreter training. Content from an earlier edition of this directory can be found at http://isg.urv.es/tti/us.html.

Web Sites

▸ http://go.compuserve.com/ForeignLanguage – This forum has message sections on careers, business, and technology.

Virtual Administrative Services

Many clerical and administrative support services that have long been done in a home business down the street or in an office across town are and will increasingly be accessible from anywhere. Virtual administrative support is the completely modern version of what small companies and professionals have turned to for decades in order to keep their costs down or to cut them back. Frequently, the independent provider offers clients a higher skill level than the clients can afford to employ and keep. Support services include secretarial, word processing and typing, desktop publishing and all types of virtual administrative support, though you're not apt to find the term "virtual administrative support" in either a print or online telephone directory yet.

You may see or hear the term "virtual assistant" (VA) which refers to the fact that a VA may never see her or his clients because they are providing services remotely, via the Internet, thus being able to serve clients who might be a continent away. VAs generally charge higher hourly rates and thus realize higher earnings. However, many potential customers do not know the term *virtual assistant;* so they look in the Yellow Pages, online, or other places for "secretarial services." So it's up to the VA to educate the prospective client as to her or his additional training and level of service.

Virtual administrative services or support is a catch-all phrase covering a wide variety of tasks, such as preparing spreadsheets or databases; word processing; transcribing; drafting correspondence, proposals, and reports; editing, formatting, and proofreading documents; bookkeeping; billing; notary services; maintaining contact management programs; desktop publishing; developing multimedia presentations; office management; making customer or patient contacts; telephone answering; sending out marketing materials and follow-up letters; Internet research; updating Web sites; travel planning; project managing; and logistics coordinating. For example, Marie Schultz, who lives in Michigan, coordinates a teleconferencing service based in Florida, owned by a woman in the DC area. It is possible to specialize in one or several of these areas or to offer all of them, depending on your skills, interests, and the needs of your clients. We describe some significant specialties under "Related Careers" below.

Clients can range from large organizations needing temporary support for projects to new businesses, small businesses, and self-employed individuals without full-time secretarial assistance. These include consultants, real estate and insurance agents, doctors, attorneys, private investigators, or any business where the owner or professional has little time or desire to do his or her own administrative work. Many independent consultants and professionals rent office space in "executive suites" and then use e-mail to send raw data or documents for formatting, proofing, editing, publishing, etc., to virtual administrative service providers.

Working from virtually anywhere is possible in this career, as most documents and information can be sent via e-mail or, for larger documents, can be uploaded to an FTP site where clients can then retrieve (download) the files or use a service such as *Send*Space (www.sendspace.com). Moment-to-moment contact can be handled with instant messaging, e-mail, and phone; Skype and other VOIP services make video communication, if desired, readily available. You and your client can have access to each other's computers with software such as PC Anywhere. On the other hand, we talked with one virtual assistant who organized the paper files for her client. The client shipped the VA a box packed with the files; the VA organized them and shipped them back.

Some clients, however, will want to work with an office services provider in the same community. For some, being able to go to where the work is being done is a necessary ingredient to outsourcing their support work. Despite being able to work at a place of your choosing, providing office support can be less flexible than other careers. You need to be available when your clients need the work done. Some clients, especially those who travel a lot, wait until the last moment to send their projects to you. You need to be able to service them, or they will find someone else. To a certain extent, you can find a balance with them, "training" your clients to give you some advance notice, but this is not always possible.

Related Careers

Desktop Publishing. Desktop publishing, according to the Bureau of Labor Statistics, is one of the fastest-growing vocations, increasing from thirty-eight thousand to sixty-three thousand by 2010. Many desktop publishers design web sites as well as print documents of all kinds. Most desktop publishers are employed by a company. Self-employed desktop publishers often specialize by creating particular kinds of documents, such as catalogs or newsletters, or by the industry they serve. Additional resources include (see end of Résumé Writing section of next page):

- ▶ www.brennerbooks.com, which sells surveys on pricing, and the portal www.desktoppublishing.com
- ▶ *How to Open and Operate a Home-Based Desktop Publishing Business* by Louise Kursmark, and there are dozens more on the subject.

> ▶ Adobe (www. adobe.com) and QuarkXPress (www.quark.com), the companies that make the major products used by professionals, offer courses, some free, in how to use their software. You will also find courses at community colleges and through continuing-education programs.

Résumé Writing. Writing a résumé might be one of the most difficult tasks a job seeker can take on. With millions of Americans changing jobs and hundreds of thousands graduating college, the need for a concise, appealing résumé often leads them to seek some assistance. Résumé writers can specialize in technology, medical, academic, or marketing fields and in the level of employment the client is seeking, (e.g., middle- or executive-level management). Résumé writers often offer other services to help their clients land the jobs of their choice. These include developing a salary history or reference list; writing cover letters and thank-you notes; designing a personalized letterhead; mailing, faxing, or broad-cast e-mailing cover letters and résumés to prospective employers; uploading résumés to online job banks; sending résumés to executive recruiters; typing applications or forms; writing telephone scripts for job seekers to use in making calls; verifying information presented on the résumé (referred to as a verified résumé); and creating Web pages where clients can direct potential employers. Of course, extra services mean extra revenue per client. Additional resources include:

> ▶ *How to Start a Home-Based Writing Business, Fifth ed.*, by Lucy Parker Globe Pequot, 2007.
> ▶ The National Résumé Writers Association offers certification: (888) NRWA-444, www.nrwa.com

Transcription. While medical and legal are the two primary types of tran-scription work, all kinds of media and events need transcribing—audio, pod-casts, WAV files, video and TV, oral histories, sermons and other church material, conference calls, training sessions, and more. Transcription may be a stand-alone specialty or offered as a service of a secretarial or word processing service. However, medical transcription is usually a specialization by itself. We believe the adoption of technology already in existence will overtake many forms of transcribing or at least reduce their work to editing, but in the meantime, legal proceedings, such as workers compensation hearings, arbitration negotiations, and police interrogations at which recorders are used need transcribing. Meditec [(801) 593-0663, www.meditec.com] offers courses in both legal and medical transcription. Additional resources include:

> ▶ The American Association for Medical Transcription is an all-around resource offering training and certification: (800) 982-2182 or (209)

527-9620, www.aamt.org. You can find dozens of other training programs on the Web.

▶ *The Independent Medical Transcriptionist,* by Donna Avila-Weil and Mary Glaccum, Lipincott Williams, and Wilkins, 2002.

VIRTUAL ADMINISTRATIVE WORK AT A GLANCE

ECONOMIC REALITY FIT

▶ Necessary vs. Discretionary	Both
▶ Replaceable with technology	No
▶ Offshorable	Technically possible but unlikely
▶ Industry Status	Established and Enduring

PERSONAL REALITY FIT

▶ Start-up costs	Minimal
▶ Overhead	Moderate
▶ Potential earnings	Moderate
▶ Flexible hours	Minimal
▶ Overall stress	More Than Most (deadline pressure)
▶ Ease of bartering	More Than Most

Durability Rating

Likely Transferable Skills, Background, Careers

Attention to detail, working quickly, meeting deadlines, and computer skills are characteristics of people who do well in providing administrative support. Because this is a service field, caring about and attending to what customers need is necessary. To meet what's expected of a virtual assistant, experience as an administrative or executive assistant, office manager, or customer service representative matters. Desktop publishing requires a creative feel for design, an eye for layout, a proclivity for problem solving, and proficiency with desktop publishing and related software. These capabilities are often refined in jobs involving graphic design and the production side of publishing.

What to Charge

Hourly rates range from a low of about $20 an hour to $50 an hour. If you are working remotely, some clients prefer a flat rate for each project. This can be a per-page rate or a simple flat rate by the job. Services such as desktop publishing, database and spreadsheet work, or writing/editing support higher hourly rates than straight keyboarding. In setting hourly rates, find out what other secretarial services located within thirty minutes of you are charging. To charge by the job, you can use the *Industry Production Standards* guide for estimating time (see "Books and Manuals"). This guide helps estimate and calculate time and charges for a wide range of services.

Best Ways to Market Virtual Administrative Work

> ► Advertise in university newspapers and church, club, and chamber of commerce bulletins, especially those published by organizations of which you are a member.
> ► Bid on projects on Web sites such as www.elance.com and www.guru.com. Your earnings will be lower, however, because of highly competitive bidding.
> ► Define and develop a specialty, which may come about because of something you do well, getting connected to an industry by a client, or obtaining special training.
> ► Get work from past employers.
> ► Solicit hotels and office business centers (often called *executive suite offices*) about offering your services to their guests and clients.

Tips for Getting Started

> ► To decide on a specialization, notice what's in demand on bidding sites such as www.elance.com and www.guru.com. Find out what other VAs are specializing in within your community to determine if there is an unmet need you can meet. Likely targets of opportunity are the health care industry, anything related to seniors and retirement, and legal support.
> ► Get certified in the Microsoft Office Suite (MOS certification) and any other software necessary for a specialization you wish to develop.
> ► Name your business to appeal to prospective customers; it might suggest your specialty or something unique about what you do. One use of a strategic business name and clever logo is using them in your signature on your MySpace pages.
> ► If you're moving to a new community, volunteer for an organization or church where you might meet people who could become customers or refer you to others.

What Next

Associations
- International Association of Administrative Professionals offers certification and local chapters: (816) 891-6600, www.iaap-hq.org.
- International Virtual Assistants Association has a mentor program and offers certification: (888) 259-2487, www.ivaa.org.
- Virtual Assistant Networking Association is an online association: www.vanetworking.com.

Books and Manuals
- *Administrative Assistant's and Secretary's Handbook*, James Stroman, Kevin Wilson, Jennifer Wauson, AMACOM/American Management Association, 2003.
- *How to Start a Home-Based Secretarial Services Business*, Jan Melnik, Globe Pequot Press, 1999.
- Nina Feldman Connections sells the *Industry Production Standards* (IPS), the Brenner pricing publications, and other helpful materials: (510) 655-4296, www.ninafeldman.com.
- *The 2-Second Commute*, Christine Durst, Michael Haaren, Career Press, 2005.
- *The Virtual Assistant's Guide to Marketing*, Michelle Jamison, Word Association, 2003.
- *Virtual Assistant*, Diana Ennen, Kelly Poelker, Another 8 Hours Publishing, 2004.

Training and Certifications
- Microsoft Office Certification: www.microsoft.com/traincert
- Certified Administrative Professional (CAP) and Certified Professional Secretary (CPS) from the International Association of Administrative Professionals: www.iaap-hq.org
- Certified Professional Virtual Assistant and Certified Master Virtual Assistant from AssistU, operated by Stacy Brice, one of the founders of the VA field: (866) 829-6757, www.assistu.com
- Graduate Virtual Assistant from Virtual Assistance U (VAU): www.virtualassistanceu.com

Web Sites
- http://us.deskdemon.com/pages/us/indexus – A British site with a special U.S. section
- www.work-the-web.com – Targeted resources for virtual teams

Web Services

Once upon a time a well-designed sign over a local shop was the essential marketing tool for any business owner. Or, as time passed, perhaps a small recurring ad in the local newspaper. Not so long ago, having a Yellow Page listing became the essential tool. Today the essential tool is a Web presence. Whether it's a multimillion-dollar business or a one-person home business, every company today knows they must have an appealing and effective Web site both to attract and to keep their clientele. Seven out of ten consumers even use the Web to search for local services; in fact, one in four searches is to find something local.

Increasingly, just having a Web site isn't even enough. One's Web presence needs to reach out to the world with the latest artistic, informative, and interactive tools, from flash screens, photos, blogs, and video clips to shopping carts, credit options, automatic e-mailed alerts and reminder notices, and, of course, appealing links and effective search engine placement. All this requires not only technical know-how but also lots of time to create and manage—much more than most small or start-up businesses can do without someone whose time is committed to just the Web site. Thus there's a growing demand for all types of professional Web service providers.

Let's start with the basics. There's the *Web designer*, who plans and then creates the look, feel, and navigation of the Web site. There's the *Web content writer*, who crafts, enters, and updates the information, descriptions, and sales messages on a site. Then there's the *Web publicist* who makes sure the target world knows about the site, can find it, and wants to come to it. There's also the *Web promotions specialist* and the *specialty programmer*, who create special features that give a site the functionality visitors expect. Every site needs to be stored in some computer, so there is the *Web host*, on whose server a site resides. The Web host makes sure the site is up and running trouble free. Finally, there's the *Webmaster*, who takes care of the day-to-day operation of the Web site. Each of these basic tasks can be a specialization, or one person or a small company can provide most or some combination of them. Even more specific tasks such as e-commerce, flash design, information architecture, interaction design, search engine optimization, and Web site reviewing can be the basis of a consultancy or career.

Each type of service requires its own set of skills, software, and equipment. Hosting, for example, requires a significant investment in hardware, such as servers, high-speed lines, and the capability to keep servers in uptime virtually 100 percent of the time. Web design requires a background in graphic design or something related, facility with design and graphic software, plus some marketing sense, because Web sites need to appeal to Web visitors who spend only thirty seconds reviewing a home page; only 50 percent of them will scroll down a Web page to see what's under the visible part of their screen. Specialty programming requires knowledge of the particular languages like CGI, Perl, Java, and new languages as they emerge, that make such wonderful features as running movies, adding animation, creating interactive surveys and polls, shopping, and payment options work.

A content writer for the Web needs a solid knowledge of the target audience, what appeals to them, and how to write concisely, clearly, and compellingly in a style between copywriting and technical writing. Web publicists and promotions specialists need to combine the creative skills one would find in a PR firm or ad agency with a working understanding of Web navigation, e-mail, links, and search engine optimization.

Whether you choose to specialize in one aspect of this field, as did Jim Hanson of Mountainpad Media (www.mountainpad.com), who specializes in database design, or decide to offer one-stop design services like Randy Caruso of Randy Caruso Web site Design (www.the7thsense.com), Web services can be appealing for someone who wants a career that is at once creative and technical in nature, presenting an unending array of engaging problem-solving challenges.

WEB SERVICES AT A GLANCE

ECONOMIC REALITY FIT

► Necessary vs. Discretionary	Discretionary
► Replaceable with technology	No
► Offshorable	Yes
► Industry Status	Established and Expanding

PERSONAL REALITY FIT

► Start-up costs	More Than Most
► Overhead	Moderate
► Potential earnings	More Than Most
► Flexible hours	Moderate
► Computer skills	More Than Most
► Overall stress	Minimal
► Ease of bartering	Moderate

Durability Rating

Likely Transferable Skills, Background, Careers

As a universal medium of communication and commerce, virtually every kind of skill and know-how can be related to the Web. For technical work, programming experience is the obvious easy transfer to this business. A mathematics background in teaching or applied math is always helpful in computer applications, and call center experience and other customer service work is a plus too.

What to Charge

Hourly rates and salaries for many Web services can be found on sites such as www.payscale.com, www.hotgig.com, and www.brennerbooks.com. However, these are often averages, and what you can charge is determined by experience, region, and what you ask. You see this reflected in the wide range of rates ranging between $25 and $125 an hour. As a rule, the more specialized the work, the higher the rate. For example, search engine optimizers get from $1,000 to $10,000 a month. You can check rates in your area by calling others doing the same kind of work. It's best neither to undercharge everyone nor to be the most expensive in starting out. Most work is usually priced by the hour or project, or with design, by the page. When pricing by the project, in addition to estimating the amount of time you think it will take, it's good practice to add an additional 20 percent to cover unforeseen problems.

Best Ways to Market Web Services

- ▶ Directly contact Web designers, Webmasters, online publications, Internet service providers, and Web hosting organizations for subcontract work.
- ▶ Search online job listings; then contact the companies and convince them to outsource the job rather than hiring someone in-house.
- ▶ Bid for work on sites such as elance.com and guru.com.

Tips for Getting Started

- ▶ Randy Caruso advises, "To be truly good and well rounded, it takes experience in all areas." So learn about the service segments you feel weakest in and identify potential subcontractors with these skills.
- ▶ Get appropriate certifications.
- ▶ Prepare a variety of service packages related to customer size.
- ▶ Use your own Web site to demonstrate what you do with links to sites of clients for whom you have done work.

► Experience shows that it's best not to rely solely on one or just a few clients for your livelihood. Even if you have solid, ongoing relationships with a core of clients, losing just one can be devastating. The fewer your clients, the more important it is to keep your marketing efforts going at some level to develop additional sources of work.

LEARN MORE

Associations

► International Webmasters Association's scope extends to Web development and e-commerce and offers many classes: www.iwanet.org

► Web Designer and Developers Association emphasizes ethical business practices: www.wdda.org

► Web Marketing Association sponsors competitions: www .webmarketingassociation.org

► World Organization of Webmasters partners with a number of colleges: www.joinwow.org

► Web Programmers Association is an invitational organization: www.webprogrammer.org

Books

► *Advanced Professional Web Design,* Clint Eccher, Charles River Media, 2006.

► *How to Be a Successful Internet Consultant,* Jessica Keyes, American Management Association, 2002.

► *How to Start a Home-Based Web Design Business,* Jim Smith, Globe Pequot, 2004.

► *Professional Web Design,* Clint Eccher, Eric Hunley, Erik Simmons, Charles River Media, 2004.

► *Search Engine Optimization for Dummies,* Peter Kent, For Dummies, 2006.

► *The Real Business of Web Design,* John Waters, Allworth Press, 2004.

► O'Reilly publishes many specific technical titles: http://oreilly.com

Training

► Hands On IT Training Nationwide offers open-enrollment classes in more than seventy-five cities: www.traininghott.com

► The HTML Writers Guild provides training courses: www.hwg.org

► Training leading to certification from Microsoft and Sun in Java is widely available. To learn more and identify providers, check out www.microsoft.com/Learning and www.java.sun.com. Several of the associations listed above offer certification.

▸ Webmonkey offers teaching tools, a how-to library, and other resources: www.webmonkey.com

Magazines

▸ *Information Today*'s online with links to a variety of magazines published by CRM : www.infotoday.com
▸ *Internet World*: www.iw.com
▸ *Web Developer*: www.webdeveloper.com

Web Sites

▸ www.pageresource.com – Offers free tutorials on Web development
▸ www.programmersheaven.com – Provides files, links, and articles
▸ www.searchengineland.com – Provides news about the search engine world
▸ www.searchenginewatch.com – Focuses on search engine marketing
▸ www.sun.com/980713/webwriting – Sun Microsystems's information on writing and content strategies for the Web
▸ www.webdevforums.com – Active Webmaster forum on Web design
▸ www.htmlhelp.com – Web Design Group offers material on a wide range of HTML-related topics
▸ www.webstyleguide.com – Offers a free basic style guide for the Web
▸ www.webmasterworld.com – Offers forums and news
▸ www.useit.com/papers/webwriting – Research on how users read on the Web

Writing for a Living

Communication is not solely a human capability, but among the species we are the only ones who write. There are many kinds of writers and writing, and there are numerous writing careers and ways to make a living involving writing. While it used to be about putting pen to paper, today it is about keyboarding, a prerequisite skill, along with reasonable knowledge of word processing software and, particularly, formatting.

Tradition would have us look at fiction and nonfiction. Subcategories under fiction would include science fiction, novella, novel, etc. Included under nonfiction might be history, technical, textbook, and business writing. Crossing into both realms are ghostwriting and coaching. At the present time, we find business writing, creative writing, ghostwriting, technical writing, and script and screenwriting most in demand on Web bidding sites such as www.elance .com and www .guru.com. A great deal of writing is destined for the Web, and writing for the Web can be a specialty unto itself. However, the Web, and particularly user-created content, like Wikipedia, is overtaking the role played by nonfiction books.

We did not forget poetry. This is a type of writing that also crosses between fiction and nonfiction, but it is a form of writing few people can earn a living doing.

Business writing is a lucrative segment of the writing field wherein you might do anything from writing company newsletters to consumer information booklets and from speeches for executives to company annual reports. A subset of business writing is the well-paying work of copywriting. Copywriters craft words to sell, market, and promote products and services to prospects and customers. You need to be the kind of person who can get inside someone else's shoes, understand him, and then provide clear and compelling copy for advertising, brochures, direct response mail, electronic promotions, packaging copy, press releases and media kits, scripts for telemarketing and infomercials, and anything intended to sell or promote.

Creative writing and script and screenwriting are skills that are not easy to develop. Creative writing careers take stamina and a stomach of steel. Writers in these genres receive many, many rejections until they find the correct piece for the right publisher, magazine, book, or producer.

Technical writing requires, in addition to writing skill, a desire to steep yourself in the material and undertake some serious research. Technical writing can be documentation for computer software or hardware, magazine articles in trade publications or journals, policy manuals for companies or government agencies, press releases, training materials, brochures, and even instruction materials. It can require a variety of writing styles and provide an array of experiences. Technical material often goes directly to the World Wide Web, and this writing demands formatting skills unlike any other. Linda G. Gallagher, Manager of the Society for Technical Communication's Consulting and Independent Contracting Special Interest Group, says technical writers are seeing a steady flow of work particularly from smaller to midsize companies. Gallagher (www.techcomplus.com) believes technology will not be able to replace the role of writers in making things understandable for human beings.

Encompassing all that we have already discussed is ghostwriting. This service is sought by a variety of potential customers: those who do not feel skilled enough to write, those with no time to write, and those with no desire or skills to do the research to produce the item they want. Ghostwriters, unlike other writers, seek no byline and get no credit for what they have written. What they get is a lucrative payday and, often, repeat customers. Ghostwriters author fiction and nonfiction, technical work and poetry, business pieces and creative efforts; they may also write for stage or screen. The work of ghostwriters is often seen on the op-ed pages of newspapers, writing what their employer wants to say in the clear and concise language favored by editors.

The wordsmith has been given many parts to play in human society. Writing is an honorable profession and can be a good business.

Related Career

Writing tutor or coach. Tutoring writers can be approached from several directions. Schools and parents share an understanding of the importance of writing, which has given rise to the writing tutor. High school students looking for help with college essays or the basic high school term paper can seek out the services of a coach. College writing requirements can be quite demanding, and the assistance of a tutor/editor will be seen as invaluable. In the business world, executives and professionals look to coaches to help improve their skills in general or for a specific presentation.

Coaching is not necessarily writing. In fact, it often requires no writing. It does require the ability to inspire others, to provide criticism in a positive and supportive manner, and to recognize the need in someone else for direction. Resources include the books *The Bedford Guide for Writing Tutors* by Leigh Ryan; *The St. Martin's Sourcebook for Writing Tutors* by Christina Murphy and Steve Sherwood; and *A Tutor's Guide* by Ben Rafoth. Also see the Coaching profile beginning on page 155.

WRITING FOR A LIVING AT A GLANCE

ECONOMIC REALITY FIT

► Necessary vs. Discretionary	Discretionary
► Replaceable with technology	No
► Offshorable	No
► Industry Status	Established and Enduring

PERSONAL REALITY FIT

► Start-up costs	Minimal
► Overhead	Minimal
► Potential earnings	Moderate
► Flexible hours	Minimal
► Computer skills	More Than Most
► Overall stress	Moderate
► Ease of bartering	More Than Most

Durability Rating

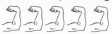

Likely Transferable Skills, Background, Careers

Teachers, particularly of English language or literature, are well prepared to use their skills in a writing field. Journalists, too, are well prepared and use their credentials to open doors in technical and business writing if they reported in these fields. Coaching is open to journalists, teachers, and retired executives.

What to Charge

The nature of the business or the project determines at which end of a very broad spectrum your work will fall. As a consultant to an executive, you can command $100 to $300 an hour while working on a public or board presentation. A technical writer charges by the page, as much as $25 a page in complex fields or thousands of dollars for a complete document. Ghostwriters charge by the page or the project; $15 per page and $4,000 to $5,000 for a novel are not unreasonable and can be much higher. Copywriters charge by the hour ($40 to $125), the day, or the project. On direct response projects, copywriters may also get a percentage of the revenue. Several Web sites, such as www.sustainable-media.com and www.professionalcopy.ca, provide rates. A writing coach working with children might charge $25 per hour, while working with an adult would command $75 to $90 an hour.

Best Ways to Market Writing Services

- ▶ Post your résumé in online job banks and search them for assignments if you want to work for an executive or a corporation.
- ▶ Reach out to local businesses that need public relations writing—press releases, newspaper articles, and mailings. Some companies and organizations post writing work they want done on their Web sites.
- ▶ Look for assignments on bidding sites like www.elance.com and www.guru.com

Tips for Getting Started

- ▶ Choose a topic or focus that motivates you to want to become an expert on it. And do develop that expertise.
- ▶ Get ahead by learning and writing about new technology.

- ▶ Offer to write something free for Chamber of Commerce members.
- ▶ As your projects come to completion, develop a portfolio you can use to promote yourself. You can also develop a portfolio from free articles you write and from class assignments.
- ▶ Don't forget the myriad of writing courses, general and specialized, that are available on the Web and in your community.
- ▶ If you're interested in coaching kids, develop a coaching brochure and circulate it through local PTAs.
- ▶ If you want to do ghostwriting, visit the sites of other ghostwriters to learn what types of writing they are promoting, and contact those with whom you won't compete to talk business.

LEARN MORE

Associations

- ▶ American Marketing Association: (800) AMA-1150, www .marketingpower.com
- ▶ American Society of Journalists and Authors: (212) 997-0947, www.asja.org
- ▶ International Association of Business Communicators: (800) 776-4222, www.iabc.com
- ▶ Public Relations Society of America: (212) 460-1490, www.prsa.org
- ▶ Society for Technical Communication has local chapters: (703) 522-4114, www.stc.org

Books

- ▶ *The Elements of Business Writing,* Gary Blake and Robert W. Bly, Longman Publishing Group, 1992.
- ▶ *Ghostwriting,* Eva Shaw, Writeriffic Publishing Group, 2003.
- ▶ *If You Want to Write*, Brenda Ueland, Graywolf Press, 1997. A classic that has inspired many to write.
- ▶ *The McGraw-Hill 36-Hour Course in Business Writing and Communication*, Kenneth W. Davis, McGraw-Hill, 2005.
- ▶ *The Online Copywriter's Handbook*, Robert W. Bly, McGraw-Hill, 2003.
- ▶ *Start & Run a Copywriting Business,* Steve Slaunwhite, Self-Counsel Press, 2005.
- ▶ *Writing the Screenplay*, Alan A. Armer, Waveland Press Inc., 2002.
- ▶ *The Tech Writer's Survival Guide*, Janet Van Wicklen, Checkmark Books, 2001.
- ▶ *Technical Writing 101*, Alan S. Pringle, Sarah S. O'Keefe, Scriptorium Press, 2003.

► *The Well-Fed Writer*, Peter Bowerman, Fanove Publishing, 2000, 2004.
► *The Writing Coach*, Lee Clark Johns, Delmar Publishers, 2004.
► *Writing Copy for Dummies*, Jonathan Kranz, For Dummies, 2004.

Training

► The Gotham Writers' Workshop offers classes both in New York City and online: www.writingclasses.com
► Learning Tree University offers short courses in various locations in North America in business and technical writing: www.learningtree .com
► Technical writing training can be found online in courses from www.technical-writing-course.com and www.online-learning.com
► The U.S. Department of Agriculture Graduate School offers courses in technical writing and writing skills in various locations: (888) 744-4723 or (202) 314-3300, www.grad.usda.gov
► Writers on the Net has been offering online classes since 1995; its offerings span fiction and nonfiction writing: www.writers.com

Web Sites

► www.publishersmarketplace.com – Offers two free newsletters: Publishers Lunch, a daily e-newsletter, and *Weekly Lunch,* a weekly that describes recent publishing deals.
► www.writersdigest.com – Offers many books and products for writers, including a magazine. The Web site annually publishes a listing of the 101 Best Web Sites for Writers. The list is organized into categories and indicates the features of each site, such as chat, classes and workshops, forum, and job postings.

*We cannot direct the wind, but
we can adjust the sails.*
Bertha Calloway

CHAPTER FOUR

14 Products and Services for New Economic Realities

Chances are, some of the careers described in this chapter are ones you may not have heard of, and it may be years before they become prominent enough to appear in another book about careers. However, we believe that to catch the next wave—the next Internet, the next computer age—one needs to get beyond what's hot today. To be certain, most of the careers in this chapter are established and, we believe, will continue to grow because of the economic, demographic, and technological forces we describe in Chapter One. Those that are less well-established now will at least evolve in other forms as people and communities deal with new realities.

Alternative Energy Installing, Servicing, and Consulting

Would you like to be in a business that is so popular you'll be scheduling appointments months ahead and have a long and eager waiting list? That's what installing—and later servicing and maintaining—alternative energy systems, such as solar panels, geothermal systems, and wind turbines, is becoming. First and foremost fueled by the escalating cost of energy derived from fossil fuels, but additionally by environmental consciousness and a growing number of people getting "off the grid," alternative energy could become the best business to be in for years to come. In 2004 solar equipment and installation ballooned into a $4.7 billion industry, and it is projected to expand to nearly $50 billion in 2015.

Futurist Harry Dent believes the United States is undergoing the greatest migration in human history. One in five Americans—at least 70 million Americans in total—will move from the suburbs over the next fifty years.[1] They're motivated by being able to get bigger homes for less money, less traffic, a greater sense of safety, better schools, and lower taxes. While most of this growth will be to what are now small towns with existing services, many of those migrating from large cities want a home in a more natural setting, such as the mountains, sea or lake shore, forest, or desert—even if it means being off the grid.

In fact, even those who aren't in the hinterlands increasingly desire to be off the grid. Being fully off the grid means having your own energy source for electricity, your own water supply, and your own sewage disposal system. Richard Perez of *Home Power Magazine* estimates that the number of people going off the grid is growing at 30 percent a year. "People just want to be separate from large energy companies," he tells us. However, most homeowners and businesses remain "on the grid," but they are installing alternative energy systems to supplement and thus reduce their energy costs.

While solar power using photovoltaic panels based on silicon remains the most popular alternative energy choice, some people are choosing hydro, wind, geothermal, hot water solar panels, or a combination of technologies. Some developers of upscale housing developments, for example, are doing what President George W. Bush did for his ranch, installing geothermal heat pumps that use heat energy from the earth to provide warmth in winter and by reversing the cycle—removing heat by sending it into the earth—provides cooling in the summer.

Some small communities are installing commercial-scale windmills and are benefiting their residents not only with significantly lower energy costs, but because production tax credits and tradable renewable energy certificates, are making money for their taxpayers. Proper siting of windmills and newer windmill technology has reduced concern about risks to the bird population. Because wind energy is responsible for virtually no air, water, or soil pollution, organizations such as the Audubon Society and the Sierra Club do anything but oppose wind power. In fact, the Audubon Society's position is "We support wind power as long as the turbines are well-sited."

When Chuck Tingstad unexpectedly got laid off from a job in the computer industry, his thoughts turned to something that had interested him since high school—how to make the world more energy self-sufficient. "I read everything I could get my hands on," he told us. He approached Eco Depot (www.ecodepot

---

[1] *TRENDS E-MAGAZINE* JANUARY 2005 PAGE 25. Projection attributed to Harry Dent.

inc.com), a Spokane store that sells renewable energy systems and green building products, and entered into a partnership to do work that enables him to evangelize about work he believes in.

Most installers specialize in one alternative system or another. Fieldstone Energy Corporation builds systems using rivers and breakwaters to power hydraulic systems. Eco Depot primarily installs photovoltaic panels, hot-water solar panels, and wind turbines. Its projects sometimes begin with an on-site consultation to assess sun patterns and wind power. The $250 fee is then credited toward purchase and installation of a system. Island Energy Solutions Inc. (www.islandenergy.net) installs photovoltaic panels. Keith Cronin, its owner, was an electrician before deciding to "make a difference in the energy field." He does not install hot-water solar panels, because that requires a different license, but he is following the development of other technologies for producing electricity, particularly wind and ocean thermal conversion.

Consulting may be especially appealing to some people because installing and servicing alternative energy systems can be physically hazardous, requiring work on rooftops and high towers. Because of the variety of energy choices that are emerging, we project a role for consultants who have in-depth expertise about multiple systems that will enable residential and commercial property owners to make good choices.

Unlike in the past, when investing ten to thirty thousand dollars for a solar installation wouldn't produce a payback until many years into the future, solar energy users are now seeing quicker returns on their investment due to the rising costs of electricity, propane, diesel, and natural gas. In addition, the cost of photovoltaic panels has decreased by 90 percent over the past thirty years.

Research underway by companies like GE to employ light-emitting plastics instead of silicon will lower the cost of photovoltaic. Thin-film solar panels, now entering production, use only one percent of the silicon of regular panels. New microturbines, fuel cells, and hydrogen storage tanks are being patented and developed, and more technologies based on nanotechnology and quantum mechanics will create new jobs and businesses.

Methane digesters on dairy and hog farms are another emerging alternative energy. The electricity, mulch, and fertilizer byproducts produced using anaerobic digesters increases farm income, reduces pollution from run-off, and eliminates the odors that foul the air of neighbors.

For people who are choosing to live in remote areas not served by utilities, alternative energy represents an immediate savings, since bringing in power lines on flat land can cost twenty thousand dollars or more a mile. In this field, you can make a good living providing people with information and technology to convert to sources of renewable energy and continued service to help them keep their systems running.

Related Careers

Greenhouse Construction. Because of the growing popularity of growing healthy food locally, greenhouses are sprouting up in backyards and side yards. Strong potential lies, too, in building greenhouses near factories that release carbon dioxide into the atmosphere. Instead of adding to the problem of global warming, carbon dioxide can be diverted to nearby greenhouses, where it works as a crop enhancer. For more information, contact the National Greenhouse Manufacturers Association at (717) 238-4530 or www.ngma.com.

Retrofitting Windows. Reducing the amount of heat loss from clear glass windows makes window retrofitting a frequent target for reducing energy costs. While many homeowners take this on as a do-it-yourself project, others turn to window contractors to ensure correct installation that will meet code requirements for egress, safety glass, and grade. Retrofitting can be done in a variety of ways, such as replacing glass windows with panes that have a low-e (low emissivity) glass coating or with panes that have a clear plastic film suspended between two layers of glass to produce a triple-pane effect. This type of plastic film, which we have in our home, will adhere to existing glass. This work, as well as other forms of weatherization, requires a contractor's license. For information about obtaining a license, contact the agency in your state responsible for licensing contractors. Links to state licensing agencies in the United States and Canada can be found at www.clearhq.org/boards.htm.

ALTERNATIVE ENERGY AT A GLANCE

ECONOMIC REALITY FIT

► Necessary vs. Discretionary	Necessary
► Replaceable with technology	No
► Offshorable	No
► Industry Status	Established and Expanding

PERSONAL REALITY FIT

► Start-up costs	Moderate, More Than Most (if stocking inventory)
► Overhead	Minimal
► Potential earnings	More Than Most
► Flexible hours	Moderate
► Overall stress	Moderate
► Ease of bartering	More Than Most

Durability Rating

Likely Transferable Skills, Background, Careers

People with technical backgrounds can more easily understand these technologies and their workings. So those who have worked with computers, telecommunications, mechanics, or traditional energy companies are well positioned to enter this field.

What to Charge

Installers charge from $50 to $75 an hour, with the higher rates going to installers with an electrical contractor's license or an electrician certificate.

Best Ways to Market Alternative Energy Installing

- ► Work with real estate agents who sell off-grid properties.
- ► Develop working relationships with builders specializing in upscale homes, which are increasingly being constructed with alternative energy systems.
- ► Provide an initial consultation or energy audit that provides property owners with an assessment that is not as comprehensive as those provided by energy raters. (See the Energy Rating and Building Performance Auditing profile in Chapter 3). The consultation or audit fee can then be credited toward the cost of installing an energy system.

Tips for Getting Started

- ► Learning is the first step in getting started. You can do this by taking one or more courses or a training program.
- ► Install a system in your own home to enable you to talk about the benefits from your own experience. Volunteering to design and install systems for neighbors will also increase your experience and enable you to garner testimonials and referrals.
- ► Some people take an apprenticeship with an installing dealer. Usually this means working for minimal pay. However, if you work for someone with an electrical contractor's license, your time will count toward what's required to get your own license.

▶ Have information available on the tax breaks available in your state. Many states, such as California, Connecticut, New Mexico, New York, New Jersey, North Carolina, and Washington, are offering subsidies such as tax credits and exemptions from sales and use taxes.

LEARN MORE

Associations

▶ The American Wind Energy Association is the trade association of the wind power industry that includes both producers and proponents: (202) 383-2500, www.awea.org

▶ International Geothermal Association provides information about the geothermal industry: http://iga.igg.cnr.it

▶ Midwest Renewable Energy Association sponsors or participates in many events every month of the year: (715) 592-6595, www.the-mrea.org

▶ Solar Energy International teaches how to design, maintain, and install alternative energy systems. While most of the workshops are offered in Colorado, some are offered in other locations: www.solarenergy.org

Books

▶ *21st Century Complete Guide to Biofuels and Bioenergy: Department of Energy Alternative Fuel Research, Agriculture Department Biofuel Research, Biomass, Biopower, Biodiesel, Ethanol, Methanol, Plant Material Products, Landfill Methane, Crop Residues,* U.S. Government, Progressive Management, 2003.

▶ *Alternative Energy: Facts, Statistics, and Issues,* Paula Berinstein, Oryx Press, 2001.

▶ *Biodiesel: Growing a New Energy Economy,* Greg Pahl, Chelsea Green Publishing Company, 2005.

▶ *Power With Nature: Solar and Wind Energy Demystified,* Rex A. Ewing, Pixyjack Press, 2003.

▶ *Real Goods Solar Living Source Book,* John Schaeffer, Doug Pratt, Gaiam Real Goods, 2001.

▶ *The Solar House: Passive Heating and Cooling,* Daniel D. Chiras, Chelsea Green Publishing Company, 2002.

▶ *Wind Energy Basics: A Guide to Small and Micro Wind Systems,* Paul Gipe, Chelsea Green Publishing Company, 1999.

Magazines and Newsletters

▶ *Home Power* covers many technologies. The magazine and its archives are fully available on their Web site: www.homepower.com

> ► *Windpower Monthly.* Past issues are archived on the Web site: http://windpower-monthly.com

Web Sites

> ► www.envirolink.org – The Alternative Fuels pages provide hundreds of links to resources in the alternative energy field—organizations, publications, government resources, articles, and more.
> ► www.dsireusa.org – Gives details on state financial incentives for renewable energy
> ► www.energystar.gov – Gives details on federal financial incentives for renewable energy

Architectural Salvage

Almost half of the 127 tons of construction debris when a two-thousand-square foot house is torn down can be salvaged and reused, and there's a ready market for what's obtained through salvage operations. In a world increasingly dominated by huge suburban superstores offering one-stop shopping solutions for everything you need, people could be forgiven for wanting to return to a time when things were a little more special and unique in their decorating. In other words, Lowe's or Home Depot might be fine, but there are other options!

Why, after all, pay full price, particularly when those prices are going up as the economies of China and India gobble up building supplies and materials? This is one way globalization is *creating* markets—many people can economize in building an addition or a home. They get materials and objects with histories!

You can take advantage of this opportunity by eliminating the one potential problem with salvage—people want the treasures that can be unearthed by architectural salvage but are reluctant to go to the effort to get the items they want. That's where you come in!

You can turn these desires into a livelihood from the two hundred thousand homes and commercial buildings demolished each year in the United States. There are a couple of directions you can go to make a living from architectural salvage. The major considerations are the amount of time and money you're prepared to invest. You can have a sideline business salvaging and selling what you acquire to other businesses. Or if you would really like to make this exciting and rewarding and build a bigger business, you can open a store yourself.

Either way, architectural salvage can be satisfying and even fun. This is a field populated by the self-employed and very small businesses, according to Brad Guy, president of the Building Materials Reuse Association. He observes, "People do this because they love it; it's very visceral."

Let's say that you have the time and start-up money to start your own architectural salvage center, a fairly fancy name for something that's essentially just a vintage clothing store, but with home supplies. An architectural salvage center, such as the Re Stores in Bellingham and Seattle, Washington (www.re-store.org), is a warehouse that buys and sells building parts salvaged from demolished or remodeled structures. The centers can be small or large; major ones can be real warehouses, with huge stocks and a large number of employees, but others are more like your ordinary antiques store. These centers purchase chandeliers, filigreed doorknobs, kitchen cabinets, bathroom fixtures, ceramic tile, bricks, door moldings, and doors, just to name a few categories, and then resell them. In every case, these items cost far less than equivalent things today, but they cost even less for the center to purchase, allowing everyone to win!

As in any antique store, there is a wide range of different kinds of settings. Some salvage warehouses resemble junkyards with broken windows and rust-stained sinks piled in untidy heaps. Others are more like museums with artful displays of architectural treasures. Some of the types of items that can be salvaged and resold include:

- architectural elements from homes and commercial buildings
- bathroom fixtures
- beams
- bricks, ceramic tiles
- building and construction materials
- doors, windows, doorknobs, and hinges
- ducting
- fencing
- flooring and baseboards
- kitchen cabinets and knobs/cabinet pulls
- lighting fixtures
- mantels
- mirrors
- molding and trim
- piping

If you don't want the intensity and expense of having a store, you can still have a fun and profitable career in architectural salvage. As we've just described, architectural salvage centers and warehouses depend on people to sell them a wide variety of items, which they can then resell to homeowners and decorators. You can have a lot of fun being a "freelance" supplier to the salvage centers and selling items that justify shipping cost from a Web site or on eBay—and support yourself at the same time.

The best way to figure out how (and where) best to make great finds is probably to go to a salvage center and ask. (A link to help you find centers near you follows.) You can also browse the net for "used building materials" or "demolition contractors," and it may also be a good idea to contact a local historical preservation society that might know of buildings or houses being renovated.

Related to being a freelance salvager but unlawful in some places is "dumpster diving." You can learn more about dumpster diving on the Web at www.dumpster world.com, which provides a message board, and www.dumpsterdiving.meetup .com, which lists groups of trash aficionados.

ARCHITECTURAL SALVAGE AT A GLANCE

ECONOMIC REALITY FIT

► Necessary vs. Discretionary	Discretionary
► Replaceable with technology	No
► Offshorable	No
► Industry Status	Established and Expanding

PERSONAL REALITY FIT

► Start-up costs	Minimal, More Than Most (store)
► Overhead	Minimal, Moderate (store)
► Potential earnings	Moderate
► Flexible hours	Minimal (store), More Than Most
► Overall stress	Moderate
► Ease of bartering	More Than Most

Durability Rating

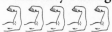

Likely Transferable Skills, Background, Careers

There are no particular skills that prepare you for architectural salvage, though any type of business experience will be helpful. What you need is an eye for a beautiful, unexpected find, and a willingness to get your hands dirty!

What to Charge

What you charge will, of course, be dependent on the items you are selling and the ease with which you acquired it. There will be a fair degree of bargaining that goes on in the selling process. This is okay and can help you as often as it hurts you. It helps to develop good relationships with customers, who will trust your prices and be less likely to attempt to lower them.

Best Ways to Market Architectural Salvage

- ▶ Develop a reputation and relationship with architects, antique dealers, interior decorators, and builders who are likely buyers of fixtures and edifice parts from old buildings.
- ▶ Sell items on the Web on auction sites like eBay and in Web galleries like www.architecturals.net. Sites for collectors can also be avenues for selling items of architectural salvage.
- ▶ As a freelance salvager, develop relationships with the buyers from local architectural salvage centers. Find them through the directory of members of the Building Materials Reuse Association and the Yellow Pages under Building Materials (Used or Salvage and Surplus).
- ▶ As a store, choose between operating a brick-and-mortar store, selling via the Web, or a combination. Location remains an important factor for a store's success, even for a trend business like this, and providing a satisfying shopping experience for customers is key. One way to do this is by providing helpful advice about installing what you sell. If you decide to have a Web-based store, see the profile on Selling Things on the Web.

Tips for Getting Started

- ▶ Consider working for someone experienced in salvage before going out on your own.
- ▶ Discuss the market with buyers of local salvage.
- ▶ Check out what liability insurance you will need. This can be a major cost.
- ▶ Explore working arrangements with contractors who specialize in rehabilitation and renovation.
- ▶ Check demolition permits issued by nearby cities and towns; talk to local historical preservationists.
- ▶ If you decide to open a store, chances are you'll be able to offer customers a wider selection and more select items if you also do the finding.

- ▶ Software that helps you to estimate the environmental benefits of salvaging and reusing building materials is available at www.decon structioninstitute.com/download.php?dow_ID=19.

Learn More

Association
- ▶ The Building Materials Reuse Association is a national association with a directory of members, training leading to certification, and conferences: (800) 990-2672, www.buildingreuse.org

Publications
- ▶ *A Guide to Deconstruction*, a HUD publication: www.huduser.org/publications/destech/decon.html
- ▶ *The Salvage Sisters' Guide to Finding Style in the Street and Inspiration in the Attic*, Kathleen Hackett, Mary Ann Young, Artisan, 2005.
- ▶ *Unbuilding: Salvaging Architectural Treasures from Unwanted Homes*, Bob Falk, Brad Guy, The Taunton Press, 2007.

Training
Training in identifying what is reusable and salable, how to maintain the value of what you find while removing it, and preparing it for sale are what you will learn from the Building Materials Reuse Association. You may also find local extension programs offering short courses.

Web Sites
- ▶ http://architecture.about.com/cs/findsupplies/a/salvage_2.htm – Jackie Craven of About.com provides information on architectural salvage from the standpoint of a buyer.
- ▶ www.wikipedia.org – See the Wikipedia topic "Deconstruction."

Elder Services

Where has the time gone?

When did we ever get so old?

I'm the only one of my friends left . . .

Within fifteen years, nearly 7 million people will be over the age of eighty-five, according to U.S. Census population projections. Following these elders will be the massive demographic wave of the baby boomers (people born between

1946 and 1964), soon to reach the early phase of their elder years. Today's boomers are finding their parents in dependent elderhood and are realizing that they are already a decade or two older than their grandparents were when their grandparents passed on.

And they are also beginning to realize that negotiating the world on a day-to-day basis is growing more challenging. They see today's dependent elders need assistance. And that is where elder services comes in.

A microcosm of the needs of the elderly can be found by simply looking inside their medicine cabinets. The number of prescriptions, vitamins, and over-the-counter medications that they take is remarkable. These medications address a long list of conditions and ailments: hypertension, enlarged prostate, CHF, GERD, arthritis, and anxiety. They take a baby aspirin a day, ginseng for memory, and vitamin E. Managing these medications and products so that they work in concert is quite a task. The different medications for all the many ailments can sometimes create as much trouble as they solve. Managing medicines is a complex thing where small errors can result in significant consequence and is itself the basis for a career or business as we discuss in the Disease Management profile on page 170.

So, too, in every aspect of life for the elderly—small errors can have significant consequence. Cataracts and slower reaction times can make driving hazardous. Difficulty driving can result in missed appointments. And so on and so on.

Elderly services covers the array of services that allow the elderly to manage their lives in a way that maximizes quality and enjoyment and minimizes the challenges that can result in annoyances, obstacles, or even worse.

If you have a background in medicine or a related field, whether in nursing, social work, or psychology, you will find that there is a tremendous demand for your services. A background in any of these fields positions you to provide elder care management—essentially organizing the "medicine cabinet" of elderly clients' lives. Your goal in this position is to allow your clients to remain independent and living at home.

If you do not have a background in the medical field, your role in an elderly client's life can still be essential:

- ► You can function as an in-home, nonmedical caregiver—helping your elderly clients manage their daily activities. These services can range from cleaning their homes to paying their bills and from laundry to personal grooming. You can learn more about these from the companies that offer franchises for nonmedical care, such as Comfort Keepers (www.comfort keepers.com), Griswold Special Care (www.home-care.net), and Home Instead Senior Care (www.homeinstead.com).
- ► You can drive seniors who can no longer get to their various appointments on their own—places like the doctors office, the beauty

shop, and the grocery store. Tricia Lee, who operates TimeSavers of Pensacola Inc., says the greatest satisfaction of her work is the relationships she develops with her clients. "We love each other. We hug when we meet and when we part. I never drag on Monday mornings—I look forward to seeing my customers."

► You can assist seniors who need to move to smaller homes or assisted-living facilities. This includes helping to sort through the senior's possessions to determine what to keep and what to sell or donate, packing and labeling boxes, arranging for a mover, and terminating and establishing new utilities and phone services. After the move, unpacking and setting up the new household is part of the service. Mercedes Gunderson started a company called Gentle Transitions (www.gentletransitions.com) in 1990 that is acknowleged as the first senior relocation service.

There was a time when family members took care of their older relatives. Distance and other life demands have eroded those family connections. Changes in neighborhoods and communities result in many elderly people finding themselves alone and isolated. Even when children live near their older relatives, their lives don't have the flexibility they would need. Tricia Martin says her clients' children tell her, "I'm going to lose my job unless I get some help." Simply being available to be a "friend"—to talk with them, play a game of cards, or assist them when they want to go out on walks—is a service that will increasingly be in demand.

Further complicating the situation elders find themselves in is the increasing difficulty in recruiting volunteers for programs like Meals on Wheels. This is attributed to the high price of gasoline and decreased levels of community participation. Energy prices are in a long-term rise at the same time there are rising numbers of seniors who need services.

The physical, psychological, and emotional challenges that increase with the years open many opportunities to assist and to establish new careers or enlarge existing careers. If you have a background in financial services, helping people to manage estates and retirements is a growing field. If you are a nutritionist, you will find that the special—and changing—needs of the elderly will give you an ever-growing client base. If you are an attorney, assisting the elderly with the myriad of decisions that they must make—things like wills, selling of assets, guardianships, and living wills—will allow your practice to grow. The growing number of elderly people suffering from senility or age-related dementia will create a growing need for anyone who is qualified—health professional to care giver—to provide dementia care.

If you live in an area where the number of elderly is growing much faster than the number of young families and small children, you may want to take your child care skills and transfer them to a day care center for the elderly. While the licensing of day care centers for seniors is more complicated than for family day care, the need is great.

Related Career

Daily Money Management. Although older adults are able to live independently longer, many need assistance with financial tasks, such as making bank deposits, paying bills, balancing checkbooks, reconciling account statements, organizing taxes and other paperwork, and filing medical claims. This business has grown from the fact that adult children often no longer live in the same community as their parents, and even when some do, they're too busy to help manage their parents' day-to-day financial affairs. Daily money managers also work with working adults whose career demands are such that they don't have time to tend to all of life's financial details. For more information, contact the American Association of Daily Money Managers Inc. at (301) 593-5462 or www.aadmm.com.

ELDER SERVICES AT A GLANCE

ECONOMIC REALITY FIT

▶ Necessary vs. Discretionary	Necessary
▶ Replaceable with technology	No
▶ Offshorable	No
▶ Industry Status	Established and Expanding

PERSONAL REALITY FIT

▶ Start-up costs	Minimal
▶ Overhead	Minimal
▶ Potential earnings	Moderate
▶ Flexible hours	More Than Most
▶ Overall stress	More Than Most
▶ Ease of bartering	More Than Most

Durability Rating

Likely Transferable Skills, Background, Careers

With enough training almost any background skill is transferable to the special needs of the elderly. You must be able to communicate clearly. You must have patience. You must be organized, as you will be assisting others with organizing *their* lives.

Older people are a perfect demographic for many of the other services we outline in this book. In a service economy, they represent a defined group that benefits from caring, considerate, and professional service providers.

What to Charge

Charging for elder services is highly variable, depending on your skill set and background. If you are providing in-home companionship without specialized care, you can charge by the hour ($15 to $25 per hour) or by the day. Driving and errand services are billed by the trip ($7 to $25 per trip) or by the hour. Day care services might function with a basic "membership" fee and then additonal fees depending on what services you provide (Medicare, Medicaid, and other grant and government monies might be available to help supplement your clients' fees). Professional, medical, financial, or legal services are lower than the prevailing rates for such services and often paid by various government agencies or insurance providers.

Best Ways to Market Elder Services

- ▶ Establish relationships with professionals and agencies that work with the elderly.
- ▶ Contact corporations in your area that are or might be providing eldercare benefits to employees caring for elders.

Tips for Getting Started

- ▶ If you are providing simple companionship and assistance services, such as driving to errands, etc., the elderly client himself will most likely hire you. However, for many services, the children of your clients will often hire you. These children find themselves caught between their own demanding lives and the responsibility they feel toward their parents. They will often feel guilty about not being able to do "more" themselves. Your ability to provide these children with peace of mind will go a long way toward your success.
- ▶ Prepare two types of brochures—one for seniors so they can seek out your services directly; the other for adult children who will refer their parents and older relatives to you.

LEARN MORE

Associations

- ▶ National Alliance for Caregiving provides a resource connection to over one thousand books and video products organized by topic: www.caregiving.org
- ▶ National Association of Senior Move Managers. Their member directory suggests there are many states lacking this service: www.nasmm.com
- ▶ National Association of Professional Geriatric Care Managers operates a chapter organization, a Listserv, and a directory of members accessible from its site: (520) 881-8008, www.caremanager.org

Licensing and Certification

Social workers, nurses, psychologists, and other professionals can obtain licenses as geriatric care managers. To be eligible for reimbursement under Medicaid or Medicare requires either becoming a certified nurse's aide or taking a training program that qualifies under the eligibility requirements.

Publications

- ▶ *The Caregiver's Essential Handbook,* Sasha Carr, Sandra Choron, McGraw-Hill/Contemporary Books, 2003.
- ▶ *The Comfort of Home,* Maria M. Meyer, Paula Derr, Care Trust Publications, 2002.
- ▶ *Eldercare 911,* Susan Beerman, Judith Rappaport-Musson, Prometheus Books, 2002.
- ▶ *Eldercare for Dummies*, Rachelle Zukerman, For Dummies, 2003.
- ▶ *Handbook of Geriatric Care Management,* Cathy Cress, Aspen Publishers, 2007.

Web Sites

- ▶ www.aarp.org/cyber/guide1.htm – The AARP Guide to Internet Resources Related to Aging and lots of valuable links
- ▶ www.aoa.dhhs.gov – Information about the Administration on Aging and the many resources of the Department of Health and Human Services
- ▶ www.ec-online.net – Offers a community for those providing elder care
- ▶ www.elderlyreview.com – Offers reviews on elderly products, businesses, people, and care
- ▶ www.caregiver.com – A bimonthly e-magazine for caregivers
- ▶ www.asktransitions.com – This Minneapolis elder care consulting firm sells a Web site and business package for people starting an elder-care business: (612) 978-1176.

Environmental Remediation

Do you wonder if there is some way you can combine your career with making an impact on the environment? Do you enjoy working with your hands in environments that might be less than hospitable? If you're also a person who understands that there is a need for identifying real environmental hazards and repairing them, this could be the business or job for you.

Most if not all commercial real estate deals today include an environmental assessment. In these examinations of a property, a prospective owner hires a professional to determine the nature and extent of risks such as lead paint, asbestos, moisture, mold, radon, contaminated soil, buried hazardous waste, etc. After the assessment is complete the buyer and seller both estimate the cost to fix the identified problems.

The same process holds true in home sales, only on a smaller scale and presently less often. In the residential real estate business buyers hire home inspectors to check the structure and seek out the obvious problems or potential problems. These will require an adjustment to the purchase price for the deal to close.

Newer homes are also candidates for environmental remediation because of mold problems caused both by construction mistakes and sealing up homes to conserve energy. The newer home problems come about because of moisture leaks resulting from mistakes made between the architect and the mechanical engineer. For example, many times architects do not leave enough room for air-conditioning ducts, so the ones installed lack ventilation, which leads to moisture building up and leaking out to eventually create the conditions for molds to grow.

Up steps the specialist in environmental remediation. You are the solution to everyone's problems. Both buyer and seller, as well as real estate broker, if one is part of the deal, want to know what it will cost to remediate the identified environmental risk factor.

Many projects are too small for the "big guys" who take on Superfund-scale projects. This is where the small business comes in. In many residential settings the problems are located in one part of the house, for instance asbestos wrap on pipes in the furnace room or an improperly ventilated laundry room spreading dampness throughout the basement.

The complicated, expensive, and regulated asbestos abatement and lead abatement projects require training and in some jurisdictions, licensing. Often the size of a project determines the expertise and training level required by regulating agencies.

Bigger businesses will have significant start-up expenses with equipment to create negative pressure environments that protect the neighboring spaces from contamination. Contaminants other than asbestos are more easily removed, and many environmental challenges can be met by relatively simple changes in structural components, such as ventilators or windows.

Remediation of environmental hazards is inherently unsafe, and you must pay much attention to your own safety at all times. Removing lead, asbestos, mold, or other environmental pollutants from one property that is being sold by a real estate broker will provide many future referrals and help grow your business.

Training is available online and through state and local environmental protection departments. When you stick with small projects, your time is your own and fairly easy to manage. Income is based on fees charged. The substance being removed or condition being corrected determines the rate you charge. Asbestos and lead abatement projects can command more than one hundred dollars per hour; billing for containment setup is at this rate.

As land in or near cities that has been used in the past to dispose of industrial waste is redeveloped for schools, commercial developments, or homes, it's not uncommon to encounter contaminants. This is another ingredient in providing a growing amount of work for remediation firms who in the future may be able to employ new techniques using nanotechnology for neutralizing contaminants. All in all this can be a very lucrative business requiring thoughtful and hard work.

An expense in start-up will be insurance. You cannot disturb toxic materials without protecting your personal and business finances. If concerns about the cost of insurance and the risk involved in handling typical remediation problems trouble you, consider necessary but less risky services, such as consulting to businesses and consumers offering practical recommendations about how to lessen their environmental impact by cutting down their energy and water usage, air duct cleaning, or worm farming (vermiculture).

The air duct cleaning industry has a national association called the National Air Duct Cleaners Association (www.nadca.com), and the worm industry has at least two newsletters—the *Worm Digest* (www.wormdigest.org) and *Casting Call* (www.vermico.com).

ENVIRONMENTAL REMEDIATION AT A GLANCE

Economic Reality Fit

► Necessary vs. Discretionary	Necessary
► Replaceable with technology	No
► Offshorable	No
► Industry Status	Established and Expanding

PERSONAL REALITY FIT

- Start-up costs   More Than Most
- Overhead   More Than Most
- Potential earnings   More Than Most
- Flexible hours   Moderate
- Overall stress   Minimal
- Ease of bartering   Minimal

Durability Rating

Likely Transferable Skills, Background, Careers

The construction trades particularly lend themselves to environment repair work. In addition, hobbyists in gardening, chemistry, and home repair will find many of their skills transferable.

What to Charge

You can set your fees according to the substance you're addressing and the complexity of the removal process. Fees can exceed $100 per hour dependent upon the perceived danger of the substance and the abatement procedures.

Best Ways to Market Environmental Remediation

- Develop relationships with an environmental testing laboratory, licensed geologists, and others who are certified to do Phase II testing and analysis for referrals.
- Work with an environmental testing company or an engineering firm that inspects residential real estate for potential purchasers.

Tips for Getting Started

- Consult your state or local Department of Environmental Protection about regulations and available training.
- Qualify for and obtain the necessary license(s) to do the work.
- Make arrangements for proper disposal of substances you remove.
- Purchase necessary equipment.

Learn More

Associations

- ▸ The Environmental Information Association offers training and certification in mold and lead paint abatement: (301) 961-4999, www.eia-usa.org
- ▸ The Indoor Air Quality Association offers training in mold remediation: (301) 231-8321, www.iaqa.org
- ▸ The National Association of Mold Professionals offers training in mold inspection and removal: (248) 669-5673, www.moldpro.org
- ▸ National Ground Water Association. Its scope includes remediation: (800) 551-7379 or (614) 898-7791; www.ngwa.org

Books

- ▸ *Asbestos,* Kenneth F. Cherry, CRC, 1988.
- ▸ *Handbook of Complex Environmental Remediation Problems,* Jay H. Lehr, Marve Hyman, Tyler Gass, and William J. Seevers, McGraw-Hill Professional, 2001.
- ▸ *Natural Remediation of Environmental Contaminants,* Michael Swindoll, Ralph G. Stahl, Charles Michael Swindoll, Stephen J. Ells (eds.), Setac Press, 2000.
- ▸ *Residential Lead Abatement,* Laurence Tasaday, McGraw Hill, 1995.

Training

Training for most forms of remediation must be approved by the Environmental Protection Agency, or in states with their own programs, by the responsible state agency. So before enrolling in a training program, ascertain that it has been approved. Three of the associations listed offer approved training.

Financial Planning

People use financial planners and counselors in uncertain and even poor financial times, according to Steven S. Shagrin, a financial planner since the mid-1980s. Over his two decades in the field, financial planning has evolved from primarily working with clients with retirement objectives to middle-class concerns, such as managing debt, buying a home, planning for college costs, and whole life planning, which includes but is not limited to retirement.

Shagrin, the author of the *Managing My Money* workbook specially produced for financial planners, asserts that part of the financial planner's role is to help clients lower their expectations so they can engage in "realistic financial behaviors." By thinking realistically, people recognize their "capacity for making financial mistakes is reduced."

Financial planners can either be generalists, such as Shagrin, or specialize on a specific need, such as college, divorce, estate, premarital, or retirement planning; helping families with children with special needs; investing; managing risks; planning for women or minority groups; protecting assets; tax strategies; or working with people in the same profession as your former one. Generalist or specialist, financial planners who wish to be self-employed need to have:

- ▶ analytical ability to do problem solving, along with good measures of creativity and flexibility
- ▶ communication skills accompanied by compassion and caring, because many clients engage in destructive behavior around money issues
- ▶ technological skills
- ▶ a keen sense of responsibility and ethics because clients rely on them
- ▶ an appetite and commitment to lifelong learning in order to be able to provide up-to-date counsel

In financial planning firms with multiple planners, the work can be divided, allowing individuals to use their main strengths. David Strege, a partner in a firm in Des Moines, breaks down the three major roles as "finding, minding, and grinding." *Finders* get clients, *grinders* produce financial plans, and *minders* hand hold clients. Stege describes himself as a *grinder* because he uses his analytical savvy and computer skills to crank out Excel spreadsheets. Solo financial planners, of course, need to perform all three roles.

Financial planning has several strengths as a career. First, most people need it but have never had it done. A 2003 Gallup survey found only about one-third of Americans prepare a long-term financial plan or use an accountant or financial planner. Second, because of the face-to-face involvement with clients, financial planners have not lost out to people choosing software instead of a personal planner, and this is the kind of work that does not lend itself to being offshored. Third, the financial planning profession seems to have high morale—practitioners feel satisfaction in helping people solve problems, and financial planners state they experience a high level of collegiality with one another.

Certification, which involves passing an exam to be a registered or certified financial consultant or investment advisor, is required in some states. However, higher earnings and added credibility are strong inducements for getting certified. A 2006 survey by CFP® (Certified Financial Planner Board of Standards) found certified financial planners earn an average of seventy-five thousand dollars a year;

noncertified planners, fifty-five thousand. Of course, if you intend to help people implement what you recommend by selling insurance products or any type of investment product such as securities (stocks and bonds), almost all states require registration as a broker or investment advisor, and the federal government also requires registration with the Securities and Exchange Commission (SEC) for certain kinds of securities sales.

FINANCIAL PLANNING AT A GLANCE

ECONOMIC REALITY FIT

▶ Necessary vs. Discretionary	Discretionary
▶ Replaceable with technology	No
▶ Offshorable	No
▶ Industry Status	Established and Expanding

PERSONAL REALITY FIT

▶ Start-up costs	Moderate (Liability Insurance)
▶ Overhead	Moderate
▶ Potential earnings	More Than Most
▶ Flexible hours	Moderate
▶ Overall stress	Moderate
▶ Ease of bartering	Moderate

Durability Rating

Likely Transferable Skills, Background, Careers

Most financial planners come from backgrounds including banking, education, insurance, investments, and stock brokerages. Licensed accountants and attorneys can become certified based on their existing licenses, although they must also take the CFP® Certification Examination, and if they wish to engage in some specialties, they need additional training for certification.

What to Charge

How planners charge for their work varies. Some charge a flat fee, such as $1,000 to $2,000 for a comprehensive plan and less than $500 for a narrower plan, such as for retirement. Others charge by the hour, typically $100 to $200 an hour. More specialized areas of planning command fees of $300 and more.

Some planners base their charge on the value of the client's assets. The percentage ranges from less than one percent to more than two percent of the assets. Commission-only planners derive their income from commissions on the investment products they sell and do not charge a fee for the financial plan. This is in contrast to fee-only planners. But then there are planners who do both. They charge for an initial plan but also derive commissions from the financial products they recommend.

Best Ways to Market Financial Planning

- ▶ Initially, get referrals from your own family and friends to help you establish a base of clients. Satisfied clients are key, from which you can use further referrals to grow a practice.
- ▶ Help clients organize their finances as part of your services. You can open the doors to potential clients by helping them overcome the largest barrier to many people using financial planners: pulling together all their financial paperwork, whether it's literally on paper or electronic. By teaming up with a professional organizer or doing it yourself, you can offer something most financial planners don't provide.
- ▶ Use personal stories, metaphors, and analogies in one-to-one presentations to help people relate financial planning to their own lives.

Tips for Getting Started

While undergraduate degree programs and employment with a financial planning firm are routes into financial planning, most financial planners enter from another occupation or profession, obtaining training and becoming certified as a financial planner. The two most prevalent certifications, which cover all aspects of financial planning, are:

- ▶ Certified Financial Planner (CFP®). Granted by the Certified Financial Planner Board of Standards, it requires a bachelor's degree, passing an exam, and experience. The College for Financial Planning specifies educational requirements. This designation is basic for someone just starting out. However, individuals with an insurance background may choose the Chartered Financial Consultant designation.
- ▶ Chartered Financial Consultant (ChFC)—Requires eight courses from

the American College and passing an examination administered by the college. After getting one of these credentials, you can obtain certifications in various specializations, of which there are more than fifteen, including:

» Estate planning (accredited estate planner)
» Insurance analysis (chartered life underwriter)
» Investment analysis (chartered financial analyst, chartered investment counselor)
» Investment consulting (certified investment management consultant, certified investment management specialist)
» Investment management (accredited asset management specialist)
» Mutual funds (certified fund specialist, chartered mutual fund consultant)
» Registered investment advice (registered financial consultant, registered investment advisor, registered financial planner)
» Retirement planning (chartered retirement planning counselor, chartered retirement plans specialist)

Related Careers

Housing Counseling. Helping people obtain housing as a certified housing counselor has become a specialized career that is licensed in many states. Housing counselors assess a client's economic ability, problems, and needs and then provide options and recommendations to buyers of first homes, seniors considering reverse mortgages, and people experiencing economic difficulty with preventing foreclosure. Housing agencies, which assist low, moderate, and middle-income families, hire housing counselors in obtaining rentals as well as homeownership education. Training for private sector housing counseling is available from organizations like the Association for Financial Counseling and Planning Education, cited below. The Department of Housing and Urban Development (HUD) authorizes private and public organizations to provide the training that leads to certification, such as the Center for Housing Counseling Training [(703) 317-9086, www.housingtraining.org] and the National Consumer Law Center (www.consumerlaw.org).

Money Coaching. Money coaches come from many backgrounds—financial planning, psychotherapy, bookkeeping—to help clients overcome limiting financial beliefs and behaviors. Through a series of steps, they help clients deal with unconscious and false beliefs and the effects money problems are having on relationships. Training and certification are available from the Money Coaching Institute: (707) 782-9044, www.money-therapy.com. *Money Magic*, a book by the institute's founder, Deborah L. Price, describes Jungian-type archetypes based on money.

LEARN MORE

Associations

The financial planning field has dozens of associations, typically organized by specialty, such as the following:

- ► Financial Planning Association (FPATM) provides a directory of member planners: (800) 322-4237, www.fpanet.org
- ► National Association of Personal Financial Advisors (NAPFA), fee-only planners: (800) 366-2732, www.napfa.org
- ► The Nazrudin Community consists of financial planners concerned with whole life planning. They communicate via a message board at www.financial-planning.com/wwwboard5/messages/7421.html
- ► Society of Financial Service Professionals (SFSP): (610) 526-2500, www.financialpro.org

Books

- ► *Deena Katz's Tools and Templates for Your Practice,* Deena Katz, Bloomberg Press, book and CD, 2001.
- ► *Getting Started as a Financial Planner*, Jeffrey H. Rattiner, Bloomberg Press, 2005.
- ► *Practicing Financial Planning for Professionals*, Practitioners' Version, Tom Potts, Leon LaBrecque, and Sid Mittra, RH Publishing, 2006.
- ► *So You Want to Be a Financial Planner*, Nancy Langdon Jones, Advisorpress, 2005.
- ► *Storyselling for Financial Advisors*, Scott West, Kaplan Business, 2005.

Magazines

- ► Keeping up with this always-changing field means reading publications, such as the *Wall Street Journal, Barron's, Forbes, The Economist, Kiplinger's Personal Finance, Money, Smart Money,* and *Worth.*
- ►► *Financial Planning Interactive* Magazine: www.fponline.com

Training and Certification

- ► American College: (888) 263-7265, www.theamericancollege.edu
- ► Association for Financial Counseling and Planning Education: (614) 485-9650, www.afcpe.org
- ► Certified Financial Planner Board of Standards (CFP®) – Their site provides a directory of college training programs: (888) 237-6275 or (303) 830-7500, www.cfp.net.

Functional Artist

Where art and function meet is opportunity! You can create a beautiful item that also functions in daily life or recreate something once functional into something beautiful. There are markets for both.

Perhaps you have seen a plain glass wine carafe that has been painted with flowers to become a vase for sale in a specialty shop. Perhaps you've seen an old window that has been painted with a view and hung as art, or a Shaker-style chair that was crafted by a contemporary fine wood hobbyist.

Let's take a look at some more possibilities. An old sink can be brought back to life as a guest bathroom basin with the application of an artisan's touch. Everyday items, like cat litter boxes and file drawers, can be designed so they look like furniture or accessories. Fabric you design can be turned into vinyl-free wallpaper. You can invent as well as reinvent. What is the latest electronic gizmo, how is it carried, what can you make a case from, and how can you decorate it? Do teenagers need a way to transport game cartridges for trading or sharing, and can you make it better or more colorful or unique?

You might consider creating canes or walking sticks that double as art, whether through carving or painting. You can start with a store-bought cane or a natural wood find. The approaches and possibilities may well be endless. Or because of the rising cost of fossil fuels, pellet stove sales are on the rise, and since wood pellets need to be kept dry, there's a need for stylish containers with covers appropriate for displaying on living room or bedroom hearths.

Two big items in the world of functional art are seating and birdhouses. The latter come in various shapes and sizes determined by the bird expected to dine or take up residence. These can be quite humble or quite elaborate. At the Web site www.naturalhandyman.com you will find birdhouses built from scraps, every one unique, many beautiful, and all functional.

Chair making is an ancient craft, and while you won't get rich making Windsor, Shaker, or other classics, you can make a living. The development of the skills involved in building furniture will take some time. There are classes and many books available. More than anything it will take experience to create a piece that will last.

Chair making is a process that can be broken down into several parts. These parts can be divided among craftsmen or completed by you alone. Trees must be harvested, lumber must be prepared and cut, and some parts may be purchased preshaped. There is assembly and finishing work, which may be left to the purchaser. Each activity brings its own satisfaction as your chair takes form and you ready it for sale.

Nina Walz's approach to pursuing her love of art was to create something appealingly practical, yet strikingly out of the ordinary. She created a line of brightly colored, gourmet ceramic serving pieces shaped like the objects they're designed to serve. They may mimic ordinary items, but they look more like sculptured works of art! Nina offers fish platters named after the fish they represent, such as rainbow trout and sockeye salmon. In addition, she sells artichoke servers, asparagus platters, corn-on-the-cob holders, and olive boats—all viewable at her Web site, www.offthewalzstudio.com. She expanded from selling directly to buyers at art fairs to selling to wholesalers and retailers at gift shows.

Even the end of life provides an opportunity for art. With the rate of cremation increasing to one out of three, survivors are choosing individually made urns and other funeral vessels. From both a Web site (www.funeria.com) and a California gallery, you can purchase creations from many artists.

Anything perceived as art that is created by hand commands a higher price than the machine-tooled version. A set of Shaker chairs made by machine can be purchased for hundreds less than a grouping completed by a craftsman. A piece of glass adorned with hand-painted flowers or a window with a hand-painted scene are found in gift shops and at craft shows; their manufactured counterparts are sold by chains and, of course, they all look alike.

If you want to sell your creations, keep the following statistics in mind. When the National Endowment for the Arts last conducted a Survey of Public Participation in the Arts in 2002, it found:

- ▶ 33.4 percent of adults attend art/craft fairs
- ▶ 31.6 percent visit historic sites
- ▶ 26.5 percent take in an art museum

If what you produce proves marketable or catches the fancy of the right person at a show, a manufacturer may wish to license it, which is a reason to sell at shows. If you wish to keep control, you can either go to a tabletop manufacturer (see the Table top Manufacturing profile on page 281) or even have a tabletop manufacturing unit of your own.

Beyond having a Web site from which you can sell what you make, the Web can be a vital way for you to produce income. Offering your work on auction sites like eBay, which has a category for functional art, can lead to commissioned work. This has been the experience of the artist Peter Gullerud, who created the marketing icons for this book. Some Web sites, such as www.etsy.com and www.functionalartgallery.com and, function as art galleries, drawing buyers to your work.

Creating functional art requires skills that can be learned and an imagination. Your rewards will be both emotional and financial.

Related Career

Inventor. If you have the knack for inventing, there's never been a better time to turn your ideas into income. While marketing is the key to getting an invention from a patent into use, the opportunities to get media exposure are growing with television shows like *American Inventor* and *Modern Marvels,* home shopping networks like QVC, and the use of the Web, blogs, and podcasts provide inventors with direct access to global buyers. In addition, corporations are shedding the not-invented-here mentality and are increasingly open to buying inventions directly from inventors. That virtually happened on-screen on *American Inventor* during the first season. If your forte is marketing more than inventing, consider turning unused patents into products.

Mom Inventors (www.mominventors.com), in addition to developing, manufacturing, and selling Mom Invented™ products, helps mom inventors to connect with one another on its site and offers educational products. Be cautious, however, of invention promotion and marketing companies that require an up-front fee for their services. As a result of the American Inventors Protection Act of 1999, you can check out complaints filed against such companies with the U.S. Patent and Trademark Office; however, because of lag time and the fact that most people are too embarrassed to file a complaint, a lack of complaints on a list is not complete assurance. The Patent Office site is also a source of valuable information (www.uspto.gov), or you can write the Patent Office at Commissioner for Patents, P.O. Box 1450, Alexandria, VA 22313-1450, or phone at (800) 786-9199.

Resources for inventors include:

- Inventionconvention.com, the home to the National Congress of Inventor Organizations
- The Kaufmann Innovation Network sponsors www.ibridgenetwork .org, where entrepreneurs can find innovations that have been created but are untapped in university laboratories.
- Nolo Press publishes several books for inventors (www.nolo.com).

FUNCTIONAL ART AT A GLANCE

ECONOMIC REALITY FIT

Necessary vs. Discretionary	Discretionary
Replaceable with technology	No
Offshorable	No
Industry Status	Established and Enduring

PERSONAL REALITY FIT

► Start-up costs	Moderate
► Overhead	Minimal
► Potential earnings	Moderate
► Flexible hours	More Than Most
► Overall stress	Minimal
► Ease of bartering	More Than Most

Durability Rating

Likely Transferable Skills, Background, Careers

Skill as an artist in permanent media like paints can be developed, but starting out with talent will make the timeline to success much shorter. When it comes to chairs, experience with wood as a professional or a hobbyist will make you exceptionally well suited for this business.

What to Charge

Individual pieces of furniture exist in a competitive environment. The best way to set prices for your creations is to window-shop retail stores with a handmade line. A well-made chair of wood will range from $350 to $2,500 depending on the wood, the type of chair, and the region of the country.

Gift shop managers will be helpful in setting prices for items you want to sell in their shops. Online sites such as those appearing in the LEARN MORE section will show you what the competition's prices are for similar items.

Best Ways to Market Functional Art

- ► Produce a catalog to distribute at shows and fairs.
- ► Rent space at gift shows for smaller items and at higher-end furniture shows for furniture. Remember that transportation of either to shows may result in damage.
- ► Try some specialty advertising for your furniture.
- ► Promote yourself as a local story of interest to nearby newspapers.

Tips for Getting Started

- To see what others are selling, visit www.functionalartcatalog.com
- Functional Art has more than one market. Approach the sale of your pieces from both the artistic and functional aspects.
- Expensive creations should be presented among other expensive items.
- Look in local shops that sell things on consignment; talk with the owners to find out what's selling and what isn't.
- If you are taking orders for items, make it clear to the purchaser that creation does take time.

LEARN MORE

Associations

- American Craft Council publishes *American Craft Magazine:* (212) 274-0630, www.craftcouncil.org
- American Ceramic Society provides a wealth of links to ceramic-related Web sites: (866) 721-3322, www.acers.org
- The Furniture Society has an internship and apprenticeship program and provides information on educational grants: (828) 255-1849, www.furnituresociety.org
- International Guild of Candle Artisans provides training and has a gallery on its Web site: www.igca.net
- The National Basketry Organization Inc.: (770) 641-9208, www.nationalbasketry.org

Books

- *The Chairmaker's Workshop,* Drew Langsner, Lark Books, 2001.
- *Functional Pottery*, Robin Hopper, Krause Publications, 2000.
- *Making Classic Country Chairs*, David Bryant, Trafalgar Square, 2002.
- *Painted Windows* by E. W. Peattie is available for free as an e-book at www.gutenberg.org/etext/1875.

Training

- For chair building training try Kentucky Rustic Furniture [(606) 346-9375, www.kentuckyrustic.com/classes.htm] and the Windsor Institute [(603) 929-9801, www.thewindsorinstitute.com].
- For many arts, there are local community courses and workshops. At virtually every workshop, you can expect to learn different approaches to your art and ways to promote it.

Web Sites

- ▸ www.potters.org – Clay art discussions provides links to dozens of topics
- ▸ www.hgtv.com – Home and Garden Television, a great source for keeping track of popular taste

Green Burial Services

Over the millennia cultures and communities have buried their dead in many ways. In ancient times, the Egyptians embalmed their dead kings, placed them in elaborate sarcophagi, and buried them in massive vaults. Less affluent families wrapped their loved ones in a skin or a cloth and laid them in the ground.

In more recent times, a funeral director is the person in charge of embalming a dead body and placing it in a coffin, which is later laid to rest by family and friends in a marked grave with a concrete lining. In the mid-twentieth century in the United States, revelations about funeral home practices and prices opened the industry to criticism and then to regulation.

Green burials encompass not embalming so bodies can naturally recycle, plain caskets, and burial in a cemetery without tombstones or alternatively using the services of a crematorium. Burials are regulated in most jurisdictions, and the services of a licensed funeral director are often required. The green burial movement has already given rise to large operations that offer fairly traditional services of a coffin, a memorial, an actual burial, or cremation. There is, however, room for people interested in providing a necessary service to people at their most vulnerable.

Among the many drawbacks to modern burial practices (and many ancient ones as well) is the rate of decomposition. Buried in a relatively simple wooden coffin, a body may take decades to return to the earth. Green burials provide a solution to this by using pressboard or cardboard coffins and having interment in open fields that reduce the decomposition time to fewer than eighteen months.

The services you provide directly, and the ones you refer mourners to, determine some of the skills required for this field. As a funeral director, usually licensed but always trained, you will be called upon to transport the deceased, prepare the body for burial, secure the selected burial container, oversee the process from beginning to end, and address the needs of the mourners. As a spiritual advisor to those who have lost a loved one, you will need to guide mourners through the process, perhaps lead the memorial service, and provide links to other service providers. A landowner willing to provide space for green burials will learn the state regulations and maintain an environment setting the tone and meeting the needs.

The direction you take will determine the investment required. If you already own usable land, the licenses and equipment will be the most significant costs. Becoming a spiritual advisor may require little or no investment. A funeral director is a licensed, trained individual with a place to conduct his or her business, including taking care of the deceased.

Green burial service providers need to be able to feel empathy, express sympathy, and simultaneously transact business. The complex feelings of survivors will give you much to respond to and much to manage. The potential rewards are not only financial but emotional as well.

GREEN BURIAL SERVICES AT A GLANCE
ECONOMIC REALITY FIT

► Necessary vs. Discretionary	Both
► Replaceable with technology	No
► Offshorable	No
► Industry Status	Established and Expanding

PERSONAL REALITY FIT

► Start-up costs	Moderate
► Overhead	More Than Most (as a funeral director)
► Potential earnings	Moderate
► Flexible hours	Moderate
► Overall stress	Moderate
► Ease of bartering	Minimal

Durability Rating

Likely Transferable Skills, Background, Careers

Social workers and those with similar skills will find themselves comfortable providing the emotional support needed for this career. Physician's assistants, registered nurses, physical therapists, and massage therapists will all bring skills to this field that make them comfortable and confident around the human body.

What to Charge

Fees for the services of funeral directors are regulated in many jurisdictions. The services of the staff alone will bring fees of $1,000, while fees for additional services can amount to thousands more when packaged. Burial plots command fees of several hundred dollars plus the services of those who do the actual interment. Spiritual support, depending on the nature and extent provided, can be priced from $100 to $1,000.

Best Ways to Market Green Burial Services

- ▶ Contact local hospitals, physicians, and clergy as sources of referrals.
- ▶ Participate in organizations dedicated to green causes, conservation, and sustainable living.

Tips for Getting Started

- ▶ State laws and local regulations need to be reviewed before making an investment in land or equipment for green burials. Also research the requirements for licenses and permits.
- ▶ Carefully examine the current providers of services postmortem. Is there a niche for green burials? Is the community large enough to support another provider?

LEARN MORE

Associations

- ▶ Association of Natural Burial Grounds offers information for many nations: www.naturaldeath.org.uk
- ▶ Funeral Consumers Alliance is a federation of Nonprofit Consumer Information Societies. The site provides a great deal of information: (800) 765-0107, www.funerals.org
- ▶ The Green Burial Council has a certification program for cemeteries and funeral providers and has a directory of providers: www.green burialcouncil.org

Books

- ▶ *Time to Go: Alternative Funerals,* Jean Francis, iUniverse, 2004.
- ▶ *Caring for the Dead*, Lisa Carlson, Upper Access, 1998.

Web Sites

- ▶ www.greenburials.org – A noncommercial site with general information about green burial

▶ www.forestofmemories.org – Provides information to support green burials in North America

Microfarming

Do you like digging in the dirt? Do you get a spiritual as well as physical feeling of well-being from gardening? Have you ever dreamed of living on a farm, raising your own food, somewhat disconnected from many of the world's troubles?

Microfarming or niche farming can provide some of those feelings along with income. A microfarm can be started in a basement, a backyard, or on a few acres. An urban microfarm, as described in Chapter 11, cannot only provide food for the family table but also bring in a full- or part-time income for the family.

The "natural" or "organic" food industry is growing at a very rapid pace. But even more notable is locally grown food. In a ten-state study in 2003, the Leopold Foundation for Sustainable Agriculture found 75 percent of consumers and 55 percent of food business proprietors say they want food "grown locally by family farmers."[2] This ranked higher than "organic" or "grown-locally organic." Major industry names have entered the organic field, too; but many shoppers shy away from these names and look for local brands or those that have already established themselves in this thriving industry segment.

Selling locally grown food has become easier with the increasing number of farmers' markets. Urban and suburban farmers' markets are attracting growing numbers of buyers who are eager for what you can grow. Some of the shoppers will be gourmet chefs, professional and not. They can offer you insights into items not currently available that you might grow. Technologies are becoming available to make growing things in a city easier, too. For example, by fulfilling its name, the Topsy Turvy Upside Down Tomato Planter (http://topsyturvys.com) eliminates the problem of weeding and ground insects.

Flowers, vegetables, livestock, herbs, and even fish can be the staple of your business. Urban aquaculture requires big tanks and a big space. Raising farm animals requires space too, but how much varies with the type of animal and the approach to raising them.

Mushrooms are perfect for a basement, urban or otherwise. Requiring darkness and moisture, the varieties possible may be endless. Like any other crop, mushroom farming will require gathering and understanding copious amounts

---

[2]http://www.leopold.iastate.edu/pubs/staff/ecolabels/ecolabels.pdf>:

of information. This phase will be followed by preparation of beds with proper soil mixtures and purchasing the spores to get your farm started. Once underway though, it should keep itself going.

If you have the space for a greenhouse attached to your own house or free-standing in the backyard, you are on your way to an income of sizable proportion. With a greenhouse you can grow herbs, hydroponically grown vegetables, and tropical plants. A twelve-hundred-square-foot greenhouse filled with six-inch pots can provide $2.50 per pot in profit. A greenhouse of this size can hold three to five thousand pots, and you can turn over what you produce every three months. So if you have four thousand pots, that's ten thousand dollars.

Growing flowers in salable quantities usually means having two to ten acres. Vegetables can be grown in backyard plots, but your climate will determine how many crops and what kind of vegetables you can grow and sell. How much you expect to earn will also figure into the acreage you will need. A full-time income will also require having adequate real estate and an investment in needed supplies and equipment.

To farm on a small or big scale, you will have to love the earth. It's ideal for anyone who wants to earn a living providing a daily necessity. You will also need a lot of energy during growing seasons to tend your crops, get them to market, and properly store them for your own future use. If you already own land and have a small plot growing, you are well on your way to bigger harvests and more income.

MICROFARMING AT A GLANCE

ECONOMIC REALITY FIT

► Necessary vs. Discretionary	Both
► Replaceable with technology	No
► Offshorable	No
► Industry Status	Established and Expanding

PERSONAL REALITY FIT

► Start-up costs	Minimal (if you own land or plan small) to Moderate (if you are purchasing land and equipment)
► Overhead	Moderate (unless you are growing small)
► Potential earnings	Moderate
► Flexible hours	Minimal
► Overall stress	Moderate
► Ease of bartering	More Than Most

Durability Rating

Likely Transferable Skills, Background, Careers

If you have worked with plants or on a farm, most if not all of your skills will be transferable. If you intend to raise animals, any work around veterinarians or livestock will be helpful, but we have met people who went from desk jobs to growing things for a living.

What to Charge

Set your retail price at four times what it costs you to grow a crop. Flowers are highly competitive, and you can learn from what others are charging. Livestock you want to sell is highly regulated at the local and federal levels. You will be a supplier in an industry where supply drives price, so it pays to track trends in consumer taste, such as for a particular herb or ethnic cuisine, but be ready to move on to the next trend when big producers move into a niche you may be doing well with. Also look for ways to add value to what you grow with packaging, processing, bottling, pickling, or drying your products.

Best Ways to Market Microfarmed Products

- ▶ Advertise "pick your own" in local papers to attract regular and new customers.
- ▶ Join together with other microfarmers to form a Community Supported Agriculture business serving member households.
- ▶ Sell directly to the public from booths at farmers' markets, swap meets, and farm stands.
- ▶ Sell wholesale to local restaurants, food cooperatives, schools, colleges and universities, supermarkets, gift basket makers, and herbalists.

Tips for Getting Started

- ▶ Check out local zoning rules to determine if you can use your land to grow things commercially as well as state regulations for any permits you may need or taxes you may need to collect (flowers, for example, are often taxable).
- ▶ Talk with the managers of farmers' markets, local restaurant owners and chefs, and natural food stores to find out what sells and what they need.

- ▶ Focus on one crop or related items for the first year or two.
- ▶ Shop around for supplies, like fertilizer, and the tools of your new trade.
- ▶ There's much to learn. In addition to the resources below, consult with your state extension service and take courses from local agricultural colleges.

LEARN MORE*

Associations

- ▶ American Community Gardening Association: (877) 275-2242, www.communitygarden.org
- ▶ International Herb Association: (717) 697-1500, www.iherb.org
- ▶ North American Farmers' Direct Marketing Association: (888) 884-9270, www.nafdma.com
- ▶ Organic Trade Association: (413) 774-7511, www.ota.com
- ▶ United Flower Growers Co-operative Association: (604) 430-2211, www.ufgca.com

Books

- ▶ *Dynamic Farmers' Marketing*, Jeff W. Ishee, Bittersweet Farmstead, 1997.
- ▶ *Four-Season Harvest*, Eliot Coleman, Chelsea Green Publishing Company, 1999.
- ▶ *Growing and Selling Fresh-Cut Herbs*, Sandie Shores, Ball Publishing, 2003.
- ▶ *Growing Gourmet and Medicinal Mushrooms*, Paul Stamets, Ten Speed Press, 2000.
- ▶ *Making Your Small Farm Profitable*, Ron Macher, Storey Publishing, LLC, 1999.
- ▶ *Micro Eco-Farming*, Barbara Berst Adams, New World Publishing, 2005.
- ▶ *Sell What You Sow*, Eric Gibson, Howard "Bud" Kerr, New World Publishing, 1994.
- ▶ *The Flower Farmer*, Lynn Byczynski, Chelsea Green Publishing, 1997.
- ▶ *The New Organic Grower*, Eliot Coleman, Chelsea Green Publishing, 1995.

Newsletters and Magazines

- ▶ Acres USA – (800) 355-5313 or (512) 892-4400; www.acresusa.com
- ▶ *Gathering Together Forum*, a newsletter for Community Supported Agriculture: (541) 929-4270, www.gatheringtogetherfarm.com

---

*Also see the resources at the end of Chapter 11

- *Growing for Market* – (800) 307-8949 or (785) 748-0605, www
  .growingformarket.com
- *The New Farm* – A newsletter from Rodale Institute, www.newfarm.org
- *Progressive Farmer* – The magazine's Web site has articles with farming
  tips, links to farm animal information and the business of farming,
  and directs visitors to U.S. rural locations, www.progressivefarmer.com
- *Vegetable Growers News* – (616) 887-9008, www.vegetablegrowersnews
  .com

Training
- Farm School Programs: www.farmschool.org

Web Sites
- www.csacenter.org – Community Supported Agriculture Center
- www.gardenguides.com – Gateway to garden guides on a variety of
  subjects
- www.herbworld.com – Herbal business tools
- www.leopold.iastate.edu – Leopold Center for Sustainable Agriculture,
  (515) 294-3711
- www.localharvest.org – An organization of farmers engaged in
  community-supported agriculture
- www.usda.gov – The U.S. Department of Agriculture supplies an endless supply of information.

Patient Champion

Have you heard or read of people getting victimized in the health care system? Maybe they were overwhelmed by a hospitalization, feeling that there is too much information to process and too many very important decisions to be made—they suffered or perhaps even died. Maybe this has happened to a member of your family, a friend, or even a coworker.

Patients of all ages and circumstances might need a patient champion. For example, Joshua Lillenstein, a twenty-six-year old University of Southern California medical student underwent extensive chemotherapy for testicular cancer. He told the *Los Angeles Times* that his experience made him realize that he needed someone with him twenty-four-hours a day to keep track of records and spot problems in care (June 28, 2007). It's not surprising that *USA Today* recommends that when speaking with a doctor when weak or ill, a patient "bring an advocate" (February 5, 2007). Particularly in need of patient champion services are aging Boomers, one out of five of whom are single with no children, and children.

So if you are comfortable in hospitals and around sick people; have an understanding of the needs of hospital patients and their families; and are tenacious, sympathetic, good on the phone, and capable of respectful firmness, consider a career as a patient champion.

Being a patient champion, patient advocate, or patient representative may be a job, a volunteer gig, or a business opportunity for you in a role becoming regarded as indispensable.

Many large medical centers have patient advocates on staff to help resolve communication difficulties between doctors and patients/family members as well as to address issues about food, environmental conditions, staff, etc. These personnel may be nurses or social workers. Hospital chaplains also serve as patient advocates. Staff positions for patient advocates are extremely rare in community hospitals and rural institutions. In these smaller health facilities volunteer patient advocates may be in use.

Patients and their families appreciate patient champion services if they are provided by someone they trust like a family member, close friend, or someone they hire for this purpose. The same extension of trust does not necessarily extend to a patient advocate who is an employee of the institution providing the health care. This is one place where the paid advocate makes an entrance. In very large urban centers, the number of advocates cannot match the need, so here, too, the paid advocate has opportunities.

A niche within this small sector is advocating for children who are ill. Advocating for them requires special knowledge about guardianship rules and child rights. Parents of these patients are often much more emotional than relatives of other patients, and dealing with them requires extra skill.

The health care industry is fraught with rules that patient champions must learn and understand. The most complex of these are the rules regarding confidentiality of information. Every hospital and every doctor follows the Health Insurance Portability and Accountability Act of 1996 (HIPAA). For anyone to discuss the health or treatment of a patient, he or she will need to be assured that you have permission from the patient or his legal representative.

When you have jumped this hurdle, you will find practitioners who don't understand your role or see you as interference or perhaps as a challenge to their authority. This is where respectful firmness and tenacity will pay off. You can be perceived as a partner, asset, and time saver, or you can be seen as a nuisance. It is not always up to you which it is, but every energy directed on behalf of your patient will move professionals in this direction.

Being a patient champion or advocate is not for the faint of heart. If you are willing to be awakened on occasion in the middle of the night and capable of dropping everything to address a crisis, this may be for you. You will feel good when a patient gets the services he or she needs and starts improving, and you may well suffer along with the patient and family as conditions cause a decline in health status. But the positives far outweigh the negatives.

PATIENT CHAMPION AT A GLANCE

ECONOMIC REALITY FIT

► Necessary vs. Discretionary	Discretionary
► Replaceable with technology	No
► Offshorable	No
► Industry Status	Emerging

PERSONAL REALITY FIT

► Start-up costs	Minimal
► Overhead	Minimal
► Potential earnings	Moderate
► Flexible hours	More Than Most
► Overall stress	Moderate
► Ease of bartering	Minimal

Durability Rating

Likely Transferable Skills, Background, Careers

Nurses and doctors have the knowledge to interpret medical information and know their way around. Others with hospital experience, such as social workers, physical therapists, occupational therapists, and others will bring their experiences dealing with other hospital personnel to the job. EMTs and other medical first responders will also transfer to the hospital setting with ease. Suzanne Steidl, founder of Your Daughter's in Town in Pittsburgh, Pennsylvania, (www.yourdaughtersintown.com) says that "while it's not necessary to have a medical background, some background in advocacy is absolutely essential. The most effective advocates have the capacity to gather and organize information and coordinate care. They are vigilant overseers and skillful, fearless negotiators."

What to Charge

Patient champions/advocates can bill for their services on an hourly basis (up to as much as $100 an hour) or on a retainer basis where you bill for as much as five or ten thousand dollars up front and take care of everything without further billing.

Best Ways to Market Patient Champion Services

- ▶ Develop relationships with emergency room personnel and the staff of critical care units to bring referrals.
- ▶ Join or even start a local association of patient champions/advocates.

Tips for Getting Started
- ▶ If you're not a skilled negotiator, take one or more courses.
- ▶ Volunteer to assist a friend, acquaintance, or relative. This can provide your first testimonials.
- ▶ Since this is a new field, you'll be a pioneer in making people aware of what you can do and when they need you. Promotion is a large part of your marketing plan.

LEARN MORE

Books
- ▶ *Advocacy Skills for Health and Social Care Professionals*, Neil Bateman, Jessica Kingsley Publishers, 2000.
- ▶ *Community Health Advocacy*, Sana Loue, et al., Kluwer Academic Publishers, 2003. This title relates to community, not individual advocacy.

Web Sites
- ▶ www.cthealthpolicy.org/toolbox – Health Advocacy Toolbox
- ▶ www.cms.hhs.gov/HIPAAgeninfo – Information from the U.S. Department of Health and Human Services about HIPAA, Title II, which sets standards for electronic health care transactions and the security and privacy of health data.
- ▶ www.info.med.yale.edu/caim/risk/patient_rights/patient_rights_2 .html – Informed Consent is an important topic when it comes to experimental treatments.
- ▶ www.patientadvocate.org – Offers extensive information on advocacy
- ▶ www.patientcenters.com – Offers copious amounts of healthcare information

- www.medicalconsumers.org – The Center for Medical Consumers
- www.childadvocate.net/index.html – Provides information on advocacy for children and their parents

Remodeling for Seniors

Most homes are ripe for remodeling around fifteen years of age according to popular wisdom. They also become good candidates for remodeling when homeowners recognize that their homes have begun to age and are becoming less and less comfortable.

You can enter this field as a contractor who does the work or as a project manager who runs the job or as a consultant/designer who helps people understand what's available to increase their comfort. You can work on many small projects through the year, or you can work on only a few major projects. If you do this right, your income potential enters the realm of six figures.

If you're looking for some larger projects that increase the comfort of a senior's home, consider jobs such as moving the master bedroom suite to the first floor and remodeling kitchens to include senior-friendly appliances and cabinetry. Another type of major project is adapting a home to multigenerational use, such as by converting several smaller bedrooms into a second master bedroom or creating a second kitchen. Smaller projects are doing such things as changing doorknobs to lever handles. Building an exterior ramp can be a big or small project depending upon the height of the entrance and the lay of the land.

Getting around inside the house is a major hurdle that many seniors must overcome. Often doorways are too narrow, bathrooms poorly equipped or laid out for a wheelchair user, and kitchen counters too high. These make for a large project you can design, manage, or build. Which approach you take will determine your start-up costs; a designer's costs are the lowest, and a builder's are the highest.

A bathroom lends itself to many small changes: a raised toilet seat, handheld showerhead, bath stool or chair, grab bars, and more. Any of these can be a major project for a senior but a reasonably simple one for you. There are similarly-sized kitchen projects: moving the microwave to the countertop, under-cabinet lighting, and friendlier cabinet hardware, to name a few.

Here are some things to keep in mind in deciding to become a designer/consultant, project manager, or contractor:

- Designing/consulting will allow you to make your own hours.
- Contracting and project management require a full-time commitment.

A contractor is on-site every day and aware of every detail as well as what comes next. If you want to take on big projects, you have to employ licensed tradespeople and have good planning skills, broad project knowledge, construction skills of your own, and people skills.

▶ To be a good project manager, you'll need to know numerous contractors with useful specialties, have an excellent planning sense, an understanding of the workflow of each job, and solid people skills for managing clients and contractors.

Whichever approach you choose, remodeling for seniors can be quite rewarding both financially and emotionally, knowing you've made someone's life more comfortable. Helping seniors stay in their own home longer is a feel-good part of any of these remodeling careers.

Related Careers

Other Remodeling Specialties. Remodeling accounts for two dollars out of five in all residential construction, according to Harvard's Joint Center for Housing Studies (www.jchs.harvard.edu/publications/remodeling). So if you do not wish to specialize in remodeling for seniors, remodeling extends to restoring homes damaged by fire and other insurable losses, condo/apartment remodeling, renovating historic residences, or specializing by architectural style or portion of a residence, such as kitchens, baths, windows, room additions, and sunrooms.

Green Construction. Green or environmentally friendly construction may soon be the type of construction most in demand. While environmental consciousness and governmental incentives provided impetus to establish green construction, its benefits, which include lower energy costs, higher productivity, and reduced absenteeism, have proven its value in offices and businesses of all kinds. This is brought about by reduced physical stress and improved employee morale as natural light and fresher air help people feel better and be more productive.

In addition to new construction, existing buildings need retrofitting and remodeling, such as replacing walks and driveways using porous pavement, and thickening walls. By planting "green roofs"—rooftops covered with vegetation that can just about halve the temperatures of rooftops—a home or business owner can reduce the building's need for air conditioning. Also emerging is installing dirt floors—yes, dirt—mixed with lime and sand, then sealed with linseed oil and beeswax. A source of information, training, and accreditation is the U.S. Green Building Council [(202) 828-7422, www.usgbc.org]. Relevant publications include *Green@work Magazine* (www.greenatworkmag.com) and *Environmental Building News* [(800) 861-0954, www.buildinggreen.com].

REMODELING FOR SENIORS AT A GLANCE

ECONOMIC REALITY FIT

- ▸ Necessary vs. Discretionary   Both
- ▸ Replaceable with technology   No
- ▸ Offshorable   No
- ▸ Industry Status   Established and Expanding

PERSONAL REALITY FIT

- ▸ Start-up costs   Moderate, More Than Most (if you're taking on larger projects)
- ▸ Overhead   Moderate
- ▸ Potential earnings   More Than Most
- ▸ Flexible hours   Minimal
- ▸ Overall stress   Moderate
- ▸ Computer skills   More Than Most (if you're designing)
- ▸ Ease of bartering   Minimal

Durability Rating

Likely Transferable Skills, Background, Careers

If you've worked in a construction trade, you have easily transferable experience.

What to Charge

Estimating is itself a specialty and, while software and books can help you do this, there's no substitute for hands-on experience. If you are managing a project or are the contractor, you have to know what you're doing. A designer/consultant can charge by the hour or the project. Fifty dollars an hour or its equivalent in project pricing is okay.

Best Ways to Market Remodeling for Seniors

- ▸ Reach out to clubs for seniors and make presentations. Seniors congregate in a number of places to which you can have access. The best of these for your purpose will be senior centers. These seniors are mostly mobile but are taking care of themselves by participating in organized programming. That's where you fit in with your presentation on home comfort and safety.

▶ Offer free consultations if you're functioning as a project manager or contractor.

▶ Hang "Pardon Our Dust" door hangers while you're working on a job and send letters to neighbors to the same effect. If your customer consents, have a "Dumpster Day" at which neighbors can retrieve items from the remodel that would otherwise be hauled away.

Tips for Getting Started

▶ Figure you'll need to cover your living costs for a year until your business is able to support you.

▶ If you're going to do the work, check state laws and local regulations to determine the kind of license and insurance you'll need.

▶ Locate outlets for the items you will recommend or need and discuss wholesale prices or discounts for multiple purchases.

▶ Contact local jurisdictions to learn about zoning requirements and local permit requirements.

Learn More

Associations

▶ American Subcontractors Association: (703) 684-3450, www .asaonline.com

▶ National Association of the Remodeling Industry (NARI) is dedicated to remodeling, and members include full-service remodeling contractors, specialty contractors, manufacturers, designers, and suppliers: (847) 298-9200 or (800) 611-6274, www.nari.org

▶ National Association of Home Builders (NAHB) offers a Certified Aging-in-Place Specialist (CAPS) designation: (800) 368-5242, www.nahb.com

Books

▶ *Best Business Practices for Builders & Remodelors,* Thomas Frisby, R. S. Means Company, 2001.

▶ *Builder's Essentials Estimating Building Costs,* Wayne J. Delpico, Reed Construction Data, 2004.

▶ *Renovating Old Houses,* George Nash, Taunton, 2003.

▶ *Renovation,* Michael Litchfield, Taunton, 2005.

Magazines

- ► *Remodeling News:* (201) 327-1600, www.remodelingnews.com
- ► Free construction magazine subscriptions are available at http://freeconstructionmagazines.com/9/categories.aspx

Training

Courses for the specialty trades can be taken at trade schools; community colleges offer suitable business courses. Certification can be obtained from trade associations.

Web Sites

- ► www.adaptiveaccess.com – Adaptive Access Company
- ► www.homeremodelingnews.net – Home Remodeling News

Repair Services

Do you like to fix things? Are you handy or a quick learner when it comes to working with your hands? Are you creative enough to mend a broken heart? A yes to these questions makes you an ideal candidate for going into the repair-service business.

That third question probably took you by surprise, but sometimes there are children with broken toys who need your services to fix their broken hearts. Toy repair might succeed in a city as a stand-alone business, but there are probably not enough children in rural areas and small towns to support such an endeavor.

However, if you live in a remote location or simply can't or don't wish to leave home, you might take a completely different approach and develop a virtual repair company. No, you are not going to repair the ether; you are going to help folks fix their bikes or lawn-mowers or lamps, using the Internet. You may have experienced remote help with your computer when the technician takes control of your computer to fix its problem. For other kinds of repair problems, there are two easily available approaches. First, you can offer repair videos, which you charge to connect to for a fixed number of hours. Second, with an inexpensive camera at both ends of the connection, there is the guided repair, your knowledge, the client's hands.

A more classic approach to fixing things is jewelry or watch and clock repair. This can be accomplished in a storefront, in a garage, or out of a truck or van. Then there is vinyl repair. Hospitals, theaters, luncheonettes, among other businesses, always need rips and tears repaired. Or how about rebuilding batteries for devices such as the Segway electric scooter, that use batteries that are no longer readily available once the device models are discontinued?

Are you old enough to remember the grinder coming through your neighborhood or down your road? Knife and scissor sharpening may be a little more high-tech today, but salons and barbershops need this service. Professional hair scissors or shears are anything but throwaway items; even ones costing $500 will get nicked when dropped on the floor. Carpenters, farmers, and lumberyard operators need their tools sharpened. Tool sharpening, particularly done from a truck at job sites, will always be in high demand; a properly sharpened tool makes the work much easier.

Repair personnel are required in many businesses if you don't want to go out on your own. Bicycle shops are the best example: they all have repair-people and assemblers. Hardware stores that sell high end tools need a reliable repair service to be available for customers in order to keep them coming back.

A man who called in to a radio show on which we were appearing in Chicago told us he was making $60,000 a year gluing things that had been broken. He'd begun his business in his garage ten years earlier charging only $3 an item. At the time we talked, he was charging $75 an hour and was specializing in serving antique dealers and collectors. Antique repair is a well-paying repair specialty requiring the development of top-notch skills and a reputation.

Another approach is the generalist or handyperson (See the separate Handyman/Handywoman profile). A retirement community will be filled with residents who need small repair jobs of all kinds. Not wanting to throw away and replace basic items is common in this sector. You can offer to spend a specific amount of time to do any fix-it work at a price per hour ($15–$25), or you can price by the project.

Fixing something is often more cost-efficient than tossing out the old and buying something new, particularly if what's new is not affordable; then comes the call for a repair service. If you choose to go down this road, you will find many smiles along the way as you redeem "treasured" appliances or heirlooms from the brink of disposal.

REPAIR SERVICES AT A GLANCE

Economic Reality Fit

- ► Necessary vs. Discretionary — Both
- ► Replaceable with technology — No
- ► Offshorable — No
- ► Industry Status — Established and Enduring

PERSONAL REALITY FIT

► Start-up costs	Minimal (if you work out of your house) to More Than Most (if you are going to hit the road in a truck)
► Overhead	Minimal, Moderate
► Potential earnings	Minimal, Moderate
► Flexible hours	More Than Most
► Overall stress	Minimal
► Ease of bartering	More Than Most

Durability Rating

Likely Transferable Skills, Background, Careers

If you have worked in a mechanical field with your hands, you are most suited to this work. A person who has repaired major appliances will slip easily into small-appliance repair. Having pursued a sport or hobby sufficiently to grasp fixing its equipment is a path in.

What to Charge :

The range is large. Repair shops price to return $15–$25 per hour of labor. Experts in antiques can charge more than $100 an hour. If you are mobile, you will most likely charge by the piece. Sharpening a tool will bring you $3–$10 each; however, one knife-sharpening service told us, as a rule of thumb, they "go by the sale price of the shear."

Best Ways to Market Repair

- ► List your services under Tool Repair, Watch Repair, Bike Repair, etc., on local search engines such as Yahoo! Local, Google Local, and Amazon's A9.com; in Internet yellow page directories, such as InfoSpace, Smartpages, Switchboard, SuperPages, and Yellowpages; and in print yellow page directories.
- ► Place flyers with telephone number tear-offs advertising your service in supermarkets and other community gathering places.
- ► Go door-to-door to stores and shops, such as salons and barbershops. Even stores with their own repair shops are apt to be short an employee and will outsource their work to you.
- ► Putting a sign on your vehicle will result in people walking up.

Tips for Getting Started

▶ Check local zoning rules if you plan to work out of your home. Noisy machinery, signage, and lots of traffic from customers frequently coming to you can trigger neighbor complaints.

▶ Search the Internet for similar repair businesses, and learn from what they offer.

▶ If you lack a skill at something that might be useful, look for and secure the necessary training.

LEARN MORE

Books

▶ *Big Blue Book of Bicycle Repair,* C. Calvin Jones, Park Tool Co., 2005.

▶ *Clock Making and Repairing,* W. J. Gazeley, Robert Hale Limited, 1997.

▶ *Complete Guide to Sharpening,* Leonard Lee, Taunton Press, 1995.

▶ *Dare to Repair,* Julie Sussman, Collins, 2002.

▶ *How To Fix Damn Near Anything,* Franklynn Petersen, Gramercy, 1996.

Business Opportunity

Thorvie International makes sharpening equipment; it offers a business opportunity in knife sharpening: (866) 497-0572 http://thorvie.com. A business opportunity offers many of the resources of franchises but without the continuing financial obligation; business opportunities, however, do not have to meet the legal requirements franchises do.

Restoration Services

Although we are often described as a throwaway society, older things have a place in everyone's life. Some have been lucky enough to keep the items that connect them to fond memories, important events, or important people in their lives. Providers of restorative services fix things that have been worn with age or damaged by man or machine. For some clients you will restore not only an item but also the feelings that accompany them.

Sometimes the reasons are not just sentimental. We left behind a 1950s-era stove a few homes back. We remember how well it cooked; new stoves just don't measure up to its performance. We would now gladly pay to get it back and have it fully restored.

Restoration services can be something you do in your garage, a storefront, or in clients' homes and offices. Restoration takes many forms: stripping, caning, staining, varnishing, porcelain repair, enameled ironwork, and more.

Restorers approach bathroom porcelain restoration in several different ways. Porcelain restoration can be accomplished (usually on-site for obvious reasons) with scratch repair or by applying a new surface of synthetic porcelain. You can own and operate a franchise in fixture restoration more easily than other restoration services.

Furniture restoration provides significant income opportunity as your skills and reputation grow. Stripping and refinishing pieces that have been painted can be a time-consuming job. Restoring or changing the appearance of a piece for a new or redecorated home will be a comfort to a client who has always known that piece as part of her environment. You can also promote restoration as less expensive than replacing a candelabra or solid piece of wood or wrought-iron furniture.

How about old radios? Have you tinkered with the one gathering dust in the basement? Were you able to get it working? This can be a fun niche. There are so many radios out there that you may never see the same model twice. For the right person, what fun! If radios aren't your thing, does restoring and repairing musical instruments appeal to you?

If you like to work with cars, auto restoration is something you can do in your backyard or garage. Collectors will pay handsomely for vehicles they covet. Some larger auto-restoration shops contract aspects of the work, such as mechanical work, leather, upholstery, and painting, to smaller independents.

Restoration work does come with safety concerns. You will often work with chemicals, and not only must you be properly protected, but so must your client and any pets they have if you do the work in their home. It is important to discuss this up front with your customer if you are going to be working in his home or office. You will also need to be aware of environmental protection rules in the communities in which you work. Disposal of chemicals is often regulated.

High-end restoration work may be done for museums. Most have controlled storage, but items stored for many years will need work, as will newly purchased antiquities. You will need a reputation, references, and top-notch skills to break into this part of the restoration business.

If you like antiques and auctions, there is a twist to this business that might interest you. An auction bargain can bring you a project that will result in a sale of your restored piece. Pricing this properly will recover your restoration time and multiply your investment in the auction price. You could also represent a restoration client at auctions once you have developed a relationship and learned their interests.

Restoration can be hard work. It will be financially rewarding and will also have its special moments: restoring a treasured memory of mom or dad, bringing grandma's chair back to life, finding and restoring furniture originally built by a well-known craftsman. You will need skills and the ability to reach back into the past to re-create the work of an earlier artisan.

Related Career

Antiquing. The passion people have for antiques arises from various motivations—some want furniture that will keep or increase its value; others acquire antiques as accents for their homes; still others find comfort in the classic; and many thrill in hunting antiques and discovering bargains. Selling antiques ranging from advertising specialties to writing instruments can be done from a Web site, on eBay, at shows, or from a store showroom. Watching bids on eBay on similar items will help you price your antique finds. Resources include:

- ▶ *How to Start a Home-Based Antiques Business,* edited by Bob Brooke
- ▶ *How to Sell Antiques and Collectibles on eBay . . . And Make a Fortune* by Dennis Prince
- ▶ Web sites such as www.goantiques.com, www.curioscape.com, www.kovels.com, and www.asheford.com

RESTORATION SERVICE AT A GLANCE

ECONOMIC REALITY FIT

▶ Necessary vs. Discretionary	Discretionary
▶ Replaceable with technology	No
▶ Offshorable	No
▶ Industry Status	Established and Expanding

PERSONAL REALITY FIT

▶ Start-up costs	Minimal (tools, if you are going to set up in your garage) More Than Most (if you are purchasing a franchise)
▶ Overhead	Moderate
▶ Potential earnings	Moderate, More Than Most (if you develop a specialty needed by museums)
▶ Flexible hours	Moderate
▶ Overall stress	Minimal
▶ Ease of bartering	Moderate (if you are building a garage business)

Durability Rating

Likely Transferable Skills, Background, Careers

If you like to tinker, use your creativity, and work with your hands, you will slip right into this career. Carpenters and plumbers will bring skills ready to apply, as will artists. Each project can be different, and you'll constantly be refining your skills.

What to Charge

You can command more than $100 an hour when you repair the heirlooms of well-to-do people, collectors, and museums. However, to begin you will either need to charge a lower hourly rate or by the project. If you charge by the hour, you will need to charge for your time at approximately $25 an hour and factor in expenses, such as tools and chemicals. So your hourly rate might then be $35 an hour. You can charge additionally for hardware, parts, and supplies. Commercial accounts, such as with antique dealers, will supply a steady income.

Best Ways to Market Restoration

- ▶ Participate in antique shows both to attract customers and to meet collectors, gallery owners, and antique dealers.
- ▶ Contact retailers of "raw" or unfinished furniture to offer your services and ask for referrals. This is one sideline to restoration: making new furniture look "older."
- ▶ Develop relationships with architects, interior designers, and contractors who do a lot of work rehabilitating older homes and buildings. Contractors who take on disaster recovery projects after natural disasters like floods, earthquakes, and fires can be a source of work.
- ▶ Take photos of special items you've restored—publicity pays.

Tips for Getting Started

- ▶ Get any special training or certification you need in addition to what you can learn from books and Web sites like those that follow.
- ▶ If you're working in your garage, contact local authorities about business permits and rules about disposing of chemicals.
- ▶ Visit museums and antiques venues to see what the standards are for refurbished items.
- ▶ Identify a specialization. Whether it's jewelry, Chinese porcelains, glass art, wood carvings, or whatever, it should be something people will pay for and you enjoy restoring.

Learn More

Associations

- The Association of Restorers is a trade association of companies that restore historical works of art, household furnishings, and architectural constructions. Their motto is "We share our secrets." (315) 733-1952, www.assoc-restorers.com
- The Association of Specialists in Cleaning and Restoration is a trade association for the cleaning and restoration of damaged buildings and their contents. (443) 878-1000, www.ascr.org/about

Books

- *Chemical Principles of Textile Conservation,* Agnes Timar-Balazsy, Dinah Eastop, Butterworth-Heinemann, 1998.
- *Furniture Repair & Refinishing,* Brian Hingley, Creative Homeowner, 1998.
- *How to Restore & Repair Practically Everything,* Lorraine Johnson, Mercury Books, 2004.
- *Repairing Pottery and Porcelain,* Lesley Acton, Paul McAuley, The Lyons Press, 2003.
- *The Complete Guide to Chair Caning,* Jim Widess, Lark Books, 2006.
- *Two Thousand Formulas, Recipes and Trade Secrets,* Harry Bennett, Feral House, 2004.

Franchises

Entrepreneur magazine lists and describes over a dozen franchises in the Franchise Zone section of its Web site at www.entrepreneur.com/franchises.

Magazines

- *American Woodworker* is a Reader's Digest publication with an index of articles in the print publication: www.americanwoodworker.com
- *Antique Trader* is a weekly with a vast storehouse of information: www.antiquetrader.com
- *The Old House Journal:* (800) 234-3797, www.oldhousejournal.com

Web Sites

- http://theantiquedoctor.com – Antique restoration tips, supplies, and hardware
- www.antiquerestorers.com – Web community with discussion groups about many specialties
- www.adhesives.com – Gluing information
- www.porc-a-fix.net – Kit Industries sells a number of porcelain repair kits

- ► www.oldhouseweb.com – Archives information about products for older homes
- ► www.bafra.org.uk – British Antique Furniture Restorer's Association offers valuable information for free

Robot Repair and Maintenance

If you're the type of person who notices technology and electronics, you may look around and feel like you're in the middle of a science fiction movie—robots are everywhere! Robots and robotics have infiltrated every aspect of our lives, in ways both obvious and subtle. To a large degree, the recent and dramatic lay-offs in the automotive industry would have been impossible a generation or two ago.

Before technology revolutionized auto assembly, placing robots in the assembly process, the task of building cars was *human* labor intensive. However, car manufacturers learned that by automating their manufacturing plants, they could increase efficiency, reduce errors, cut costs, and become more competitive. Rather than human workers, robots began to weld metal to metal, fit engines to chassis, and connect transmissions to drive trains.

The same dynamic that changed the automotive industry soon revolutionized other manufacturing as well. Worldwide, it's estimated that one million industrial robots are working on assembly lines. And then, as robots have evolved, they are rapidly finding roles in our personal lives. They are in hospitals, homes, and schools. We could no longer make cars, movies, or computers without them. They dispense medicines without error in hospitals. RP-7, a robot whose head is a screen, enables twenty-four-hour attention by specialists even in remote medical facilities. Robots can assist in taking care of our children and our aged parents.

Glenn Dantes, a partner in a firm called ICR Inc. (www.industrialcontrolrepair.com) that has created several niches for itself in the growing robotics field, says, "Anywhere a person is doing a physical task, a robot can do that task." Dantes notes that vision systems that provide feedback are resulting in an increasing number of industries converting to robots. Japan is a driving force in developing these new technologies because of high labor costs and its aging workforce. There's no end to the types of robots or the capabilities that will be developed. Within the next five years, experts anticipate that robots will clean homes and offices, wash clothing, provide plant and lawn care, and teach dancing.

This growing rush to robotization is part of a larger trend that futurist Arnold Brown calls "othersourcing." Othersourcing includes outsourcing and offshoring. Some people decry the many jobs being lost to increasingly smart and capable robots, thus taking a "glass half empty" perspective, but there is a clear "glass half full" story here. Robots are high maintenance—in more ways than one—and being trained to perform that maintenance could provide you with many years of steady income.

What's more, the confluence of millions of people living longer and the availability of robotic assistants like the "Nursebot" and the "Carebot" that "live" in the homes of elderly people have enabled seniors to continue to live independently. This means that when something goes wrong with their robotic caretaker, those robots will need immediate attention. We foresee self-employed technicians providing this on-call care as well as company or franchise crews like "Geek Squad" or "Geeks on Call®." We think the edge will go to the independents because of their pricing advantage and their motivation to retain customers and build their businesses.

The more precise the robot, the more regularly it will need to be adjusted and tuned up. The more demanding the task, the more regularly circuitry will have to be replaced. The more dangerous the circumstances of its function—from bomb and chemical sensors to "handling" molten steel—the more its "limbs" will require repair. As robots continue to play a more prominent role in our economic and personal lives, the need for qualified robot repair technicians will only grow.

Robot repair technicians install, service, troubleshoot, maintain, and repair robots and automated production systems. Robot technicians employed by robot manufacturers also assist in the design, manufacture, and testing of robots. In short, as a robot repair technician, you could easily find yourself called upon to perform important, demanding, and creative maintenance on robots.

Ironically, in order to do well in this field, you will need to have reasonable communication skills. Inevitably, before you work on a robot or robotic system, you will have to speak with a person who will describe the initial problem. However, beyond communication skills, you will need to have a good technical sense and a strong, basic understanding of electronics and circuitry. An associate or bachelor's degree in electronics or a related field (or equivalent experience) is required to get started in this field. You should have a background in computer programming languages. If you train yourself in the basics of this field, you will be able to work in a broad range of environments or specializations.

You will need to have the patience of a "tinkerer"—one who enjoys playing with something until it is perfect. However, depending on the specific robot and its function, you will have to work under time constraints. This means that you will have to be competent enough to efficiently assess, diagnose, and correct any problems you find.

While it is possible to repair a broad range of robots, it is likely that you will become expert in a narrow field of repair as robots become more specialized. For some, that might be computers, manufacturing robots, automotive robots, or medical robots. You might focus on home-use robots—from caretaking robots to electronic butlers.

ROBOT REPAIR TECHNICIAN AT A GLANCE

ECONOMIC REALITY FIT

- ► Necessary vs. Discretionary — Discretionary
- ► Replaceable with technology — Not Completely
- ► Offshorable — Possible
- ► Industry Status — Established and Emerging

PERSONAL REALITY FIT

- ► Start-up costs — Moderate
- ► Overhead — Moderate
- ► Potential earnings — More Than Most
- ► Flexible hours — More Than Most
- ► Overall stress — Moderate
- ► Ease of bartering — Minimal

Durability Rating

Likely Transferable Skills, Background, Careers

A background in electronics, computer programming, or computer services provides a ready basis for robot repair and maintenance.

What to Charge

The hourly rate for robot repair and maintenance is higher than for computer consultants, whose median rate is around $75 an hour. Larger firms are now charging hourly rates of $115 to $150. Specialization, community size, and location are factors that will influence the rates you establish. Some repair services charge a minimum, like four hours, and/or for travel time; others do not. Those who charge for travel or drive time either charge a flat fee for a service call, such as the equivalent of two hours, or their hourly rate "port to port."

Best Ways to Market Robot Repair

Tips for Getting Started

► Obtain training and certification. Glenn Dantes, whose firm provides training, among other services, advises avoiding colleges and training programs with antiquated equipment. The major manufacturers such as ABB and Fanuc, donate recent equipment to colleges and universities. Also, find out if the equipment at the school is the type you are likely to be working with.

► If you haven't acquired field experience, work for a company that provides robot repair services. Once you feel comfortable and know what you are doing, you are ready to go out on your own.

► Either cast a very wide net and do a broad range of repairs or a very narrow net at the outset.

Related Career

Computer Repair. Despite "plug and play" simplicity and software to enable wholesale migration of programs and data when you get a new computer, technicians who help install, upgrade, and repair computers remain in demand. Most computers need something from a pro at some point during their time in our homes, offices, or stores. Like a paramedic arriving in an ambulance, a computer repair specialist comes with the problem-solving skills to troubleshoot and fix whatever needs to be repaired. That person will also spend the time (and have the patience) to sit on the telephone with the support personnel of the hardware or software maker.

Computer repair technicians are also called upon to perform data recovery, remove viruses from systems, repair networking problems, get the multimedia applications to work, and more. Corporate and other sophisticated customers expect certification, and the necessary training is widely available at community colleges, trade schools, and online in the form of self-paced training. You can learn more about certification at sites such as www.certification.net and www .certification-crazy.net or in the following books:

► *Computer Certification Handbook* by Michael McCallister
► *The Complete PC Upgrade and Maintenance Guide* by Mark Minasi
► *Upgrading and Repairing PCs* by Scott Mueller. Others written by Mueller are well-regarded guides as well.

LEARN MORE

Associations

► Robotics International Tech Group of the Society of Manufacturing Engineers holds conferences, is developing a certification program, and publishes *Robotics Today,* a technical quarterly: www.sme.org.

- The Robotics Industry Association's Web site, www.roboticsonline.com, provides lots of archived articles for beginners, a listing of print resources, a message board, and a wealth of links.

Magazines

- *Robotics Daily* provides news about industry developments on a daily basis, plus an extensive archive of past stories: www.roboticsdaily.com.
- *Robot Magazine* – Though primarily for hobbyists, this print magazine's Web site provides links to industry sites and to local chapters of robotic societies: (203) 431-7787, www.botmag.com.
- *Robotics World* describes itself as the "End Users Magazine of Flexible Automation." Available in both print and electronic form: www .roboticsworld.com.

Training

- Learn About Robots – This site was created by a professional engineer and provides succinct explanations of robotic specialties: www .learnaboutrobots.com
- iRobot, the maker of Roomba, offers a Create kit, which comes with a course enabling developers to use the basic hardware and software to develop their own variations of household robots: www.irobot.com. The site has a discussion board for those working with Create.
- This site lists colleges and universities with training programs in robotics: www.robotics.com/universities.html

Web Sites

- www.robotcafe.com – A portal to directories, a gallery, discussion forums, and more.
- www.microsoft.com/robotics – Hobbyists, educators, students, and anyone not using the software for commercial purposes can download and use the kit for free. Businesses can too. However, if they want to license the runtime and use it to drive robots in a commercial endeavor, they'll have to pay $399 per seat.

Tabletop Manufacturing

Can you wait a few years to get your new business up and running? The future is coming fast, but it's not quite here. If you've got patience, vision, and a few bucks to stash away, you will soon be able to enter the world of *tabletop manufacturing*.

Put your plan in the PC, and almost magically you have your item built t
If you place an object on the tray of a tabletop manufacturing unit, you will get a
duplicate.

You can actually build prototypes today, but costs are still fairly high.
VersaLasers are now available that can transform images on your computer into
things made from wood, plastic, fabric, paper, glass, stone, ceramic, or rubber.
Prices for these desktop devices begin at less than eight thousand dollars. Most
machines do "rapid prototyping" work in plastics, which is the most complicated of multiple materials, including metals. You will be able to build almost
anything in just a few more years, particularly as systems employing nanotechnology become available. *Star Trek* had to wait until the twenty-fourth century
to get replicators; we anticipate getting them much sooner—possibly mid-
twenty-first century.

There is a growing list of companies already using these technologies: Align
Technology, makers of Invisalign orthodontic appliances; Cynovad, makers of
crowns and bridges; and Interpore Cross International, builders of spinal
implants. If you're seeing a theme, there are actually two in this list. First they are
all medical companies, and second, they are creating one-of-a-kind items. These
items remain expensive, yet costs have come down and continue to drop as more
companies with equipment like that developed for these companies come online.

Tabletop manufacturing, which we think the accepted term will be when
the equipment is produced in numbers, is called "Rapid Prototyping" in
Wikipedia and is defined as:

> The automatic construction of physical objects using solid freeform fab-
> rication. The first techniques for rapid prototyping became available in
> the 1980s and were used to produce models and prototype parts. Today,
> they are used for a much wider range of applications and are even used
> to manufacture production quality parts in relatively small numbers.
> Some sculptors use the technology to produce complex shapes for fine
> art exhibitions. http://en.wikipedia.org/wiki/Rapid_prototyping

If you stick only to plastics you will be amazed. Today, there are plastics that
can withstand heats of more than two hundred degrees centigrade. Auto parts
and who knows what else can be built of materials like these. In fact, luxury car-
makers are already using this technology as they build their cars one or two at a
time.

Where might you go with this technology? Bill Griffin (www.grifftek.com),
a machinist who's been using this technology for sixteen years, told us, "The
price of the machines, while still high, is coming down. I believe the first 'affordable' machines to be available to the general public will be the inkjet-based

machines." In a local community, the person providing tabletop manufacturing might become a "Mr. or Ms. Make-It," kind of like the role a "Mr. or Ms. Fix-It" plays in some places. Also look for things you can export to developing countries. The ability to manufacture many different parts for assembly of small numbers of completed items according to preestablished plans would enable growth in economies where little growth has been. Building pumps to bring water to parched fields, right there in the field, would be revolutionary in its impact.

Keeping an eye on this technology as companies such as 3D Construction, Universal Laser Systems, Stratasys, Z Corporation, and others develop it will provide you with the opportunity to take the jump when you and the technology are ready. We have looked into the future—will you be ready?

TABLETOP MANUFACTURING AT A GLANCE

ECONOMIC REALITY FIT

► Necessary vs. Discretionary	Will Be Both
► Replaceable with technology	Yes
► Offshorable	No
► Industry Status	Established and Emerging

PERSONAL REALITY FIT

► Start-up costs	Moderate (if you wait)
► Overhead	Minimal (but hard to know)
► Potential earnings	More Than Most (if you get in at the right time)
► Flexible hours	Minimal (if you get in early, it will take a lot of hours)
► Overall stress	More Than Most
► Computer skills	More Than Most
► Ease of bartering	Moderate

Durability Rating

Likely Transferable Skills, Background, Careers

Drafting skills will no doubt be helpful if you go for a CAD-driven system. If your focus will be the laser-guided system that copies an item that already exists, mechanical skills to adjust and maintain fine equipment will be needed in the early stages, when equipment is new to market.

What to Charge

While there is no way to determine today what to charge tomorrow, we expect the pricing will enable many items to be locally made rather than imported. Consider that what can be made locally will not have shipping costs, and by making things on demand, the cost of warehousing and distribution disappears too.

Best Ways to Market Tabletop Manufacturing

- ▷ Specialize in making prototypes for new inventions or parts or whole products for items corporations no longer sell or support. Where patents or trademarks cover designs, you will need to purchase plans or obtain releases and pay royalties.
- ▷ Fabricate your own designs for items serving local, national, and worldwide markets.

Tips for Getting Started

- ▷ You can build your own tabletop manufacturing devices using Cornell University's Fab@home design that can be assembled for about $2,400 in parts – essentially a 3-D printer that can create objects such as bottles and watchbands. The parts can be obtained from Koba Industries (www.kobask8.com).
- ▷ Follow the companies listed above and the popular journals of mechanics. These will help keep you up on the technology and its falling costs.
- ▷ While you're waiting for this equipment to become affordable, begin thinking of applications for this technology. At www.emachineshop.com and www.ponoko.com, you can find how some people are already implementing tabletop manufacturing technology.

Learn More

Associations

- ▷ The Global Alliance of Rapid Prototyping Associations: www.garpa.org
- ▷ The Society of Manufacturing Engineers offers dozens of resources about rapid prototyping: www.sme.org.

Book

▶ *FAB: The Coming Revolution on Your Desktop—From Personal Computers to Personal Fabrication*, Neil Gershenfeld, Basic Books, 2007.

Magazines

▶ *Desktop Engineering:* (847) 559-7581, www.deskengineer.com
▶ *Time Compression Technologies*, www.timecompress.com

Web Sites

▶ http://home.utah.edu/~asn8200/rapid.html – the Rapid Prototyping site will help you understand the technology and keep up with the latest information.
▶ www.rapidprototyping.net – Discussions of rapid prototyping
▶ Learn more about fused deposition modeling at www.stratasys.com, 3-D printing at www.zcorp.com, and laser technology for engraving, marking, and cutting at www.versalaser.com. Smaller machines will now work without the need for special venting or office modifications.
▶ See what can be done with desktop scanning now from companies like NextEngine (www.nextengine.com) and Rapidform (www.rapidform .com).

PART III

Safeguarding Your Quality of Life:
Nine Off-the-Map Lifestyle Choices for Increasing Satisfaction While Lowering the Cost of Living

The quality of life for those of us in the United States and other affluent countries is sufficiently varied, so it's difficult to say just what a "typical" middle class lifestyle is like. But Nina Fuller captured a flavor of what it's become for many in *Stanford Magazine* when she spoke of our dominant culture as "the eight-to-whenever work world, commute attached; the gadgetry, always-on, five-hundred-channel, thirty-six-button" lifestyle. To that we would add—everything from our calendars to our "to do" lists and each and every nook and cranny of our closets, drawers, and cabinets packed to the gills.

It would be fair to say our typical middle-class way of life is busy, overstuffed, and costly to maintain. Costly in terms of how much money we need to earn to support it and costly in terms of how much time and energy we have to devote to earning that money. Of late, it requires more work than most of us expected. So many of us are falling behind, hanging on, or just plain getting tired of the pace and lengths we must go to in order to maintain that way of life.

But who says we need to do it this way? It's what we've been accustomed to, and certainly what we're encouraged and expected to do by the culture at large. It's what we see on TV and in the movies and what we hear from parents, counselors, advisors, peers, colleagues, and mentors. Of course, it's how things are done. It's what "everyone" does, if they can. Or at least that's how it seems to most of us.

So it's not unusual that in the past only a rare few have set off to find another way to live. It may still not be commonplace but now more and more middle-class folks of all ages, intent upon restoring and safeguarding the eroding quality of their lives, are finding some interesting and creative alternatives to our usual overly crowded way of life. Part III provides an opportunity to explore nine choices others are making and consider if any of them, or some combination or modification thereof, might be a way for you to improve and safeguard your quality of life.

Discovering the new freedom—the less
you need, the freer you become.
E. F. Schumacher,
Less Is More

CHAPTER FIVE

Simply Simplifying—
Eliminating Stuff That Drags You Down

So much has been made of the need and desire to simplify our lives that a "movement" has grown up around the idea. Gerald Celente, director of the Trends Research Institute in New York, estimates some 20 million people have been attracted to what is called the Voluntary Simplicity Movement. Contrary to stereotypes, these 20 million folks represent a wide range of ages, from twenties to sixties, and live in a wide swath of locales, including rural, small town, urban, and suburban. Just what "simplicity" means for one's daily life, though, varies greatly, says Cecile Andrews, one of the pioneers of the movement and author of the book *Seeds of Simplicity*.

On one end of the spectrum, Andrews explains, are those who are simply making more deliberate choices about how they invest their time, money, or energy, like eating out less or not buying a new car every four years. Near the center of the movement are people who have switched to less stressful jobs, cut back their work schedules, or downshifted to a smaller home in order to have more time to enjoy those things in life that are most important to them. At the other extreme are those who are opting to wear secondhand clothes, sell their cars, recycle everything, and either raise their own food or cart home bruised leftovers from the grocery store.

Many books have been written about how to simplify our lives (see LEARN MORE at the end of the chapter), but some fail to acknowledge this wide range of what "simplifying" means. The first book we read on the topic, for example, had pages of suggestions, many of which would have made our lives as professional speakers and hosts of a network television talk show far more complicated than they already were. Ideas like "don't use dry cleaners" and "throw away your cell phone" made us shudder. We were supposed to trash our professional wardrobes, buy new ones, and start doing laundry? Were we to return to waiting in line for pay phones at airports or exiting unfamiliar freeway off-ramps in rush-hour traffic to find a phone when we were late for an important meeting?

Other ideas, like "sell the yacht," just made us laugh. Like we have a yacht? While selling the yacht has never been an option for us, now that we've simplified where we live and the kind of work we do, we rarely need to use dry cleaning or a cell phone (there isn't cell service in our mountain community). But I'm sure plenty of other people, maybe you included, would find working at home in the mountains, as we do, far from a simple choice.

In other words, "simplifying one's life" is not only highly personal but also may change as one's circumstances change. The other eight lifestyles featured in this section all reflect choices people are making to simplify, improve, and safeguard the quality of their lives. But the choices we're talking about here to *Simply Simplify* don't involve replacing or substantially changing your existing life. Here we're talking about cutting away the excess that's *complicating* your life—whatever it might be—so that your life is more rewarding and not as financially or personally costly.

Excess is expensive and complicating, not only financially, but also in terms of the time and energy it consumes. Still, the list of possibilities for what constitutes "excess" would more than fill this entire book. Just about anything and everything can go into the mix, as long as it fits *you*—your situation, your values, and your needs.

There was a time in U.S. history, less than a hundred years ago, actually, when we were not attracted to excess. At that time, the word *consumption* referred to a disease. In his book *The End of Work,* Jeremy Rifkin explains how consumption went from a vice to a virtue beginning in the early twentieth century. Around that time, he carefully documents, "economists noted that most working people were content to earn just enough income to provide for their basic needs and a few luxuries, after which they preferred increased leisure time over additional hours and extra income."

Our preference for free time over working more for additional income became a grave concern for manufacturers and retailers whose inventories of merchandise were piling up in factories and storerooms. What followed was a concerted marketing effort to draw workers into what industrial relations consultant Edward Cowdrick called "the economic gospel of consumption." This is a concentrated drive, that continues today, to convince people to want things they had never previously desired. As Charles Kettering of General Motors proudly called it, "the organized creation of dissatisfaction." While not initially an easy task, within less than a decade, a frugal, producing culture was becoming the consumer culture we know today.

So in a very real sense *simply simplifying* is about welcoming aspects we appreciate from the past back into our future and focusing on what we actually want and need to be happy and secure—instead of on the excesses we accumulate because we're enticed into thinking we want more than we actually would if left to our natural inclinations. We had begun to notice this proclivity in our own lives well before we moved to the mountains and changed the type of work we do. The excess belongings and activities in our lives were becoming oppressive. They were feeling more like a burden than a blessing, and we'd already found many ways we could simplify our lives right where we were, in busy, bustling Santa Monica.

We began focusing on what was most important to us versus what was consuming more time and money than it was worth, and was just plain unnecessary. One obvious answer for us was to find local merchants or farmer's markets closer to our town house so we didn't have to drive through Santa Monica traffic to shop. We found a hairstylist, a dentist, and a farmer's market in walking distance, all of which not only saved time and aggravation but also cost less than the services we had been using.

Another decision we made was to consolidate trips out of the area to one day of the week during a time that avoided rush hour traffic. Still another was to take the required continuing education courses I need to complete each year online, or through home-study courses, instead of traveling to live workshops and seminars.

We also started to look at where we were spending our money. Did we need five hundred satellite stations? Clearly not. We never watched more than a handful. Did I need yet another pair of shoes, even if they were really attractive? Not really. My closet was already past full. Did we have to take business guests to an expensive restaurant, or might they be just as entertained, if not more so, to share a meal at home with us?

Cumulatively these little things made a big difference in our time, energy, money, and quality of life. Again, they are personal choices. Our choices may seem perfectly ridiculous and totally inapplicable to you. You may thoroughly enjoy having five hundred TV stations and treasure going out to eat at fancy restaurants. Or you may never have made these particular choices in the first places.

The question for each of us is, *what excesses are dragging me down?*

Where Most People Start: Baby Steps

We've found most people start by making little shifts that make their lives easier, less costly, and a lot more enjoyable. Too often when our lives start to feel crowded, we automatically think first of expanding: "We need a bigger house." "I've got to get a bigger car." "I need a job that pays more." "I need to increase business."

That's what DC residents Lindsey Lowell and her husband, Ken, thought at first. They wanted to have their first child but thought their house was too small and, although both were working at well-paying jobs in telecommunications, they believed they would need to increase their income before they could afford a bigger house and start a family.

To accomplish this, Lindsey wanted to start a part-time home business as an event planner. That's what prompted her to call us for phone counseling. But as we talked, it became clear Lindsey was far too exhausted after commuting to and from a ten-hour workday to start a sideline business. Instead she decided to apply for a higher-paying yet more responsible job with the same company. But even as she explored the parameters of that job, she realized her existing job was already stressful enough. She didn't need more responsibilities, especially if she wanted to have a baby.

In one conversation, she paused and said, "If we didn't have so much debt, we'd have plenty of income. In fact, without all this debt I could probably just work part-time at home." Their credit card debt was substantial and growing. Lindsey had to admit shopping had become her one pleasure in life. "You know, though," she told us, "I buy tons of new things every weekend, and I'm so excited when I come home with all the bags and boxes of new things, but it's like eating a bag of potato chips. That good feeling never lasts. It always leaves you wanting more." So she decided she would start applying the money she usually spent each weekend toward bringing down their debt and start doing other things she enjoyed on weekends, such as reading, spending time in nature, and rearranging areas of the house to make room for a nursery and a home office.

This plan didn't require Lindsey and her husband to make many changes in their existing lifestyle. They already had just about everything anyone could need. It was simply a shift in values. Instead of automatically assuming, as so many of us do, that they had to have more new, bigger, and better things, they were starting to believe less is better. "Each week I watch our debt shrinking, and I feel like I am freeing myself from a prison of my own making. We've cut up our credit cards, and we've never been happier."

Breaking the Shopping Habit

Are you addicted to shopping? Do you buy stuff you don't need? Are you spending more than you're earning? Is your debt piling up? Well, if so, you're not alone. In fact, it's become All American to "shop 'til you drop," and companies spend billions of dollars every year to entice you to do just that. Their goal is to get you to shop and buy on impulse. They want you to buy without thinking, without regard for whether you need, want, or can afford what they are selling. After all, you can always put it on your credit card. Everything from advertising to store layouts, aisle arrangement, displays, product placement, and the unsolicited catalogs you receive in the mail are designed to draw you in and make you believe you will be happier, better looking, and more successful. You just must have what they're selling. The techniques they're using are based on highly sophisticated brain research that enables them to structure their enticements to bypass your conscious mind. This is not a paranoid delusion. It is documented fact. Advertising industry leaders proudly speak openly about these techniques and train extensively in how to apply them. So here are ten tips for how to avoid these ubiquitous spending traps by becoming a Conscious Shopper:

1. *Always shop with a list.* Before heading out to the mall or store, make a list of what you intend to buy based on what you actually need.
2. *Have a budget.* Your budget need not be a straightjacket but should keep your purchases in the ballpark of your income.
3. *Shop like a hunter, not a tourist.* Whether you're walking through a mall, shopping at a store, or perusing a catalog, have your list in hand and use it as a set of mental blinders. Find the items you need; ignore the rest.
4. *Only buy the "right thing."* If you don't find what you need or truly want to invest in, don't settle for less just to buy something. Often you will just be disappointed and end up buying what you really want later. Remember, *if it's not what you want, need, or will use, then no matter how good the price, you've lost money.*
5. *Have a mental wish list.* We all have things in the back of our mind that we'd like to have, need, or could really use, but we haven't found just the right thing yet. Keeping a mental list of these things allows you to shop in stores or catalogs with an eye for what you want. You can ignore the rest without fear that you might miss something you've been wanting.
6. *Give your purchases a screen test.* If you get attracted to something that isn't on your list, ask yourself, do I really need this, or is this something I can do without? How and when would I use it? Where would I put it? Is this really how I want to spend the money I have? Are there other things I'd rather apply it to? Do I want to work to earn the money to pay for this?
7. *Apply the twenty-four-hour test.* If something isn't on your list or anything you really need but still seems appealing, think the purchase over for twenty-four hours. See if it still holds the same appeal to you. If so,

and it passes your screen test, put it on your shopping list for next time. Or look for it on the Internet, where you might even get a better deal anyway.

8. *Toss.* If catalogs or direct mail pieces don't sell the kind of items on your current shopping lists, throw them away without looking at them. These ads and catalogs just create desire for things we don't need or want. Often something they offer will appear so very appealing, and it might even be great, but it's not really a priority for you.

9. *Tell the truth.* Do you use shopping as a form of entertainment, a way to cheer yourself up, reward yourself, or escape from problems? If so, it won't work. As Lindsey found, the shopping high is short-lived. Whatever is bothering you will still be there when you get home, so you'll get hungry to shop again soon. As debt mounts, you'll feel guilty after your purchases, and the added financial pressure will bring even more problems to face.

10. *Don't deprive yourself.* Your shopping lists should always include things you enjoy. Don't let simplifying become sacrificial punishment. Buy things within your budget that please you. In fact, reserve your money for what pleases you, rather than buying substitutes that appease but never fulfill.

Gail Sullivan was also feeling cramped in her Baldwin, Georgia, home, but taking a look around quickly revealed that the problem was not about having enough room. The problem was that all the rooms were filled up to the brim, mostly with things she no longer used or needed.

A collector since childhood, she had hundreds of books she hadn't read and wasn't going to read, including over five hundred cookbooks. She had dozens of sets of pillowcases, jars of trinkets she had saved because they were pretty, a collection of thirty ceramic cats, and many glass and trinket boxes, only a few of which she treasured. Stashed away in a storeroom, she had several discarded television sets that didn't work and a couple hundred videotapes she and her husband rarely watched. Her closet was full of clothes ranging in size from tiny to big, some she hadn't worn in years.

Gail decided she had to do something to take back her home, but the enormity of it seemed overwhelming until she found www.flylady.com, a Web site that provides tips on how to organize our homes and lives in fifteen minutes a day. She decided to start with her books and found http://freecycle.org, a site with local chapters where you can offer things you no longer need and can ask for things you do need—all for free. "I joined their online community in my area," she explained, "and offered some books, bagged up about one hundred, and a sweet girl came to pick them up. I can't describe the feeling I had when she left. I felt so proud that I had begun my journey of decluttering my home." (We talk more about Freecycle Networks™ in Chapter 14.)

But that was just the beginning. Setting a timer for fifteen minutes a day, Gail chose one very small area of her home and went through just that spot, getting rid of anything she didn't truly love or need. "I chose only my very favorites," she explains, "and put the rest in a box to give away on www.freecycle.com, donate to a local shelter, or sell at a yard sale. My new rule is if it hasn't been used or worn or needed in the last year, then why is it here in my house?"

These small, consistent changes have already made a difference in the quality of Gail's life. For example, when it's time to dust, it now takes minutes instead of hours because there aren't as many things to dust or move. "I can actually see my shelves again!" she declares. When she vacuums, she doesn't have to pick up a dozen things first. She has access to all areas. Under the bed isn't even loaded with stuff. Cooking has become a breeze, too, because everything has a place, so when she needs a certain utensil or dish, she doesn't have to dig through dozens of things to find it. The empty "storage" room now serves as a large closet where she can see everything she has.

Best of all, freeing up time from cleaning has allowed Gail more time to do the things she loves, such as playing with her animals, feeding the birds, and working in her flower gardens. "My spirits have soared. It's amazing what a weight has been lifted from my shoulders in just this short time," she concludes. "The effect has carried over to every aspect of my life. The laundry stays caught up and is always put away as it is folded. Life is so much simpler without a lot of stuff around."

Simplifying with Kids

From the time our children begin watching TV, advertisers bombard them more than a million times a year with campaigns specifically designed to get them to beg their parents for enticing products they just *must* have. No parents today are immune to pressure from their children to buy, buy, buy. Often it grows more intense year by year, culminating with the teen years, when kids may feel that their entire identity hangs on having the latest "in" stuff from moment to moment.

In his book *No: Why Kids—of All Ages—Need to Hear It and Ways Parents Can Say It*, psychologist David Walsh calls this "the gimmies." He points out that media advertising promotes a yes culture of more, easy, fast, and fun, that implies more is better and that we should be able to instantly have everything we want whenever we want it. This makes saying no to our children harder than ever. But rather than leading our children down a path of happiness, this approach to life takes them down a path to disappointment and failure. Sooner or later they will be faced with the reality that they can't always have every thing they want. Walsh believes this lesson is best taught sooner than later because children's brains are primed to learn the concept of no early in life.

While Walsh admits that saying no is harder now for parents than ever, he claims that having the courage to do it is vital if our children are to learn how to manage the six drives the human brain comes hard-wired with and grow into self-disciplined, well-adjusted adults. Fortunately, he also offers a lot of practical advice on how to say no to the yes culture.

Six Hard-Wired Drives We Need to Help Our Children Manage

1. Fight/Flight
2. Seek Pleasure/Avoid Pain
3. Social Connection
4. Seek Approval/Avoid Disapproval
5. Empathy
6. Guilt

Next Steps: One Thing Often Leads to Another

Wherever one starts to simplify, be it by reducing debt, like Lindsey and Ken, or getting rid of excess stuff, as Gail did, we find the decision to simplify one area of your life usually spreads to other areas. For example, simplifying their spending habits led Lindsey and her husband to reassess how they could make better use of the rooms in their home to accommodate their plans without buying a new house. After simplifying her home, Gail's buying and collecting habits began to change, too. She and her husband go to a lot of yard sales and always used to buy something just because it was a good price. But now Gail only buys something if she absolutely loves or needs it. "I'm very selective now. When I'm tempted to buy something at a yard sale or anywhere, I really look at it and ask myself, will it break my heart to leave the piece where it is? If I say no, then it stays, and I go home without it. My goal is to only replace what's necessary."

What is your next step? What detracts from your peace of mind? Where is your life overcrowded? What could you easily do without to make elbow room for what serves you well? What shifts could you make in how you use your time, money, and energy that would make your life easier, less costly, and more enjoyable?

Living a simple life had been part of a lifelong personal philosophy for Daniel Nign. "We wanted Mary to be able to stay home with Sean, and that reinforced our goal to live simply," Daniel told us. For them this means not getting caught up in feeling they need to have lots of material possessions. "We focus on what we need, not necessarily on all we might want, and we go about what we buy in mindful ways," Daniel explains. For example, they have one newer car but keep a second car longer so they are never paying on two new cars. "We just want to meet our basic needs and have a little left over for special, small treats, like a book or CD, so we never feel deprived."

Lately his interest in simplifying has spread to a deep, personal concern for the plight of the middle class as a whole. Having seen a building boom in his once suburban, now urban neighborhood focus chiefly on attracting wealthy new residents, Daniel worries about what will become of what was once a predominately middle-class community. Gasoline and energy prices are squeezing the life out of those that remain. The poor in the community are in desperate straits, but at least they can qualify for various supplemental programs, while the middle class can't. When he and his wife look at "affordable" housing, they make too much money to qualify for any programs, but not enough to afford an "affordable" house.

Still hoping to buy a home someday, Daniel, who was working as a bookkeeper for a Methodist church, applied for a job as a business manager with another institution where he could earn far more. After an extensive interview process, he was offered the job but found to his surprise that whether to accept the offer was a tough decision! Finally, he decided to remain at his present position because of his coworkers and the caring, fun atmosphere where he works. "I would *never* have turned down such an offer a few years ago," he told us, "but with my changing attitude more toward simplicity, the decision to stay was much easier to make!"

 OUR ADVICE

Dos

- ► Feel free to experiment, adjust, and change the decisions you make.
- ► Find and associate with others who want to simplify their lives
- ► Only make changes that actually make your life simpler.

Don'ts

- ► Don't eliminate things that are really important.
- ► Don't expect perfection. You don't have to simplify everything at once.
- ► Don't assume your family and friends will share or even support your efforts to simplify. Let them find their own ways.

Many people we interviewed emphasized how important it is to find and associate with others who want to simplify their lives. "It can be hard to do this by yourself," was a frequent refrain. "Many people feel somewhat isolated in their journey to simplicity," Linda Breen Pierce explains in her book *Choosing Simplicity*. In an extensive study of 211 individuals who were simplifying their lives, she found 40 percent had mixed support from others in their life; 26 percent found others were outright disapproving; but 34 percent found others to be generally supportive. You can learn more about Breen's extensive research in her book which is listed in the LEARN MORE section at the end of this chapter.

Disapproval is a typical reaction, of course, to anyone who dares to step out of the mainstream. When we first began working from home, many people thought it was a really peculiar thing to do. They thought we were nuts. But it wasn't long before so many people saw what our lives were like and knew that's what they wanted to do, if only they could. You will likely have the same reaction as others begin to see how much you enjoy your simpler life.

Slow Cities

While many people in the United States are joining or forming Simplicity Circles to support one another in living more simply, whole cities in a number of other countries are joining the Slow City movement. Slow City, or Citta Lente, as it's called in Europe, is an offshoot of Slow Food, a movement that began in 1989 in Italy when a McDonald's opened up in one of Rome's most historic piazzas. The purpose of Slow Food was to counter the rise of Fast Food by encouraging people to relish the joy of traditional cuisine and long, leisurely meals.

Slow City began in 1999, when the mayors of four small Italian towns drafted a manifesto that includes pledges to take fifty-five steps that will encourage a simpler, more leisurely way of life. Cities of fewer than fifty thousand people can join, but the principles can be valuable for any city. So far eighty cities have become members, from Brazil, Croatia, England, Germany, Greece, Italy, Japan, Norway, and Switzerland. There are none yet in the United States, but there are signs of the movement here. Small towns like Floyd, Virginia, that have been bypassed by industrialization and rampant growth are beginning to capitalize on their slow and simple way of life. They are closing streets to cars; reducing noise; encouraging mom and pop shops, farmer's markets, and restaurants that serve locally grown food; and establishing art and music events. The goal is to preserve their way of life by drawing burned-out city dwellers to come and experience it and enjoy a much-needed respite. And maybe they can even take a little bit of the slow and simple back to the Fast City where they live.

Bigger Steps: When a Little More Is Needed

Sometimes shifting the details of one's life just isn't enough to provide the desired sense of well-being and security. In that case, a little remodeling may help. Nothing wildly different, but more than making minor rearrangements. Hillary and Josh Schriver are a good example. Both health care professionals, this two-career couple with three children ages nine, twelve, and fifteen were feeling quite squeezed financially even though they'd been cutting back on excesses for some time. They considered relocating to a more affordable part of the country but hated the thought of taking the children away from friends and having to invest the time, money, and energy in obtaining professional licenses in another state.

After reading *Your Money or Your Life* by Joe Dominquez and Vicki Robin, they took a more comprehensive look into their finances to see if there was a less drastic solution. Using a software program to chart where their money was going, Hillary was astonished to see that a big blue area of the pie chart that popped up on the monitor represented more than a third of their expenses! "What is that?" she asked, moving closer to the screen. It was state and federal income taxes!

Both Josh and Hillary were stunned. As they delved into their tax situation, they were even more surprised to discover they would have a lot more income to live on if Hilary didn't work. Their dual income was pushing them into a higher tax bracket that was costing them more than her salary was adding.

Deciding If You Can Live on One Income

1. Calculate the cost of both parents working, e.g., taxes, transportation, child care, clothing, meals, and household services you pay for that you could do yourself if one of you stays at home.
2. Calculate each parent's real hourly wage after deducting all the costs. Be sure to factor in any health benefits, bonuses, or retirement plans when calculating actual wages. Employers offering health insurance, for example, are paying an average of $11,500 for a family health plan.
3. Determine if the "actual" wage of either parent is adding to or subtracting from the family's physical, emotional, and financial well-being.
4. For 25 percent of two-career couples, the wife is earning more than the husband, so don't just assume it would be the wife who will stay home. Explore fully both parents' earning power as well as who is most interested and best suited to continue working versus staying at home. Sometimes it will be the mother; sometimes it will be the father.

At first this was quite upsetting to Hillary. She'd spent years obtaining an advanced degree and becoming licensed in her field. Now her income was a detriment! It was an ego-bruising experience. But looking at the situation in terms of what mattered most to her, she realized that basing her self-worth on having a salary was inconsistent with what she valued most—contributing to their family and making a positive difference in the world. She could do both by working part-time as a sole practitioner and volunteering her services through local charities.

"I've been surprised at how much less stressful our lives are now that I have more flexibility in my daily schedule," Hillary admits. "In the past, with us both working, every day was always so rushed. Oddly, by having more time to volunteer in my profession, my stature in the field has gone up too! That was totally unexpected. I can still make a difference in the lives of many people while taking the financial pressure off our family."

For Becky Kowalski, whom we mentioned before in Chapter One, simply simplifying involved yet a bit more extensive remodeling. A recently divorced, single mom, Becky was at her wit's end. She had a good job with an adequate salary. But every weekday she rousted her eight-year-old daughter, Cassie, from bed at 5:00 AM to get her ready for school. Then she drove through heavy, rush-hour traffic to her daughter's special education private school in another part of the city. Then she headed off, still in rush-hour traffic, to her job in yet another part of the metro. After work, she reversed the trip back to pick up her daughter and out to the stylish, suburban neighborhood where they lived.

Unable to find a comparable job near her daughter's school, she could see no way to simplify her arduous week. But with gas prices soaring and private school tuition going up, the situation was becoming unbearable. The stress was affecting her relationship with Cassie, whose school performance was deteriorating. So, at the urging of a friend, Becky began looking at possibilities she'd previously refused to consider.

 MAKING THE CHOICE TO SIMPLY SIMPLIFY

Pros	Cons
▶ Less disruptive	▶ Can be misconceived as deprivation
▶ Maintains continuity	▶ Requires thinking about yourself and your relationship to time, money, and things in a new way
▶ Allows for making incremental or gradual changes	
▶ Changes can be relatively easily adjusted to find what actually works.	▶ Habits are harder to break when you are still in the same settings or social circles.
▶ It's possible to stop and start again as needed.	▶ It may put you at odds with family and friends.
	▶ Sometimes it's not enough.

TIP

Based on her three-year study of people who have simplified their lives, Linda Pierce Breen found that we can work less, want less, spend less, and be happier and more fulfilled in the process. But she warns, "Don't try to simplify your life in a few weeks or months; most people need an initial period of three to five years to complete this transition. Small, gradual steps are best." We agree.

She found a roomy apartment above a mom and pop grocery store within walking distance of her work. It didn't convey the kind of image she'd been used to, but it was comfortable and offered all the amenities she needed. In addition, there was a public charter school in the neighborhood, where her daughter could get the kind of individualized attention she had been getting in private-school. To her surprise, the mom of the mom and pop store downstairs was even happy to pick Cassie up from school and take care of her until Becky got home from work. "How odd," she reflects, looking back, "that I was letting my image-conscious pride stand in the way of making sense of my life! These two changes have given me my life back, and my daughter has a mother again. I even have money left over now to do special things with Cassie—and the time and energy to do them!"

When Simply Simplifying Doesn't Do It

Sometimes "simple" solutions or rearranging the pieces of your current life will not get you where you want or need to be. We were a case in point. We thought we had it down. We'd simplified our Santa Monica life to the point that things were running smoothly. Well, we were still pretty stressed out. We were still working awfully hard to maintain a Santa Monica lifestyle. And, yes, I had become ill, but I was recovering and still keeping up with the pace we were accustomed to.

It's hard to miss what you don't remember, or never had, so we weren't even considering other options. Paul had wanted to live in Santa Monica all his life. We'd both wanted to have successful careers and to enjoy the many material benefits such careers can provide. We'd finally gotten there. So why weren't we enjoying ourselves?

Although our Santa Monica lifestyle was just about as simple as it could get, it wasn't simple enough to feel really good. We were still panting with exhaustion at the end of the day, but we didn't know how worn-out we really were until we took off for a long weekend to visit with friends who'd moved to the mountains an hour and a half outside of Los Angeles. As we drove into the little mountain village where they lived, we felt something very different taking place. Our muscles were relaxing. We were breathing deeply. We were feeling refreshed, alive, and invigorated.

When our friends greeted us from the front porch of their log cabin that sat beneath a stand of giant Jeffrey pines, they looked like completely different people from the people we'd known in LA. They looked relaxed and calm, yet vibrant and energetic. As the weekend passed, everything about their life and this mountain village seemed to be running in slow motion. Wow! What a relief! We actually caught our breath. Right then and there we realized we weren't going to find the peaceful, easy feeling we'd been missing unless our lives got *a lot* simpler. And that wasn't going to happen until we made some much bigger changes in the way we were living.

We'd learned firsthand what others have since told us: sometimes simply simplifying things as they are just takes you so far. Certainly that was true for Tim Berry. He, his wife, son, and two daughters were living what he thought was a simple, good life. He was working from home as a software engineer in their modest home in Silicon Valley. But as good as life was, Tim and his wife were growing increasingly concerned about the values their children were picking up in the increasingly chic and upscale public schools in the community. Materialism ruled. Classmates were literally having TRW credit reports run on their friends' families to find out how well they were doing financially. Tim knew there was no simple way to simplify that. They needed to make a more drastic and fundamental change to secure the lifestyle they wanted for their children.

Of course, the fundamental changes both we and Tim would soon be making could still be considered "voluntary" simplicity. None of us *had* to change. We could have kept going as we were. But we *wanted* to recapture a way of life that had slipped away from us. For a lot of the middle class, however, simplifying not only isn't enough, but it doesn't feel "voluntary." They are recognizing they *must* make some major life changes if they hope to achieve or preserve security and a comfortable middle-class life.

For example, Megan Edwards and Mark Sedenquist lost everything in a house fire just as they were launching a new business from home. Martina and Burton Knutson had just moved to their dream home when both were laid off from their jobs unexpectedly within the same month. Shelly and Markus Cole ran out of options for continuing their successful two-career lifestyle when a life-threatening illness put Shelley in the hospital for several months. Paying the bill after their medical insurance ran out sent the couple into bankruptcy. Ed and Gertie Miller, both in their sixties, were wanting to retire, but health complications and the rising cost of living in Southern California left them wondering if they'd need to keep working into their nineties.

We've noticed that in times like these, people are becoming quite creative about inventing positive, new choices, be they from personal choice or unexpected circumstance. In the chapters that follow, you'll discover more "off-the-map" alternatives that are attracting folks like these, including us, as ways to improve and secure a satisfying middle-class life.

LEARN MORE

Books

- Breathing Space: Living and Working at a Comfortable Pace in a Sped-Up Society, Jeff Davidson, Mastermedia Publishing Company, 1999.
- *Choosing Simplicity: Real People Finding Peace and Fulfillment in a Complex World*, Linda Breen Pierce, Gallagher Press, 2000.
- *The Circle of Simplicity: Return to the Good Life*, Cecile Andrews, Harper Paperbacks, 1998.
- *Greed, Inc.*, Wade Rowland, Thomas Allen & Son, 2006.
- *How Much Is Enough?* Jean Illsley Clark, Connie Dawson, and David Bredehoft, Marlowe, 2004.
- *The Joy of Simple Living*, Jeff Davidson, Rodale Books, 1999.
- *No: Why Kids—of All Ages—Need to Hear It and Ways Parents Can Say It*, David Walsh, Free Press, 2007.
- *Prodigal Sons and Material Girls How Not to Be Your Child's ATM*, Nathan Dungan, Wily, 2003.
- *Take Back Your Time: Fighting Overwork and Time Poverty in America*, John de Graff, ed., Berrett-Koehler Publishers, 2003.
- *Shattering the Two-Income Myth: Daily Secrets to Living Well on One Income*, Andy Dampen, Brier Books, 1997.
- *Slow Is Beautiful: New Visions of Community, Leisure and Joie de Vivre*, Cecile Andrews, New Society Publishers, 2006.
- *The Stay-at-Home Dad Handbook*, Peter Baylies and Jessica Toonkel, Chicago Review Press, 2004.
- *Staying Home: From Full-Time Professional to Full-Time Parent*, Darcie Sanders, Martha M. Bullen, Spencer & Waters, 2001.
- *Work to Live: The Guide to Getting a Life*, Joe Robinson, Perigee Trade, 2003.
- *Your Money or Your Life*, Joe Dominquez and Vicki Robin, Penguin, 1999.

Web Sites

- www.debtorsanonymous.org – Doing away with debt
- www.flycatcher.com and www.freecycle.org – For giving away stuff you don't need
- www.simpleliving.net – Includes many resources and information about joining or forming a Simplicity Circle

- ▶ http://shorterworkweek.blogspot.com – Includes many links and resources
- ▶ www.usaweekend.com/98_issues/980719/980719income_calculator .html – Automatic calculator for deciding on one income or two

*Living in a small town will allow you to stretch
to reach different parts of yourself
professionally and personally.*
Wanda Urbanska,
Moving to a Small Town

CHAPTER SIX

Moving to a Small City or Town—
Farewell to City and Suburb

Midlife José Juarez, a single building maintenance manager, realized the only reason he was living in suburban Houston was because of his job. But the metro area was growing larger by the year, becoming more costly and ever more congested, and for José, the suburbs were lonely and isolating. He decided to return to his prairie hometown in Nebraska, a historic Victorian community of about three thousand warm and welcoming people. To some, a small town in rural Nebraska, 110 miles from the nearest small city, would be isolating. But to José it was home, and he wasn't the only one heading home again. Others were trickling back to his hometown as well, nostalgic for the easy pace and charm that's hard to find in a big city. José is hoping not too many will move there, though. He wants it to retain its small-town feel.

He is one of many who are opting for the second most common choice people are making to improve and safeguard their quality of life: fleeing the high costs, congestion, and hassle of big cities. In fact, the desire to escape the pressures of city life is fueling the third great migration in U.S. history. This shift is presenting many attractive choices for where to live, from small, rural towns to high-tech small cities, quaint art villages, and scenic resort communities with natural amenities such as lakes, ocean views, forests, mountains, and deserts.

For most of the twentieth century, millions of people, especially young men and women, poured in droves from rural areas into cities. Rural areas were in decline decade after decade. But no more. Today that migration has reversed. This shift, which began in the 1970s, faded briefly in the '80s, and reemerged in the '90s, has been called the "rural rebound," the "nonmetropolitan turnaround," or more recently, "population deconcentration," a long-term gradual dispersal of the population from metro areas into smaller, less densely settled locales.

Yes, cities are still growing, especially from a continuing influx of immigrants, but more people are moving away from urban to rural areas, and fewer people are leaving rural areas. The 2000 U.S. Census reported that two million more Americans have moved from metro centers to rural areas than migrated the other direction. And, no, it's not just retirees fleeing city life. It's people from all age groups, especially people in their thirties with families, and boomers in their forties and fifties. Nor is this migration reversal happening in just a few "desirable" areas. Demographers tell us the rural rebound is occurring in virtually every part of the United States (with a few exceptions, like a narrow swath down the middle of the Central Plains).

Exurbanites are attracted away from cities primarily by:

- ▶ lower cost of living
- ▶ higher quality of life, including more space, less congestion, lower crime, and proximity to nature
- ▶ newfound opportunities to live where they choose

While nearly 80 percent of the U.S. population still lives in metro areas (cities and their suburbs), studies show that, given a choice of where to live, more than 80 percent would prefer to live in a small city, town, village, or rural area. But for decades that has not been a feasible choice for most people. The best jobs, services, amenities, and other opportunities were in cities or, if you were willing to commute, their suburbs. That was true for us.

Years ago we traveled the Oregon coast on vacation and fell in love with tiny, remote Otter Rock, where the mountains meet the sea. How we wished we could live there, but there was no way. Our jobs were in the city, and there were no jobs for us there. But since then, advances in technology and transportation make it possible for more people to live where they choose instead of where they must. That includes us. We long ago left behind the city life we'd known since birth and moved to Otter Rock.

But moving to a nonmetropolitan area today doesn't necessarily mean moving to an isolated or "rural" area. Today there are many other nonmetro choices. So if you are hungering to get out of the city to save your sanity and/or your pocketbook, don't think you have to give up everything you value about living in the city. Begin by asking yourself: *Just how far from city life do I want to get, not only in terms of miles, but also in terms of the type of life I'm seeking?* Check off which of these best applies to you:

❏ Do you want or need to stay near the metro area where you now live but would love to escape the costs, congestion, and hassle?

❏ Do you love city life but just wish it were less expensive, less congested, or more convenient?

❏ Are you hungering to get away from city life and find a smaller, simpler, friendlier, more laid-back community with stronger personal ties?

❏ Would you love to find a simpler way of life but fear you would be bored without the amenities, cultural attractions, and intellectual stimulation of the city?

❏ Are you wanting to get away from populated areas altogether and live closer to nature, yet still be part of a villagelike community and have access to urban services?

As you explore the following nonmetropolitan possibilities, you'll see there are options for just about any answers you come up with.

Metro-Adjacent or "Fringe" Communities

If you have family, friends, a valued job, or other important ties to a metro area that makes leaving difficult, you may be able to engineer a partial escape by moving to an adjacent area. Every metro area has a "fringe"—a region between ten and forty miles outside, where the urban suburbs end and where traditional rural industries are giving way to residential, commercial, and industrial development. Often along highways, the fringe consists of what we would consider countryside, although it may also include small, outlying towns or villages.

Of course, it can be difficult to know just where the suburbs end and the fringe begins, but one way to recognize an adjacent metro area is a shift in the size of land parcels from fairly small lots to property with acreage. The attraction of such fringe areas is immediately noticeable: open space, cleaner air and purer water, and the lack of congestion, noise, and crime. Such locales offer affordable housing and, to many, a better environment to raise a family. City amenities such as shopping, services, entertainment, and even the ability to commute to a job are within reach, yet distant enough to enjoy the slower pace of nonmetropolitan living.

Futurist Harry Dent predicts that 20 percent of the U.S. population will move away from the suburbs over the next fifty years, and many, maybe even the bulk of them, will simply move to adjacent nonurban areas. This is especially true of couples in their thirties with children.

 MAKING THE CHOICE TO LIVE IN A FRINGE CITY

PROS

- ▶ Proximity to metro jobs, resources, and amenities
- ▶ Lower-cost housing
- ▶ More space; less congestion, cleaner air and water
- ▶ Ambience of country living
- ▶ Prospect of raising property values

CONS

- ▶ Limited nearby jobs may require someone in the household to commute
- ▶ Need to drive to city for services and shopping and pay city prices
- ▶ Fringe areas ripe for development and surrounding countryside may soon become suburbs

 OUR ADVICE

If the idea of "fringe living" appeals to you:

1. Take a drive around the outlying areas of your own metro area. Explore the highways and byways.
2. Hop online and search around to learn more about the outskirts of other metros of your choice. Check out the details of areas you find appealing on their Web sites.
3. Visit such as like www.hometownlocator.com and www.city-data.com to find a wealth of information.
4. Go explore a few fringe communities firsthand. Visit with local real estate agents, service providers, and residents who share your interests.

That's how Ed and Gertie Miller found the right metro-adjacent place for them. Unable to afford to retire in Southern California, Ed and Gertie began searching on the Internet for a more affordable locale away from the city, but not too far as to be isolated from urban amenities. "I'm too old to be working this hard," Ed, a construction contractor, told us when he reached his late sixties. Gertie, who had already retired, was a year and a half short of qualifying for Medicare when health complications cost them thirty thousand dollars in out-of-pocket medical expenses and took a large chunk out of their savings. They toured the United States online. "We looked everywhere," says Ed.

Their search led them to Sapulpa, a hundred-year-old fringe community sixteen miles south of Tulsa, Oklahoma. It has been the perfect choice for them. "It's close to the city, but," Ed assured us, "there's plenty of open space and farmland between us and Tulsa." The far lower cost of living, coupled with a commensurately high quality of life, astonished the couple. They bought a stone house on 5 acres of land with a 1.5, acre stock pond, three bedrooms, and hand-hewn oak trim throughout for less than half the median price of a house on a tiny lot in Southern California.

They're reaping savings on more than housing, though. At the nearby superstore, eighteen eggs are $2.00, a gallon of milk is $1.00, and gasoline, well over $3.00 a gallon in California, has yet to reach $3.00 in Sapulpa. A three-course meal for four at one of three upscale restaurants in Sapulpa will set you back only $22.00. "This is America like it used to be," Ed, who describes himself as semiretired, "People are friendly, and everyone, from little kids to grandparents, is involved in the community." Ed was puzzled, for example, when he saw folks with gray hair in the local high school band. "What's this?" he asked. In Sapulpa, he learned anyone of any age who can play an instrument can join the high school band. But only minutes away Ed and Gertie can also enjoy concerts in the city. "We completely love it here!"

Consider Edge Cities

If you're looking for good job opportunities nearby when you relocate, you might want to begin by exploring the fringe areas outside of what Joel Garreau calls "edge cities." Edge cities are full-blown cities that have grown up on the perimeter of metro areas, but which have their own unique and separate identity. They have a strong commercial base and usually have more office buildings than residential homes. Midsized office towers, malls, and shopping centers dot the landscape and provide all the accoutrements and services associated with city living.

Many were once suburbs that have morphed into cities with their own suburbs. Others grew up at urban highway intersections around malls, industrial parks, and clusters of commercial office centers. The rapid growth of edge cities attests to the livability of metro-adjacent fringe locales.

As long as an edge city has not been swallowed up by masses of surrounding suburbs and other edge cities, their presence makes living in an adjacent nonmetro area easier. Edge cities offer those in fringe areas closer job opportunities, shorter commutes with less traffic congestion, ample shopping outlets from box discount stores to malls, and a full range of medical and other services without having to travel all the way into the urban core.

A Sampling of Edge Cities

ATLANTA
- Marietta-Cobb County
- Gwinnett
- Sandy Springs/Dunwoody

BALTIMORE
- Owings Mills
- Columbia

CHICAGOLAND
- Algonquin/Elgin
- Aurora/Naperville
- Deerfield/Northbrook
- Oak Brook
- Rosemont
- Schaumburg/Hoffman Estates

DALLAS/FORT WORTH
- Arlington
- Irving
- Plano/Frisco

DENVER
- Aurora
- Centennial/Littleton

DETROIT
- Auburn Hills/Pontiac
- Southfield

HOUSTON
- Sugar Land
- The Woodlands

INDIANAPOLIS
- Carmel

LOS ANGELES
- Santa Clarita (Valencia)

MILWAUKEE
- Wauwatosa

PHILADELPHIA
- King of Prussia
- Cherry Hill

SAN FRANCISCO BAY AREA
- Pleasanton
- Walnut Creek

SEATTLE
- Bellevue
- Federal Way
- Redmond

ST. LOUIS
- Clayton

WASHINGTON DC
- Arlington, Virginia (Crystal City)
- Tysons Corner

Small Cities – Population 25,000 to 150,000

Most of us have grown up and lived in cities the majority of our lives, so leaving behind the jobs, services, and entertainment available *in* the city may not appeal to you. Lots of folks hate congestion, hassle, and high prices but still would prefer green space, good schools, affordable housing, low crime, and good jobs *without leaving* the city. For decades, moving to the suburbs became a way to have all that. But as the suburbs have burgeoned and commutes have lengthened, suburbia has become as expensive and congested as the city, and for some, even more isolating.

Today small cities promise the best of possible worlds—city life and amenities with lower prices and human-scale ambience. Nearly one in every three people would choose to live in a small city or its suburbs if they could live anywhere they wish. While definitions of just what constitutes a "small city" vary, we've settled on cities under 150,000 as large enough to have urban amenities but small enough to avoid many of the problems of large metro areas.

JoAnn and Kevin Collins, who had lived in the Washington DC metropolitan area for more than fourteen years, were eager to escape the long daily commute, traffic congestion, and high cost of living. They also longed for a sense of community, time for lasting friendships, and the freedom to earn a living on their own terms with clients who would recognize and appreciate their hard work. They recently chose to relocate to downtown Harrisburg, Pennsylvania.

With a population of just under fifty thousand, Harrisburg is large enough to support the specialized law practice JoAnn wanted to open, yet close enough to DC for both her and Kevin to maintain contacts in the DC area. Although they've only lived in Harrisburg for a short time, already they have met wonderful neighbors and friends whom they can rely upon. Kevin found a position with a Harrisburg-based university, and JoAnn explains, "While I'm just beginning my law practice, I've met many individuals who are willing to assist me in meeting potential clients. It took longer than we thought it would to find the right home, sell our old home, and make the move, but we're very pleased now to have made the change."

Cole Thompson had grown up in the city and couldn't imagine living anywhere else. But of his decision to leave he says, "The crime was increasing, and it pained me that our children had to live in a protected compound. It was not even safe to walk to the corner store as we had done as children. I was also saddened that they would not have the opportunity to play in a stream or explore an open field as I had done." His wife, Dyan, who had grown up in Ashland, Oregon, had never really appreciated the city. They also shared a concern about raising their five children in a place with such materialistic values.

Cole and Dyan spent a couple of years looking for the perfect place to live, concentrating their search in smaller towns in the West and Midwest. "We had certain criteria, such as a population around one hundred thousand, preferably a college town, and near a major metro area and airport. Very important was that we had sunny, reasonable weather with distinct seasons. Fort Collins, Colorado, a city of 128,000 at the foot of the Rocky Mountains and sixty miles north of Denver, was the clear winner."

It boasts nearby hiking, boating, and swimming, has the highest-ranked high school in the state, and is home to many thriving high-tech companies. It was a winner financially for the Thompsons, too. While the average price of a home in Orange County, California, is in the $500,000s, a comparable home in Fort Collins is $125,000. These facts are among the many reasons *Money Magazine* also chose Fort Collins as the Best Place to Live in 2006.

But Fort Collins is not the only small city under 150,000 to make *Money Magazine*'s Best Places to Live list. Also included, to mention a few, were Fairfield, Connecticut, population 57,800; Olathe, Kansas population 112,100; Sandy, Utah, population 89,700; and Bellevue, Washington, population 117,100.

Inc. Magazine compiled its own list of what their readers consider to be the Hottest Small City Boomtowns in 2006. Their list of top cities features St. George, Utah, known for its scenic beauty; For Walton Beach-Crestview, Florida, known for great weather and low taxes; picturesque Coeur d'Alene, Idaho, a top vacation spot; and Bellingham, Washington, known as a progressive community at the foot of Mount Baker.

Each year Relocate-America.com, an extensive relocation website with a directory of more than six thousand national community profiles, selects its Top 100 Places to live based on demographic analysis and evaluations of people who lived in their communities. Among their top ten in 2006 included these four towns under 150,000: Cary, North Carolina; Ithaca, New York; Columbia, Missouri; and Bend, Oregon.

We noticed that with the exception of Ann Arbor, Michigan, and Cary, North Carolina, no other small cities appeared on more than one of these lists. This demonstrates the significance of knowing what's most important to you in terms of your livelihood and quality of life. For example, the *Money Magazine* list featured livability factors such as jobs, low crime, quality schools, open space, reasonable home prices, and lots to do. On the other hand, the *Inc. Magazine* list, focused on job growth and living in an up-and-coming place. Naples, Florida, makes their list but has the most overvalued property in the nation, according to the National Association of Realtors. But if you're looking for the affordable, the National Association of Home Builders has yet another list that features the lowest-cost cities with a population at less than 250,000. Among its top ten were Bay City, Michigan; Cumberland, Maryland; Davenport, Iowa; and Lima, Ohio.

This list is made up predominantly of cities in the upper Midwest, but there are still many affordable locales in other parts of the country where you can purchase a home less than the median national housing price, which as of this writing is $230,000. For example, consider Tallahassee, Florida; Cedar Rapids, Iowa; Pueblo, Colorado; College Station, Texas; Yakima, Washington; and Boise, Idaho.

In the book *Best Places to Raise a Family*, Bert Sterling and Peter Sander researched the top one hundred most affordable places to raise a family and narrowed it down to the neighborhood level. They based their list on standard of living, education, health, safety, and lifestyle. Their best of the best list includes some of the cities we've mentioned from other lists, such as Fort Collins, Colorado, and Cary, North Carolina. But other small cities in the top ten aren't among the top of the other lists, such as their first choice Louisville, Colorado; Rosewell, Georgia; Flower Mound, Texas; and Noblesville, Indiana. Notably, none of their top ten are on the most affordable list.

Sterling and Sander also list their choices for best small cities to earn an independent income from home. Some were not mentioned at the top of other lists, for example Bethlehem, Pennsylvania; Sheboygan, Wisconsin; and Winters, California. Bellingham, Washington, and Fort Collins were at the top once again.

AARP hired a team of researchers to come up with the best places to retire based on cost of living, taxes, climate, recreational opportunities, and livability issues, such as access to health care, transportation, and special perks for seniors. Their top ten choices of small cities includes several we've mentioned already as well as several we've not mentioned yet like Fayetteville, Arkansas; Asheville, North Carolina; and Ashland, Oregon.

The real estate prices in a couple of the places on the AARP list, such as Santa Fe, New Mexico, and Charleston, South Carolina have become pretty steep. And then at any age, there is the weather to consider. Charleston, South Carolina, would be way too hot for us, for example, and Bellingham, Washington, would be way too rainy. But they might be perfect for you. So, clearly, as these lists demonstrate, we each need to create our own list of criteria for what makes for the "Best Place to Live." Then we need to explore any small city we're considering in depth, making sure to visit in person at the *most unpleasant* time of the year—the very time when most people there will tell you, "Oh, don't come then!"

Keep in mind, too, most of Best Places to Live lists we've mentioned are done annually. Today's small city could well be tomorrow's large city, and as they grow, they change. So be sure to check the Web sites of the Best of Lists in LEARN MORE to find the places that will interest you if you're ready to relocate to a small city.

In fact, by the time you read this, some of the small cities we've listed may have fallen off the "Best of" lists. Others may have already outgrown our 150,000 criteria. As the Natural Resources Defense Council points out, sprawling land development is gobbling up the American countryside at an alarming rate—around 365 acres per hour according to government figures. In most communities the amount of developed land is growing faster than the population.

When Cole and Dyan Thompson moved to Fort Collins, for example, they only had two concerns: could they get used to snow and cold winters, and could they stand living in such a small city? Turns out they found the weather to be wonderful. They loved the four-season climate. But to their surprise, the city wasn't too small; it was growing too big. After living there for several years, they moved to Laporte, population 1,000, which is seven miles from the northern edge of Fort Collins.

The Thompsons learned that, like a kid who's outgrowing his clothes, popular small cities can quickly outgrow their infrastructures. As more people attracted by the amenities move in, existing streets get clogged with increased traffic. Schools become overcrowded. Services get stretched to the limit. So roads are widened, new schools are built, and new businesses open. Health and welfare services are added, often at taxpayer expense and with considerable inconvenience in the interim.

Along with congestion, growth also brings many of the very things we wish to escape in moving away from big cities, for example, air and water pollution, crime, and higher taxes. So if you want a small city that will stay reasonably small, you will need to check the state and local growth policies before moving in. Check out www.sustainablelane.com to research the growth direction and policies of some communities. Often you will be able to observe a city's growth policy in action—look for construction and new development everywhere, especially on the outskirts. While you're visiting, you can also hear it in the things real estate agents and local residents will say in praise of their city, for example, "This is a great place. We're growing fast. New residents are flocking here from all over the country!" versus, "We are trying to preserve the small-town quality here. We want to keep our city livable."

Eugene is a small city in the "smart growth"-oriented state of Oregon. It is also the small city where Tim Berry and his wife moved when they realized that, if they wanted their children to grow up in a simpler, more family-oriented environment, they would need to relocate from California's Silicon Valley. Tim's experience illustrates the double-edged sword of growth and what small cities must deal with if they want to both protect their small-town feeling and remain economically healthy.

Tim was delighted with the family's move to Eugene. The family-oriented atmosphere was as wholesome as the couple had hoped. One of the first things he noticed was that his teenagers' friends were not alienated from their parents and other adults, but to the contrary, enjoyed interacting and did so eagerly. What he really didn't expect, though, was the effect the move had on his career.

You may recall Tim had been working from home in his own one-man firm as a software engineer. While his income was adequate, salaries in Silicon Valley were such that there was no way he could afford to hire anyone else to work with him. He'd never really entertained the idea. But in Eugene he met people who were eager to work with him at salaries he could afford. The result was that through his company, Palo Alto Software, he went from selling his time to selling his own award-winning Business Planning Pro software. Quickly outgrowing his garage where it began, the company required that he rent office space, which he has needed to expand eight times to house his now thirty-five employees.

This is a wonderful success story for Tim personally, for Eugene, and for those who can live there because of the new jobs he has created in Eugene. But this is also how growth occurs. Reasonable prices create opportunity, and opportunity creates new jobs. New jobs attract more people who can move into the thriving community. More people need more services, which creates more opportunity, which creates more growth.

The downside of success, though, is that without foresight and planning, growth can lead to rising prices—especially rising home prices. So once affordable, livable cities get priced out of reach for the middle class, and the gap between rich and poor neighborhoods widens. In Vail, Colorado, and Santa Barbara, California, the people who are needed to work in the city can no longer afford to live in the city. Thus, the need for city planning toward "sustainable growth." Friends of Eugene (www.friendsofeugene.org), for example, is a coalition of individuals and organizations who are working toward this very goal. "We value the high quality of life that we enjoy here," their mission statement reads, "and believe that the small-town atmosphere and outstanding natural environment contribute greatly to the livability of our city. We wish to preserve these qualities."

MAKING THE CHOICE FOR A SMALL CITY

PROS

- ▶ City services and amenities with small-town feeling
- ▶ More job and self-employment opportunities than small towns and more remote areas
- ▶ Less congestion, shorter commutes, cleaner air, more open space, and fewer problems associated with large cities
- ▶ Often lower costs of living than metro areas

CONS

- ▶ You are still in a city.
- ▶ Great small cities often grow into large cites more quickly than you might expect.
- ▶ Small cities don't have the services and infrastructure to accommodate the rapid growth popularity brings.
- ▶ Cost of living goes up as small cities become popular, especially housing costs and taxes.

Coalitions like this are forming in small towns and cities all over the country. If there is no "smart" or sustainable growth policy in the small city of your choice, you will need to get actively involved with others in creating one, or you could once again be looking for someplace else to live. *This Is Smart Growth* by the Smart Growth Network provides an excellent explanation of "smart growth." You'll find it and organizations dedicated to helping cities create sustainable growth policies in LEARN MORE at the end of this chapter.

 OUR ADVICE

1. Shop for a small city as you would shop for back-to-school clothes for your kids. Choose one you can grow into because the city will probably grow over a period of only a few years.
2. Be clear on your criteria for what makes quality city life for you.
3. Absolutely visit any cities you are considering. Real estate brochures and public relations fact sheets can be very misleading. Go there at the seasonally "worst time of year."
4. Connect with groups you would be participating in, and talk with members who have moved there from larger cities. How happy are they? What do they miss?
5. Check growth policies, and be prepared to get involved to help your new small city retain its size and quality of life.
6. If you want to live in a small city for a good number of years, you might want to consider moving to a fair-sized small town you like with, a population around 25,000 that's growing and likely to keep growing. Soon you'll have your small city.

To-Dos for Investigating Any Small City or Town

We often take our state and local governmental regulations and protections for granted. They exist primarily in the background, but they vary greatly from one state and community to another, as do homeowner association Covenants, Codes and Restrictions (CC&Rs). So be sure to check:

1. Zoning regulations, e.g., can you have a home business? What kind?
2. What is the tax rate? What is and isn't taxed?
3. Who are the licensed health insurance carriers, and what will and won't they insure?
4. Are there restrictions on what you can do with your property?
5. What licenses or taxes are required for the type of work you plan to do, if any?

Small Towns and Rural Areas – Population up to 25,000

Where would you live if you could live anywhere you wish? At least half of the people in the United States say they would choose to live in a small town or rural area. While for decades it was looking as though small towns surrounded by rural areas were going the way of covered wagons and typewriters, advances in technology and globalization are revitalizing nonmetro areas. Fortunately, this trend provides us with a wealth of small-town choices. Using calculations from U.S. Census Bureau data, we estimate there are about twenty-two thousand small towns spread out across the United States, populated collectively by more than 50 million Americans. And many of these small towns come with their own unique character, from university and college towns to art communities, resort centers, and down-home county towns.

First, high-speed Internet access and other telecommunications are making it possible to work from just about anywhere there's a cell tower, satellite, or cable access.

As Jonathon Schechter, executive director of the Charture Institute, a nonprofit organization that studies small recreational towns points out, there is "a transformation taking place in once rural communities. The same processes that led to suburbanization in the United States after World War II," he explains, "are now producing virtual suburbanization in places like Jackson, Wyoming, and Steamboat Springs, Colorado."

On a similar note, "There's an enormous change taking place because of the internet and information technology," says Eric John Abrahamson of the Institute for Applied Economics and the Study of Business Enterprise at John Hopkins University. "It's affecting the Great Plains and all of rural America." The internet is enabling young people who have fled small towns and rural areas in search of jobs to return, he points out, and for others to move to new locales they have no other connection with other than liking it.

Thom McAnally is an example of what's possible. Like so many executives these days, Thom was downsized when the manufacturing operation he ran was eliminated. Using his savings, a severance package, and credit cards, he not only started his own company, but he also decided to do it from his own little house on the prairie.

Thom and his wife, Renae, wanted to start a family and were looking for an alternative to fast-paced Southern California, so they moved their new home business from Orange County to Conrad, Montana, a small town of a little under three thousand people in and around it on the east slope of the Rocky Mountains. There McAnally set up TheJobLine.com, a nationwide placement registry for the manufactured building and component industry.

The McAnallys chose Conrad because not only does it have beauty, low crime, and a low cost of living, but also because the Conrad Economic Development Corporation was actively seeking new small and home-based businesses and welcomed the McAnallys and their new company with open arms. For less than twenty thousand dollars, they sold him twenty-five acres of land with a two-thousand-square-foot modular metal Butler building that was part of an abandoned missile installation. They also financed the purchase 100 percent.

Thom built his six-hundred-square-foot high-tech office in the Butler building and added on a twenty-one-hundred-square-foot manufactured home. "Our customers can't believe our large-scale operation is only a two-person home business in a rural location." He routinely has to notify three to five hundred clients about a candidate's availability. But with multiple computers, laser printers, phone lines, a dedicated fax server, and high-speed modems in their home office, that is no problem. Three years after moving to Conrad, their home-based company was doing well, and they were enjoying their newfound country lifestyle with toddler Christopher, age twenty-seven months, and newborn Stefani.

Another reason small towns and rural areas are rebounding is that with improved telecommunications and transportation, major companies find they can operate more cost effectively by relocating all or part of their operations outside metro areas, creating job opportunities and, in turn, a demand for people to fill them. Also, growing complaints from customers about services that have been offshored are driving companies to improve their service by bringing jobs back home to low-cost small towns. Lebanon in southwest Virginia, population around 3,200; Rock Port in northwest Missouri, population around 1,400; Portales in eastern New Mexico, population around 11,000; and Valley City, eighty-three miles east of Fargo, North Dakota, population around 7,000, are a few examples of ideal low-cost towns.

This phenomenon is called *farmshoring.* It enables companies to operate at up to 40 percent below the cost of locating in metro areas. For the small towns where they are locating, it means offering jobs to the area's graduating students, who would otherwise have to move to the city. It also means attracting highly trained, high-tech professionals from the city who are eager for a simpler lifestyle where they can actually enjoy a *higher* standard of living despite lower salaries.

In addition to place-based companies moving into nonmetro areas, other companies, such as Arise Virtual Solutions (www.arise.com) are outsourcing call center work to independent virtual agents who are trained to provide customer service, tech support, or sales from their homes for thirty-seven different U.S. companies. To date Arise Virtual Solutions has thirty-two hundred independent home agents who live in forty-three different states. They determine their own schedule and work hours. Such opportunities make it possible to work from anywhere in your own home if you have a high-speed Internet connection.

As Angie Selden, CEO of Arise Virtual Solutions, points out, nonmetro areas sometimes have better access to residential high-speed connections than many urban areas. A growing number of small towns like Powell, Wyoming, population 5,300, and Windom, Minnesota, population 4,500, for example, are installing fiber-optic networks throughout the community as part of their economic development efforts. UTOPIA is a consortium of fourteen Utah communities bringing such services to its members, which include a number of small towns with populations under 25,000, such as Brigham City, Cedar City, Cedar Hills, Centerville, Lindon, Payson, Perry, South Jordan, and Tremonton.

Maine was the first state to make fiber-optic-based networks available to all its communities, both large and small. This statewide effort intends to give nearly every Maine resident the opportunity to plug into the global economy. The goal is to ensure that 90 percent of Maine communities will have broadband access by 2010 and 100 percent will have quality wireless service by 2008. Similar efforts in Kentucky (Connect Kentucky) are raising the bar for other states and regions to join in such efforts or lose out.

Access to high-speed services opens small-town doors for those of us wanting to relocate to smaller communities, both in terms of creating more local jobs and making it possible to bring or start small businesses or telecommute from urban jobs. *Forbes* magazine has selected 150 small towns and small cities and divided them into six categories, based on amenities and quality of life. Here's a geographically dispersed cross-section of some of their top Small Town Telecommuting Havens.

Wired Small-Town Havens

EAST
- Burlington, VT
- Freeport, ME
- Stockbridge, MA

SOUTH
- Blacksburg, VA
- Clemson, SC
- Savannah, GA
- White Sulphur Springs, WV

CENTRAL
- Branson, MO
- Durango, CO
- Hot Springs, AR
- Michigan City, IN

NORTHWEST
- Anacortes, WA
- Astoria, OR
- Bend, OR
- Sandpoint, ID
- Sisters, OR
- Whitefish, MT

SOUTHWEST
- Angel Fire, NM
- Mariposa, CA
- Moab, UT
- Sedona, AZ

(For more information on these small towns, see Wired Small Towns in LEARN MORE) **at the end of this chapter.**

In addition to farmshoring, three large population groups are also driving the new ruralism. These groups desire to live in or near recreational areas with natural amenities, such as lakes and ocean shorelines, forests and mountain-sides, sunny winters and temperate summers. These groups include working-age couples with young families, early retirees who are still economically active, and traditional retirees.

From 2000 to 2006 population in the 297 counties rated highest in natu-ral amenities by the United States Department of Agriculture grew 7.1 percent, ten times the rate for the 1,090 rural communities with below average amenities.

A frequent concern these eager exurbanites have about moving to a small town could be called culture shock. Used to the cultural riches of the city, some fear they will become disappointed by the slow pace and limited cultural ven-ues associated with many small towns. Thus the growing attraction to particu-lar types of small towns: recreational areas, art centers, and university towns, where residents can enjoy a year-round schedule of cultural events, from music and live theater to stimulating classes, festivals, and outdoor sports.

For example, the McAnallys, who moved to Conrad, Montana, loved the community but eventually hungered for more stimulating activities. Five years later, they moved to the resort community of Seeley Lake, Montana. Named after the 1,025-acre lake at its front door, Seeley Lake has a year-round population of about 2,000 people. In summer months its population swells to more than twice that as seasonal residents come home to enjoy the fishing at their mountain cabins. It's also a popular winter sports resort. And, most appealing to Thom and Renae, Lake Seeley is only forty miles to Missoula, a small town of about 63,000 that is home to a University of Montana campus, which offers a wealth of courses, workshops, art exhibits, wilderness pro-grams, and concerts.

An intellectually and socially stimulating atmosphere is drawing many others to small university towns. That's what drew Hector Kiminsky and his wife, Brenda, back to Chadron, Nebraska, where they had met during under-graduate school. Like so many other baby boomers, once their children were grown and it came time to retire, they wanted to get away from suburban Detroit but just weren't interested in a traditional retirement community in Florida. They had many fond memories of their college years and were attracted to a community with the stimulation of academia and the dynamic energy of a vibrant college-age population. "We loved being here from the very first day," Hector told us.

Recognizing their allure, many university towns are actively courting retiring alumni with educational, volunteer, mentoring, housing, and social programs. Due in part to the size of the student-body population, college "towns" often fall somewhere between our criteria for small towns and small cities. Lawrence, Kansas; Columbia, Missouri; Boulder, Colorado; Berkeley, California; and many other university towns are in the eighty to one hundred thousand population range and larger. But drawing on lists from Sperling and Sander, www.cnnmoney.com, and www.epodunk.com, we've identified some inviting small college towns. The Web site www.epodunk.com rated college towns not just from the perspec-

Best College Towns	
Bronxville, NY	Hanover, NH
Brunswick, MA	Hays, KS
Coralville, IA	Middlebury, VT
Conway, SC	Menomonie, WI
Deforest, WI	Oneonta, NY
Durango, CO	Rolla, MO

tive of students seeking a place to go to college but also from the perspective of someone looking for a place to live that's a mix of urban amenities and small-town charm. They were looking for the spark that bookstores, cafes, jazz clubs, literary events, and intellectual, art, and cultural hubs bring to a small town.

Some of the most appealing small towns and art communities, such as Ashland, Oregon; Santa Fe, New Mexico; Carmel, California; and Taos, New Mexico, have become too expensive for the middle class, but if one is at the top of your list, look for adjacent small towns. For example, Deborah Durham, who operates her own specialty PR firm that requires little direct client contact, was ready to escape the high costs and hassles of Los Angeles. Santa Fe, New Mexico, charmed her with its unique geography, history, museums, opera, award-winning restaurants, overall beauty, and sunny, four-season climate. "It has all the good stuff a big city offers . . . without the downside," she explains. Housing costs in Santa Fe are high, though, so she chose to move to Galisteo, population 275, only eighteen miles outside of Santa Fe.

Arts-driven economic development is another national trend that is revitalizing smaller communities. In his book *The 100 Best Art Towns in America,* New Mexico author John Villani profiles towns known for their strong sense of support for the visual arts, the performing arts, and music. Interestingly his top art communities are all located in college or university towns. Here's a sampling by region:

Best Small-Town Art Communities

EAST

Beacon, NY (16,059):
  Mount Saint Mary College
Brattleboro, VT (12,005):
  School for International Training
Great Barrington, MA (7,527):
  Simon's Rock College of Bard
The Hamptons, NY (4,075):
  Southampton College

CENTRAL

Marfa, TX (2,029):
  Ross State University
Grand Marais, MN (1,427):
  Stetson College
Saugatuck, MI (1,037)
  Hope College
Traverse City, MI (14,466)
  Northwest Michigan College

SOUTH

Berea, KY (11,259):
  Berea College
Beaufort, SC (12,376):
  University of South Carolina,
  Technical College of the
  Lowcountry
Carrboro, NC (16,747):
  University of North Carolina
  Chapel Hill

SOUTHWEST

Bisbee, AZ (5,957):
  Cochise College
Durango, CO (14,741):
  Fort Lewis College University
Ruidoso, NM (8,270):
  Eastern New Mexico University –
  Ruidoso
Mendocino, CA (824):
  Mendocino College
Shepherdstown, WV (803):
  Shepherd College

The Internet, technology, and a well-established reputation in her field made moving possible, and she finds living eighteen miles away hasn't hindered her social life. "I've found the people here very open to newcomers and have made lots of friends," she tells us. "One LA friend couldn't believe I knew eighty-four people who came to my holiday open house last year after living here only three years!" She cautions, though, in moving to somewhere outside a larger locale you love, "find at least one person you know who lives there. Failing that, find an organization with people with similar interests and investigate. Secondly, rent for a year first. It's different being a local versus being a tourist. Hang on to your current place while you rent. It minimizes the risk. Then if you like, make the move permanent."

Of course, growth is nipping at the heels of small towns, too. Before you can turn around, they may have become small cities. The population of Lawrence, Kansas, for example, has nearly doubled in the past thirty years and is still growing. Other popular university towns have already outgrown our criterion of a population of 25,000 or less. So again, be sure to check the growth history and actually visit any small town you are considering. Find out what is and isn't included in the population statistics. When we were considering moving to the small town of Pagosa Springs in south central Colorado, www.city data.com listed the population as 1,628. Local residents and real estate agents we contacted by phone confirmed that. That seemed small enough to us. They also said it was a "mountain" community. Just what we were looking for. So off we headed to take a look.

Well, that population statistic was only half-right. The 1,628 figure referred to the population within the original limits of what was once a quaint town with a long history for its hot springs mineral baths. That is still there, but it is surrounded now by suburban developments that more than double the population. We saw huge additional residential developments underway, and our real estate agent kindly pointed out to us many additional ones already approved but not yet underway. Not to mention, the mountains in the distance were beautiful, but a full forty miles away.

The Micrometro or Micrometropolitan Areas

Increasingly, we won't need to worry about being too isolated from urban amenities if we choose to move to a smaller town, rural, or metro-adjacent area. After the 2000 census, the Census Bureau noticed an interesting population pattern. Our country was no longer just urban and rural. There are a lot of small communities clustered in areas that fall somewhere in between. So in 2003, to account for this large segment that isn't truly rural, but certainly isn't urban, the Census Bureau unveiled a new classification: "Micropolitan Statistical Area" (MSA).

A micropolitan area has a core designated as the "principal city" that has from 10,000 to 49,999 people residing there. Surrounding the principal city are adjacent communities of fewer (often *far* fewer) than ten thousand residents. These small towns, while distinct geographically, have a high degree of social and economic integration with the principal small city. Additionally, MSAs are spread out over one or more entire counties, so they are definitely not densely populated. As of this writing, more than 28 million people, or one in every ten Americans, live in such an area.

For example, Roanoke Rapids, North Carolina, one of the 565 MSAs, anchors an area of small towns such as Halifax, Northampton, Gaston, and

Weldon that together consist of 76,000 people. That's plenty to collectively support a wealth of services and amenities such as hospitals, schools, shopping areas, and entertainment, even with no nearby metro area. As Wal-Mart discovered years ago, it doesn't take a big city to create an urban economy.

MAKING THE CHOICE FOR A SMALL TOWN

PROS

► Lower housing prices. Often you can buy a larger and/or higher-quality home for far less.
► Lower cost of living, especially for essential services.
► Slower pace.
► Friendly neighborhood atmosphere and willingness of residents to help one another.
► A strong sense of community.
► Greater opportunity to take a role that is welcomed and appreciated in one's community.
► Usually less crime and less traffic, noise, light, and air pollution.

CONS

► Small towns can grow into big towns or can be swallowed by a nearby metro.
► Fewer nearby jobs, services, amenities, and government resources.
► Possible culture shock with small-town ways. (See "Our Advice, which follows.")
► Possible seasonal influx of residents or visitors and off-season drop in residents and services.
► New people moving in may bring urban life with them.
► Growth can be disruptive, e.g., construction, labor shortages, etc.
► New developments may have property owners associations with yearly fees and restrictions on use of property.

People living in MSAs are often surprised when they learn their community is so designated. The city clerk in Sheridan, Wyoming, is one of them. Micro, yes, he can get that. Sheridan's population is a little more than 15,000. But metro? Well, only if you include the nearly 12,000 other people who live in nearby small towns like Ranchester and Big Horn.

The advantages of such clusters of small town networks are obvious: access to basic services, jobs, and amenities. But again, growth is a factor to heed. Some MSAs have been swallowed up by one of what the Census Bureau now calls "Combined Statistical Areas" (CSAs). CSAs consist of micropolitan areas adjacent to a metropolitan area. In such a population area, you can lose any sense of the "micro." Consider Seattle-Tacoma-Olympia, Washington, for example. Or much of Southern California. Dozens of small cities now comprise one seamless back-to-back metro area from the Mexican border to the northernmost edge of Los Angeles. The only apparent separations between them are the "Welcome to Our Town" signs along the freeway.

So in exploring a small town, always look not only at the town itself but also at the surrounding area. Is it part of an MSA? (See the list in LEARN MORE.) If so, how close are the other towns? Or the nearest metro? What is the regional plan for growth? Are there efforts to achieve regional sustainability, or will helter-skelter housing and commercial growth soon close any gap between what are now distinct locations?

 OUR ADVICE ON MOVING TO A SMALL TOWN

If you are thinking of moving to any of the previously mentioned types of small towns, here are ten things we recommend doing first:

1. Before you start exploring small towns, consider how you plan to maintain a secure income away from a more populous area. Thom McAnally advises anyone moving to a small town not to plan on being able to earn a living there, but instead to bring a job (commuting or telecommuting) or your own business, as both we and the McAnallys did. We agree this is the safest choice but would add that since many small towns are now attracting new residents, some may be ideal places to provide a local service that isn't currently available but may soon be in demand. (Check out the profiles in Part II for more information.) This option is definitely worth investigating, particularly as relocalization becomes more prevalent.

2. Make a list of all the basic services and activities that are important to you. Do not assume they will be readily available in a small town. Be sure to include things one takes for granted in the city, such as trash pickup, medical services, newspaper delivery, Internet access, fire and emergency service, cell service, and nearby, adequately funded schools.

3. Also list the kinds of personal services, organizations, groups, and other activities you value, e.g., specialized health practitioners; civic groups; church denomination; beauty services, such as hairstylists, manicurists, or aestheticians; clubs or organizations you want to belong to; and social and cultural activities you (and others in your family, if applicable) value.

4. Do a preliminary Web search to ascertain the availability of the items on your lists. You can do this through the community's Chamber of Commerce Web site or online Yellow Pages.

5. Contact the church, groups, or other organizations you would hope to participate in by phone and/or e-mail to see if they are welcoming and helpful and what insights they can provide you about the community.

6. Spend as much time as possible in any town you are considering. Ideally you would vacation or visit there for several years, but at least spend several weeks there over a variety of seasons, especially during the most extreme weather seasons. Do this even if you are thinking of returning to your hometown or college town. Don't assume it will be the same as you remember. Return for one or more extended visits to see if the things you valued most are still there.

7. Do not rely on real estate agents to provide you with all the information you need. While they can be quite knowledgeable and helpful, they are intent upon selling property. So visit the schools, medical facilities, shopping areas, restaurants, etc., you are interested in yourself. Ask local personnel questions about the items on your list by phone or in person.

8. Make personal contact with others who share your interests and values through clubs, churches, or other organizations, not only to get the inside scoop about the things on your list but also to see if there is a "social fit."

    Social fit is especially important when moving to a small town, because a small population usually doesn't offer the wide range of social, ethnic, political, and religious groupings that larger metro areas do. As a result, small towns are alternatively stereotyped as being warm and friendly or closed-minded and set in their ways. What is more likely the case is that small towns are warm and friendly to people who "fit in" with their way of life, but maybe not so welcoming to those who do not.

    If you move to a small town because you like the people who live there and enjoy their way of life, you will probably feel at home and welcomed. On the other hand, if you move to a small town with the hope of remaking it into your idea of what it could be, you will probably meet with resistance and feel like an outsider. So in addition to actually meeting local residents and attending some of the kinds of activities you think you would enjoy, read up on the history of town, learn about its roots, and discover what type of community it was and is now, i.e., tourist, farming, mining, forestry, college, retirement, etc.

9. Determine if the town is in transition from one type of community to another. Many small towns that are attracting people today are undergoing big changes in their demographic and commercial bases. Farming and logging towns are morphing into tourist centers. Retirement communities are attracting young families. Moderate-income, down-home country locales are drawing upscale urbanites with lots of money and fancy tastes. Ethnic immigrants are moving into small communities that once had few if any minorities. Such shifts offer opportunities for new services but can lead to social and political conflicts that can make for an uncomfortable period while new and old either accommodate one another or move elsewhere. Of course, such periods also offer a chance to make a valuable contribution if you find facilitating healthy community change appealing.

10. Finally, be prepared to either live as a hermit or accept that everyone may know your business. Small towns do not offer the anonymity a metro area provides. Things you say or do can spread like wildfire throughout town. Think back to high school. Small towns are like high school for grown-ups. There are circles of friends, gossip, and rumors. But also lots of fun, camaraderie, and community spirit.

If you don't do your homework in the fashion we just described, you could well be putting your new home on the market within a year or so. There is a high turnover in our community, for example, because often people come in the summer, love the mountain beauty, and buy before winter. Sometimes they don't even find out they need four-wheel drive vehicles to live here in the winter until they slide down the hillside and off the road during the first snow. They don't learn that their driveway isn't accessible in ice and snow until the first time they can't get up or down it. They don't realize there aren't any four-star restaurants or that it takes a half hour for an ambulance to reach you and an hour's ride to the hospital in case of an emergency.

When Joy Laskin and her husband moved from Chicago to a small town in South Carolina, she found the people delightfully welcoming and very social, but all they talked about was golf and gardening. Her husband loved both these activities, so he was happy there, but Joy wasn't interested in either of these activities and was bored at social gatherings. Nor did she care for the community's popular pastime of potluck suppers. "I'd rather eat out or entertain at home," she told us. "But worst of all, when winter comes, half the friends I've made head back to the city and I'm quite lonely."

These are the very kind of surprises you don't want and won't need to face when you thoroughly research your decision upfront.

LEARN MORE

Books

- *Where to Retire: America's Best and Most Affordable Places*, John Howells, Globe Pequot, 2006.
- *Best Places to Raise a Family*, Bert Sperling and Peter Sander, Frommers, 2006.
- *Making Your Move to One of America's Best Small Towns: How to Find a Great Little Place as Your Next Home Base*, Norman Crampton, M. Evans and Company, 2003.

▸ *Life 2.0: How People Across America Are Transforming Their Lives by Finding the Where of Their Happiness*, Rich Karlgaard, Crown Business, 2004.

▸ *America's Most Charming Towns and Villages*, Larry Brown, Open Road, 2003.

▸ *The 100 Best Art Towns in America: A Guide to Galleries, Museums, Festivals, Lodging, and Dining*, John Villani, Countryman Press, 2005.

▸ *101 Best Outdoor Towns: Unspoiled Places to Visit, Live & Play*, Sarah Tuff and Greg Melville, Countryman Press, 2007.

Web Sites
Exploring Possible Locations
▸ www.findyourspot.com
▸ www.relocate-america.com
▸ www.bestplacestolive.net

Art Communities
▸ www.americanstyle.com

Best Rural Living
▸ http://progressivefarmer.com/farmer/bestplaces/

Best Places to Retire
▸ www.aarp.org – American Association of Retired People
▸ http://money.cnn.com/best/bpretire/index.html
▸ www.neamb.com/lifeplan/retresctr/lin210.jsp

Best Small Towns
▸ www.bizjournals.com/edit_special/18.html
▸ Guide to small towns by state: http://smalltown.freeservers.com/hometown.html

Best Small Cities and Towns
▸ *Money Magazine* Guide to Best Small Towns by state: http://money.cnn.com/magazines/moneymag/bplive/2006/index.html
▸ www.findyourspot.com
▸ *Inc Mazagine* annual list – www.inc.com/magazine/20060501/boomtowns-small.html
▸ http://bestcities.milkeninstitute.org/bc179_2005.html
▸ Relocate American Annual Top 100 – www.relocate-america.com

Reasonably Priced Places to Live
▶ *Forbes* Magazine's 150 Cheap Places to Live: http://www.forbes.com/
2005/10/25/cheap-places-to-live_05life2_land.html
▶ National Home Builders Association – Most Affordable:
http://www.nahb.org/fileUpload_details.aspx?contentID=535s

Micrometro Areas
▶ Lists all 116 CSAs alphabetically by city:
http://geography.about.com/gi/dynamic/offsite.htm?zi=1/XJ&sdn=geo
graphy&zu=http%3A%2F%2Fwww.census.gov%2Fpopulation%2Festi
mates%2Fmetro-city%2F03mcsa.txt

Small College Towns
▶ Lists college towns by state: www.collegetownlife.com/us_small
_town_colleges.htm
▶ www.epodunk.com/top10/colleges/index.html
▶ www.cnnmoney.com

Wired Small Towns
▶ www.forbes.com/technology/2005/10/31/telecommuting-havens
-communities_cz_rk_1101liverich.html

Demographic Information on Locales
▶ www.hometownlocator.com
▶ www.city-data.com

Information on Smart Growth and Sustainability
▶ "This Is Smart Growth" by The Smart Growth Network: www
.smartgrowth.org/pdf/this_is_smart_growth.pdf
▶ www.smartgrowth.org
▶ www.sustainlane.us/overview.jsp – Provides sustainability ranking of
various cities
▶ www.sustainable.org – Sustainable Communities Network
▶ www.smartergrowth.org/nga_smart_growth.htm – Lists the National
Governors' Association Smart Growth Principles Guidelines

What are the natural features which make a township handsome and worth going far to dwell in? A river with its waterfalls, meadows, lakes, hills, cliffs, or individual rocks, a forest and single ancient trees— such things are beautiful.

Henry David Thoreau,
Natural History of Massachusetts

CHAPTER SEVEN

Nestling in a Nearby Faraway Place—
Back to Walden Pond

Despite all the small-town options we've just described, what if you want to really get away from metro areas without being totally cut off from services and amenities? Or what if you're concerned about moving to the small town or village, only to have it be swallowed up in no time by encroaching suburban, metro, and micro-metro growth? Well, then what we call a "nearby faraway place" may be the perfect way to protect your middle-class lifestyle.

A nearby faraway place is a remote small, community setting within an hour to ninety minutes of an urban, suburban, or micro-metro area that is likely to remain small and remote because, due to its geographical location, it either cannot grow or presents barriers to ready access.

For some, moving to a nearby faraway place to live in a cabin, ranch, or cottage offers a low-cost way of life with the unencumbered beauty of woods, ocean, desert, river, or lake, without totally disconnecting from the conveniences of modern life. For example, a Chicago-based speech coach moved to a small adobe home surrounded by chaparral twenty-five miles outside Santa Fe, where he has a small office. Two editors left New York City to start a small publishing company from a home office overlooking the Hawaiian surf outside of Paia, Maui. Two Midwestern urban planners retired to rural southeast Arkansas, not far from Joplin, Missouri, where they raise alpacas.

We, too, live in a nearby faraway place. Our community of about twenty-three hundred people is surrounded by the Los Padres National Forest. Thus, it cannot expand, and getting to it involves traveling over dangerous, curvy roads.

These roads are especially hazardous in the winter, when snowfall can be up to three feet. So the people who move here have to really want to be here. Prices aren't extraordinarily high for California, because there aren't that many people who will put up with the barriers involved in getting here. But for those who appreciate our truly remote location, within an hour of Bakersfield to the north or an hour of the northernmost suburbs of Los Angeles to the south, it is truly worth it.

When our community was built in the 1970s, the population was mostly early retirees and people who came up on weekend getaways from the city. Over the years, however, it has become attractive to many families with young children, as well as to singles and empty-nest couples who can work from home or are willing to commute. Many families homeschool, but we now have a charter school for grades K–6, so young children don't have to be bused to schools thirty minutes away.

Eureka Springs, Arkansas, is also a nearby faraway place. An art and resort community, it's a quaint, nineteenth-century Victorian village, population around 2,400, nestled in the Ozark Mountains in northwest Arkansas. Yet it's only thirty-six miles from Fayetteville, a small town of around 67,000; sixty-four miles to Joplin, Missouri, another small town of around 45,000; and two and a half hours from Tulsa, a small city of around 400,000. But Barbara Harmony, who has lived in Eureka Springs for twenty-eight years, tells us, "It's the difficult winding roads that keep us from growing."

Concrete, Washington, population 800, is another community that qualifies as a nearby faraway place. As the I-5 corridor from Seattle to Bellingham fills in with micro-metros, what was once a long drive to and from this quaint mountain community is only about twenty-one miles to Burlington, forty-six miles north to Bellingham, and sixty-three miles south to Seattle. With magnificent Mount Baker and Shannon Lake as neighbors, Concrete is a rich draw for hikers, campers, birdwatchers, and boaters.

Marion Weeks moved there from San Francisco with her husband and two young children when she was in her late twenties. Her husband secured a full-time job, and she worked part-time as a consultant for the local school system so she could devote time to raising her family. Marion's description of life in Concrete well summed up the blessings and the challenges of living in a nearby faraway place:

"The Bay area was getting crazy with people and prices," she explained, "and I didn't want my kids to grow up in a place like that. In Concrete we could afford to buy a four-acre farmette, whereas we could not buy *anything* in California. I love the rural, small-town community. We all know each other, fight, gossip, and pitch in the minute someone needs help. It's like a very large extended family. I love the trees, the water, the mountains, and no neighbors breathing down my neck. The drive in town for shopping and other services is worth the solitude.

"For those wedded to such urban landmarks as Starbucks, McDonalds, and malls, living here, with a forty-minute drive to such spots, is a culture shock. Gossiping can be difficult. You are not so anonymous as in the city. Emergency services are good, but the nearest hospital is twenty minutes away. The schools are not so good, but not so bad. They don't have a lot of frills and extras in small schools like ours, but my daughter got into medical school coming from little old Concrete, so I think schools are what you make them.

"Weather can be an issue, too. We are in a remote, rural area. So we're not the first to be dug out in a snowstorm. You need to have four-wheel drive vehicles to live here and the ability to live without power for a number of days. You need to plan ahead a little. This is really not a problem, though. My mom lives in a major city, and she has lost her power more than we have.

"But it is rustic. Wild animals abound. This is *not the city*. People really need to understand that fact before heading off into any remote area. For me it's fun and beautiful. I am so grateful I got to raise my kids in a small town community. They can choose to go live in the city, but the country ethics and lifestyle will always be in their hearts."

Marion touches on many of the same things we enjoy and contend with, living here in the Los Padres National Forest. You have to have four-wheel drive here, too, and having a generator helps a lot when there's an electrical outage. Also, it was quite an adjustment to discover that everyone knows everyone else's business here. In LA we didn't know anyone's business, nor they ours, unless we went out of the way to let someone know. In fact, that was something I often worried about, living in LA. If something were to happen to us, I was concerned everyone I knew would be too busy or too far away to call upon for help. But here, we all take care of each other. We are a family.

Friendlier from Afar

The friendly community feeling so commonly mentioned about living in small towns in remote locations is no surprise to researcher and economist Jan Brueckner of the University of California–Irvine. In a study of fifteen thousand Americans, she found that living away from the city or other congested metro areas is better for people's social life. The less crowded a neighborhood is, the friendlier its residents become, the report says. For every 10 percent drop in population density, the likelihood of people talking to their neighbors once a week goes up 10 percent, regardless of race, income, education, marital status, or age. Involvement in hobby-oriented clubs also soars as population density falls, the study found.

We have more friends and participate in more activities than we ever did in LA. Getting to and from activities was such a hassle there that we usually just stayed home. Here we can be anywhere in town in five minutes. And we create our own activities. Local theater, writer's groups, concerts with local bands, movie clubs, book clubs, and lots and lots of parties. While we have our share of hermits, there are plenty of opportunities to participate in the community. In fact, participation by everyone who's willing is really needed.

While Marion and her husband found jobs in Concrete, Thom McAnally's advice to bring your income with you when moving to a small town is even more important when moving to a nearby faraway place. It's harder to commute to and from a job, and often there are minimal local services and very limited job opportunities. Most jobs outside the construction industry pay around minimum wage. But again, as more people from urban areas find these special spots, they want and need additional local services, so exploring the potential for independent careers in Part II is worth considering.

Here in our mountain community, the daily commute to Bakersfield or LA gets old really fast, so a number of people who thought they would commute have changed their minds and created successful independent careers. Three women we know, for example, have become licensed massage therapists. One has become a manicurist. Another is now a financial planner. Two men have become mortgage brokers, and two others have started Web design businesses. Several have become real estate agents. Each of these individuals had to take classes or become certified to enter his or her new careers.

Others, of course, brought established Web or virtual businesses with them, for example, a PR firm, a travel Web site, a handmade jewelry site, a Web design company, and a small record label. There is only a tiny commercial area, however, so most businesses must be operated from home.

Sarah Jane Owen, for example, had planned to keep her job at an LA design school, but the commute quickly become exhausting and detracted from the peace and beauty she so enjoys in the mountains. So having both a passion for and skill at yoga, she has converted the lower level of her mountain home into a yoga studio where she offers yoga classes. Gradually her classes have grown, and she has added a line of various herbs and essences that she creates and offers at her studio. Collectively these activities are making it possible for her to drive into the city only two days a week now.

Of course, because nearby faraway places are usually off-the-radar spots, and since people who live in them are rarely excited about letting others know about them, finding some to explore can be a challenge. It's hard to say where or how many there are. We'd lived in the LA area for twenty-two years and had never heard of Pine Mountain until some friends invited us to visit their weekend cabin here. Get the map of your urban area, or one that appeals to you, and look for the out-of-the-way places within an hour's drive. Here's our summary of the pros and cons of this unique way of life.

MAKING THE CHOICE TO MOVE TO A NEARBY, FARAWAY PLACE

Pros

- ► There are stars, darkness, open space, silence, wildlife, a wealth of outdoor activities, and nature, nature everywhere.
- ► Prices are lower.
- ► Lots are larger and often have acreage.
- ► There are no traffic jams or stoplights, and few stop signs.
- ► There is a strong sense of community with the choice to hole up on your own or participate in maintaining and creating your community.
- ► Taxes, insurance, and cost of living are lower.

Cons

- ► They are difficult to identify.
- ► The wilderness is wild.
- ► Jobs and services in the immediate area may be limited.
- ► Getting to and from nearby urban areas is inconvenient.
- ► Portions of the population may be weekend or seasonal residents.
- ► Schools may have fewer resources, and teenagers may get discontented unless you provide interesting activities for them.

OUR ADVICE

1. All our prior advice for moving to a small town applies here, only more so. Being remote and more cut off from ready access to other locales means you will be even more dependent on your local community for your physical, social, and psychological well-being. This is especially true if gasoline prices continue to rise.
2. Look particularly closely at health and emergency services, as well as available schools, if applicable, to be sure you will not be disappointed with what is available.
3. Don't move to a nearby faraway place unless you are willing to be flexible. Even if you find the things that are important to you are available when you investigate, you can't be guaranteed they will remain that way. In small, remote areas the resource pool is shallow. If someone becomes ill or dies, for example, there may not be anyone to step in to offer what that person was providing. Service providers may also find the community unprofitable and pull out. In our community, for example, when the woman who delivered the *LA Times* quit her job, the delivery service could find no one else to take her place, so we no longer have home delivery. The manicurist who was here when we came moved away a few years later. There is no manicurist

here now. The closest one is seventeen miles away. The cable company that provided high-speed dial-up went out of business. We now have a slower wireless service.

4. Then, of course, nature is king in remote places, so again, patience, flexibility, and a willingness to go with the flow are the alternative to ongoing frustration. You may well have to share your property with wild creatures. They will be your neighbors. Weather could be unpredictable and prevent egress to and from the area. We no longer make irrevocable commitments between November and April because if there is a big snow, we won't be leaving the mountain, and only the most daring or well prepared will be coming in.

5. Beware of the negative side of escalating housing prices. Prices in a small, remote locale that cannot grow are prone to rise sharply should it be "discovered." Of course, it's nice to have the value of your home go up and up, but if prices get too high, it becomes very difficult and costly to get services because most service workers, from teachers to plumbers, won't be able to afford to live there anymore. And, of course, your property taxes will rise too, increasing your costs of living.

LEARN MORE

The benefit of living in a nearby faraway place is that you really don't have to depend on the wilderness to live unless you choose to (see Chapter 12). You are in or very near the wilderness but have some of the amenities of society there, and the rest reasonably close by. So, as of yet, we could find no resources specifically focusing on this rather rare hybrid lifestyle. The most appropriate resources for adapting to this lifestyle are quite similar to the resources we listed in the previous chapter.

Those of us who live in the west have the privilege of living in another country. In human history this kind of mass migration is an extremely new idea.

Darren Barefoot,
Living Abroad Makes You a Better Human

CHAPTER EIGHT

Living in a Foreign Land—
A Good Life Abroad

Bob Doumouchel fell in love with the Bahamas when he began to vacation there annually from Kansas City and then later from the Berkshires in Massachusetts. He loved the people, the culture, the waters and beaches, and the tropical climate. It was the perfect getaway, and he dreamed of living there. But his work for the government took him to Morocco instead, which he also enjoyed, and then back to DC, where he eventually left government employment to write an annual reference book on government resources. Living in the Bahamas appeared destined to be one of those lifelong unfulfilled dreams we all harbor until several years later when he met and fell in love with his wife, Mary. Serendipitously, Mary was from the Bahamas, where she and Bob now live. With the help of telecommunications, Bob has been able to continue updating and expanding his book, working only blocks from the soaring palms, white sand, balmy breeze, and azure sky of the Caribbean seashore.

Like Bob, many of us yearn for the romance, novelty, and adventure of living in a foreign land, be it in a mountain cabin, a Swiss chalet, a Parisian pied-à-terre, a Tuscan villa, or an Argentinean ranch house. In the past such dreams were destined to be passing fancies or simple daydreams, but today they are becoming a practical reality for many. The rate at which American citizens are leaving for foreign lands has risen sharply over the past years to a record of 6.6 million, says the State Department, and the migration seems to be accelerating.

Since we are now more of a global village, a portion of this six-plus million are employees of international companies. But a growing portion consists of people who are choosing to live outside the United States specifically because they want to preserve the quality of life once equated with middle-class America. Americans are discovering a variety of affordable, exotic locales, from Costa Rica, Mexico, and Panama to Canada, Croatia, and Bulgaria, where they can live for less while enjoying a comfortable middle-class life and a little adventure in the process.

This choice is indeed for the more adventuresome. Leaving one's native country is not something most do without considerable thought and preparation. It can be a challenge on many levels, from legal and financial to social and psychological, but several things make it easier. Bob Doumouchel's story is an excellent example of when it works ever so well.

Five Ideal Criteria for Living Successfully Abroad

1. **Experience.** It will be easier if, like Bob, you've already had an experience of living in one or more foreign countries, even if it's not the one you are considering now. You will have already gone through the learning curve of adjusting to a "foreign" way of life and know the kind of ups and downs to expect.

2. **Familiarity.** It's also easier if you've already spent considerable time in the country you want to move to, so you're acquainted with their customs, language, weather, amenities, and drawbacks (every country has them).

3. **Appreciation.** You'll have fewer difficulties if you love the customs, language, weather, people, and amenities of the country *as it is*. Granted, in some countries now you can buy into developments that are populated almost entirely by other American expats, to the point that you can forget at moments that you're not still in the United States. But, you aren't, as you will inevitably be reminded sooner rather than later.

4. **Contacts.** It helps if you have friends, family, colleagues, or other personal contacts in the community to assist you in navigating unfamiliar territory. Sometimes being able to enter a country or to be employed there will depend, or at least be advantaged by, having a relative who is a native.

5. **Independent income** (or an existing job). Most countries require immigrants to demonstrate that they will be bringing their means of support along with them and will not be depending on the local economy. So having already established an independent source of income you can do virtually, like those profiled in Chapter Three, opens more options for living abroad and makes doing so easier.

Of course, having all five of these criteria in place is ideal, but it's the rare person who has all five. So, if that includes you, it doesn't mean you can't successfully live abroad. It just means you'll need to do more preparation, starting with exploring just where you'd like to relocate. Maybe, like Tom Richards, author of

The Survivor's Guide to Living in Ireland, some foreign land has already won your heart. Richards went to Ireland for a four-week vacation after graduating from UCLA. He was so smitten that he only came back to pack up his wife and first-born, and they've lived in Ireland ever since.

If you've been smitten too, you may worry that your dream locale is no longer affordable, and that is possible, but don't close any doors as you begin to explore. There are many wonderful places to live on this planet. Start with what's motivating you to consider living abroad, whether it's a passion for somewhere you've already been or a need to find some place new.

For example, coming from the East Coast, with its bone-chilling winters, Al and Chris Kocourek were looking for somewhere with a comfortable year-round climate. They also wanted the cosmopolitan atmosphere of the East Coast but with a kinder, gentler, more affordable lifestyle. They searched the Web for possible locales to visit and explore. They chose a small, picturesque city with cobblestone streets and colonial architecture in central Mexico. It's known for its thriving cultural center of writers, musicians, and artists and its near-perfect year-round climate. Al and Chris are among the one million Americans now living in Mexico. While San Miguel de Allende is one of the most expensive places to live in Mexico, as in any other country, the cost of living there varies from region to region. *Newsweek International* magazine reports North Americans and Europeans can live in Mexico at one-fifth the price of living in their homelands.

The Kocoureks are most pleased with their choice. "It's like Santa Fe used to be," Chris explains, "only at half the price. There are virtually no real estate taxes. No state income tax there either. Labor is very inexpensive. You're expected to have a maid and a gardener. It's a kinder, gentler way to live. We go to the States as infrequently as possible, and when we do, we can't wait to go back to Mexico. It's just a slower and much more gracious way of life. You say hello to everyone on the street. Good manners abound, and the health care is excellent and very cheap."

For the Templetons the quest was to find respite from the desert heat of Arizona. They wanted a home in one of New England's many seaside villages, but property there was too scarce and too pricey. Then they discovered Nova Scotia, with its forty-six hundred miles of coastline, hundreds of lakes and rivers, and rich Celtic and Acadian heritage. They found life there to be more like New England fifty years ago, wholesome and slower paced.

Jorli McClain was looking for a remote natural setting where she could afford to buy some acreage and run her thriving Web-based business, www.everythingforlove.com. She and her partner explored the western United States, but again, found sky-high prices. Seems all the bargains had already been snatched up. But then they found Costa Rica. There she was able to buy six acres of land with a house for two hundred thousand dollars on the Oso Peninsula in a little village called Ojochal, so small you can't find it on the map. "It is so unbelievably beautiful here," Jorli told us. "The air is so pure in the jungle, and you can live for so little money. They have a beautiful standard of living, and there are many Americans and French Canadians living here. It's our American fantasy of the American dream of yore."

As midlife arrived, Linda and Horatio Scheinbaum were ready to do something totally different. Because Horatio had lived in Argentina early in life, they traveled there to explore possibilities and soon decided to sell the small businesses they operated in the United States to buy fifteen acres of land in Argentina, with two homes and a vineyard. The purchase price for their new homestead was forty-five thousand dollars, and it's a perfect place to raise olives and garlic. "We've been surprised to learn," says Linda, "that not only are other Americans moving nearby, but they're doing so with the help of U.S. real estate agents who specialize in working with expatriating Americans." Linda is busy learning Spanish while her neighbors are eagerly taking English immersion classes so they can communicate with their new neighbors, too. "We've felt very welcomed by Argentineans," adds Linda.

Panama is one of the hottest spots for Americans living abroad. Although there is no official count of U.S. citizens living there, the U.S. Embassy estimates around twenty-five to thirty thousand. Why Panama? Because it's known as the place to live better for less. It's considered safe, uses U.S. currency, and because of the canal, has an American-built infrastructure and lots of the amenities Americans are familiar with. So it's a place that's similar to Florida or Arizona, where one can live for far less. It's becoming so popular, though, that prices are rising in areas such as Baquete and Panama City, where the new home and condo markets are booming.

Affordability played a role in each of these decisions and made it possible to pursue otherwise impractical dreams. So drawing from a variety of sources, we've gathered a list of countries that have been attracting middle-class North Americans to go for their dreams. They each have, or are developing, a reputation for providing an affordable quality of life. Of course, cost of living can shift quickly once a country becomes popular or as economic circumstances change, so think of this list simply as a jumping-off place to begin your search.

Affordable Best-Bet Countries

1. Belize	8. Hungary
2. Czech Republic	9. Malta
3. Costa Rica	10. Nicaragua
4. Croatia	11. Nova Scotia, Canada
5. Ecuador	12. Panama
6. Etruscan Italy	13. Poland
7. Honduras	14. Portugal

Of course, there is so much more to choosing a country than affordability. If affordability was the only criterion, some of the countries lowest on *International Living*'s annual livability index would top the list, for example, Laos, Pakistan, Afghanistan, Haiti, and Saudi Arabia. Of the 193 countries they evaluated, the countries ranked in the top ten for livability also tended so be some of the more costly.

Top Ten Most Livable Countries Outside the U.S.

1. France	6. Austria
2. Switzerland	7. Sweden
3. Australia	8. Finland
4. Denmark	9. Italy
5. New Zealand	10. Netherlands

htttp://www.internationalling.com

Surprisingly, although we fear that many of idyllic places we dream about, like France, Switzerland, Australia, New Zealand, and Ireland, have long ago become too expensive, they still offer affordable choices if one locates outside of the most popular high-cost areas. Ruth Holcomb, for example, founder of Network for Living Abroad, reports that in locales outside of Paris, an American could live in France on forty thousand dollars a year. And *International Living* claims that one can still buy small properties in the French-speaking mountain areas of Switzerland for around the median U.S. housing price.

Although both Australia and New Zealand are experiencing rising housing costs, they both still hold promise. Housing costs in western Australia's Adelaide are close to the U.S. median, and the cost of living there is one of the least expensive in the world, according to global economics consultants Mercer Consulting Group. New Zealand, remains at this time, one of the more affordable developed nations.

Nonetheless when it comes to the best places for middle-income America to migrate, *International Living* has its own list of favorites. As you can see, it's a composite of countries from the other two lists.

International Living's Favorite Places to Move

1. France	6. Ireland
2. Italy	7. Panama
3. Uruguay	8. Ecuador
4. Argentina	9. Nicaragua
5. Mexico	10. Honduras

http://www.internationalliving.com

In considering the possibilities for living abroad, clearly there are many factors to consider. Here is a checklist to consider carefully in exploring if there's another country in your future.

Checklist for Choosing If and Where to Live Abroad

❏ *Cost of living.* Cost of living comparisons between the United States and other countries are available on such Web sites as www.internationalliving.com. Often, you will note that quality of life and cost of living are juxtaposed. For example, Austria, Denmark, Sweden, and Finland all rank in the top ten of *International Living*'s Quality of Life Index because they score so highly in health care, infrastructure, safety, freedom, and strength of economy, but they lose points on cost of living. These countries are expensive. While France, Switzerland, Australia, and New Zealand are certainly not bargains, they have a higher quality of life for about the same or somewhat less than the United States. Of the Affordable Best Bet Countries we've listed above, Costa Rica, Ecuador, Honduras, Hungary, and Panama have the lowest cost of living compared to the United Sates.

Of course, the cost of living is constantly shifting with changes in the global economy. Also, as a country becomes known as a bargain, the cost of living tends to go up as more people rush to get in on a good deal and create demand for more services and infrastructure. So in calculating what your cost of living will be in a country, focus specifically on what you will be paying for: basic essentials, such as housing and utilities, and those things you will be spending money on. And remember to take into account taxes, the exchange rate, and cost of money transfers.

❏ *Residency requirements and work permits.* Most countries have requirements for allowing foreigners to live in, as opposed to visit, their country. Such laws specify, for example, under what conditions and for how long someone can reside there. In some countries there are particularly severe limitations on who can work there, and work permits are granted for a period of time and then must be renewed repeatedly. Both residency and work restrictions most often relate to demonstrating that one is in good health, has no police record, and has an adequate ongoing source of income that will not depend on the local economy, take away jobs native residents could fill, or become a burden on their tax system.

In keeping with the theme of this book, our recommendation would be, prior to relocating, to establish an ongoing source of income you can rely on that does not depend on earning a living within the country. It might be from retirement income, a successful virtual independent career that does not depend on serving local residents, or some combination thereof. Even if you have a successful virtual business underway, though, you may still need to obtain a work permit.

In the Bahamas, for example, Bob Doumouchel must have a work permit, even though as a writer all his income is earned outside of Nassau. Because he is married to a Bahamian citizen, he has a permanent work permit. Were he not, he would need to renew his permit every few years. In Costa Rica, however, Jorli McClain didn't need a work permit to live there as a self-employed U.S. citizen operating her online company that drew no income from within Costa Rica.

 Tips for Making Your Move Official

1. Apply for your visa directly from the embassy or nearest consulate of the country in which you plan to reside, before you leave the United States. The Department of State's Web site lists foreign embassies and consulates at www.state.gov/s/cpr/rls/fco.
2. Determine whether or not you need a work permit, and obtain one if you do. This will depend on the laws of the particular country to which you are moving. If you do need a work permit, apply for it at the same time you apply for the visa.
3. Be prepared to prove your residency status to obtain many basic services, such as banking, utilities, library privileges, etc.

Lining up a job abroad is not usually an easy task, although certainly not impossible everywhere. It will be easier if you have professional or technical skills that are sorely needed in a country. Shortages in health care workers and information techs are obvious areas of expertise often in demand, but countries have differing needs for specific workers. For example, at this time electricians, auto mechanics, film animators, and cabinetmakers are in demand in New Zealand. There are many find-a-job-in-foreign-lands scams to beware of, but sites such as www.internationalliving.com and www.workabroad.monster.com provide information on actual job opportunities in various countries around the world.

Starting up a business, as opposed to bringing along a virtual one, is yet another matter. Some countries like Nicaragua and Panama welcome and offer incentives for foreigners to own and/or invest in a local business. For example, if you build or buy a new house in Panama, you will not owe income taxes on that property for up to twenty years. In Nicaragua you can start a tourist-related business and pay no taxes for ten years and import all needed supplies tax-free.

Your U.S. Rights

1. You will not need to relinquish your U.S. citizenship even if you obtain permanent residency elsewhere.
2. You will not be eligible for Medicare, but you will most likely still be able to receive U.S. Social Security. There are certain countries where the United States is not allowed to send Social Security payments. For rights and responsibilities under Social Security while living abroad, visit the Social Security Web site at www.socialsecurity.gov/pubs /10137.html, or call (800) 772-1213 [TTY (800) 325-0778] and ask for the publication "Your Payments While You Are Outside the United States."

So, in exploring a country, before all else ask these questions:

1. What type of visas are available to you, and which one best meets your needs?
2. If you need to continue earning an income other than from Social Security and investments, what type of work permit would you need, and what would be required to obtain one?
3. What is the process for applying for needed visas and work permits?
4. What is the waiting time for this process?
5. If renewal is required, how often and under what conditions will it be renewed?

Hiring an attorney in the United States and/or the country you are seeking to live and work in can make answering these questions and navigating your way through the necessary processes much easier than attempting to sort through all the requirements by yourself. Such requirements change frequently and have many nuances, so you may find yourself acting on contradictory or incomplete information. Of course, the more homework you have done before contacting an attorney to familiarize yourself with the requirements and gather and prepare the needed information involved, the less costly such services will be.

 OUR ADVICE: MAINTAINING AN INCOME IN A FOREIGN COUNTRY

Be sure you have a stable source of ongoing income before relocating to another country. Others are doing this in a variety of ways, some of which enable them to live in a country for six months or more to explore opportunities there and to find out for sure if it's somewhere they actually want and could immigrate to. Some of these options might include:

> ▶ Living on Social Security or other retirement income
> ▶ Relying on an existing successful virtual business
> ▶ Joining the Peace Corps
> ▶ Doing missionary work through one's church
> ▶ Finding a position with a U.S. company that has a workforce abroad
> ▶ Obtaining a position or contract to teach English and/or American business practices with a company in the country
> ▶ Providing a needed service to other expats
> ▶ Taking a position where you live on and care for someone else's property in the country of your choice (for more on Caretaking see Chapter 9)

❏ *Real estate laws, ownership restrictions, and fees.* Countries may also have restrictions as to when, where, and under what conditions people emigrating from another country can own property. In Argentina, Canada, and France, for example, there are few restrictions on foreign ownership of property. In Belize and Croatia, government approval is required for any property purchase by noncitizens, but there are few restrictions. In some countries like New Zealand, it depends on how much land you buy. In Bulgaria and Romania, you can buy buildings, but not land. In Honduras and Panama, there are certain locations where you cannot buy property. This is true in Switzerland, as well, where local *cantons,* like counties, decide who can buy property, and some exclude or set quotas on foreign ownership. In countries like Poland, there are restrictions related to the number of years one has been a permanent resident before one can buy property. In the Czech Republic, only Europeans can buy property until 2009.

 Tips for Buying Real Estate

1. Most countries outside the United States do not have multiple listing services. Thus you need to meet with many agents to see a wide selection of available property, though some U.S. real estate agents sell property in nearby countries like Mexico.
2. Mortgages may not be available or feasible in some countries, so expect to pay cash to buy a home. Usually you will be better off selling a U.S. home and buying foreign property with your equity.
3. In some countries, real estate prices for nonresidents will be higher than for residents, so you may want to buy through a local intermediary.

Other issues to check carefully are add-on fees, commissions on real estate purchases, and taxes at time of purchase as well as annual property taxes. Such costs can vary widely from country to country, as well as from locale to locale within a country. Getting a clean title and title insurance can also be an issue. Especially in Eastern European countries, someone from generations past could contest your title.

OUR ADVICE: A WARNING

Don't let anyone talk you out of getting title insurance. A notary, or *notrios*, who specializes in verifying legal documents, can help read a title history to see if there are any gaps in the property's history or numerous property claims. Or you can access the services of a U.S. title company that issues policies in foreign countries. The security from such an investment can be worth its weight in gold.

❏ *Tax and Financial issues.* Stability of the national economy and its currency, the value of the dollar against the local currency (the exchange rate), and the money transfer process and fees are just a few of the financial issues you will want to explore as you consider a particular country. Generally speaking, such issues are easier in countries where the U.S. dollar is the official currency (see next heading) or where the local currency is pegged to the US dollar, such as in Argentina, the Bahamas, Barbados, and Lithuania. Otherwise you need to carefully investigate and weigh the country's economic stability, as well as the risk presented by the volatility of the exchange rate, because you will most likely be receiving your income in U.S. dollars and paying for many local products and services in the currency of the country where you live.

Officially U.S. Dollarized Economies

- British Virgin Islands
- East Timor
- Ecuador (uses its own coins)
- El Salvador
- Marshall Islands
- Federated States of Micronesia
- Palau
- Panama (uses its own coins)
- Pitcairn Islands (also uses the New Zealand dollar)
- Turks and Caicos Islands

Laws that govern how much tax one must pay and for what varies widely from country to county, including whether you can bring household possessions or a car into the country tax free. Individual income tax rates and value-added taxes can vary widely from low-tax countries like Panama and Nicaragua to high-tax countries such as France and Netherlands. You can check the prevailing tax rates by country on various Web sites such as www.worldwidetax .com and www.internationalliving.com

If you will be operating a virtual business and earning most or all of your income from outside any country you are considering, also check to see if you will be taxed only on income earned within the country, as in Honduras or Ecuador, or if you will be taxed on worldwide income, as in Argentina and Ireland. Consider also that the United States has tax laws, including tax exemptions that apply specifically to Americans living abroad. So, of course, if possible you will want to avoid being double-taxed on the same income. The United States has double taxation agreements with many countries, including at this time France, Ireland, Italy, and Mexico. Some countries also allow tax credits to immigrants on taxes paid to the country of origin. Others have progressive scales depending on income:

Australia	Indonesia	Poland
Austria	Ireland	Portugal
Barbados	Israel	Romania
Belgium	Italy	Russia
Canada	Jamaica	Slovakia
China	Japan	Slovenia
Cyprus	Kazakhstan	South Africa
Czech Republic	Korea	Spain
Denmark	Latvia	Sweden
Egypt	Lithuania	Switzerland
Estonia	Luxembourg	Thailand
Finland	Mexico	Trinidad
France	Morocco	Tunisia
Germany	Netherlands	Turkey
Greece	New Zealand	Ukraine
Hungary	Norway	United Kingdom
Iceland	Pakistan	Venezuela
India	Philippines	

Of course, income tax is by far not the only tax to explore and compare, and U.S. tax treaties cover other types of taxes as well.

Common Types of Taxes to Consider

- ► Capital gains taxes
- ► Income tax
- ► Inheritance/gift tax
- ► Sales Tax, VAT, UVA, or SST
- ► Transfer tax
- ► Wealth tax

Of course, tax laws are ever changing, so information on the latest tax implications is available from the nearest American consulate or the consular services department of the embassy. We also strongly advise consulting with an international tax planner in the U.S. and a tax professional in any country you are considering who has experience working with expats and foreign residents.

 OUR ADVICE: A TAX WARNING

The United States is the only developed country that taxes it citizens while they live overseas. Beginning in 2006 the United States sharply raised tax rates for citizens living abroad with incomes of more than $82,400 a year. "The administrative costs of being an American and living outside the United States have gone up dramatically," Zurich tax lawyer Marnin Michaels told the *New York Times*. This recent development is only one of many reasons to consult with two international tax planners when weighing a decision to live in another country: one from the country you are considering and one from the United States.

❏ *Infrastructure.* We take reliable power and water, roads and transportation, phone, cable, satellite, and Internet services for granted. But in some countries they are not assured. In moving to Costa Rica, for example, Jorli McClain was promised phone service would be available before she arrived. Eventually it was, but not until after she had to leave. "Without the phone I was helpless to run my business," she explains. "I also needed a high-speed Internet connection. Now you can have this through a home satellite system, but not while I was there. Still, though, the infrastructure is fragile, very hit-and-miss, so I can't afford to live there. I need these services to be up and running all the time to keep my business going. That is the reason I had to leave and why I can't go back."

Infrastructure refers to basic facilities, services, and installations that are needed for the functioning of a community or society. It includes such things as roads, transportation and communications systems, water and power lines, and public institutions, including schools, post offices, law enforcement, courts, and prisons. In *International Living*'s Quality of Life Index, the United States scores third only to Finland and Switzerland for the quality of its infrastructure, so don't assume you will have all the facilities and public services you're used to. Check them out before you decide to move elsewhere.

OUR ADVICE: A WORD OF CAUTION

Don't buy based on promises of things to come unless they don't matter to you. Only buy when the basic facilities and services you need to live securely and comfortably are already functioning to your satisfaction.

❏ *Accessibility and proximity to the United States.* If you want to return to America to visit with family, shop, obtain medical or other services, and so forth, then distance, cost of travel, and ease of entry and egress are all important issues to consider. Aside from affordability, proximity is a key reason Mexico and Central American countries have become popular places for Americans to locate. You might love Italy or Australia, but do you really want to be that far from your homeland? Calculate how often you think you want or need to return home and check the availability, cost, and convenience of travel to and from there. Also, if you wish for family and friends to visit you as well, ask how they feel about their travel options.

❏ *Language.* If you are considering a country where English is not the native language, it is preferable to learn the language. Many language programs and language schools include home stays with families. The latter is also a good way to get to know the local culture. A list of many such programs is available at sites such as www.transitionsabroad.com and www.languageskillsabroad.com.

Learning a new language is a challenge and not an easy task for those without an ear for language. This is particularly true of Slavic-speaking countries, like as Bulgaria, Croatia, the Czech Republic, Poland, Slovenia, and Baltic nations, such as Estonia, Latvia, and Lithuania. These languages have a different alphabet and very few sounds common to English. So ask yourself, do you really want to learn a new language?

If learning a new language is not for you, you don't necessarily have to rule out all non-English-speaking countries. In many countries, like Germany, English is widely spoken as a second language. Other countries, such as France, Panama, and Mexico, have large English-speaking expat communities, where you can live without speaking the native language. There are entire French villages dominated by English-speaking expats, for example. In Costa Rica, Jorli McClain found she could get along fine with a few phrases, hand gestures, and general goodwill.

This doesn't mean, however, that you will necessarily be welcomed in these countries as a non-native speaker. The French populace is renowned for resenting foreigners who aren't willing to learn their language. In some French villages where as much as a third of the population speaks only English, English-speaking residents have been harassed and had public protests waged against them. It is our view that even in more welcoming countries, you will always be somewhat handicapped and isolated from the culture if you don't speak the native language.

Tips for Learning a Slavic Language

If the beauty, opportunity, and lower cost of living in a Slavic or Baltic country appeals to you, but language is a barrier, you might consider learning Slovio. Known as a constructed or planned language, Slovio is an international simplification of Slavic languages that can be used on an immediate daily basis to communicate with some four hundred million people around the world. Unlike traditional Slavic languages, it uses only the most basic Latin alphabet without any accents or special characters, and it can be typed on any keyboard—including U.S. keyboards. Its grammar is simple and logical, it uses simple phonetic spelling, and it is compatible with all European languages—only simpler. You can find out more at www.slovio.com.

❏ *Safety.* Safety is one of the motivating reasons retirees and younger people in the United States seek to move to another country. In fact, drawing from a variety of statistics on crime, militarism, and gun-related crimes, the United States ranks twenty-fifth, third, and eighth respectively in NationMaster's worldwide analysis of safety issues (www.nationmaster.com). This massive central online data source derives its statistics from sources such as the *CIA World Factbook,* United Nations, World Health Organization, World Bank, World Resources Institute, UNESCO, UNICEF, and IECD. Still, when it comes to the thought of moving to a foreign country, we often tend to feel safer "at home." And many countries are, in fact, known to have high incidents of violent crime.

Safety is related to economic and political stability, however, so countries once reputed to be highly dangerous may now be quite safe and visa versa. So the current and projected safety of a nation, and particular locales within a nation, is definitely something to explore in depth.

At this time many of the countries we have listed or discussed are considered to be safe or safer than the United States. Exceptions are Mexico, Costa Rica, Poland, and Bulgaria, which are reported by NationMaster to have a higher crime rate than the United States. In calculating the best ten places for the non-rich to retire, *US News* rated Ecuador and Panama as poor, although they scored well or tops in real estate, health care, and taxes. *International Living* disagreed, scoring Panama high for safety in 2006, but they listed Ecuador, Nicaragua, and Honduras as less safe than the other countries we've discussed.

Tips on Safety

For the best source of international safety information:
1. The *CIA FactBook* has individual profiles by country: www.odci.gov/cia/publications/factbook/index.html.
2. The U.S. State Department (www.state.gov) offers background information and current safety alerts by country: www.state.gov/r/pa/ei/bgn/.
3. NationMaster, which allows you to graphically compare countries you may be considering, is at www.nationmaster.com.

Of course, crime and violence are not the only measure of safety. Freedom from repression is clearly another aspect of how safe one feels living in any country. By this measure Croatia, Argentina, and Mexico scored below the United States, with Ecuador, Nicaragua, and Honduras scoring lower yet, but still with nearly seventy out of one hundred points.

What legal rights and responsibilities one has vary quite widely across the world. Don't assume you will have the same legal protections we take for granted. As the Kocoureks pointed out to us in discussing their move to San Miguel de Allende, "There are a lot of differences between U.S. and Mexican laws. There is no automatic right to inheritance for a wife, for example, and you are guilty until proven innocent." Or as Jorli McClain found out, the air in the jungle region of Costa Rica where she lived was pristine clean, but there are no pollution controls in that country, so on the roads and in the towns and cities where she had to shop, she found pollution levels nearly unbearable.

So, as Chris Kocourek advised, when it comes to legal protections, "don't take things for granted." Consult with a legal expert to get a short course in how the legal systems vary from that which you are familiar.

The threat of natural disasters is another safety issue to consider. The United States certainly has its share of tornadoes, hurricanes, floods, earthquakes, and forest fires. They occur virtually everywhere, but some places are clearly more prone to certain types of disasters than others. So it's a good idea to at least know which potential disasters you might encounter, determine how you feel about living with those types of risks, and what type of insurance protection, if any, you would have access to. General information about natural disasters by country is available at http://en.wikipedia.org/wiki/Category:Disasters_by_country, but you will need to investigate the specific areas you're interested in for particular risks and resources.

❑ *Health services and insurance.* Many have long thought of the United States as having the world's best health care, but these days fewer than 50 percent of

Americans are satisfied with the health care they receive. Many U.S. companies are even offering incentives to their employees to have major surgery and other health care needs handled in other countries because it costs far less and is of high quality. Still, we were surprised to learn that despite not being able to take advantage of Medicare when one moves to another country, none of the "Best Bet" countries we listed score low on health care. Half actually rated as tops.

The World Health Organization analyzed healthcare systems in 191 countries using five performance indicators. It found France provides the best overall health care, followed by Italy, Spain, Oman, Austria, and Japan. The report also showed the United States spends a higher portion of its gross domestic product on health than any other country, yet ranks 37 out of 191 countries on performance. The United Kingdom, on the other hand, spends just 6 percent of its gross domestic product on health services but ranks eighteenth for performance. Several small countries, San Marino, Andorra, Malta, and Singapore, rated close behind second-place Italy.

 Tips on Getting Health Insurance

Most U.S. health insurance companies won't cover U.S. citizens living abroad. You may be able to get government coverage in the country you choose or private insurance from companies there, usually quite reasonably. The following companies offer international coverage:

- ► Allianz Worldwide Care: www.allianzworldwidecare.com/EN/index.php
- ► AllNation Insurance Company: www.allnation.com
- ► Bupa: www.bupa-intl.com
- ► InsuranceToGo: www.insurancetogo.com
- ► Expacare International: www.expacare.net
- ► HI Denmark: www.ihi.com
- ► Goodhealth Worldwide Ltd.: www.goodhealth.co.uk
- ► Expatriate Health Insurance: www.expatriateinsurance.com

In Europe, health systems in Mediterranean countries such as France, Italy, and Spain are rated higher than others in the continent. Norway is the highest Scandinavian nation, at eleventh place. In Latin America, Colombia, Chile, Costa Rica, and Cuba are rated highest: twenty-second, thirty-third, thirty-sixth, and thirty-ninth in the world, respectively.

The upshot is that depending on your circumstances and the country you choose, you may well be able to obtain as good or better health care abroad for less cost. Consistent with these findings, those we interviewed for this book were satisfied, if not very pleased, with the health care available to them. Those we spoke to in Mexico and Panama, for example, reported that most of the doctors there were American trained. Some locales there and elsewhere have outstanding state-of-the-art medical facilities nearby.

Some expats told us they didn't need health insurance because they could pay for whatever health care they needed, including surgery, out-of-pocket for less than their monthly premiums had been in the United States. Others were able to participate in a state-supported health insurance system like Mexico's, which costs only a few hundred dollars a year. Nonetheless, explore the health service and insurance options thoroughly in any locale you are considering.

❑ *Red tape and convenience.* The United States is reputed to be the most convenient country in the world. We're pretty used to being able to do just about whatever we want when we want. We can even open a business by simply printing up a business card. This is not so everywhere. Not that we never encounter any bureaucratic governmental or institutional red tape in the United States. We do, but compared to many places, it is insignificant. In the first study of its kind, the World Bank looked into the relationship between bureaucratic red tape, corruption, and poverty and found that in general the more heavily regulated a country was and the more red tape required, the more corruption and poverty.

 Tips on Staying in Touch with Home

1. Some people discover the cost of making calls to U.S. family, friends, or business contacts becomes their biggest expense, so one way to enjoy staying in touch without breaking the budget is to use Internet telephony. Check out Vonage (www.vonage.com), Delta Three (www.deltathree.com), Net2phone (www.net2phone.com), or Skype (www.skype.com).
2. The United States is undoubtedly the easiest place in the world to get reasonably priced financing. In other places it's not so easy. In Latin America it's rare. So consider securing an equity loan on your U.S. home or using funds from an IRA or other retirement account as a means to finance the costs of your move.
3. For ordering online and through catalogs, it may be easier to keep a U.S. street address and have your mail forwarded monthly. This could be a friend's address or a street address provided by a mail-receiving service such as the UPS Store (www.theupsstore.com/index.html).

Countries where small businesses can be created the most quickly and cheaply, for example, tend to also be the most prosperous and the least corrupt.

Australia, Canada, New Zealand, Denmark, and the United States are ranked as the quickest, cheapest, and easiest places to start a new business and also rank among those with the least corruption. On the other hand, countries that make starting a business the most difficult and expensive, like Haiti, Indonesia, Brazil, Angola, and Venezuela, also rank highest for corruption.

But of course, regulations and fees relate not just to business, but also to what you must go through to become a resident, to bring a pet into the country, to buy property, to set up financial accounts and transfer money, or to make long-distance calls.

❏ *Climate.* Climate preferences are personal. One person's oasis or Shangri-La is another's Hades, be it too hot, too cold, too wet, or too dry. Those wishing to escape the long, cold, snowy winters of our northern-most states probably won't be happy with the six months of long, bitter, cold, dark winters of Estonia, Lithuania, and Romania—no matter how great the cost of living. On the other hand, countries like Belize, Brazil, and Panama may be too hot and humid for someone used to California's Mediterranean climate. Those who relish the four seasons may not be happy in Argentina's mostly year-round temperate climate. Costa Rico's seven-month rainy season may be just too much for some, while Bulgaria's hot, dry summers and cold, damp winters may be too wide an extreme for others.

You will find a short synopsis of the climates of countries around the world at www.ed-u.com/climate-of-countries.htm. But the only real way to know how you will feel about a country's climate is to experience it live and in person. Often that will mean arranging to be there at various times of year.

❏ *Culture.* U.S. culture is infiltrating many countries, so it's possible to buy into a new development or locate in an area of a foreign city where you'll feel like you are still in the United States with our many malls, golf courses, condos, and all. But for some, this is not the desired experience, and for everyone, it's not wise to assume you'll feel at home in another culture. We are all one world, but we don't all live the same way in "our" world. Each culture is unique.

Some countries, like Germany we hear, can be slower to warm to foreigners, for example. Others are less open to Americans and American culture. So it is important to learn as much as you can about a country's history, culture, traditions, institutions, values, and political orientations. Of particular importance are the customs, manners, and other definitions of proper and improper behavior, so you will not unintentionally offend your new compatriots.

❑ *A country's imperfections.* As you've seen from the examples in this checklist, choosing a country is like choosing a marriage partner. No one is perfect, but some are a much better match than others. So be sure to identify the imperfections of any country you are considering, and then decide if they are things you can live with.

Take Croatia. It has been dubbed the Tuscany of the Adriatic and is often compared to St. Tropez, with breathtaking beaches, beautiful untouched natural scenery, quaint villages and towns, one thousand islands reminiscent of Greece, and a reputation for a cuisine that rivals Italy's. As a tourist Mecca, outdoor sporting opportunities abound, from winter skiing to boating, biking, mountain climbing, and white-water rafting. Crime is low, and people are friendly. Many types of income from abroad are exempt from taxes, and once you are a resident, you can obtain the same inexpensive health care as local citizens. The coast of Croatia has a Mediterranean climate, with mild winters and dry summers. Financially it is positioned to be part of the European Union in 2007, so its economic future is promising.

Sounds ideal, yes? But concerns about a resurgence of political instability remain, the language is challenging (although more Croatians are speaking English), and you need to obtain permission from the government to buy property (this can take three to twelve months.) Travel conditions about the country can be patchy, property rates and taxes are rising, and continental Croatia has hot summers and cold winters.

Similar to finding a marriage partner, you shouldn't think you'll be able to change the country into the place you wish it to be. Make sure you can enjoy it *as is!*

❑ *Psychological barriers.* All the experts on living abroad, and all those we've spoken to who've done it, emphasize that moving to another country requires one to be open to adventure, flexible, determined, persistent, patient, comfortable with being something of an "outsider," and able to welcome the unexpected. For this reason most people find actually making the move and adjusting to a new way of life psychologically more difficult than they expected. Not that they regret their decision to move, just that it's more of an emotional challenge than moving from Kansas to California. So after you've done your homework and gathered all the information, advice, and firsthand experience you need, be honest with yourself. Are you up to this? If so, ride out the panic attacks we're told are inevitable at first and enjoy your new country.

Seven Steps to Gathering the Information You Need

Obviously there is a lot of information to gather when moving to another country. If it's not already a second home to you, where do you find all this info, and how do you go about gathering it? Here's what we recommend:

1. *Do an Internet search.* Review and collect as much information as you can about each of the issues we just named. Many sites feature articles and general information about a variety of countries, so you can compare and contrast a number of possibilities and narrow down your favorite(s). Most of these sites also abound with links to sites that contain detailed info about specific countries. In LEARN MORE at the end of this chapter, we list links to several of these general sites. They are an excellent place to begin your search. Look for the most often recommended books, tours, and other resources. Read the stories people have posted about their personal experiences living abroad. But be sure to check the dates of posted material, as much of the kind of information you need changes frequently and is time sensitive.

2. *Read the most popular books about countries you're interested in.* Amazon.com reviews a plethora of books on most of the popular countries where people are moving. Again, check the publication date to be sure a book is current. In LEARN MORE we list books with general information about moving abroad. All have been written since 2000 and have a four-star or above Amazon rating. They include overviews of many countries.

3. *Take a relocation or destination tour.* Of course, you can always find vacation tours to most countries, but there are also tours that are specially designed to acquaint people who are considering immigrating. *International Living* (www .internationalliving.com), for example, offers many such tours and conferences each year, featuring one or more of two dozen countries, such as Honduras, Croatia, Mexico, Panama, New Zealand, and Belize. Their tours and on-site workshops include presentations from tax specialists, immigration experts, real-estate companies, health care professionals, lawyers, and seasoned expatriates, as well as on-site tours of available real estate. Other destination tour companies specialize in a particular country, for example, Christopher Howard Costa Rica and Latin America tours (www.1costaricalink.com/eng/tours/relocation/ retirement.htm) and Red Beard's Tiki Tours of New Zealand (www.redbeard stikitours.com).

4. *Talk via e-mail with others* who have moved to the countries you are considering.

5. *Contact professionals* who specialize in dealing with the above issues in countries you're considering. You can locate them via the Internet, through tours, or by referrals from others who have moved there.

6. *Visit the country.* Need we say anything more about this?

7. ***Arrange to live there for a while,*** if possible, before making a permanent move. As Jorli McClain points out, visiting a country is not the same as living there. "Don't do what I did. Stay in the country a long time before actually moving there. Hang out; house-sit. Get to really know a place!" Here are a variety of ways to get that kind of firsthand feel for a country:

- ► Consider taking an extended vacation or a series of shorter vacations over a period of time.
- ► Rent your home to cover your mortgage or other costs while visiting.
- ► Do a housing exchange, or house swap, with someone from that country (www.homeexchange.com, www.homelink.org, www.intervac.com, www.digsville.com).
- ► Take a caretaking position (www.caretaker.org or www.property-caretaking-jobs.com). Also see Chapter 9: "Living Rent Free."
- ► Volunteer for the Peace Corps (www.peacecorps.gov/index.cfm?shell=learn).
- ► Do missionary or other volunteer work through your church.
- ► Take a short-term or summer job, find an internship, or arrange to study there.

Tips for Renting or House Swapping

If you rent out your home or do a house swap, be sure to take these protective steps:
1. Talk to others who have done it, to glean firsthand tips.
2. Let neighbors know about your plans, leave their numbers for your guests, and provide neighbors with contact information so they can contact you if they observe unusual activity at your home.
3. Leave emergency numbers for your guests, e.g., hospital, fire department, and household repair personnel, and written directions for operating various home appliances, heating, air-conditioning, etc.
4. Be sure your car and homeowner's insurance covers others using them.
5. Place valuables or private information in a locked closet or other area of your home.
6. Password protect computers, movie channels, or other equipment you do not want guests to use.

Guidelines for Creating an Independent Career Abroad

If you are thinking of starting or moving a business to another country, virtual or otherwise, here a few key suggestions from Ruth Holcomb, who founded the Network for Living Abroad (www.livingabroad.com):

Profile: A Butterfly Paradise

Ten years ago, when Costa Rica was suffering its most devastating economic crunch, resulting from dependence on agricultural exports such as coffee, bananas, and sugar, none of which are indigenous to the country, Joris Brinckerhoff, then a Peace Corps volunteer in Costa Rica, thought, *Why not export the best of Costa Rica—its beautiful natural history—in a way that doesn't destroy the environment but actually enhances it?* With his wife, Maria Sabido, Brinckerhoff converted a two-and-a-half-acre horse pasture into one of Latin America's first butterfly farms specifically intended to supply butterfly houses.

Stressing the importance of preserving the butterfly habitat, the couple trained local people in conservation methods and assembled a work force of native Costa Ricans. Eventually fifteen of these people started their own butterfly farms. The Brinckerhoffs also helped women in the area start a cottage industry making replicas of butterflies to sell to tourists.

Brinckerhoff manages the farm as much as possible for the benefit of wild butterflies, planting thousands of nectar and larval food plants, yet allowing most of the land to revert to functional rainforest. "It's a butterfly paradise," he explains. "The adults come in to get nectar, they fly a short distance, and they find a larval food plant to lay their eggs on." To maintain genetic diversity in his breeding stock, he brings wild adults into the netted breeding enclosures. The netting is not there to keep the butterflies in, but to keep predators out. In the wild, birds, lizards, spiders, ants, and parasitic wasps kill more than 90 percent of a butterfly's potential offspring by attacking eggs, larvae, and pupae, as well as adults. Within the farm, Brinckerhoff reverses the odds, losing only some 10 percent of his butterflies to the food chain.

For adult butterflies inside, it's business as usual as they fly about, feeding, mating, and laying eggs. Farm workers meticulously scour the plants daily to collect the eggs—some of them the size of a comma on this page—which will be sorted into labeled boxes. When the caterpillars hatch a few days later, they are placed on their species-specific food plant. Fresh cuttings are provided each day as the caterpillars alternately outgrow their skins and molt until they're ready to enter the chrysalis stage. At this point, most of the pupae are shipped to a distributor in England, while the rest are kept for breeding or released back into the wild. You can find out more about their butterfly farm at http://centralamerica.com/cr/butterfly/bflyfarm.htm.

1. *Choose your region or country as carefully* as you choose your type of business. You'd better have a passion for both to get past whatever obstacles and barriers you may encounter. It will be a definite asset to speak the language or to have studied or done volunteer work in the country.

One of Ruth's and our favorite examples is Joris Brinckerhoff, a Peace Corps volunteer in Costa Rica who stayed to develop a butterfly farm that sells to zoos and museums all over the world. Ruth also points out that from the Philippines to Poland, U.S. citizens are choosing to return to places where they, their parents, or grandparents were born, where the legalities of starting a business may be easier because of their roots or ties to their country of origin.

2. *Resolve to educate yourself about and adhere to the laws of your host country as well as those of the United States.* You probably won't need to become a citizen of another country, although the United States now allows dual citizenship, but most likely, you will need to become a legal resident. Early on, research regulations by contacting the embassy, the nearest consulate, trade commission, or the Chamber of Commerce. To remind us of the difference in national laws regulating business, Holcomb points out that in some countries, like the Czech Republic, you will need to have a local business partner.

3. *Forge personal relationships and connections at all levels.* Make contacts among officials, locals, and expats. Holcomb finds that in small countries like Belize, which has just three stoplights in the entire country, it's easier to have access to and relationships with ministers and other officials. Get to know other expats there, she urges, and seek their recommendations for the local professionals you'll need to know. Develop relationships with local tradespeople, potential neighbors, and as many people as you can. Outside of the United States, *whom* you know usually counts more than *what* you know.

4. *Bring more money than you think you'll need, and manage it wisely.* Think twice about having checks sent via the mail. Local banks may require you to be a legal resident of the country before you open an account, so you may want to use a mail-forwarding service, wire transfers, or a service such as PayPal (www.paypal .com). On the upside, Holcomb has found that the lower cost of living in many foreign countries allows more time to get a business up and running. Still, the cost of permits, legal fees, delays, or increased shipping, postage, and mail charges can eat up your capital.

5. *Be flexible.* Seems this is the living-abroad mantra. Holcomb urges that you have a backup plan, so if your first idea doesn't work out, you can readily move to something else. She also points out that the country of your dreams may not be the best setting for your business and suggests that the next best place may be a country bordering the one you fell in love with. Overall, learn to live with uncertainty of all kinds, and be open to new ideas.

6. *Be prepared for a different pace and different values.* Many Americans find it hard to appreciate that even in the business world, for many countries "mañana doesn't mean tomorrow. It just means not now." In much of the globe, people see no reason to be punctual or to hurry. Time isn't money. So adjust your attitude accordingly or you'll be unhappy. After all, isn't taking time to enjoy life a key aspect of the quality of life you want to attain?

7. *Respect the local language.* Memorize the words for "hello," "please," and "thank you," even if the language is as challenging as, say, Hungarian. A cursory attempt is better than nothing. Learn gestures, table manners, and proper behavior in the home and office. Don't wear resort wear where business attire is expected, and do learn to appreciate local food. Know something of the country's history, holidays, and national heroes.

Of course, even if you do everything perfectly, Holcomb reminds us, don't expect to blend in. Accept that you'll be seen as an outsider, perhaps even "the crazy foreigner" whom nobody really understands. Just remember the reasons you moved there in the first place and *"viva la difference!"*

 MAKING THE CHOICE TO LIVE ABROAD

When it comes to deciding to live abroad, what some people consider to be a pro may be a con for someone else, and vice versa, so put more weight on your own reactions to where you would place the items on this list than to where we've placed them.

Pros

- You may well be able to enjoy a higher standard of living while working and/or earning less.
- Life may be slower and less hectic.
- You may be able to afford property surrounded by astonishing natural beauty that only the rich can enjoy in the United States.
- Living abroad is an extended adventure for a lifetime.

Cons

- Moving to another country is a very big change and involves adapting to new laws, a new culture, and a new way of life.
- Life may not be as convenient.
- You most likely will have to bring your own income with you and still need to obtain work permits that must be renewed.
- You may have to learn a new language and yet remain somewhat of an outsider.

LEARN MORE

Books

- *Retiring Abroad*, Ben West, Cadogan Guides, 2005.
- *Work Abroad: The Complete Guide to Finding Work Overseas*, Clayton A. Hubbs, Transitions Abroad, 2002.
- *The Work Overseas Kit: Starting Your Own Overseas Business,* available only from www.ibookstore.com.
- *The World's Best, The Ultimate Book for the International Traveler,* available only from www.ibookstore.com.

Magazines & Newsletters
- *Escape from America*: www.escapeartist.com/efan/efan.htm
- *Transitions Abroad*: www.transitionsabroad.com/publications/magazine/archive.shtml
- *Living Abroad Magazine*: www.shelteroffshore.com/index.php/living/more/living_abroad_magazine

Organizations
- American Citizens Abroad, located in Arlington, Virginia, assists Americans abroad with information, advice, useful links, and country contacts: 1051 N. George Mason Dr., Arlington, VA 22205; Fax (703) 527-3269; jacabr@aol.com, www.aca.ch
- The Association of Americans Resident Overseas (AARO), 34 Avenue de New York, Paris 75116, works to secure, protect, and improve basic American rights for U.S. citizens overseas. Offers a group medical insurance plan and a quarterly newsletter. Active in facilitating absentee voting in U.S. federal elections. Phone 011-33-1-47-20-24-15, Fax 011-33-1-47-20-24-16, www.aaro.org

Agencies
- Consular Affairs: www.co.custer.id.us/Bureau%20of%20Consular%20Affairs,%20US%20Department%20of%20State.htm
- US Embassies, Consulates, and Diplomatic Missions: http://usembassy.state.gov

Web Sites
General Exploration
- www.contactexpats.com
- www.escapeartist.com
- www.expatreunion.com
- www.internationalliving.com
- www.liveabroad.com
- www.nationmaster.com
- www.transitionsabroad.com
- www.workandliveabroad.com
Worldwide Quality of Life Index
- www.shelteroffshore.com/index.php/living/more/living_abroad_magazine

Worldwide Tax Summary
- www.internationalliving.com/free_reports/03-02-06-world-tax.html
- www.worldwide-tax.com

Property Laws
- A Global Guide to Property Ownership Rules and Restrictions: www.internationalliving.com/free_reports/07-01-06-guide-to-property-ownership.html

Work Permits/Visas by Country
- Going Global: www.goinglobal.com/topic/work_permit.asp

*Caretaking is much more than a job—it is an attitude,
an ethic, a way of relating to all of life.*
Glen Horton III, Caretaker

CHAPTER NINE

Living Rent Free—
Room and Board in Inviting Locales

What if you could live rent free, or even get paid to live and work in one of the most exotic or exciting places in the world, the very place you've always dreamed of living? Sound too good to be true? Well, it's not, says Gary Dunn, publisher of the *Caretaker Gazette*, a newsletter that puts people in touch with caretaking opportunities across the globe.

Just imagine for a moment that you didn't have to worry about making rent or mortgage payments. What would you really like to do with your life? Write, paint, draw, sculpt, garden, care for animals, travel the world, farm the land, visit with friends, volunteer for a worthy cause? And where would you like to do that? In a tropical island paradise, a Mexican villa, a nature preserve, a lakeside fishing or hunting lodge, amid a national forest, in a coastal lighthouse, on a ranch in big sky country, a rural farm, an equestrian center, a natural healing center, an historic Spanish mining town turned resort, a riverside cabin, or maybe a nice home in your own hometown? Or would you rather sample a bit of all such lifestyles, never having to settle down to just one?

These are but a few possibilities the intriguing lifestyle of a caretaker offers. At times called home tenders, property managers, or inn sitters, caretakers mind and otherwise manage various and sundry aspects of someone else's property. The caretaker works in exchange for room, board, and utilities and, depending on the scope of responsibilities involved, often also receives a stipend, fee, or salary ranging from several hundred dollars to, in rare cases, six-figure incomes. Some positions include health and other standard benefits.

Dunn points out that about 50 percent of caretaking positions are long-term, while others are for shorter periods and require greater flexibility. But caretaking is not the same as house-sitting for a weekend here and there. It is an increasingly popular career and way of life. In some positions you can run your own virtual business from a home office where you're working, and usually you will have ample free time to pursue personal interests.

Dunn, who is without question the leading authority in this field, points out that this way of life is best suited to reliable, mature individuals. But it's ideal for dependable singles, couples, and in some cases even families who want to escape the fast-track job world to enjoy and concentrate on other things that are more important to them. For example, Patricia Roukens and her partner, Pat Frost, lost their jobs in the electronics industry, but Patricia didn't really want another job. "I've always wanted to be an artist," she explains. They both wanted to live in Arizona, so when the couple saw an ad seeking a caretaker and handyperson for property five miles into the high mountain woods of Arizona, they applied and got the position. They have lived there now for fourteen years, and Patricia also works as a sculptor and stained-glass artist. "I'm living my dream," she says.

A passion for writing led Cynthia Morgan to caretaking. After graduating from college with a degree in education, she wanted to try her hand at writing a novel before taking a teaching position. *Who can write their best*, she thought, *after a long day of working and commuting*? So when the placement office suggested caretaking, it seemed like a good way to have a year or two to write. Her wages were only three hundred dollars per month, but, as she points out, it doesn't take as much money to get by if you don't have to pay for rent or a mortgage. Little did she know that taking this simple job would change her way of life.

Since then, thanks to listings in the *Caretaker Gazette* and on www .caretaker.com, where you can read more about Cynthia, she has lived in many lovely locales she would never have been able to afford on a teacher's salary: a cottage on a vineyard, a mountain cabin, a mansion, and a riverside resort in California's Big Sur. Her tasks as caretaker have included housecleaning, cooking, taking phone reservations, greeting guests, banking, shopping and other errands, and gardening and mowing the lawn, among others.

The caretaker way of life has also afforded her access to swimming pools, hot tubs, tennis courts, and even a complimentary country club membership. But for Cynthia, the biggest benefit is time, blocks of time to think and write without interruptions. "I get to own my own brain!" she says. Even the work itself can be a benefit, because interspersing physical activities with writing clears the mind and provides a needed shift from sitting at the computer.

Don Cole was a successful architect who'd grown weary of the administrative demands of his profession. "I'd become a slave to my practice," he remembers, so he started to look for ways he could continue to live well while keeping his expenses low enough to close his practice. His solution was to house-sit vacant properties in the Houston area where he lives. Don deals only with owners of vacant investment properties or owners who have moved away without having sold their homes. He requires that the house be emptied of belongings and then fills the house with his own furniture and artworks. He pays for utilities and takes care of upkeep.

Since Don doesn't have a home of his own, in between homes, he uses a storage warehouse for his belongings and finds the ebb and flow of "stuff" he owns to be less stressful than the responsibility of owning a houseful of things. "I look at this as a lifestyle, a way of living well for less," he says. It also provides time to take on choice creative architectural projects and to do some writing, golfing, and socializing. "Consider me a vagabond," he says of his lifestyle.

Dave and Sumana Harrison McCollum needed a break from the rat race, so they phased out their catering and bookkeeping businesses and left for an extended RV vacation through Mexico. They loved Mexico's beauty, charm, and friendliness and really didn't want to leave. Stumbling upon the *Caretaker Gazette*, they subscribed and in the first issue found a listing for a position managing a forty-acre property in the mountains nearby the colonial city of Casa Raab. Like many caretakers, their roles are varied. "Living here is like taking care of your own home. You see what needs to be done, and you do it," says Sumana. They love the slower pace of Mexico, where "people generally have less, but give more. Here in this village it's like turning back the clock one hundred years." No phones ringing, no schedules, and always time to visit with guests.

Virginia Doser is one of the few professional inn sitters in the United States. She began her career fourteen years ago as a favor for two friends in their hometown of Emporia, Kansas. Like most innkeepers and B&B owners, her friends needed a vacation, so Virginia stepped in to help. She enjoyed the experience so much that she signed on for an intensive inn-sitting workshop to see if it might be a possible new career. Having been a librarian for twenty years, she decided it would be a refreshing change. She's been inn-sitting ever since.

On any given day, Virginia's duties might include all or some of the following tasks: greeting guests, taking telephone and in-person reservations, sending out confirmations, giving brief tours of the inn to people who stop by, cooking and serving breakfast and afternoon snacks, shopping and banking, housekeeping, laundry, pet care, and light gardening, if needed.

Over the years Virginia has managed small inns with no guests, larger inns with twelve to fifteen guests, and has traveled the world from the United States and Canada to Europe, China, Australia, and New Zealand. During quiet times, she indulges her interests in collecting and using unique and vintage cookbooks, embroidery and needlepoint, early Renaissance music, writing short stories, and yoga. But her favorite part of this itinerant lifestyle is the interesting and diverse people she has met around the world.

For some, caretaking is a way to get back to nature. For example, for the Chamberlands, father Les, son Richard, and daughter-in-law Earleen, it means managing the Boise National Forest, known for its hot springs and kayaking heaven. This involves checking campsites, looking for fires, collecting visitor fees, bookkeeping, checking pumps and testing water supplies, and responding to and calling in emergencies in primitive woods. The family lives out of their own RV and pays their own expenses, but they receive a monthly salary and overtime pay at time and a half. Best of all, says Les, it means meeting new friends every day. For others, caretaking can be an opportunity to learn self-reliance and survival skills for the time when they will be able to acquire land of their own and become self-sustaining.

Hopefully this brief collage of caretaker stories illustrates how varied the types of work, tasks, and opportunities are that this lifestyle offers. But truly, this is only the smallest taste of the range of interesting possibilities. You can read more about some of the people we've mentioned and many others on www.caretaker.org.

Caretaking Is Ideal For Individuals and Couples Who are self-directed, dependable, honest, and flexible, especially those who:

- ▶ need time to create without becoming starving artists (like painters and writers)
- ▶ want to live on acreage but can't afford to buy land
- ▶ seek a slower, more natural way of life
- ▶ yearn to live and work close to nature
- ▶ need free time for family or community, that traditional employment doesn't allow
- ▶ yearn to live in lots of different places

- ▶ want to try out living in a new locale or another country before committing to moving or purchasing property
- ▶ wish to pursue activities for a living that they would otherwise have to squeeze in as a hobby
- ▶ want to pursue a home business that can't produce a dependable full-time income
- ▶ prefer to do a variety of work and learn to do a lot of different kinds of things
- ▶ are RVers who'd like to take periodic breaks from life on the road

[This] field is growing, attracting recent college graduates and refugees from the rat race, as well as artists, writers, and craftspeople—all of whom like to do their own thing when the day's chores are done.

Kiplinger's Personal Finance

Growing Caretaking Possibilities to Consider

A number of trends are feeding an expanding demand for caretakers. One is a recent surge in second home sales. In 2005 alone Americans snapped up a record number of 3.4 million second homes for vacation and investment purposes, says the National Association of Realtors (NAR). Second homes now account for over 40 percent of all residential sales. As NAR chief economist David Lereah points out, the baby boom generation is driving these sales. Boomers are at their peak of earnings, interest rates on mortgages are historically low, and many want and need to diversify their investments.

As Gary Dunn, publisher of the *Caretaker Gazette,* explains, with "Baby Boomers entering and nearing retirement, we see more are opting for multiple homes and properties, not only in the United States but also internationally." Such properties may be everything from a condo in Vail, a house in a middle-class resort development, or a mansion on a vast spread of land that backs onto a national forest, lake, or river. Mansions, of course, are not the majority, but modest or majestic, they are almost always in geographically interesting locales. As we've described in previous chapters, yet another major trend is the growing preference to vacation and retire away from urban congestion and bad weather in favor of out-of-the-way, naturally desirable places.

Whether multiple property owners have opted for farms, ranches, retreats, investment, resort, or vacation property, they often need someone to take care of and protect their additional homes when they're not there. This is especially true with the recent rise in security concerns and the upswing of rural crime. In the aftermath of 9/11, many insurance companies will no longer insure unoccupied property. But as Gary Lebo of Gypsum, Colorado, knows, there is plenty else homeowners need help with as well. Lebo once sold second homes but had so many buyers ask him to help care for their new homes that he opened Alpenglow Property Management, which he describes as a kind of do-everything local concierge service. Lebo claims to have seen and heard just about every request imaginable, from chartering planes to pet-sitting.

A growing concern for the environment is yet another trend fueling caretaking opportunities. Both individuals and public and private institutions are buying land to reclaim and restore to its natural habitat, as well as to provide research and education on land reclamation.

Such trends all contribute to the growing list of differing kinds of caretaking opportunities, including:

- B&Bs, lodges, and inns
- Farms
- Camps
- Elderly households
- Fisheries
- Homesteads
- National and state parks
- Nature and ecological preserves
- Ranches
- Vacant realtor properties
- Retreat centers
- Real estate investment properties
- Second homes and other holdings of absentee landowners

Where to Start in Deciding if Caretaking Is for You

So before beginning to look for a caretaking position, consider just what kind of caretaking lifestyle would best suit you. As in any position, experience and references can be important, so you may not be able to start off in your *ideal* caretaking situation. Many positions are seeking individuals with specific skills, some need generalists, and others are open to honest, dependable newcomers. Use the following checklist to clarify where you want to end up so you get as close to your goals as soon as possible.

❏ *Type of locale.* What type of geographical and demographic area would you prefer? For example, do you want to live and work in an urban, rural, wilderness, or resort-type setting? Do you want to live in the United States or other countries? What type of climate do you prefer?

❏ *Type of work.* Do you want to work primarily indoors or outdoors? What are your skill sets? There are positions for such varied skills as driving; housekeeping; maintaining and repairing things; hauling; tending, training, or husbandrying animals; gardening and farming, organic and traditional; construction; planning and coordinating activities or tours; operating heavy equipment; stewardship; cooking; bookkeeping; undertaking capital improvements; budgeting and financial management; and more.

So usually there is a way to find a fit for your particular interests and talents. One position can lead to another that's either similar or quite different. Bruce Weaver, for example, was a personal trainer. His first caretaking position involved providing physical training, nutrition guidance, and meal preparation for a handicapped man in Cuernevaca, Mexico. Since then he has worked as a groundskeeper and mechanic for a spiritual retreat center and year-round manager of a Jewish summer camp.

❏ *Amenities.* Are you looking for comfort, luxury, and convenience, or are you happy with a more Spartan way of life, or even roughing it a bit? And just how much roughing it can you take? How about privacy and space? Just how much do you need, and what amenities are important to you? Ohioans Cynde and Pete Pangas's first caretaking position was tending a twelve-acre botanical garden in Hana, a secluded Hawaiian village paradise on the island of Maui. But their tiny tin cottage was forty feet from the restroom, and the only shower was outdoors. They loved it!!! Would you?

❏ *Financial considerations.* With the cost of housing (mortgage payments, taxes, and utilities) eating up a fifth to a third of most people's incomes, caretaking can dramatically reduce how much income one needs and free up a lot of time or money to pursue other activities. But actual financial arrangements for caretaking vary greatly. Fees are usually commensurate with duties required and may take the form of a stipend, a monthly fee, or hourly wage. If you are simply occupying the house or doing very light care, for example, compensation may be room and board only. But when considerable responsibility is required, a fee, salary, or wage is included.

Bruce and Kristen Weaver, for example, work as year-round caretakers for a Jewish summer camp in the biggest Ponderosa forest in the world. They live rent-free in a large home and receive a full salary with benefits and an annual bonus. Some positions will include utilities and use of a car; others leave that up to you. Household managers can earn thirty-five to seventy-five thousand dollars a year; estate managers eighty-five to more than two hundred thousand a year. Long-term, higher-paying positions usually require experience or a specialized background.

So just what do you need? Do you have access to medical insurance? Student loans to pay off? Alimony or college tuition to pay? How little or much do you *need*?

❏ *Isolation or socialization.* Do you want to work with guests and visitors? Or do you prefer solitude? Unless you are working strictly off-season, caretaking at camps, inns, lodges, national parks, and retreat centers usually involves interacting with guests, visitors, and other staff.

❏ *Duration and scheduling.* Are you truly a vagabond? If so, you can take a number of shorter-term positions, moving from one kind of off-season facility to another. Or would you prefer longer-term positions from a year to a dozen years or more? Do you need large blocks of free time each day for other activities, or can you enjoy a flexible schedule? Will there be periods when you must vacate, as in when the owner comes for holidays? Where can you arrange to go during such times? Are there times of year you need to be elsewhere?

❏ *Physical stamina and special needs.* The more unencumbered, physically fit, and flexible one is, the greater number and types of caretaking possibilities that will be open to you. But, as there is such a wide range of tasks needed, it's important to weigh what type of tasks you have the physical strength to undertake and how many possessions you want or need to bring with you. Do you have pets or children? Do you plan to have a home business while caretaking? Do you have special dietary, health, or communication needs?

Worried about just how many possessions you really need? Take a weeklong cruise, or talk with others who have, and find out. When most of life's necessities are provided by the facility where you live, you will be amazed at how few possessions you need.

Best Ways to Find a Caretaking Position

1. *Word of mouth.* Once you have a track record of being a capable, reliable caretaker, it's possible that you will have opportunities for other positions presented to you. It can still be a challenge, though, to line up a new position at the precise time you are completing another one, so even with an outstanding reputation, you may not be able to rely completely on word-of-mouth referrals.

2. *Local ads, placement, and employment agencies.* Like Patricia Roukens and Pat Frost, you may sometimes find a position advertised in the classifieds of a local newspaper, or like Cynthia Morgan, you may find one through a placement office. Such listings, however, are usually more limited and/or sporadic.

3. *Subscribing to the* Caretaker Gazette. This unique newsletter contains listings for property caretaking and house-sitting opportunities, as well as advice and information both for those seeking a position and for property owners who are seeking caretakers. Published since 1983, it's the only publication in the world dedicated just to the property caretaking field. New listings come in through their Web site, www.caretaking.org, on a daily basis, and they now also send out e-mail updates to subscribers almost daily.

We find this is the most dependable source of positions, because it features such a continually wide range of fresh national and international listings. Even well-established caretakers subscribe and follow these listings, especially when a current position is ending, but also because any day a more desirable position may beckon. Here's a taste of the many kinds of positions you can find listed there:

ALASKA

CARETAKER NEEDED late September to May on a self-sufficient, comfortable Aleutian homestead. Free housing and stipend. Orcas, eiders, sea otters, caribou, hydroelectric power, Internet, loom, hot tub. Writers and naturalists have prospered here.

AUSTRALIA

HOUSE SITTERS needed on the Great Keppel Island to look after a holiday house. Live in flat available, perfect for a couple.

CALIFORNIA

HOUSE GUEST(S) wanted to occupy a mountain cottage(s). Full-time. Located in the foothills, one hour from Sacramento. Bottom of canyon. Four miles from freeway. You can fish off the porch. Keep all gold found in the river. Must love outdoors, remoteness. Pets permitted. References required. No job. No addictions.

MEXICO

HOUSE SITTERS of adventuresome spirit, Europeans, jet setters, retirees, caretakers. Discover unspoiled Alamos, Sonora's city of silver in semitropical Sierra Madre Mountains. Live in 250-year-old Spanish colonial mansions. Experience a unique community. The Santa Fe of Mexico. Little theater, tennis courts, bridge club, poker, chess, municipal airport.

NEW MEXICO

HELP WANTED year-round to caretake home, property, and pets (one dog, six cats). Thirty-seven-acre property halfway between Santa Fe and Taos, bordered by the Rio Grande. Two-bedroom, recently remodeled home (unfurnished), plus utilities offered, as well as negotiated salary.

U.S. VIRGIN ISLANDS

CARETAKER positions available on St. John in a hillside community. Free housing and a 40 percent meal discount are available. Anyone aged eighteen to eighty is eligible to apply. We have short- and long-term time frames available.

WASHINGTON

NEED CARETAKER or handyman or woman or couple to help on 8.5-acre farm and inn on Orcas Island. Person or persons need their own tools to do fence mending, landscaping, light plumbing, light electrical. Lots of landscaping and gardening in small orchard garden. Have just purchased property and need help getting it into shape. Have some tools but not for carpentry jobs, etc. Person will work with animals, ducks, geese, miniature horses, etc. Will exchange room or guest cottage for work.

AND OUR PERSONAL FAVORITE!!

HORSE FARM MANAGER needed in Colorado. Salary: based upon experience and résumé. We are searching for a caretaker couple to manage a two-hundred-acre hay and tree farm and twelve-horse barn and arena. Must be avid horse people with experience in all aspects of general horse care, including vet care and purchasing and maintaining stock, supplies, and tack. Riding instruction experience. This position will entail some traveling and trailering to Wyoming. Other duties include, but are not limited to: maintenance and upkeep of ranch houses, barns, and owner's homes, with experience in landscaping; maintenance and repair of farm equipment; mowing, haying, and tree farm upkeep; and supervision of day laborers. Modern four-bedroom home provided on-site, with vehicles included. Room for two personal horses. Health care and 401K benefits provided. A background check will be preformed prior to employment. Long-term experience and references required.

4. *Checking Internet ad sites.* There are other sites such as www.craigslist.com, www.monster.com, and www.jobster.com where you can place positions wanted and search for help wanted opportunities. Also, retreat centers, camps, and ecological preserves may place ads on their own Web sites, so you can Google for such facilities and look for opportunities. Interim Innkeepers also links its membership to inn-sitting positions at www.interiminnkeepers.net.

5. *Marketing yourself as an independent professional.* While you may obtain salaried positions as a caretaker, you needn't think of yourself as "in the job market." Caretakers are best cast as independent professionals. As such, you aren't so much job hunting as you are seeking clients to serve. That is certainly how Virginia Doser approached her new inn-sitting career. She set herself up as an independent business. To get started she created an attractive, informative brochure and began mailing them directly to inn and B&B owners.

Don Cole does hometending for owners of investment properties or people in the Houston area who have moved away without selling their homes. He launched his new career by working directly through local realtors and other owners. Of course, as a professional caretaker, you can and should take advantage of all the options we've mentioned.

OUR ADVICE

1. Identify a niche or specialty you can capitalize on based upon your experience, background, and interests. It might be a particular type of work, setting, or expertise, from gardening or organic cooking to leading nature tours or maintaining electrical engineering systems. And remember, in this field, being a generalist, or jack-of-all trades, is itself a specialty. Of course, unless you choose, you need not allow this niche to limit the type of positions you take, but when you are getting started, it can be helpful in targeting whom to contact and how to reach out to them.

2. Invest in a notebook computer you can take with you wherever you are located to keep your own personal and financial records and to set up a Web site featuring your experience, background, and interests. You can send prospective clients or employers to your site and keep in touch with past and present contacts through blogs, e-zines, or e-mail.

3. Have an attorney draw up a general contract template you can customize and present to an owner who doesn't present you with one. Usually if your position is for other than the briefest period, the owner will provide you with a contract covering the duties and responsibilities of both parties. But remember, such contracts will be written from the perspective of protecting the owner. So by having a template contract your lawyer has drafted to protect *you*, you'll be able to compare and contrast any contracts with this basic one and can negotiate any important issues. For other than short-term positions, one such protection you'll want to be included, for example, is a thirty-day cancellation notice that will allow you time to find another position and to relocate. You are within your rights to make modifications or additions to contracts presented to you. Your changes or additions will, of course, have to be reviewed and accepted by the other party, and at times you may have to negotiate these details. A written contract seals on paper the details that have been discussed and agreed upon in personal conversations.

   Be willing to go to the location beforehand at your own expense. Verbal and written descriptions, even Web photos, can never provide the full picture you'll get from firsthand experience.

4. Owners for longer-term positions may want to obtain, or have you obtain, a performance bond. A bond provides assurance to clients that work you contract for will be satisfactorily completed or that they will be compensated for any losses arising from your inability to complete agreed-upon work. It is *not* an insurance policy. This is an important distinction. For example, a bond will not pay for property damage or personal injury resulting from your being on a client's premises. For this, you or the owner will need other conventional insurance coverage. Usually bonding companies will only provide bond coverage in an amount that can be covered with the existing liquid assets of the person being bonded. Speak with a qualified insurance agency as to what is available to you and review other types of insurance you should consider. A less costly way to protect yourself is to be sure the owner has obtained a performance bond and homeowners insurance that covers accidents and inadvertent damage to their property arising from your living there.

5. Obtain a storage locker for belongings you cannot take with you or need to store in-between placements.

MAKING A CHOICE FOR CARETAKING

PROS

- ► Caretaking can be a temporary or long-term way to afford the particular kind of life you dream of.
- ► There are many possible ways to use your unique skills, background, and interests.
- ► Flexibility abounds as to place, hours, type of work, and payment possibilities.
- ► There are many opportunities to learn new skills if you desire.
- ► You are freed from the encumbrance of buying, taking care of, and becoming enslaved to supporting lots of material possessions.

CONS

- ► You will be living in/on someone else's property, and he can decide he no longer needs your services.
- ► You will need to have a "service first" orientation to enjoy this lifestyle.
- ► Generally you will have to be present on the property much of the time.
- ► Unless you find a long-term position, you will need to have an eye out for future placements.
- ► You may not be able to have all the possessions you value with you. Pets, family, and other personal needs may limit what positions you can take.

Learn More

Books

- ► *Innkeeper to Innsitter Manual*, Sallie Clark and Lynn Mottaz, Innsittter Consultants, 1999.
- ► *Innsights: An Innsitter's Tale*, R. J. Riggs, PublishAmerica, 2004.

Newsletter

- ► *The Caretaker Gazette*: (830) 336-3939, www.caretaker.org. Subscriptions are $29.95/year.

Seminars, Training, and Certification

- ► Meadows Bed & Breakfast Inn-sitting Seminars: www.bbonline.com/innkeeper/meadows
- ► Professional Domestic Services and Institute is a home study program: (614) 839-4357, www.housestaff.net
- ► Starkey International Institute for Household Management Inc.: (800) 888-4904, www.starkeyintl.com
- ► The International Butler Academy (www.butlersguild.com), located in the Netherlands, can be contracted through the International Guild of Professional Butlers. They also have a reading list.

Organizations

▸ Interim Innkeepers Network (www.interiminnkeepers.net) is a
   nonprofit organization of professional innkeepers who are available
   for short- or long-term posts.

Web Sites

▸ www.caretaker.org
▸ www.craigslist.org/about/cities.html
▸ www.housecarers.com
▸ www.jobster.com
▸ www.thinklocal.com

We are the vagabonds of time,
Willing to let the world go by,
With joy supreme, with heart sublime,
And valor in the kindling eye.
William Bliss Carman,
The Vagabond

CHAPTER TEN

Traveling the Land or Sea—
Dashboarding, Workamping, and Live-aboard Boating

Like so many couples, Rick and Terry Russell were working seventy to eighty hours a week, busily climbing the ladder to success. As they describe in their *Gypsy Journal,* www.gypsyjournal.net, they already had all the toys that come with success: a beautiful home with a sunken hot tub, a huge collection of antiques, a minivan, a four-wheel-drive pickup truck, and a classic car collection in a custom-built garage. With a bit of gypsy in both their souls, the Russells' ultimate dream was to someday buy a motor home and travel full-time.

But someday seemed awfully far away until the end of one particularly exhausting day. Sitting across from each other at the dinner table, they asked themselves, "Why are we doing this?" Rick had already had one heart attack at age forty-six. What, they wondered, was the use of working for all these possessions if they didn't have the time or energy to enjoy them? And what fun would it be to end up as the richest people in the graveyard?

That's how Rick and Terry decided they would join the over one million people who are full-time RVers and become one of growing numbers of what the site www.trendwatching.com calls *transumers,* folks who are living an increasingly transient lifestyle and freeing themselves from the hassles of permanent ownership and possessions.

After careful soul-searching and ample preparation, Rick and Terry traded their big house full of stuff for a thirty-six-foot motor home with all the comforts they enjoy most in a home, including a satellite dish TV, washer and dryer, and side-by-side refrigerator and freezer. With Rick's experience as an editor for several small-town community newspapers, Terry's background in commercial windshield repair, and their shared knack for antiquing, the couple was confident they could earn a living on the road. In 1998 they closed their two businesses and began traveling full-time. They're still on the road and share their expertise in the RV travel newspaper the *Gypsy Journal.*

But, no, they didn't retire. Like so many of today's full-time vagabonds, they live and *work* on the road. They are what Steve and Kathy Jo Anderson call *workampers.* The Andersons, publishers of *Workamper News,* coined this term in 1987 to refer to the rapidly growing number of adventuresome souls choosing a lifestyle that combines some kind of full- or part-time work with traveling and living in a motor home.

Note there is no mention in this definition of either the word *retirement* or the word *camping.* A full-time life on the road is no longer just for those who can afford to retire. In fact, less than half of full-time RVers consider themselves retired. Their average age is forty-nine. They are families, singles, and couples of all ages, with an average income of fifty-six thousand dollars, which means they are both living and working on the road, sometimes with young children, pets, and even horses.

Megan Edwards and Mark Sedenquist refer to themselves as *dashboarders,* a word they coined to describe working on the road, using wireless Web access. They hit the road full-time thirteen years ago after their home, their business, and everything they owned went up in smoke in a devastating California wildfire. Traveling the country from coast to coast with their dog in a custom, seven-ton, four-wheel-drive mobile home/office, Megan remade herself as a writer, columnist, and publisher; Mark founded his own marketing company, designing and producing national public relations tours for corporate clients. Together they launched www.roadtripamerica.com, a premier dashboarding site.

Eight years ago, Ed and Cheryl Nodland began traveling full-time in their thirty-two-foot RV with their two sons, Mitch and Max, now thirteen and eleven, and their dog, Cocoa. In their midforties, Ed and Cheryl both worked, Ed for Boeing Company, Cheryl as a software developer in her own freelance computer services business. They had a beautiful home, and by most any definition, a successful life. But after twenty years it seemed that every day had become the same. Get up, go to work, come home, and repeat the process. It was as if life was passing them by. Over a two-year period they decided there had to be more to life than routine. They wanted to live more, spend more time with their children, and be more involved with their educations.

Ed left his job, and Cheryl took her business on the road. "All I need is a phone and satellite link," explains Cheryl. "Our cost of living is lower, so we can easily live on one paycheck." So Cheryl has become a traveling telecommuter and employs three other moms who work from home. Together she and Ed "road-school" their boys, otherwise known as homeschooling, all in the comforts of an up-to-date life/work/education center that includes three networked Pentium computers, a dual satellite dish with two receivers, and built-in stereo with three-way speakers throughout their living room, kitchen, bath, and bedrooms. Cheryl's office is in one of their three extensions, or slide outs, that expand the living space when their mobile home is parked.

The Nodlands believe life is the best classroom, so what better way to learn than to travel the country? They are proponents of what is called *unschooling*, a natural learning method promulgated by pioneering educator John Holt. As described in *Live Free Learn Free* magazine, www.livefreelearnfree.com, unschooling involves trusting children to learn what they need to know from the real world when they are ready and helping them find and follow their own interests, forge their own paths, and pursue their innate abilities. Natural learning is thus unhindered by curriculum, lunch bells, standardized tests, schoolyard bullies, and tedious homework.

Eager to share what they've learned about their mobile family life, the Nodlands also operate a Web site for other families living or wanting to live on the road, www.road-school.com. Their Web site also includes information on how they had their RV prewired with solar panels to operate their home on the road more efficiently (www.road-school.com/acintro.htm).

For Janine and Jim Wilder, the irresistible call of the road came from their two greatest loves: horses and travel. Over the past twenty years, they've ridden their horses over thousands of miles throughout all of the lower forty-eight states and trailered them for hundreds of thousands of miles. Five years ago they decided to pursue these passions full-time. Jim retired from his job; sold their North Carolina home; bought a Class A motor home, a pickup truck, and horse trailer; and they hit the road full-time. When they move from place to place, Jim drives the motor home, and Janine drives the truck. They keep in touch with each other through CB or ham radios.

"Our home is literally where our horses are," says Janine, author of *Trail Riding—A Comprehensive Guide to Enjoying Your Horse Outdoors*. "Our life is a great equestrian adventure." Together Janine and Jim share their experiences through their Web site, www.horsetravel.com, and offer clinics, lectures, book signings, and trail rides along the way.

For Maria Santa Cruz and Chris Van Over, the call of the sea drew them from their jobs in Southern California to the Pacific Northwest. They are live-aboard boaters. Both are cancer survivors, and their illnesses played a large part in the decision to quit their jobs and live full-time in a twenty-three-foot, six-by-seven Drifter. Initially, Chris thought he was probably dying. That being the case, he wanted to cruise the Washington coast, where he could die with the orcas and eagles.

Using 401K funds, they began simply cruising without renting a slip where they could dock their boat. But Chris didn't die. In fact, he recovered, so they rented a boat slip in Anaconda, Washington, where they work part-time locally and sail the rest. "Living on the boat took some adjusting to," says Maria. She missed having space and all her "stuff." "It gets cramped at times," she admits. "We get in each other's face sometimes." Learning to cook on a two-burner propane stove and Coleman folding oven was a challenge too. Storage is really tight, and Maria finds it hard to have hobbies on a boat. But it's been more than three years now, and this couple loves their life on the sea. "It's very cozy in our boat and very spiritual being so close to nature," they explain.

Janet and Barry Acker live aboard a boat, too, but not in the relatively warm waters of the Pacific Northwest. They are East Coast boaters, Portland, Maine, to be precise, where, as they explained to KTLA news and the *Los Angeles Times* (4/16/06), frigid weather means "shrink-wrapping" a forty-two-foot sailboat in the winter. Janet manages a chain of drive-through gourmet coffee shops almost entirely by phone and laptop at their dinner table. Barry is an educator and president of the Landing School, a vocational education program offering career opportunities as designers, builders, or systems technicians of both recreational and commercial watercraft.

Like other full-time boaters, they find marine life to cost less than conventional living onshore. Like RVers, boaters either own their boats or pay mortgage payments. Instead of park fees, they pay slip or mooring fees, which vary by length of the boat. The Ackers pay fifty-six hundred dollars a year for their spot at South Port Marine in Maine.

As Maria points out, space can be tight, but cozy and comfy, with electricity, plumbing, heaters and primitive galleys, sometimes just a hot plate and cooler. Galleys in larger boats, while rarely as spacious as the typical kitchen in a single-family home, come equipped with the typical culinary basics of stoves, refrigerators, and microwaves. Janet says that maneuvering in their galley is like dancing skillfully with one's partner. But she bakes pies and cookies in the microwave and has even cooked dinner parties for eleven on their propane stove. Like other live-aboarders, the Ackers love being outdoors and at one with the ocean and the elements of nature. They enjoy the smell of ocean breeze, the beautiful sunsets, and most especially—the nonstop motion of the tides, whether they're rocking gently or rockin' and rollin'.

Whether they call themselves dashboarders, workampers, full-time RVers, or live-aboard boaters, all these folks have decided they don't want to wait until someday to follow their dreams to travel. And they're finding that life on the road not only allows them to visit places they've always wanted to go, but also frees them from the burdens of supporting so much stuff, allowing them to work less and live more. And, say Steve and Kathy Jo Anderson, editors of

Workamper News, this lifestyle comes with some pretty neat perks, such as tax-free RV spaces or, if you operate a business while on the road, many of your traveling and living expenses may be tax deductible.

Interesting Trend Predictions

Real estate professional Marguerite Hampton predicts a future she already sees unfolding. Growing numbers of people, she predicts, will pay cash to purchase a full-time recreational vehicle, situate it in an attractive locale, and set up very low-maintenance lives for themselves, with lower taxes and little overhead to worry about. As she points out, outfitted with solar panels, a composting toilet, and a swamp cooler, one can camp almost anywhere there is a food supply and fresh water. She predicts motors will be reengineered to run off either gas or biofuels, thus eliminating the full-time RVers' high fuel costs.

Hampton also predicts others will be purchasing boats, outfitting them for living aboard, and setting out to navigate coastal waterways. She even foresees a time when merchants will establish large sailing vessels that can be anchored conveniently offshore to service the needs of live-aboards who will congregate nearby to avail themselves of needed services.

"The fortunate ones," says Hampton, "will be those unhampered by a permanent residence and mortgage, leaving them fluid, flexible, and prepared for almost anything."

Her view of the future may not be so far away. The Web site www.boatstogo.com already reports a growing demand for livea-board boats among first-time home buyers who can't afford to break into the all-time-high cost of the housing market.

Supporting the Journey

People who are living on the road or at sea fall into several categories:

1. those who keep moving most of the time, living on retirement income or income from their own virtual businesses
2. those who stop between travels and live locally for varying periods of time, usually taking short-term local jobs
3. those who live in their RV or boat but work year-round in one location, such as a national park, resort, marina, aquarium, camp, nature preserve, racetrack, ranch, etc.

If like most folks, you can't rely entirely or at all on savings or retirement income, you'll find the types of work one can do while living on the road are surprisingly varied. For some, doing what they most love and do best can actually be done more easily and profitably from the road. If, for example, you are an entertainer or performer of any kind, for example, singer, musician, storyteller, and so forth, you can not only save a lot of money by traveling full-time but also take gigs you couldn't otherwise afford. This is also true of public speakers, trainers, and on-site consultants, especially anyone wanting to serve nonprofit or religious organizations and other clients who cannot afford expensive airfare and lodging but can otherwise pay for expert services they need.

Artists who exhibit at expos and fairs can also benefit from living on the road, although they will have to make special space accommodations for a workshop, storage, and collapsible displays. Living on the move is enabling not only for travel writers, but also for freelance writers, journalists, and photographers who wish to cover interesting, unique stories. Think also of the benefits for authors and ghostwriters who need to interview people for their books, as well as for those who wish to do workshops, media appearances, and book signings across the country. Book tours, highly expensive when done traditionally by flying from city to city, become feasible when you are traveling full-time. If you have an existing business back home, you may be able to manage it via cell phone and the Internet while traveling.

But if your current career isn't suited for the road, many independent careers featured in Part II can be done while traveling. Some businesses are, by their very nature mobile, for example, mobile food service, mobile RV repair/maintenance, mobile notary, mobile screen repair, or mobile dog grooming. But Steve and Kathy Jo Anderson of *Workamper News* believe literally any business can be run from the road. Certainly many of the independent careers we feature in Part II can be as easily run from a mobile home as a fixed one.

With the proper equipment and connections, for example, most of the virtual careers profiled in Chapter Three can be done from the road. Also, keep in mind that RVers and live-aboarders are themselves a community you can serve virtually or in person. As you travel from place to place, you will meet many fellow travelers, some of whom may need services you can provide. Repair services, restoration, tutoring, pet services, and résumé writing are just a few possibilities you might consider from among the careers profiled in Chapters Two or Four as useful services for fellow travelers or for residents of local communities where you will be staying.

Alternatively, of course, you can always take temporary or short-term jobs along your route, staying for several weeks or months in one place. Jaimie Hall's book *Support Your RV Lifestyle* lists 295 ideas for on-the-road jobs. They range from positions at RV parks, resorts, or marinas to seasonal jobs with the National Forest Service, public parks, or other government agencies, as well as special seasonal or annual events and festivals. Other local work can be found as utility inspectors, field reps, carnival/circus crew members, ad salespeople, NASCAR ushers, and souvenir vendors.

For example, when Jaimie and husband Bill decided to take to the road full-time, they worked their way through the tedious application process for jobs in a dozen different national parks and were hired to work in Grand Teton

National Park for a season. Since then they have reapplied for other seasons and been hired to work in seven national parks from Colorado and Utah to California, Arizona, and Alaska. In between they have taken other seasonal jobs as well, from selling Christmas trees and remodeling houses to providing help with tax preparation and working in the tourist industry.

Keep in mind, though, when you are employed in a state, you may need to pay income taxes in that state, as well as in the state you've chosen as legal residence, or domicile. Some states will even expect you to pay taxes on a proportional share of all your income, based not upon how much you earned there, but on the percentage of the year you spent there. Many full-time travelers choose to domicile in a state with no income taxes, like Alaska, Florida, Nevada, South Dakota, Tennessee, Texas, Washington, or Wyoming. But if you move around quite a bit, you'll still end up having to file a number of state tax returns each year, and rules as to which state is owed what vary. So you will want to get some expert tax advice as part of preparing for how you want to structure your work and travel plans.

Such tax complications are a key advantage of establishing an independent or self-employed career instead of taking a multiplicity of temporary local jobs. Generally, as a self-employed individual, corporation, or partnership, you will only owe taxes in the state where you've established your business. This is particularly true of any virtual business where your clients or customers could be anywhere in the world. But some states, like Wisconsin, are quite strict about collecting income and sales taxes on work done or products sold within their state to local buyers, for example, consulting, speeches, or workshops provided, art pieces sold at fairs, or books sold at expos or signings. Organizations hiring us to speak in Wisconsin, for example, were required to withhold state taxes from our fees. Arranging to have a sponsoring organization, local gallery, or bookstore to handle sales can simplify sales tax requirements, but this will cut down on how much you can make on sales. So it's important to get good tax advice as you plan how you'll be earning a living while you travel.

Checklist for Living a Mobile Lifestyle

Of course, how you will support your journey is only one of many decisions you will need to make if you choose to live on the move. As we've become an increasingly mobile and wired society, one's options for living on the move have become simpler and easier. Here's a checklist of the kinds of issues you will need to consider if you decide upon a mobile lifestyle.

❏ *Is this really for you?* Even an avid boater like Mark Nicholas, author of *The Essentials of Living Aboard a Boat*, admits this kind of lifestyle is outside most folks' comfort zones. While there was a time when most of us lived as nomads, traveling from place to place with very few possessions, that was long, long ago. As romantic and adventuresome as you may imagine living on the road or at sea would be, all those we spoke with who love doing it had a ready list of routine tasks that could be major detractors to some if they knew what's really involved.

So if you're not already an experienced RVer or boater, the first question is, are you ready to learn about and master a whole lot of routine tasks you've probably never concerned yourself with? For example, you're probably not used to thinking about things such as: stabilizing; leveling; hooking and unhooking utility connectors; replacing propane cylinders; turning on and off your refrigerator, water pump, and water heater; making sure nothing in your home is sitting about loose; connecting TV cables and Internet cables before you can use them; dealing with gasoline fumes; cleaning bilge pumps; and handling regular waste removal.

The list of things you must learn, master, and do regularly that aren't part of a place-based life is quite long. This is just a sample. Not to mention learning to steer, park, and navigate a large vehicle or boat. You'll have to invest time, energy, and money to learn all such things *before* you set out.

Also, how about your friends and family? Are you ready to leave them behind? You will most likely meet lots of new people, and hopefully make new friends, but they may be short-term in nature or become long-distant contacts. Regular contact with ongoing friends and loved ones will be limited to phone calls, e-mail, and occasional visits. And are you ready to leave behind the comfort and convenience of the hairstylist, dentist, medical specialists, and other professionals and service providers you rely upon and turn to instead of whatever services you can find hither, thither, and yon?

What about space? Are you really ready to live in much less? Are you ready for a little kitchen and bedroom, a tiny bath, a teensy bathroom? While motor homes and boats come in lots of sizes, unless you're thinking about buying a massive yacht, they are going to be smaller than most small houses or apartments.

How about your stuff? Storage, even in a well-designed motor home or boat, is limited. What happens to all your furniture, clothes, shoes, purses, artwork, collections, kitchen utensils and supplies, tools, books, and hobby materials? A good way to help answer that question is to imagine that you had to evacuate your home in the face of a natural disaster and could only take what would fit into a couple of vans. Go through your home and, leaving all furniture and decorative art pieces behind, itemize the things you would need to take, want to take, and like to take. (Don't forget the attic, basement, and garage. Motor homes and boats don't have any.) That's it. There won't be room for much more. So imagine you'd have to part with or store everything else and live only with what remains.

If, after answering these questions, you're still motivated to explore this way of life, then explore the resources in LEARN MORE, and try it out before you decide. See if you can do the tasks required and will enjoy the benefits of living on the move.

❏ *How much do you want to travel, with whom, and to where?* Do you intend to travel or cruise most of the time, with stopovers of only one week or less? Do you want to settle in one place for part of the year and travel the rest of the time? Or would you prefer to live long-term in one location and travel else-where occasionally? For example, some boaters, referred to as *floaters*, don't cruise at all. They live on their boat in a marina full-time and drive their car to and from work every day, just like someone in the suburbs. They don't even need a boat with an engine. Others want to live on their boats in port most of time but take short jaunts at sea on weekends and vacations.

Will you be traveling alone, with a partner or spouse, with children, or with pets? And where do you plan to travel? What kind of weather conditions can you expect to face in the locales you will visit? What kind of terrain or water conditions might you encounter?

You need to be able to answer questions like these in as much detail as possible to select the right motor home or boat. For example, because Janine and Jim Wilder travel all across the country into remote locales with their horses, it would be difficult for most motor homes large enough to live in full-time to navigate the back-road trails they seek out, especially when they're also pulling a horse trailer. So they chose to buy two vehicles: a Class A (bus-size) motor home and a pickup truck with horse trailer. This way, they can each drive a vehicle to the campsite and then head off together with their horses in the truck and trailer onto trails off roads too narrow, windy, or poorly maintained to accommodate a motor home.

The Nodlands, on the other hand, are traveling with their two boys. They rarely stay in one place too long, but they want to take the boys on historical, cul-tural, or recreational outings without having to unhook every time they drive about the area. So they chose a thirty-four-foot fifth-wheeler, which they can detach from the truck base and leave in camp while they shop and explore the environs. In hindsight, after traveling in Alaska, they wished they'd had their water lines routed and fastened under the flooring near the warmth of the inte-rior or run all the water lines in a heated duct, because with nighttime winter temperatures as low as minus 26 degrees Fahrenheit, their water lines froze solid several times.

Not having this kind of information in mind when you buy a boat or mobile home can not only be inconvenient, but it can also be very expensive, as Mark Nicholas discovered. Unprepared when he bought his boat, *The Morning Fog,* he ended up having to rebuild and reinstall all the electrical lines and plumbing systems, replace the holding tank, add a diesel heating system, update the engine, replace the alternator, and on and on. Some of these things he was able to do himself, but most he had to pay to have done at a hefty price.

❏ *What amenities do you want and can you afford?* Just what kind of life do you want to live on the move? Is your goal to live as inexpensively as possible? Do you want to live the simple life? Or do you really want as much luxury as possible without having to work as hard, and if so, just what does luxury mean to you?

With each passing year, RVs come equipped with more and more options. You can have nearly every imaginable comfort of home: satellite TV; Jacuzzi; a kitchen with granite countertops, built-in appliances, and lighted dining hutch; all-leather seating; hardwood floors; wood paneling and cabinetry; a king-size bed; and a private bath with a full tub or even heated shower floors. Some RVs come with "basement storage" or "garages" known as "toy haulers," which could also be used for workshop or business equipment. Others come with sports utility trailers for those who want both comfortable living quarters and a cargo area for transporting motorcycles, ATVs, snowmobiles, a small car, or needed equipment.

Obviously, as we've all seen on TV shows, boats can be equally luxurious and elaborate. But of course, the more space and amenities, the higher the cost to purchase, maintain, and, due to added weight, to drive, not to mention the added difficultly of navigating a larger, heavier boat. So there is no need to go fancy. The choice is yours. If your goal is to preserve the comforts of a middle-class lifestyle or scale back to a simpler way of life, keep this goal front and center in your mind when shopping. Sales personnel and displays are hoping to entice you into buying more than you may want or need. As you will see below, prices can range from as low as fifteen thousand dollars for small, minimally equipped boats to nine hundred thousand dollars for large, deluxe models.

Being clear on your goals is important not only in deciding on what size and kind of boat or RV you want but also in deciding where you will stay when not on the road or at sea. There are stunningly beautiful campsites, for example, near pristine wilderness, that cost next to nothing, but you won't find any hookups there. That means you will either literally be camping or running your generator for electricity, water, heat, air-conditioning, etc. At the other end of the spectrum, you can find elegant, country club–like RV parks with swimming pools, saunas, libraries, and entertainment halls.

The same can be said of buying a boat. While it's commonly thought that a boat one could live on would cost a celebrity-level fortune, Mark Nicholas points out that the cost of a forty-foot, preowned, dock-bound wood boat or rafthouse (which can't be financed) could run as low as $10,000 to $15,000. Or a new thirty- to forty-foot boat (which can be financed usually with a 20 per-cent down payment) could cost anywhere from $35,000 to $150,000 on up.

❏ *What type of vehicle or boat do you want?* Think of shopping for an RV or boat you're going to live in the way a woman thinks about shopping for a wedding dress. The type, kind, and size of vehicle you choose will make or break your ability to fully enjoy a life on the road or at sea. Fortunately, you have lots of choices, and no one size fits all. That means doing a lot of investigation and "trying on" your options.

For example, there are two types of RVs: towables, which are pulled by a sep-arate vehicle; and motorized, which are self-propelled. Towable motor homes are either travel trailers or fifth wheels. Travel trailers have been around since the 1920s. Owners tow them with a truck, van, or a hearty family car. Fifth wheels are the elite towables. They have a raised forward section that allows a bi-level floor plan, and owners tow them with a pickup truck equipped with a special hitch in the truck bed.

Motorized motor homes come in three classes: Class A vehicles are built on a bus chassis and resemble busses; Class B vehicles are van conversions; and Class C vehicles are built on a truck chassis and resemble trucks.

Each of these choices comes in various shapes and sizes: larger, smaller, longer, shorter, rectangular, or more streamlined. All have models with options for slide-outs whereby part of the rooms can be expanded outward when the RV is parked, thereby providing additional living space. Newer models have three and even four slide-outs. Slide-outs are especially desirable when one needs extra space for oper-ating a business on the road or living with a family. They do add weight, however, and are yet another mechanical part to deal with. Also, some campsites may not accommodate the additional space for slide-outs, and with slide-outs you may have to give up some "basement" storage room beneath the RV.

All five RV types we've mentioned can be found at different price ranges and with a variety of floor plans, although fifth wheels generally have the bed and bath areas in the raised portion with the living, kitchen, and dining areas on the lower level. Class C RVs often have a bed above the driver/passenger area. Each has its pros and cons. In choosing a model and floor plan, think about the activities you'll be doing. Will you be primarily on the go, or will you be spend-ing most of your time at a campground or dock? Will you be working as well as living in your new home? Will you want room to host social gatherings or to entertain? What special space and activity areas will family members or pets need? Clearly you don't want to pay for more than you need, but you do want the room and amenities to live the comfortable life you plan.

Considerations in Comparing Types of RVs

Styles, models, and prices of RVs are constantly changing in the direction of increasing options that make an RV as comfortable and enjoyable as most any home. At the time of this writing, here's a summary of your options, including size, price, pros, and cons:

Style	Pros	Cons

Travel Trailers
Size:
  Length 14 – 36'
  Width 72 – 96"
Price:
  $10,000 – $65,000
Average:
  $15,000 – $30,000
	1. The least expensive.
	2. Can be towed by a family car and thus unhitched and left at the campsite.
	3. Trailer or towing vehicle can be replaced or repaired separately.
		1. More difficult to park than others.
		2. Longer, larger ones may be less stable and more susceptible to wind problems.
		3. No access or use of them while driving.

Fifth Wheels
Size:
  Length 21 – 40'
  Width 96 – 102"
Price:
  $15,000 – $100,000
Average:
  $20,000 – $35,000
	1. Most luxury and space short of the cost of a Class C vehicle.
	2. More stable on the road and easier to park than a travel trailer.
	3. Can also be unhitched and left at campsite.
	4. Truck and trailer can be replaced or repaired separately.
		1. Cost more than a travel trailer. There's a double cost—the fifth wheel and the specially tailored truck.
		2. They are still harder to park than self-propelled models.
		3. You will be driving and riding in a truck not a car.

Class A Motor Homes
Size:
  Length 21 – 45'
  Width 96 – 102"
Price:
  $24,000 – $900,000
Average:
  $80,000 – $150,000
	1. Crème de la crème of RVs in terms of living space and comfort.
	2. Drive more like a very large car than towables do.
	3. Fully self-contained, only steps inside to your living quarters.
	4. Newer, smaller 21' diesel-powered models can get 36 mpg.
		1. The most expensive.
		2. Like driving a small house. Hard to maneuver, steer, park, and stop, especially in congested traffic or low, tight spaces.
		3. Usually poor mileage—can be less than 7 mpg.

Style	Pros	Cons
Class A Motor Homes Continued	5. Easy to insure and finance. 6. High resale value.	4. Two engines required. 5. When your motor home is in the shop for repairs, so are your living quarters. 6. Many owners tow a car.
Class B Motor Homes Size: Length 16 – 23' Width 78 – 85" Price: $37,500 –$71,000 Average: $40,000 – $60,000	1. Self-contained with benefits of larger vehicles. 2. Drives like a van: fast on the road, easy to maneuver, park, and get in and out of most places. 3. A second vehicle isn't necessary. 4. Generally better gas mileage, e.g., 13–20 mpg. 5. Easy to find parts and mechanics.	1. Less room. 2. Cost per square foot is high. 3. Because of size, probably not as suit-able for most couples or families. 4. Specially sized appliances may be hard to replace. 5. When your motor home is in the shop, so are your living quarters.
Class C Motor Homes Size: Length 20 – 32' Width 60 – 102" Price: $48,100 – $139,000 Average: $60,000 – $80,000	1. Most RV for the money. 2. Almost as easy to maneuver through traffic and camping areas as Class B motor homes. 3. Larger Class C motor homes can tow a small vehicle if desired. 4. Can enter or exit without walking through the coach.	1. Smaller storage compartments. 2. Depreciate faster. 3. Look more like a camper/truck. 4. Passengers sitting in the living space can't see out the windshield.

There are similar choices in selecting a live-aboard boat, the first being that not just any boat is suitable to living on full-time. The one choice that all live-aboard boaters seem to agree upon is that you should not consider living on a boat that's smaller than thirty feet long, although some people do. On the other hand, it's important to avoid the "bigger is better" trap, as every linear foot of boat brings added expenses. Aside from size, two key choices are sail vs. power and wood vs. fiberglass. Again, each has its pros and cons, and the final choice is highly personal.

Style	Pros	Cons
Sailboats	1. Quiet. 2. Greater stability in difficult situations. 3. Unlimited range when there is a wind. 4. When running efficiently, less expensive to operate. 5. Low fuel usage and little engine maintenance.	1. Slow and dependent on wind conditions. 2. Considerable skill, experience, and manual labor required. 3. Rigging and sail require ongoing maintenance. 4. Must weave toward an intended direction. 5. Tighter living conditions.
Powerboats	1. Faster. 2. Easy—push a button and it heads straight in the desired direction. 3. Larger, higher, and more comfortable interior living space with more storage. 4. Ideal for fishing as they can trawl. 5. No rigging to maintain 6. Less complex skills required.	1. Louder. 2. Range and expense depends on fuel usage. 3. Fuel is very costly. 4. High engine maintenance required. 5. More uncomfortable in wind and bad weather and more likely to roll.
Wood Boats	1. Much lower cost, especially used ones. 2. Provide more living space for less money.	1. Require more care. 2. Not as easy to finance, insure, or sell.

Style	Pros	Cons
Wood Boats (continued)	3. Look and smell lovely.	3. Not all travel lifts will haul wooden boats
Fiberglass Boats	1. Strong yet lightweight. 2. Versatile 3. Easier to finance, insure, and resell at higher value. 4. Easy to maintain and repair. 5. Doesn't rust, corrode, or rot.	1. More expensive to buy and operate. 2. Unpleasant fuel fumes. 3. Fiberglass is a heavier material than wood. 4. If fiberglass is bonded with composite to lighten the weight, it may not be as sturdy.

Without a doubt, living on a boat, especially when at sea, is considerably more dangerous and involved than living in an RV. So much so, in fact, that Mark Nicholas, who is also an attorney, points out that if one were to live on a boat with small children and any of many possible disasters were to occur, a parent might be charged with child abuse, even if all turned out well. Not that it can't be done safely, though. Tom Neale, author of *All in One Boat: Living Aboard and Cruising,* and his wife, Mel, left for a life at sea with their two pre-school-aged daughters, Melanie and Carolyn, whom they raised and home-schooled aboard their GulfStar Sailmaster 47, cruising an average of three to five thousand miles per year. Both from boating families, the Neales are boating people. They left behind their careers as a trial lawyer and a teacher for the freedom of life at sea. Now, with their two daughters away in college, they write and speak about cruising and conduct a cruising school in various U.S. locales (www.tomneale.com).

But knowledge and safety are clearly musts for this lifestyle. Nicholas also points out that not a year passes without some live-aboards dying from their efforts to heat their homes. Fire resulting from inadequate ventilation and flammable items onboard, such as propane, cooking alcohol, cleaners and thinners, and so forth, are the most typical causes.

Both safety and sanitation are concerns that require forethought and attention to select a properly equipped seagoing home. Also, both the boat and those living on it need protection from weather, humidity, condensation, and the corrosive effects of seawater. The prevalence of such concerns is clearly evident in the list of top ten reasons marine technician Chris Birches tells Nicholas for why people stop living aboard:

Top 10 Reasons People Stop Living Aboard

1. The smell
2. The motion
3. The clutter
4. The expense
5. The work involved
6. The sewage
7. Deck leaks
8. Not enough room for valued items
9. Boat sinking
10. A partner who says "no more!"

For more top 10 lists by Birches and others, see Nicholas's *The Essentials of Living Aboard a Boat,* listed under LEARN MORE at the end of this chapter.

So it's especially important in shopping for a boat to check on the safety features, ease of use, and maintenance required on a boat's support systems, for example, electrical, water, sewage, climate control, ventilation, and materials used to operate each. Nicholas points out that taking care of these concerns allows liveaboard boaters to savor the joys of the sea, including living in locales one couldn't otherwise afford, traveling to other countries, a ten-foot commute, no more traffic noise, a better-organized and less-cluttered way of life, lower living expenses, and the chance to live the dream of millions of others.

Clearly, selecting the right RV or boat makes a big difference, and that means considering many little details one easily takes for granted when buying a land-based home. Here are few key things you will need to become familiar with (and later learn how to use and maintain safely) when making your choice to buy either an RV or a boat:

What to look for When Choosing an RV or Boat

- Battery capacity and compartments
- Capacity and operation of fresh- and gray-water holding tanks
- Climate control
- Detectors for smoke, propane, and carbon monoxide
- Ease of driving or sailing and handling
- Ease of refilling propane cylinder compartments
- Fuel requirements
- Headroom
- Living space and arrangement
- Leveling methods
- Sewer size and accessories, fittings, and adaptors
- Storage space
- Warranty limits and sources for repairs and service
- Water sanitation system
- Weight and weight carrying capacity
- Trailer carrying capacity
- Weatherproofing
- Windows: number, size, location, and view obstruction

❏ *How much will it cost?* There seems to be general agreement that one can live on the road or at sea more inexpensively than in a traditional home. Some expenses, of course, such as food, will remain constant. Others like a second car or dry-cleaning bills, will automatically go down. Some expenses, like health insurance and taxes, may go up, down, or stay the same depending on your circumstances.

Based on a 2001 survey by Stephanie Bernhagen and Jaimie Hall, adjusted for inflation, nearly 60 percent of full-time RVers spend an average of fewer than twenty-three hundred dollars per month living on the road, with 11 percent spending as little as eight hundred dollars a month. In estimating monthly expenditures for live-aboard boaters, Nicholas projects annual expenditures, excluding personal living costs, to be from around nine thousand dollars for pre-owned, forty-foot dock-bound options to forty-three thousand dollars for a forty-five-foot cruising sailboat and fifty thousand for a forty-foot cruising powerboat.

Of course, depending on how much time one spends actually traveling versus residing in camp or at dock, these costs could be more now, given the rise in the cost of gasoline and all oil-based fuels.

AVERAGE MONTHLY EXPENDITURES
(for full-time RVers)

Under $800	11%
$800 – $1,600	21%
$1,600 – $2,300	27%
$2,300 – $2,800	17%
$2,800 – $3,300	5%
Over $3,300	18%

Can you do it for less than the lowest end of these estimates? Jaimie Hall says no; Mark Nicholas says yes, possibly. (See our tips on saving money on the pages that follow.) Can you do it for more than the upper ranges? No question about it. Absolutely. Any one person's actual costs of living on the road or at sea will depend on a myriad of personal choices and preferences. For example:

1. *How ready you are to hit the road.* If you are already fully equipped with a suitable RV or boat that will meet the needs and demands of full-time living, your initial costs will be minimal. You'll save if you buy a trailer or fifth wheel and already own a suitable tow vehicle. Your costs will also be less if you already have all the computer, office, and telecommunication equipment you need.

2. *If you buy new or pre-owned.* Regardless of what size or type of RV or boat you choose, your initial investment will be far less if you buy a used one. Of course, to be worth the savings, a pre-owned vehicle needs to be relatively new and in excellent working order and condition. Pre-owned motor homes

and trailers can cost one-third to one-half the cost of new ones, and there are plenty on the market. For a wide variety of reasons, from illness and financial setbacks to family considerations, time constraints, or personal preferences, some people purchase an RV or a boat (sometimes equipping it to the hilt), only to decide soon after to sell it. Remember, most RVs and boats aren't purchased for full-time living. They are used for vacations or weekend jaunts. So some are essentially brand-new, with little actual wear and low mileage. This can be true even if they are several years old.

One advantage of buying an almost-new RV is that during the first year of ownership, dealers and manufacturers will usually rectify or repair defaults and bugs. Nicholas says "ditto" for boats. Boats depreciate quickly, he says—just look at www.yachtworld.com to see how quickly. You can save twenty-five thousand dollars on a near-new boat, and year-old boats are more likely to have worked out their quirks and bugs. He goes further to claim that if logic dictated, there would be little need for any new boats because there are already a million boats on the market.

3. *Whether you buy your RV or boat outright or finance it.* Of course, if you finance, you will have the equivalent of a monthly mortgage payment. RV interest rates are tied to auto car loan rates. Your interest payments will be deductible, as with any other home you buy, and if you are working from your RV or boat, you can also take a home-office deduction on your income taxes for storage related to your business or slide-out space devoted strictly to business use. Always check the tax laws to make sure these deductions are still valid. As you know, the tax code changes every year. Banks, credit unions, and independent finance companies all offer RV financing. A list of RV financing companies is available on the Recreational Vehicle Industry Association (RVIA) Web site at www.rvia.org. In the search box just enter "loans."

Many people choose to sell their homes and a substantial portion of their belongings when they choose this way of life, thereby freeing up cash to purchase their RV or boat outright, eliminating the burden of monthly payments. This also eliminates the cost of annual property taxes and other costs involved in maintaining a home, thus greatly reducing one's monthly cost of living. Others who aren't sure if this will be a permanent lifestyle prefer to rent out their homes, thereby reducing if not eliminating the costs of having a dual dwelling.

4. *Where you camp or dock.* Campgrounds, RV parks, and marinas come in all price ranges, from nothing at all to pretty pricey, but then again, the services they offer vary substantially as well. If you pay nothing, you get nothing but a place to park. There are a variety of different types of sites, each more or less appropriate for the type of stay you need:

- ► Low or no-cost overnight stop spots. Highway truck stops and Wal-mart parking lots (Wal-mart welcomes traveling RVers) are plentiful and cost nothing, but offer little other than lighted parking and restroom facilities. State and national parks, national forests, Bureau of Land Management facilities, U.S. Army Corps of Engineer campgrounds, and municipal camp and fairgrounds are other low-cost options. Some offer hookups for electricity, water, etc., but others don't.

- ► Associated campground networks. Private campgrounds that are affiliated throughout the United States have specific quality standards and offer discounts and many services to members. They include Good Sam's and RV clubs such as Family Motor Coach Association, Escapees, and Kampgrounds of America (KOA), a collection of affiliated independent private parks usually near tourist spots.

- ► Membership sites. Members join an organization such as Coast to Coast, Thousand Trails, and Resorts Park International, where for anywhere from several hundred to several thousand dollars of initial investment and an annual fee, members have a home site they can use as often as they wish. But they also can take advantage of special discounts and cost-savings programs for staying at other sites, some-what similar to owning a time-share condo. Members can resell their memberships.

- ► Discount camping clubs. In organizations like Recreation America, Passport America, and Happy Camper, members buy into a network of sites for a low annual fee, for example, fifty to one hundred dollars, entitling them to pay low overnight fees around ten dollars per night. There is no contract agreement and renewal is optional.

- ► Premium resorts. Large high-end resorts with equally high costs offer RVers every possible amenity. RVers can purchase or rent a site on a long-term lease. Sometimes these resorts are restricted to newer, larger motor homes.

As with most things in life, you get what you pay for. So selecting sites involves finding a balance between budget, convenience, and comfort. Overnight rates are the highest. Weekly, monthly, or long-term rates are lower. Sometimes there are additional charges for various services, such as electricity, phone, Internet WiFi, or cable TV.

As for where to park your boat, well, renting a slip in a marina is the most common choice but not the only one. You can also live at anchor (on a hook) or at mooring (on a ball). Some live-aboards literally live *underway*, cruising without ever pulling into a marina. This presents challenges, though, as you need to use a water taxi or have an inflatable dinghy to go into ports for food, fuel, and supplies. Also, there are limitations on how much fresh water a boat can store, so live-aboarders must regularly replenish their water supply and charge batteries as well.

---

10 Great Places to Float Your Houseboat
USA Today 10/20/2006

1. Lake Ouachita, Hot Springs, AR
2. Don Pedro Lake, Modesto, CA
3. Smith Mountain Lake, VA
4. Dale Hollow Lake, TN
5. Lake Sidney Lanier, GA

6. Lake Mead, NV
7. Table Rock, MO
8. Suswap Lake, British Columbia, Canada
9. Green River, UT
10. Center Hill Lake, TN

At the other extreme are those who live on their boat in a marina and never get their boat underway. In between are folks who take cruises over weekends or longer ones over a season and dock in a marina the rest of the week or year. It is possible, for example, to live aboard one's boat and have a full-time, nine-to-five job. Of course, if you plan to pursue your own business while living aboard, you will be able to do this more easily if you have a "home base" for your boat that can serve as your address.

Campsite and RV Park Essentials

Peggy McDonald, author of *RV Living in the 21st Century*, recommends ensuring for these basics when selecting a campsite or RV park:

1. Level ground
2. Easy access to the site
3. Conveniently located, quality hookups for water and electricity
4. Steady, properly wired power

5. Well-maintained grounds
6. Sufficient space to park and maneuver
7. Pure, odor-free water
8. Safe and secure premises

See LEARN MORE at the end of this chapter for a list of campsite directories where you can find all the details about campsites and their locations, including price, services, amenities, and add-on fees. You can also visit the Web sites of the various camping organizations we've mentioned.

Marina Essentials

Like campgrounds, marinas come in all flavors and prices. Some are right in the heart of a city; others are remote. Some prohibit live-aboards; others cater to them. Some are geared to recreational boaters, others to long-term residents. Some provide more services than others, such as restrooms, showers, shore power, telephone, cable, Internet access, and city water connections. Some are for transient boaters; others are for very tight-knit social communities. Some are members-only, with exclusive country-club–like atmospheres and amenities, such as golf courses and five-star restaurants.

In his book *The Essentials of Living Aboard a Boat*, Mark Nicholas recommends considering these basics when selecting a marina:

▶ Location: urban, rural, suburban, proximity to services and jobs, etc.

▶ Atmosphere: quiet and private, social and bustling, luxurious or sparse, etc.

▶ Rules and attitude of management and employees who enforce them

▶ Protection from weather

▶ Safety and security of premises

▶ Services and amenities: water and electrical hookups, phone jacks, parking, showers, pool, lounge, etc.

▶ Access to conveniences: stores, restaurants, haul-out facilities, or business services

▶ Culture, i.e., sailboaters, powerboaters, golfers, etc.

▶ Costs, based on season and size of boat

5. *Your lifestyle.* As with any other way of living, if you have big spending habits, you could find life on the move becomes just as expensive, and thus pressured, as the life you were trying to escape. Your basic costs of living may go down, but if you *must* have every new gadget for your RV or boat, prefer to eat out, stay at expensive spots, go to high-priced entertainment events, buy lavish gifts for family and friends, etc., you could find yourself having to earn as much money as ever to support your new lifestyle. On the other hand, if you want to lower your cost of living, live simpler, and enjoy a comfortable middle-class lifestyle, RV or boat living can make it easier.

Typical Costs to Budget for When Living on a Boat or in an RV

Here is a list of things to investigate and consider in estimating what your expenses will be:

- Cost of vehicles: any down payment, monthly finance charges, and towing costs
- Fuel: gasoline and propane
- Campground or docking fees
- Insurance
- Taxes: local, state, and federal
- Maintenance
- Repairs
- Cell/telephone and Internet service
- Mail service

- Satellite or cable service
- Storage facility fees for household items
- Vehicle registration fees
- Emergency services
- Membership club fees
- Health and life insurance
- Other medical costs
- Personal and household supplies
- Food, clothing, and personal services
- Entertainment

Be sure to add to this general list special monthly or annual expenditures, such as college tuition payments for children; professional licensing fees; business expenses; child support payments; vet bills, if you are traveling with a pet; home-schooling fees and materials, if you are traveling with children; etc.

 OUR ADVICE: KEEPING COSTS DOWN

Obviously if your goal is to work less and enjoy life more, it's desirable to keep costs as low as possible without making unappealing sacrifices. Here's a list of money-saving tips:

1. Don't maintain a separate home. Sell or rent out your previous home before taking to the road or sea.
2. Avoid buying a gas-guzzling vehicle. Gasoline will be one of your highest costs, so weigh size and weight against higher fuel mileage.
3. Register your vehicle in a state with no or low sales, wheel, or personal property taxes. As a full-timer you can choose where you buy and register your vehicle.
4. Choose a state with no income taxes as your domicile (more on this later).
5. Be a do-it-yourselfer. The more maintenance and repair work you can do yourself, the lower your cost of living will be. So if you're not "handy," read up and/or take courses on basic handyman skills and RV/boat maintenance. See LEARN MORE.

General Do-It-Yourself Repair and Maintenance

▸ Book: *Handyman's Handbook* by David Koenigsberg (2003)
▸ Guide and CDs: www.handyman-business.com
▸ The Natural Handyman: www.naturalhandyman.com

6. Many campgrounds offer one day free if you stay for a week, and monthly rates are 30 to 40 percent less than daily fees, so plan to stay awhile.

7. Avoid high-priced resort campsites, and if feasible, arrange your itinerary so you are traveling or cruising in locales off-season, when both fees and fuel costs will be lower.

8. Make sure your RV or boat is well insulated.

9. Set your water heater for most efficient operation.

10. Order special amenities and add-ons for your RV or boat at the time of purchase, as they will be more expensive if you add them later.

How will you handle legal, tax, and insurance issues? Our legal, tax, and insurance systems aren't designed for folks to be permanently on the move. They are built upon the unquestioned assumption that, while we may relocate from time to time, we are basically a settled population, and the place where we settle determines our legal residence, or domicile. *Black's Law Dictionary* defines one's domicile as "that place where a man has his true, fixed, and permanent home and principal establishment, and to which whenever he is absent he has the intention of returning."

In our increasingly mobile society, this assumption presents legal, tax, and insurance problems for the full-time traveler who no longer chooses to have a "true, fixed, or permanent place" to which he or she intends to return. Vehicle registration, driver's licenses, taxes, insurance, annual vehicle inspections, proof of insurance, and voter registrations are issued or levied based upon where you live and require a street address to which bills, renewal notices, and other official communication will be sent.

Of course, if you are living on a boat that is dock bound, or have a slip you travel in and out of, this won't be a problem for you. That boat slip is your legal residence. If, while traveling about full-time in your RV, you continue to maintain a home somewhere, then it can be your legal residence, even if you're not there very often. But what if, like the Nodlanders, the Russells, and the Wilders, you don't have a permanent home anywhere?

Well then, you get to choose and declare your domicile. You might even buy your RV in one location and have a driver's license somewhere else. This can be advantageous, as you can choose a domicile that provides you with the greatest tax advantages. You can also buy, insure, and register your vehicle in a different state where there is no sales tax. Such choices can save thousands of dollars a year. The latest edition of *State Residency Requirements: Selecting an RV Home Base* by the editors of *Travel Life and Motorhome Magazine* is an excellent resource for making such choices. It details legal and financial liability by state, including tax advantages, vehicle licensing and registration, voting requirements, etc. It's available at http//:rvbookstore.com and elsewhere. See LEARN MORE.

A legal or tax advisor familiar with full-time travelers can assist you in making the most advantageous choice of a domicile. But tax savings and legal requirements should not be the only criteria to consider. Think also about such things as:

- Where you might want to spend time each year
- Proximity to family and friends you may want or need to see
- Limitations and costs of qualifying for and changing health insurance companies
- Medical services you've come to rely on and might wish to continue getting treatment from
- If you have a virtual business, you may need to meet with associates or suppliers periodically in person during the course of running your virtual business
- If your children will attend college someday, you may want to establish residency in a certain state so they can qualify for in-state tuition.
- If you want to vote, you'll need to be a resident of somewhere for voting purposes.

Health Insurance Alert!

Before selecting a legal domicile be sure to give careful thought to your health insurance options (see "How Will You Obtain Health Insurance?" on page 394).

Being able to choose the most advantageous domicile is quite an advantage—one that placed-based folks don't have. But it's not always simple. For example, states have varying definitions and requirements for what constitutes establishing and maintaining a domicile. It can be determined by your permanent mailing address, where you are licensed to drive, where you register your vehicle, where you own property, where you're registered to vote, or where you're employed, etc. Also, if you are changing your domicile, for example, you might have to live in your new location for a six-month period.

Thus, if you don't establish one domicile, other states where you work or live temporarily may determine they are your domicile, in which case you will need to prove otherwise. Of course, the state you've chosen will expect to collect taxes from you, but so may other states where you work. A state where you live and work for a while may expect you to register your RV or obtain a driver's license while you're there. Also, wherever you're registered or domiciled will be sending regular renewal notices or other communication to your "official" street address, sometimes in envelopes marked "Do Not Forward."

Full-time workampers, dashboarders, and live-aboard boaters handle these challenges in various ways. If they travel half the year and remain in a park or boat slip the rest of the time, they may use that address as their domicile. Or, like Bill and Jan Moeller, who move to various sites throughout the year, they may use the address of whatever campground they are staying at, changing mailing addresses, licenses, registrations, etc., as they move from place to place. This, however, involves a lot of paperwork and can get complicated at renewal time. Changing addresses over and over can also be a challenge for any full-timer who wishes to have a virtual business while traveling. Even in this virtual age, many clients and customers need or want to know where to send contracts, checks, or other land mail communication, and they don't expect it to be someplace different each time.

 OUR ADVICE: ESTABLISHING A DOMICILE

The easiest way to avoid domicile issues is to choose where you want your legal residence to be and transact most of your legal, tax, insurance, financial, and business matters from that address. That includes where you:

- register your vehicles
- get your driver's license
- register to vote
- get professional licenses
- obtain insurance policies
- file your state and federal taxes

- open your bank account
- store household items
- have your passport issued
- file a will
- obtain needed business licenses and DBAs*
- obtain your cellular or satellite service

*Use this address on your letterhead, cards, stationary, Web site, etc.

You probably won't have an actual residential address in your legal domicile for applying, obtaining, and renewing such things, but fortunately there are a variety of other options, from very low cost on up:

- Use the address of a friend, relative, or business associate who lives in your chosen domicile.

▸ Rent a small room or office in that locale to use as your legal residence. Sublease it to an affiliate who will forward your mail.

▸ Rent a mailbox with a physical address within your chosen domicile. The U.S. Post Office cannot forward mail to various addresses. Also, other carriers, like Fed Ex and UPS, will not deliver to a USPS postal box, and a physical street address is required for most official legal transactions and desirable for many business purposes. A mail-receiving service, such as UPS Stores (www.theupsstore.com), with thirty-three hundred locations across the United States, will provide you with a permanent physical street address and forward mail when and where you specify. There may be an additional charge for forwarding above the standard box rental fee. You may also need to provide the mailbox company with a street address for their records; however, this could be the address of the campsite or marina where you are currently residing or the address of a local friend, family member, or associate.

▸ Sign up for a mail-forwarding service located in your chosen domicile. There are many private mail-forwarding services, with experience in forwarding mail to RV travelers that will send your mail to you as often or as little as you'd like, anywhere you might be in the United States. Most RV clubs also offer this service (see RV Clubs in LEARN MORE). The best services will forward your mail for the actual cost of postage plus a flat handling fee that includes the cost of the envelope used and all other supplies, but watch out for hidden costs—some forwarding agencies tack on "low" handling fees.

 Tips for Sailing in International Waters

1. Always have passports with you for everyone aboard.
2. Have all registration and other needed documentation, i.e., certificates and proof of vaccinations, etc., on board.
3. Be aware of the laws of the jurisdictions into which you will be cruising. Rules vary for such things as use and possession of drugs, firearms, alcohol, plants, and agricultural products. There may also be restrictions on pets, including strict quarantines.
4. Determine if you will need visas to enter port in advance of arrival.
5. Learn entry procedures, and follow them carefully, as penalties can be extreme.

How will you stay connected? Once upon a time, staying connected while traveling cross-country or offshore was a problem. Today the problem is more about choosing between all the available options, so most anyone who wants to be connected by phone, Internet, or mail while traveling can do so. Cellular, satellite, and wireless telecommunications technology is changing so rapidly we can only provide a snapshot of what's available today and invite you to explore the new possibilities that will most likely be available when you start your quest. You may be surprised. When Mark Nicholas bought his boat, he thought he'd spend less time on the phone and the Internet, but it didn't turn out like that. With the options he has now, he discovered he could spend about as much time as he did when he was land-based.

So, while tax, legal, and insurance demands are still quite place-based, communications technology is anything but. This is especially good news for full-timers wanting to have an independent career on the road. As Cheryl Nodland explains in running her computer services business, "All we need is a phone line . . . and a satellite link." And actually those are only two of many options.

 Tip for Being Self-Employed While Living on the Road

If you want to run a business or have an independent career while on the road, you must be easily reachable by phone, e-mail, and mail at a permanent phone number, mailing address, and e-mail address. Your phone will need to be answered in a professional manner in person or electronically during regular business hours, and you will need to respond to calls and e-mail within twenty-four hours.

Phone service. At this time, there are four basic choices for phone service: cellular, landline, satellite, and Internet. In addition, for live-aboard boaters, ship-to-shore radio communication is a requirement, not an option.

▶ *Cell phones:* For most full-time travelers, cellular is by far the most common and advantageous phone choice at this time. There are, of course, places where you can't get cell phone service. Far out at sea, naturally, but also in more remote countryside. We live in such a spot. We have to drive about ten minutes southwest before we can make or receive calls on our cell phones, but even here in this off-the-beaten-path village in the Los Padres National Forest, a cell tower is in the works and probably will be up by the time you read this.

We have traveled all over the country, however, with our cell phones, only losing service in the most remote of places. Even live-aboard boaters who opt to have landlines at their marinas usually have a cell phone, too.

In 2005 nearly eight percent of U.S. households had given up their landlines for wireless-only telephone service, and more than half of these households have family incomes of less than thirty thousand dollars. Price is not the barrier it once was, and the advantages of cellular service are many. So, the number of those choosing cell-only service is growing rapidly every year. There are so many different models and service plans, all at varying prices, that one can tailor cell service to meet preferences, budget, and needs.

Why Cellular Phone Service?

1. You can use a cell phone both in and off your RV or boat.
2. The cost is now about the same as a landline.
3. Plans often provide Internet and e-mail access both on the phone and with your computer.
4. Long distance rates are usually not different from local calling.
5. Cell phones can be charged and operated from any 12-volt connection, such as a car adapter.
6. You don't have to use battery power when you're connected to an electrical source.
7. The only disadvantages are that you can't use cell phones while cruising the open sea and in certain locations on land or near shore where there is no signal.

► *Landlines:* If you really don't want cellular, or you will consistently be offshore or in a remote location, phone jacks and hookups are available at some RV camps for outgoing calls. You may even be able to install a landline in your RV if you will be camped in one location for an extended period of time. If you do this while running a business from the road, though, we'd recommend using an answering service that will take or forward calls from colleagues, clients, and family and friends. There are many private answering services and some mail-forwarding services. RV clubs offer this service as well. Just be sure your calls are being answered professionally.

► *Satellite:* Most people are not yet aware that with a portable and handheld satellite, you can make calls, surf the Internet, and do e-mail from your boat or RV even in the middle of nowhere. Satellite phones do not require "cells" or cell towers, but they are still quite expensive and require a monthly fee and per-minute charges. They can be cost-effective for international travel, however, where phone rates are high. Just as cell phone costs have dropped greatly in past years, satellite phone prices could well come down over time.

▶ *Internet Phone Service:* Software such as Skype (www.skype.com) enables you to talk to anyone anywhere who is a Skype user from your computer for free. As of this writing, you can also call landline or cellular numbers in the United States and Canada for free. This will be changing, however, to a low, per-minute rate, which you prepay. For international calls you open an account online, prepay for time, and are credited at 2.1¢ per minute to more than twenty countries. You receive a real phone number that others use to call you, and Skype stores messages when you're busy or offline.

The software is reportedly easy to download and use without the assistance of a technician, but at this point, the voice quality is not so hot. Also, you need headphones and a mic. This technology holds promise, though, for RVers and live-aboard boaters and may already be improved by the time you read this.

Additional Requirement for Live-aboard Boaters

Full-time boaters who cruise will need ship-to-shore radio communication equipment, which can be either a VHF or SSB radio. VHF radios are economical, easy to install, and reliable at short ranges from shore. SSB radios are expensive and complex to install but provide communication over long distances and, once installed, require no additional fees. Some also permit e-mail data transfer.

▶ *Internet access.* Only a few years ago, techies on the road were quick to say that there wasn't a really good solution for mobile Internet access, but once again, technology is progressing so quickly that even the workable solutions we present here will undoubtedly be outdated quickly as we become an increasingly mobile society. Already more than eight in ten campers get online while camping, and RVers are leading the pack, especially full-timers.

Assuming you want to connect from the comfort of your RV or boat and not trek to local libraries, computer cafés, or campground and marina rec rooms, there are four* ways to connect to the Internet at this time: wired connections, cellular, satellite, and WiFi. The benefits and limitations of each depend on your needs and preferences. Here's a summary:**

---

*There is another Internet option for offshore boaters: e-mail services may be performed over SSB radio for a fee comparable to dial-up service
**Of course, any type of Internet access also requires a Web-based e-mail service, such as Yahoo, AOL, or Hotmail, that enables you to get online, send, and retrieve e-mail.

Internet Options

Options	Pros	Cons
Wired Connections (Dial-up phone line, DSL phone line, Coaxial cable) *Requires:* ▶ Computer ▶ Modem ▶ Account with an Internet provider with local access ▶ Working phone or cable connection	▶ Dial-up is inexpensive. ▶ DSL is a high-speed connection providing quick upload of information, including photos, movies, TV and music clips, etc. ▶ Familiar technologies ▶ Cable is three times faster than DSL. ▶ Cost of cable and DSL are more expensive but relatively comparable in price ▶ Same line can be used for voice and Internet	▶ Campground, marina, etc. must have hookups and may charge a usage fee. Or you must be in a location long enough to have a phone line installed, if it is allowed. ▶ In the latter case, provider may require long-term contract with cancellation penalties. ▶ Dial-up is too slow for most people; virtually precludes large files. ▶ Speed can be reduced based on local usage.
Cell Phone Service Best as a backup for checking messages briefly en route *Requires:* ▶ Computer ▶ Cell phone with built-in modem ▶ Cell service with Internet access ▶ Cord to connect phone to computer ▶ ISP with access number local to your cell phone	▶ Least expensive. ▶ Can be part of or an add-on to your regular cell service. ▶ Wide area of coverage. ▶ You can be on the Internet while on the road or at sea as long as you have cell reception. ▶ You can send and receive e-mail without connecting to your computer.	▶ Slowest speed. ▶ Too slow for sending or receiving large files. ▶ You need to be in a location that has cell reception. ▶ The screen and keyboard are small if you are using only the cell phone. ▶ ISPs that require their own dialing software may not work.

Options	Pros	Cons
Satellite Excellent for the self-employed, who need to be within reach of the Internet at all times *Requires:* ▶ Computer ▶ A two-way satellite, preferably mounted ▶ Subscription to a broadband satellite Internet service	▶ High-speed access wherever you are in the continental United States with unobstructed southern sky. ▶ Fast download speeds. ▶ Roof-mounted units are completely automated, connect within a few minutes. ▶ LRV batteries can provide all the electrical power that's needed; no cell phone, landline, or other transmission assistance necessary.	▶ Some campsites don't have unobstructed views. ▶ Slow upload speeds. ▶ Higher cost. ▶ Real-time applications not practical. ▶ You can't be moving.
WiFi *Requires:* ▶ Computer with built-in WiFi connection or a PC card that plugs into your PC's PCMCIA slot ▶ SSID and password to get on the WiFi network, if required by provider	▶ Fast speed. ▶ Easy to use and connect. ▶ Truck stops, coffee shops, restaurants, and bookstores (sometimes even entire towns) are WiFi "hotspots." ▶ Some campgrounds and marinas offer it free.	▶ You have to be within about three hundred feet of a WiFi "hotspot."

Business Meetings. If you are running a business or independent career from the road, there may be occasions when you will need to meet with clients, customers, and colleagues. Of course, you have the advantage of being able to travel for face-to-face meetings when you wish, and fortunately there are many possible meeting locations depending on the nature and purpose of the meeting and the number of people who will be present. Here are a few suggestions:

1. You can arrange to meet on the contact's premises. Many companies are eager for those they work with to see their offices and facilities.

2. If your RV or boat is roomy enough and the campground or marina is attractive, inviting, and easy to navigate, you can invite contacts to meet in your "home office."

3. Meeting over a meal in a restaurant of your contact's choosing can be pleasant if privacy or noise levels are not an issue.

4. Hotel lobbies are usually quiet and pleasant, or some campgrounds and marinas have lobbylike meeting areas.

5. If you will be meeting with a larger number of people, you can rent a conference room at a hotel or office suite company such as Regus, HQ Global Workplaces, Stratis, and Business Meeting Places. This network of office suite companies has thirty-seven hundred locations in sixty countries. Meeting-room facilities come in different configurations, such as boardrooms, conference rooms, interview rooms, training rooms, data rooms, and rooms suitable for audio, video, or Web conferencing.

6. Office suites are a valuable resource if you have the opportunity to obtain a contract with an organization that requires a physical office. For a reasonable monthly fee, you can rent a shared office with an address and answering service that will take your calls and provide conference facilities.

How will you obtain health insurance? Health care has become so costly that insurers are becoming much more particular about who and what they will cover. They are also charging more while offering less. This means obtaining quality, affordable health insurance could be a challenge when you leave your job, change domiciles, or take your business with you to travel full-time. Here are several possibilities:

1. **You could already be covered.** If you're on Medicare and don't want supplemental Medigap coverage or are a veteran receiving medical care through the VA, you already have nationwide coverage.

2. **If you'll be taking jobs, future employers might cover you.** Be aware, though, that fewer companies are offering insurance to their employees, especially short-term ones, and there can be waiting periods before employee coverage takes effect.

3. **You may be able to retain your existing coverage**, but be sure to check out if, how, by whom, and for what you will be covered while traveling. Some HMOs and PPOs in particular provide limited coverage when you are out of the area.

4. **COBRA may offer coverage.** When you leave in good standing from a job where you had health insurance through an employer, you can be covered on an

eighteen-month interim basis by COBRA, but you will need to keep your current domicile, as an employer is not required to offer a plan in a new area. Also, your payments will go up substantially during this period, as you'll be paying the full group amount. At the end of your COBRA coverage, you can apply for an individual policy with that company, but depending on your current and past health, you may not be accepted, or the premiums, co-pays, and coverage offered may not be desirable.

5. You may need to start fresh with a new individual or group policy. In this case, you should give careful forethought to both your choice of legal domicile and the various health insurance plans available to you.

When you change domiciles, you need to qualify for health insurance with an insurance company licensed to write policies in that state. Insurance laws and regulations as to who can be covered, for what, and at what cost, vary greatly from state to state and from company to company. Since Medigap and the Medicare prescription drug policies are also sold through private insurance by state, rules governing these plans also vary from state to state and plan to plan. Some states, such as Massachusetts, Minnesota, and Wisconsin, for example, have more advantageous coverage than others.

When you apply for a new policy, your premiums may well be higher and your coverage less. Preexisting conditions will most likely be excluded, and you may be denied coverage based on some minor past or existing health issue. Because the cost of individual policies is so high, self-employed, or pre-Medicare-age individuals usually find that the best way to get decent health coverage at a reasonably affordable cost is to get into a group plan. Here are several places to look:

Sources of Group Health Insurance

1. RV Clubs, like Camping World, Good Sam's, Escapees RV Club, and Coast, to Coast offer group health insurance, Medicare supplements, dental insurance, and long-term care plans.
2. College alumni associations
3. Business and professional associations
4. A union you may be eligible to join
5. If you've incorporated your business or have employees, another possible way to get group coverage is to lease your employees, including yourself, from an employee leasing company. Employee leasing companies hire the employees you select and for a fee provide health care and other payroll-related services for you. You can identify such companies by occupation or state at the National Association of Professional Employer Organizations' Web site.

If you have a preexisting health problem, like a lower-spine injury or a chronic illness, finding a good group plan will be a bigger problem, because most groups screen individuals applying to join. Even if you can get into a plan, it's apt to exclude your condition. In this case, you may be able to buy a separate policy covering just that risk. In either case, consider locating your domicile in a state that mandates guaranteed issue. Many states do, and some states, such as California, Colorado, Connecticut, Maryland, and Texas, have specific provisions for the self-employed. Some require that you have an employee, but a husband and wife may qualify. Rates for guaranteed issue policies may be between 10 and 50 percent higher than regularly issued insurance, and there may be a waiting period before preexisting conditions are covered. In cases like these, we advise working with a knowledgeable agent to get the best possible coverage you can.

 Tips for Finding Health Insurance

Begin looking for the largest group plans available to you. Evaluate them carefully for reliability, quality, choice of providers, limitations on geographic coverage, and price. Once you've identified several plans, compare their costs and benefits. Beware of "bargain" rates—you may find that the companies offering them are either outright scams or have received many complaints about nonpayment of claims.

Always check these two things with the state insurance agency. First, make sure the company you get your health insurance from is registered to sell insurance in your state. Second, check out its record of complaints. When claims are unreasonably denied and medical bills go unpaid—as happens to too many people every year—"bargain" insurance is no bargain. One of several Web sites that will link you to your state's insurance department is the National Association of Insurance Commissioners at www.naic.org. (Click on NAIC States and Jurisdictions.) Finally, work with a knowledgeable agent to arrange for the best coverage available to you. You can find a broker in your area through the National Association of Health Underwriters.

 OUR ADVICE

1. *Do extensive homework and preparation first* Granted, it may seem romantic to act on impulse and hit the road or sail the seas without a log of arduous and time-consuming planning. But the tasks involved in living in an RV or on a boat are quite different from those of living in a house. If you take time to study thoroughly before you leap, you will notice that most of the available materials on this way of life are written by people who didn't plan adequately, had to learn the hard way, and want to be sure you don't have to endure the travails they did. So unless you have already had ample prior experience RVing or boating, you will have a considerable learning

curve to master, not only in determining which type of vehicle will best meet your goals, but also, and most especially, with all that's involved in operating and maintaining the myriad of systems that keep your new home running. To begin the learning process do these things:

- ► Attend RV and boat shows.
- ► Go to dealer open houses.
- ► Take workshops they offer.
- ► Take training programs, such as those offered by the American Sailing Association.
- ► Read books by workampers, dashboarders, and live-aboard boaters.
- ► Scour the Internet for information.

2. *Try out this way of life part-time before you move into an RV or boat.* If you don't already own an RV or boat, and it fits within your budget, buy one just for short trips or extended vacations before deciding to live on the move. You might even want to rent one of the models you're interested in first and take a few travel trips before you buy. Renting is a great way to compare types and models of RVs and boats before deciding which one to buy. Rentals are offered in a variety of forms from hourly and daily rentals to weeks-long charters. Not all models may be available, but you'll find a range of types to try.

   Of course, short trips and vacation, can never be the same as full-time living, but at least it will give you an idea. Unfortunately, we bought before we tried RVing. Blessedly, we hadn't sold our home. We planned to use our RV for book tours and nature excursions. We *quickly* learned it was *not* for us. We're not the slightest bit mechanical. We don't like having to do even simple technical things. We want equipment to work the way our car does. You get in and drive it, someone else maintains it, and should something go wrong—heaven forbid—a trained mechanic fixes it. Even though our RV was relatively small, we didn't like driving a larger vehicle, nor did we care for the RV park facilities that were convenient to where we needed to be. They were crowded, noisy, and most unattractive. We couldn't wait to get to a motel, where someone else cleaned the bathroom. Even a Motel 6 would have seemed like a palace.

3. *Avoid older vehicles and equipment in disrepair.* During the period we were trying out our RV, we caravanned a few times with friends. One couple had purchased an older RV with lots more space than we had, but it was constantly breaking down. These were short trips, so we can only imagine what our friends would have faced on a long journey and if the husband hadn't been a contractor with over twenty years of experience fixing all types of household and auto systems. So have any used RV or boat thoroughly checked by a knowledgeable, independent mechanic.

4. *If you plan to rely on income from a business or independent career* while traveling, we suggest getting it up and going before going mobile, if possible. At least have done as much research and developed the outline of your business and marketing plan before hitting the roadways. Otherwise you may have so much on your mind adjusting to your new way of life that your business will have to wait until you get settled in. It usually takes at least six months to launch

a new business. You would need to have other means of support on hand to tide you over through both the adjustment and the start-up period.

5. *Bank electronically with a bank that has as many branches as possible across the country.* Although banks are still chartered by state, some like Bank of America and Citywide, have bought up many once-independent banks all across the country. Bank of America, for example, has sixteen thousand ATMs and fifty-seven hundred banking centers across the country. You can find addresses, maps, driving directions, phone numbers, and business hours at http://bankof america.via.infonow. net/locator/atmbranch. With a bank like this, you'll be more likely to find and use a convenient branch or ATM without additional charges. Doing the rest of your banking electronically is easy now and will save time and the hassle of mailing or finding a branch for making deposits and bill paying.

 MAKING THE CHOICE FOR TRAVELING FULL-TIME

Pros

► You can explore places you've always wanted to see, unlimited by the pressures of "vacation" time. This is the #1 reason people take to the road or sea.

► You can live as close to nature as you wish, yet enjoy most of the comforts of civilization you're accustomed to.

► If you make prudent choices, it can be a very economical way of life. Shopping sprees are no more. There's no room. You discover how to live well for and with less and have more time to do what you want.

► It can be the ultimate in freedom, flexibility, and variety. You can set your own schedule. You can be where you want, doing what you want, when you want.

► Some careers, such asentertainment, public speaking or selling one's artwork at shows become more feasible.

► Your life choices aren't constrained by the whims and the ups and downs of the housing market.

Cons

► You need to be adventuresome at heart, unattached to a place, and welcoming of the unpredictable. Home must be wherever you are, rather than somewhere specific.

► On the road or at sea, contending with nature must be addressed on a daily basis in transit.

► Although you will meet new friends and interesting people on the road, you will be leaving behind the friends, family, and services you've come to depend upon.

► There probably won't be room for everything you currently own. You'll need to live with fewer things without feeling deprived.

► There may be legal, insurance, and tax issues to deal with regarding the various jurisdictions where you live or earn income.

► Providing consistent, simple, and seamless ways for people and institutions to reach you by mail, phone, and Internet still takes some effort.

Making the Choice for Traveling Full-time continued:	
Pros continued:	Cons
► With the right vehicle, properly equipped, there are fewer household chores and less need to invest time, money, and hassle in ongoing home maintenance. You may even have more luxuries in your home than you could otherwise afford.	► Driving or sailing live-aboard vehicles requires skill, technical knowledge, and experience that may not come easily to those who aren't mechanical, creative problemsolvers. Lack of these can be dangerous, or at least quite frustrating.

LEARN MORE

There are an utterly overwhelming number of resources for full-time RVers and live-aboarders. This is undoubtedly a reflection of the level of passion and interest in these lifestyles. We've included a small number that we found helpful, each of which will lead you to many more.

Books

RVing

▶ *Complete Guide to Full-Time RVing: Life on the Open Road,* Bill and Jan Moeller, Trailer Life Publications, 1998.

▶ *RVLiving in the 21st Century: The Essential Reference Guide for All RVers,* Peggie McDonald, Authorhouse, 2004.

▶ *RV Owner's Handbook: Do-It-Yourself Maintenance and Repair,* Gary Bunzer, Woodall's Publications Corporation, 2005.

▶ *RV Repair and Maintenance Manual,* Bob Livingston, Trailer Life Publications, 2002.

▶ *Selecting An RV Home Base, State Residency Requirements, Taxes, Licensing, Voting Regs & More,* editors of *Trailor Life* & *MotorHome Magazines,* Trailer Life Books, 2007 or latest edition. Available at http://rvbookstore.com and www.workamper.com.

▶ *Support Your RV Lifestyle! An Insider's Guide to Working on the Road,* Jaimie Hall, Pine Country Publishing, 2002.

Living-aboard

▶ *All in the Same Boat: Living Aboard and Cruising,* Tom Neale, International Marine/Ragged Mountain Press, 2003.

▶ *Changing Course: A Woman's Guide to Choosing the Cruising Life,* Debra Ann Cantrell, International Marine/Ragged Mountain Press, 2003.

- *The Essentials of Living Aboard a Boat*, Mark Nicholas, Paradise Cay Publications, 2005.
- *The Practical Encyclopedia of Boating: An A-Z Compendium of Seamanship, Boat Maintenance, Navigation, and Nautical Wisdom*, John Vigor, International Marine/Ragged Mountain Press, 2003.
- *Boatowner's Mechanical & Electrical Manual: How to Maintain, Repair, and Improve Your Boat's Essential Systems*, Nigel Calder, International Marine/Ragged Mountain Press, 1995.

Campsite Directories

- *Trailer Life Directory for Campgrounds, RV Parks, and Services*
- *Woodall's North American Campground Directory*

Web Sites
General RVing

- www.fulltimerver.com
- www.rvia.org – Recreational Vehicle Industry Association
- www.roadtripamerica.com
- www.rv.org – RVConsumer Group offers rates on new and used motor homes.
- www.rvclub.com – Offers a newsgroup and lists members
- www.rvnetlinx.com/index.php
- http://thervsite.com – Lists used and new motor homes for sale by owners and dealers
- www.workersonwheels.com

General Live-aboarding

- www.americanboating.org – American Boating Association
- www.boatus.com – U.S. Boat Owner's Association
- www.livingaboard.com
- www.livingaboard.net
- www.sailnet.com
- www.sleepingwithoars.com
- www.latsandatts.net -– the Internet's Cruising Center

Singles on the Road

- http://rving-singles.com – RVing Singles Association
- www.napanet.net/~mbost – Loners of America
- http://autos.groups.yahoo.com/group/rvingsingles – Yahoo RVing

Singles
- www.lonersonwheels.com

Families on the Road
- www.familiesontheroad.com

Homeschooling on the Road
- www.homeschool-wealth.com – *The Homeschoolers' Income Makeover,* Tisha M. Silvers, 2007.
- www.familiesontheroad.com/life/homeschooling.html
- www.nhen.org – National Home Education Network
- www.home-school.com – Home Life Inc. features a magazine, *Practical Homeschooling,* and Mary Pride's *Big Book of Home Learning* series with reviews of curricula and other homeschooling products.
- www.nheri.org – The National Home Education Research Institute
- www.homeschoolnewslinks.com
- www.road-school.com

Pets on the Road
- www.familiesontheroad.com/life/pets.html

Finding Jobs on the Road
- www.roadtripamerica.com/dashboarding/working.htm
- www.workamper.com/WorkamperNews/WNIndex.cfm – Includes a résumé service
- www.housecarers.com
- www.workersonwheels.com/working/property_caretaking.html – property caretaker choices

Women on the Road
- www.rvingwomen.org – Includes a magazine

Campsites Network and Membership Sites
- www.goodsamclub.com
- www.fmca.com – Family Motor Coach Association
- www.escapees.com
- www.KOA.com
- www.coastresorts.com
- www.1000trails.com
- www.resortparks.com

RV Club Sites
- www.camphalfprice.com – Happy Camper
- www.passportamerica.com
- www.campingandcampgrounds.com – Recreation USA

Road Services
- www.campingworld.com
- www.goodsamers.com

Mail Receiving Services
- www.goodsamclub.com
- www.escapees.com
- www.fmca.com
- www.explorer-rvclub.com – Canada's largest RV club
- www.vmfs.com – Voyagers Mail Forwarding Service

Internet Access
- www.rvinternetacccess.com
- www.wififreespot.com/rv.html

Newsletters and Magazines
- *Gypsy Journal* – www.gypsyjournal.net
- *Latitudes and Attitudes, The Cruising Lifestyle Magazine* – www.latsandatts.net/magazine
- *Living Aboard* – www.livingaboard.com
- *MotorHome Magazine* – www.motorhomemagazine.com
- *PassageMaker, The Trawler & Ocean Boat Magazine* – www.passage maker.com
- *Power Cruising* – www.trawlerworld.com
- *Sail Magazine* – www.sailmagazine.com
- *Trailor Life* – www.trailorlife.com
- *Workamper News* – www.workamper.com

CHAPTER ELEVEN

Bringing Country Life to Town, City, and Suburbs—
Urban Thoreaus

If given a choice, four out of five people want to live in a small town, rural area, or some other natural setting. The emerging lifestyle trends we've been discussing so far reflect this desire. But, fact is, the United States gained one hundred million people in the past thirty-nine years, topping the 300 million mark in October of 2006, and most of these 300 million live in large cities. What's more, the U.S. Census Department estimates that we'll top 400 million within the next thirty-six years. Accommodating this massive rate of growth will require 70 million new homes and 73 million new jobs, according to Arthur C. Nelson, codirector of the Metropolitan Institute at Virginia Tech in Alexandria, Virginia. Where on earth will they be? According to Anthony Flint, author of *This Land: The Battle over Sprawl and the Future of America,* most of them will be in even larger, more densely populated cities.

Of course, as we've already discussed, people have been fleeing big-city life in droves for decades. Towns are rapidly transforming into small cities, and small cities are morphing into big cities. Obviously we can't all live in small communities, remote areas, or natural locales. There are just too many of us. By the late 1990s, 1.7 acres were developed for every person added to the U.S. population. That's the equivalent of building 220 parking lots or sixteen basketball courts for each of us in the form of housing, schools, stores, roads, and so forth. But now such sprawl is drawing people back into the cities. When you have to leave home at 6:00 AM to get to work on time and head back again after 5:00 PM along traffic-clogged roadways, living "in town" is becoming more appealing to many.

Suddenly the city promises new financial and personal benefits for young professionals, empty nesters, and retirees. Eliminating the commute is a big attractor, of course, but the cost of gasoline is making the commute not only unpleasant and time-consuming, but also expensive. Savings on a bigger suburban house can get lost at the pump. Often profits from the sale of a pricey suburban home can buy a comfortable city condo with money left over. The city offers other attractors, too. Closeness to where the "action" is, such as, entertainment, cultural, and social activities; medical facilities; and career opportunities. The freedom of having no grass to cut or landscaping to maintain or meals to cook if you'd rather grab some food at, or order in from, a nearby restaurant or fast-food place.

But does this mean we must resign ourselves to crowded, noisy, smoggy, alienating, barren, high-rise living that's devoid of any sense of peace, tranquility, nature, and close-knit community? Since most of us are going to be living in cities, we had better hope not. Much of what could make our cities truly livable will depend upon the foresight of politicians and city planners, so visionaries are giving considerable thought to how we could create more natural, human-scale urban environments. Several scenarios have emerged. Might one of these four scenarios be attractive to you?

Four Scenarios for Urban Living

Scenario One: Organic Human Scale Cities

Richard Heinberg, author of *Power Down* and *The Party's Over*, sums up his perspective quite simply: "We have known for a long time," he asserts, "that the status quo—a society that is machine-oriented, globalized, monocultural, and corporate-dominated—is deadening to the human spirit and unsustainable." He believes what's needed is a new urban infrastructure that's "organic, small-scale, local, convivial, cooperative, slower paced, human oriented rather than machine oriented, agrarian, diverse, democratic, culturally rich, and ecologically sustainable."

We're seeing some indications toward this scenario in both cities and suburbs. In cities such as Denver and Santa Monica, older downtown commercial buildings have been razed and replaced by low-rise, pedestrian-friendly urban town centers that combine condos, shops, and offices. In an effort to lure people back to the city, Cincinnati neighborhoods, such as College Hill, Columbia Tusculum, and Clifton, are embracing the town-square model of yore to give their neighborhood a community focus and feel.

Realizing people increasingly want to shop where they live, suburban areas like Fairfield, Ohio, and Valencia, California, are seeking to create town centers that provide an identifiable gathering place that counter their image as somewhere best described by American author Gertrude Stein's quip, "There is no there there." Such low-rise developments often allow people to live, work, shop, and recreate on foot should they choose.

Top Ten Most "Walkable" Cities

1. Portland, OR
2. Colorado Springs, CO
3. Madison, WI
4. Boise City, ID
5. Las Vegas, NV
6. Austin, TX
7. Virginia Beach, VA
8. Anchorage, AK
9. Fremont, CA
10. Raleigh, NC

Prevention Magazine & American Podiatric Medical Association (2006)

For the current year's top te,n see www.prevention.com.

"Walkable" cities and neighborhood communities within cities are an increasingly popular choice as evidenced by the rapid growth of the communities known for their walker-friendly character. Architect and planner L. Gene Zellman goes so far as to contend that "maximum livability can only be achieved if a town's circulation is pedestrian—no cars—and everything is within a short walk." Many must agree.

AAA's Top Ten Most "Walkable" Cities

1. Old Town Alexandria, VA
2. Boston, MA
3. New Orleans, LA
4. Downtown Los Angeles, CA
5. Washington DC
6. Charleston, SC
7. St. Augustine, FL
8. Old Québec City, Québec, Canada
9. Greenwich Village, NY, NY
10. San Francisco, CA

www.aaanewsroom.net

There are hundreds of new, small-scale urban infill projects underway at this time aimed at restoring the urban fabric of cities and towns by reestablishing walkable streets and blocks.

Most Walkable Medium and Smaller Cities and Towns

1. Eureka Springs, AR	7. Naperville, IL
2. Clayton, CA	8. Portland, ME
3. Boulder, CO	9. Annapolis, MD
4. Glenwood Springs, CO	10. Orion, MI
5. Dunedin, FL	11. Duluth, MN
6. Savannah, GA	12. Lincoln, NE

PBS Home www.pbs.org/americaswalking/travel/travelmost.html

The big challenge, though, with this scenario now, is that many of these "walkable" urban areas have become so highly desired that few people can afford to consider them. As Robin Rosen, who lives an hour outside of Washington DC, told us, "My husband loves the stimulation of the city. We've looked at moving to some of the low-rise urban developments in DC, or even Baltimore, but even though we both have good jobs, these places are just too expensive. We're stuck in the suburbs and still driving to and from every day."

Scenario Two: Ambient Hight Density Cities

In his book *Eco-Cities*, Richard Register proposes a different possibility. While Heinberg advocates shrinking the scale of metro life, Register proposes compacting our cities into bigger, denser, multistory, urban neighborhoods with "walkable centers and transit villages" that rise over wildlife corridors or tunnels beneath them with agricultural areas close to the center.

Register advocates concentrating on tall buildings around public spaces, with large trees floating high over the city in rooftop arboretums, supported by pillars built into high-rise apartment and office buildings. He sees these structures linked with pedestrian passageways and adorned with movable greenhouses perched a dozen or two dozen stories above the streets, and planted with fruit trees, flowers, and berry bushes.

Indeed, high-rise residential urban development is underway. Many consider it an inevitability, given the predictions for massive population growth coupled with increasingly stringent growth restrictions to curb sprawl and preserve rural and wild land. While what's being developed is not nearly as fanciful as Register envisions, they are moving somewhat in that direction. Some, for example, are integrating loft aesthetics into the unit mix—huge windows, open spaces with few walls, exposed concrete ceilings and mechanical ducts, expansive wood or stone floors, etc. Others are providing generous courtyards, rooftop gardens and terraces, and decks or walking areas, where urban dwellers can enjoy having plants and flowers with little maintenance. Still others are fostering a sense of community within the high-rise, offering alcove doorways for each unit and community gathering places with natural flora in lobbylike plazas and terraced garden areas, not unlike the proverbial "town center." The high-rise "city-within-a-city" may even have needed services within the building itself from banking and dry cleaning to fast-food outlets and even room service.

Again, though, these high-rise units with lovely views are not inexpensive. But some singles and couples without children can save enough on transportation costs to live affordably in these reengineered high-density areas.

Scenario Three: Traditional Neighborhood Design

David Korten, author of *The Post-Corporate World*, proposes village and neighborhood clusters of "modest row houses of varied design . . . clustered around courtyards, with lawns, playgrounds, and flowerbeds. Spaces between housing units would be for small gardens, composting, and raising small animals, such as chickens and goats for food." Housing clusters would bring together all generations, he explains, with older folks helping with housework, gardening, and child care, and families sharing in turn with elder care. Basic food and convenience items would be available from local shops owned and operated by local residents. All this, including medical facilities, schools, library, and entertainment, would be in easy walking distance and adjacent to green spaces and agricultural enterprises.

Characteristics of Traditional Neighborhood Design

- An identifiable neighborhood center with a transit stop.
- Dwellings mostly within a five-minute walk to the center.
- A variety of dwellings, e.g., houses, townhouses, and apartments to accommodate young and old; poor, middle class, and wealthy; singles, couples, and families.
- Shops and offices in the neighborhood of sufficiently varied types to supply the weekly needs of a household located within walking distance of homes.
- An elementary school close enough for most children to walk to and from school.
- Ample green spaces, recreation areas, and community-wide meeting facilities accessible to all dwellings—not more than a tenth of a mile away.
- Narrow streets shaded by trees and arranged to provide a variety of pedestrian, bicycle, and vehicular routes to any destination.
- Parking relegated to the rear of buildings, usually accessed by alleys.
- A self-governing body that decides matters of maintenance, security, and physical changes.

Again, while not as visionary as Korten's scenario, New Urbanism, or Traditional Neighborhood Design, is a growing movement among architects, planners, and developers that coalesced in the 1990s and has a flavor of what Korten is advocating. It focuses on incorporating pre–automobile age characteristics into new urban developments and into redevelopment areas. Homes of various types are clustered in villagelike arrangements along narrow streets that discourage auto traffic. They are lined or interspersed with greenbelts and open common areas that allow for social interaction, children's activities, and integration with commercial and agricultural uses.

Reportedly more than six hundred new towns, villages, and neighborhoods are planned or under construction in the United States using these principles of Traditional Neighborhood Design.

Some Urban and Suburban New Urbanism Communities

- Legacy Town Center, Plano, TX
- Haile Village Center, Gainesville and Miami Lakes, FL
- The Peninsula Neighborhood, Iowa City, IA
- The Village of Ponderosa, West Des Moines, IA
- Harbor Town, Memphis, TN
- Kentlands, Gaithersburg, MD
- King Farm, Rockville, MD
- Addison Circle, Addison, TX
- Orenco Station, Hillsboro, OR
- Mashpee Commons, Mashpee, MA
- The Cotton District, Starkville, MI
- Celebration and Avalon Park, Orlando, FL
- Cherry Hill Village, Canton, MI
- Baxter Village, Fort Mill, SC

Redevelopers of historic areas are adopting this model in some cities, too, such as Beerline B in Milwaukee, Crawford Square in Pittsburgh, Highlands Garden Village in Denver, and Park DuValle in Louisville. Most of these developments have Web sites to explore, and many claim they offer "affordable housing," but too often this phrase has become an oxymoron, especially considering that the value of these properties tends to escalate with each resale.

You can find profiles and additional information on "smart growth" developments like these around the country on the EPA Web site, www.epa.gov/smartgrowth/case.htm.

Scenario Four: Individually Initiated Urban Countrification

Richard Manning, author of *Against the Grain*, claims the last place we should turn for providing ways to live more naturally are the politicians, academics, real-estate developers, or professional urban planners. As William J. Mitchell, architect and author of *E-topia*, points out, "given the enormous inertia of cities we can expect the city of the next fifty to one hundred years to look a lot like the city of today." So what Manning suggests is yet a fourth scenario that appears to be more feasible and affordable for individuals to undertake right now. In this scenario, our future way of life in metro areas will depend upon individuals working independently or coming together to define and create new ways to bring the aspects of the country life they yearn for back into their existing neighborhoods.

For better or worse, the planned developments we've been discussing from Scenarios One through Three may make urban life more convenient and tolerable, but they tend to be expensive and, so far, still feel pretty much like urban or suburban life as we know it. Certainly traditional rural activities, like farming, owning livestock, and nature corridors, have yet to make their way into the typical development. But a growing number of maverick metro dwellers we call Urban Thoreaus are, as Manning advocates, taking matters into their own hands and simply undertaking more countrylike ways.

Douglas and Anita Brownfield, for example, work from home in the heart of the downtown area of a midsized city where they can walk to most of the services they need. They're restoring a comfy old house with recycled and environmentally safe materials and replanting their degraded lot with native plants, fruit trees, and a food-producing garden. They are working with neighborhoods to create a mini-community, where everyone knows one another and helps each other out when needed by pooling talents and abilities.

Lisa and Laird Schlockman are urban farmers. They live in a house on a standard-sized lot in a small city that's part of an extended micropolitan area. They use permaculture techniques to grow most of their own fruits and vegetables, from squash and watermelon to beans and strawberries, all in their backyard. "The more time you invest in providing for yourself," Lisa explains, "the less time you have to spend earning money to pay others to do it for you." They've been surprised to learn that it takes only about an hour and a half a week to plant, maintain, and harvest their urban homestead. Within this year, Lisa and Laird expect their urban lot will provide nearly twenty thousand dollars in vegetables, fruits, and nuts.

But money isn't all or even most of what's motivating Urban Thoreaus. Many are part of a trend called *urban homesteading*, composed of a growing number of people who enjoy city living, but don't see why that should stop them from engaging directly with nature, even growing their own food. From reforestation and permaculture to backyard sanctuaries and patio or community gardens, Urban Thoreaus are finding a whole continuum of ways to enhance city life by brining the best of country living to the metropolis.

Telecommuting or Working from Home

Only in the past hundred years or so have most people had to travel to their work. Throughout history, most people have lived on farms, above their shops, or had workshops behind the house accessed through alleys. The Industrial Revolution took work out of the home and had a deleterious effect not only on air quality and the general ambiance of the city but also on the cohesion of family, personal, and community life. Telecommuting or working independently from home makes an enormous difference in the quality of urban life, eliminating or drastically reducing daily commutes and freeing up the equivalent of two weeks of extra time per year usually spent driving to and from work. It also provides greater flexibility to set one's schedule around personal and family needs and priorities.

Toni Benvenuti works from home and enjoys what he calls a "boutique" lifestyle. After driving LA freeways for years, he took an unexpected downsizing as an opportunity to start his own consulting company, and although he lives in the heart of a busy, noisy urban suburb, his home and office are as tranquil and pleasant as any rural locale. Every morning he gets dressed professionally for work and walks down a lovely, shaded stone pathway to his office one hundred feet away in a converted detached garage off the backyard of his home. The walkway and most of the yard are canopied by an ancient live oak tree so large and lush that Benvenuti and his clients don't even get wet walking to the office on a rainy day.

The tree and lush foliage that fills the yard, combined with a high fence, buffer the sound of heavy street traffic only blocks away. The large windows in his office look directly onto the garden patio. A small waterfall in the garden adds to the office ambience, as does the gurgling fish tank he's turned into a novel coffee table.

Benvenuti finds his work-from-home lifestyle not only enables him to be more creative than when he worked downtown an hour away, but it also makes getting himself off to work in the mornings easier. While he once dreaded Monday mornings, he now looks forward to his short walk to the office, and he never has trouble motivating himself to start the workweek.

Working from home not only frees up jam-packed, rigid schedules and reduces the hassles of commuting, congestion, and noise and air pollution, but it also cuts expenses for eating out and wardrobe purchases and maintenance. And it can reduce the amount owed on federal and state income taxes because, if you qualify, many household costs can be deducted as legitimate business expenses.

To qualify for a home-office tax deduction, you must meet two principal criteria:

1. The deductible portion of your home must be used *exclusively* and *regularly* for your independent career or business. There are two exceptions to the criteria for exclusivity: storage of inventory or product samples and space used for a day care facility.

2. The deductible portion of your home must be *your principle place of business,* where you meet with clients or customers in the normal course of your work, or a separate structure that's not attached to your home used in pursuit of your independent career or business.

If you meet these criteria, you can not only deduct your regular costs of doing business but also a portion of the indirect expenses equivalent to the percentage of your entire home that is being used for your work, such as:

- rent
- mortgage
- security system
- housekeeping

- household supplies
- condominium association fees
- trash collection
- utilities (gas, electric, etc.)

Tip

If you are working from home in a suburban or remote area where no one else is at home or nearby during the day, be sure to connect with others through online communities or establish colleague groups to meet with regularly in person so you don't feel isolated.

Personal Nature Sanctuaries

Like Benvenuti, whether they're working from home or away, many metro residents are creating personal outdoor sanctuaries on their property. Fortunately you don't need a great deal of space, or even a yard, to create a natural retreat. Small lots, balconies, side yards, or roofs can become natural havens. Homeowners can use various combinations of color, texture, and size of foliage; waterfalls; streams; pathways of flagstone, brick, or pebbles; and curved or terraced open spaces to create an illusion of substantially greater depth and spaciousness. High, vine-covered fencing can block otherwise less-than-restful or unsightly views and reduce noise levels.

Stephanie Harrold's town-house garden off Lake Michigan in Chicago is tiny, only forty feet by twenty-five feet, but she has made use of every inch to create a charming outdoor garden and patio that can be viewed from both the living room and the kitchen. She used a trellis, fountain, and staircase to lead the eye to a circular seating area the entire family enjoys. She lightened the brick walls of her 1890 townhouse and garden to create a more spacious feel, and the fountain masks the street and air-conditioning noise. The circular brick pattern on the patio floor is set in sand, so it's softened by moss growing between the bricks.

Creating and maintaining such a sanctuary can in itself be refreshing, getting you out of doors and reconnected with the natural world. But if doing it yourself is not for you, there are natural gardening designers in most cities now who specialize in creating ambient low-maintenance, pesticide-free environments in even the tiniest backyards, side yards, decks, patios, and balconies. Most will also gladly teach you how to maintain and care for them if you wish. Some specialize in patio gardens, roof or balcony gardens, and container gardens.

Jan Goldfield (www.pondlady.com) specializes in water gardens. Discovering this passion began as a hobby in 1986. Once she completed her own garden, it was such a showpiece that friends encouraged her to offer her skills to others, and from then until her retirement in 2006, she designed, installed, and maintained aquatic gardens throughout the southern United States. She still teaches others how to bring their backyards to life with everything from ponds in pots to streams and waterfalls, large and small.

A wealth of information on creating natural urban gardens is available from shows on the Home and Garden Television (HGTV) and Do-It-Yourself (DIY) networks, each with its own informative Web sites, as well as many books and other urban gardening sites. There's even a book on welcoming wildlife to your backyard or balcony garden. See LEARN MORE.

Backyard Farms and Orchards

About 800 million people are currently involved in urban agriculture and it is estimated [that] urban agriculturists will provide up to 33 percent of the world's food production.
                                        International Conference on Urban Horticulture

Of course, vegetable gardens have long been a popular hobby, but for Urban Thoreaus it's more than that. It's a way of life. Urban homesteaders like Douglas and Anita Brownfield and Lisa and Laird Schlockman, mentioned previously, are permaculturalists. Permaculture is a set of principles and techniques for designing holistic, human-friendly landscapes modeled after nature and organic systems. It involves treating one's outdoor environment not as a separate piece of land with lots of separate elements in it, but as an ecosystem where all the elements interact cooperatively in mutually nourishing and self-sustaining ways.

Will Yeager of Venice, California, invests the time and money one might ordinarily spend to maintain a lawn in growing his own fruits and vegetables. So far he has planted sixteen fruit trees on his city lot in Venice and converted the front yard into an edible vegetable, herb, and flower garden. There he has corn, sunflowers, tomatoes, zucchini, tomatillos, radishes, onions, leeks, mustard greens, rosemary, cilantro, sage, lemon balm, sorrel, mint, curry, oregano, and marjoram, to list only a few of the plants growing in his yard on a major city boulevard. "The neighbors love the yard," he explains, "and I am always giving away herbs and veggies," he explains.

By producing much of his own food, he is not buying as much from the grocery store. He's substituting his own produce for foods imported to the city from California's Central Valley and Mexico. "Thus, for every dollar I have not spent at the grocery store I have a dollar that I can spend in other ways. And I am eating healthier food that is locally grown." Just as there is no waste in nature, no organic material leaves Will's yard, as it is all composted. The only input imported is the water.

Each element of his orchard and garden also interacts supportively with the others. The pineapple sage attracts hummingbirds with its red flowers, for example. The squirrels get real fat off the sunflowers; they tear through them, but he doesn't mind. There are always birds, butterflies, and all sorts of insects in the yard, as there are no pesticides to harm them. "Yes," he admits, "the aphids and snails can be a problem at times, but you learn integrated pest management, and by having a diversity of flora, I don't have the infestations that monocropping allows." Further, since he is always out weeding, shoveling, and engaging in physical activity, he reports that his physical health is better now. His psychological health has improved, too, thanks to the exercise he gets in the garden, a sense of connection with the land, and the wealth of positive interactions he has with neighbors.

 Tip: Saving on Water Costs

Will Yeager warns that until urban gardeners convince their city water companies to provide an allowance for garden water, you will probably be paying sewer fees on the water you use in your garden, even though it will never make its way into a sewer. Since you'll be paying both for water in and water out, having an edible garden will increase your water bill. You can minimize this, however, by having a rainwater harvesting system (see http://rainbarrelguide.com) and/or, if allowed in your community, having a gray-water recycling system for watering your garden (see www.greywater .com). Gray water, also spelled greywater and grey water, is washwater that has been used for doing dishes, laundering clothes, or bathing. While unacceptable for drinking or cooking, it can be reused, if done properly, in the garden and other purposes, thus reducing the amount of freshwater you need and reducing the amount of waste water entering sewer or septic systems. You'll save even more by harvesting rainwater and reusing gray water in your home as well as your garden.

Jim Montgomery and Mateo Rutherford also have an urban farm. On their six-thousand-square-foot yard in Berkeley, California, they, too, grow their produce, some quite esoteric, as well as apples, Asian pears, apricots, Santa Rosa plums, Satsuma tangerines, kiwi, gooseberries, and olallieberries. They also produce their own eggs, milk, cheese, and meat. While most urban areas ban livestock on city property, Berkeley does not, so they have goats, chickens, ducks, rabbits, and pigeons in their dense residential neighborhood on a busy boulevard.

The goats produce two gallons of milk a day in summer and a half gallon in winter, which Montgomery and Rutherford drink and bundle into feta cheese. The chickens lay eggs. The ducks are killed, plucked, and smoked; chickens are roasted when the flock needs culling. The pigeons serve as food, too. When goats born on their property can't be placed with other farms, Montgomery takes them to a butcher in another town, where slaughtering is legal, and watches the process to acknowledge how meat gets to our tables.

Montgomery and Rutherford have full-time jobs, and they also started a newsgroup, the Network of Backyard Urban Gardeners.

Now, before you think Urban Thoreaus can thrive only in sunny climes like Southern California, check out Greening Gotham's Green Rooftops Initiative in New York City (www.greeninggotham.org). This project demonstrates how gardens, farming, and even meadows can exist in the density of New York City.

Four-Season Greenhouse Growing

Weather needn't be a barrier for Urban Thoreaus. You can grow crops in your yard, or possibly on your roof depending on its construction, by installing an energy-efficient greenhouse. A geodesic solar greenhouse, such as those offered at Growing Dome (www.geodesic-greenhouse-kits.com) in Pagosa Springs, Colorado, provides a four-season growing environment.

Such greenhouses can be as small as twelve feet in diameter, and because they are sold as kits and use solar energy, they're not expensive to buy or operate. The interior space is heated or cooled as needed by using solar energy in conjunction with fans, venting, and a water tank. The principle of cold weather growing is to capture the heat of the sun in the day and store it inside the greenhouse, then slow down the heat loss at night, thus maintaining an ambient temperature throughout the night. In hot weather, hot air escapes through top vents in the greenhouse, and cool air comes in through the lower vents.

With their dome greenhouse that's eighteen feet in diameter, Dolores and John Swatzki are able to have a year-round growing season in their suburban yard outside of metropolitan Denver in Thornton, Colorado. Dolores built it herself with the help of her kids. "It was really easy," she explains. Even though it can get as cold as nineteen below, she's able to grow tomatoes, figs, and various herbs. She told us, "I could grow a lot more than I do." Although many of the functions, such as sprinkling, can be automated, Dolores prefers to do all the garden care herself, because it is a joy to her.

And we might add, a small greenhouse makes a very nice year-round natural urban sanctuary as well.

Community Gardens

Not all Urban Thoreaus have the space or the desire to plant and cultivate an edible garden or orchard on their own property. Some find it both more practical and more enjoyable to participate in a community garden. Residents in many urban and suburban neighborhoods are coming together to create a food-producing community garden on a vacant lot, open space, or even a rooftop. For example, according to Libby J. Goldstein, president of the Food & Agriculture Task Force, Philadelphia has 501 community vegetable gardens that have produced $1,948,633 worth of fruit and vegetables. A total of 2,812 families and 12,093 individuals are involved in these community gardens.

In 1973 artist Liz Christy gathered friends and neighbors together to create a community garden in New York City's Lower East Side of Manhattan. They found a large rubble-strewn lot that had potential as a garden and gained approval from the city to rent the site for one dollar a month. Volunteers hauled out the garbage and rubble, spread donated topsoil, installed a fence, and began planting. Their garden became New York's first community garden. Still thriving year-round, it now includes a pond, a beehive, a wildflower habitat, beautiful wooden furniture, a grape arbor, a grove of weeping birch trees, fruit trees, a dawn redwood, vegetable gardens, berries, herbs, and hundreds of varieties of flowering perennials. Members of the garden community design and tend their own individual plots, and overall maintenance is shared. (Take a peek at www.lizchristygarden.org.)

Calling themselves the Green Guerillas (www.greenguerillas.org), this group's efforts have spurred a community garden movement throughout the city. They have helped forty other community garden groups get the materials and expertise they need, and they run workshops on how to plant and grow a wide variety of plants in hostile conditions.

According to Diane Relf, a horticulture professor at Virginia Polytechnic Institute, research shows that activities like personal or community gardening provide three distinct roles in urban development:

1. They provide a more livable environment by controlling physical factors, such as temperature, noise, and pollution.

2. They help create a community image that is perceived as positive by both residents and outsiders.

3. They provide opportunities for people to work together to improve their communities.

The results translate into tangible economic and social benefits, like reduced crime, higher property values, more green areas, nutritious locally grown food, and increased business activity in attractive neighborhoods . . . not to mention the peace that being outdoors provides to the human soul.

 Tip

As permaculture activist Andrew Millison points out, native people and early European settlers chose to locate their communities in fertile floodplains or along creeks and rivers, so often older, more affordable urban neighborhoods have some of the greatest potential for growing residential crops.

Of course starting a community garden is considerably more involved than growing one on your own property. It not only involves finding and creating a proper site, but it also means working cooperatively with others and deciding collectively how you as a group will set up and maintain your garden. Sometimes there are local zoning or CC&R's (Covenants, Codes & Restrictions) present that must be overcome or changed. The American Community Garden Association Web site outlines the steps a group needs to take and provides basic information for getting underway.

Starting a Community Garden

- ▶ Form a group of interested parties to determine if there is interest, select a leader, decide what will be grown and how (organic, permaculture, etc.), select a name for your garden, raise needed funds or establish a membership fee structure, serve as work crews, and schedule needed activities.
- ▶ Choose and gain permission to use a site that gets at least six hours of sunlight a day for vegetables, is accessible to water, and contains suitable nontoxic soil. Some sites require creating suitable topsoil. Two neighbors in our community have donated use of garden sites on their property. Other groups work out a lease agreement for their land.
- ▶ Clear, clean, prepare, design, and develop your site. Ask for donations or raise funds to obtain the needed materials and tools. A secure, dry space will be needed for storing tools and equipment.
- ▶ Organize how the garden will operate. Some community gardens are run quite informally. But as workloads grow, issues and questions may need to be addressed more formally. For example, will there be members? Dues? Meetings? How will the money be collected and used and produce distributed? Will the land be worked cooperatively or divided into plots to be developed and cared for by individuals? Will there be rules for gardeners to follow and, if so, how will they be enforced? Who will perform regular maintenance, and when will it occur? What happens when people decide to drop out or others wish to join?

Ecohoods

The Lincoln-Dameron neighborhood of Prescott, Arizona, is a well-known *eco-hood*, an urban neighborhood where a certain percentage of the residents have decided to live more naturally, farming on their property and otherwise bringing traditional rural values like self-reliance, caring for and living off the land, and fostering a strong sense of community. Located in a middle- to low-income neighborhood comprised of roughly two city blocks, it includes two apartment buildings and thirty mostly small (one thousand to fifteen hundred square feet) 1930s houses. Seven separate households in the neighborhood are Urban Thoreaus. Using permaculture principles, these residents have developed six gray-water systems, two rainwater systems, five organic gardens, twenty-five heirloom fruit trees, and several dozen chicken coops in the neighborhood.

Each household decides what projects to develop, according to their personal interests and skills. But they share ideas and expertise with each other. One goal they all share is to be able to eat a significant amount of food right from their own yards. More information on the Prescott EcoHood is available on the "Projects" page of Millison Ecological (www.millisonecological.com).

Ecohoods are popping up in other urban areas, too. Sustainable Bellingham (www.sustainablebellingham.org), for example, is working at both a citywide and local neighborhood level to provide support and educational opportunities for existing neighborhoods of Urban Thoreaus. These residents can jointly develop their own ideas and models for creating self-sustaining minicommunities based on such natural principles as permaculture.

 Tip

To obtain a lease from a landowner may well involve obtaining public liability insurance. Garden insurance is still rather new to many insurance companies, so work with an agent that represents many different carriers and look to the larger, well-established carriers.

The Phinney Ecovillage Project in North Seattle's Phinney Ridge Community was founded by Cecile Andrews, author of *Circle of Simplicity: Return to the Good Life*. As their site (www.phinneyecovillage.net) points out, ecovillages are often cohousing or communal arrangements, but like Prescott, the Phinney Ecovillage is emulating the elements of such communities within a typical metropolitan neighborhood, where people may have moved for location or lifestyle reasons rather than to live in an intentional community. (See Chapter 12 and 13 for more on ecovillages.) They're looking to create "greener, healthier lifestyles, more vital inner lives, and a stronger community life." Their motto is "Simpler, Slower, Smaller. Phinney Ridge Community." Some of their many community projects include a Buy Local program, a Work at Home Group, and a compact fluorescent bulb campaign, for which they've received a grant from the City of Seattle. There is a list of other urban ecovillages at www.phinneyecovillage.net/otherecovillages.

There are many advantages to turning one's neighborhood into an ecohood:

1. First, no one is required to carry out specific shared tasks or undertake a joint project like a community garden. This enables everyone to work on their own time schedule on projects of interest to them.

2. Second, since everyone is developing projects on their own property, there's no need to locate a site or negotiate with and pay rent to a landlord.

3. Third, by sharing the benefits of each other's expertise, ideas, and experience with doing their own projects, all can enjoy a shorter learning curve.

4. By being in existing urban neighborhoods, opportunities for jobs, health care, and services are readily available.

5. Since there is no need to tear down existing structures and rebuild, there is no large initial financial investment for those participating. Thus, individuals already living in or wanting to move into existing middle- and low-income areas of a city can develop an ecohood.

Of course, again, organizers must investigate zoning and CC&R restrictions and, if necessary, may need to challenge these restrictions via political or legal means. Also, organizers must consider the soil, water, and weather conditions of the neighborhood. In Prescott's Lincoln-Dameron, for example, such conditions happen to be ideal. They have water at twelve to twenty feet, with old wells throughout the neighborhood. They sit atop an average of eight feet of topsoil and are sheltered by the topography and large, established cottonwoods.

Other factors to consider include whether the area is affordable for middle-class families and their friends, how existing residents who are not interested in participating will feel about their neighborhood becoming an ecohood, and whether the neighborhood is conveniently located within the metro area.

Relocalization Communities

Urban community efforts like those in Bellingham and Seattle mentioned previously are also part of a much larger movement called *relocalization* that's taking place across the country. This effort is arising primarily from a growing concern about the effects of dwindling natural resources and escalating energy costs, particularly fossil fuels. Growing numbers of middle-class individuals are realizing that they're almost totally dependent upon the automobile and other means of transport to get to and from work, as well as for their food or other basic supplies that must be shipped into their area from other parts of the country or abroad. This, of course, is the circumstance in most metro areas, and it's leaving many feeling quite vulnerable to economic forces far beyond their control.

So local groups are looking for ways to enable their neighborhoods and communities to become more geographically self-reliant, providing for their basic needs from sources within their own locales. They work on projects such as cooperative transport and food networks, local renewable energy production, community assessment inventories, and municipal action plans. We'll be mentioning such community efforts again in Part IV because many relocalization groups are also developing alternative means of exchange in addition to money.

The Relocalization Network (www.relocalize.net) based in Vancouver, British Columbia, was created in 2003 by Julian Darley and Celine Rich as part of the Post Carbon Institute (www.postcarbon.org). The goal of the network is to provide community groups with "support, knowledge, tools, experience, connections, working models, relationships, and plans to develop and implement relocalization strategies." They do this by providing Web-based communication tools for groups around the world to pool resources, share ideas and strategies, and collaborate on initiatives.

At this time there are 128 local groups, or outposts, in the network. They are located across Canada, the United States, and some parts of Europe, Australia, Japan, and other nations. Each group posts updated information about the steps they are taking in their community. The Web site has many resources for any group wishing to reduce their dependence on costly fossil fuels and live a more community-centered life.

Ten months ago, a decision to live locally changed Heather Gwaltney's life dramatically for the better. After commuting for ten years to a downtown job where she worked as one of 165,000 employees for a nationwide bank, she was beginning to experience physical symptoms related to stress. When she learned about the relocalization activities in her community, she quit her job to live and work locally. Her new position, which included organizing a community garden, pays 30 percent less than what she'd been earning. But her locally focused life has allowed her to slow down and recover from the physical symptoms of stress. "It's a whole different world," she says. "You go from bottom-line thinking about money to focusing on social well-being."

A year and a half later Gwaltney is studying to become a certified permaculturist. Soon she'll be teaching permaculture to others. "Living locally is very liberating," she tells us. "I've gone from using only about 40 percent of who I am as a person to 90 percent. I've found my own voice and my creative power. I've made many local friends and have a greater sense of connectedness. I'm happier."

Communities like Excelsior, Minnesota, and Humbolt County, California, represent a separate trend toward relocalization. These and many other smaller communities are concerned about losing their local character and control of their community's economic well-being to outside companies, national franchises, and big chain stores owned by international corporations. So they are taking political action to reestablish local control by creating laws and ordinances that support businesses of local residents and limit or prohibit businesses with ownership strictly outside the community. To keep a strong local commercial district and anchor the local businesses, still other towns like Anita, Iowa; Houston, Minnesota; Iron River, Wisconsin; and Scott's Bluff, Nebraska are transforming their local grocery stores into co-ops.

The Business Alliance for Living Local Economies (BALLE) is a growing US- and Canadian-based network of businesspeople who are dedicated to ensuring that economic power resides locally to sustain healthy community life as well as long-term economic viability of locally based economies. BALLE is currently comprised of forty-three locally operated business networks representing more than eleven thousand business members overall. For more on BALLE see www.livingeconomies.org.

Don't Know How?

As you can see, many of the things involved in being an Urban Thoreau, like growing seasons, planting, soil conditions, and harvesting rainwater, while once common knowledge, are now quite unfamiliar to most urban- and suburbanites. Other things, like harnessing solar or geothermal power to heat and cool our homes, require learning about new technologies.

The lack of such a knowledge base presented a challenge for us and our community as we began to contemplate such things as getting a greenhouse or starting a community garden whereby we could grow a substantial portion of our own food. We didn't know how to do it, especially in our high mountain community. When we lived in Kansas City, Missouri, Paul grew tomatoes in a small backyard garden each summer, and we had many fruit trees and some vegetables in our yard when we lived in Sierra Madre, California. But these were hobby efforts, and they contributed only marginally to our annual food needs.

A number of people where we live now are interested in having their own organic gardens or a community garden using permaculture. But the key word is "interested." There is interest but not much knowledge about how to do these things in our short, high-mountain growing season. It has also been difficult translating interest into time. Most of the interested people don't have much time to invest in such projects, often because they are spending long hours commuting.

So we've started with educating ourselves. We have brought permaculture experts in to speak to interested community members. We've joined the Post

Carbon Institute to gain access to what other communities are doing. We hold documentary film discussion groups on the need, potential, and means for establishing a more self-sustaining lifestyle within our local area. We also hope to organize a tour of local existing yard gardens.

To get around the problem of having lots of sympathetic residents with available land or fruit-bearing trees but no time or interest in cultivating or harvesting them, we hope to employ a novel solution devised by a local permaculture club in another community. First, they identified who has potential garden areas or fruit trees but no time or desire to tend them and who has the time and desire to tend a garden or orchard, but no place to do so. Then they matched up the two groups. Those willing to work do so for free and get half the produce for personal use or to sell at the local farmers' market. This arrangement seems to be working well.

If you and your group are also novices at personal and community food growing, sites like www.thegardenhelper.com, which offers a free gardening encyclopedia for beginners, and the gardening section of www.almanac.com can provide basic gardening information, as can books like those under LEARN MORE at the end of this chapter. University extension programs often include courses on gardening, sometimes including organic and permaculture gardening methods. They may also have county agents who provide on-site help to your group.

Applying for a Variance for a Community Garden

Variances are exceptions granted by a zoning, planning, or appeals board. They are escape valves built into the system. No one has an inherent right to one, and boards don't usually like granting them. Some boards will consider variances only under certain circumstances.

You start by making a request to the board. Filing fees are charged to initiate the process. These fees may range from hundreds to thousands of dollars, whether your application is approved or not.

Demonstrating that your request will cause no harm to the neighborhood or larger community, and will even enhance it, will help. A public hearing is required, so find out how people in the neighborhood feel about having a community garden. Honor their concerns, and get them to come out to the hearing to speak on your behalf.

Most areas also have private individuals who offer courses on gardening, permaculture, and organic gardening. You'll find a listing of local permaculture courses throughout the United States and in some other countries on www .permaculture.net. Lost Village, www.lostvillage.org, offers intensive residential winter and summer permaculture courses. The LEARN MORE section that follows also includes a list of specific resources for starting a community garden.

OUR ADVICE

1. If you enjoy the benefits of living in a city or suburb but are finding it harder and harder to cope with the costs and drawbacks involved, make a list of what specifically is bothering you. Is it the long commute? The noise? The cost of living?

2. Explore options like these we've discussed for how you could modify the way you live and where you live and/or work to capitalize on the pros of city life and avoid the cons.

3. If you decide to work from home, grow food on your property, or otherwise modify your property in some way, check zoning and CC&R restrictions to be sure what you wish to do is allowable. If it isn't, you can apply for a variance or work with others to changelimiting regulations that prevent residents from having more affordable and ambient ways to live.

4. If you want to enjoy any of the gardening options we've discussed, be sure that the soil, sun exposure, and other conditions will support what you want to do. Check with local landscape and gardening experts to help you determine what you can grow and when.

5. If you discover you cannot do what you want to do where you currently live or that your metro area is simply becoming too expensive, consider moving to a less costly area of the city or to a lower-cost city that has many of the urban amenities you enjoy.

Profile

Adam Gordon loves city life. But after completing law school and planning where he would sit for the bar exam, he realized that as a public-interest lawyer, he was not going to be able to afford a home in his favorite East Coast cities: Boston, New York City, or Philadelphia. So he purchased a home in Haddon Township, an older New Jersey suburb, just twelve minutes outside Philadelphia. Gordon explains that we underestimate the quality of life older, less well-known suburban or urban areas have to offer. Some such areas have many of the same amenities, including a wealth of cultural and community activities, but at a significantly lower cost. Also, like Haddon Township, such metro areas are often within easy access of a larger city for the occasional work or pleasure-oriented excursions.

---

6. If you decide you'd like to start growing your own food or creating a personal outdoor sanctuary, start small. Begin with the basics before undertaking extensive projects or buying a full range of the latest tools and equipment you think you might need. Find out if you'll like doing what's involved. In the meantime, consider sharing tools with others or borrowing as you explore what will best suit your needs.

7. If you enjoy the options you've chosen and they make your metro life more pleasurable, consider the time, money, and effort to implement your plans as a long-term investment that will reap ultimate savings and a more secure and comfortable life.

 MAKING THE CHOICE TO BE AN URBAN THOREAU

Pros

- You will be able to live more cost effectively and naturally, yet retain the many benefits of urban life.
- You will most likely master new skills and learn how to become more self-reliant and versatile.
- As you become more self-reliant and/or community based, you'll be less dependent on the whims of the consumer price index, job market, and the global economy.
- There should be more time for home and personal life and an opportunity to be more involved in your local community. You may make new friends.
- Becoming an Urban Thoreau is usually not disruptive of your existing way of life. You may be able to stay where you are now and maintain the support systems you rely on. Many physical and financial benefits will accrue over the years.

Cons

- You will still be in the city and will undoubtedly still need to contend at times with the negative aspects of city life.
- There will most likely be a learning curve to go through as you master living and working in new ways.
- There will probably be new tasks to carry out that add to your daily routines. Some of these tasks may be time-consuming and feel like hard work.
- By spending more time at home and in your community, you may be confronted with neighbors and community issues you used to more easily ignore.
- There will be an initial outlay of time and money to pursue most of the Urban Thoreau options, but this initial investment is usually considerably less than relocating and pursuing the other more drastic lifestyle changes we've discussed in other chapters.

LEARN MORE

Background on Future Urban Scenarios
Books
- *This Land: The Battle over Sprawl and the Future of America*, Anthony, Flint John Hopkins University Press, 2006.
- *Power Down: Options and Actions for a Post-Carbon World*, Richard Heinberg, New Society Publishers, 2004.

- *The Party's Over,* Richard Heinberg, Temple Lodge Publish, 2005.
- *Eco-Cities: Rebuilding Cities in Balance with Nature*, Richard Register, New Society Publishers, 2006.
- *The Post-Corporate World*, David Korten, Berrett-Koehler Publishers, 2000.
- *Against the Grain,* Richard Manning, North Point Press, 2005
- E-topia, William J. Mitchell. The MIT Press, 2000.
- www.cityfarmer.org – The Urban Agricultural Network

Backyard Farms and Orchards
Books
- *The Sustainable Vegetable Garden: A Backyard Guide to Healthy Soil and Higher Yields*, John Jeavons, Ten Speed Press, 1999.
- *Welcoming Wildlife to the Garden: Creating Backyard & Balcony Habitats for Wildlife*, Catherine J. Johnson, Susan McDiarmid, and Edward R. Turner, Hartley & Marks Publishers, 2004.

Catalogs
- Peddler's Wagon – http://pathtofreedom.com/peddlerswagon

Web Sites
- www.cityfarmer.org
- www.oasisdesign.net/faq – ecological design systems
- www.growing – gardens.org

Apprenticeships
- Soil Born Farm Urban Agriculture Project, 3000 Hurley Way, Sacramento, CA 95864; (916) 486-9687, soilborn2@earthlink.net

Basic Home and Gardening How-Tos
Books
- *Gardening All-in-One for Dummies*, The National Gardening Association, Bob Beckstrom, Karan Davis Cutler, Kathleen Fisher, Phillip Giroux, Judy Glattstein, Mike MacCaskey, Bill Marken, Charlie Nardozzi, Sally Roth, Marcia Tatroe, Lace Walheim, and Ann Whitman, For Dummies, 2003.
- *Organic Gardening for Dummies*, Ann Whitman and the Editors of the National Gardening Association, For Dummies, 2001.
- *Herb Gardening for Dummies*, Karan Davis Cutler, Kathleen Fisher, and The National Gardening Association, For Dummies, 2000.

Associations

▸ The National Gardening Association, 1100 Dorset Street, South Burlington, VT 05403; (802) 863-5251, www.garden.org

TV Shows

▸ DIY: The Do-It-Yourself Network – www.diynetwork.com
▸ HGTV: Home and Garden Television – www.hgtv.com

Web Sites

▸ www.almanac.com
▸ www.thegardenhelper.com

Community Gardening
Books

▸ *Growing Communities: How to Build Community Through Community Gardening*, Jeanette Abi-Nader, David Buckley, Kendall Dunnigan, and Kristen Markley. Available through www.communitygarden.org/growing.php
▸ *How Does Our Garden Grow? A Guide to Community Garden Success*, Laura Berman, FoodShare Metro Toronto, 1997. See also www.foodshare.net/garden
▸ *Urban Gardening Program: The Coordinator's Book*, Pennsylvania State University Cooperative Extension Service, 1990. Available through www.cityfarmer.org/gardenrules.html

Associations

▸ American Community Garden Association, c/o Franklin Park Conservatory, 1777 East Broad Street, Columbus, OH 43203; (877) ASK-ACGA or (877) 275-2242, www.communitygarden.org

Web Sites

▸ http://celosangeles.ucdavis.edu/garden/articles/startup_guide.html – Community garden start-up guide
▸ www.cityfarmer.org – Considered the most comprehensive site on the Internet about urban agriculture, community gardening, and sustainable agriculture
▸ www.mindspring.com/~communitygardens – urban community Gardens

Ecohoods

▸ *Superbia: 31 Ways to Create Sustainable Neighborhoods*, Dan Chiras and Dave Wann, New Society Publishers, 2004.

Greenhouses
Books
- ▶ *Greenhouse Gardener's Companion: Growing Food and Flowers in Your Greenhouse or Sunspace*, Shane Smith and Marjorie C. Leggitt, Fulcrum Publishing, 2000.
- ▶ *Home Solar Gardening: Solar Greenhouses for Your House, Backyard, or Apartment*, John H. Pierce, Key Porter Books, 1992.

Greenhouse Designs and Dome Kits
- ▶ www.geodesic-greenhouse-kits.com
- ▶ www.greenhouses.org

Web Sites
- ▶ www.backyardgardener.com/greenhouse
- ▶ www.cityfarmer.org – Includes City Farmer TV

Permaculture
Books
- ▶ *An Introduction to Permaculture*, Mollison and Reny Slay, Tagari Publications, 1997.
- ▶ *Gaia's Garden: A Guide to Home-Scale Permaculture*, Toby Hemenway, Chelsea Green Publishing Company, 2001.
- ▶ *Permaculture: A Practical Guide for a Sustainable Future*, Bill Mollison, Island Press, 1990.
- ▶ *Permaculture: Principles and Pathways Beyond Sustainability*, David Holmgren, Holmgren Design Services, 2002.

Magazines
- ▶ *Permaculture Activist*, www.permacultureactivist.net
- ▶ *Permaculture*, www.permaculture.co.uk

Training, Workshops, Certification, Consultation
- ▶ The Food Forest – http://foodforest.com
- ▶ Listings of local workshops and training programs by state – www.permaculture.net
- ▶ Residential training, camps, and certification in permaculture and EcoCertification – www.lostvalley.org/epcp
- ▶ University Extension Programs Nationwide – www.csrees.usda.gov/Extension

Web Sites
► www.millisonecological.com
► www.permaculture.net

Raising Chickens, Goats, Etc., in the City
Books
► *Barnyard in Your Backyard: A Beginner's Guide to Raising Chickens, Ducks, Geese, Rabbits, Goats, Sheep, and Cows*, Gail Damerow, Storey Publishing, 2002.
► *Keep Chickens! Tending Small Flocks in Cities, Suburbs, and Other Small Spaces*, Barbara Kilarski, Storey Publishing, 2003.
► *Natural Goat Care*, Pat Coleby, Acres USA, 2001.

Web Sites
► www.naturalfamilyhome.com/livestock.html

Relocalization
► The Business Alliance for Local Living Economies (BALLE) – www.livingeconomies.org
► The Post-Carbon Institute – www.postcarbon.org
► The Relocalization Network – www.relocalize.net

Rooftop Gardening
► www.cityfarmer.org/rooftop59.html
► www.cityfarmer.org/roofmonica61.html
► www.cityfarmer.org/roofthesisIntr.html

Water Gardens
► *Complete Guide to Water Gardens: Ponds, Fountains, Waterfalls, Streams*, Kathleen Fisher, Creative Homeowner, 2000.
► *The Master Book of the Water Garden: The Ultimate Guide to the Design and Maintenance of the Water Garden*, Phillip Swindells, Bulfinch, 2002.
► *Water Gardens, Pools, Streams & Fountains*, Better Homes and Gardens, 2006.
► *Encyclopedia of Water Garden Plants*, Greg Speichert and Sue Speichert, Timber Press 2004.

Working from Home

- ▶ *Working from Home*, Paul and Sarah Edwards, Tarcher/Penguin, 1999.
- ▶ Also available in eBook form:
    - » Is Working From Home for You? Working for Yourself? On a Salaried Job?
    - » Setting Up The Professional Home Office
    - » Working From Home: Legal, Tax, and Insurance Matters
    - » Working From Home: Managing Your Time, Money & and Your Stuff
    - » Working From Home: Avoiding The Four Most Dreaded Pitfalls. Pine Mountain Institute, 2007

Can the average American begin to move away from traditional
energy sources without pulling out of society? The answer
is yes! There is a revolution afoot, and it's happening
quietly across the country.

Christine Woodside,
award-winning environmental writer

CHAPTER TWELVE

Living Off the Grid—
Powering Down

Our homes are connected by a vast grid, or infrastructure, that most of us pay little attention to but depend upon for the lifeblood of our households. This grid is a system of poles, wires, towers, dams, cellular nodes, and pipes that link us all together and provide heat, cooling, water, light, communication, and sanitation. There was, of course, a time long ago when each of us had to provide for such things ourselves. For rural families, it has only been several hundred years since they were still responsible for digging wells for water, making candles from animal fat for light, cooking and heating their homes with wood fireplaces, and disposing of their own waste.

Most of us living today have no personal memory of doing such things, nor do we think of how these services are provided to us . . . until we get our monthly utility bills. For a variety of reasons, however, some 180,000 U.S. families have decided to disconnect from the grid they've depended upon for so long. That figure has jumped 33 percent a year for a decade, says Richard Perez, publisher of *Home Power* magazine. Thanks to utility company incentives, another twenty-seven thousand grid-connected houses supplement the utility's power with their own energy systems, mostly with solar power. As bills for electricity, heating oil, or propane energy inch up to levels once equivalent to one's monthly rent or mortgage payment, as is now often the case during the winter where we live, the decision to disconnect is primarily a financial issue for many.

For others, like Janaia Donaldson and Robyn Mallgren, who wanted to buy a remote 160-acre swatch of land and build a new home, it was a necessity. Most land without utility lines can be purchased for 25 to 40 percent less, but their location was a mile and a half to the nearest power pole. Bringing in a line would have cost thirty-eight thousand dollars. Installing alternative forms of energy and living off the grid made buying and living on the land possible.

To some, getting off the grid provides a sense of independence. Still others are motivated by a concern about dwindling natural resources and the effects our heavy use of fossil fuel is having on the environment. By turning to renewable sources of energy, such as sun, wind, and water, they're choosing a more natural, self-sufficient way of life that leaves a smaller environmental footprint.

Usually it's some combination of reasons like these that attract people to live fully or partially off the grid. We've already mentioned several examples in other chapters. In Chapter One we wrote about Katy and Rick Blanchard. If you recall, Katy, a fifty-seven-year-old fiber artist, and Rick, a sixty-two-year-old landscape architect, decided to escape the high cost of their San Diego lifestyle for life off the grid on fifty-six acres outside tiny Abiquiu, New Mexico, where they are now self-sufficient, relying on solar power and the well water on their property. Their motivation behind the move was multifaceted. Partly financial, as supporting a San Diego life left little time for anything other than work, but also because they wanted to live closer to nature, focus more on the work they love, and still have ample time for the personal and civic activities they value. They are involved with others, for example, in efforts to redevelop a local arts-based economy in northern New Mexico so artists can afford to continue living and working there.

Rising Utility Costs over Last Twenty Years	
Energy	132%
Fuels	81.9%
Electricity	53.0%

U.S. Department of Energy's Energy Information Administration
www.eia.doe.gov/emeu/aer/pdf/perspectives.pdf

In discussing living on the road, we mentioned that when Ed and Cheryl Nodland began traveling on the road full-time with their two sons, they had their thirty-two-foot RV prewired with solar panels for greater energy efficiency. They feature the details of their power system on their Web site at www.road-school.com/acintro.htm. Many of the Urban Thoreaus we wrote about in Chapter 11 keep the costs of their urban homesteads down by using solar panels and energy-efficient appliances, including a solar oven and biodiesel processors. Dolores and John Swatzki, for example, chose a solar greenhouse so they could use the sun's power to grow year-round. The Lincoln-Dameron ecohood in Prescott, Arizona, is developing gray-water systems and doing rain harvesting.

Contrary to common misconceptions, it's possible to live off the grid, either fully or partially, whether you live in the city, on a farm, in an RV, or on a boat. This is true regardless of whether you are buying or building a new home or adapting an existing one. And you don't have to give up the many comforts of modern life we depend upon and enjoy. As with the other lifestyles we've featured, there are many choices, e.g., just how off the grid you want to be, which utilities you take off grid and to what extent, and whether you also choose to live a low-energy lifestyle.

What to Take Off the Grid

Here, for example, are a number of the systems one can consider powering with alternative forms of energy:

- Cooling
- Cooking
- Communication
- Driving
- Heating

- Lighting
- Powering household tasks and appliances
- Water supply
- Waste disposal

How Off the Grid Should You Go?

Off the grid is not an all-or-nothing prospect. There's a wide spectrum of choices, from simply conserving and supplementing traditional household utilities to disconnecting altogether. The choice is yours, and it needn't be made all at once. Here are some ideas to get you started:

- You can supplement or augment your existing utilities to reduce costs and live more efficiently, for example, using solar panels to heat your water heater.
- You can convert one or more functions to off grid and leave others on the grid, for example, heating your home in winter with a woodstove but otherwise remaining connected to electricity, water, and sewer systems and continuing to drive a gasoline-powered car.
- You can progressively take as many systems as possible off the grid, for example, beginning by simply composting your food waste; then deciding to install some form of alternative energy to power your home; later developing a gray-water system; and eventually taking your phone off the grid and converting your car so that it operates on something other than gasoline.

▶ You can buy or build a brand new "green" home where off-the-grid alternatives come with the house or building. You can construct your new "green" home with the usual "stick" or wood framing we're all familiar with or some alternative method that will greatly reduce energy costs and make low-energy living easier and more convenient, such as, straw bale, insulated block cordwood, concrete block forms (CFS's), rammed earth, earth berms, or "thick shell" construction.

▶ You can buy a home, rent, or join in an ecovillage community, such as Village Homes in Davis, California (www.villagehomesdavis.org), or EcoVillage in Ithaca, New York (www.ecovillage.ithaca.ny.us). Ecovillages are sustainable living communities with options such as small-scale organic farming, land preservation, green building, energy alternatives, hands-on education, and cohousing neighborhoods. They can be urban or rural. Some resemble a traditional housing development except that the homes are built with "green" materials, come with solar or other alternative forms of energy, and usually have ample green space. Others are intentional communities with an explicit set of values where residents share many community functions and facilities. (See the LEARN MORE section that follows this chapter and Chapter 13 for more on ecovillages, including a list of such communities.)

Whichever choice you make, you can usually continue using most of the modern appliances and amenities to which you've been accustomed, or you can choose to adopt a low-energy lifestyle and slightly or dramatically reduce your energy usage.

Homesteaders, like some of the Urban Thoreaus we described in the previous chapter, are choosing to not only live off the grid but also to produce much of their own food. People sometimes confuse powering down with homesteading, but homesteading is actually only the most extreme example.

Homesteading

In pioneering days in the United States, the term "homesteading" referred to staking a claim to land on the frontier. This was the most common way land was settled in the late nineteenth century. Homesteading pioneers settled on rural land and generally raised their own food. Today, the term *homesteading* refers to what's alternatively called the back-to-the-land movement, and it generally refers to living off the land in a sustainable, self-sufficient way. Most homesteaders are locating in rural areas on at least several acres of land. The Urban Thoreaus we described in the previous chapter are part of a more recent movement, called "urban homesteading," bringing sustainable living and small-scale agriculture and home food production into metro areas.

Most homesteaders, be they urban or rural, make an effort to be as self-sufficient as possible, and often that means cutting energy usage and getting off the grid to whatever extent possible.

Unhooking from the Grid

Although almost every aspect of powering our current lives depends upon fossil fuels such as electricity, heating oil, propane, and gasoline, there is an array of alternatives, all of which are and will become more and more desirable as fossil fuels rise in price. Following is a list of some of the more commonly discussed options. Many are simple and cost little; some are more complex and require an investment; a few are too cutting-edge to be practical at this time but hold promise for the future.

Various Off-the-Grid Options

- Biodiesel
- Composting food wastes
- Compost and waterless toilets
- Energy-efficient appliances
- Hydrogen fuel
- Insulated windows
- Internet telephony
- Geothermal heat pumps
- Green building and materials
- Gray-water systems
- Low-wattage light-bulbs
- Native plant landscaping
- Rainwater harvesting and wells
- Root cellars
- Solar energy
- SunFrost refrigerators
- Wind-generated electricity
- Window coverings
- Wood

Udgar and Puja Parsons live off the electric grid in a valley situated along the edge of the San Juan National Forest near the town of Pagosa Springs, Colorado. Living "lightly on the land and using natural energies" are among Udgar's primary values. Amazed by the power of sailing ships, waterwheels, and windmills, he's inspired by their practicality. "There is free energy all around us!" he points out. But his way of life isn't only a practical matter. "There's a spiritual aspect to caring for life and living in relationship with the land, too," he says. He and his wife, Puja, still enjoy most of the electric appliances one would find in any middle-class household. They still have satellite TV, a DVD player, a juicer, a boom box, toaster oven, hair dryer, a variety of electric saws and other power tools, as well as computer systems with which they run their business, Growing Spaces (www.geodesic-greenhouse-kits.com).

They're able to live comfortably off the grid because they use many of the low-energy alternatives you will read about in this chapter. The electricity that powers their home is generated by PV solar panels, stored in batteries, and then converted for use in the household from DC to AC power. They started out with only four 50-watt solar panels at a cost of three thousand dollars. As they remodeled and expanded their cabin, they grew to using ten 50-watt solar panels. They heat their home using propane and a woodstove. They also have a backup propane generator, but they've only needed it four or five times in eleven years.

Like others in Pagosa Springs, their ground water is full of sulfur, so they haul in one thousand gallons of fresh water every three months and store it in an underground cistern. Other water comes from a rain catchment system that collects and filters rainwater that runs off the roof. After using their low-energy washing machine, they send their wash water out to fertilize the land. Their refrigerators and stove run on propane. Much of their produce (greens, spinach, beans, tomatoes, onion, chard, kale, potatoes, beets, and so forth) grows year-round in their two Growing Dome® Greenhouses.

"We're not disconnecting from ordinary life," Puja explains. "We're entrepreneurs who live off grid. We consider ourselves progressive, not regressive." They have vehicles that run on gasoline, a normal telephone line, and a satellite dish. But at night, they turn off the TV and computers by flipping the switch on a power strip the appliances are plugged into. This means that during the night these machines no longer draw what's called "phantom load," the electricity consumed by devices while they are switched off but plugged in.

The one appliance they don't have that most folks do is a clothes dryer. Their dryer is the wind, or normal daily indoor heat. "I love the experience of hanging our clothes out to dry," Puja reports, "noticing the smell of pine and the blue Colorado skies." They both like the fresh smell of sun-dried clothes and haven't missed the dryer.

For Udgar, continually watching the gauge for energy usage is fun. It's like a game. He likes knowing how many resources they are using and finding ways to conserve. But Udgar's son, Nick, who also lives off grid in his own home isn't so enamored with monitoring usage; he prefers to have more solar panels. With more power in his system, he doesn't have to be so mindful of what he uses, only checking usage after a series of cloudy days.

Udgar admits, though, that cleaning and maintaining the water level in the batteries and keeping them aligned each month can be a challenge. "That's a small price to pay though," he explains, "for the peace, silence, and beauty of living more naturally."

Janaia Donaldson and Robyn Mallgren live off the grid, too, but they choose also to live a lifestyle without many of the appliances most people take for granted. Sixteen years ago they were well-paid techies living and working in fast-paced Silicon Valley. Janaia cherished the lifelong goal of being financially independent by the age of forty-five, and she had begun to wonder if she was going to achieve this goal. They were also growing weary of the long hours and the treadmill-like quality of their life. So she and Robyn signed up for a Your Money or Your Life course, a nine-step program for changing the way you earn, spend and save money, based on a book by the same name, we mentioned in Chapter Five. They had the money; they were ready for the life. They began to question, *just how much money (and all the things it can buy) is enough?*

Shortly after the end of the course, they visited a friend in Nevada City and were taken by the beauty and the leisurely pace of life there. A new, shared dream began to form in their hearts that Christmas of 1988. One year later, they purchased land outside Nevada City, and by 1999 they were living off the grid in a twelve-hundred-square-foot manufactured home, telecommuting to their Silicon Valley jobs. They're still there now and working in their own business, Yuba Gals, a TV production company. Here's how they do it.

They have a well on their property with a two-hundred-foot water level from which they can pump one gallon a minute. A three-thousand-gallon underground water storage tank keeps water ready for their use. A separate pump moves the water out of the tank into their house. They use about fifty gallons of water a day and fill the tank once a month.

Their home is powered by twenty-four 60-watt PV solar panels that feed electricity into a set of eight six-volt L-16 batteries. Their water pumps, ceiling fans, and SunFrost refrigerator run on DC energy and are powered directly by these batteries. An inverter enables their other electrical devices to run on regular AC power like in traditional homes. Altogether the entire system—PV solar panels, batteries and chargers, inverter, and propane backup generator—cost twenty-five thousand dollars.

Because they were telecommuting and now work in their own business, they have computers, monitors, and printers, as in any other up-to-date home office, as well as a telephone line with ISDN Internet access. But to keep their energy use and costs down, they have no electric kitchen appliances, for example, no waffle iron, toaster, or toaster oven. They prepare their meals on a propane stove or the top of a wood stove. In good weather they cook outdoors in an outdoor solar oven. Like the Parsons, they have a washing machine but no dryer. Their iron runs on butane.

The house is lit by windows and skylights in the daytime and with compact fluorescent bulbs at night and on overcast days. While they're asleep they turn off the inverter, so there is no AC running at all!! "No hums, no EMFs (Electromagnetic Force) in walls—very healthful effects," says Janaia. To combat the cold winter weather, Janaia and Robyn covered their windows with Warm Window insulating window shades (www.warmcompany.com). The shades immediately cut the amount of wood they need by a half to a third.

They don't have a satellite system, but they do have a stereo system, VCR, DVD player, sewing machine, and vacuum sweeper, but they only vacuum on sunny days. They do their wash on days when the propane generator is charging the batteries. The batteries can run for five or six days of cloudy, gray weather before they need to be recharged. "There is a lot of maintenance and new habits to develop when you live off the grid," Robyn explains, but Janaia adds that they don't feel the time-exhaustion they felt on their jobs. "This is our choice, and it enables us to feel more connected to our environment, for example, watching for sunshine and the clouds. I love doing the things I do for the house. It's not a burden."

Unlike Udgar and Puja, they don't grow any food on their land, but evidently there is something quite special about drying one's clothes outdoors, because Janaia also mentioned how much she enjoys it.

Both Udgar and Puja's and Janaia and Robyn's homes are outside small towns on multiple acres of land, but Julia Russell's off-the-grid home is quite distinct from theirs. Her Eco-Home™ is located in Los Feliz, a quiet residential neighborhood of Los Angeles, California. Her home is literally a living demonstration of how one can live off the grid in the heart of an urban area. It's a restored And retrofitted California-style bungalow, circa 1911, that incorporates solar hot water heating, photovoltaic panels, ultralow-flow water systems, and other energy and water conservation measures. Beginning in 1988, Russell opened Eco-Home to the public (www.eco-home.org), offering Sunday afternoon tours by reservation only. Now internationally known, it has attracted thousands of visitors. You can see it, too, on the DVD *Going Green*, which shows how one can live off grid on a limited budget in the middle of a city. It's available from www.greenplanetfilms.org.

A Glossary: Just What Are These Things Anyway?

In describing these three homes, we've mentioned a lot of alternatives, some of which you might not be familiar. We weren't. While we can't go into detail as to how they each work, here is a glossary of terms and a brief synopsis of their benefits and limitations, along with how you can find out more about the alternatives you might like to consider.

▶ **Biodiesel:** Plant and animal waste or vegetable oils used as fuel. With modification, diesel-engine automobiles can be fueled with biodiesel or waste vegetable oils. Also, most residential furnaces and boilers designed to burn No. 2 heating oil can be modified to burn either biodiesel or filtered, preheated waste vegetable oil. Biodiesel is generally not as clean burning as petroleum oil, and although there are eighty-five biodiesel refineries in the United States as of this writing and sixty-five others under construction, you can't go to many service stations and say "fill 'er up." There are a few truck stops, mostly in Texas and the southern United States, that sell BioWillie, a biodiesel blend of clean burning renewable fuel developed and promoted by the singer/songwriter Willie Nelson. It's made from soybeans and other vegetable oils and can be burned without modification in diesel engines. Existing locations selling BioWillie are listed at www.wnbiodiesel.com.

For most of us, though, biodiesel is still mostly a do-it-yourself project. But if processed properly at home, it can result in a considerable cost savings. The United States produces over 11 billion liters of waste vegetable oil annually from deep-frying potato processing plants, snack-food producers, and fast-food restaurants. Many restaurants will give away their used cooking oil either for free or at minimal cost; otherwise they pay to have it hauled away by a renderer. Processing biodiesel at home is fairly simple and inexpensive. Those we've spoken with who are doing it also claim it takes very little time. Although thousands of drivers are producing pure biodiesel at home without difficulty, there can be problems using vegetable oil when converting some of the more recent diesel engines.

Clean Diesel Cars

While at this time biodiesel isn't readily available commercially for most cars, Mercedes-Benz, BMW, and Volkswagen have an agreement to share what's called BlueTec diesel technology that will enable diesel-powered cars and SUVs to meet the toughest auto emission standards. Diesel-powered cars get mileage some 30 percent higher than a gas-powered equivalent. GM has announced what they call a "serial-hybrid project" to develop an electric car with a small diesel engine to charge batteries. Keep an eye out for these and many other gas-saving vehicles, including GM and Ford's planned plug-in hybrid gas/electric cars and the rumored Visionary Vehicles' Chery car, a 100-mpg plug-in hybrid that could be priced 20 to 30 percent less than gasoline-powered vehicles.

▶ **Composting food wastes:** turning household waste into fertilizer and organic soil matter. Basically, composting is recycling one's garbage. All organic matter eventually decomposes, but composting speeds up the process by creating an ideal environment for microorganisms to do their work. The result looks and feels like garden soil. It's dark, crumbly, and makes an excellent fertilizer for gardens, lawns, and landscaping. One can simply create a compost pile, mixing and turning the compost regularly, or one can purchase a compost tumbler or bin, which is routinely turned and then emptied into the soil when it's full. If done properly, it's not smelly and need not be unattractive. It does involve taking your garbage outside. However, if you're like us and have meat-eating wildlife in your area (e.g., bears, bobcats) composts may attract them, so we don't compost animal waste such as meat bones, fat, or eggshells. This means taking a few minutes to sort out garbage.

▶ **Compost or waterless toilets** (sometimes called *biological toilets* or *dry toilets*): compost human excrement, biodegradable paper, carbon additive, and, optionally, food wastes. Since toilet flushing normally accounts for up to 50 percent of indoor water use, a compost toilet results in a considerable reduction in water usage and cost. Several kinds are available. Electric toilets burn the waste. Others use a very small amount of water or a chemical foam to assist the passage of waste to the composting chamber. When properly installed, none of them create odor or health problems, and some models require only minor maintenance. The end product is a stable, soil-like material called "humus" that, in the United States, must be either buried or removed by a licensed seepage hauler in accord with state and local regulations. Also, some communities do not allow compost toilets in a home. In other countries, humus is used as a soil conditioner on edible crops.

▶ **Energy-efficient appliances:** appliances designed to use less energy. The price you pay for any appliance you buy is only the beginning of what that appliance will cost. The operating cost over its lifetime can be many times greater than the initial investment. The amount of energy appliances use varies, even model to model. So an easy way to save money without giving up the convenience and comforts of the many appliances we depend upon is to buy energy-efficient models. ENERGY STAR is a joint program of the U.S. Environmental Protection Agency (EPA) and the U.S. Department of Energy to identify efficient products and practices. An Energy Star rating on an appliance or new home indicates that it meets strict energy-efficiency guidelines set by the EPA and Department of Energy. So look for an Energy Star label, and review the tips, lists, and guidelines on www .energystar.gov. Also, check out the Consumer's Guide to Home Energy Savings at the American Council for Energy Efficient Economy Web site at www.aceee.org/consumerguide. When shopping, note specifications and compare products. In the United States the amount of energy an appliance uses appears on the product, usually on the back or the bottom.

Also, consider replacing older appliances. Many were manufactured before there was interest in saving on energy costs. You might be surprised how much money you can save. Older refrigerators and freezers especially are energy gluttons.

► **Hydrogen fuel cells:** Combine hydrogen (stored in a tank) with oxygen in the air to make electricity. Predicted by many to be the fuel of the future, major auto manufacturers have been rushing to develop and test fuel-cell cars. Honda has recently introduced the FCX fuel-cell sedan. Fuel cells power an electric motor, which ultimately propels the vehicle. Water is the only by product from the tailpipe. The challenge has been finding a way to produce hydrogen from something other than some other fossil fuels, such as gasoline, natural gas, or propane. GM is developing what's called a Hy-wire fuel-cell propulsion system for their concept car, Chevrolet Sequel. Fuel cells also hold promise for fueling one's furnace or air conditioner. They are definitely an emerging technology to watch.

► **Geothermal heat pumps:** a system for heating and cooling one's home by tapping into the earth's natural thermal energy. Also called geo-exchange heating, this alternative energy system is composed of a heat pump and diagonal or horizontal loops of copper coil filled with refrigerant that are drilled into the ground. Heat is exchanged between the house and the ground for cooling and between the ground and the house for heating. The heat pump moves heat by evaporating and condensing the refrigerating fluid. Although installation can be costly, geothermal heat pumps can be used in virtually every region of the United States and can significantly reduce energy usage without decreasing comfort. Depending upon the size of one's home, it can provide a 30 to 40 percent savings over conventional heating systems. There are limitations, however. It can't be used on property that sits on rock or on soil that is laced with thick tree roots. There also must be ample space for drilling downward or outward thirty feet. The pump requires considerable electric power, but this can be supplied by installing solar panels.

► **Green building and materials:** using design, siting, and construction materials that increase the efficiency with which a home or building uses energy. Also known as "sustainable building" or "environmental building," the benefits of green building are reduced operating costs from increased productivity and less usage; fewer toxic substances and thus better indoor air quality and a healthier home environment; and reduced environmental impact. At this time, green construction and green materials are still generally more expensive than traditional ones, but not always, and yield considerable cost savings in terms of energy usage over the lifetime of the home.

Some of the more nontraditional green construction methods include:

- **Straw bale:** using bales of straw for walls, insulation, or both. Its advantages include the ready availability, the low cost of hay bales, and their very high insulation value for keeping in heat or cool air. In some areas it is difficult to find contractors who know how to build hay bale homes. This can raise the cost, but often people save on construction by building a hay bale home themselves. Some counties or cities do not allow them under the local building codes. See LEARN MORE.
- **Insulated block cordwood:** using short-length pieces of debarked tree laid crosswise with masonry or cob (a mixture of clay, sand, straw, water, and earth) for walls of a home. This material has much greater thermal mass, making the home easier to heat and cool. Western red cedar is especially good for this use, as it is resistant to rot and insects, but almost any softwood species can be used. It is a third the cost of standard building materials and has been used for more than one thousand years in other parts of the world.
- **Insulated Concrete Forms** (ICFs): walls that consist of concrete poured into permanent frames or blocks that are filled with foam and reinforced with ties that allow for any type of exterior or interior finish. ICFs are so airtight that you can save up to 50 to 80 percent on energy bills. How much you save will depend on many factors, such as the number and type of windows in the home, the roof structure, the heating and cooling system, and weather conditions in the locale. ICFs are also exceptionally fire, earthquake, and wind resistant, so insurance for ICF homes can be considerably less. However, adding or moving external doors, widows, or plumbing is difficult once a house is complete.
- **Rammed earth:** construction material composed of earth in suitable proportions of sand, gravel, clay, and sometimes an added stabilizer, like cement. Rammed earth evens out daily temperature variations and reduces the need for air-conditioning and heating. It heats up slowly during the day and releases its heat during the evening. But it's not a good insulator, so like brick and concrete in a colder climate, it often requires insulation. It's naturally soundproof and virtually fireproof.
- **Earth berms:** the piling up of earth on the sides and sometimes the roof of a structure to provide a thick surrounding insulation. Usually

used in cold climates, earth-bermed structures commonly use rustic posts and beams, stacked logs, stacked stones, steel arches, or ferro-cement shells. They provide improved energy efficiency and greater insulation for rather simple, cheap, and quickly built structures. Windows tend to be few and small except on south-facing walls to make optimal use of passive solar heating. Some designs use an earth-covered roof rather than a side berm. This allows for more windows and exits but requires a structure of much greater load-bearing strength.

▸ **Gray-water systems:** recycled wash water, also called *graywater, grey water,* and *greywater.* Gray water is water that's been used for washing dishes, doing laundry, and bathing. Since it constitutes 50 percent or more of household water usage, it can be reused for garden and landscaping purposes if properly filtered and treated. Although they are not allowed in all communities, a gray-water system reduces the amount of freshwater needed as well as the amount of wastewater entering sewer or septic systems. At this point gray-water treatment systems are still not in high demand, so you may well have to design and build a system that meets your needs. Options to consider for gray water treatment include settling tanks, disinfectants, and filters.

▸ **Internet telephony:** eliminates the need for a land phone line or cellular service. As we've mentioned previously, software such as Skype (www.skype .com), Vonage (www.vonage.com), Delta Three (www.deltathree.com), and Net2phone (www.net2phone.com) enable you to talk by phone to anyone anywhere for far less than typical landline or cellular phone services do. The software is easy to download and use without the assistance of a technician, although at this point, the voice quality is variable. Features such as call waiting, call forwarding, and voice mail are available, and some packages are available for use with all the touch-tone phones in your house.

▸ **CFLs and LEDs:** low-wattage light bulbs. Compact fluorescent lamps (CFLs), often called low-energy bulbs, use much less energy than the common tungsten filament bulbs. CFLs work much like a fluorescent strip. The inside is coated with a phosphor that gives off the light, and there is an electronic ballast to start the lamp operating. They plug directly into normal light fittings and come in a variety of shapes and forms, including short glass sticks or tubular loops, producing either warm or cool light. Sometimes, they are enclosed in a glass bowl to look like a traditional bulb. CFLs should not be confused with low-voltage bulbs, which do not offer significant energy or cost savings. As these U.S. Department of Energy figures demonstrate, the energy savings are considerable:

Incandescent vs. Compact Fluorescent Light Bulbs		
Bulb type	100W Incandescent	23W Compact Fluorescent
Purchase price	$0.75	$11.00
Life of the bulb	750 hours	10,000 hours
Number of hours burned/day	4 hours	4 hours
Number of bulbs needed	About 6 over 3 years	1 over 6.8 years
Total cost of bulbs	$4.50	$11.00
Lumens produced	1,690	1,500
Total cost of electricity ($.08/kwh)	$35.04	$8.06
Total cost over three years	$39.54	$19.06
Total savings over three years		$20.50

Like traditional bulbs, CFLs are sold by wattage, but because they produce more light per watt, you don't need to buy CFLs with as much wattage to obtain the same degree of light.

Ordinary Bulbs	CFLS Equivalents
40W	7–10W
60W	15–18W
100W	20–25W
150W	32W

 Warning!

Compact fluorescent bulbs contain small amounts of mercury, and even though they can be disposed of with regular trash, they are categorized as household hazardous waste. They pose no threat while in the bulb, but if one breaks, do not inhale the mercury. Use a wet rag to clean up breakage and put all of the pieces and the rag into a plastic bag. Do not incinerate.

On the down side, CFLs are more expensive to buy, but their life cycle and energy savings more than make up for the initial cost. Other drawbacks include that they do produce what some find to be the irritating hum of fluorescent lighting, although it has been reduced, and personally we've found that there are areas they simply don't light adequately, particularly in the kitchen and bathrooms.

Light-Emitting Diodes (LEDs) are even more energy efficient. Until recently, small, solid lightbulbs had limited uses, but recent improvements have lowered their cost, and they're now available in arrays of bulbs that fit standard AC and DC receptacles, lamps, and recessed and track lights. They last 10 times as long as compact fluorescents and 133 times longer than typical incandescent bulbs. Because they also don't have a filament, they don't break as easily as other bulbs. They are cool burning because there is no heat buildup, and they use a fraction of the wattage of incandescent bulbs. Because of the low power requirement for LEDs, using solar panels becomes more practical and less expensive. But on the downside, although their cost keeps coming down, they are still expensive. They also don't radiate light in 360 degrees the way an incandescent bulb does. Their light is focused, that is, bright where it's pointed, so they're best for task lighting, such as reading lights, desk lamps, night-lights, spotlights, security lights, etc.

Although you can find CFLs and LEDs at local stores that sell lightbulbs, you'll find a greater selection and better prices from online sources. Prices for the same bulb vary widely, so shop around. At this time, our picks for the best-priced sites are www.bulbs.com, www.1000bulbs.com, and www.lightbulbsdirect.com.

▶ **Microhydropower sources:** making electricity from falling water. We're all aware of hydroelectric power from large dams, but microhydropower involves capturing the power of water on one's own property. There are severe limitations as to when this would be feasible, because you must have a stream or river running through your land, and there are a variety of conditions for the way the water needs to drop or otherwise flow through your system. There must be enough flow to make efforts to harness it worthwhile. Then you must find a contractor and a turbine that is specifically designed for the condition of your stream or river. You will also need to get a permit to do the work. This could be the most difficult step. There are many limiting regulations involving various local, state, and federal agencies as to what one can and cannot do with streams and rivers on your property. Also, microhydro systems are expensive, so much so that even microhydro dealers may discourage anyone from pursuing this route if it's possible to generate electricity some other way.

▶ **Solar energy:** using the radiant energy of the sun for hot water or electricity. Solar energy is the quietest form of energy. There are two methods for collecting and using the sun's power: 1) solar thermal systems, which can provide up to 80 percent of a home's hot water needs, including heated pools, spas, and saunas; and 2) photovoltaic technology, which converts light into electricity using silicon cells to provide all or part of a household's electrical needs. Both methods involve having some number of panels on your roof to capture sunlight. More recently, companies such as Oksolar (www.oksolar.com /roof) have started manufacturing photovoltaic roof shingles.

Using a solar thermal system to power a household's water heater can reportedly save two to three hundred dollars in electricity costs per year for a family of four whose average usage is seventy gallons of hot water per day. A solar thermal system can be either active or passive. Active systems use electric pumps and valves to circulate water (open-loop or direct configurations), or heat-transfer fluids, such as diluted antifreeze (closed-loop configurations) to transfer heat to household water. Passive systems move water or heat-transfer fluids through the system without pumps and are less expensive than active systems. A conventional backup system is usually necessary for both active and passive systems in nearly all applications.

Photovoltaic or PV panels contain rows of cells, usually thirty-six per panel. The solar energy collected in the cells travels down wires into your fuse box and into your electric lights, appliances, and so forth. First, however, it must go through an inverter box to convert it from DC power to AC power that is used in household wiring (although some appliances, if so designed, can run off DC power). If the energy coming in from the panels is not needed at the time, it can be stored in batteries for later use or more commonly, tied into your electric company's grid, where it will be used for other customers. At such times your electric meter will be running backwards! The utility company will "pay" for the excess power you generate by crediting your account at wholesale rates. Of course, when you are not storing your own electricity, during the night or on cloudy days, your electricity will be coming from the grid.

According to the U.S. Department of Energy, the amount of solar energy that hits the surface of the earth about every hour is greater than the total amount of energy that the entire human population requires in a year. But it may not hit the surface of your home. While solar energy can dramatically reduce the cost of electricity and fossil fuel usage, in order to benefit from it, the roof where your panels are mounted needs to get sunlight most of the year and preferably be positioned so the panels are facing south.

Also, although the cost continues to drop, an installed PV solar system large enough to power a modest-sized home is still expensive. But most states provide rebates to offset the costs. Costs can also be reduced if a local bank offers low-interest loans for the purchase of a solar PV system. Alternatively, your bank might extend your home loan or mortgage. That could be the lowest-cost way to finance a solar system. If your goal is to save on monthly expenditures, though, you'll need to calculate how much equipment and what level of energy usage will save you enough on utility bills to more than cover the costs of your payments. While you're researching, look into individual DC solar appliances or fixtures, such as attic fans, pumps, ovens, refrigerators, and sidewalk or driveway lights. They're more affordable than installing an entire solar system and may be a good place to start.

To find out if solar power would be cost-effective for your home, contact a local solar energy installer to help you determine how much electricity you could generate compared to how much you need and what the cost would be for installation. Look for listings of installers in the Yellow Pages and search engines such as http://local.yahoo.com, or search for a prescreened installer on www.findsolar.com.

States That Offer Incentives for Solar Installation*

Arizona	Maryland	Oregon
California	Massachusetts	Pennsylvania
Connecticut	Michigan	Rhode Island
Delaware	Minnesota	South Carolina
Florida	Nevada	Texas
Hawaii	New Jersey	Washington
Illinois	New York	Wisconsin
		Wyoming

▶ **Native plant landscaping.** Native plants are plants that were growing naturally in the area where you live before people introduced other plants from distant places. Because they have evolved and adapted over thousands of years to the local soil, moisture, weather conditions, and other species in the area, they are vigorous and hardy, and once established, require no irrigation or fertilization. They're also resistant to most pests and diseases. Thus *xeriscaping*, which means landscaping with drought-resistant native plants and using water-conserving methods, can dramatically reduce water usage, as well as the need for toxic pesticides. It also provides a more naturally attractive setting for your home and requires far less care.

---

*As of this writing. For an up-to-date list of state, local, utility, and federal incentives in your area that promote renewable energy, see the Database of State Incentives for Renewable Energy at www.dsireusa.org.

For details on landscaping with native plants, see the many resources at www.for-wild.org, which includes local chapters and contacts for others who share an interest in native plants and natural landscaping. Also see LEARN MORE for a list of books on this topic.

 Tip

The traditional "turf grass" lawn is one of the most unnatural of landscaping choices. It is expensive to care for and guzzles water, using six hundred gallons of water an hour. There are natural grasses and other natural land covers that will thrive in your local weather conditions. For natural lawn alternatives, see "Low-Maintenance Lawn Alternatives" at www.lesslawn.com.

▶ **Rainwater harvesting and wells.** A well is an ideal off-grid option, but unless you have or are buying property with a well, it's not an option for most homeowners. Collecting rainwater for garden and household use, however, is an option for nearly everyone. It can reduce your water bills, relieve pressure on the municipal water supply, safeguard your water supply, and increase self-sufficiency. The simplest water harvesting method is a rainwater tank made of plastic (polyethylene), concrete, galvanized steel, or fiberglass that is rust and chemical resistant, where you collect and store rain runoff, typically from rooftops. You can then use the stored water for flushing toilets, washing clothes, watering gardens, washing cars, or for drinking, although for drinking, it will need to be filtered. Tanks are covered and screened to exclude animals, bird droppings, debris, insects, etc. The tanks often come with a plastic inner lining that increases the life of the tank and protects water quality. If your water utility charges a fixed fee, there will be no cost savings. To prevent health risks, tanks do require maintenance, for example, checking roofs and rain gutters for vegetation and debris, cleaning and replacing screens around the tank, and periodically draining and cleaning the tank to remove sludge or sediment.

▶ **Root cellars, cold rooms, and cold boxes.** A refrigerator/freezer is one of the most expensive household appliances to operate. One way to cut this cost is to have as small a fridge as possible or to buy a SunFrost (see below) and store larger quantities of fruits, vegetables, and other items that don't need to be kept at a very low temperature in a root cellar, cold room, or cold box. These each use nature to keep fruits, vegetables, and other things cool. Root cellars, like storm cellars, were once simply holes dug into the ground or into a hillside, with a door on top. They still can be built just that way, although to keep rodents and insects out, you'll want to enclose the cellar with some material, such as cement or pressure-treated wood. The floor can be dirt, gravel, or cement. You can also turn a corner of your basement into a root cellar. (See "Building a Root Cellar" at www.organicgardening .com.) A root cellar needs to be dark, humid, clean, and well ventilated, but without drafts.

Tips

If you are generating your own energy or trying to keep your electricity costs down, consider the advantage you would gain by placing your refrigerator and/or freezer in a root cellar's fifty-five-degree winter environment instead of in a kitchen that's at least sixty-eight degrees. Just this thirteen-degree difference can make a significant reduction in electrical usage.

We have one room in our house that's not heated, so we use it year-round as a cold room for storing fruits and vegetables. In the summer, it remains cool, but not cold. Still, it's adequate for most fruits and vegetables.

Cold boxes ("cool closets") work on a similar principle as our cold room. Before the 1950s, they were a standard feature in homes. A cold box is built into a shaded, north-facing wall of the house. It's insulated and ventilated to outside air. A black-painted metal vent pipe siphons off hot air and continually pulls cooler air into the box, making a perfect place for storing fruits and vegetables year-round. In colder months, from October through May, cold boxes can safely store milk, butter, cheeses, and salad dressings. During subfreezing winter months, they can also safely store meat.

▶ **SunFrost refrigerators.** Electric refrigerators are the biggest electricity-suckers in the average home. The SunFrost refrigerator is six hundred times more energy efficient than a standard fridge. Typically, in a home using conventional utility power, this device can cut energy consumption for refrigeration use by a factor of five! The walls of a SunFrost have four to six inches of insulation, compared to two in standard refrigerators. You can purchase a stand-alone refrigerator, freezer, or a combination refrigerator/freezer model in various sizes. The SunFrost compressor is so efficient that it runs on 12 volts of DC current (that means you could run it off flashlight batteries). The compressor is quiet and fanless, with only one moving part. Also, it's located on the top, so it doesn't siphon heat back into the box.

On the downside, although every SunFrost is custom crafted so that you can choose the hinge side and finish (laminate, wood, or stainless steel), they are still pretty basic. For example, they are not frost free. At least the ice does not need to melt for the freezer to be defrosted. To defrost, the contents of the freezer are transferred to the refrigerator section to remain frozen, and the refrigerator is turned off for about twenty minutes until the ice is easily removed in large pieces. An add-on advantage is that SunFrosts can be equipped with a noninterruptible power supply should there be a power outage. Take a look at www.sunfrost.com.

▶ **Insulated windows.** Windows with low-emissivity coatings are one example of windows that are more energy efficient. Called Low-E for short, these windows are mainly transparent and reduce the amount of long-wave infrared thermal radiation that's both absorbed and emitted by the glass pane. This way, heat loss is greatly reduced, with almost all reemission taking place toward the interior of the home in cold climates (if the coating is on the outside face) or reflected back out into the environment in a hot climate (if the coating is on the inside face). Thus, homes with high-performance low-E glass use less heat in the winter and less air-conditioning in the summer. Low-E coatings are commonly used in double-glazing units. The coating on either face is fully protected and may also enclose gases such as argon or krypton between the panes to further reduce heat loss.

To learn more, there are videos on Guardian Industries' Low-E Glass, and information is available in the "How to Library" section on Windows at http://www.bobvila.com/HowTo_Library/Guardian_Industries_Low_E _Glass—V20523.html. This library has a wealth of other information on windows and how to keep one's home cool or warm naturally.

Laminated glass, similar to glass in car windshields, and Heat Mirror® glass, which suspends a thin sheet of clear PVB between the panes, can also enhance energy efficiency. Triple-pane windows can reduce heat loss by 30 percent, but while they sound appealing, they aren't generally considered cost-effective. Usually all these types of low-energy windows cannot be placed into existing single-pane frames, so unless you are building a new home, installing them would mean replacing all windows and frames. That's costly. But single-pane or even double-pane windows can be retrofitted with Low-E solar control window films. These films can reportedly reduce heating and cooling energy demands by as much as 10 percent annually. The films come in various degrees of transparency from virtually clear to slightly tinted and are available in various models for hot or cold climates.

Window films for hot climates reject up to 79 percent of incoming solar energy and 99.9 percent of ultraviolet rays. Films designed for cold climates reflect 35 percent of the heat back into the room that would normally be lost through windows. Window films can also correct temperature imbalances between sunny and shady areas of the house and reduce harsh glare. Window film is usually best installed professionally to ensure against bubbling and peeling. This is what we had done and have been most satisfied. There are, however, also do-it-yourself installation kits. For more information, see the Window Film listing guide at www.window filmlistings.com.

We've learned, though, that what matters most in having energy-efficient windows is the frame material of the window, the methodology of construction, and then the actual installation process. To reduce cold air seeping in through our window frames, we hired someone to remove the window and doorframes and caulk the openings. We were astonished to discover how little effort had been made by the original builder to seal the window frames.

To check the air tightness of your window's weather stripping, hold a lighted candle or stick of incense near your window frames on a windy day and watch the smoke trail for signs of leaks.

 Tip

In 2006–2007, there is a two-hundred-dollar maximum tax credit on 10 percent of the costs of making windows more energy efficient. This tax credit does not apply to labor costs, so it's actually 10 percent of material costs, up to two hundred dollars.

The National Fenestration Rating Council provides unbiased information on different brands and types of windows on their Web site at http://nfrc.org. It also provides information on federal and state rebates, under Documents, www.nfrc.org/documents/TaxCreditFactsheet_000.pdf. The Efficient Windows Collaborative (www.efficientwindows.org) provides illustrated information about saving energy on windows and skylights, including a step-by-step guide to selecting energy-efficient models.

▶ **Wind-generated electricity.** You may have seen a "wind farm" along a highway where hundreds of huge whirling wind turbines that look like airplane propellers harvest the power of wind for utility companies or communities that produce their own electricity. Home-sized wind generators for personal use are fairly recent. The conditions required for even these smaller turbines, though, make them of limited practicality for most homes. First, your home must be sited in a windy locale where the wind blows strong and steady with an average annual wind speed of at least nine to ten miles per hour. Also, you should have at least an acre of land. The turbine, which runs off a magnetic generator, must sit atop a tower at least sixty feet high. The higher the turbine, the faster it will turn, and the larger the blades on the turbine, the more power it will generate.

If your property meets these requirements, and residential wind turbines are allowed in the area, you can choose whether or not to link the wind generator into the grid. If you do, your home will run off wind power until the turbine exceeds your demand; then, as with PV solar panels, the power will run into the grid for others to use. Similar to solar energy, wind power will need to be inverted from DC to AC power. But unless you get a lot of high and steady wind, it probably won't power an entire household. Residential wind turbines are expensive, but the payback is quicker than with solar.

► **Window coverings.** The typical single-family home loses 25 to 35 percent of its heat through windows. There are a variety of window coverings that, if installed and used properly, can make getting off the grid easier or at least reduce one's dependency on it. Roller shades, draperies, insulating Roman shades, Venetian blinds, insulating panels, and shutters can all be helpful, although some are more efficient than others. To be energy efficient, a window treatment needs to trap and hold the air coming off the window. That means it must fit tightly at the edges of the window, about an inch from the glass. The best choice depends on the location of the window, how the room is used, the effectiveness of the material itself, and the cost.

Cellular shades, also called honeycomb shades, are among the most effective at reducing energy costs. They consist of accordion-style, honeycomblike cells. Each cell traps air, and the trapped air acts as an insulator, limiting the air that leaves the home and buffering the home to prevent outdoor air from coming in. The shades come in single-, double-, and triple-cell construction. The more cells, the more energy efficient they are.

Tight-fitting interior storm windows are yet another option that can reportedly save 30 percent on heating and air-conditioning bills without the high cost of replacing existing windows. Interior storm windows are particularly suited to historic or older homes, where it's desirable to retain the original windows, yet also improve energy efficiency—without altering the home's exterior appearance. They can be customized to fit any size rectangular window, and some manufacturers also advertise the ability to fit a variety of geometric-shaped windows. You can leave them in place year-round or remove them so that windows can be opened in milder weather. Do-it-yourself kits like Window Savers (www.windowsaver.com) are similar in insulating power, durability, and appearance to custom interior storm windows but cost three to five times less.

▶ **Wood.** Traditional wood-burning fireplaces warm only a small nearby area and actually draw as much as 90 percent of their heat out of the house. But woodstoves and pellet stoves, either freestanding or fireplace inserts, are fuel-efficient. Larger models can heat entire homes if the construction of the house is open enough so that heat can travel throughout. Many homes in our community are heated entirely by wood or pellet stoves. Smaller models can be used to heat rooms that have no other heat source. Some models also have cooktops.

Woodstoves are the least expensive heating system. They burn wood far more efficiently and slowly than a traditional fireplace, but not as efficiently as a pellet stove. They come in three basic types: radiant woodstoves, the simplest and least expensive type; circulating woodstoves, which are double lined so they do not become hot to the touch; and combustion woodstoves, which allow the doors to be opened while burning, thus turning the stove into a fireplace. Radiant and circulating woodstoves have 70 to 80 percent efficiency, but combustion stoves lose heat when the door is open, dropping the efficiency to 50 to 60 percent.

Woodstoves are a flexible option because they can be safely located almost anywhere in the house if there is enough space for proper clearances and a properly routed chimney. As with any space-heating system, they provide the best performance and require the least maintenance if installed in the center of the main-floor living area of the house, with the flue pipe running straight up from the stove flue collar into the chimney. But they do require a lot of work—bringing in, tending, and cleaning up after the wood fire. They also produce a dry heat that can be rough on sinuses, and smoke escaping from the stove can cause unhealthy indoor air.

Introduced only ten years ago, pellet stoves look similar to woodstoves or fireplace inserts, but they burn compressed wood pellets that are fed automatically from a storage hopper into the combustion chamber. They burn a renewable fuel and are the cleanest burning of all wood-burning stoves—so clean, in fact, that the EPA does not regulate their chimney emissions. They provide greater control over the heat output, because you can set the rate at which the pellets are dropped, and, of course, there is no wood to chop or haul. There is an electric-powered fan that disperses the heat into the room and two other small motors, so pellet stoves do increase electrical usage. Some models come with automatic thermostats so a home can stay heated even when one is away. There are also pellet-fueled furnaces and boilers designed to take the place of, or supplement, conventional forced-air heating systems.

Pellet stoves cost more than fuel-efficient wood-burning stoves, ranging from about $1,700 to $3,000 or more for the stove, and $150 to $400 for installation, but they don't require installation of a full-height conventional chimney or flue, which is the most costly part of some fireplace and wood-stove installations. Pellet stoves require regular maintenance, particularly of the refractory and burner holes. Maintenance may need to be as frequent as daily if the stove is used as a primary heat source, and it is a messy matter. Also, due to the rapid growth in popularity of pellet stoves, there is currently a severe nationwide shortage of pellets, so prices have risen to as much as nine dollars a bag, up from three dollars only a year ago. Industry representatives project this shortage will be temporary. Also, while using higher-quality pellets, like Atlas pellets and Bear Mountain Golden Fire pellets, costs more per bag, using these premium brands saves money in the long run because they burn considerably more efficiently and also reduce the frequency of maintenance.

Wood and pellet stove installers can be found in your local Yellow Pages or through local online directories.

 Tip: Using Pellet Stoves

- ▶ Before buying a pellet stove, check the availability of pellets and the current price per bag in your area. Then compare the cost of heating your home with a pellet stove versus other forms of energy at www.pelletheat.org, and click on "Compare Fuel Costs" at the bottom of the page.
- ▶ Since both demand and prices for pellets are lower in the summer, buy a ton (fifty forty-pound bags) of pellets early in the summer. This will last most households for the entire winter and cost far less.
- ▶ To burn most efficiently, pellets should be stored in a sealed bag or a covered container in a dry location away from the fire.
- ▶ Locate the remote thermostat away from the stove in the coolest area of the room.
- ▶ To make maintenance easier, cleaner, and safer, use a warm-air ash vacuum like the Cougar or Cheetah, instead of a standard indoor-outdoor vac or vacuum cleaner.
- ▶ Wear plastic gloves while cleaning the stove if you don't want to get your hands really dirty.

Powering Down While On the Grid

These many options can help you to power down significantly, even if you can't or don't want to go fully off grid. Here are two examples: Jan de Leeuw built a new home that's off grid while remaining connected to the grid. He actually returns more energy into the grid than he draws out of it. The other example is of our own experience in trying to power down our existing on-the-grid home.

Being Off Grid While On Grid

Although building a new home with the idea of powering down is always easier than working within the constraints of an existing house, Jan de Leeuw can attest that, even with new construction, there are still many decisions and an investment of time and money to make. De Leeuw, a UCLA professor, bought five acres in a sunny meadow a little over an hour outside LA. First, he chose to have his home built using Reward Wall Systems (www.rewardwalls.com), a type of ICF (see Insulated Concrete Forms, earlier in chapter) that is so airtight that it can save from 50 to 80 percent on energy bills right from the get-go. He also had a woodstove installed in his living room/kitchen/dining room.

When the house was complete and he had moved in, de Leeuw installed a geothermal heating and cooling system and a PV solar system to provide the electricity he needs. The geothermal system is composed of a heat pump and twelve loops of copper coil drilled diagonally thirty feet into the ground that are filled with refrigerant. Heat is exchanged between the house and the ground for cooling and between the ground and the house for heating. The heat pump moves heat by evaporating and condensing the refrigerating fluid. He admits the system was expensive and difficult to install, particularly because his house sits on land with quite a bit of rock. The installer broke a number of drill bits.

Eighteen PV solar panels on his roof generate the electricity he needs, including the electricity needed to run the pump for the geothermal system. But he is not off grid. To obtain energy rebates, he's required to remain on grid, but he only draws from the grid if he needs to. During the day de Leeuw's panels generate about 20 kwh, which flow back into the grid for others to use. This system was also expensive to install. It will take a considerable period of time to repay his investment; however, his electric meter runs backwards, and 30 percent of his installation costs were covered by government subsidies. Because his electricity isn't stored, if he generates more than he uses over the year, he is not reimbursed for that surplus. To cook and heat with the geothermal system instead of using propane, he will need to install more panels. He could get more electricity from his existing solar panels if they faced south, but because of the construction of his roof, they must face east.

Three years later, his system is working, and he's planning to add an electric tankless (on demand) water heater, which can save up to half of one's water heating costs; switch from propane to electric conversion cooking; and generate more electricity using sun and wind. "I didn't do this for the money," de Leeuw explains. "It's a good thing to do, and as the cost of fossil fuel rises, hopefully, my energy costs won't go up, and my house will increase in value."

Converting an Existing Home

Of course, when you already own a home and you don't want to move, powering down can be more of a challenge. Few existing homes were built with energy conservation or off-the-grid conversion in mind. That was certainly true of our house. Here's our tale.

We live in a three-story four-thousand-square-foot house in a small village located in the Los Padres National Forest in California, about an hour from the nearest shopping areas. Although our home is retrofitted for earthquakes, it is not energy efficient. There are many windows and many rooms heated by a radiant heat furnace that runs on propane. We work from home, so we are usually here twenty-four hours a day. When we purchased our home, neither propane nor electricity was a significant portion of our monthly expenses, but as our propane bills began to top five hundred dollars a month in the winter and our electricity bills inched upward to nearly two hundred dollars a month, we became interested in the idea of getting off the grid.

At first we considered moving to a smaller home on land where we could be more self-sufficient. We explored many different communities throughout the western and midwestern United States, from urban areas and small towns to remote locations, looking for property. We almost moved on three different occasions, but the options we found were not cost-effective, nor did any of the communities we found offer the kind of natural beauty and close community ties we enjoy right where we are. Ultimately we decided to stay here and see what we could do to get off grid and become more energy efficient. We figured if we could do it in this house, then certainly almost anyone else could, too.

Over the next year we explored various options for getting off grid and became quite discouraged. Our home sits under a grove of old-growth Jeffrey pines, with sun hitting the house only part of the year and only from the north. So, no solar. The Jeffrey pines have a very dense root structure. So, no geo-thermal. There is no stream and, although there is quite a bit of wind, our property isn't large enough for a wind turbine, nor would installing one be permitted. Fact is, we won't be able to get off the grid. But we remained determined to dramatically power down our energy use and cost. Here's what we've done over the past year:

1. Replaced 90 percent of our light bulbs with CFL low-wattage lightbulbs
2. Routinely disconnected from much of our "phantom" power, leaving our TV and other appliances unplugged until we need to use them.

3. Closed off two rooms on the first floor that are not heated, for use as cold or cool rooms for storing fruits, vegetables, and other items.

4. Installed a pocket door at the top of the stairs to the second floor so no heat from the first floor escapes up to that floor. Since this floor is only rarely used for guests, this reduces the area we're heating by a third.

5. Replaced our wood-burning fireplace with a pellet stove that heats the first floor, more than one-third of our home, all of which was previously heated with propane. Our hope was to reduce both our costs and use of fossil fuel by one-third. This effort, however, has to date been disappointing. We had a lot of difficulty getting the pellet stove installed properly, there is more maintenance than we expected, and it has boosted how much time we've had to spend cleaning the house. Also, the fan has raised our electrical usage, and due to the nationwide shortage of pellets, we've had a difficult time keeping enough pellets on hand. The last straw, however, was when pellet prices rose to nine dollars a bag. At that point we were actually spending more money than ever on energy every month. So for now we've returned to heating the house with propane and hope this will change within the next year. The upside has been that while we were using the stove, we became acclimated to a lower winter room temperature.

6. Had all window and door frames removed and sealed the many gaps where air was moving freely in and out before replacing them.

7. Had Vista Low-E window film placed on all our north-facing windows. This has made a dramatic difference in how much heat we must use to keep rooms comfy during winter.

8. Bought a Prius hybrid car. Driving the Prius cut our gasoline costs in half immediately. Given road conditions here, we can't drive it during the snow season, but it has been great the rest of the year.

As you can see, becoming more energy efficient has been a long and frustrating process for us, but we are definitely making progress, and we're not done yet. Our next step will be to replace our freezer and refrigerator that came with the house with SunFrost or Energy Star models.

 OUR ADVICE

1. *Expect a long learning curve.* Even Udgar Parsons, who lived in self-sustaining communities before going off the grid on his own, urges patience. Before he undertook creating his off-the-grid home, he spent a winter studying every aspect involved—land, solar, electric, gray water, etc.

Next he put his office, then located in Aspen, Colorado, on a PV system to try it out. The *Real Goods Solar Living Sourcebook* became his bible as he proceeded. He says it is *the best* source of technical information for off-grid living, guiding you step-by-step through the process. It is even tailored to what part of the country you live in. Still, as his experience and that of the others in this chapter illustrate, living a life of lower energy use will be a work in progress. Everyone we interviewed, including those who started going off grid years ago, not only had tales of what they'd learned along the way but also each had plans for what they would be doing next.

2. *Be ready to spend time "hands-on."* Living off the grid is a hands-on experience. As Yuba City gals, Robyn and Janaia, point out, there are things you must do around the house when you're off grid, or even, as in our case, only powering down. There is a lot of monitoring, maintaining, and experimenting involved. Udgar was quick to point out that one needs to have a natural ability and enjoyment for learning and doing physical things.

    This is an easy question for those of us who have been "tinkering" with things since childhood, but for those of us who have grown up in a highly professionalized, information-driven era, you may not really know if you have what we call a "builder" aptitude. So visit an off-the-grid or powered-down home in your area. Talk in person, or online, to others who have energy efficiency as a goal. Then start taking a few tiny steps to see how you react. You may be surprised to discover just what is involved and may decide this is not for you. Or, even if it seems foreign at first, you may be surprised to discover that you love doing things with your hands and putting your mind to work to solve physical challenges.

3. *Check your timing.* Don't add powering down to an already jam-packed, hectic, fast-paced, overscheduled life. We speak from experience on this point. When we were pressed by deadlines and juggling a hundred balls in the air, there just wasn't time to take on the tasks involved in powering down. We had to power ourselves down before we had the time and energy to power down our home. If you recall, Janaia and Robyn powered down in order to power down from their stressful jobs. Had they still been leading a Silicon Valley life, they could not have accomplished what they have. So start by simplifying your life enough to make room for the time and space to read, study, try, and experiment—and then organize to set up and maintain a more energy-efficient life.

4. *Expect to make major choices.* Since our culture and predominant way of life is not set up to make powering down a natural and easy thing, if this is a way of life you yearn for, you may have to make some difficult choices. Julia Russell's off-the-grid home demonstrates that we can live a powered-down life in the city. The Urban Thoreaus featured in Chapter 11 prove you can even homestead in the city. But you may not be able to do as they have done where you live. We certainly couldn't have done so in our Santa Monica town house, where the homeowners' association managed all the utilities and there was no yard in the front or back. You, too, may need to move to another home or a locale with less restrictive zoning or

Covenants, Codes, and Restrictions (CC&Rs). Or, like Janaia and Robyn, you may need to change your work situation, either in order to move to a more receptive location or to have the time to live in a slower-paced, more self-sustaining way.

5. *Weigh your values.* Most likely this way of life is not going to be as "convenient" as what you're used to. Most of us have become addicted to convenience. We want our technology to be quick and easy, with no mess and no fuss. We're accustomed to automatic and remote controls, fast-food establishments, instant microwaved meals, and a host of other out-of-sight, out-of-mind systems that take care of us without us having to think about them. But powering down or going off the grid is not an instant lifestyle.

When fiber artist Katy and landscape architect Rich Blanchard moved from San Diego, California, to an off-the-grid life on fifty-six acres of land outside of a tiny town in northern New Mexico, Katy told us, "The hardest thing was the necessary shift in consciousness it requires. This way of life was quite an eye-opening experience. Our society is a consumer-oriented, high-energy one. You don't realize how much you're consuming until you're generating it yourself. Then you become very aware of how much you're using. I was shocked to discover how much energy even one 60-watt bulb draws."

The Blanchards placed most of their household possessions in storage to live and work in a five-hundred-square-foot trailer and two studios—one thirteen hundred square feet, the other one thousand square feet—where Rick telecommutes and Katy does her artwork. All the structures are powered by a PV solar energy system they installed themselves. The solar system also powers the pumps that get two to three thousand gallons of well water to their cistern. Because some seasons can be cloudy, they have a backup gasoline generator, which they soon hope to replace with a diesel generator. They also hope to build a straw bale home on their property. As they learned just how much power they were using, they made additional changes, adding low-voltage fluorescent bulbs and placing their computer and the other limited electronics they own on a power strip that's off at night, or when not in use. For them the adjustment in their values these changes have inspired have been worth the effort. "It's magical here," Katy exclaims.

Not everyone is willing to make the kind of value shifts Katy and Rick have made, even to enjoy a more self-determined life. So in considering this lifestyle choice, look carefully at your values. What's really important to you? Would this lifestyle support or hinder your life goals?

Will you enjoy the many do-it-yourself maintenance tasks involved in living a low-energy lifestyle? For some people, it may feel like a cultural step backward; but for those who enjoy learning, exploring, and actively creating a more self-sufficient life, it's a step forward.

6. *Get help!* You probably noticed that most of the people we discussed did all or much of the work involved in powering down themselves, to keep costs down. That is what Janaia and Robyn did, but even they were adamant that *"you have to have a good advisor or installer."*

Robyn has a mind for understanding electricity. She has a background in physics. Still, they knew enough to know they didn't know enough and turned for help to an expert renewable energy installer who had been working in the field for many years. They also relied on an uncle who is a retired contractor. He came to help and to work with them. And like Udgar, they studied and read, and they visited a local solar home before proceeding. So even if you enjoy do-it-yourself projects, get the help you need. The LEARN MORE section that follows has a wealth of resources. Also review "Alternative Energy Installing, Serving, and Installing" in Part II for the type of professionals working in this field.

Shifting Values

Here are several of the shifts in values we've noticed among the people we've talked with who are adopting a lower-energy way of life. They prefer:

- self-reliance, or reliance within the context of a small community of like-minded folks, vs. dependence on large established institutions and social groups
- achieving self-directed goals vs. competing with others
- hands-on and face-to-face activities vs. a virtual world through electronics
- experimenting and learning on their own and with others vs. having someone else take care of whatever needs doing
- relating to people vs. accumulating possessions
- cherishing the joys of being at home vs. getting out and about
- spending time with family and community vs. working to make more money
- working outdoors with their hands vs. primarily working indoors
- thinking of electronics as tools vs. necessities
- valuing flexibility and freedom vs. convenience and comfort

 MAKING A CHOICE TO GO OFF GRID OR POWER DOWN

Pros
1. A lower cost of living in the long run that reduces the need to keep earning more, thus allowing greater freedom and flexibility in one's daily life.

Cons
1. Not all locales or homes are well suited for many off-the-grid or lower-energy options, e.g. solar, geothermal, wind, or hydropower.

Pros continued:

2. Once changes are in place, one can enjoy increased disposable income that once went to paying for basic utilities.
3. Greater independence and control over daily life and increased security that one's basic needs will be provided for.
4. A healthier and more comfortable home environment while placing less of a toll on our natural resources and the environment.

Cons continued:

2. There are usually initial financial investments involved. Some can be quite costly.
3. Many of the changes involve ongoing operation and maintenance tasks that were once done automatically.
4. Benefits may not be immediate. Often it takes considerable time to explore, choose, and then make the needed changes.

LEARN MORE

General Resources for Powering Down or Going Off Grid
Books

▶ *The Homeowner's Guide to Energy Independence: Alternative Power Sources for the Average American*, Christine Woodside, Lyons Press, 2006. Discusses taking an existing home off the grid.

▶ *The Homeowner's Guide to Renewable Energy: Achieving Energy Independence Through Solar, Wind, Biomass, and Hydropower*, by Dan Chiras, New Society Publishers, 2006. Discusses retrofitting an existing home for renewable energy.

▶ *New Complete Self-Sufficiency: The Classic Guide for Realists and Dreamers*, Charles Long, Dorling Kindersley Publishers, 2003.

▶ *The New Ecological Home: A Complete Guide to Green Building Options*, Dan Chiras, Chelsea Green Publishing Company, 2004. An overview of green building techniques, materials, products, and technologies.

▶ *The Renewable Energy Handbook: A Guide to Rural Energy Independence, Off-Grid, and Sustainable Living*, William H. Kemp, Aztext Press, 2006. Discusses designing and creating a green home in a rural area.

▶ *Smart Power: An Urban Guide to Renewable Energy and Efficiency*, William H. Kemp, Aztext Press, 2006. Offers many ideas for how energy efficiency can improve urban lifestyle, lower operating costs, provide a more comfortable environment, and increase disposable income.

Magazines

- ► *Home Power*, P.O. Box 520, Ashland, OR 97520; (530) 475-3179, (530) 475-0830, or (800) 707-6585. The magazine is fully available on the Internet at www.homepower.com.
- ► *Mother Earth News, The Original Guide to Living Wisely*, 1503 SW 42nd Street, Topeka, KS 66609; www.motherearthnews.com.

Web Sites

- ► www.off-grid.net
- ► www.nef.org.uk/greenenergy – The National Energy Foundation
- ► www.greenchoices.org/index.html

Catalogs

- ► *Ecobusinesslinks Green Directory* – www.ecobusinesslinks.com
- ► *Real Goods Solar Living Sourcebook–12th Edition: The Complete Guide to Renewable Energy Technologies & Sustainable Living*, John Schaeffer, 2005. Although this is actually a catalog, it is a premier source of information and the classic resource on sustainable living technology, including an extensive selection of the necessary hardware, planning worksheets, and detailed information and guidance on renewable energy, sustainable living, alternative construction, green building, homesteading, off-the-grid living, and alternative transportation.

Films

- ► Green Planet Films (www.greenplanetfilms.org) is a nonprofit distributor of nature and environmental DVDs from around the globe.

Homesteading
Books

- ► *Country Wisdom & Know-How: A Practical Guide to Living off the Land*, The Editors of Storey Publishing's Country Wisdom Boards, Black Dog & Leventhal Publishers, 2004.
- ► *The Self-Sufficient Life and How to Live It,* John Seymour, DK Adult, 2003. Discusses all aspects of homesteading, including

basket and cloth weaving, beekeeping, raising and butchering animals, fishponds for food, and food preservation techniques.

Web Sites
► www.offgrid.homestead.com

Directories and Catalogs
► www.homestead.org
► www.naturalfamilyhome.com
► www.homesteadingtoday.com

Native Plant Landscaping
Books
► *Natural Gardening in Small Spaces*, Noel Kingsbury, Timber Press, 2004.
► *Landscaping Revolution: Garden with Mother Nature, Not Against Her*, Andy and Sally Wasowski, Contemporary Books, 2000.

Web Sites
► www.for-wild.org
► www.lesslawn.com

Solar
Books
► *Passive Solar House: The Complete Guide to Heating and Cooling Your Home*, James Kachadorian, Chelsea Green Publishing Company, 2006.
► *The Solar House: Passive Heating and Cooling*, Daniel D. Chiras, Chelsea Green Publishing Company, 2002.
► *Solar Water Heating: A Comprehensive Guide to Solar Water and Space Heating Systems*, Bob Ramlow, New Society Publishers, 2006.

Catalogs
► Backwoods Solar Electric Systems, 1395 Rolling Thunder Ridge, Sandpoint, ID 83864; (208) 263-4290, www.backwoodssolar.com. A well-done and comprehensive catalog that includes the personal commentary of the owners, Steve and Elizabeth Willey.

Magazines
► American Solar Energy Society, 2400 Central Avenue, G-1, Boulder, CO 80301; (303) 443-3130, fax (303) 443-3212,

www.ases.org. Publishes *Solar Today* magazine covering all solar technologies, policies, and regulations.

Web Sites
▶ http://energy.sourceguides.com – Lists solar energy installation companies in the world by business name

Root Cellars
Books
▶ *The Root Cellar*, Janet Lunn and N. R. Jackson, Puffin, 1996.
▶ *Root Cellaring: Natural Cold Storage of Fruits & Vegetables*, Mike and Nancy Bubel, Storey Publishing, 1991.

Water
Books
▶ *Create an Oasis with Greywater: Your Complete Guide to Choosing, Building, and Using Greywater Systems*, Art Ludwig, Oasis Design, 2000.
▶ *Composting Toilet System Book: A Practical Guide to Choosing, Planning, and Maintaining Composting Toilet Systems*, David Del Porto and Carol Steinfeld, Center for Ecological Pollution Prevention, 2000.
▶ *Rainwater Collection for the Mechanically Challenged*, Suzy Banks and Richard Heinichen, Tank Town Publishing, 2006.
▶ *Rainwater Harvesting for Drylands: Guiding Principles to Welcome Rain into Your Life and Landscape,* Brad Lancaster, Chelsea Green Publishing Company, 2006.

Wind
Books
▶ *Wind Power: Energy for Home, Farm, and Business,* Paul Gipe, Chelsea Green Publishing Company, 2004.
▶ *Renewable Energy Handbook: The Complete Step-by-Step Guide to Making and Selling Your Own Power from Sun, Wind, and Water,* William H. Kemp, Hushion House Publishing Ltd., 2004.

Magazines
▶ *Windpower Monthly* – Published by The International Journal of Wind Energy Development, P.O. Box 4258, Grand Junction, CO, 81502 [phone and fax: (970) 245-9431, www.wpm.co.nz]

Other

- *Biodiesel Basics and Beyond: A Comprehensive Guide to Production and Use for the Home and Farm*, William H. Kemp, Aztext Press, 2006.
- BioWillie diesel fuel locations – www.wnbiodiesel.com
- *Cutting Your Car Use: Save Money, Be Healthy, Be Green!*, Randall Howard Ghent, Anna Semlyen, and Axel Scheffler, New Society Publishers, 2006.
- *Serious Straw Bale: A Home Construction Guide for All Climates*, Paul Lacinski and Michel Bergeron, Chelsea Green Publishing Company, 2000.
- *Composting for All*, Nicky Scott, Green Books, 2003.
- *Microhydro: Clean Power from Water*, Scott Davis and Corrie Laschuk, New Society Publishers, 2006.
- *Composting Toilet System Book: A Practical Guide to Choosing, Planning, and Maintaining Composting Toilet Systems*, Carol Steinfeld and David Del Porto, EcoWaters, 2007.
- *The Humanure Handbook: A Guide to Composting Human Manure*, Joseph C. Jenkins, Jenkins Publishing, 2005.

*True community is not simply an aggregate of people . . .
but people who have made a commitment to
communicate more authentically, more
intimately, more vulnerably.*
M. Scott Peck, *A Different Drum*

CHAPTER THIRTEEN

Living Together—
Shared Homes, Shared Communities

In 2006, for the first time in U.S. history, households headed by single individuals outnumbered those headed by married ones, the Census Bureau reports. Once the norm, the nuclear family (mother, father, and their children) is on the decline from a high of nearly half the population to less than a quarter today. The percentage of households with someone living alone, however, has leaped from less than one in five to more than one in four in just the past ten years. Other countries are seeing this population trend, too. The reasons for such a dramatic shift in living arrangements are many. They include a divorce rate that has swollen the ranks of single parents, a tendency for young adults to postpone marriage in the face of college debt, escalating costs of living, and highly demanding work schedules, as well as an aging population that includes many widows and widowers.

But a countervailing shift is already underway. The past decade has seen a resurgence of shared living arrangements. The number of people who are sharing homes with friends and family or creating new intentional communities of like-minded folk is on the rise. Laird Schaub, the executive secretary of Fellowship for Intentional Community, sees this as a growing trend. Diana Leaf Christian, author of *Creating a Life Together* and editor of *Communities* magazine, agrees, but she says, unlike the 1960s, when communal living last became the rage, today's interest in sharing one's home with others centers on equity ownership, egalitarian relationships, cooperative decision making, and clearly defined boundaries.

In other words, the desire for personal privacy, personal space, and personal ownership remains high, but many people are beginning to rethink what constitutes a family and entertain new ways of sharing living arrangements. Four primary motivators are drawing people to live less insular and singular lives, either under the same roof, in nearby or adjacent homes, or under a broader roof of community. Might any of these goals apply to you?

Goals Drawing People to Live with Others

1. *To reduce expenses.* The rising cost of basic living expenses, most particularly the cost of housing, utilities, household maintenance, health care, and child care, is spurring interest in sharing the cost of living. This is a motivating goal for both singles and families, but especially for young adults who are burdened with large college loans to repay while working in lower-wage entry-level jobs and for singles of retirement age who face living on a fixed income. It is also appealing to anyone who is faced with caring simultaneously for both young children and aging parents.

2. *To have an opportunity for closer relationships.* Living alone, while fine for some, is lonely and isolating for others who yearn for companionship, socialization, and community. Although most people spend the bulk of their day at a job, the work milieu often can't meet all of our needs for affiliation. Within the hierarchical, competitive culture of a work environment, coworkers often have a range of personal interests and live in places distant from one another throughout a metro area. So they may not be readily available to socialize, share intimacies, and offer psychic support the way a family or shared household can.

3. *Share the workload.* Many folks are feeling unduly stressed and pressed by the demands of daily life. This is particularly true of single parents, dual-career couples, and widows and widowers who have to somehow "do it all." Many are eager to find ways to share some of the workload of running a household and caring for children, the sick, or the elderly.

4. *To find an alternative.* As concerns about the future in a rapidly changing and globalizing economy grow, some individuals are driven by political, spiritual, and/or ecological values to seek alternative ways of life that can be a model for a more secure and fulfilling future. The United States has a rich history of such quests, from the Puritans who came to the New World from abroad to the utopian social experimentation of the transcendentalists in the 1830s and '40s and the idealistic youth of the 1960s Flower Power communes.

Sharing a Home with Family and Friends

Time to be with family and friends is always high on the list when people are polled as to what they miss most in their overly busy lives. Financial pressures and crowded schedules make finding time to relax and enjoy leisurely relationships with others more difficult. But ironically the very financial pressures that have been pulling us away from those we miss are now drawing us back together. The rising cost of housing, education, and quality health care (or its unavailability) are making it both more practical and more comfortable to share housing with other adults.

The family "compound" and shared family home have long been a common way of life. We *Homo sapiens* have been a tribal species throughout most of our existence. Only in recent history has the nuclear family or single-person household become a predominant living arrangement. Even in recent times, grandparents and single relatives often came to live with other family members. The norm was that extended families would live together or nearby one another. In the nineteenth century, for example, before the decline of the family farm and the exodus of young adults into the city to find jobs, it was customary for a family to buy land where all the adult members would establish their households.

In Europe and many other countries, extended families living together, and providing intrafamily care has always been a cultural norm. Now such solutions are once again becoming popular in North America. Parents are living with their adult children; adult children are returning home to their parents, or never leaving home; and siblings, cousins, grandparents, and friends are sharing an apartment, town house, or single-family home.

These days the decision to live with other family members or friends often accompanies some major life change or crisis. A son or daughter graduates from college with no job in hand, gets a divorce, loses or changes a job, or decides to go back to school. One parent leaves the other to raise their children alone. An older parent dies, leaving his or her spouse behind. Or illness strikes. At times like these, it suddenly makes sense to share household costs and tasks. Most often two or more incomes in a household will go much farther than one, so everyone is able to enjoy a fuller life with a higher standard of living by moving in together than by struggling to make it on their own.

Shared housing is so hot right now that the construction industry is featuring homes designed specifically for multigenerational households. Such homes have features such as separate bedroom suites with private entrances, bigger kitchens, extra storage, wider hallways for wheelchairs, and light switches that are reachable by children or someone in a wheelchair. When we were looking at houses a couple of years ago, we could hardly find a new home that didn't have what's called a guesthouse, *casita*, or mother-in-law suite. Usually on the basement or ground floor, these suites are like separate apartments, with a full kitchen, bedroom, bath, and living room.

Multigenerational households include any household where three or more generations live under one roof. They are becoming so commonplace that they even have their own nickname, "multigens." It's estimated there are only about 4.2 million such families right now, but their numbers have grown by 38 percent over the last reported ten-year period. They represent the fastest-growing type of living arrangement. Grandparents lead 62 percent of multigen households.

Gail Sullivan of Baldwin, Georgia, is an example. When her daughter's marriage broke up, Gail's daughter and two granddaughters, ages three and fifteen months, moved in with Gail and her husband until her daughter could get back on her feet. Gail, who has her own home-based business, cares for the girls during the week while her daughter works in Atlanta, an hour and a half away. "I want to help my daughter any way I can," Gail explains, "and I always wanted to spend more time with my grandchildren, who I never got to see often enough. Now I get to take care of them. It can be tiring, but also very fun and rewarding. And my daughter can go to work knowing her children are safe and being taken care of by someone who would give her life for them if necessary."

It's quite common these days for grown kids from middle-class families to move back in with their parents upon graduation from college, and sometimes repeatedly through their twenties, thirties, and forties. Some 39 million adults ages twenty-five to thirty-four are living in a parent's home. That's up more than 50 percent since the 1970s, when young people were expected to leave home after college and not return except to visit. There is no longer an assumed cutoff age for when one "should" have moved out on one's own. The typical undergraduate enters the workforce with nearly nineteen thousand dollars in student loans to repay, and a recent survey reports that 57 percent of college graduates expect to move back in with their parents. The entry-level positions open to them are lagging behind inflation, so paying the nine to thirteen hundred dollars a month in rent that's common in many large metro areas is a considerable challenge, especially for anyone who's hoping to save money to get married or buy a house.

When Chris Angeletti, forty-one, retired from his career in the military, he decided to settle down in the San Francisco Bay area, so he took a job there and moved into his mother Linda's comfortable two-bedroom apartment while he saved to buy a home. "I was glad he wanted to live in this area," Linda remembers. "It felt good to be able to help him out." At first, it was going to be a temporary arrangement, but then Chris was laid off during the dot-com bust. Since then, mother and son have settled into a comfortable routine.

"Chris and I are friends," Linda says of why they're able to get along so well. "We each have our own lives. We do our own laundry and prepare our own meals, but we share a meal if we're both there at the same time." Chris pays rent and contributes to the utilities and cable service. They each have their own set of friends, although over the past year they've gone together to several Bo Bice and Sugar Money rock concerts. "When I tell people my son lives with me, sometimes they look at me askance," Linda admits, "but Chris is a responsible person. I trust him. This works well for us."

Young adults like Chris and parents like Linda are defying the stereotypes. While living with one's parents may once have been a stigma, today's young adults—and their parents—tend not to see it that way. For them it's about making wise financial decisions and establishing a solid footing for the future. Usually deciding to live with mom and/or dad is anything but a hardship. The alternative would be sharing a tiny apartment with two or more other people and just scraping by. Instead they're contributing to the household, saving money, and continuing to enjoy a middle-class lifestyle until they're able to duplicate it in a home of their own.

 Tip: Living with Your Parents or Your Kids

1. Living with one's kids or one's parents is not for everyone! Some parents and some kids are more difficult to live with than others or simply have personalities that don't mesh. So if the idea of living with a grown child or parent doesn't appeal to you, don't do it.
2. Get money issues straight. Will kids or older parents pay rent? Contribute to household expenses? Live rent free but help out with household chores? Let grown kids or parents propose how they want to handle their contribution, and make sure everyone is satisfied with, and committed to, the arrangements. Otherwise resentments are guaranteed to arise.
3. Be sure you can accept and accommodate each other's lifestyles. It works best when parents and kids both treat each other as grown adults and behave as grown adults. Granted, habitual ways within a family may die hard. But living together will present fewer problems if you treat each other as you would another adult whom you're not related to. For example, would you assume another grown adult would do your laundry every week without your offering to do something in exchange? Would you feel free to tell another grown adult how to live his or her life?
4. Talk this decision to live together through with others in the household, as well as significant others in one's life, such as boyfriends and girlfriends. Everyone close to you will be affected by this decision.
5. Don't expect your new living arrangement to be conflict free. Conflicts are inevitable from time to time. To prevent them from becoming problems, though, keep lines of communication open. Don't let slights or unpleasant feelings pile up. Find mutually agreed-upon ways to resolve inevitable conflicts and disagreements.

Psychologists are noticing that, as with Linda and Chris, today's grown children also have very different relationships with their parents than previous generations. They are far more likely to get along with their parents. There is no generation gap, so to speak, in these relationships. They consider their parents to be their friends, and their parents are accepting of them and enjoy having them at home.

Older parents living with their grown kids is also on the rise among middle-class families. "It's an age-old concept," Lynne Shane told us, speaking of her decision to have her mother, Anne, come to live in her mountain cabin with her. "Parents raise their kids, and kids step in to care for their parents when they get old." A divorced, single mother of six children, Lynne, fifty-eight, had raised her family teaching private music lessons. Once the children were grown, she sold her suburban house and bought a log cabin here in Pine Mountain, where we live. She had just settled into an idyllic life, teaching music in LA three days a week while building a local clientele. Then her brother, who had been living with and caring for their ailing mother in the city, died unexpectedly.

Lynne became one of 9 million people who are living with and looking after an older parent. For Lynne it was an easy decision. Aside from the astronomical expense of long-term care, having performed as a musician at many nursing homes over her lifetime, she didn't want to place her mother in a facility. As her mother's health deteriorated, caring for her wasn't always easy, Lynne remembers, especially given that she was Anne's sole caretaker, and the nearest medical care was an hour away.

Ten Home Safety Ideas for Multigenerational Homes

1. Have plenty of lighting.
2. Avoid throw rugs.
3. Use night-lights along dark hallways.
4. Keep stairways free of clutter and well lighted.
5. Secure electric cords out of the way.
6. Keep furniture out of household traffic patterns.
7. Place a board under soft cushions to make sitting down and getting up easier.
8. Keep the water heater temperature set to 120 degrees or lower.
9. Have a lamp in easy reach of the bed.
10. Use a nonslip pad in tubs or showers.

The hardest part, she recalls, was not having a social life. Also, it was a lot of work and very isolating. But living in a close, small community like ours, friends and neighbors came forward to help when they could. Also, Lynne started "Lunch with Lynne." Each week on Thursdays until Anne passed away, three or four of Lynne's friends would come over for a potluck lunch. We would talk about life, share favorite readings, commiserate, and celebrate with each other. "Looking back," she says, "I treasure that time with my mother. Even the most difficult times I had to work through with my mother were a valuable experience in learning about life and death."

 Tips: Caring for Aging Parents in Your Home

1. It may feel as though parent and child roles are reversing in subtle and not-so-subtle ways, but living together will be easier if one keeps in mind that parents still consider themselves to be parents. So while there are times grown children will have to step in to make decisions, set ground rules, and provide care for elders, this is best done with respect for their elder status and with the intentions of allowing them to be as independent as possible.

2. Make sure everyone in the household has some privacy. Ideally, there would be rooms everyone in the household shares, such as the kitchen, dining area, and family room, and also private bedrooms for parents, kids, and grandparent(s).

3. Don't expect young children to stop being kids, but do set ground rules as to how the household can function best. Ideally, everyone would be involved in developing these rules. This may require compromise, but if it means everyone willingly abides by the ground rules, making accommodations will avoid innumerable hassles.

4. The needs of children and grandparents living under the same roof may conflict at times. Bottle caps on medication are a simple example. It may be impossible for a grandparent to open a childproof cap on medication. So think through how to best accident-proof the household for everyone.

5. Recognize that a parent who is closing down her household will want to bring some of her favorite things with them. Such belongings, whether it's a favorite chair, a family heirloom, or a treasured dish, are usually quite significant to anyone who is moving into someone else's home. Accommodating as many of these items as possible, even if they don't match your décor or suit your taste, will help make the adjustment less unsettling.

6. Caring for an ailing or declining parent can be exhausting, so be sure to arrange to have time for yourself, even if it means paying someone to come in and help you.

Of course, adult children have always cared for ill elders, but a number of factors are making doing this more compelling. More than 6 million seniors need help with basic activities, such as getting out of bed, bathing, cleaning, dressing, handling finances, and preparing food. This number is expected to grow. An estimated 5 million Americans already spend some time caring for an aging parent, but we are living longer, so the number of "super seniors," people over eighty-five years old, is expected to double in the next twenty-five years. That means more sixty-five-year-old "children" will be providing care for their octogenarian parents.

Also, 60 percent of grown children who care for their parents are still working full-time. Many still have children in the home. And they are not only women. Men account for 40 percent of those who have significant caregiving responsibilities. So as health care costs, especially long-term health care costs, increase as expected, and health care benefits upon retirement continue to decline, caring for an aging parent in one's home will be an increasingly appealing choice, if not a necessity. What's important is to do this in a way that, to the extent possible, doesn't detract from one's quality of life.

Of course, not all parents moving in with their kids need caretaking. Not by far. Many senior parents step into vital household roles, remain active in their community, and have a busy social life of their own. The Everson household in suburban Birmingham, Alabama, is one such active multigen family. Linda Everson, fifty-nine, found herself worrying about her eighty-one-year-old mother, Jane, living alone in Memphis. She knew her mother was sad and lonely there. So she and her husband, Tillman, sixty-three, who operate an executive recruiting company together, decided to add on a one-thousand-square-foot addition to their home so Jane could move in with them. Now Jane is a busy and greatly needed part of the household. She watches her two great-grandchildren, who live nearby, during the day and helps out with the laundry and cooking while Tillman and Linda are at work. "She hasn't been this vital in ten years," says Linda.

Since the Eversons' three grown children and grandchildren live nearby, it's not unusual on a typical afternoon to find four generations racing around the Everson's split-level house. They're hoping to add on an additional eight-hundred-square-foot suite so Tillman's eighty-five-year-old mother can join them in the future. So far, though, she's committed to staying in Memphis. She says there's too much going on in the Everson household for her.

Most people who are sharing homes live a conventional lifestyle similar to any other household in an urban, suburban, or small-town setting, but sometimes the decision to live with adult family members comes about in conjunction with the decision to pursue one of the other lifestyles we've discussed in Part III. You may remember the Cumberlands, for example, from Chapter 9. Father Les, son Richard, and daughter-in-law Earleen live together in their RV and work as caretakers managing the Boise National Forest.

For Sylvia Lyn, a successful nature writer, pooling resources with her eighty-four-year-old mother made it possible to pursue her dream to live in a rustic nearby faraway place. "I wouldn't have been able to do this alone," Lyn told us. While recovering from an unpleasant divorce, she had moved in temporarily with her mother in suburban Omaha, Nebraska. She was hoping to buy a home on some forested land in Idaho but couldn't afford to do so on her own. Sensing that living alone would soon be difficult for her mother, she proposed that they pool their resources and go in together on an acre of land with a twelve-hundred-square-foot home in southern Idaho.

"This was strictly a financial decision," explains Sylvia, who lives in a separate suitelike area of the home. "My mother is a difficult person to live with, so from an emotional standpoint this arrangement is a strain, but the benefits for both of us outweigh the drawbacks. I am able to live where I do the kind of creative writing I love. Otherwise, I'd be living in a tiny apartment somewhere in a big city. I can't write under those circumstances. I need to live in a small, quiet place, close to nature."

Three years later, despite the emotional challenges, she is happy with the decision. "I look at this long term. There is a plan, a goal, a future to living as we do that makes sense for us." Soon she and her mother will be adding a five-hundred-square-foot suite to their home for Sylvia and her soon-to-be husband. "That wasn't in the plan," she says with a smile. "By spring we will be adjusting once again to a new living arrangement."

Living with Friends

The trend toward home sharing is by no means limited to family members. Friends and colleagues are also making homes together. Single parents, for example, are finding that sharing a home with another single parent can be a real lifesaver, as are many divorced and single baby boomers who are retired or approaching retirement. They and others are asking, "Why do I need to do this stage of my life all alone?"

The number of single-parent families is on the rise in many countries such as Australia, Britain, France, Germany, Greece, Ireland, Japan, and Mexico, often doubling in recent years. In the United States, where 53 percent of first births are to single women, there are some 13 million single moms, nearly three times the number only years ago. But life as a single is often difficult and exhausting. It usually involves taking a serious cut in income. Single mothers are often forced out of the middle class, typically living on one-fourth the income a two-parent household has. It means shouldering nearly overwhelming responsibilities from which there is virtually no respite. As a professional artist and early childhood educator Carmel Sullivan can attest, it can also be lonely and frightening.

"I found it hard to deal with the sudden isolation," says Sullivan. "It was like living in a vacuum." Raising her son alone didn't seem natural to her. "We need to stop worshiping privacy and realize we are tribal by nature," she points out. "We're social creatures who need to connect and nurture each other." So Carmel reached out to see if there were other single moms who felt as she did, and found that indeed there were.

She decided to buy a home in Highland Park, New Jersey, that's large enough for two families. She placed notices at her son's school and elsewhere in the neighborhood, seeking another single mom to room with. Eighteen mothers replied, all from her own small neighborhood. Among them she found the perfect roommates for herself and her son.

What a difference this has made! "It wasn't just about money," she explains. "For the first time in my life, I felt powerless and utterly alone, plagued with worry and doubt." But forming a new family with another single mom restored her confidence and gave her a personal life again. The experience also impressed upon her just how many single mothers are hungry to join a household with another single parent and convinced her to create Co-Abode (www.co-abode), an Internet site where single mothers can find support and links to others in their own communities they could share a home with. Co-Abode now has twenty thousand members across the United States, many of whom are sharing homes. Their comments about their new living arrangements are heartwarming.

Benefits of Home Sharing for Single Parents
based on comments from www.co-abode.com

Single mothers report that living with another single-mother family makes it possible to:

1. Have a larger, more comfortable home in a safer school district.
2. Cut monthly costs for rent or mortgage and other household expenses in half.
3. Split the costs of essentials such as rent and utilities, so there is money to provide nicer things for your children.
4. Escape the stress, fatigue, and pressure of having to do everything oneself by sharing chores, such as cooking, grocery shopping, laundry, homework, carpooling, housecleaning, and child supervision.
5. Have newfound time and energy to devote to oneself and one's children.
6. Trade babysitting nights so one can have a social life, take evening classes, or get out to a movie every so often.
7. Hold on to a family home after a divorce.
8. Leave an abusive marriage knowing one will have the emotional and financial resources needed to care for oneself and her family.
9. Build strong bonds among "surrogate" siblings. Children feel less lonely because they're part of a larger family and have other kids and another parent they can confide in, play with, and be entertained by.
10. Do away with loneliness a single parent often feels, because there is a companion who understands and shares the same challenges.

Together these factors result in a significantly higher quality of life. As some of the parents on www.co-abode.com put it, life is "Simpler. Better. Happier. Easier. Cheaper." Others said, "I'm a better mom," and "It's priceless!"

MAKING THE CHOICE TO LIVE WITH OTHERS

Pros

- ▶ Multiple wage earners in a household can combine incomes to purchase a nicer, roomier home.
- ▶ Everyone can save money on basic costs of living and thus need to work less and/or have more income for other activities.
- ▶ Many hands make light work. Everyone can share in the tasks of maintaining a household.
- ▶ Often household items and equipment can be shared, thus cutting down on living expenses.
- ▶ A home that's designed, remodeled, or expanded with shared housing in mind adds square footage and value to your property.
- ▶ Shared living arrangements usually make going through life transitions and personal crises easier.

Cons

- ▶ There is less privacy and more noise in the house.
- ▶ Personality difficulties can arise, because everyone has his or her own preferences and habits, pet peeves, likes and dislikes.
- ▶ Time schedules and house rules need to be explored, agreed upon, and coordinated.
- ▶ There is a risk that not all parties will contribute equitably to the costs and work of the household.
- ▶ More people living in a home adds wear and tear on furniture, carpeting, flooring, countertops, etc. Your housemates may not feel as respectful of your belongings as you do.
- ▶ Shared living arrangements may be temporary, as kids get married and have children, older parents need more intensive care or die, or single mothers remarry.

Retiring and preretiring singles are also discovering the benefits of home sharing. When career teachers and best friends Heidi Conners and Deana O'Dell of Pittsburgh, Pennsylvania, turned fifty-five, for example, they began looking forward to the time when they could retire. They weren't looking forward to living alone on a fixed income. "I was worrying about how I'd make ends meet without a salary if I lived to ninety-five, like my mother did," Deana admitted. "Having been divorced for five years, I know how lonely it can get, living by yourself all the time. So when Heidi raised the idea of selling our homes and pooling our funds to build a dream home we can retire to and live comfortably, I leapt at the idea."

"Deana and I had taught at the same school for twenty years," Heidi points out. "We've been through lots of ups and downs together. I lost my husband.

She'd been through a tough divorce. I knew we would get along fine. Because we were building a new home, we were able to design the house the way we wanted it. We each have our own bedroom suite with a fireplace, small living area, and side porch. There's a big kitchen, dining area, and living room where our families can gather. And a nice-sized hobby room that we share. She sews. I weave. I'm really glad we did this while we are both healthy and well. I think it's ideal."

Because women tend to live longer than men and have lower incomes upon retirement, they often have a harder time making it on a retirement income. Also, since women tend to be more social than men, it's not surprising more women retirees seem to be home sharing with friends and colleagues than men. When considering a shared living arrangement, men seem to prefer rooming in a house where a number of other people are also living. Harking back to boarding house days, with more than half of women and nearly half of men living without a spouse today, many find that renting a room, floor, or suite in a large shared home can be a cost-effective and enjoyable way of life.

For example, when Allison and Dave Ewoldt bought a large home in downtown Bellingham, Washington, where they could operate their nonprofit foundation, they moved in with Allison's young son, Kyler, and shared their roomy home with three boarders—two single men and a single woman, all of whom were working full-time. Normally they each prepared their own meals, but they often shared movie nights in the comfy living room and periodically enjoyed sharing potluck supper nights.

Some couples are also becoming more open to sharing a home. Linda and Ed Reines, of Santa Fe, New Mexico, are in their mid-forties. "We always wanted to live in Santa Fe after our kids got off to college, but housing there had become so expensive that we'd all but given up on the idea until we met a couple at a party who shared our dream," Linda remembers. "They were semiretired and a little older than us, but we got to talking and decided to take a trip there to see if, by pooling the equity we each had in our home, we could buy a house that would accommodate all four of us."

They now share a twenty-eight-hundred-square-foot adobe house just outside Santa Fe. "I think we tend to close off options for ourselves out of habit," Linda told us. "I was afraid I wouldn't like sharing a home with anyone other than Ed, but we remodeled the house slightly so that each couple has their own private bedroom, bath, and sitting area on opposite ends of the house. This provides plenty of privacy when I need it, and to my surprise we're not crowded. You don't need as many things when you're sharing tools, cleaning supplies, kitchen utensils, and other equipment with someone else. We don't need two sets of everything." But they do have three entertainment centers: one large new one for the living room and two smaller ones for their personal quarters that they brought with them when they moved from St. Louis, Missouri. Each couple also brought their own dog with them, but now it's hard to tell whose dog is whose. Their pets seem to think they're all one pack.

OUR ADVICE : LIVING WITH FRIENDS AND FAMILY

If the benefits of sharing a home with friends or family are appealing to you, here are several factors to explore:

1. *Motivation.* What's most appealing to you about sharing a home with someone else? Lower expenses? Companionship? A larger home? Help with the tasks of daily life? Something else? How important are these things relative to other things you value in life? The answers will help you define if and what type of shared living arrangement will meet your needs. If you are in the midst of a personal crisis, such as a divorce, the loss of a spouse, or a serious illness, you probably won't be as objective about your decisions as you will at a later time. Approach your decision to share a home as an interim one you can reevaluate once you get your bearings.
2. *Attitude.* Do you have concerns about how friends or colleagues will perceive you when you say you're living with others? In Western countries we tend to place a high value on independence and individualism. We think adults should be self-sufficient and live on their own terms. But many of us are beginning to rethink these attitudes. What about yours? People will afford you as much respect in a shared lifestyle as you afford yourself.
3. *Comfort.* Take a comfort assessment. What makes you feel comfortable and happy in your home? What are your sacred routines, your favorite places to sit, your treasured belongings, the special things you like to do around the house? How flexible would you be in regard to these things if you needed to accommodate someone else's habits? What are your "must haves" and your "must keeps"? Knowing these things will help you weigh decisions about whether and under what circumstances you will enjoy sharing a home with others.

Tip

Most people find that having a separate bedroom and bath for each individual, couple, or family whenever possible makes for the best arrangement.

4. Compatibility. Being able to get along well with the others you will be living with is probably the most important ingredient for enjoying a shared living arrangement. Even if you will be living with friends or relatives whom you think you know well, it's important to explore similarities, differences, preferences, expectations, and pet peeves before deciding to live together. Here are a few topics to consider:

- ▶ Are you neat or messy?
- ▶ What is your idea of clean? Do you like surfaces kept clear and everything put away, or are you fine with having a lot of clutter around the house?
- ▶ What music do you like?
- ▶ How much noise can you tolerate or not tolerate, and what kinds?
- ▶ Are you a morning person or a night person?
- ▶ Do you like a warm house or a cool house?
- ▶ What are your eating preferences? Frequency? Special foods you prefer?
- ▶ What is your daily schedule? Your routines?
- ▶ How much space do you need? What kinds of space?
- ▶ How much and what type of privacy do you need?
- ▶ Do you want to have pets?
- ▶ What tasks will need to be done around the house? Cooking, shopping, cleaning? Who is willing to do what? When?
- ▶ What are your views on religion, drugs, smoking, drinking, having guests of the opposite sex stay overnight, and, if there will be children in the house, what are your parenting philosophies?
- ▶ What are your financial expectations or requirements, and do you each have the ability to meet them? Consider monthly rent, utility bills, and household expenses.
- ▶ How do you deal with money? Are you a spendthrift, a miser, or somewhere in between?
- ▶ What is your approach to handling things that need to be done? Do you put things off until the last minute, or do you like to have everything done well ahead of time?
- ▶ What common interests, backgrounds, and experiences do you share?

You don't need to agree upon on all such points, of course. You probably won't. But you will need to be able to accept, accommodate, and understand where you're each coming from in regard to such issues and have agreements and ground rules that will prevent unpleasant conflicts.

5. *Equitability.* To live successfully with others, most people need to feel that the relationship is an equitable one. No one wants to feel he is being taking advantage of or is contributing disproportionately to household responsibilities, be it around finances, housework, or who decides what. Of course, what one can contribute depends on many things. An ill parent cannot do an equal share of the work around the house, but hopefully no one would expect that. Nor can a son who is right out of college and still without a job pay an equal share of the costs of running his parents' home. What's important is to know what seems equitable to each of you under the circumstances, to have clearly stated and understood agreements about who will do and pay for what, and then, of course, to keep or reevaluate your agreements. Open and honest communication will be the key to ensuring that everyone continues to feel they are being treated fairly.

Creating Intentional Communities

It's not only kinship or close personal relationships that are bringing folks together these days. It's also about coming together with small groups of people who want more than a cursory relationship with their neighbors. The term "intentional community" is an inclusive one. It embraces a variety of living arrangements, including cohousing, residential land trusts, communes, student co-ops, urban housing cooperatives, ashrams, ecovillages, collectives, and other projects that are formed around shared social, political, spiritual, or professional interests, goals, values, or common vision. An intentional community might be located on rural acreage, in a suburban development, within a residential urban neighborhood, or in a converted apartment complex. Members of the community may share a single residence or live separately in a cluster of private dwellings.

At Ashland Vineyard, north of Richmond, Virginia, for example, six families are living together on forty rural acres of land with a commitment to living by Quaker principles. In the Seattle Urban Intentional Community, young adults live together in urban neighborhoods and work with urban churches and ministries to provide programs like after-school tutoring, outreach to homeless kids, and ESL classes. On Blue Heron Farm in Pittsboro, North Carolina, an old, tin-roofed house, a one-hundred-year-old sharecropper's cabin, and an assortment of other homes that were once destined for demolition are now home to a group who came together after reading Scott Peck's book, *A Different Drum*. They have taken up Peck's suggestion that the way to world peace is through individuals coming together to share their lives, work out their differences, and find resolution to life's problems through community building. Brindledorl, an 1880s farmhouse in Silver Spring, Maryland, now houses an intentional community for schoolteachers. Cheesecake is a cluster of communal buildings on nineteen acres of land in Mendocino County, California, created by a group of longtime friends who decided to retire together.

YOUR CHOICE?

- ▶ Live in a community of others under one roof or in separate households.
- ▶ Own your own property or share ownership in property.
- ▶ Live in an urban or rural environment.
- ▶ Join a diverse community or join a community of like-minded members.
- ▶ Share in the tasks of each other's daily lives or share only in tasks related to common interests such as grounds or selected social activities.
- ▶ Earn a separate income of your own or produce an income together with others.

So there are a rich variety of choices when it comes to living in an intentional community, but the desire for community is the one distinction that binds them together. Shared living is about personal relationships. When living with room-mates you may have close personal relationships, but community is still something separate, something outside your personal life, something you come home to retreat from. In an intentional community, that's not the case. Intentional communities are about community relationships. Community becomes a central part of your personal life, not something you leave behind when you go home. Just how much of a social, economic, and philosophical connection one shares in an intentional community is a matter of how each group collectively chooses to define their relationships.

It is this self-determining character that makes intentional communities distinct from each other, so distinct that chances are you won't find any two quite alike. Even their legal and ownership structures vary. They may be organized as associations, partnerships, corporations, limited-liability companies (LLCs), or cooperatives. Whether you are buying into a community or participating in forming one, discussing the legal structure of the project with a knowledgeable attorney is essential, for as you can see from the following section, each choice has important financial implications for the future of the investment you will be making.

Legal Options
1. Association: ▶ People can form associations without incorporating them, even without having formal documents or organizational papers. Of course, this level of informality has definite risks. An association can be created by CC&Rs (Covenants, Codes, and Restrictions).   ▶ Having liability insurance is important for an association, particularly one that is not incorporated.

- ► Examining the association's insurance policy should give you an idea about how it's been organized.
- ► State law determines whether an association needs to register with a local government.

2. Partnership:
- ► Partnerships also can exist without formal documents.
- ► Each partner shares in the risks and benefits of the partnership.
- ► Liability insurance can be even more important than it is for corporations.
- ► The are two common types of partnerships:
  - » Equity partnerships – Partners share responsibility and risk equally. Each partner can bind the partnership legally, and each partner becomes responsible for the actions of every other partner.
  - » Limited partnerships – Run by a general partner. This limits the risks of other partners to the amount they invest; however, they have no control over how the partnership is operated.

3. Corporation:
- ► These usually protect association members from personal liability.
- ► Corporations need liability insurance and must comply with federal and state laws.
- ► Lenders prefer to deal with corporations.
- ► There are two types of corporations:
  - » For-profit – Ownership takes the form of shares. Such corporations may or may not earn a profit.
  - » Not-for-profit (nonprofit) – Activities are limited by the nonprofit's declared purposes, which are narrowly defined by law. A nonprofit's members are not "owners."

4. Limited-liability company (LLC):
- ► Requires formal organization, like a corporation, but costs less to form and maintain.
- ► Limits liability of its owners.
- ► Frequently used form of ownership for cohousing projects.

5. Cooperative (Co-op):
- ► A Co-op is a form of corporation that's similar to both a for-profit corporation (it issues shares to owners) and a nonprofit (it also has a purpose: the cooperation of its owners).
- ► Residents own shares in the cooperative, but do not own an individual dwelling.
- ► Lenders are more skeptical of co-ops than other corporations.
- ► Two types of co-ops are:
  - » equity in which shares are sold at market value
  - » limited equity in which shares are sold at a fixed value

If the idea of living in a shared community appeals to you, you'll find there are over six hundred existing intentional communities listed in the fourth edition or online edition of the *Communities Directory: A Guide to Intentional Communities and Cooperative Living*. The key will be finding one that suits you. Or, if you are so inclined, you can always create your own. Here we'll describe two general types that fall along a continuum from more to less private autonomy:

1. *Cohousing*, in which residents design and operate their own neighborhoods, allow for privately owned homes and economically independent households that contain all the features of a conventional home, yet also provide commonly owned areas and services shared, and paid for by all residents, such as open spaces, courtyards, playgrounds, and a common house. Neighborhoods are usually composed of ten to forty households.

2. *Communes*, today more commonly called collectives or egalitarian communities, are groups in which members may or may not live in separate housing. Members agree to live in accordance with a certain motivating philosophy, and to that end, pool their resources, including income, share their expenses, and own their property collectively. Sometimes they produce their income through collective activities as well.

Cohousing

Cohousing is a way of life that balances the need for privacy with the need for community. It originated from the needs of a group of two-career couples in Denmark who were searching for a way to share child care and meal preparation. Since that time the concept has attracted families, singles, and especially the elderly across Europe and now North America. Currently there are more than sixty small residential cohousing communities in the United States. Many more are under construction, and others are in early planning and developmental stages. Architect Charles Durrett and his wife, Kathryn McCamant, who popularized this way of life in the United States, coined the term "cohousing" in their 1988 book by that name.

Cohousing projects attract people who are consciously committed to living as a community and are willing to plan, design, develop, and run a community that meets their needs. Cohousing communities usually contain single-family homes or attached private residences, shared common grounds, and a common house that serves as a social center for the community. Individuals buy their own residences and contribute both time and money to the operation of the shared facilities, which include such things as a large dining and kitchen area where all residents can gather, a lounge, recreational facilities, children's play spaces, a guest room, workshop, and laundry room. Communities usually serve optional group meals in the common house several times a week.

Cohousing communities are typically characterized by:

1. **Resident participation in project planning.** Significant participation by the residents-to-be in the planning and development stages is integral to the concept of cohousing. This enables residents to tailor their future community to their particular interests and needs and to develop a shared vision of the goals of the community, what it will be like, and how it will operate. This gives each community its own personality and flavor. Some communities are inter-generational, composed of residents of all ages. Others are family focused or feature a singles' lifestyle. The fastest-growing projects in the United States are oriented toward elderly couples and singles who see cohousing as a way to age noninstitutionally. Glazier Circle in Davis, California, is the first self-planned housing development for the elderly. It was conceived, planned, and designed by twelve friends with an average age of eighty and took five years to complete. Four couples and four singles live in eight individual townhomes. A seventy-six-year-old former nun named Dene Peterson founded ElderSpirit of Abindon, Virginia. It was ten years in the making. Six more are in development, including one in St. Petersburg, Florida, and one in Wichita, Kansas.

In an effort to streamline development, some of the recent cohousing communities have been built by a developer who brings a group of future residents into the process after the structures are built. Eldershire in Sherburn, New York, is an example. It was actually built before the owners were consulted, but once completed, the community was turned over to residents to run.

2. **Structures and streets arranged for neighborly interactions.** Developers and cohousing residents design the layout of private homes and common areas to encourage community relationships. Homes typically face each other across a pedestrian street or courtyard; owners park their cars on the periphery. Often, every home looks onto the common house. Foot traffic is emphasized over motor vehicles.

3. **Common facilities secondary.** Common facilities in cohousing projects are tailored for daily uses desired by the residents and integral to the community. Unlike communes or collectives, where common areas are predominant, they are always supplemental to private homes in cohousing communities. Structures are usually grouped together to allow for as much undeveloped open space as the site allows.

4. **Residential management.** The residents manage their own community and perform much of the work required to maintain the common property. They share in preparing optional common meals and meet regularly to identify and

solve problems and to develop policies for the community. Some communities, especially those for the elderly, choose to pay someone to come in and do community tasks such as yard work, maintenance, and preparation of shared meals.

5. Egalitarian decision-making. While residents assume leadership roles in the community, no one person (or persons) has authority over the others. Usually there are several highly motivated individuals who take the lead on the initial tasks, but as others join the group, each person takes on roles consistent with his or her skills, abilities, and interests. Many cohousing groups make their decisions by consensus, although some allow voting if the group can't reach consensus. Most rarely resort to voting, however, because when there is a vote, some people win and others lose. This creates divisiveness and antagonism and forms factions. This is one reason these communities remain small and focused on a shared vision. The larger and more diverse the needs of those in the community, the more difficult it is to manage by consensus.

6. No shared production of income. Unlike communes or collectives, cohousing communities do not produce a source of income for their members. Sometimes a resident will be paid to do a specific time-limited task, but more typically that kind of work is counted as that member's contribution to the shared responsibilities.

 Tip

Some intentional communities have condominium ownership, but a condominium is not a form of legal organization. A condominium is a way an established association, partnership, LLC, corporation, or cooperative can use to separate legal ownership of their land or building into smaller units to be made available to various owners.

Allison and Dave Ewoldt believe cohousing is a good choice for them. As you may recall, the Ewoldts shared their large downtown Bellingham home with three other adults. Allison found this to be a beautiful ideal but a personal hardship in reality. She struggled with the lack of privacy and the fact that not everyone did his or her share of cleaning and upkeep. "I'm not a Material Girl," she told us, "but it was depressing that my personal belongings with which the house was furnished weren't respected."

Last year, the Ewoldts sold their home and moved with Allison's twelve-year-old son into Stone Curves, a new cohousing community in Tucson, Arizona. It's an urban, environmentally oriented intergenerational community of about fifty people who live in their own private homes but share in many community activities. Of their new community Allison says, "Cohousing is great!" She enjoys the community meals, the holiday events, the projects (like building a community tree house), and the workshops offered in the common house. She also likes having a support network of neighbors who can help you out in a pinch.

Dave and Allison admit that running the community involves major responsibilities for everyone, but they both agree that having private living quarters gives cohousing a big advantage. Dave also values the ability to share things that not everyone needs on a regular basis, such as a library, workout room, a garden, meeting rooms, and large kitchen for community events. Best of all, though, he adds, "You actually know your neighbors, and we share a purpose to live more sustainably. People don't need to be under one roof to be in community."

Gina and Dan Kruse would agree. Before coming to Stone Curves from Massachusetts, they also lived in shared housing and enjoyed it, but they hoped cohousing would provide a more balanced, middle-of-the-road approach to blending private and community life. Gina admits living in Stone Curves took some adjustment. The setting is very urban. The streets are noisy, and there is crime in the area. She gets frustrated at times with how long it takes to get anything done with consensus decision making, and sometimes she has difficulty following her diet at the community dinners. But after two years there she says, "I enjoy the spontaneous activities with neighbors and living in a diverse community of all ages, ethnic backgrounds, and interests. I can hardly imagine living any other way now."

 Tip

If you are a person who can't say no, you may find yourself overcommitted in a cohousing community. Living in community with others is an excellent way to learn how to know your limits and define your boundaries.

Everyone seems to agree that what makes cohousing a great choice is that there is so much choice. If an urban area isn't for you, there are communities in rural areas. If you don't enjoy having children around, there are communities for the elderly and for singles. Cohousing is like the Burger King of housing arrangements—you can have it your way!

If living in a cohousing community sounds appealing to you, there are three ways you can get involved:

1. *Bring together others you know* who share your vision for a cohousing project, and develop a cohousing community together. This is how most of the early projects came about. For example, a group of four couples created Milagro,

a cohousing community of twenty-eight energy-efficient, passive-solar adobe homes on a forty-three-acre site in the Tucson mountains. The idea for Milagro began in 1994. All twenty-eight homes were fully occupied in 2003.

The major advantage of initiating your own cohousing project is that you'll be able to shape your community to your group's wishes and vision. But it is an expensive, complicated, and long process, involving many steps that can take from three to six years or more to complete, including:

- forming a group
- developing a process for how you will proceed
- defining your collective vision
- finding and buying the land
- lining up the professionals to design and build the community
- Setting up a legal and financial structure

- securing financing
- obtaining building permits and approvals
- marketing and selling the properties
- overseeing construction
- defining ground rules for the community
- moving in and getting underway

On their Web site, the folks at Milagro (www.milagrocohousing.org) summarize the lessons of their twelve years in development this way:

- It can be done.
- It will take twice as long and cost twice as much as you think.
- By the time you figure out what you're doing, the project is complete.

If this is too much for you to take on, there are development and consulting companies that work with groups wanting to create cohousing communities. They underwrite the financing and work with you step-by-step through the process. (See LEARN MORE.) Another alternative is to consider converting an existing apartment, condo, warehouse, campground, farm, or other facility into a cohousing community.

2. *Become involved in a project that is in development.* There are many cohousing communities already in various stages of development that are seeking other community members. Some are being developed by groups of individuals working on their own or with a developer. Others are being built by a developer who plans to sell the properties and turn the management over to the residents upon completion. The Web site www.cohousing.org lists many such as projects at various stages of development throughout the United States.

This is surely a quicker and less personally time-consuming option, but keep in mind, if a project is developed without resident participation, it is not technically a cohousing community, because being involved in the planning is a core feature of cohousing. Unless care is given to establishing a shared vision among those who buy into these developments, the community may end up simply being another typical homeowners' association, where people live in proximity of each other but not truly as a community.

3. *Buy into an existing community* that isn't filled yet or has a member who is selling his or her home. Since everyone in a cohousing community owns their own home, homes will become available whenever residents sell their property and move elsewhere. This is without doubt the quickest way to become part of a cohousing community, but it will be important to explore carefully if an existing community is well suited to you because you won't have played a role in formulating the vision or determining the design, layout, policies, and ground rules you will be living with.

Boston's Beacon Hill: A Virtual Retirement Community

If you would like to stay in your own home and love your neighborhood, but also desire the mutual support and connections living in an intentional community can provide, there's another option you can consider. A group of two hundred residents in their sixties in Boston's Beacon Hill, not relishing the prospect of a future move someday to a retirement home, banded together to form the first virtual retirement community, Beacon Hill Village (www.beaconhillvillage.org), which brings shared services they need to their homes. For five hundred dollars per year, members of their nonprofit village share the benefit of group discounts, in-home health services, group rates on long-term care insurance, and access to a concierge service that takes care of things like errands and excursions to cultural events. Similar communities may soon be started in New York, Los Angeles, and Las Vegas.

 MAKING THE CHOICE FOR COHOUSING

Pros

▸ You can have both closer relationships and a sense of community camaraderie around a shared vision without losing privacy or control over your personal space.

▸ There is mutual support for dealing with the work, challenges, and crises of life.

Cons

▸ Creating a cohousing development is a long process. It can take three to six years to form and develop one. Buying into an existing one, though, requires fitting into a community others have established.

▸ There are many legal, zoning, financial, and building codes to deal with in the beginning.

Pros continued

- ► You save money by sharing community resources, such as tools and equipment.
- ► You own your own home, so you can sell it at any time you desire to do so.
- ► You can enjoy open space and amenities such as a spa, pool, or garden that you might not otherwise be able to afford if you had to purchase them by yourself.
- ► By sharing common spaces and community resources, you don't need as large a home or as many belongings to care for and maintain.

Cons continued

- ► There are ongoing shared costs in terms of fees or dues. Residents may have differing abilities to pay for amenities.
- ► Residents commit to share duties and responsibilities, but if some shirk theirs, others get burned out.
- ► Participating in committees and making community decisions by consensus with various personalities is often time-consuming and tedious.
- ► Unless new people buying homes are screened, those who move in later may or may not share the original goals and values of the community.

 OUR ADVICE

1. If developing a cohousing community with a group of your friends or colleagues appeals to you and others you know, we recommend partnering with a development company (See LEARN MORE) to save hours of work and a large up-front financial investment. Even with the help of a development company, though, this will not be something you can do short of the expenditure of several years of time and energy.

2. If you don't have the time and energy to be involved in developing a project, then buying property in an existing community or becoming involved in the development already in the planning process will be your best option. But when buying a home in an existing community, don't assume the developer or real estate agent has the inside scoop. They will be eager to sell to you, so they may gloss over details or simply not know much about the cohousing way of life. Instead, thoroughly explore with residents the vision and expectations for the community.

3. Living in a cohousing community requires a significant commitment, so before settling on this choice, visit a variety of communities to find out if it's a commitment you would actually enjoy making. You'll find they are all different. So explore the directories of cohousing communities in LEARN MORE at the end of the chapter. In these directories, communities can be located by state, and most cohousing communities have Web sites listed, so visit their sites to see if you'd like to make a trip there to experience it firsthand. The Cohousing Association of the United States (Coho/US) sponsors daylong tours of cohousing communities in several areas around the nation. The Fellowship of Intentional Communities lists cohousing conferences and other events in various local areas.

4. As you visit communities, review with residents what would be expected of you. Arrange to attend some of their community meals and to sit in on some of the committee meetings. Observe their decision-making process. Compatibility with your possible new neighbors will make or break your experience, so meet as many of them as you can before you make a commitment.

5. If you're still not sure, it may be possible to rent a home or unit in the community you are considering before you commit to buying.

6. When you find a community that is to your liking, check out how the community goes about ensuring that new people who buy homes there are committed to the vision and way of life you've fallen in love with.

7. Expect an adjustment period. As Dave Ewoldt of Tucson's Stone Curves points out, although there were times in the past when humans lived quite naturally and comfortably in much more communal lifestyles, most of us in the Western world today are accustomed to a high degree of privacy. We take it for granted, so we may feel out of our comfort zone at first in a cohousing arrangement.

8. Be ready to give a lot of time to your new community and to have more close relationships than ever.

 Tip

Stone Curve's Gina Kruse recommends that communities have a membership team composed of residents who are willing to talk with prospective buyers, answer their questions, and explore feelings about the community vision, roles, expectations, and commitment.

 Tip

Since affordable land for an urban cohousing project can be challenging, consider locating in one of the world's "shrinking cities. This is a growing movement in realizing that a city needn't be large or growing to be a good place to live. In the United States, more than half of the one hundred most populous cities in 1950 have fewer residents today. About 6 million fewer people live in sixteen of the twenty cities that were the largest then. Eleven of the one hundred largest cities fifty years ago have fewer than one hundred thousand people today.

Some of these cities, such as Richmond, Virginia; Youngstown, Ohio; and St. Louis, Missouri, are rethinking their identity and taking on a new view of city life. They are targeting declining neighborhoods and redesigning them in a variety of creative ways, including allowing homeowners to buy abandoned lots next door to create gardens, relaxing zoning rules to allow small farms or apple orchards, and turning abandoned areas into parks, wildlife refuges, and green spaces. See the Cleveland Urban Design Collaborative's Shrinking Cities Institute at www.cudc.kent.edu/d-Service-Learning/Shrinking to learn more.

Communes, Collectives, or Egalitarian Communities

In the United States the term commune comes with a lot of baggage. It's still associated with communes of the 1960s. Images of hippies, antiwar protests, cults, free love, and pot come to mind. As a result, most cooperative communities in the United States shy away from using the term, choosing instead to refer to themselves as *collectives*, *cooperatives*, or *egalitarian communities*. But by whatever name, today's intentional communes are quite different from those of the '60s and should not be confused with their midtwentieth-century past.

Like other intentional communities, communes are usually organized around ideological beliefs, but the one belief that sets them apart from other communities is their view of ownership and income. While members of a commune may or may not share housing, they do share ownership of community resources, meaning that members own little or no personal property, and, most importantly, they share in producing an income for the community and its members. At first glance sharing ownership of property and income with others, or "income sharing," as it's called, may sound odd. It's not so strange, though, if you think of it as an extension of a two-career or other multiwage-earning family. The difference is simply that in a commune the "family" extends beyond relatives and is larger than in most blood-related families.

"Income sharing is an arrangement where the group as a whole assumes responsibility for the needs of its members, receiving the products of their labor and distributing these and all other goods equally, or according to need. In other words, forgoing private income in favor of shared wealth."
—SHANTAGANI, FREELAND, MD

The Farm, located off the Natchez Trace in Tennessee, was once a classic '60s commune, but it abandoned such ways long ago. Today, no longer referring to themselves as a commune, the Farm defies the stereotypes. Home to a two-hundred-member cooperative where families live in single-family residences and pay monthly rent, it's still a rural farm with woodstoves and mandalas, but it's also a high-tech entrepreneurial center of several multimillion-dollar industries, such as a $2.5 million company that produces satellite radiation detectors, a publishing company, and a video production business.

Of course, most of the six hundred such collective settlements in the United States are not that entrepreneurial, but they do produce income. They earn their collective living in various ways. For example, like many egalitarian communities, Sandhill, which is located on 135 acres in northeast Missouri, earns its living by farming. They produce and sell sorghum syrup, tempeh, honey, garlic, mustard, and horseradish. Acorn in Mineral, Virginia, runs a mail-order seed business, selling heirloom and endangered varieties of seeds mostly grown on their own seventy-two acres of certified organic land. They also have a tinnery where they recycle functional arts and crafts from tin cans. Residents of Skyhouse, also in Missouri, are telecommuters; they provide computer consulting. Some operate home-based businesses. Meadowdance, a community of fourteen adults and children in Walden, Vermont, for example, operates Wordsworth, a typing/editing/graphic design home business.

Terra Nova in Columbia, Missouri; Emma Goldman Finishing School in the north Beacon Hill neighborhood of Seattle (home of www.amazon.com); and Shantagani in Freeland, Maryland, outside of Baltimore, support the community by having salaried jobs outside of the community. Gana on New York's Staten Island owns five nearby commercial buildings where they recycle and resell furniture, clothing, and household goods. Innisfree, in the Blue Ridge Mountains of Virginia, runs a boarding school for disabled children. Sunrise Ranch in Colorado runs a retreat and conference center.

Principles of The Federation of Egalitarian Communities

Each Federation Community does the following:

1. Holds its land, labor, income, and other resources in common.
2. Assumes responsibility for the needs of its members.
3. Practices nonviolence.
4. Uses a form of decision making in which members have an equal opportunity to participate, either through consensus, direct vote, or right of appeal or overrule.
5. Actively works to establish the equality of all people and does not permit discrimination on the basis of race, class, creed, ethnic origin, age, sex, sexual orientation, or gender identity.
6. Acts to conserve natural resources for present and future generations while striving to continually improve ecological awareness and practice.
7. Creates processes for group communication and participation and provides an environment that supports personal development.

—From www.thefec.org

Clearly, today's communes, by whatever name, are not withdrawing from life. They are contributing to and supporting themselves within Western culture in a very different but compatible way—their way. Most have Web sites describing their community, and invite visitors. Many have marketing managers, health plans for members, and newsletters for those interested in learning more about their lifestyle, and members actively contribute to civic and humanitarian causes. There is an association of such communities, The federation of Egalitarian Communities (FEC) and a thick national directory.

So with the hippie counterculture misconception clearly set aside, another false impression about communes is that they center around a charismatic leader who establishes and directs the community and holds the group together. Not so today. Today's collectives share a common philosophy, are equalitarian in nature, and focus on consensual decision making. Tim Miller of the University of Kansas, who studies communal life, estimates there are as many as 150,000 people living in U.S. collectives. While they consist of families and singles of all ages, they seem to be an increasingly popular choice for baby boomers who are fifty and older.

The Trends Research Institute, a network of interdisciplinary experts who forecast developing trends, says that one of the hottest trends they see is a rapidly growing desire among people to be more self-reliant and less dependent on mainstream society, choosing "for example, ecovillages, sustainable intentional communities, and organized neighborhoods."

Cooperative communities such as these may be located on small or large agricultural homesteads, in villagelike community settings, and urban buildings and homes. Some live in a shared home; others live in separate homes, townhomes, or apartments on shared property. Some are small groups of five or six adults like Sandhill; others are larger groups, like Gana, where eighty-five people live in ten well-maintained buildings on New York's Staten Island. But unlike cohousing, one cannot just buy into a collective. Collectives have limited membership. There is an application process, and one must be interviewed and accepted by the group before becoming part of the community. At any given time many are closed to new members.

They can operate under any one of the legal structures described in the cohousing section, but since the communities are run by the members, just how the community is run varies. They all have some way of contributing "labor equity" (the work tasks) and distributing income within the community. In some, duties and responsibilities are clearly defined, and hours contributed are carefully tracked. Others are run entirely by people who are volunteering to do whatever they do. Generally income is pooled, and whatever is left over after the expenses of the community are paid is then distributed equally between the members. Sometimes participants receive a monthly allowance. Each member usually receives housing, food, health care, and personal spending money in exchange for working an assigned number of hours in any of the community's businesses or domestic roles. Labor is not always measured only in terms of income-producing activities but also includes time contributed to the household.

MAKING THE CHOICE FOR COMMUNAL LIVING

Many of the same pros and cons we identified for making the choice for cohousing apply here as well. Here are a few others:

Pros

- ► Community, person-to-person relationships, kinship, and personal support can be central to daily life instead of squeezed into special occasions.
- ► Sharing of equipment, appliances, cooking, cleaning, and child care saves time and money.
- ► You have a voice in determining how your community will operate.
- ► The group works together to provide the basic necessities of life, i.e., comfortable housing, good food, medical care, clothing, and some extra spending money.
- ► You can live more simply, get out of the rat race, and spend less time earning a living while still living comfortably.

Cons

- ► Since this is an unconventional way of life, you may face misconceptions and even prejudice at times by people who don't understand your lifestyle.
- ► There is decidedly less privacy and autonomy than is customary and, depending on physical arrangements, it may be crowded.
- ► If you are in the minority, you may have to live by the rules of the majority.
- ► Without a solid economic model and income base, these communities flounder. If some don't do what others feel is their part, hard feelings will arise.
- ► A high degree of commitment is required, and group decision making takes considerable time. Conflicts can arise, especially when romantic or marital relationships end.

OUR ADVICE

In addition to our advice under cohousing, most of which applies equally to communal living, we also suggest:

1. Evaluate carefully if this way of life is actually suited to you. It might sound idyllic in concept, but to fit into a collective, you need to be self-motivated, conscientious, tolerant, willing to share, a

good communicator and problem solver, capable of handling conflict, and willing to participate in making group decisions about how you will live. If you like privacy, love to compete, and enjoy having lots of your own money to spend as you wish, this is clearly not for you.

2. Absolutely visit any collective-living situation you are considering. There is a list of FEC member communites on their Web site (www.thefec.org). Be sure you know what will be expected of you financially, socially, and emotionally. Far more participation will be required than in a cohousing living arrangement. Find out about the rules and agreements among members for handling income contributions and household duties, how decisions are made, and how conflicts and concerns are handled.

3. If possible, arrange for an extended stay of several weeks or more. Some communities will require this, but we recommend arranging to do this when possible even if it's not required. Here's a list of things to consider:

   ▶ Is there a clearly defined mission? The most successful communities see themselves as having an urgent mission in the world. Anyone who doesn't share and want to work diligently toward this mission should not be in the community. So when you visit, check out if the community's mission is clear, if everyone seems to be fully on board with it, and if you share it passionately, too.

   ▶ Does the community have a solid economic base? The most common reason collectives fail is not having a strong enough economic base to keep going. So make sure the community has ways of producing a reliable and sufficient income to provide a secure lifestyle for all the members. Is each person expected to contribute an income in the form of an outside job/independent career, or is everyone able to work within the existing business(es) of the community?

   ▶ How does the community deal with members who do not contribute their share or otherwise adhere to community agreements? In successful communities, everyone is expected to adhere to every decision the group makes. Thus it's important to determine if the community has the courage to enforce their decisions. How is this done? There should be some recognized means of authority, even if it's simply a group decision.

   ▶ How compatible are the community members? Get to know community members personally, and observe their interactions. While there will always be conflicts to resolve when humans come together, the more compatible the group, the less conflict and discord there will be. Also, how compatible are they with your personality, needs, and preferences? Consider such things as work ethic, political and religious views, attitudes toward money and spending, space, degree of privacy, and other issues raised on the compatibility checklist in the "Our Advice: *Living with Friends and Family*" section of this chapter.

4. Banks will not extend loans for single-family homes without an individual title, but if a collective is organized as an LLC, corporation, or cooperative, it is possible to own shares that can be sold

when you leave a community. These shares can be set at market value or a fixed value. So check carefully into the legal and financial arrangement structure of any community you are considering so you know up front what your situation would be should you decide to leave the community.

5. If you don't find a community that's suited to you, consider drawing together a group of your own. All the existing communities were born by bringing together like-minded people who want to live cooperatively. The FEC has many resources for setting up and operating a collective.

Ecovillages

Ecovillages are intentional communities of like-minded individuals who are devoted to creating and demonstrating an ecologically, socially, economically, and spiritually sustainable way of life, often including growing their own food in permaculture gardens and having their own power, water, and sewage systems. Participants may or may not share housing and may or may not be economically independent of one another. They may be a community of private residences, such as EcoVillage at Ithaca, in the Finger Lakes region of upstate New York, and Stone Curves, the cohousing project we discussed in Tucson, Arizona. Or they may be collectives, such as Earthhaven outside of Asheville, North Carolina, where residents build jointly owned, earth-friendly homes and develop their own sustainable careers or businesses that serve the community.

Wildroots is a thirty-acre "radical" ecovillage located in western North Carolina where the members live off the grid, carry their water, and practice "earthskills," or an earth-based way of life, such as permaculture, natural and primitive shelter building, hide tanning, herbal medicine, nature crafts, and wild food foraging. They see these skills, often as old as mankind itself, as essential survival skills that are rapidly falling into disuse in a throwaway culture. They intend to help keep them alive.

According to the Global Ecovillage Network (GEN) there are more than fifteen thousand identified sustainable community experiments in the United States. Generally speaking, urban-based ecovillages focus on restoration of land and community. Los Angeles Ecovillage, for example, is composed of restored old apartment buildings that are retrofitted with environmentally friendly materials and fueled by alternative energy and off-grid arrangements when possible. The community also nurtures organic gardens and fruit trees.

Rural ecovillages focus on preservation. For example, Wildroots reintroduces and propagates endangered native plants and animals into the local ecosystems from which they have been displaced. Using conservation and alternative energy, EcoVillage at Ithaca consumes only 41 percent of the natural gas and 22 percent of the water used by the average household in the northeast United States. See LEARN MORE for information on ecovillages.

LEARN MORE

Cohousing and Intentional Communities
Books
▶ *Builders of the Dawn: Community Lifestyles in a Changing World*, Corinne McLaughlin and Gordon Davidson, Book Publishing Company, 1990.
▶ *Creating a Life Together: Practical Tools to Grow Ecovillages and Intentional Communities*, Diana Leafe Christian, New Society Publishers, 2003.
▶ *The Cohousing Handbook*, Chris and Kelly Scott Hanson, New Society Publishers, 2004.
▶ *Cohousing: A Contemporary Approach to Housing Ourselves*, Kathryn McCamant and Charles Durrett, Ten Speed Press, 2003.
▶ *Senior Cohousing*, Charles Durret, Ten Speed Press, 2005.

Magazines
▶ *Communities* – Features information, issues, and ideas about intentional communities in North America, from urban co-ops to cohousing groups to ecovillages to rural communes: http://communities .ic.org

Directories
▶ "Directory: A Comprehensive Guide to Intentional Communities and Cooperative Living" by the Fellowship for Intentional Community (FIC). Published in 2005, this directory describes more than seven hundred intentional communities in North America and around the world, including contact information, core values, availability for visits, and a synopsis of their unifying vision.
▶ The Intentional Communities Directory Online by the FIC: http://directory.ic.org
▶ U.S. Cohousing Communities: http://directory.cohousing.org/us_list/all_us.php

Organizations
▶ The Cohousing Association of the United States (CO/US): www.co housing.org

- The Federation of Egalitarian Communities: www.thefec.org
- The Fellowship for Intentional Community: www.ic.org
- Seculife International Ltd. – Online support service center for senior citizens wishing to be part of a virtual retirement community: www.seculife.com

Consulting and Development Firms

- The Cohousing Partners, 241 Commercial Street, Nevada City, CA 95959; (530) 478-1970, www.cohousingco.com. A full-service real estate development firm that specializes in partnering with future residents to create neighborhood and environmentally sustainable cohousing projects.
- Wonderland Hill Development Company, 4676 Broadway, Boulder, CO, 80304; (303) 449-3232, www.whdc.com. Handles cohousing development details from beginning to end, or any particular phase of development, including locating the site, purchasing the land, financing, construction, and closings.

Ecovillages

Books

- *Ecovillages: A Practical Guide to Sustainable Communities*, Jan Martin Bang, New Society Publishers, 2005.
- *Ecovillage Living: Restoring the Earth and Her People*, Hildur Jackson and Karen Svensson, Green Books, 2002.

Organizations

- Ecovillage Network of the Americas – Includes a directory of ecovillages in North and South America: www.en.ecovillage.org
- Global Ecovillage Network: www.gen.ecovillage.org

Training Programs

- Ecovillage Training Center – www.thefarm.org/etc

Living with a Parent

- *Boomerang Nation: How to Survive Living with Your Parents . . . the Second Time Around*, Elina Furman, Fireside, 2005.
- *Coming of Age with Aging Parents: The Bungles, Battles, and Blessings*, Gail Goeller, Patina Publications, 2005.
- *Taking Care of Parents Who Didn't Take Care of You: Making Peace with Aging Parents*, Eleanor Cade, Hazelden, 2002.
- Children of Aging Parents (CAPS) – www.caps4caregivers.org.

Living with Your Grown Children

- *All Grown Up: Living Happily Ever After with Your Adult Children*, Roberta Maise, New Society Publishers, 2001.
- *Family for Life: How to Have Happy, Healthy Relationships with Your Adult Children*, Kathy Peel, McGraw-Hill, 2003.
- *Mom, Can I Move Back in with You?* Linda Perlman Gordon, Susan Morris Shaffer, Tarcher, 2004.

PART IV

Safeguarding Your Ability to Afford the Life You Seek—Nine Cashless Ways to Extend Your Income, Work Less, and Live More

"I don't want my life to be about working for money," Kevin Krieger told us. "There is so much more to life." Kevin is a software engineer. He would have no problem getting a high-paying job. In fact, he had one after graduating from college, but after a few years on the job, feelings of resentment and depression were nipping at his heels. "I like the work and had the money to do what I love, like travel, ski, and climb mountains, but there was so little time to do them." At thirty-four he quit his job. Since then, he works exclusively through a job shop, taking on programming projects they refer to him when he needs to earn some money, saving up as much as he can, then taking off again for several months to enjoy life.

Lisa Mainiero, sociologist and author of *Opt-Out Revolt,* would say Kevin's choice supports her findings that show both men and women are feeling trapped in our money-based economy that forces us to choose between working and having the resources to enjoy a personal life. Even those who are self-employed or pursuing one of the lifestyle options we described in the last section can get caught in this dilemma. Whether you're living on the road, in the city, out in the country, in an ecovillage, or abroad, if your lifestyle is heavily dependent on having to earn a lot of money, you can still find yourself working too hard to fully enjoy the fruits of your labor.

But in writing this book we've noticed that as people get a taste of a simpler, saner life, the less time and energy they want to devote to overworking and making money. Even if they enjoy their work, they want to work less and enjoy their lives more, so they're turning to cashless alternatives to multiply, supplement, extend, or stretch their primary incomes. Some are even finding they can live with very little cash at all.

As consumers, we've come to think that money is the only way to obtain almost anything of value we want or need. This means that to keep up with inflation and rising costs, we have to continually earn more just to maintain a decent standard of living. But money is only one means of exchange humankind has used throughout history. Recently many people are updating and adapting a number of alternatives that were common in the past as a way to:

- cut costs
- work less
- simplify life
- reduce debt

- start and expand an independent career
- escape rising financial pressures
- reduce stress on the environment
- build stronger communities

Barbara Harmony, for example, was working for the city of Hoboken, New Jersey, when she became disenchanted with the hassles of city life. She decided to pack up what belongings she could fit into her Volkswagen convertible and drive southwest in search of a simpler way of life. En route to nowhere specific, she was invited to the wedding of a friend in northwest Arkansas and decided to stay. There she and her former husband remodeled a small home north of Eureka Springs, where they raised their son. Twenty-six years later, Barbara, a gentle, soft-spoken woman with a generous laugh, still lives in her home on that wooded lot with her cat, Alice, and her rooster, Koko-da.

She refers to her lifestyle as "purposeful simplicity" because it enables her to devote the majority of her time to the nonprofit causes she loves. She does this by living simply, providing a variety of income-producing services she enjoys, and participating in cashless alternatives. "I heat the house with a woodstove and have a compost toilet," she explains. "I collect water from my roof into a cistern and enjoy my garden and locally grown food." By bartering and exchanging services for things she needs, she's able to live on very little money. She earns what income she needs by conducting outdoor weddings and teaching a peer counseling method called *reevaluation counseling*.

These choices have freed Barbara to devote the majority of her time to her passion for community service without financial concerns. She has cofounded the National Water Center and serves as its coordinator. Through the center she has published two books on water resources and the environment. She also actively spearheads water preservation efforts, such as One Clean Spring to reconstitute one of Eureka Springs's sixty-six freshwater springs, and conducts an online class on natural springs for Eureka Springs Online Learning (www.eurekaol .com).

So while living on less money than most would consider a middle-class income, Barbara is by no means deprived. Her home is comfortable and includes an efficiently equipped home office. She dresses attractively, travels, speaks at regional and national conferences, and has been awarded grants to support her water conservation projects. Nor did her son suffer from their new, simple lifestyle. He graduated from college and is currently completing his studies to become a lawyer. Barbara believes her lifestyle encourages others to live in a more aware manner than our predominantly nonthinking consumer society. "When people come to visit me," she says, "they see there is a different possibility." Having been a guest in her home repeatedly, we would agree.

Raymond Powers of Ojai, California, hasn't worked for anyone in fifteen years and for six years has paid no rent. Over this time he has been invited to live on and steward property for people he meets. "My life is devoted to service," he explains. "If I can do something someone needs I say yes." He rejects what he calls our exchange economy—I pay you this, and you give me that. He prefers what he calls a gift economy in which people "gift" each other with what they need. He's able to save significant amounts of money by bartering and swapping. For the limited cash he needs, he does personal coaching and Web design from his home on the land he's restoring.

Nine Alternatives to Money

- Do-it-yourself
- Helping one another
- Community Co-ops
- Lending and sharing
- Exchanges and swaps
- Regiving networks
- Barter
- Time banks
- Local currency

Raymond is quick to point out that using cashless alternatives requires a shift in consciousness. In today's consumer-oriented culture, many of our values and even our very identities are often tied to how much money we have. Earning money is how we "pay our way." So at first the very thought of living without as much money, even if we could be perfectly happy without as much, may make us feel uncomfortable. But then constantly overworking, worrying about money, and not having time to do what you want most is uncomfortable, too. So as you read in the next chapter about nine cashless alternatives to money that others are embracing, ask yourself how you would feel about dipping a toe or taking a step into a way of life that relies less on cash and more on sharing and exchanging resources with others.

CHAPTER FOURTEEN

Getting Out of the Money Game

There is an element of our culture that suggests life is a game in which money and the possessions we buy with money are the way we keep score. Playing this game keeps most of us quite busy working and consuming. But that wasn't always the case. It took time, a lot of effort, and millions of dollars in advertising and promotion to entice us into devoting our lives to this game. As recently as the early twentieth century, most people were content to have their basic needs for food, shelter, and clothing met, plus a few extras. After that there wasn't much that could tempt them to work harder or longer. Economic anthropologists tell us that in preagrarian cultures, nothing could tempt tribal people to willingly do boring or unpleasant work in exchange for anything they didn't absolutely need, and they needed very little.

As we mentioned in Chapter Five, beginning in the early 1920s, as the general level of affluence in the United States rose, manufacturers began to realize that people preferred leisure time to increasing their income by working additional hours. Merchandise began to pile up in warehouses, and they were desperate to find some external motivation that would keep people working and buying their backlog of products. What could they do to convince people to work longer and harder at generally unappealing jobs, in decidedly unappealing environments, and forego saving for a rainy day to spend more so that the economy could keep growing? Over the first half of the twentieth century, business leaders undertook a concerted effort to find the answer.

Local chambers of commerce launched "Buy Now" and "Put the Money Back to Work" public relations campaigns. Retailing giants initiated massive advertising programs to entice people to want things they'd never thought of needing. These campaigns focused on denigrating "homegrown," "natural," and "handmade" items, while extolling the superiority of "store-bought" and "factory-made" ones. Within less than a decade, a nation of frugal working people had become a nation of status-conscious consumers. Historian William Leach, who documented this process in his book *Land of Desire: Merchants, Power, and the Rise of a New American Culture,* describes the result as a culture of unlimited desire.

I, Sarah, experienced the results of that campaign when I was in school in the 1960s. I remember kids making fun of classmates whose mothers sewed their clothes. I also remember being glad I didn't have a big sister, because my best friend was so embarrassed that she had to wear her older sister's hand-me-downs. If you didn't have the latest fashion each year when school started you were really "out of it." We were being groomed as steadfast consumers.

Efforts to create a culture of limitless desire have been successful beyond what anyone could have imagined. A recent Pew Research Center survey found that the number of gizmos and gadgets people now consider necessities rather than luxuries has accelerated over the past decade even faster than a similar survey conducted in 1996 by the *Washington Post,* the Kaiser Family Foundation, and Harvard University. "New technologies not only give us something new we can covet and feel like we can't live without," Robert Thompson, a professor of media and popular culture at Syracuse University, told *USA Today,* "they transform the way life is organized. What used to not be a necessity because nobody had it first becomes a luxury, and then it becomes a necessity. Things that you lived without before they were invented really do become necessities."

Necessities
(to Nearly Half or More of Americans)

► Car	► TV set
► Clothes washer	► Car air conditioner
► Clothes dryer	► Home computer
► Home air conditioner	► Cell phone
► Microwave	

Necessities
(to Nearly a Third or More)

► Dishwasher	► High-speed Internet
► Cable or satellite TV	

Pew Research Center Survey, 2006

Anyone who operates a small business knows how true this last statement is. The fax, Web site, or CD burner once clearly a novelty or available only to large companies, quickly becomes a necessity when prospective customers count on your having one because everyone else in your line of work does. This endless imperative to upgrade and consume the best and latest in order to succeed is the engine that drives the treadmill that so many of us are trying to escape.

What things in your life do you consider to be necessities? Were some of them once luxuries? Has convenience been a stepping-stone from luxury to necessity? Are there things you wouldn't need if you didn't have to work so long and hard to earn your income?

As we've talked with people in writing this book over the past year, we've noticed that once people get a taste of what life is like off the treadmill, they never want to get back on. They're taking a serious look at how "the money game" is impacting their lives and then reevaluating their values. Here are a few of the materialist values people are beginning to question:

- a large income
- social status that impresses others
- many expensive possessions, e.g., expensive homes, cars, clothes, and other luxuries
- the admiration, recognition, fame, and praise of society
- the "right" image according to the latest fashions, trends, and technologies

Surprisingly, a considerable body of research, comprehensively summarized by psychologists Tim Kasser and Richard Ryan in their book *The High Price of Materialism,* shows that these values correlate negatively with attaining the financial security, personal expression, autonomy, relationships, and community ties that most of us seek. To make matters worse, Kasser and Ryan's findings also show that these values actually diminish the qualities one needs to define, create, and enjoy a self-chosen lifestyle, such as:

- a strong sense of inner security and deep sense of self-worth
- the ability to take independent action with confidence
- an enthusiasm for the challenge of problem solving and innovating
- relating well to others' needs
- itrinsic enjoyment of chosen work

Research by psychologists at the University of Minnesota published in *Science* magazine, October–November, 2006, tells us that the mere thought of money changes us in ways we might not prefer. For example, subtle suggestions of money caused those participating in the study to act more selfishly, give less to charity, fend more for themselves, expect others to do the same, offer and ask for help less frequently, choose solitary activities over social ones, and maintain greater physical distance between themselves and others.

Most alarming, though, are results from a Pew Research Center poll of eighteen- to twenty-five-year-olds. It found that 81 percent of the participants said getting rich is their generation's most important or second most important life goal; 51 percent said being famous was their first or second life goal. Another study by the Higher Education Institute reports that 75 percent of U.S. college freshman believe being very well off financially is essential or very important. Yet having enough money is by far their most important current problem. One in three report having financial concerns. The incongruity of these realities both reflects and foretells how much discomfort the money game places on us. There is little to suggest that 81 percent of young adults are going to be rich, but there is every reason to believe that if we're willing to step out of the game, we can not only pay our bills but also live comfortably and provide an enjoyable life for our children.

In light of these findings, it's not surprising that people from across all age groups are choosing alternatives to a life driven by money and possessions. They are shifting their views of what's important and returning to simpler, cashless ways of living so they can be more directly involved with their personal daily lives and with the lives of their families, friends, and communities.

 Warning

With a few exceptions, most of these alternatives don't blend well with a fast-paced, 24/7, high-pressured life. In fact, they would probably make things worse or just not be feasible. That's why they've fallen into disuse over the past decades. These are ways to safeguard the steps you're taking or will be taking to preserve your quality of life by stepping out of a high-pressure lifestyle. They can help you to reduce the time and energy you must invest in earning a living so you can go about living.

Do-It-Yourself (DIY)

Since the advent of the Gilded Age, or Progressive Era, around the turn of the twentieth century, virtually every endeavor once carried out by families and community volunteers has morphed into a professional or commercial service. The effects of this change have been far-reaching. First, we no longer consider ourselves capable of taking care of whole swathes of life we once managed quite successfully for ourselves. As philosopher Alan Watts observed, our educational system trains us to be sales personnel, administrators, bureaucrats, or some other kind of "cerebral character." It does little to give us any kind of material competence for doing the most fundamental things in life, such as cook, make clothes, build houses, etc.

We're encouraged instead to turn to experts for help with everything from how to plan a wedding, choose a career, and raise our children, to how to decorate and repair our homes, save our marriages, and invest our money. But, as if that isn't disempowering enough, this also means we have to spend most of our time and energy earning enough money to pay for all this help and expertise. A forty-something couple we know are a prime example of this conundrum. They were both high-powered management consultants, earning a good income, but they complained mightily about the long hours they had to put in to stay afloat. To manage their overly busy lives, they relied regularly on the services of:

- ▶ a virtual assistant to arrange their schedules
- ▶ an errand service to pick up and deliver their dry cleaning, groceries, etc.
- ▶ a cleaning service to clean their condo
- ▶ a caterer to cook for and serve at their parties
- ▶ a dog walker to walk their dogs on weekdays
- ▶ a massage therapist to rub away their tensions
- ▶ an aesthetician to care for their skin
- ▶ a chiropractor to control their repetitive strain injuries
- ▶ a professional organizer to keep their home offices neat and efficient

The list goes on to include more customary services like home repair, auto detailing and maintenance, landscaping, hairstyling and coloring, manicures, pedicures, nutrition counseling, fitness training, and yoga classes. In talking about how they might simplify their lives so they wouldn't have to work so hard, they were horrified at the idea that maybe they could do some of these things themselves! They couldn't possibly do that! They'd never have the time. Also, they took pride in their ability to afford all these services. It was evidence of their success and meant that they were living the "good life."

Granted, this couple's situation was extreme, but less-dramatic versions abound. A middle-class audience at a permaculture workshop in our community, for example, had a similar response to the leader's offhand comment that the more things we do for ourselves, the freer we become to do something with our time other than produce an income. But the group found it hard to imagine how they'd have time to do any additional routine tasks. They already felt overworked. So it was a catch-22. "We work so much that we don't have the time or energy to do the things that need to get done in our personal lives, so we work still harder so we can pay others to do them."

This conundrum was especially frustrating to another friend of ours who is a communication specialist and single mother. She found that after deductions, her hourly wage was only slightly more than what she had to pay for child care and, other than on weekends, she rarely got to see her kids in daylight. She decided it would be far easier to work from home on her own and take care of her kids herself. She might end up making less money overall, but she would save enough to actually have more money to live on. Many people, including the couple we mentioned above, are making similar decisions to "do-it-themselves."

They are taking over tasks they once paid others to do in exchange for working less overtime or fewer hours per week. The do-it-yourself movement has become so popular in Europe that no one takes the time anymore to say "do-it-yourself." It's simply called DIY. They are returning to traditional patterns of personal involvement, caring for their homes, cars, computers, Web sites, children, and personal grooming/pampering. After taking over many of the tasks they used to pay for, the couple we mentioned earlier, who had delegated so much of their lives to others, told us, "Our expenditures had gotten completely out of hand, and the problem wasn't just how much they were costing us. We were losing control of our lives. Everything was in someone else's hands, and all we did was work to pay for it. Because we're working less, we're earning less, but it's hard to explain the freedom we feel to be taking care of our own lives. It's fun to walk the dogs. We get outdoors and get more exercise. And doing errands takes us out of the office. It's like there's a whole world out there we were missing!"

Nowhere has the DIY trend caught on more dramatically than in home decoration and repair, where the savings can be big. Both men and women are painting and wallpapering; installing new floors, countertops, doors, windows, and lights; and adding rooms, decks, and more. Home improvement stores like Home Depot, Ace Hardware, and Lowe's have taken note of this trend and are providing the materials, tools, workshops, and assistance to scores of eager do-it-yourselfers.

As you probably noticed in the previous chapter, often the willingness and ability to do things yourself make it financially feasible for people to pursue and enjoy one of the lifestyles we described. Living on the road or at sea, living rent free, going off the grid, or participating in a cohousing project, for example, are all more feasible if you're able to do much of what's involved yourself, instead of having to pay others to do it. But whether one of those lifestyles appeals to you or not, if you're looking for ways to afford the lifestyle you have without having to earn so much, make a list of all the services you now pay others to do, and explore how much less you'd need to earn if you did those things yourself.

For each item, ask yourself:

► How many hours do I have to work each day, week, or year to pay for this service?

- ▸ Is this something I can do myself or could conceivably learn to do with help from a friend, book, video, short course, or workshop?
- ▸ How many hours would it take me to do it myself?
- ▸ Would I be advantaged by doing this myself, i.e., would I save time, money, or enjoy life more? Or would I rather work for the money to pay for it?
- ▸ What would I do with the time or money I'd save?

Here are a few examples of what others have found:

- ▸ One couple discovered they could earn more than twelve thousand dollars less a year if they did their own home repairs and cleaned their own home instead of using outside services.
- ▸ A single mother found she could spend sixty-five hundred dollars less a year if she worked from home independently instead of paying for child care so she could work away from home.
- ▸ A fifty-four-year old divorcée found she could afford to quit her job and do freelance writing, something she'd always wanted to do, if she stopped paying for someone to color her hair, used a yoga video instead of paying for triweekly classes, and bathed and groomed her dog herself.
- ▸ Another couple who wanted to start a family calculated that one of them could afford to stay at home with a new baby for a whole year by foregoing the thirty-thousand-dollar wedding they'd been saving for and held a smaller DIY gathering of family and friends in a nearby park.

Of course, "work" means different things to different folks. Some people would rather do just about anything than clean house. Others find it's a good way to get rid of stress and tension. Some take great pride in keeping their house spick-and-span, or would if they gave it a try. Landscaping and gardening or changing the oil and washing the car are a joy for some and a misery to others. Then, of course, there are things we might prefer to do or be willing to do but simply do not have the knack, know-how, or strength to do. I, Sarah, for example, have many friends who color their own hair, but that's a task I would never dare undertake. We've also tried doing our own plumbing repairs but failed miserably, even with guidebooks. So we gladly work to pay for these services.

On the other hand, we used to eat many meals out every week but find we enjoy fixing our own meals and preparing healthier foods. We also now do our own housecleaning and yard work. It's good exercise, and we believe we can do a more thorough job. So the question for each of us is what can we do or learn to do that will actually enhance our lives and at the same time free us from having to work so many hours at a job?

Just don't jump too quickly to the conclusion that you can't do something yourself if you'd rather not pay for it. Talk with others you know who are doing it themselves. See if with their help or suggestions you might give it a try. You might be surprised!

Helping One Another

There are many things we can't do ourselves, but with a little help from our friends, we can get them done without paying a penny. Helping out is all about doing needed favors for our friends and neighbors and their doing favors for us. In his book *Bowling Alone, The Collapse and Renewal of American Communities*, Robert Putnam points out that the proclivity to help one's neighbors has been on the decline in our culture for some time throughout the United States. In fact, too often we don't even know our neighbors. Here's a line from the movie *Garden State* that captures how unpopular doing favors for one another has become: "Favors are bad news, and the only thing worse than favors is a favor for money." Fortunately this attitude is changing, and not just in cohousing projects, ecohoods, ecovillages, and communes. Helping out is on the rise wherever people are seeking a stronger sense of community, because wherever there is community, people spontaneously help one another.

Be it in an apartment or condo complex, neighborhood, church congregation, homeowners' association (of which one-fifth of all American homes are now a part), or in small communities like ours, we see people reaching out to help each other when they can with many tasks one would otherwise have to pay for.

We first experienced this when we moved here from Los Angeles. We discovered that residents here do all kinds of things for one another with nary a thought of being "paid" for it. For example, during one of our first winters here, Paul broke an ankle and couldn't shovel the driveway. I was going to hire someone to do it for us (we have a very long driveway), but before I got to make the call, I heard some noise out front. To my surprise, two friends of ours were busily shoveling our driveway! They just came over to help. Also, before moving here we had to hire a pet sitter for our dogs or leave them in a kennel when we went out of town on business trips. We expected to do that here, too, but to our surprise, a friend offered to have our dog Billy stay with them whenever we have to go out of town. We offered to pay, but they said, "Absolutely not! We like having Billy come to visit."

It's not that folks here don't pay for services. Residents rely on many local businesses, but it is also the norm to help when you can. Mention a home maintenance problem at a party, and often someone will offer to share his expertise or volunteer to come by to see if he can help. In turn, people frequently call Paul for advice on running a local political campaign. I, Sarah, am often asked to write articles or to help edit materials someone in the community needs.

When we are replacing or otherwise don't need something, we offer it to friends, as they do to us. We've found happy homes among our friends for a DVD, printer, TV, and computer. When a friend outgrew a shearing coat, she offered it to me. I love it. Recently when we were unable to buy wood pellets for our stove due to a nationwide shortage, a neighbor whose pellet stove is broken gave us the ten forty-pound bags of pellets she wouldn't be using.

On a grander scale, because another of our neighbors, Linda Madden, is someone who's always ready to help friends in need, when her day spa burned down right after a stressful divorce, her friends rushed forward to rebuild the spa, paint her new home, and help her move in. When construction began on the other side of our next-door neighbor's house, they decided they needed to put up a fence to define their property line. A friend volunteered to build one for them. When a local couple lost their home to fire, everyone chipped in to help them out. Someone donated a temporary place where they could live. Others brought clothes and food. Some gave cash contributions.

Usually no one needs to ask for this kind of help. Nor does anyone expect anything particular in return. Help within a community is freely given, no strings attached. Reciprocity is engrained in the human brain and arises naturally within communities. When someone invites us to dinner, for example, most people feel inclined to reciprocate. This innate sense of reciprocity applies to favors and help of all kinds. Of course, if we're culturally conditioned to think we have to pay for the help we need, then our tendency for reciprocity declines. Instead, an attitude of "you get what you pay for" emerges. So reciprocity is reinforced or extinguished by cultural norms. But shifting our personal perspective from "pay as you go" to "how can I help?" goes a long way toward making life simpler and easier.

We can each initiate efforts to encourage a norm for reciprocity within our own community circle by offering to help when the occasion arises. Obviously if you are the only one helping, you will soon feel used and resentful. Whenever helping out is too one-sided, we stop offering. But as Daniel Goldman, PhD, articulated so well in his latest book, *Social Intelligence,* human beings are social creatures. Our built-in sense of empathy and fairness leads us to reciprocate unless our natural tendencies are too deeply buried under negative experiences, a pay-as-you-go attitude, or overwhelming distress. Usually, as people see there are truly no strings attached, no hidden agendas, they're willing to accept or offer help to those within their community when circumstances call for it.

Helping out is a matter of extending to a broader community what family members routinely do for each other. But it requires having a community or creating one where everyone knows one another well or comes to know each other well, sees one another regularly, and shares positive, amicable relationships. The ability to enjoy the benefits of most of the moneyless alternatives we'll be discussing is one of the many advantages of being part of a community. Fortunately, many people are hungry for community and ready to get involved with other like-minded folks. Here are some of the elements we can encourage that contribute to a healthy community.

Creating and Preserving Community

Com-mun-ity: a group of people who are united in the desire to give of themselves in service to what they collectively hold dear.

Robert Putnam of Harvard University and author of *Bowling Alone* has documented the decline of community and civic participation in the United States, as well as the many negative effects of this decline on individuals, families, and our society. The following six elements of healthy communities have been extrapolated from his findings. They appear as a central theme in the novel, *Sitting with the Enemy*. Through the characters in the book, readers are invited to ask key questions about how they can create, preserve, and strengthen their own communities. You can use these questions as a guide in your community:

1. Face Time: Is there ample opportunity to interact with one another in our community? Do we see each other often and say hello even to those we haven't met yet? Or do we think of those we don't know yet as strangers? Do we talk to people we know when see them, or do we look down and continue on our way? Do we get together at least once each week to socialize with friends and participate regularly in community events, or do we stay home and watch TV?

2. All Crew: Are we participating in our community, or are we going along for the ride? Do we roll up our sleeves and pitch in like members of a crew to help with community responsibilities, or do we sit back and let others do it? Do we share leadership, or do we try to amass power or privileges for ourselves and our friends?

3. Solid Level Ground: Are we working to create a level playing field for all members of the community? Do we spend our money to support our local businesses? Are we doing what we can to help everyone be secure and live well? Are we tolerant and respectful of others' opinions and needs, or are we living simply to get ahead personally and have our way prevail? Do we take pride in doing better than others, or do we relish in everyone achieving prosperity?

4. Harvest Hands: Are we willing to help each other when in need? Are we trustworthy and trusting of others in our community? When we see someone in need do we ask how we can help? Or do we assume everyone can or should handle their own lives? Or that someone else will step in?

5. Common Bond: Are we acting from a common bond, or are we thinking of what we can get for ourselves regardless of how it might affect others and the community as a whole? Are we open to hearing about others' needs and views? Do we make an effort to find ways to accommodate as best as possible what's most important to everyone?

6. Rich Soil for New Seeds: Are we doing what we need to do for our children? Do we volunteer for school activities and support family-friendly policies and facilities throughout the community? Or do we think of kids as a nuisance and assume it's up to their parents to keep them neither seen nor heard?

Cashless means of exchange are common in any community rich in the above elements. Over time helping out saves everyone a lot of money and provides a much-needed sense of camaraderie, peace of mind, and security. As long as you don't overdo your requests and do your share to help others, you'll even be able to ask for help within your community when you're in a pinch. You'll often find it forthcoming even if you don't ask. But a norm for helping out must be continually cultivated and encouraged. It's not something anyone can take for granted, expect, or have at your beck and call. There are other cashless ways to accomplish that.

 Tip

We've observed that unless you earn your living from outside the community, it's best to avoid offering or accepting help related to your own or others' livelihoods. Because we live in a cash-based economy, many people are uncomfortable accepting free help when it is something you would usually be charging for. They're not sure if something is or should be expected in return and may fear they're depriving you of income. It also puts you in the awkward position of having to charge some people while giving freely to others; yet, giving to everyone in need can jeopardize your ability to earn a living. You can offer a sliding scale or special price for local residents.

Of course, giving a gift for special occasions or under special circumstances is an exception, e.g., when a neighbor who is a professional photographer offers to take the photos for a local friend's wedding as a wedding gift. Also, if you do need to pay for a service, you can support your neighbors by turning to local service providers first whenever possible.

Community Co-ops.

In the sense we are speaking of here, co-ops are not a business or housing venture, such as a farm co-op or co-op apartment. We're talking about a more organized or formal version of helping out. Whereas helping out is strictly voluntary and arises spontaneously, a co-op in this sense is when a group of individuals or families join together to share or reduce the time and costs of doing or buying things they all need. Such cooperative activities can be done formally or informally as one-time efforts or as ongoing activities. Some of the kinds of things people can co-op to do include:

- babysitting or child care
- pet sitting
- buying food or supplies in bulk
- preparing a week's worth of meals
- caring for invalid or ill neighbors
- home repair
- carpooling
- forming a shopping pool to share the task of routine shopping trips
- maintaining a community garden

Any activities that members of a co-op must depend on regularly, such as buying food, carpooling, maintaining a community garden, or providing child and invalid care, are best operated on a more formal basis where the individuals each commit to participating on a set schedule. In a successful child care co-op, for example, participating families commit to provide needed child care on a regular schedule for the children of all the families. Each family contributes a fixed number of hours or days a week. Child care co-ops are particularly popular with work-from-home parents who need to have times in the workday or workweek when they can concentrate uninterrupted or attend meetings with clients and customers.

It was a perfect solution for Nancy and Mark Pollack. They run a successful herbal gift basket company from a workshop behind their garage and sell their gift baskets to health-food stores in their metro area. At first they took turns watching their two preschool-aged children, but as their business grew more successful, they needed time when they could work together on certain projects and orders. "We really hated to put our kids in a day care program though," Nancy remembers. "We left jobs so we could both work and be home with our children. What good does it do if we still can only see them evenings and weekends?" Sharing child care with two other neighbors who work from home has solved this dilemma. "We each have shifts when we take care of the kids during different times of the week. This means we all have parts of the week when we are with the kids all day," Mark explains, "but we also have times of the week when we get to work together on the business. It's a good balance."

Other shared activities like pet sitting or shopping groups, might be organized more informally. Our shopping co-op, for example, is quite informal. We have a list of interested participants, and before one of us heads off to shop in town we check with others on the list to find out what they might need from one of the three or four stores we all routinely shop at. Or if someone needs something and can't get into town, he or she checks to see if anyone will be going in and could stop by to pick up the needed item. This has been particularly handy when someone is sick and needs to have a prescription picked up.

Benefits of Co-ops

1. Saves money.
2. Saves time, although everyone must donate some time to running the co-op.
3. Builds and strengthens community relationships.
4. Encourages useful exchanges of information.
5. Supports and strengthens the local economy.

In a food-buying co-op, a group of people chips in to buy food collectively at wholesale prices from distributors or growers who normally sell to supermarkets or grocery stores. The co-op is then able to purchase food in bulk at lower prices. Food clubs are run on a voluntary basis, with members sharing the tasks of taking and placing orders, collecting payments, paying growers and distributors, keeping records, and sorting and distributing food. Alternatively, a group can approach a local grocer or health-food storeowner about placing bulk orders for their group. Although prices will not be as low as buying directly from distributors, members can save money, support local merchants, and invest somewhat less time.

Our fledgling shopping co-op for buying fruits and vegetables from local growers also operates very informally. Whenever someone is going out to a local farm or orchard, he or she e-mails those of us who are participating to determine if we want to place an order.

We're currently organizing a wood pellet co-op for next year. By going in with a number of others, we can purchase the multiple tons of wood pellets required to get us all through the winter at a lower bulk price and share, or even eliminate, delivery costs. With the rising cost of fuel, we are also considering starting a propane co-op and a gasoline co-op. The latter would be run through our property owners' association. Another interesting "co-op" we're initiating is for scheduling services and deliveries. By arranging to have a certain provider come to our community to service several households on the same day, we're able to get service more quickly and share the cost of charges for travel to the area.

We also have a shared Netflix subscription. It seems rather silly for all of us to sit in our separate homes to watch the same rented movies when we could periodically make a social evening of watching them together. So everyone in our Movie Pals group chips in for the annual cost and we have movie nights at least once a week. Anyone can request a movie be placed in our queue, and generally we watch the movies together with whoever wants to see a particular movie.

Small Business Co-ops, Alliances, and Networks

Owners of small local businesses, such as those we featured in Chapter Two, are securing their success by participating in or forming various collaborative affiliations. For example, to keep costs of doing business down and prices affordable, producers' cooperatives or purchasing groups bargain, buy, store, and distribute in bulk, making it possible to get better prices and reduce overhead. Artists, self-employed individuals, and small business owners are joining together to share advertising and marketing projects, hold expos and fairs, print neighborhood directories, and launch "Buy Local First" or "Made in _____" campaigns.

The Business Alliance for Local Living Economies (BALLE) and the American Independent Business Alliance (AMIBA) both have dozens of chapters where local self-employed and small businesses promote local ownership and work to promote public policies that support community self-reliance. Members of local networks like Business Network International make personal referrals to one another. To find a local affiliate or chapter in your area, see their Web sites in LEARN MORE.

To start a co-op in your neighborhood or community, begin by identifying something you see as needed and ask around to see if there are others who would be interested in going in with you to provide or collectively buy it. This is obviously easier if you are already part of a community, circle of friends, or organization where you and others know each other well, e.g., a church, school, cohousing project, business group, property owners' association, or close, well-defined neighborhood.

If you're not already a part of a community, though, you can post flyers on grocery store or other local bulletin boards or place a small want ad in a community newspaper. Once you've identified a group of interested parties, hold a meeting and develop a plan for how you might go in together to provide the service(s) you need. If you will be providing something those participating will need to depend on, be sure to get firm commitments from everyone as to who will be able to provide what when.

Tip

Yes, coordinating cooperative activities does take a commitment of some time by everyone, and someone has to take the initiative to be sure everything is running well. Sharing this commitment equally is key. If all the work falls on one or two people, they will get burned-out, and the co-op will dissolve. Having a group e-mail list everyone can use is a quick and easy way to facilitate decision making, manage communication, and coordinate tasks.

Lending and Sharing

There are dozens of appliances and other equipment that any one person uses only periodically. Why should everyone in a community go to the expense of buying one of their own for it to just collect dust in a closet, garage, basement, or attic during most of the year? Of course, owning something is usually cheaper than paying someone to come in and do it with their equipment, but why not go in with others and share equipment you all will be using only periodically?

We do a lot of informal tool sharing here in our community. We borrow tools from one another all the time. In a more formal community program, though, those interested list the tools or equipment they have and use only occasionally, such as a rug-cleaning machine, a power washer, snow plow, or heat gun (for removing wallpaper), and then lend them out to other participants on the list when they're needed. Still another approach is for a group of folks to chip in to buy certain equipment or tools together. Doing this, though, means you'll need to find and agree upon a place to house the equipment and, like a lending library, have a system for tracking who has borrowed what.

Another time when lending and sharing comes in handy is when hosting large parties. Large parties may require more chairs, plates, glasses, platters, serving dishes, table cloths, eating utensils, etc., than one household may have. But it's costly to buy or rent large numbers of these things, and if you do buy them, you need lots of space to store them in. Cohousing communities, or other intentional communities with shared facilities, can easily handle such needs by going in together to equip the community building, workshop, or garden with the needed items. But anyone who lives in a community with close relationships can simply call on others to contribute needed items for particular events. For example, when our next-door neighbors host a Fourth of July yard party for fifty to sixty people, friends contribute lawn chairs, long folding tables, extra utensils, glasses or cups, and, of course food! Also, there's always a group who's willing to make and put out the decorations, help set up, and then clean up afterwards.

Obviously there needs to be a high degree of trust when sharing and lending, the kind of trust that comes from living in a community where people know one another and where one's reputation precedes him. In such communities people who can't be trusted to take care of shared and borrowed items, or who won't contribute to rectify any damage that should occur to the items they've used, are no longer invited to participate.

Exchanges and Swaps

We all have things we outgrow, no longer need, replace, or simply grow tired of. It's a pity to toss them out or stash them away on attic and basement shelves. Of course, many people donate such items to charities or hold garage and yard sales. But holding community exchanges is a great way to not only pass along things you won't be using but also to pick up things you will use . . . all at no cost. The most popular annual exchanges in our community are clothing exchanges and book exchanges.

On one Saturday in the fall we've held a clothing exchange at our club-house. Anyone who wishes to can bring by clothes he or she has outgrown or grown tired of. The clothes are folded or on hangers. The day of the exchange any member of the community can come by, browse through, and take whatever clothing he likes, whether or not he or she contributed anything to the exchange. We donate whatever clothing is left over at the end of the day to charity. This is a very popular event with people coming by as early as they can before the best things have been taken. I, Sarah, contribute regularly and have gotten some great clothes from these exchanges, including a pair of cowhide boots, a see-through beaded jacket that's perfect over a little black cocktail dress, some brand new white jeans that fit perfectly, and two denim sundresses.

On a Saturday in the spring we've held book exchanges. People cull through their bookshelves and drop off boxes and sacks of books in every possible genre. We arrange them by department, just like in a bookstore; mysteries in one area, children's books in another, etc. Usually those who bring books can't resist browsing through the tables and end up going home with nearly as many books as they brought. But anyone can come and take as many books as they wish. At the end of the day, we donate any leftovers to our nearest library.

Other exchanges might include:

- ▶ kids' toys
- ▶ music CDs and/or movies on DVD or VHS
- ▶ sporting goods
- ▶ homegrown fruit and vegetables
- ▶ a "Take Potluck," where folks bring whatever they might otherwise put out at a garage sale for whoever wishes to take it and, if they wish, can pick out things others have brought to give away

Like any community activity, the primary challenge of organizing an exchange is locating a place to hold it and finding volunteers to staff it. You will need some energetic workers to collect, set up, oversee, clean up, pack up, and deliver remaining items. Usually the opportunity to pick their favorite items when they arrive early to help is enough incentive to get needed volunteers. You will also need to promote the exchange so everyone knows it's coming up well in advance. You can do this by posting flyers on community bulletin boards, notices on community Web sites, organizing a telephone tree to spread the word, and getting a write-up in the local community newsletter or newspaper. Because no money is exchanged, most small newspapers will do an article or post a notice about upcoming events like these.

Community Drop-Off Exchanges

At our recycling center there is a designated place where anyone can leave items they would like to make available to others. On a given day you might find a box of books, a printer, computer software, a toaster oven, a lamp, or who knows what. Most items aren't there for long. Someone is glad to give them a home. After a period of time, items no one takes are deposited in the recycling bins. In Telluride, Colorado, their drop-off exchange is called a Freebox. It's a collection of wooden bins in the center of town where people swap such things as CDs, concert tapes, alpine gear, and so forth.

Regiving Networks.

Regiving networks are essentially Web-based community recycling programs. They are ongoing ways for local community groups to give away unwanted durable household items for reuse by others in the community without any exchange of money. The benefit of a regiving network over local exchanges such as those we just described is that there's no need to organize, schedule, set up, and put on periodic events. Instead, computer software matches givers and receivers in the community 24/7. The first such program, Twin Cities Free Market (www.twincitiesfreemarket.org), was created in 1997. Since then it has facilitated more than thirteen thousand exchanges of durable goods, preventing nearly two thousand tons from the waste stream. They currently have more than seventy-five thousand active users nationwide.

Facts from Freecycle Network

- It takes twenty times the raw materials to produce new consumer products than the weight of the product itself.
- Reuse a sofa and you save one hundred pounds from going to a landfill and two thousand pounds of raw materials from being taken from Mother Earth.
- Freecycle's three million members reused two hundred million pounds of stuff in 2006, keeping four piles of garbage trucks the size of Mount Everest out of landfills.

Many other online regiving networks quickly emerged. These global networks have facilitated the formation of tens of thousands of local regiving groups, some independent and others affiliated or part of a wider network. (See LEARN MORE for a list of such networks). Freecycle Network (www.freecycle.org), a nonprofit organization started in Tucson, Arizona, in 2003, is one of the largest and most popular networks. It has more then three million members in seventy-five countires. On their Web site, Freecycle founder Deron Beal points out that "one person's trash is truly another person's treasure." So he emphasizes, regiving networks like Freecycle "are *not* a place to get free stuff for nothing." They are a local mechanism to "give or receive what you have and don't need to get what you need and don't have."

Here's how they work: Each local group is moderated by a local volunteer who requests to start a local group. This volunteer must meet certain qualifications, such as living in the area, having time to run the online network, and having a computer, computer skills, and Internet access. Then members of the community can join the local group for free. You join a group in your area, if there is one, by logging on to www.freecycle.org, clicking on the region to locate your community, and then going directly to the group nearest you. You become part of the local e-mail group by providing your e-mail address and registering as a member. You will receive information via e-mail on how the local group works.

In keeping with the stated goal, your first post must be an offer of something to give to someone in the community who might need it. After that you can post offers and review offers for items you're looking for. On some sites you can also post what you are looking for. When someone replies to an offer it's up to the giver and receiver to arrange how to pick up their gifts. All items must be "free, legal, and age appropriate." If there is no group yet in your area, there is a link on www.freecycle.org for how to "Start a Group."

Tax Tip

There are no tax implications for participating in regiving networks. You don't owe taxes on the gifts you receive, nor can you claim a tax deduction for the items you give away.

You may recall from Chapter One that Gail Sullivan of Baldwin, Georgia, joined the Freecycle Network in her county as a way to simplify her life. She gave away about one hundred books, clothing, a matching set of sheets and pillow cases, VHS tapes, a full-length mirror, and more. Since then she has also responded to offers and put up requests. She's received clothing for her grandchildren, some furniture, and a roll of chain link fence for her husband. "All the people I met for pickups were always on time and had what they promised to have," she reports. "It has been a wonderful experience. People here have given away cars and all kinds of cool stuff. I tried to get the car, but someone else beat me to it. It's a great thing!"

Barter

So far the cashless options we've been discussing have been about sharing, not trading. In other words, there hasn't been any tit-for-tat exchange involved—as in "I do this for you if you do this for me." No need to ascribe measure or track the value of the items, time involved, or effort involved in what's being offered. Bartering, however, is different. Barter involves directly trading goods or services of equivalent value without the exchange of money. It's the oldest form of trade and the basis of all early commerce. Metals, produce, grains, livestock, hides, furs, arms, or anything of value, even other humans (as in slaves), have all been used as barter at some point in history, always determining the value of what's being exchanged via negotiation or prescription by some social authority.

Barter, also referred to as reciprocal trade, is still a common informal means of exchange both among individuals and businesses, e.g., "I'll trade you a month of yoga lessons if you'll paint my kitchen." It can come in very handy anytime one is short of cash but needs something people would usually expect to be paid for. That's another difference between barter and the other cashless methods we've been discussing. Whereas in helping out, exchanges, and co-ops, you're not usually contributing things your livelihood depends on, in bartering that's usually exactly what you are exchanging. If you are a graphic designer, for example, you might design a new logo, letterhead, and stationery for an event planner in exchange for her organizing an open house to introduce clients and referral sources for your business.

Here in our community, as is too often the case, lots of people suffer from sore, aching neck, shoulders, and lower back pain. This makes it easy for Linda Madden, a massage therapist, to barter for many of the personal and business services she needs. For example, an artist was eager to trade the painting of two floral murals on the walls of Linda's spa for a series of weekly massages. Linda also regularly trades services with the hairstylist and manicurist next door to her spa.

Because of the freedom bartering offers to line up whatever kind of products or services one needs, regardless of one's cash on hand, we encourage everyone in the new economy to identify something they can offer for barter. "Barterability," that is, something people will gladly trade for, is one of the criteria we used in selecting the careers in Part II of this book. Barter doesn't have to be limited to what you do for a livelihood. You can barter anything someone else wants to exchange, from homemade pies to babysitting, tutoring, or house-cleaning to Web site development, public relations, plumbing services, or marketing advice. If someone needs it, you can offer to work out a trade for it.

As you may already be thinking, there are limitations, though, to trying to barter informally on a one-to-one basis with those you know. Those you need services from may not need your service, at least not when you need them. I, Sarah, get my hair styled regularly at a particular salon, so I am happy to barter with my stylist in exchange for writing a series of advertorials for her salon whenever she needs one. It's a win/win arrangement for us both. But what if she doesn't need my particular service?

This quandary is precisely what gave rise to the need for some form of paper currency. Money makes it possible for anyone to exchange whatever of value he or she contributes to society for whatever is available from anyone else in society, regardless of whether any particular person needs it. But, participating in a barter club, barter exchange, or online swap site also provides this advantage.

A bartering exchange or barter club is a company or Web site that serves as a clearinghouse for businesses of all sizes who want to barter services with one another. The barter club is similar to a bank that tracks barters using points or credits, so you're not limited to bartering with any particular person. Members can trade for goods and services with any of the other members. A Web designer, for example, can provide services to an optometrist and use the trade credits he earns to obtain auto repair services from another member. The auto repair company in turn can exchange its trade credits for yet another member's service, such as for legal advice.

There are more than five hundred barter exchanges in the United States alone. Some focus on large companies; others on small businesses. Some are entirely Web-based and global. Others operate offline with a local focus. But barter exchanges are not completely cashless. Some like www.u-exchange.com are free, but many barter organizations and barter Web sites are for-profit businesses that charge a membership fee for joining. There may also be an exchange charge fee of 12 to 15 percent per transaction. Both these fees are to be paid in cash. Some exchanges also charge monthly fees. Even so, you can save considerably on costs, as Giles Tessier of Moncton, New Brunswick, can attest. His lawn care business was, as he described it, "barely surviving." His truck had broken down, and he didn't have the funds to replace it or to print much-needed flyers to attract more customers. At this low point he saw a news story on TV about a man who had put his son through flight school by bartering. Giles, who has a college degree in small business management, immediately contacted a local barter exchange.

After paying an initial membership fee of $375, Tessier was able to replace his truck with a van and print the flyers he needed by bartering his lawn care services. Since then his business has grown. He's hired four employees and continues to barter to save money and avoid cash flow crunches. During the long Canadian winters, he uses his van to pick up and deliver goods for business customers in Canada and down the eastern seaboard of the United States. Through the barter exchange, he's gotten his van repaired and hasn't had to pay for a hotel room in five years while delivering goods to customers down the eastern Canadian and U.S. seaboard.

Tessier pays the exchange a fee both when he uses the services of other members and when others use his service. He pays cash for 10 percent of the value of what he receives in barter. Then when his services are used, he provides the equivalent of three percent of his services to the exchange in barter credit. So when he receives barter goods or services worth ten thousand dollars, he pays the exchange one thousand dollars. If he provides one thousand dollars of his services to another barter exchange member, the exchange credits itself with an additional thirty dollars worth of his lawn care. He observes, "When you first start a business, you have little cash flow. You must depend on your customers to pay you on time, and if someone doesn't, you have to phone to ask for payment. By bartering, I can keep cash in my business by borrowing from other businesses, as they do, also by using his services.

You can find barter exchanges in your area through your local Yellow Pages, in *BarterNews* magazine (www.barternews.com), or through the International Reciprocal Trade Association (IRTA) and the National Association of Trade Exchanges (NATE). Both of these associations' Web sites enable you to search their online directory listings for member barter exchanges in your area (www .irta.com and www.nate.org). IRTA also has a checklist of things you should consider before joining a bartering exchange.

Tip

Since barter exchange groups are often for-profit entities, be sure to compare groups you're considering, examine their benefits, the membership costs, and obtain member references.

If you don't want to pay the costs involved in joining a membership-fee barter exchange, you might be able to find barter partners on www.craigslist.org, for which there is no charge. Other Web sites also post a notice that they'll barter. Or you can use a consumer swap site like www.swapace.com, www.swaptree.com, or www.peerflix.com. At this time the items that can be swapped are quite limited, for example, CDs, books, and games, but many consumers prefer swapping to selling because it eliminates the bidding, negotiating, fee structures, and ratings systems on sites like eBay. When social networking sites like MySpace expand to offer swap capabilities, we predict that before long there will be a wealth of online consumer swapping opportunities. Also, keep an eye on the horizon for online group buying. By the time you read this it may already be available.

Warning: Tax Implications!

For tax purposes barter is considered a form of income. So it is not a way to avoid paying income taxes. The same rules of taxation apply to barter as would to a cash transaction.

According to the IRS Web site, "Income from bartering is taxable in the year in which you receive the goods or services. Generally, you report this income on Schedule C, Profit or Loss from Business Form 1040."

Whether you join a bartering exchange or not, you must report the fair market value of goods and services exchanged as income in the year in which you receive the goods or services, but you may deduct costs you incurred to perform the work that was bartered or the costs of services you receive that qualify as standard business deductions. Barter exchanges are required to comply with their own reporting requirements on Form 1099-B for all transactions.

Time Banks

Time banking is an additional formalized way of helping one another. The time bank tracks the time members of a community spend doing something for one another. Each member accumulates "time credits" that they can "spend" to get help they want or need from others.

In bartering, whatever one exchanges is valued at market price, but in a time bank, all time is valued equally. Each one hour of service provided equals an hour of credit one can use for another service. Time banks overcome one of the common problems of bartering. Sometimes what we need is more expensive than the standard value ascribed to what we have to offer. We may not be able to afford to devote an equivalent amount of time to barter for a service we need. For example, a math tutor who charges $35 per hour may need advice from a local attorney who bills out her services at $250 per hour. So the tutor would have to contribute more than twenty weeks of hourly tutoring sessions to get just three hours of legal services.

But in a time bank, the tutor who contributes three hours of time tutoring a child in math can use her "banked time" for three hours of any other person's service, for example, lawyer, doctor, plumber, and so forth. Granted, in our status-conscious culture, this may seem odd. How could an hour of a lawyer's time be considered equal to an hour of a tutor's time or a plumber's time? But valuing all contributions equally is at the core of what makes time banks a uniquely useful alternative to cash.

As Time Bank USA points out on their Web site (www.timebanks.org), time banks "aren't meant to replace standard dollars. They are designed to counterbalance the market economy where people may have invested in special training to make their time more valuable." While there's nothing wrong with specialized training, as we've mentioned, it's just that we've grown to depend on specialists for many things we can do for ourselves and each other. As Time Bank USA goes on to point out, "Almost everything is monetized. Putting a price on people's time separates us by making some people more valuable than others." Instead, time banks are a parallel economy where people take care of each other as they would those in their families. You wouldn't ask your cousin to give you two hours of dog walking for every hour you spend fixing his computer. We build extended families by geography, not bloodlines."

Benefits of Time Banks

- They help save you money.
- They allow you to enjoy services you could otherwise not afford.
- They contribute to your community.
- They build and strengthen the community.
- They reduce isolation.
- They help build trust with and get to know your neighbors.
- You can participate without tax implications.

Time banking arose in 1980 when Dr. Edgar S. Cahn, author of *Our Brother's Keeper* and founder of the Antioch School of Law, created Time Dollars™. On his Web site (www.timebanks.org) Cahn states that the goal of this movement is to build community. In our formal economy, he explains, we only value things through their cash value. As a result many important things have lost their value. So programs like Time Dollars™ are locally based ways people can come together to help out in a formal, equalitarian way where everyone's contribution is valued equally.

Time banking is now a global movement in twenty-two countries on six continents with two hundred programs worldwide. For a sample of how it's working in several communities in Maine, watch the video at www.timebanks.org. We find it quite inspiring and are planning to create a time bank program here in our community. We especially like the idea of including an "expertise exchange" in our time bank. We want to identify who knows how to do what so we can exchange our wisdom and know-how among ourselves.

Time exchanges are an excellent way for professionals such as doctors, lawyers, and businesspeople to give back to their community. For example, they can set aside 10 percent of their appointment calendars for time bank members. Of course, no one needs to contribute more time than they wish to a time bank, so there is never a need to feel burdened by participating.

To find out if there is an existing time bank program in your area, search the community listings on www.timebanks.org/directory.htm. If not, you can join with others to create one. Individuals, neighborhoods, community groups, churches, and organizations can easily create their own time bank. There is a comprehensive start-up kit available through www.timebanks.org. Your group can either select a local coordinator to oversee membership and set up time exchanges, or the group can use software such as that available through www.timebanks.org or Local Exchange from www.sourceforge.net. Some time banks charge an annual membership fee to cover costs of administration.

Tax News on Time Banks

Unlike bartering, time banking is tax exempt. What you give and receive from time banks is not taxable for three reasons:

1. Everyone's time is valued equally.
2. Time dollars are not "legal tender." You cannot sue a person or a time bank if someone refuses to take your time dollars for goods or services they are offering.
3. There is a general charitable intent behind time dollars. They exist to help people live more wholesome lives of meaning and connection. They are not intended to provide luxury goods.

But as www.timebank.org points out, if you were to use a formula such as one hour of credit equals ten dollars and then price things accordingly, you would be directly violating the principles that make time dollars tax exempt. Otherwise each person would have to make a fair and accurate assessment of the value of the goods or services they receive each year from a time bank and report that as income to the IRS.

Unlike bartering, time banking is a "pay-it-forward" system. You don't have to pay back the person who does you a favor. You contribute what you want to, when you want to. Also, no one is calculating equivalent monetary values for the time contributed or received. This not only makes it tax exempt to bank time, but it also makes it simpler and easier to use. When someone contributes an item instead of a service, the time credit is based on direct costs of the item and the time it takes him or her to make it.

 Tip: Don't Know What You Could Contribute?

If you're wondering what you might offer to a time bank, check the kinds of services commonly offered through a time bank at www.timebanks.org/services-exchanged.htm and download their self-assessment questionnaire at: www.timebanks.org/documents/TimeBanksSkillsAssessment.doc. You'll see the list is quite long. Everyone has something of value to offer. In fact, you may find many of the things you're already doing in the community can be credited as time dollars, from driving kids to soccer games to helping a neighbor repair the porch. You can also use the www.timebanks.org questionnaire to help recruit participants for a time bank in your community.

Local Currency

Local currencies, also called *complementary currencies*, are an alternative to money. We may think that only the government can issue money, but this is not the case. Anyone can create money as long as it is redeemable for something of value, for example, gold, oil, time, or services. Historically, people all over the world have issued their own money to trade for needed products and services. Right now there are some nine thousand alternative community currencies in circulation all over the world. The Swiss Wir is one of the oldest, introduced in 1934 to fund small businesses through bartering. It now circulates about $1.2 billion each year. Others are scattered throughout Argentina, Australia, Canada, France, Germany, Holland, Ireland, Japan, Mexico, the United Kingdom, and some communities in the United States. In the 1930s community currency was quite popular in the United States and is becoming more so again in recent years.

In the United States, local currency, or what is often called *script*, usually involves a hand-to-hand exchange of currency in the form of coins, tokens, notes, or some other type of printed "dollars." It is issued by a nonprofit or co-op community organization instead of by the national government. Script does not replace regular currency, but operates in combination with, alongside, or parallel to the national currency. It is usually valued and exchanged in relation to the national currency, for example, one unit of script in the United States is often valued at ten U.S. dollars. Thus, unlike in the case of time banks, different services can have different values. So an hour of an accountant's time may cost more in local currency than an hour of home repair services, just as it would in standard dollars.

Tax Alert!

Note, like barter, community script is not a way around paying taxes. It is taxable when traded for goods or services.

People use local currency to buy goods and services from participating local businesses and professionals who are willing to accept payment from clients and customers in local script, or some combination of money and script. But if a dollar is still worth a dollar, why, you might ask, would they do this? Here's why. The more a dollar is spent, saved, or invested within a local community, the more services and jobs it creates there. For example, Michael Sherman, author of *Local First: Creating Self-Reliant Communities in a Global Age* and *The Small-Mart Revolution*, explains it this way: Say you spend one hundred dollars at a Borders bookstore in Austin, Texas. Just thirteen of those one hundred dollars stay in Austin. On the other hand, if you spend that same one hundred dollars at a locally owned independent bookstore (though there aren't many of them left), forty-five dollars remain in the local community. Since local currency can only be spent within the local community, though, it can't go anywhere else, so none of the money is lost to the community.

This makes local currencies attractive to both consumers and local businesses for many reasons:

> ▶ Those who use script have more national dollars left over each week that they can spend, invest, or save.
> ▶ It provides an incentive for residents to shop locally.
> ▶ As residents spend more of their earnings locally that they once spent elsewhere, local businesses, especially small and home-based businesses, have more customers.
> ▶ With added customers and "income," local businesses can hire others in the community, live better, and provide more services and resources.

- As the local economy becomes more stable, other individuals can start new businesses and provide services one once had to go elsewhere to buy.
- As existing new and local businesses thrive, fewer people need to commute outside the community.
- In such an economy, the middle class expands.
- Increased commerce increases the local tax base so communities can add and/or improve services and infrastructure.
- Local communities have an alternative to letting corporate conglomerates that have no connection to the community move into the area.
- Jobs are more stable because local employers are less likely to offshore jobs or to leave the area to relocate someplace with cheaper labor.
- Control moves from the boardrooms of distant corporations and back to the community where it belongs.

Those are economic benefits. But there are other social and personal benefits to local script as well. Here are just a few:

- By doing business locally, neighbors get to know neighbors.
- Commerce is no longer faceless. People do business with people they know outside of their job roles.
- Residents feel a stronger sense of community.
- People can earn credits doing community tasks that are not usually compensated for.
- Residents who are freed from commuting by working locally can spend more time with family and volunteer in the community.
- Self-esteem grows as people are able to earn a living by contributing directly to the welfare of their immediate community and people they know.
- Members of the community who might otherwise have to depend on welfare or charity can be contributing participants.
- Each community reaps the benefits of the skills, talent, knowledge, and energy of its residents.

There are at least seventeen U.S. communities with local currencies. You can find and read about them in the directories listed in LEARN MORE. They each differ somewhat. Some require an annual membership fee, others time-date their script to keep it circulating, and each has a unique name for their script: Bay

Bucks in Traverse City, Michigan; Burlington Bread in Burlington, Vermont; and Equal Dollars in Philadelphia, Pennsylvania. Also, some are launched strictly by community volunteers while others receive public or private start-up grants. Most, though, are based on the model from Ithaca, New York, the highly successful Ithaca HOURS, a local currency that Paul Glover started in 1991.

Glover became interested in the idea of creating a community script because, as is common to many rural areas and small towns, many people can't rely on well-paying, steady jobs with companies that may pull out willy-nilly to relocate somewhere they can pay lower wages. He focused first on talking with self-employed individuals and couples who were running small businesses from their homes providing the kinds of local services we've featured in Part II, for example, pet sitting, tutoring, home maintenance, and landscaping services. Most of the business owners he spoke with were undercapitalized, underpublicized, and in need of more customers. So Glover asked various owners if they would agree to accept a local script for their goods and services. Since they had little to lose, they signed up.

Here's how it works: Each Ithaca HOUR, or note, is valued at ten dollars, because that was the average wage in the community in 1991. Ithaca HOURS are backed by the time, skills, and products of people who have committed to accept them. They are printed in five denominations. Everyone who agrees to accept HOURS is paid two complementary HOURS (twenty dollars) for listing in the directory as a business that accepts HOURS. During the year, they can then spend and receive as many HOURS as they wish. Each year they renew they receive another two complementary HOURS. This is how they have built their "money" supply. Once a note is issued, just as with regular money, anyone in the community may earn or spend it whether they signed up to be in the business directory or not.

Since 1991, from its modest beginning, Ithaca HOURS Inc. has issued over $110,000 of their own local paper money to thousands of residents who have used them to make tens of thousands of local purchases. Over nine hundred businesses accept Ithaca HOURS for products and services. Residents have used them to buy food at grocery stores and farmers' markets, pay their rent, get haircuts, take dance lessons, buy computer supplies, have their shoes repaired, get a massage, pay for day care, have their plumbing fixed, rent movies, buy eyeglasses, have dental work done, get legal advice, eat out at a fine restaurant, go to a movie, have someone do their bookkeeping . . . the list goes on and on. Residents even use Ithaca HOURS to pay wages, hospital bills, and make mortgage and loan payments. Ithaca HOURS Inc. also makes interest-free loans and provides grants to nonprofit community organizations.

To protect against counterfeiting, Ithaca HOURS are printed in multiple colors, some with locally made watermarked cattail (marsh reed) paper or handmade hemp paper, others with nonxeroxable thermal ink, and all with serial numbers. Paul Glover describes the effect of their community currency this way: "We're making a community while making a living. As we do so, we relieve the social desperation which has led to compulsive shopping and wasted resources."

As Glover also points out, having a local currency involves a lot of work and responsibility to launch and maintain. In addition to tracking and issuing script, some of the key ongoing tasks include recruiting participants, promoting the program, letting people know what's available in the community through script, and promoting the use of products and services offered. All the local currency organizations publish and distribute a directory of members either online, in print, or both. Most have Web sites. Other outreach methods include: publishing a newsletter; having a booth at festivals, trade fairs, and other community events; making personal visits; holding auctions, hosting potluck suppers or musical events; circulating a calendar of events; and obtaining publicity in local print and broadcast media.

Local Exchange Trading System (LETS)

LETS is a type of local exchange system that enables the purchase of local goods and services without the need for coins, tokens, notes, or any form of printed money. With a LETS system, there is no need for script. Instead, transactions are simply tracked and recorded centrally by members of the system, usually by computer software that's available specifically for this purpose. A bookkeeper may earn credit, for example, by providing his services to another resident and then use that credit to purchase a product or service from someone else.

Michael Linton developed this system in 1982 and ran the first such exchange in Courtenay, British Columbia. Since then it has been gaining in popularity around the world, although more slowly in the United States, where communities still tend to prefer hand-to-hand exchange. We anticipate that, as electronic banking becomes the norm, LETS will become more acceptable in the United States, too, as it saves much of the time and energy involved in running a community currency. Less oversight and fewer volunteers are needed.

Despite the effort involved, this is one of the most empowering cashless options available to us as middle-class individuals. It empowers us personally by providing options for rewarding work right in our own communities and makes it easier and less expensive to enjoy our lives. But it also empowers our local communities to become more self-sustaining and supportive of all their residents.

To help with the many tasks involved, those organizations underwritten by grants or donations usually have one or more full- or part-time staff. Others add paid staff as they grow. To raise funds some sell ads in their directories, charge an annual membership fee, or do fundraisers. Of course, project and salary costs are often paid fully or partly in script.

From what we surmise, though, launching and maintaining a local currency requires the efforts of a dedicated champion, either a determined local community organization or an energetic and committed individual, who, along with a cadre of others, will spearhead, recruit, and motivate others to get and stay involved. The Ithaca HOURS Web site, www.ithacahours.org, is a helpful resource for those wishing to explore developing a program in their area. Ithaca HOURS Inc. is developing a start-up kit for other communities that's scheduled for publication in late 2007.

Also, to help groups learn more about the Ithaca program, Paul Glover's book *Homemade Money* provides additional information for starting and operating an HOURS system. His book includes forms, applicable laws, pertinent articles, important procedures, and useful samples. Glover has a video as well that is useful for introducing others in your community to the possibilities for community currency. Software is becoming available that makes running a community currency system easier. The software in essence acts as a bank, lowering the cost, time, and effort of managing local currency (see LEARN MORE).

LEARN MORE

Background
- *Bowling Alone: The Collapse and Renewal of American Communities,* Robert. D. Putnam, Simon & Schuster, 2000.
- *Sitting with the Enemy,* Sarah Anne Edwards, Pine Mountain Institute, 2007.
- *Social Intelligence: The New Science of Human Relationships,* Daniel Goldman, Bantam, 2007.

Do-It-Yourself
- *Be Jane's Guide to Home Empowerment: Projects to Change the Way You Live,* Heidi Baker and Eden Jarrin, Clarkson Potter, 2006.
- *Do-It-Yourself Home Improvement: A Step-by-Step Guide to Home Improvement,* Julian Cassell, Peter Parham, and Theresa Coleman, DK Adult, 2006.
- *Complete Do-It-Yourself Manual: Completely Revised and Updated,* Family Handyman Magazine Editors, Readers Digest, 2007.

Helping Out
- *Sitting with the Enemy,* Sarah Anne Edwards, Pine Mountain Institute, 2007.

Regiving Networks

- ▶ Don't Dump That (www.dontdumpthat.com) has groups in the United Kingdom and Europe (formerly known as Freecyclers).
- ▶ Freecycle Network (www.freecycle.org) has nearly four thousand communities with more than 3 million members worldwide.
- ▶ FreeSharing Network (http://freesharing.org) currently has 630 groups in the directory, serving more than two hundred thousand members in the United States, Canada, United Kingdom, and around the world.
- ▶ Sharing is Giving: http://sharingisgiving.org
- ▶ Worldwide Free Share: http://finance.groups.yahoo.com/group/WorldwideFreeShare

Co-ops

- ▶ *How to Create a Neighborhood Food-Buying Club*, a short e-book produced by Yes We Can!, available at www.wkkf.org/Pubs/GreaterBC/Food_Buying_00254_02998.pdf, 2003.
- ▶ National Cooperative Business Association provides information about cooperatives and distributors: (202) 628-6222, www.ncba.org.
- ▶ Food Club (www.foodclub.org) offers software for running a local food co-op as well as useful information on starting a local group.

Local Business Networks and Alliances

- ▶ American Independent Business Alliance (AMIBA): www.amiba.net
- ▶ The Business Alliance for Local Living Economies (BALLE): www.localeconomies.org
- ▶ Business Network International: www.bni.com

Time Banks

Books & Kits

- ▶ *No More Throw Away People*, Edgar Cahn, Essential Books Ltd., 2004.
- ▶ *Time Bank Start-Up Kit* by TimeBanks USA – a manual, DVD, forms, and three-month free trial of their Community Weaver software: (202) 686-5200, ext. 34; www.timebanks.org/startup-package.htm

Web Sites

- ▶ TimeBanks USA: www.timebanks.org

Exchange Management Software

- ▶ Community Weaver: www.timebanks.org
- ▶ Local Exchange: www.sourceforge.net

Barter and Swap

- *BarterNews* magazine – www.barternews.com
- International Reciprocal Trade Association (IRTA) – www.irta.com
- The National Association of Trade Exchanges (NATE) – www.nate.org
- www.swapace.com
- www.u-exchange.come
- Worldwide Buy, Sell, Trade, Barter – http://finance.groups.yahoo.com/group/WorldwideBuySellTradeBarter
- XO Barter Software – www.barter-software.com/home/index.asp

Community Currency

Books

- *Going Local: Creating Self-Reliant Communities in a Global Age,* Michael H. Shuman, Routledge, 2000.
- *The Small-Mart Revolution: How Local Businesses Are Beating the Global Competition,* Michael H. Shuman, Barrett-Koehler, 2006.

Web Sites

- The E. F. Schumacher Library – www.schumachersociety.org
- Ithaca HOURS – www.ithacahours.com
- LETSystem – www.gmlets.u-net.com

Manuals

- *The LETSystem Design Manual* by Landsman Community Services – www.gmlets.u-net.com/design/home
- *Hometown Money and Starter Kit* by Paul Glover, 2006. Available with a video from Tompkins County Workers' Center, 115 The Commons, Ithaca, NY 14850, www.tclivingwage.org. Click on the "Make a Donation" button on the page, make a twenty-five dollar donation, and specify in the comment box that you want to receive the starter kit.
- *New Money for Healthy Communities* by Thomas H. Greco Jr., 1994. A how-to manual for local trading systems. The first seven chapters are downloadable without charge as a PDF file from www.ratical.org/many_worlds/cc/NMfHC.

Directories

- Directory of LETS programs in the U.S., Canada, and other countries – EcoBusiness Links – www.ecobusinesslinks.com/local_currencies
- E. M. Schumacher Society – Provides a directory of community currency groups in the United States, Canada, and Mexico: www.schumachersociety.org/local_currencies/currency_groups

Software

- ► Cclite: http://sourceforge.net/projects/cclite
- ► MySQL: http://en.wikipedia.org/wiki/MySql
- ► CES: www.ces.org.za/
- ► Cyclos: http://project.cyclos.org/site.php

All great masters are chiefly distinguished by the power of adding a second, a third, and perhaps a fourth step in a continuous line. Many a man had taken the first step. With every additional step you enhance immensely the value of your first.

Ralph Waldo Emerson

CHAPTER FIFTEEN

What's Your Lifeboat?

We don't get to choose the era into which we're born, yet every era presents its own set of challenges. In his book *The Small-Mart Revolution,* Michael Shuman writes of many hardships his grandparents had to endure and overcome to escape persecution in Czarist Russia and immigrate to the United States—exhausting ocean voyages, anti-Semitism, and the Great Depression. On the other hand Shuman's father, born in another era, was able to obtain an advanced degree after, World War II, take a job with Western Electric, and enjoy a life of security that has since virtually disappeared from the economic landscape, as foreign to us as turn-of-the-twentieth-century czarist Russia, from which his parents escaped. The deal in his father's time, Shuman explains, "was simple: work hard and stick with the company, and we'll give you a middle-class salary for the rest of your life with periodic raises, decent health care, and a generous pension."

Today the deal is not that simple. Today we're charged with creating our own deal in an era replete with its own set of challenges, fortunately not as stark as living in Czarist Russia but also not nearly as comfy as post–World War II America. A once dominant and affluent industrial nation is faced with learning to share all forms of wealth with the rest of the world, including jobs and natural resources. While the past sixty years have been about growth and expansion, this time in history is about reevaluating the costs of more, bigger, and faster, focusing instead on enough, smaller, and slower and reclaiming many of the human-scale pleasures we've lost in our rush to material comforts and riches.

Just as the deal Sherman's father enjoyed served as the economic lifeboat for his future and that of his family, the deal we will craft for ourselves today will provide whatever lifeboat we are to enjoy in our futures. Today our challenges are about answering the questions we've addressed in this book:

- ▶ How can we safeguard our livelihoods?
- ▶ How can we safeguard our quality of life?
- ▶ How can we safeguard our ability to afford to pursue a new simpler, slower, and less stressful life of our choice?

After reading about the many choices those on the cutting edge of meeting these challenges are making, what are you thinking your lifeboat will look like? What deal are you working out for yourself, and what steps will you need to take to build and launch your lifeboat? Are you thinking about:

- ▶ establishing an independent career?
- ▶ choosing a new lifestyle?
- ▶ finding new ways to extend your income with alternatives to cash?

Having begun the quest to find, build, and launch our own personal lifeboat seven years ago, and having interviewed many others who are doing the same, we can attest it usually isn't something you'll be able to do overnight. As you've probably noticed, most people emphasize that it's a difficult task to do alone and have found that joining with a community of friends and like-minded folks helped make their choices clearer and launching them easier.

Others are finding that their choices would be still easier to launch if there were certain changes in local, state, and national laws, policies, and practices. Certainly having access to affordable health insurance, whether you're able or willing to continue in a certain job, is one such step. Another is creating incentives that level the playing field for small, locally and personally owned businesses or independent careers. Changes in local zoning restrictions to allow home businesses or lessening the tax burden on living abroad are still other examples that might need to be addressed.

Of course, making institutional changes such as these that support middle-class self-sufficiency is something else we cannot do alone. For these two reasons, we urge you to get together with others you know who are thinking *I just can't keep this up* or *There has to be a better way*, and form a "lifeboat discussion group" in your neighborhood, workplace, church, or online community. Here are some suggestions:

- ▶ Invite the group to explore the options we've presented in this book.
- ▶ Assist each other in making new choices that are right for each of you.

- Support one another through the process of designing, building, and launching your own lifeboats.
- Join together to reshape local, state, and national policies to make launching your lifeboat choices easier. To assist you in exploring and discussing policy directions, you will find our suggestions and ideas on middle class policy matters as well as updates to this book at www.middleclasslifeboat.com.

Now, as you prepare to launch your lifeboat for this new era, we want to personally wish you bon voyage!

Learn More

- *The Small-Mart Revolution: How Local Communities Are Beating the Competition,* Michael Shuman, Barrett-Koehler Publishers, 2007.

About the Authors

PAUL and SARAH EDWARDS have been called the "gurus of the work-at-home movement" by publications such as the *Christian Science Monitor*. They are the authors of the best-selling book *Working from Home: Everything You Need to Know About Living and Working Under the Same Roof*, which Dennis Wholey of *Late Night America* called "the bible of the business."

Paul, educated as an attorney, and Sarah, a licensed clinical social worker and Ph.D. ecopsychologist, brought their careers home in 1974. Before becoming authors, they enjoyed individual careers, Sarah as a psychotherapist, and Paul as a lawyer, CEO, and political consultant. In 1980 they began researching the work-at-home phenomenon at a time when working at home was considered unusual. As authors, they have written sixteen books that have more than 2 million copies and have been published in eight languages.

Always interested in trends, the Edwardses became increasingly concerned about the squeeze being experienced by so many people to fulfill their dreams as the global economy changes. Thus they decided to write *Middle-Class Lifeboat*^{sm} as a way of providing people with positive career and lifestyle choices/alternatives.

Since their first book was published in 1985, the Edwardses have been the subjects of scores of articles in such publications as the *Wall Street Journal*, the *New York Times*, *Los Angeles Times*, *Business Week*, and *Newsweek*. A number of their books have become audio titles.

They've hosted their own radio shows for twenty years, and for four years they hosted *Working from Home with Paul and Sarah Edwards* on HGTV.

Paul and Sarah have consulted the White House and been retained by such corporations as Ameritech, Avery-Dennison, Bell Atlantic, Canon, Compaq, DuPont, Epson, Fuji, Hewlett-Packard, Intuit, Mail Boxes Etc, Microsoft, Northern Telecom, Okidata, Sears, Symantec, US West, and Xerox. As keynote speakers for many professional and trade associations, the Edwardses were named "Consummate Speakers for 1996" by *Sharing Ideas*, an international newsmagazine. They have appeared on radio and TV, both on national shows as well as in nearly one hundred U.S. cities. Their advice has also been featured on *Oprah*.

The Edwardses write a print column *Costco Connection*, from 1988 until 1998 were contributing editors and columnists for *Home Office Computing* magazine, and until recently wrote a column distributed through the Los Angeles Times Syndicate and several columns for *Entrepreneur* magazine. In 2006 they were recognized as the U.S. Small Business Administration's (SBA) Region IX "Small Business Journalists of the Year."

Paul and Sarah are now focusing on middle-class issues and have three Web sites, www.MiddleClassLifeboat.com, www.PineMountainInstitute.com, and www. WhatIWishThe DoctorToldMe.com.

Acknowledgments

We wish to express gratitude to Kristen Parrish, our editor; Victor Oliver, our acquisitions editor; Joel Miller, our publisher; Dave Schroeder, our marketing director; Jennifer Hesse, our copy editor; **Heather Skelton, our managing editor; Mike McDaniel, our designer;** and the others at Nelson who have helped to make this book come to life.

We owe special appreciation to Dave Fuller, Tim Talevich, and Anita Thompson of the *Costco Connection,* who enabled us to use our column to identify a number of the people whose stories appear in this book.

Many kudos to Mar Preston for her expert help in polishing and refining the last drafts of the lifestyle and income-expansion sections. Our gratitude to Peter Gullerud for doing the icons for the marketing methods in the book and the sketches that illustrate Chapter 11 on the Middle Class Lifeboat Web site. Thanks to David Wolfe and April Durham, who helped us organize truckloads of information for the career profiles. We also acknowledge the helpfulness of our agents, Marilyn Allen and Colleen O'Shea, who united us with Nelson and have encouraged us along the way in taking this book from concept to hardcover.

Finally, we thank the hundreds of people we interviewed who shared their experience and expertise as well as their insights, wisdom, cautions, and inspiration so others can fully appreciate the possibilities for living more rewarding, sustainable lives.